Advance praise for *Cross-Cultural Filmmaking:*

"Here is the definitive A-Z of documentary filmmaking. No stone is left unturned, no truth unshared, and fresh insight informs every chapter. Student fiction filmmakers should also savor this book, because only if your dramatic film achieves a real sense of actuality, no matter what your style may be, can you begin to convince your audience."

MIKE LEIGH, director of *Secrets & Lies*

"Anthropology needs an up-to-date manual on filmmaking. Fifty years ago Margaret Mead and Gregory Bateson demonstrated what film can do for ethnography. It was daringly novel then, but times have changed, the technology has changed, and now every fieldworker expects to be able to work in this new medium. In presenting the new technology and the history of ethnographic filmmaking together, *Cross-Cultural Filmmaking* represents a coming-of-age for anthropology."

MARY DOUGLAS, author of *Purity and Danger*

"*Cross-Cultural Filmmaking* is the ideal 'how to' companion for the serious documentarian and ethnographic filmmaker. Informed by theory, seasoned by experience, and sensitive to issues of cultural difference, this book enlarges our understanding of documentary production as both creative art and social praxis."

BILL NICHOLS, author of *Representing Reality* and *Blurred Boundaries*

"This is an extraordinarily valuable work that many of us have been waiting for. Gracefully integrating the most progressive ideas about what ethnographic media could still be, this volume provides a thorough account of the use of film and video as a mode of ethnography as well as a nearly irresistible enticement to give it a try."

GEORGE E. MARCUS, Professor of Anthropology, Rice University

"Barbash and Taylor have created a thinking-person's guide to documentary filmmaking. Not only is it required reading for any student who wants to learn production techniques, but it offers an indispensable refresher course for seasoned documentary filmmakers who want to catch up on the latest critical thinking about their practice. *Cross-Cultural Filmmaking* even makes enjoyable reading for a determined non-producer like myself."

B RUBY RICH, Professor of Film Studies, University of California, Berkeley

"*Cross-Cultural Filmmaking* is the definitive guide to making an informed and savvy contribution to the 'photochemical permeation of the world.'"

PAUL RABINOW, Professor of Anthropology, University of California, Berkeley

"*Cross-Cultural Filmmaking* is an excellent book. It provides a wealth of sensible and perceptive advice in a calm, jargon-free style. Beautifully organized and filled with instructive examples, it deals with the whole range of visual, financial, ethical, and aesthetic issues in documentary filmmaking in considerable depth. It will immediately become the standard manual for teachers and filmmakers."

ALAN MACFARLANE, Professor of Anthropological Science, Cambridge University

Cross-Cultural Filmmaking

Ilisa Barbash and
Lucien Taylor

Technical illustrations by
SANDRA MURRAY

Figure drawings by
CHAD VAUGHAN

Cross-Cultural Filmmaking

A HANDBOOK FOR

MAKING

DOCUMENTARY

AND ETHNOGRAPHIC

FILMS AND

VIDEOS

University of California Press
Berkeley, Los Angeles, London

Front cover: Still from *A Wife among Wives* (1981) by David and Judith MacDougall, courtesy Fieldwork Films. Front insets (top to bottom): Trinh Min-ha behind the camera, courtesy Women Make Movies, Inc.; Lorna Marshall interviewing !Kung San men, courtesy Documentary Educational Resources; Helen Van Dongen and Robert Flaherty editing *Louisiana Story* (1948), courtesy Museum of Modern Art; David MacDougall and Thomas Woody Minipini, working on *Goodbye Old Man* (1977), photograph by Judith MacDougall, courtesy Fieldwork Films. Back cover: From *The Nuer*, photograph by Robert Gardner, copyright the Film Study Center, Harvard.

University of California Press
Berkeley and Los Angeles, California

University of California Press, Ltd.
London, England

Library of Congress Cataloging-in-Publication Data

Barbash, Ilisa, Cross-cultural filmmaking : A handbook for making documentary and ethnographic films and videos / Ilisa Barbash & Lucien Taylor.
     p.   cm.
    Includes bibliographical references and index.
    ISBN 0–520–08759–3 (alk. paper).—ISBN 0-520-08760-7
(pbk.: alk. paper)
    1. Motion pictures in ethnology.   2. Motion pictures—Production and
direction.   I. Taylor, Lucien.   II. Title.
  GN347.B37   1997
  305.8'00208—dc20   96–17662

Printed in the United States of America
9 8 7 6 5 4 3 2 1

The paper used in this publication meets the minimum requirements of American National Standards for Information Sciences—Permanence of Paper for Printed Library Materials, ANSI Z39.48–1984.

For Joseph and for Jasper

Ethnographic film is the documentary's avant-garde. Who is more self-conscious than an anthropologist with a movie camera? The ethnographic film's most scrupulous examples don't simply document alien cultures, they necessarily question the nature of filmmaking itself. For, even more than conventional documentarians, visual anthropologists are compelled to consider the relation of the filmmaker (and the film process) to the filmed.

—*J. Hoberman*

[A]t a time when modernist experimentation is old hat within the avant-garde and a fair amount of fiction-filmmaking, it remains almost totally unheard of among documentary filmmakers, especially in North America. It is not political documentarists who have been the leading innovators. Instead it is a handful of ethnographic filmmakers like Timothy Asch (*The Ax Fight*), John Marshall (*Nai!*), and David and Judith MacDougall who, in their meditations on scientific method and visual communication, have done the most provocative experimentation.

—*Bill Nichols*

There is the rest, the most difficult, the most moving, the most secret: wherever human feelings are involved, wherever the individual is directly concerned, wherever there are interpersonal relationships of authority, subordination, comradeship, love, hate—in other words, everything connected with the emotive fabric of human existence. There lies the great *terra incognita* of the sociological or ethnological cinema, of cinematographic truth. There lies its promised land.

—*Edgar Morin*

[T]he movies are peculiarly suited to make manifest the union of mind and body, mind and the world, and the expression of one in the other.

—*Maurice Merleau-Ponty*

CONTENTS

INTRODUCTION

This handbook is for anyone who wants to make a documentary or ethnographic film. You may be a student, a professor, or out on your own, working independently. You may be a budding filmmaker or an emeritus anthropologist. You may have a burning desire to shoot a feature-length movie about a revolution in a remote spot of the globe, or have long hoped to make a ten-minute video about your grandmother. You may want to learn the technology simply to shoot research footage, or to improve your home video style. In any of these cases, this handbook contains the background information you'll need to work with moving images.

Making Films and Writing Texts

Since the early 1960s, documentary makers have been able to shoot films with synchronous ("sync") sound almost anywhere in the world. From the mid-1970s, portable video cameras have been widely available too, and they're getting cheaper, smaller, and better by the day. They're used by Yanomamo and Kayapo in the Amazonian rain forest as well as by hi-tech national television stations around the world.

Film brings people and cultures alive on the screen, capturing the sensation of living presence, in a way that neither words nor even still photos can. The cumulation of successive film frames evokes the sensation of movement over time quite literally *through* movement over time. Film language is the language of moving, seeing, and hearing. More than any other medium or art form, film uses experience to express experience.

This is why film is such an absorbing medium to work in. With documentary, additionally, the filmmaker enters other people's lives, their hopes and fears, their loves and hates, and then goes all out to resurrect them on the screen. The challenge is engrossing and often intoxicating. While it lasts, it can take over your every waking moment. It can change your and your subjects' lives forever—for the better or for the worse. If you are writing a book or an article, you can go home and write it all up afterwards. With film, you have to shoot events and activities at the time they occur. If you don't catch them then, they're lost forever. That's what is so special about film: it's linked absolutely, existentially to its object, a photochemical permeation of the world.[1]

Film also has the possibility of reaching a far vaster audience than most academic writers could ever imagine. The subjects of your film are better able to judge your representation of them than if you write a book about them in another language. Your films can be seen and evaluated by all sorts of communities to which you'd otherwise have no access. And this can be a two-way learning experience.

As you start out to make your first films, and as you use this handbook, try to watch as many documentaries as you can. But look at them with new eyes. Look at the shooting style. Look at how they're constructed. Look at how cuts establish relationships that are not inherent in the images themselves. Look at how they build up characters and tell stories. Look for structures that don't revolve around straightforward stories. Look, too, at how films fail, at how much they leave out, and for other stories that could have been told. And think about what kind of a film you would have made instead.

Film and Video

This handbook covers both film and video. The basic principles are similar but the technologies are different. Film is still preferred by people with the resources or expertise, but most of us are now shooting video. Video doesn't yet have the same image quality as film, but it's the medium of the future. Because low-end video is relatively cheap and compact, it has a democratic potential that film lacks. People all over the world are buying or borrowing video cameras to document their own and others' lives. You may want to shoot some of your movies in video and others in film, depending on your budget and your aesthetic.

You don't have to choose one medium or the other, once and for all. Except where the context demands precision, "film" is used in the pages that follow as a shorthand for both film and video.

Practical and Theoretical

This handbook smuggles in a little film theory here and there. Apologies in advance! By contrast, most documentary film manuals are exclusively practical. But there's a problem with this. Styles of filmmaking, like styles of writing, change over time. Filmmaking conventions are continually conceived, used, abused, exhausted, and then recuperated. These conventions have assumptions built into them, often quite profound ones. As the ethnographic filmmaker David MacDougall has noted, "Implicit in a camera style is a theory of knowledge."[2] This may sound a bit terrifying, but it's true. It doesn't mean that we have to go around thinking "Gee, what's my theory of knowledge today?" every time we turn our cameras on. But it does mean there's a mixed bag of assumptions that affect the way we shoot. These assumptions have to do with our relationships both to the realities we film and to our prospective viewers. Some of the assumptions we're aware of, others we're not. The more we can bring them out into the open, the better. That way, we'll have more of an idea what we're doing, and be less likely to repeat blindly the errors of the past. In addressing some of these assumptions, this handbook tends to pose more problems than it solves. This is because when "film language" is learned by rote and applied formulaically, without regard for subject matter, documentary is invariably diminished.

But who wants film theory? Most of it is unreadable to the uninitiated. In fact, it often sounds like gobbledygook to filmmakers themselves! So, when we've slipped it in, we've done our best to dispense with the jargon by using plain English. Feel free to skip over passages you think are overly pedantic. But if you can bear with us, it'll probably repay the effort, as we raise issues that are usually swept under the table.

As well as being practical, documentary film manuals also tend to be prescriptive: they tell you how you should write, shoot, and edit your films. That is, they tell you *how* but not *why*. Unfortunately, many of their prescriptions are derived from conventions established for fiction filmmaking. But fiction and documentary have a different relationship to the worlds they depict, and there are difficulties involved when you shoot a documentary with the liberties you would take for a work of fiction. Quite a few manuals even talk about "directing" your documentaries, as if you can direct what happens in front of the camera: this suits some styles, but it doesn't suit all. While we try to get away from this talk about directing, it's still a tension you'll have to deal with yourself when you shoot. And though this handbook gives you advice about shooting and editing styles, feel free to take such suggestions with a grain of salt. What's important is that you evolve your own style and that it's born out of your encounter with your subject.

Ethnography and Documentary

This handbook covers documentary and ethnographic filmmaking of all kinds—at home or abroad, within your own community, subculture, or class, or about other ones altogether. There's no precise distinction between ethnographic and documentary films. All films, fiction films too, contain ethnographic information, both about the people they depict and about the culture of the filmmaker. And some documentaries are richer and reveal more about human experience than films that call themselves ethnographic. Though ethnographic films have characteristics of their own, they can't be weeded out from the broader documentary traditions from which they have borrowed, and to which, in part, they belong. So, unless the context demands a distinction, we use "documentary" to refer to both explicitly ethnographic and not-so-explicitly ethnographic documentary.

(Cross-)Cultural?

Is this handbook restricted to "cross-cultural" documentary? Not really. The chapters that follow should be helpful for anyone wanting to make any kind of documentary about human beings in society. But the handbook does take cross-cultural differences seriously, asks what they're like in the contemporary world, and addresses the possibilities and problems of putting them on film.

Some people used to say that ethnographic films were about strange rituals in "exotic cultures" and documentaries were about modern life in industrial nations (and their rural provinces). But the world has changed, and anthropology and filmmaking have changed with it. The world, though far from unified, has become increasingly interdependent. People, like corporations, are on the move, and they take their identities with them. Members of the First, Second, Third, and Fourth Worlds now intermingle and intermarry. The colonial expansion of the First World has been succeeded by its postcolonial implosion through a demographically expanded Third, and this, in turn, has been followed by the post–cold war fragmentation of the Second. The world's inhabitants, in short, are tumbling all over each other, and it's only natural that filmmakers should try to keep up with the times. Just as documentaries are now made at all ends of the earth, ethnographic filmmakers are "coming home" to study their own societies, showing their customs to be just as curious and conventional as anyone else's.

Cultural Differences?

So what's happened to cultural differences? They're being ceaselessly de-formed and re-formed on your doorstep, wherever you are. Cultures are now less bounded and homogeneous and more porous and self-conscious than ever before, and cultural differences—of religion, gender, language, class, ethnicity, sexual orientation, and so on—are no longer contained within old geopolitical boundaries. Subcultures, cultures, and supercultures merge and emerge anew, ceaselessly. In the rough-and-tumble of transnational migration and capitalism, what was exotic yesterday may be domestic today. And what is domestic today may be exotic tomorrow. Cross-cultural filmmaking, then, can be as easily undertaken at home as it can in Timbuktu or up the Orinoco.

But cultural differences in documentary are more various than you might think. This of course only makes them more interesting. In fact, they may be at play in at least six different sites, any (or all) of which are worth highlighting in your films:

1. You (the filmmaker) may belong to a different culture from the people you film. You may be a Sri Lankan making a film about the maize or motel culture of the American midwest, or you may be an American midwesterner making a film about the Tamil Tigers. Many ethnographic films, but not all, continue to depict differences at this level.

2. You may make a film about people from more than one culture. Films about tourism (like Dennis O'Rourke's "*Cannibal Tours*" [1988] or, in part, David and Judith MacDougall's *Photo Wallahs* [1992]) depict at least two cultures or subcultures. Jean Rouch's *Madame L'Eau* (1993) is set on the canals of Amsterdam, in Holland, and also on the banks of the River Niger, in West Africa. Robin Anderson and Bob Connolly's *First Contact* (1984), *Joe Leahy's Neighbors* (1988), and *Black Harvest* (1992) are a trilogy of films about the intercultural fallout from the encounter between Australian gold prospectors and Papua New Guinean highlanders.

3. You may belong to a different culture from (some of) your spectators. If you do, it's possible that film subjects, filmmakers, and film spectators may all be from different cultures. (How many languages can communicate in such conditions?) Just as peoples are moving around the world, so are their films. And it's not only big-budget Hollywood films that are shown in buses, on walls, and in movie theaters on all the world's continents. Ethnographic and documentary films are there too.

4. There will probably be cultural differences among your spectators. Even if you make a film that's only shown in classrooms in the U.S. or Britain, it's already reaching an audience with a tremendous degree of cultural diversity. If you make a film abroad and your film is shown in the country where you shot it as well as at home, the spectators will be more diverse still. If your film is screened at festivals around the world, or broadcast on television in a few countries, you'll lose control over its reception altogether: there's no way you'll know what kinds of people are watching it.

5. If you work with a film crew, there could be cultural differences among your crew members: they may come from various backgrounds. When you collaborate with your subjects (for example, ethnographic filmmakers often work with a sound recordist from the community they're filming in), then your crew is inherently diverse. As you go about filming, you and your crew may respond in various ways to the scenes you shoot. Wittingly and unwittingly, these different perspectives may be incorporated into the film itself.

6. Finally, even you, in and of yourself, may, in a sense, be cross-cultural. Whether through your life experience or your genealogy, you may span more than one cultural tradition. You may be Hopi and Irish-American; you may be Chicana; you may have dual citizenship (legally or illegally) in Canada and Chile, India and Indonesia, or Britain and Bolivia; you may have an American father of African descent who grew up in Paris and a Japanese-American mother who was interned in California during World War II; you may be considered white when you go home to Liberia but black when you're living in exile in London; you may be a Guadeloupean descendant of French slaveholders, African slaves, Carib (West) Indians and indentured (East) Indians, but live in Pondichéry and be married to an exiled Anglo-Tibetan; and so on and so forth. "Fragmented" identities and multiple affiliations of this kind (as the academics like to call them) are the way the world is going, and films are being made that reflect them.

So, whether disenchanted or just discombobulated, today's world is no less fascinating or stupefying for it. We hope this handbook gives you the incentive and resolve to represent it on film.

The Terms We Use

On top of using "film" indiscriminately for film and video, and "documentary" to encompass ethnographic as well as non-ethnographic films, a few other words require explanation right off. There are two groups of people who appear so often in this handbook that we use various terms for them. These are the people you make your films about, and the people who watch them. The people you feature in your films are usually called "subjects," but this can get a bit cumbersome after a while, so we also talk about "actors" and "characters." These terms typically refer to fiction film actors, but they're pertinent for documentary too. "Actors" points to the performative quality of documentary, in which social actors are for a time, for better or worse, also film actors: they act out their lives, more or less self-consciously, in front of your camera. "Characters" hints at how you, the filmmaker, have to construct and develop your characters on the screen, and at how documentary conventions of character development over the course of a film are uncannily close to fictional ones. Additionally, the people who watch your film are also referred to so often that it would be repetitious to stick with just one word. "Viewers," "spectators," and "audience" are all used interchangeably.

Finally, there are two words of nasty but unavoidable jargon that crop up now and then. The first is "pro-filmic" or "pro-filmic event." This basically means whatever takes place in front of and around the camera, as it's rolling. The term is important because documentary is not just a presentation of reality (i.e., it's not reality itself), it's also a representation of it. Filming is as much a process of selectivity and interpretation as writing; there's some distance between the actual film and what it depicts. The "filmic," then, is what is on the film itself, after it's been mixed and edited. It's the *re*-presentation of reality that the film makes. As such, it exists apart from the pro-filmic, which is the multitude of processes and activities that *actually* happened in the shooting of the film, some of which were recorded, others of which were missed, ignored, unknown, concealed, or denied. So if you used special lights to illuminate a scene but kept them out of frame because you didn't want your spectators to know you used them, they'd be part of the pro-filmic but not the filmic. Or if you cut between two shots of your main protagonist that were filmed on two different days, but manage to make it look as if the two shots represent a continuation of a single action, set at the same time and same place, the two different events ("what really happened") would be part of the pro-filmic, and the synthesis into a single event as implied by the cut would be the filmic: it would be a connotation of the film.

Documentary has a different relationship to what's in front of the camera from fiction. Fiction films generally negate the pro-filmic; that is, as spectators we suspend disbelief and forget about all the lighting, staging, acting, and makeup that we know is there "behind the scenes." But when we watch a documentary, we usually assess it as a record of the pro-filmic events we see magically projected on the screen. When we describe a documentary as good or bad, complete or incomplete, objective or biased, we're evaluating it in terms of its faithfulness to the reality it has recorded. And because different documentaries represent reality in different ways, they have different relationships to the pro-filmic.

The second word also comes from the world of film criticism. This is "diegesis," or "diegetic." A film's diegesis is its story: the universe it constructs on the screen, everything that the events and characters signify. One has only to look at the films of Robert Flaherty or Jean Rouch to see that documentaries can tell stories. The concept of diegesis is closely linked to the pro-filmic. A fiction film's diegesis (i.e., story) denies its status as a record of the pro-filmic (the actors and set), while documentary diegesis stakes some claim to affirming it. "Extradiegetic," then, means elements of your film that aren't supposed to be a natural part of the story, that are somehow outside your narrative yet are integral to the film. For example, if you linked two sequences with a montage of short shots of your protagonist engaged in various activities (say, growing older in her teenage years) and added a music sound track over the montage, the music would be extradiegetic. That is, the viewers would realize that it wasn't recorded in sync with the images, that you're not pretending that the music was actually playing along while your subject was aging. You may be using the music to "make a statement" about the montage images, or just to add feeling to them, in order to bring them alive.

Images can be extradiegetic as well as sounds, though this is relatively uncommon in realist documentaries. For instance, in his personal film about Paris in 1962, *Le joli mai,* Chris Marker condenses a conversation by cutting in images of cats and sounds of harp music that have no narrative relation at all to the discussion. They are rather an editorial commentary, however ambiguous, on the conversation itself. Images and sounds can also be viewed as simultaneously diegetic and extradiegetic—that is, part of the narrative but also a "statement" by the filmmaker. Equally, too, it may be hard for a spectator to tell whether the filmmaker intended a shot or some sound to be considered as integral to the story or as their own statement about it. As a filmmaker, you'll find you have the power to play on this ambiguity.

So, to sum up, your diegesis is the story you construct in shooting and editing (be it real or fictional), and the pro-filmic is what was really going on when you were shooting. With these two words defined, this handbook should be accessible to filmmakers and non-filmmakers and anthropologists and non-anthropologists alike.

How To Use This Handbook

This handbook can be used as an introductory textbook for instruction in documentary and ethnographic film. Whether for classes given in anthropology, film, art, sociology, ethnic studies, or journalism, it provides basic information about all aspects of documentary, theoretical and practical.

The book is also meant as a guide for the independent film- or videomaker, as well as for anthropologists who want to try their hand at a camera. Half a century ago, just before he was appointed to the chair in Ethnology at the Sorbonne, André Leroi-Gourhan lamented the untold opportunities lost by anthropologists who had "turned the handle of a film camera for the first time in the field, with only the vaguest ideas on lighting and angles, and no serious notion of how to construct a film."[3] Now's the time for things to change.

There are three parts to the book. "Getting Going" begins with a brief account of documentary styles, from the scripted to the spontaneous (chapter 1). It then discusses the kind of preparation you need to undertake before actually filming, the ethics of image-making, various forms of collaboration, and how you can home in on a suitable subject for a film (chapter 2). You should read "Getting Going" first.

The second part of the book, "Nuts and Bolts" is the densest and most difficult. But it contains crucial information both about how filmmaking equipment works and about the aesthetic principles you put into play when you use it. Chapter 3 is about the film picture, and chapter 4 about film sound. Parts of chapter 3 will seem familiar if you're a still photographer, and you may be acquainted with some of the information in chapter 4 if you've already recorded sound or are an ethnomusicologist. Chapter 5 then runs through the differences between film and video, and their respective formats, to help you decide what medium and equipment to use.

If you can, read through these chapters in order. But if you find the technical sections too laborious at first, try skimming over them, and come back to them later. If you already have your equipment and know how to use it, you may be able to skip chapter 5 altogether. But if you're starting your first filmmaking venture, you'll need to refer back to details in all these chapters at various points throughout your production.

The last part of the book, "Stages of Filmmaking," describes the different steps of filmmaking itself: preproduction (chapter 6), production (chapter 7), postproduction (chapter 8), and finally distribution (chapter 9), what you can do with your film once it's finished. These chapters are relatively straightforward, and you should read them all before actually starting to film. How you envisage distributing your film, and how you edit it, will also affect how you shoot and prepare for your locations.

Of course, no handbook will ever replace hands-on experience. Much of the technical information will only really make sense when you have the equipment and instruction manuals in front of you. Most people can learn to shoot (low-end) video by themselves. High-end video and film are often thought to require instruction, even though it's actually a lot easier to shoot *well* on film or with a professional video camera than it is with a consumer model. Real film aficionados often manage to teach themselves anyway. In any case, the more practical experience you can have, the more helpful this handbook will be.

Good luck!

Getting Going

PART ONE

1. Documentary Styles

Documentary is evolving constantly. As you take up a camera you're coming in on the heels of over a century of documentary experimentation. What are the styles that have been spawned and spent over the years? Which will inspire you and which infuriate you? Which will you want to draw on and which to reject, which to use and which to abuse? You have an almost infinite variety of stylistic options to choose among. All of them are revealing about their filmmakers and their times, and all of them are interesting, in different ways, about their subjects. This chapter will give a brief (and inevitably selective) outline of documentary styles from Lumière to our day.

THE BIRTH OF DOCUMENTARY

Though the camera obscura extends back to the mid-sixteenth century, it wasn't until 1816 that the first paper negative was produced, and 1839 that the first positive image appeared on a silver plate (the "daguerreotype"). As the nineteenth century drew to a close, a Frenchman, Louis Lumière, conceived of a way to project one image after another. For the next few years, from 1895 on, Louis and his brother Auguste, along with their camera operators, churned out film after film about apparently inconsequential moments of daily life: workers leaving their factories; a train arriving at a station; gondolas going down Venetian canals; a baby learning to walk; and blacksmiths, firemen, and lumberjacks all going about their work. Incredulous audiences from all over the world flocked spellbound to the public screenings of these first films, in some cases astounded to see themselves on the screen, filmed in the streets only a few days earlier. Cinema was born, and it was born with the documentary.

The early Lumière films were only a minute long—that was all the reels could hold. Louis Lumière thought that cinema should draw back from the dramatic conventions of theater. Motivated by "scientific curiosity," he was convinced that cinema should seek to capture real life *sur le vif*—on the fly. He wanted spectators to witness "nature caught

◄ **FIGURE 1** Longole filming the filmmakers in *A Wife among Wives* (1981) by David and Judith MacDougall.

in the act" and enjoy such simple pleasures as seeing "the ripple of leaves stirred by the wind."[1]

But even the early films reveal ambiguities about the camera's relationship to what it records. Once people on the streets recognized a camera for what it was, they began to wonder how they should react to it. Should they acknowledge it, or should they ignore it? Soon enough, people affecting to ignore it were doing so with a concentration of the mind that rivaled that of the people who were approaching and gesticulating self-consciously, or posing as if for a still photograph. Hidden within these various responses to the camera lies an important question, one that you'll also have to address yourself: should documentary depict life as it would have been had the camera not been noticed, or life as it actually goes on before and as affected by the camera? Different documentary styles implicitly answer this question in different ways.

As the Lumière cameras were catching life on the fly, they were also beginning to tell stories, and some of these stories were told either *for* or *by* the camera. The comic *L'arroseur arrosé* (Waterer Watered, 1895) depicts a mischievous boy stepping on the hose of a gardener while he's watering his flowers. As the gardener turns the nozzle to his face to see what's wrong, the little boy takes his foot off and leaves the poor man drenched. The boy runs away, but the gardener catches up and spanks him. Some people think this film was the first to tell a "found story," that is, a story that exists in nature or real life, outside of the film.[2] But it's difficult not to see it also as a specifically filmic story, one equally narrated by the filmmaker who recorded the images. Not surprisingly, other people feel it's the first fiction film. Here, too, there is a tension that has stayed with the documentary form ever since: if we are storytellers, are we telling our own stories or those of our subjects? Can documentary stories ever be completely "discovered"; are they not also always at least partly "contrived"? The Scottish documentary filmmaker John Grierson defined documentary as the "creative treatment of actuality," but what liberties are we allowed to take as long as we remain tied to documentary as something other than pure fiction? Again, different styles have their own answers.

There's a third way in which the early Lumière films prefigure debates that are still raging among documentary filmmakers today. Their cameras were hand-cranked, which meant that the operators could create special effects by speeding them up or slowing them down. Equipment operators also sometimes projected film in reverse, so that spectators would watch people walking forward and then all of a sudden retracing their steps. Playing with space and time in this way can reveal detail that goes unnoticed when film is projected forward at the "real time" speed. In fact, as soon as you, the filmmaker, make a cut, you're changing time, and as soon as you adjoin one shot to another, you're re-creating space. As the French anthropologist-filmmaker Jean Rouch has said, "Cinema allowed intervention into *time,* for the first time ever, permitting the construction of a wholly different object. It is this that has always appealed to me most about film."[3] But other filmmakers have felt that documentary should not reassemble the fragments of recorded reality in a mixture of its own making. In order not to distort or synthesize, they shoot long, uninterrupted sequences. This tension around manipulating space and time has also been with documentary since its conception.

Documentary styles since the time of the Lumière films can be categorized in umpteen different ways. For the sake of simplicity, this chapter distinguishes between four main styles. This framework is meant more as a rough guide to certain labels that filmmakers and critics use (labels that reappear in the following chapters) than as a hard-and-fast historical or theoretical taxonomy. The four basic divisions are expository, impressionistic, observational, and reflexive.[4]

EXPOSITORY

Expository documentaries typically address the spectators directly, through either an on-screen commentator or a voice-over track (a narration by someone we don't see that's laid over the images). Neither the voice-over nor the on-screen commentator necessarily speak in the second person, literally *to* the spectators, but they both implicitly address an audience, and they both tend to be somewhat set apart from the rest of the film. They seem to comment on the action or the scene, rather than to constitute it or be part of it.

The meaning and point of view of expository films is thus elaborated more through the sound track than the images. Whereas the images in fiction films tend to articulate a continuous time and space with the help of conventions of continuity cutting (see chapter 3), images in expository documentaries are edited as a complement or counterpoint to an argument being articulated in voice-over. The visuals are thus structured in accordance with a sound track which has a certain priority.

Expository documentary is sometimes called Griersonian, after John Grierson. Grierson looked on cinema as a "pulpit," and urged documentary filmmakers to consider themselves propagandists, making socially engaged films about "the drama of the doorstep" in the service of national culture. The documentary, he said, is not a mirror but a hammer. However, the films of Grierson and his disciples were as impressionistic as they were expository. Grierson's silent first film, *Drifters* (1929), depicted Scottish herring fisheries of the time as "an epic of steam and steel." *Drifters* stunned spectators with its dignified representation of a heroic working class. "Men at their labour," said Grierson, "are the salt of the earth,"[5] and indeed his films were lauded as the first ever to show "a workingman's face and a workingman's hands and the way the worker lived and worked."[6] Louis de Rochemont's *March of Time* series from the 1930s, John Huston's war documentaries of the 1940s (including *The Battle of San Pietro* [1944]), along with innumerable contemporary National Geographic and other nature films are more obviously examples of expository documentary.

Most of the documentaries that are still broadcast on television are, like TV news, expository. Since the 1960s invention of portable equipment able to record a sound track in sync with the picture, the expository style has accommodated itself to the interview format, enabling people other than the filmmaker-commentator also to address the audience more or less directly. Interviews, voice-over, and archival images are often combined in contemporary mainstream television documentaries, such as Ken Burns's *The Civil War* (1990) and *Baseball* (1994) series. However, as a style, expository documentary has fallen into disuse among ethnographic and independent documentary filmmakers, who want the visuals to have more autonomy and breathing space.

The arguments elaborated by expository documentary tend to be didactic; they seek to inform and instruct. Expository documentary is popular among television programmers because it presents its point of view clearly, and leaves little room for misinterpretation (or interpretation for that matter). But this is exactly what some filmmakers have reacted against, describing disembodied voice-over as authoritative, "colonial," "an enemy of film," the "Voice of God," and even "the (nonexistent) view from nowhere." They have reacted against the tendency of expository documentary to explain what the images mean, as if they don't explain themselves, or as if viewers can't be trusted to work the meaning out on their own. Indeed, the voice-over often seems to attribute a reduced meaning to the visuals; that is, it denies them a density they might have by themselves. Moreover, because the visuals are edited to the (non-synchronous) sound track, their meaning is determined by extrinsic elements. Left to themselves, expository visuals typically lack not only continuity but also cogency. This is why some people have described expository documentary as equivalent to an illustrated lecture.

But if, aside from television, infomercials, and industrial films, the expository style is no longer much in favor, that doesn't mean that it is all bad, or that you can't make good use of its elements in other ways. After all, there is nothing *inherently* didactic or authoritative about voice-over. Films as diverse as Luis Buñuel's *Land without Bread* (1932), Alain Resnais's *Night and Fog* (1955), and Chris Marker and Resnais's *And Statues Also Die* (1953) show that you can as easily write narration in a style that undercuts itself, that is enigmatic or unsettling, or that offers a wry, self-reflexive commentary about the visuals, as you can in a style that pontificates pretentiously about the world. Likewise, voice-over needn't be moralistic: you can as easily write a voice-over track that is ambiguous and ambivalent about ethical matters as one that naively divides up the world into victims and villains, or heroes and antiheroes. Moreover, the visuals may be used, not just redundantly, to illustrate the sound track, but also as a counterpoint to or even a refutation of it: you don't have to say and show the same thing.

Thus, as you consider your stylistic possibilities, it helps to remember that even if you don't want to make a didactic or propagandistic film, and even if you want to make a film that is more evocative than it is argumentative, voice-over is not *verboten*. You may still want to edit your images at least partially to a non-sync sound track.

Impressionistic films tend to be lyrical rather than didactic, poetic rather than argumentative. They imply more than they inform, and evoke more than they assert. They may be as socially engaged as expository films, but are less level-headed, hard-hitting, or solemn. They also tend to be more self-consciously stylized, more aestheticized. Their meaning may be oblique, even obscure. At times, though, the distinction between impressionistic and expository films is fuzzy, and, in fact, a number of the early films in the Griersonian tradition may be as properly described as one as the other.

Night Mail (1936), directed by Harry Watt and Basil Wright, was one of the most aesthetically acclaimed films of the Griersonian era. Like their "chief" Grierson, Watt and Wright sought to ennoble workers, in this case postal workers on the "Postal Special" night train from London to Glasgow. W. H. Auden wrote the narration and Benjamin Britten composed the score. The combined sound track was so powerful that it dictated the pacing of the picture—shots of mail pouches, mechanized pick-ups, and teams of efficient workers. Much of the drama and poetry of the picture stems from its being paced to the musical rhythms.

Another impressionistic film of the time that experimented with sound was Basil Wright's *Song of Ceylon* (1934), sponsored by the Ceylon Tea Propaganda Board. The film had a multivocal sound track that articulated a complex and at times ironic counterpoint to the beautiful and impressionistic images of Ceylonese life and landscape. The voices that are laid over the images implicitly call the supposed benefits of Westernization into question. (The Ceylon Tea Propaganda Board was nonetheless gratified with the film because it was let off the hook: the film conveyed the board's esteem toward Ceylonese culture.)

Recent impressionistic documentaries often celebrate their own subjectivity to such a degree that they form a hybrid genre somewhere between documentary and fiction. Many of Jean Rouch's ethnopoetic films (like *Moi, un noir* [1957], and *La pyramide humaine* [1958–61]) blend his own and his subjects' playacting, so much so that it's hard for a spectator to separate out fact from fantasy. Rouch is an anthropologist and ethnographic filmmaker, but he describes these films as works of "ethno-fiction." Trinh Minh-ha's *Reassemblage* (1982) and *Naked Spaces: Living Is Round* (1985) combine gnomic sound tracks with stunningly beautiful visual fragments of West African architecture and landscapes. Much of the most interesting filmmaking today is happening in a fuzzy area between objective and subjective. *The Passion of Re-*

FIGURE 2 While shooting his film *Frantz Fanon: Black Skin, White Mask* (1996), director Isaac Julien reads on-camera from the Martinican revolutionary-psychiatrist's book *Black Skin, White Masks*. By interweaving studio dramatization and actuality footage, archival images and improvised acting, and interior speech and evocative music, Julien's films have rehabilitated an impressionistic style with hybrid forms that fuse fact and fantasy and blur the boundary between documentary and fiction.

membrance (1986) by Maureen Blackwood and Isaac Julien, *Testament* (1988) by John Akomfrah, *Dreaming Rivers* (1988) by Martina Attille, *Tongues Untied* (1989) by Marlon Riggs, *I'm British But* (1989) by Gurinda Chadha, *Imagining Indians* (1992) by Victor Masayesva, and *Fronterilandia/Frontierland* (1995) by Jesse Lerner and Rubén Ortiz-Torres—all these films combine poetry and performance with auto-biography and archival footage in ways that sublate traditional distinctions between fact and fiction.

An impressionistic style gets away from the earnestness and argumentative qualities of expository documentary, and tends to highlight people's subjective feelings more than other styles. However, it is not without problems of its own. Documentary stakes some claim to representing the historical world, and it may be unclear what relationship an impressionistic documentary has to reality. Robert Gardner's work, particularly *Forest of Bliss* (1988), which depicts funereal rites in Benares, India, is not stylistically complex, but it has been particularly controversial in its impressionistic quality. Are the subjective states of mind evoked in an impressionistic documentary the filmmaker's, or are they attributed to the characters, or even to the viewers? Early impressionistic films (before the invention of portable sync sound) often reflected the artistic sensibility of the filmmakers more than the actual lived experience of the people they depicted, who were at times transformed into arresting patterns of light and shade, composition and movement, at the expense of their own particular humanity. These documentaries were often shot in part in studios, set up by an "art director." Indeed, a few impressionistic films are so stylized that some spectators, unsure of the films' relation to "reality," find them frustrating.

OBSERVATIONAL: DIRECT AND VÉRITÉ

Observational cinema was a movement of the 1960s that took advantage of technical developments in the recording and editing of sync sound. A reaction against both expository and impressionistic styles, it sought to be a mirror to the world rather than a propagandistic hammer, and in this it had precursors both in the first Lumière films, catching life "on the fly," and in Robert Flaherty's work.

Prehistory: Robert Flaherty's "Slight Narratives"

Flaherty's most important film is *Nanook of the North* (1922), about the Hudson Bay Itivimuit Eskimos' struggle for survival. The film strings together a series of loosely linked vignettes. Each vignette tells a story of sorts—the building of an igloo, the spearing of a seal—but Flaherty doesn't try to fabricate one overarching, continuous narrative, as a fiction film would and as other documentaries of the period did. As Paul Rotha, a British documentary filmmaker and critic of the time, put it, Flaherty "prefers the inclusion of a slight narrative, not fictional incident or interpolated 'cameos,' but the daily routine of his native people."[7]

Flaherty did, however, partly adopt a film "language" that had been developing in fiction films ever since the days of the early Lumière documentaries: a language consisting of diverse camera angles, shots and reverse-shots, establishing shots and close-ups, pans and tilts. (Chapter 3 explains these terms, in case they're new to you.) These are cinematic codes that had been created to articulate a continuous time and space. However, all the various camera angles spliced together in the editing room and the final film bear more of a resemblance to the perspective of a superhuman spectator than to that of an individual on the scene at the time. They let the film spectator be everywhere, all at once. But there are also quite a few long takes in *Nanook,* shot from an "objective" position that doesn't tie the viewer to the optical perspectives of the characters. While many filmmakers—then and now—use short close-up shots of fragments of details and then create a sense of continuous space through montage, Flaherty at times follows action with long takes that include all of the relevant detail within the frame. (Later observational and neorealist filmmakers celebrated his work for this quality.) There is, for instance, a long and hilarious sequence of a seal hunt. Whereas other filmmakers might have cut between short close-up shots of various details of the hunt, Flaherty keeps the camera rolling and shows us Nanook, the ice hole, and eventually the seal, all in the same frame.

Flaherty was also quite a master of suspense, or what is sometimes called "slow disclosure." The film begins by introducing us to Nanook and his family as they emerge, one at a time, out of what looks like an impossibly tiny kayak. It's almost as if we're watching a magic trick in a circus. And in the seal hunt sequence, we see Nanook tugging on a line going through an ice hole, but it is only at the end that we see what he was fighting: a seal. These suspenseful moments are what gives *Nanook* drama, and what holds the spectator's interest.

Nanook was remarkable not just for its style but also for its subject matter and approach to its subject. Never before had a non-Westerner been brought alive on the screen with such sympathy and humanity. "A story," said Flaherty, "must come out of the life of a people, not from the actions of individuals."[8] Flaherty was a mining engineer and had lived among the Hudson Bay Eskimo for much of the decade before embarking on the film, and was there for a year during the making of the film itself. He was convinced that he had to live among his subjects for a long time before he would know them well enough to make a documentary faithful to their lives.

Flaherty also screened at least some of his rushes (the developed footage) for his subjects, eliciting their feedback and suggestions for future scenes that they could film. Although he may have transformed his subjects into actors in the process, he also actively collaborated with them to a degree that is still rare today. This kind of acting out was an inspiration to Jean Rouch, who has coined the concept of *anthropologie partagée* (shared anthropology).

Why the enduring appeal of *Nanook?* What was Flaherty's secret? "Non-preconception," his wife Frances said, "a method of discovery as a process of filmmaking . . . "[9] Rather than scripting all the filming in advance, Flaherty would take each day as it came. At night he would write out in his diary the ideas he had for future sequences, and he would revise them as he went along. This is also a practice of observational filmmakers today. Moreover, while expository documentary seeks to impart information or make a case for some position or another, Flaherty filmed simply in order to explore and depict life itself. As Frances Flaherty suggests, his films "do not argue. . . . What they celebrate, freely and spontaneously, simply and purely, is the thing itself for its own sake."[10]

Of course this is only true up to a point, for Flaherty's films (like anyone's) celebrate *his conception* of "the thing itself." Within our conceptions are hidden arguments, and this is as true of an observational

FIGURE 3 Building an igloo for *Nanook of the North* (1922).

style as of any other, even if it is less obvious. Flaherty was a romantic, and has been called a rhapsodist of backward areas. The American documentary filmmaker Emile de Antonio even charged that "[t]he charm and power of his camera are marred by distortions, lies, and inaccuracies which pander to a fake romantic, fake nature-boy view of society." [11] Flaherty wanted to make a film about the majesty and nobility of the Itivimuit as they were in the olden days. His camerawork disguised some tricks: the igloo in the film was not only built especially large so that it could accommodate the camera, it was also initially too dark to film in, so they knocked one side down. Nanook and his family shivered away as they pretended to sleep in the half that still stood. The Itivimuit at the time used rifles more than they used harpoons, but the film gives no hint of this. Nanook may have tried to bite a gramophone record in the film, as if it were a novelty, but in reality gramophone players were already common in the Hudson Bay. John Grierson had this to say about Flaherty's brand of romanticism: "Consider the problem of the

Eskimo. . . . His clothes and blankets most often come from Manchester, supplied by a department store in Winnipeg. . . . They listen to fur prices over the radio, and are subjected to fast operations of commercial opportunists flying in from New York." [12]

As a mining engineer, Flaherty was well aware of this, but he found contemporary Eskimo life depressing, and its Westernization sullying. Because he collaborated with Nanook, it's possible that the nostalgia for old times was as much Nanook's as it was Flaherty's. Perhaps Nanook should have shared credit as filmmaker. That would have been difficult, however, as his real name was not Nanook at all. It was actually Allakariallak. Even his family was not in fact his own. It was cast by Flaherty. [13]

While these distortions discredit the film in many people's eyes, *Nanook* is still considered a seminal film in both ethnographic and documentary film traditions. In part this is because Flaherty showed more interest in the lives of indigenous people than any Western documentary filmmaker before him, and he collaborated with them to a degree that would still do many filmmakers credit today. But it is also because of his proto-observational shooting style and his attempt to allow events on the screen to unfold as far as possible at their own pace.

Technological Developments

Observational films were born in the late 1950s and early 1960s out of technological developments that affected both shooting and editing. Previously, sound had been edited using an optical track that ran alongside the picture. But in the 1960s, most documentary editors replaced the optical track with magnetic sound stock ("mag"). Because mag is separate from the picture, it can be cut and recut without affecting the picture, and may be laid over any part of the picture a filmmaker wants. For the first time it became easy and affordable to lay people's words over other images as voice-over. Previously this was so expensive and cumbersome that it was rarely undertaken. Now, if you interviewed someone, say, about a crucial local football match but didn't want your spectators to have to look at the person talking all the time, you could simply cut a few seconds of something else into the picture track (such as shots of the game). This use of mag sound was immediately liberating for the editor and filmmaker, but it has had very different implications for film subjects, whose words could henceforth be combined with images of the filmmaker's rather than their own choosing. As documentary editor Dai Vaughan says, "Already the participants in a film are one step further from knowing what is being done to them." [14]

When you shoot film, the picture is recorded on one substance (a roll of film) and the sound on something else (a separate audio tape). However, while film moves at a constant speed, audio tape stretches and contracts, slows down and speeds up. This means that if you want to film and record someone speaking and for the spectators to both see and hear them at the same time, then you need to be able to sync the picture and sound up very precisely. Otherwise, the subject's lip movements and words will fail to match. Up until the 1960s, sync sound could only be recorded well with massive and extremely expensive equipment. This equipment was regularly used in fiction film studios but rarely wheeled onto a documentary location. Even when brought out for a documentary, it was so obtrusive that it usually transformed the social dynamics of the situation it was there to record. But within the space of a couple of years, a silent-running 16mm camera and a high-quality lightweight sound recorder had been invented. (If a camera isn't silent-running it drowns out dialogue in quiet settings.) This meant that documentary filmmakers no longer had to bring their subjects into a studio and interview them on a set; they could go anywhere in the world and record people speaking in their own words. As film historian Erik Barnouw has put it, "field footage began to talk." [15]

The result, all of a sudden, was a very different kind of documentary. Because we could at last hear people's words, commentary was felt to be reductive and restricting. Extradiegetic music fell out of favor for the same reason. Consequently, images and their sync sounds were given more freedom. Formal interviews were avoided, as the filmmakers were more interested in looking at people rather than simply listening to them, and they wanted to wait and see what people would say to one another rather than to the filmmaker. The idea was to film lived experience itself instead of summaries or reports on it as condensed in interviews. People were to be represented not as social types or aesthetic patterns, as in some expository and impressionistic films, but as flesh-and-blood individuals. Films were edited to be more faithful to real time, with digressive long takes being left in the film rather than automatically shortened or cut out. Wide-angle lenses were used and apertures closed down to maximize depth of field and convey the impression of what it was really like to have been on the scene at the time. Because the new equipment was so portable, new arenas of human experience were opened up to scrutiny—in particular, people's private and domestic lives. Cameras were often handheld, both because tripods are intrusive, and because a wobbly, handheld image somehow seemed less mediated, more authentic. As one advocate of observational cinema, Colin Young, has put it, in the 1960s it was "almost as if 'talkies' were starting all over again, but this time in the right way." [16]

Observational filmmakers initially saw themselves as reacting both against expository documentary and against the "Olympian omniscience" with which fiction films are edited. However, surprising as it may seem, most observational films are edited in a style that is closer to classic fiction films than to earlier documentary. Though they rarely have a single tight narrative, they are usually structured around a series of semiconnected scenes, which are individually often cut loosely according to the codes of conventional continuity. Observational filmmakers make a point of leaving jump cuts in their films (cuts that disrupt continuity), but their films are still shot and edited to fabricate a homogeneous space, more so than most expository films, which are designed instead to further the logic of the commentary or interview testimony. As with fiction films, observational documentaries let the spectators put the pieces together for themselves: they proceed by implication rather than demonstration, and so demand a more active viewing experience.

There are different schools of observational filmmaking. Direct Cinema is a movement that began in the 1960s in the U.S., with filmmakers like Frederick Wiseman (*Titicut Follies* [1967]), the Drew Associates, Robert Drew, Richard Leacock, and D. A. Pennebaker (*Primary* [1960], *Don't Look Back* [1966]), and Albert and David Maysles (*Salesman* [1969]). Films by the Drew Associates in particular typically build toward a crisis, not only because such a structure is inherently dramatic, but also because in critical moments people reveal aspects of their character that are normally hidden in day-to-day life.

Direct Cinema filmmakers tend to be relatively noninterventionist and self-effacing, at times aspiring to be invisible flies-on-the-wall. By contrast, the French Cinéma Vérité of Jean Rouch and Edgar Morin (*Chronicle of a Summer* [1960]) is actively interventionist. While the Drew Associates waited around until a crisis happened, Rouch and Morin tried to use the camera itself as a catalyst to induce a crisis. The filmmakers deliberately provoke moments of self-revelation. As such, Vérité is much more interactive than Direct Cinema.[17]

An observational style has long been popular among ethnographic filmmakers. David and Judith MacDougall are extremely sensitive observers of daily life (e.g., *Nawi* [1970], *Lorang's Way* [1979]), concentrating on moments of informal conversation, interaction, and self-reflection that elude almost everybody else's cameras. They are equally sensitive to the manifold and subtle effects of their influence on what they film, and deliberately leave (or introduce) traces of this in their finished films. Although their style is much more relaxed than Rouch and Morin's, they too have modified an observational style by making it not only more participatory but also mildly self-revelatory.

John Marshall (*The Meat Fight* [1957–58]) and Timothy Asch (The "Yanomamo" Series [1969–76]) also adopted an observational style in shooting chronologically edited "sequence films" around "discrete events." The problem with this is that events are rarely discrete, and that most of social life is not made up of "events" anyway. Nonetheless, their sequence films reveal an attention to the lived world of non-Western people that is still rare today. Marshall's first feature-length film, *The Hunters* (1958), was rather more synthetic. It follows four !Kung hunters as they track a giraffe in the Kalahari Desert. While the film presents it as a single hunt, the footage is actually a pastiche of shots taken over several years. (If you look carefully you may notice that the number of giraffes sometimes changes between shots; occasionally even the number of hunters!) Its ethnography has since been shown to be wanting too: the film is very much a Flahertian struggle for survival, but we now know that the !Kung were more gatherers than hunters at this time, and were not as short of food as the film implies. It was, however, an important film, for although Marshall's voice-over attributed thoughts to the hunters that may sound patronizing and improbable to an audience today, it displayed an interest in the subjective lives of indigenous people that surpassed both anything in its day and Flaherty's *Nanook* a quarter of a century previously.

As a way of conveying the rhythms and texture of everyday life, a (modified) observational style is still unsurpassed. Like the other styles, however, observational filmmaking runs into difficulties of its own. Some of these turn on its relationship to reality. Direct filmmakers were often naive about their (lack of) effect on what they were filming, and spoke as if it really was possible to be flies-on-the-wall in intimate settings. At times they seem to have assumed that what occurred while they were there is what would have occurred had they not been there. More interactive (and Vérité) filmmakers have a slightly different problem. By conceiving of the camera as a deliberate provocation, they conflate social actors and filmic actors, and deflect attention from what life would have been like without the camera. Since the films are decreed to be about life in front of the camera, life as it would go on without a camera present is not a question that is even raised.

Moreover, although many observational filmmakers dispense with voice-over, claiming that they want a more democratic style in which the images speak for themselves, even images are shot, selected, and set in a sequence by the filmmaker. While sync images may *seem* to be objective or transparent to their object, they, too, display the invisible hand and authorial perspective of the filmmaker: they are not automatically elevated to some higher ethical ground.

Observational films are also largely confined to the cinematic present, except insofar as screen subjects reflect out loud on the past. They are sometimes criticized for not providing an historical or other context to the events they show. One response to such criticism has been an increasing use of interviews in documentary films. Interviews allow witnesses to say things to the camera that they wouldn't think of saying to their friends or family. They can also add a personal dimension, lacking in some observational films where the filmmakers seem to be very much outsiders to the lives they're depicting. A few innovative filmmakers, like Emile de Antonio and Errol Morris, play with interview testimony, showing it to be partial and at times misleading. In many cases, however, the taking up of interviews has meant a return to an earlier expository style, with the interview segments standing in for the now forsaken commentary.

REFLEXIVE

Another response to the limitations of the observational style was already evident in Vérité. Rouch and Morin's *Chronicle of a Summer* begins by asking people on the streets of Paris, vox pop style, whether they're happy (it's 1960, in the middle of the Algerian War). It goes on to show the subjects sitting in a theater, watching and criticizing an early version of the film, and ends with the two filmmakers walking the corridors of the Musée de l'Homme evaluating the making of the film as a whole. This self-conscious, or self-reflexive, style addresses the process of representation itself and foregrounds the relationship between the filmmaker and the spectators as well as between the filmmaker and the subjects. Though it extends back beyond the Russian revolutionary filmmaker Dziga Vertov's *The Man with a Movie Camera* (1929), reflexivity has only recently become popular, with films like Jean-Pierre Gorin's *Poto and Cabengo* (1979), Trinh Minh-ha's *Reassemblage,* and Errol Morris's *The Thin Blue Line* (1987).

Some reflexive films accentuate the interactive qualities of Vérité, and set them in the first person: the filmmaker may either appear on-screen, or talk to us (or him- or herself) in voice-over. Many autobiographical films, such as Ed Pincus's *Diaries* (1971–76) or Ross McElwee's *Sherman's March* (1985), seem to be fashioned as filmic analogies to a diary, conveying a similar feel for the contingent, personal, and meditative qualities of our emotional lives. Other films are more formally than personally reflexive, showing themselves to be constructed texts or highlighting the relationship between cinema and the world.

Tim Asch and Napoleon Chagnon's *The Ax Fight* (1975) was one of the earlier explicitly reflexive ethnographic films. It is structured into five parts: (1) the sync "rushes" of a fight in a Yanomamo village; (2) a black screen over which three bewildered men (Asch, Chagnon, and the sound recordist) try to make sense of what they've just seen, and Chagnon suggests incest as a cause; (3) intertitles and kinship charts explaining that the filmmakers' speculations were wrong and that the fight had to do with a lineage conflict; (4) the rushes are shown for a second time, though now with a voice-over commentary, slow motion, and pointers identifying individual protagonists; and (5) a shortened, edited version of the fight. *The Ax Fight* is subversive of mainstream documentary practice because the fifth section would normally be all that would make it through to the final film. By including the first four parts, the film highlights the condensation and reduction inherent in the editing process. The second part reveals the conjectures and refutations of the anthropologist-film team as they struggle to make sense of what's going on.

While a reflexive style fills in a gap that other styles tend to ignore, it has its own problems. It is occasionally accused of intellectual elitism and even narcissism. If a film is more formally than politically reflexive, it may lose sight of the historical world of which documentary tries to provide a record. Also, if all a film does is to remind spectators that they're watching a representation of reality rather than reality itself, then the filmmaker would seem to suppose, as film critic Louis Comolli has suggested, that spectators are "total imbeciles, completely alienated human beings, in order to believe that they are thoroughly deceived and deluded by (filmic) simulacra."[18] Moreover, reflexivity does not provide the unassailable assurance of the filmmaker's morality or sincerity that some viewers might hope for. In Mitchell Block's *No Lies* (1973), a student filmmaker mercilessly interrogates a friend about her recent rape. Her seeming insouciance finally cracks under his barrage of questions, and she breaks down before his (still rolling) camera. It is not until the end credits that we learn that, despite the observational style of the camerawork, we have just watched a work of pure fiction. As this example shows, it's as easy (if not easier) to stage a reflexive scene as any other kind. There's nothing to stop you from scrupulously setting up a Vérité-style scene featuring yourself on-camera, listening to apparently innocent bystanders talking, supposedly spontaneously, about anything under the sun. You might even get away with it.

Movements and styles come and go. What is exciting initially soon becomes commonplace and exhausted, and other innovations are in order. But all four of these styles are still in use today, in countless different configurations. The challenge is to invent and improvise new twists to old styles, not for their own sake, but as you wrestle with and respond to your subject. Documentary is on an impossible and unending quest to depict the depth of life as it is actually lived. Life will always run away from our films, and exceed our grasp, but the task, however vain, is to run after it again.

2. From Fieldwork to Filming

As an academic, I had assumed that I
could learn about anything by reading
about it. Long ago I thought that being
told "how to film" would be all I
would need in order to produce a
satisfactory film. But film . . . is a
complex medium. If we come from
an academic background, we are not
trained in its use to the extent that we
are trained in the medium of words.
Instead, we are taught to move
"quickly and efficiently" from the
realm of observation to the realm of
words. These words are simply markers
of the mental constructs with which we
work. We are hardly taught to work
with images or to broaden our ability
to observe.

—Allison Jablonko

Documentary films are made for all sorts of reasons: an ardent wish to communicate ideas about people on film, a heartfelt need to commit a long-term project to a visual medium, an accidental encounter with a remarkable individual. Producing films involves a mixture of intellectual, emotional, and practical concerns, any one of which may override the others at different points. As a filmmaker, you will probably ask yourself more than once: Can I make this film? Why do I want to make this film? What do I want to show, or to say? Making documentaries is a constant process of self-examination and reevaluation.

Along the way, you'll be making many choices. Not the least of these are how to begin: where to make the film, what to make it about, and who to focus on. If you're an anthropologist, and have an established field site, you may have already made these choices. Feel free, then, to skim over the following pages if they seem redundant. But remember that choosing a film site is only a small part of deciding on the subject for a film. Certain concepts, too, may be more easily and economically communicated in words than on film. At the same time, film offers possibilities of its own, such as the portrayal of living experience, in ways that are unavailable to writing.

TOPIC

It's important that you make committed choices and that you care about what you film. This doesn't ensure you'll make a better or more emotionally engaging film (although you probably will). It's just that making films is such a difficult and all-encompassing endeavor that if you're not wholeheartedly committed to what you're doing, you may not make it through the long haul—the inevitable sticky moments on location and the seemingly endless days and nights in the editing room.

Not all topics can be explored easily in film; or rather, not all ways of conceiving topics lend themselves to film. Although film is capable of

◀ FIGURE 4 American anthropologist Annette Weiner and Trobriand friend take a stroll during the production of *The Trobriand Islanders of Papua New Guinea* (1990).

abstraction, and its construction is usually complex, it's important to remember that it is a concrete, experiential medium. Part of the attraction of film is its affinity with life itself—the movement on the screen evoking the movement we ourselves experience outside the cinema, the seeing evoking our own seeing, and hearing evoking hearing. To label a film "documentary" is to assert that it has a specific, indexical relationship to its pro-filmic subject. Thus, whether you want to make a film about legal disputes, gender relations, or colonialism, about an individual, a personal relationship, or an institution, it's important to remember that film is essentially an audiovisual medium. It can *show* as well as simply *say*. Why not use the medium to its and your best advantage? Rather than relying only on written documents, narration, and interview testimony to tell your or your subjects' stories, try imagining the sorts of images that could tell the stories. Consider filming events and conversations, rather than monologues: life as it is lived rather than as it is reported upon. And bear in mind, too, that landscapes and cityscapes, physical interactions and spatial relationships, gestures and objects can all speak to an audience in ways that spoken dialogue cannot.

As you focus on a topic, there are some practical considerations to remember, above all its feasibility. There's always a danger to setting out to make a film about a single, short-lived event, especially if you're working within a tight schedule. One group of student filmmakers at the University of California, Berkeley, planned to make a film about a transgender beauty contest in San Francisco, only for it to be postponed until after the end of the semester, by which time their project had to be finished. They were forced to refocus their film completely, following two people they had met during their research. Since both were at different stages of a sex change, they had a provocative film topic.[1] As you get caught up in preproduction and production, you can forget that life very rarely coincides with your imagined script.

LOCATION

Many of you will start with a location, and decide what to shoot once you see what emerges during your preproduction research or fieldwork. Quite a few documentary (and especially ethnographic) filmmakers have had a long-term dedication to one locale, or to a single group of people. Both Jean Rouch and John Marshall have worked (on and off) with the same people over a thirty-year period. Robert Gardner's latest film, *Roads End* (in progress), was shot among the Dani, with some of the individuals featured in his earlier film *Dead Birds,* which he completed in 1963. In each case, they were able to produce additional films, either because of changes within the community, or because of changes in their own perspectives and interests.

Others of you may cast about for locations, wondering both where and what to film. When Paul Hockings and Mark McCarty set out to film *The Village* (1968), their goal was simply to produce "a general ethnographic account of life in one Irish village."[2] Hockings drove through 300 villages in western Ireland, in a quest for the ideal site: a small village with a pub, church, and crossroads! His problem was that he had an image of a "normal" village in his head which eluded him on the ground. As he says, almost none of the villages "had a close clustering of houses that could *look* like a village in some establishing shot."[3] Finally, they settled on Dunquin, such a scenic spot that it was featured the following year in the narrative film, *Ryan's Daughter.*

The Village is a fine film, but there are problems inherent in seeking out "perfect locations." There's a danger of imposing preconceptions on a particular place, rather than allowing your ideas to emerge from real experiences there. To an outside viewer, Dunquin might have looked like a quintessential Irish village when in fact it was quite atypical. So, as you're on the lookout for a location, ask yourself whether it needs to be "typical" or representative at all, and if so, of what?

Plan as you might, film locations often seem to pick themselves, sometimes for arbitrary, sometimes for practical reasons. The setting for David and Judith MacDougall's Turkana Conversations Trilogy (*The Wedding Camels* [1977], *Lorang's Way, A Wife among Wives* [1982]) was almost accidental. In 1968 they had shot *To Live with Herds* (1972) and *Under the Men's Tree* (1974) among the pastoral Jie in Uganda. Their interest in East African herding societies stayed with them, and they wrote grant proposals to return to make more films. By the time they received their grants, however, Idi Amin was in power in Uganda, and the long-term filming they envisaged was too dangerous. Instead, in 1974, they decided to relocate their project just over the border to Kenya, among the neighboring Turkana.[4] Likewise, we had planned in

1991 to make a film on tourism among the Dogon in Mali, but there was a coup d'état a couple of months before we were to leave, and a civil war ensued. There weren't going to be many tourists around. We still had the following months earmarked to make a film, and ended up collaborating with Gabai Baaré, an art dealer, and Christopher Steiner, an anthropologist, to make *In and Out of Africa* (1992). Shot in the Ivory Coast and the U.S., it addresses questions of authenticity, taste, and racial politics in the international African art market. Though we'd been interested in these themes for some time, we hadn't originally planned to make a film about them.

Quite a few films are shot in more than one location. Jean Rouch's *Jaguar* (1954–67) and *Madame L'Eau* both depict journeys—from Niger to the Gold Coast (Ghana), and from Niger to the Netherlands, respectively. These journeys provoke psychological and social as much as physical transformations. Jorge and Mabel Preloran's *Zulay, Facing the 21st Century* (1993) is about an Ecuadorian woman called Zulay. Zulay is living with the filmmakers, Argentinean expatriates, in Los Angeles, but her family is back in Otavalo. The film moves back and forth between Zulay's family talking to her through the camera in Otavalo, and Zulay screening their "letters" in L.A. The film ends with Zulay, wearing traditional Otavaleño costume, watching the latest message from her mother. She bursts into tears on hearing her mother say that perhaps it would be best if she stayed in Los Angeles and didn't return home. Our own *In and Out of Africa* follows a Muslim Hausa art trader from Abidjan, in the Ivory Coast, to Long Island, New York, buying art objects in Africa and selling them in America. In places it was edited so that you can't be sure whether you're in Africa or America. We did this in a deliberate attempt to get viewers to wonder what kind of associations they may have unconsciously invested in the very distinction.

Films set in more than one location are becoming increasingly common. They are an inevitable response to the complicated conditions of social life in the contemporary "world system." Societal structures are increasingly a reflex of a more or less global and transnational economic system and are no longer either conceivable in terms of local knowledge or accessible to everyday lived experience. Multi-locale documentary is one kind of attempt to represent these conditions and to come to terms with the modern-day deterritorialization of culture.

Even if you wish to make a film that highlights such processes of globalization, there is no compulsion to set it in more than one location. After all, globalizing forces are manifested locally, and you can visualize this same interplay of presence and absence in a single place. The MacDougalls' *Under the Men's Tree,* for instance, depicts East African Jie men telling tales about motor cars (something few of them have any firsthand experience of) as they casually craft leather objects. And their *To Live with Herds* makes the impact of exogenous development policies on the Jie plain to see. Marilu Mallet's *Unfinished Diary* (1983) uses her own first-person voice to depict her life in Canada—exiled from her native Chile and estranged from her Australian-Canadian filmmaker-husband. All the dislocation that she experiences is immanent in her Montreal apartment.

A final question to ask yourself as you choose your location(s) is a practical one: *can* you film there? Technically, films can be made almost anywhere these days, from the flanks of K2 to the depths of the Atlantic. Regardless of where you will film—even if it's at home or just down the block—you should remember that making a film is much more cumbersome and conspicuous than doing fieldwork with a notepad and pencil, or even a still camera. The equipment is usually heavier and requires more care and additional crew. When you come to record picture and sound, light and noise will disturb you more than they ever have before. If you're unprepared, adverse weather conditions can ruin your equipment and film or tape stock. Moreover, the days when a filmmaker or anthropologist could walk blithely into an area with a camera are gone. First of all, anthropologists and other outsiders never really were inconspicuous. Secondly, in these days of global media awareness, many people around the world are conscious of what a camera can and cannot do, and are likely to have strong feelings about whether or not they want to be in your film. The chances are they will make this quite clear, either with vocal refusal or enthusiastic assent whenever you start rolling. Additionally, if you're filming in an urban or densely populated area, you may find, not only that you're unable to cut out unwanted background noise, but also that your recording is subject to electric interference. You may need as well to watch out for the security of your crew and equipment. Finally, many national governments and regional representatives may require that you get special permissions to shoot in their jurisdiction. (See "Travel" in chapter 6 for more detail.)

PEOPLE

Finding the people to be in your film (your "subjects") may take some time and work, even if you're a seasoned fieldworker or filmmaker. Flaherty cast his films by mixing and matching stereotypes. The families featured in *Nanook of the North, Man of Aran* (1934), and *Louisiana Story* (1948) were not real families: they were Flaherty's conception of an ideal-typical Eskimo, Irish, and Cajun family.[5]

While casting (and narrating) of this kind is certainly problematic in a documentary, it is quite widespread. Just as the narrative structures of most documentaries are curiously conventional (beginning with an introduction to characters and locale, telling a story oriented to a goal and climax, and ending with some kind of resolution), the relationships they depict tend to be equally familiar. Relationships within and between families, and between generations, are the subject of as much documentary as fictional representation. They derive their resonance from real relationships that the viewers can relate to in their own society.

When James Blue and David MacDougall set out in 1972 to make *Kenya Boran* (1974), they searched for a family that exemplified the rapid social and economic change that Boran society was undergoing at the time. In the end, they couldn't find one. Instead, they structured the film around four characters, two fathers and their sons. The fathers were from different villages, but knew each other already. The sons came to know each other during the filming. *Kenya Boran* ends up exploring relationships both between and within generations. It is an interesting hybrid between observational and participatory cinema. Although some of the conversations involve subjects suggested by the filmmakers—such as education or population control—for most of the time Blue and MacDougall were simply sitting around waiting to see what would happen.[6]

The process of casting usually involves choosing not only relationships that will resonate for the viewer but also subjects with particular personalities. Much of the charm of Flaherty's films comes from his engaging characters. David MacDougall has noticed that ethnographic filmmakers often "either seek out exotically interesting types in other societies or people who conform to familiar figures in their own, at the expense of people more characteristic of the society being filmed. One thinks immediately of those 'stars' of the ethnographic cinema—among them, Nanook, Damouré, N!ai and Ongka."[7]

Certainly these four celebrities fit the bill of the classic hero or heroine, someone slightly apart from his or her own community, on a quest of some kind. Nanook is the romantic hero, battling the forces of Nature in order to feed his family, traveling miles to find an appropriate place to build his igloo. Damouré also embarks on a journey: in Rouch's *Jaguar* he's one of three young men off to seek his fortune in the Gold Coast, and in *Madame L'Eau,* he's one of three older men, off in search of the bittersweet benefits of applied technology in Holland. In John Marshall's *N!ai, the Story of a !Kung Woman* (1980), N!ai strives to make a living for herself and her family, fighting against the forces of cultural change. In Charlie Nairn's *The Kawelka—Ongka's Big Moka* (1974), a film about the Kawelka of Papua New Guinea, Ongka pools his resources in order to hold a *moka,* a ritual gift-giving ceremony, only to have it continually postponed. These are goals and struggles Western audiences can relate to, and plots whose basics they already know by rote. Add a little humor, a climax, and a resolution and you have the trappings of a film that will play in Peoria (or at least in Peoria schools).

Of course there's nothing wrong with filming people who will appeal to your audience. But you should ask yourself why they have that appeal: if their personality conforms to your conception of an engaging or extraordinary individual, does it have the same resonance in their own society? Are they indeed representative in the way you suppose? Of course, no one is ever wholly representative, nor do you have to make films about individuals who are more so than others. But you need to query why it is you want to cast someone.

Some filmmakers have known their subjects for years. Jean Rouch had been friends with Damouré for over a decade before they collaborated on *Jaguar.* John Marshall has worked among the !Kung Ju/'hoansi since 1951, and knew N!ai when she was a little girl. Ethnographic filmmaker Tim Asch taught scores of aspiring visual anthropologists, telling them countless times, "Know your subject. . . . Spend time with them, cultivating a relationship. If you can't do that, then collaborate with an anthropologist who has."

FIGURE 5 While filming among the Ju/'hoañsi (!Kung), John Marshall worked with
N!ai for over twenty years. The top image shows N!ai as a young girl in the early
1950s; the bottom image shows her in 1978.

Often the first people you meet when you start a project end up not being involved at all. People have their own personal and political motivations to gravitate toward the camera, just as you do toward them. Social life itself has performative elements, and filmmaking fits right in to them. (Warren Beatty takes this to its logical limits in *Truth or Dare* [1991] when he discloses to the camera that Madonna "doesn't want to live off camera, much less talk. . . . There's nothing to say off camera. Why would you say something if it's off camera? There's no point in existing.") Since each contact you make can lead to another and may provide you with deeper insights into your subject matter, you're not necessarily wasting your time by getting to know the people you meet right off. At the same time, it makes sense to be wary of people who are overly enthusiastic about being in your film. Ask yourself what's in it for them.

Bear in mind that film has the power to make ordinary people look interesting and celebrities appear mundane. You'll wield an extraordinary amount of control over your material while shooting and editing. You don't need a star like Madonna to make a compelling film. (Nor does a star guarantee that the film will be interesting.) As producer Craig Gilbert says of *An American Family* (1972), his documentary series about the Loud family of Santa Barbara, it "was based on the belief that there is considerable drama in the daily lives of ordinary citizens. The citizens themselves may be unaware of this, as the Louds were, but it is there just the same, waiting to be captured by the peculiar alchemy of the camera in the hands of anyone with the ability to see and the patience to wait."[8] While the filmmakers waited, a number of significant events occurred in the lives of the Loud family: the parents, Bill and Pat, decided to divorce; the oldest son, Lance, revealed that he was homosexual; and the oldest daughter, Delilah, fell in love for the first time. Yet Gilbert says that these developments had not been anticipated. He insists that "*Whatever happened* would have revealed, within the context of the Louds' daily life, as much about how men and women feel about each other as those events that actually did occur."[9]

One final point about casting. Quite aside from the kind of representation you will go on to make, the very act of filming is a political endeavor. In a small close-knit society, who you choose to feature, and who not, may have significant repercussions, even changing the balance of power. Try to be as sensitive as you can to how your filming might affect people's lives and relationships to each other.

RAPPORT

> What is now so clear to me is that you can tell people a thousand times that you are making a film or writing a book about their village, you can show the film to them or have it programmed on television but what is essential for them is you as a person. They said it to me quite clearly: "We agreed to collaborate with you on your film through the friendship that we developed with you."
>
> —Colette Piault

The kind of personal investment by your subjects in your film that Colette Piault is talking about is truer of ethnographic film than your typical television documentary. If you will be on location for a substantial period of time, or engaged in any long-term interaction with your subjects, it's important to build rapport. Observational filming, in particular, can be very intrusive and demands considerable cooperation and trust. This is not to say that once you're all committed to making a film, you're going to live together happily ever after. That is rarely the case. Your relationships will probably fluctuate over time. Even if you build rapport slowly and conscientiously, it may not always progress as surely as you might like.

It's important to start off by establishing trust. People are often suspicious about outsiders coming into their community, and may be curious about what you're up to. Making a documentary is probably (but not always) more innocent than many other hidden agendas they might imagine. You should be both honest and tactful in explaining your curiosity about their lives. You're better off telling people at the start why you want to talk to them, rather than letting them find out accidentally or at the end of your project. Be careful how you describe your interests. If you want to make a film about "gender relations," and come in to a community announcing as much, they may think either that you're off your rocker or that it has nothing to do with them. It helps to articulate

FIGURE 6 Timothy Asch being kissed by a Yanomamo friend.

your interest in individuals, or at least types of individuals, in a way that
expresses a concern for the specific community itself. As Craig Gilbert
notes, "Human beings do not like to be treated like guinea pigs. If you
tell the subjects of a documentary that their behavior and their lives are
being used to make a larger statement about human behavior and human lives in general, they are more than likely going to be highly in-
sulted. We all tend to think of ourselves as special and unique, with
problems, fears, likes, and dislikes different from those of every other
person in the world." [10]

Paul Hockings describes how he began work on *The Village:*

> The best way to get started was to tell everybody we could, ex-
> actly what we were up to. We emphasized that we were from the
> University of California and not Hollywood; hence our relative
> poverty. We visited the parish priest in a neighboring village,
> wrongly believing that an audience with him would win us ac-
> ceptance in Dunquin. We allowed people to watch us filming
> the most innocuous things, cows and hedgerows and hillsides,
> so that they could see that the camera was not really threatening

even though it looked like an elephant gun. And most importantly, McCarty and I began taking Gaelic lessons every morning. I can't say we made very great strides in what is perhaps the
most difficult of all Indo-European tongues, but we could make
small talk in the bar.[11]

While mastering Gaelic is hardly a prerequisite of cross-cultural documentary, knowing at least a little of the language of the people you're
filming can go a long way toward building rapport. Ideally, we would
be fluent in all of our subjects' languages, but this is not always realistic.
Even if you still need to rely on an interpreter part of the time, learning
a few words of someone's language testifies to your interest in and respect for their community.

If you're going to be on location for any stretch of time, you may
need to be self-conscious about the role you set up for yourself. This
doesn't necessarily entail establishing fictive kinship ties with everyone,
but it does mean forming an identity in the community. The most honest and perhaps the easiest is to present yourself as the filmmaker(s) you
are. David MacDougall usually wears his camera brace and camera constantly when he's on location. Even when he and Judith are just "hanging out" with their subjects, they're ready to roll with a minimum of
fuss. As a result, from the point of view of many of their subjects, they're
always filming. Their subjects know that they are there to film, that this
is their "job." Because the camera is always attached to the frame in
front of David's eye, the dynamics of their social interactions change
little when they start rolling film.

If you come into a community with a crew, crew members, too, become involved in local life (whether they like it or not). Anthropologists
Mariane Ferme and Colette Piault both recount stories of how their
sound technicians have been prized for their ability and willingness to
fix villagers' broken electronic goods. According to Ferme, the sound
recordist on *The Mende* (1990) "fixed countless radios, cuckoo clocks
and just about anything, you name it. Within a few days . . . the rumor
had spread in the chiefdom that this guy could fix. And people started
traveling. . . . People came from the neighboring chiefdom—a day's
walk away—to bring their old grandfather's clocks which had long since

stopped working. And big ghetto blaster radios; . . . they came with all their electronic equipment. He was probably the most adored person on the whole film crew." [12]

Any number of anthropologists warn against "going native." This may be easier said than done, and obviously depends on your own personality as well as the kind of community you'll be filming in. (If you're filming in your own community, you're already a native.) During the filming of *An American Family,* Craig Gilbert had to transfer one member of his film crew, Susan Lester, from location to the office, because she developed too close a personal relationship with the mother, Pat Loud. Apparently the two spent much of the time talking to each other. As Gilbert was shooting Direct Cinema-style, these interactions were unusable. As Gilbert says, Lester felt that his "early admonition not to get involved with the affairs of the Loud family was not only unworkable but inhuman. . . . She added that if there had to be a choice . . . between maintaining a friendship and the integrity of a film, she would opt for the friendship every time." [13]

Situations like this involve difficult decisions and it may not always be clear which way to go. There may be other contexts in which you find your participation with your subjects leading you (consciously or not) to make a puff-piece—an advocacy film. If you find that happening, ask yourself if it's compatible with your conception of documentary. After all, advocating—like attacking—a cause or a person is not the same as documenting them and can lead to easy, and potentially propagandistic, moralizing. As one ethnographic filmmaker exhorts:

> I want to warn us (myself included) to withstand the temptation to make "nice" films. One hazard which accompanies our general ideology of cultural relativism is that we tend to make "nice" films about people who are not very "nice" at all. We will too often film the wedding ceremony with all its colorful gaiety, and shy away from showing the conflicts, confusion and contradictions which often precede and more often follow the ceremony and feasting. Clearly, showing what the culture demands necessitates a focus on both big and small events and on people and activities which are both "nice" as well as not "nice." [14]

Ethical issues are rarely discussed in film production manuals. Ethics make us uncomfortable. They seem to demand a hard-and-fast code of right and wrong. But right and wrong are culturally and contextually, personally and professionally relative. Documentary filmmakers often find themselves performing a balancing act between their ethical responsibility to their subjects, to themselves, and to their viewers. Also, unless you already have a long-standing relationship to the community you'll be filming in, you may well be identified in some sense as belonging to the "media." The journalistic search for the spectacular, as well as the topical requirements of broadcast "news," has pushed the limits of the ethical in ways that implicate us as documentary filmmakers too.[15]

The American Anthropological Association has tried to clarify the professional responsibility of anthropologists with a Statement on Ethics. Currently under revision, the statement does not specifically address filmmaking. Here is an excerpt:

> Anthropologists' relations with their discipline, with the individuals and groups among whom they conduct research or to whom they provide services, with their employers and with their host governments, are varied, complex, sensitive, and sometimes difficult to reconcile. In a field of such complex involvements, misunderstandings, conflicts and the need to make choices among apparently incompatible values are constantly generated. . . .
>
> Anthropologists' first responsibility is to those whose lives and culture they study. Should conflicts of interest arise, the interests of these people take precedence over other considerations. Anthropologists must do everything in their power to protect the dignity and the privacy of the people with whom they work, conduct research or perform other professional activities. Their physical, social and emotional safety and welfare are the professional concerns of the anthropologists who have worked among them.[16]

As with any code, this is more abstract than practical. How do you define or determine "the interests" of other people? How do you protect them? Above all, if there are conflicts of interest between various of your subjects, how do you balance them? In short, each case has to be evaluated separately.

When you're faced with concrete ethical dilemmas, as you inevitably will be when making a film, a code can't provide you with the answers. Ethical problems will arise despite your best intentions. They may even emerge after your film is finished and in distribution. One of the most famous examples is Tanya Ballantyne's National Film Board of Canada film *The Things I Cannot Change* (1966). Intended as a sympathetic portrait of poverty in Canada, the film was approved of by its participants after a screening. Yet when it was publicly shown, the family it focused on was criticized by the community.

IMAGE-MAKING

Some ethical issues are specific to filmmaking. Regardless of the filmmaker's intentions, filmic representations are often perceived as the Truth: since you see it, it must be so. By the time you get to edit your own films, you'll see that nothing is further from the case. Cinematic representations are as constructed as any other. But, paradoxical as it may seem, film seems to connote both immediacy and timelessness. Events captured on film seem to be locked in time, virtually repeating themselves at every screening. As film critic Brian Winston points out, "these texts have extended, perhaps nearly indefinite, lives. Paul, the failed salesman in the Maysles film of that name, is constantly exposed as such wherever documentary film classes are taught or Maysles retrospectives are held. The anonymous midwestern boy who spews his heart up as a result of a drug overdose in Wiseman's *Hospital* (1970), spews away every time the film is screened. Should it be played in the community where he is now, one hopes, a stable and respectable citizen, there is nothing he can do about it." [17] Similarly, the Yanomamo of Mishimishimaböwei-teri erupt into violence every time Asch and Chagnon's *The Ax Fight* is shown, and the !Kung fall into drunken disputes during each screening of John Marshall's *N!ai*. While Asch and Marshall probably never intended such a narrow interpretation, their films are often shown in anthropology classes as films about these peoples ("the Yanomamo" or "the !Kung"), rather than as films about certain individuals in a particular place at a particular time.

Some of these ethical issues stem not just from the public nature of cinema but also from film's indexical, lifelike qualities. The print-based reports of journalists, historians, and anthropologists may also be read years later, time and again. Some occasionally have undesirable repercussions in the communities they represent. But on film, the impact of representing a human being is very different. The midwestern boy in *Hospital* might be unnamed in the film and named in a newspaper report, but as we actually watch him throwing up, can he really be said to be anonymous at all?

The ethics of the making of a film are manifested in various ways in the film's aesthetics. Most viewers sense the filmmaker's attitude toward their subjects—be it contempt or respect, compassion or cynicism, arrogance or humility. Even a documentary reveals qualities of its maker as well as its subject. The way subjects are framed, the shots they're juxtaposed to, the images their voices are laid over, how long they're allowed to talk for and what about, the revelation of a camera pan or tilt, whether the style disguises or discloses the filmmaker's authorial presence—in all these ways an audience pieces together clues about the filmmaker's intellectual and behavioral point of view.

Among the questions, then, that you should ask yourself are the following: If you edit an interview tightly, are you cutting someone off? That is, are you not giving them the time they deserve? Are you deliberately omitting lines that would round them out as a person or complicate their position but diminish the dramatic impact when they are juxtaposed to another person saying something different? Are you editing them to say something that you know is not their opinion? Conversely, if you shoot and edit in long takes, are you allowing your subjects to speak their piece, or are you letting them ramble on long enough to embarrass themselves? If you reassemble significant events in someone's life in a quick montage, are you trivializing? Or might you be "aestheticizing" them? If you show shots of a person in extreme poverty next to a shot of a rich person, are you implying that one is exploitative of the other? Or are you simply saying that one's class is exploitative of the other's class? Even if you don't deliberately intend either of such possibly reductive readings, is it right to leave such a potential connotation available to the spectators? If so, how do you decide what's fair? Fair to whom?

When considering issues like these, you need also to have your audience(s) in mind. In the later stages of editing *In and Out of Africa,* we sought to counter the reactions of some American anthropologists (of diverse backgrounds) who had seen earlier rough cuts. They had hissed, booed, or laughed contemptuously when certain characters reappeared on the screen. We tried to foreclose such a moralistic reading, which would divide the film's subjects into two camps—good guys (Africans) and bad guys (Americans)—and which impeded further reflection on the issues we hoped the film would raise (one of which was precisely to render such banal binary oppositions problematic). Thus, even as you may struggle against classic conventions of dramaturgy, you need to be aware that certain viewers will still try to project drama of that kind onto your film.

At the same time, you shouldn't forget that viewing should be an active experience. Films are always susceptible to unanticipated interpretations, and there's no way you could or should prevent all alternative responses to your material. As editor Dai Vaughan has insisted, "We cannot boast of leaving our films open-ended and at the same time complain if people draw from them conclusions we dislike."[18]

RESPONSIBILITY TO SUBJECTS

In photographic interactions, what do subjects consent to? To have their pictures taken or to have them used in some way?

—Lisa Henderson

Much of the debate around how best to protect screen subjects revolves around a principle of informed consent: what are the conditions under which consent may be given in which it is truly informed about the contexts in which the material will be screened and the consequences thereof? Your subjects may be "media literate"—that is, recognize fleeting two-dimensional motion pictures for what they are—and their understanding of your film about them has as much validity as any other, but they probably won't be in a position to gauge how your representation of their lives will be received by others. Of course, none of us (subjects or filmmakers) can ever be exactly sure, unless we sign a release form limiting the viewers to those few people we personally know so well that we can predict with absolute certainty how they'll respond. Even then we might be surprised. When a documentary is broadcast on television, how many of us feel confident in predicting how viewers will react? When a film about people from one culture is shown to an audience from another, the cultural distance between subjects and spectators is such that your characters' ideas about the context of the film's reception may be hazy, impressionistic, and perhaps altogether wrong.

How, then, to decide whether consent is informed or uninformed? Documentary film critic Calvin Pryluck suggests the following:

> In the scientific literature, there is wide consensus that consent is not valid unless it was made (1) under conditions that were free of coercion and deception, (2) with full knowledge of the procedure and anticipated effects, (3) by someone competent to consent. The requirement that consent be truly voluntary is a recognition of the fact that there is typically an unequal power relationship between investigators and subjects; the disproportion of status and sophistication is subtly coercive. . . . Considerable argument has developed over what constitutes "informed consent" but one point is clear. *Consent is flawed when obtained by the omission of any fact that might influence the giving or withholding of permission.*[19]

It's easy to assume that we will all make films that are "free of coercion and deception." Or will we? The release forms that filmmakers typically ask their subjects to sign usually give the filmmakers the right to use (or *not* use) the subjects' image and words as they like, and bugger the consequences. (For examples of release forms, see appendix 1.) Intended principally as a protection for the filmmaker (in case of a subsequent lawsuit), a release form also theoretically lets your subjects know what their involvement in your film legally entails. But, in the U.S. at least, release forms tend to be written in such complicated legalese that few people actually read them before signing. If they were to read them, they might find that they had very nearly signed their life away. Indeed, in much of the world, particularly in countries of absolutist state power or political corruption, simply signing a sheet of paper could be extremely dangerous. In such contexts, even asking someone to sign a release could be an unethical act. Moreover, standard release forms do not take into account the fact that notions of property—"intellectual," image-based, and otherwise—are culturally variable. In cross-cultural contexts, your subjects' conception of morally acceptable uses and abuses of their image may in fact be unreconcilable with your own. Additionally, as a practical matter, release forms are usually in the language of the filmmakers, and not necessarily in those of the subjects. Some subjects may not even understand what they're being asking to sign—hardly a guarantee of informed consent.

Numerous documentaries, for instance, have been made over the years about the police in the U.S. Often the filmmakers establish initial contact with the police and then enjoy access thereby to all the people the police come into contact with. Many such films have been shot "over the shoulders" of law enforcement authorities. Few people entangled with the police have the time or presence of mind to turn to a camera operator and ask them to stop shooting. And if a film crew, buttressed by the police, asks them to sign a release, they probably won't call a lawyer to look over the form. Can we really say that they were not coerced?

Coercion can take more subtle forms. When Albert and David Maysles shot sales customers in their documentary film *Salesman*, they'd show up at the door with the salesman and explain what they were up to. "That took me maybe thirty seconds," says Albert. "Most people at that point would then say they understood, even though perhaps they didn't; but we would try to explain honestly what we were really about, and that was enough. Then when the filming was over . . . they would say, 'Tell me once more what this is all about,' and then we would explain and give them a release form which they would sign." [20] Clearly, the aura of film equipment and the presence of a crew can frighten people into signing.

Going back to the American Anthropological Association's Statement on Ethics, and wondering how you can reconcile the various interests of your subjects, you may have an analogous problem with consent. Often some subjects agree to sign immediately, while others are more circumspect, even suspicious. Your willing participants, either of their own accord or with your encouragement, may try to persuade their skeptical friends and relatives to sign. In cases of true misunderstanding or when there's a need for translation, you may require the help of some of your subjects. But there's also a danger of a particularly insidious kind of coercion in this, so beware.

Just as competence to consent is an issue whenever there is cultural distance between production and reception, it is also an issue with minors, the mentally challenged, the terminally ill, and substance abusers. Despite your efforts to explain yourself, these people may not be in a position to make a decision that is in their best interests. You will have to judge for yourself. Parents usually sign a release for minors, but you may not always have access to parents. Who is there to represent the others? Rightly, a release form may not always be legally binding in these situations.

Deception is another matter altogether. Yet it, too, is more complicated than it may seem. Deception can occur quite surreptitiously. For example, suppose you embark on a film with promises to portray your subjects honestly. They will most likely assume that this means that you will film them in a relatively flattering, or at least impartial light. What happens if you find that a subject is not as scrupulous as you initially supposed? Do you concentrate on someone else? Do you stop filming altogether? Do you confront that person with your reassessment of their character? Or do you continue filming as you have been? And if you don't say anything, does that constitute deception? Can deception ever be justified? Most ethical codes would say no. But what if you're deceiving someone whom most people would call unethical anyway? If you don't reveal your bias to your subjects are you deceiving them? Suppose you wanted to make a film about neo-Nazis in Europe or about the militia of Montana in the U.S.; do you try to "keep an open mind"? You could film them in a plain observational style, with no obvious editorializing of your own, knowing very well that they would "undo" themselves before an "outside" audience. If you intend from the outset to be critical of them, or at least anticipate that your viewers will be, do you tell them this? Do you feel morally obliged to be as honest with them as you would be with anyone else? Are you certain that you're faithful to a higher ethical imperative than they are? On the other hand, if no one ever filmed acts that they considered immoral, imagine what an impoverished record one would have of human existence. There are surely situations in which the most ethical response to an immoral act is to bring it to the attention of the public. Clearly, all these questions have to be considered very carefully on a case-by-case basis.

Even if you are completely honest about your intentions, the next question is, do both you and your subject have, as Pryluck puts it, "full knowledge of the procedure and anticipated effects" of your filming? When people consent to be in a film, they may not anticipate that every aspect of their lives will be open to scrutiny, assuming that they will be able to maintain a certain amount of privacy. Observational filmmaking can be intrusive in the extreme, and if your subjects are to have confidence in you, it's important to be clear about that from the outset.

Unfortunately, you may also have to make certain concessions if you are to gain access to people in positions of power. When, in the mid-1970s, Roger Graef made his documentary series "Decisions" about three large British corporations, they all agreed to the following rules:

1. The filmmakers would shoot only what had been agreed on by both sides.
2. No scoops to newspapers. This was essential when a great deal of confidential information was being disclosed.
3. The films would be released only when both sides agreed to it. In other words, the filmmakers weren't setting out to embarrass the subjects.
4. In return for the above, the filmmakers asked for total access to one or two subjects they had agreed to film—that is, the right to film them at any time and walk in on any conversation.
5. The filming would be done without lights and without anything being staged.[21]

However well you prepare, documentary filmmaking is in part a process of discovery, and you're bound to have some rude ethical surprises along the way. Filming may affect current relationships. By choosing someone as your subject, are you likely to stir up any (public or private) rivalries? On the other hand, some film subjects happily bask in the prestige of being followed around by a documentary crew. What about your personal relationship with your subjects? Given the often confessional nature of filming, will you awaken symptoms or memories better left buried? And if so, how will you and your subjects deal with that? And what happens to someone when you, the engaged and interested filmmaker, are no longer there to watch and listen? The effects of the finished film are even more difficult to predict. Once it goes into distribution, it often leaves your control. The broadcast of *The Things I Cannot Change* is just one example of a score of films that have had negative repercussions on their subjects. On the flip side, many films have happy real-life endings: people usually attribute Errol Morris's documentary *The Thin Blue Line* with helping Randolph Haines go free, after years of imprisonment for a murder he did not commit. Nevertheless, as Calvin Pryluck cautions, "Ultimately we are all outsiders in the lives of others. We can take our gear and go home; they have to continue their lives where they are."[22]

REPRESENTING AND INTERVENING

While it's impossible to be completely objective about the people and events you film, it helps to maintain a certain amount of distance. Observational filmmakers in particular try to minimize their interference with their subjects. But this is easier said than done, as the example of a team of anthropologists/filmmakers dedicated to the principle of non-interference shows.

The film *A Country Auction* (1984) follows the Leitzel family in Pennsylvania as they prepare for and conduct an auction of their family estate. It was made collaboratively by four men who had an equal share in decision-making: Robert Aibel, Ben Levin, Chris Musello, and Jay Ruby. Just before the auction, the Leitzels were sorting through the estate, setting aside items they deemed worthless to be burned. At one point Aibel intervened, advising them to save some papers that he thought were historically and financially valuable. Musello objected to this interference because he felt that it imposed the values of outsiders upon the family and that the family should be permitted to make such decisions according to their own symbolic values. As Aibel puts it, "While my actions were motivated by a sense of responsibility to the family and community, Musello felt that I was potentially encouraging the economic and historical aspects to dominate the symbolic aspects of the family process." In other words, Aibel was caught between what he perceived to be the best interests of the Leitzels and what he imagined to be best for the film. Irreplaceable "historical" documents were at stake, but the filmmakers were dedicated to recording and representing as faithfully as possible the social values of the Leitzels as they were manifested in their estate auction. Eventually Aibel decided that active intervention "would inevitably lead to an undesirable level of distortion, but . . . that we should be willing to give advice in response to a request—a form of passive involvement."[23] Another possibility would have been to highlight this clash of values within the film itself, and to feature the dissent among the filmmakers.

In human affairs, the principle of non-intervention is more or less a myth. Filmmakers influence events by their very presence. With Vérité filmmaking, where the camera becomes a catalyst, a stimulus to action (and acting), the problems are only compounded. In Jean Rouch and Edgar Morin's *Chronicle of a Summer,* the boundaries between filmmakers, technicians, actors, and subjects all blur. The kinds of provocation at play in the film cannot be monitored from afar, because they are being improvised and lived as they are being filmed; they are inseparable from the act of filming itself. Rouch has expressed horror at how everything, all of a sudden and with no warning, can run out of control when the camera incites subjects to expose themselves, whether to themselves, to you, or to unseen others—at, for example, Marceline's visceral response when remembering her deportation to a concentration camp.[24] The literary and cultural critic Walter Benjamin compared the camera to a surgeon's knife, opening up what he called the "optical unconscious." In documentary, the *caméra-stylo* ("camera-pen") can unleash the psychic unconscious, the "soul," and the filmmaker has a lot less control over it than the surgeon has over the body. That's not to say that you should recoil from such moments. They provide unparalleled flashes of revelation, intimacy, emotional intensity, and self-consciousness. However, you should always be on the look out for psychosocial repercussions of the camera; it is an instrument of trauma as much as therapy.

Debating whether or not to interfere actively takes on a different turn if you witness behavior that you find ethically problematic. If you recognize that the camera or your own presence is an incentive for the behavior, then you are clearly implicated. The easiest way out might be to stop filming, for the time being or for good. You may have to leave. But it may be too late. And it's not always easy to tell if you're an active agent in it all. Tim Asch tells us that Napoleon Chagnon once shot a 2½-minute sequence of a Yanomamo man beating his wife. Asch and Chagnon decided not to use the footage in a finished film; they felt it was too distressing to watch.[25] Asch admits that, personally, he would not have shot such a sequence, and that he suspects that in some cases a camera may even encourage such behavior.[26] There may also be occasions when you decide the most ethical response is to make a filmic record of your observations. How then do you edit the footage? If, like Asch and Chagnon, you leave it on the cutting room floor, why did you bother shooting it in the first place? (Besides, the camera can always be a provocation in ways hidden to you.) If you leave it in, are you implicitly condoning it, or simply opening it up to the scrutiny of others? Can you, or should you, be culturally relative in such cases? How can you convey your point of view in the editing?

Robert Gardner's film *Rivers of Sand* (1974) is about, among other things, gender relations among the Hamar of Ethiopia. It shows women being whipped by men. At the beginning of the film, Gardner contextualizes the practice by talking in voice-over of the women's "familiarity with both physical and psychic abuse." While this is certainly problematic, we should also ask what the whipping *means* to the Hamar women and men, and how is it experienced by them. Much of the film concentrates on the scarification of women's bodies for adornment. The scarification is performed by other women. We see some girls having teeth extracted, also for aesthetic reasons. It is plain to see that there is a degree of sexual desire and gratification involved in such practices. One young woman smiles radiantly at the man who is whipping her. The images make it apparent to a sensitive viewer that these women—at least the ones that we are shown—initiate this activity, and also that the whipping is ritualized. However, one of the two anthropologists who worked on the film with Gardner, Ivo Strecker, protests that neither the ritual nature of the whipping nor the fact that it was "initiated by the girls themselves" is made clear in the film. *Rivers of Sand* is narrated in part by a married Hamar woman, called Omalleinda, and she talks about the subordination of wives. Strecker tells us that she had never been beaten herself. Moreover, he says, "[l]ike Omalleinda's account, the ritual whipping belongs to the realm of the ideal, rather than everyday reality . . . [while the film] presents the ideal as if it were reality."[27] One might ask: whose ideal? We *see* the whipping; it is real enough, whether or not it happens every day. Admittedly, although the film does not state that women are whipped daily, it does highlight the whipping and other corporeal practices, so most viewers probably *would* go away thinking they were relatively common among the Hamar.

Part of the confusion here derives from the different orientations of a textual anthropologist and a filmmaker. If Strecker feels that the ritual nature of the whipping and its initiation by the women themselves is not evident in the film, this is probably because, so far as he is concerned, nothing is considered clear until it is stated in words. But the images "speak for themselves," at least to the majority of viewers.[28] (It is always possible that a foreign audience, new to Hamar physiognomy, would mistake grimaces of pain for expressions of pleasure, but neither Strecker nor the film seem to imagine this to be so.) As with all your material, then, but particularly when it is ethically explosive, you should be aware of the ambiguity of images, and also of the diversity of possible responses in your viewers. Estimations of morality and immorality are themselves extremely complicated. In addition, how you choose to contextualize your representation is also indeterminate and, like life itself, will always admit of a plurality of interpretations.

CONTEXTUALIZATION

How, practically speaking, can we contextualize our films? One way is to admit that our representations are partial, and limited to our own perspective. Jay Ruby takes a forceful approach to the ethics of image-making:

> I believe that the maker of images has the moral obligation to reveal the covert—to never appear to produce an objective mirror by which the world can see its "true" image. For in doing so we strengthen the status quo, support the repressive forces of this world, and continue to alienate those people we claim to be con-

cerned about. So long as our images of the world continue to be sold to others as *the* image of the world, we are being unethical.[29]

Filmmakers (like writers) can hardly maintain control over every aspect of the way their images are "sold" and "received." First of all, at a certain stage we lose control of the distribution process. Moreover, spectators are active agents of their own, and it is their understandings of our films that constitute the films' meanings. Additionally, if we try to fashion films that are open-ended—that may be understood in a variety of ways—this doesn't mean that we are aware in advance of what all these interpretations will be, and that we confer equal weight on each and every one of them. In fact, nothing can prevent a spectator from deducing from a film a singular and definitive "image of the world," one that may or may not go against the grain of the distributor's or filmmaker's intentions.

Of course, the meanings we filmmakers affirm in our work may just as easily subdue the status quo, counteract repression, and empower our subjects, as the opposite. However, this does not absolve us from our ethical responsibility in contextualizing our films. After all, films *are* constructed so as to authorize certain readings and to discredit others. (To be impartial does not mean being equally partial to every viewpoint.) Anthropologist and filmmaker Karl Heider has suggested that filming and editing "whole bodies and whole people in whole acts" is the preferable style for ensuring a representative, complete, and fair picture.[30] One problem with this is that close-ups, fragments as they are, reveal a whole lot more detail than relatively disinterested long shots. If the camera is to provide a record of human events, it needs to get close and be involved, for that is how we experience life itself. Another problem is: what is to count as a whole body, a whole person, or a whole act? At a certain point the estimations become arbitrary. A precondition to Heider's holism is his exteriority, for wholes from one perspective are fragments from another. Something is whole only if it is both closed and viewed from the outside.

Tim Asch and others have suggested that films be accompanied by written study guides. Such guides can provide important background information about the content of a film and how it was made. They can be useful in academic contexts, for ethnographic films in particular, but they will hardly be adopted by all documentary filmmakers, and it would in any case be a shame to limit our audience to scholars and students. It is also more of a cinematic challenge to try to contextualize *within the film itself.*

Many filmmakers today feel that being reflexive addresses some of the ethical problems inherent in other styles of filmmaking. That is, the filmmaker tries to make his or her position vis-à-vis the subjects manifest within the film itself. The audience may, for example, see them (or at least the sound recordist) in the frame, or hear them on the sound track, making it clear that they are not some invisible master puppeteer. But self-reflexivity is no more an assurance of authenticity or sincerity than any other style. If, as Ruby says, we have "the moral obligation to reveal the covert," it is quite possible to dream up a reflexive moment or scene in order to dramatize, quite duplicitously, some such divulgence. On news shows we often see reporters introducing themselves to people who evidently already knew they were coming. Only their bad acting gives the game away. This staged self-revelation is antithetical to the earlier promise of reflexivity.

Some filmmakers have responded to the ethical quandaries of documentary filmmaking by collaborating with their subjects. Although there are different degrees of sharing authorship and power with your subjects, the idea is to level the playing field and admit the creative contribution of film subjects to the film itself. However, like reflexivity, collaboration has problems of its own. If you want to collaborate in any substantial way, are you ready for your filmmaking method, and even your conception of the film itself, to be drastically altered? And are you sure that collaboration is not a conceit? Perhaps your and your subjects' perspectives really do not coalesce into some synthetic voice, and you would be better off trying to make a film that also reflects the differences between you. Collaboration is a complicated issue. It is discussed in more detail later in this chapter.

Finally, even if you're not considering any formal authorial collaboration, one of the most important ethical issues you have to address is whether and how to compensate your subjects for sharing their lives with you on camera.

> From the beginning I fitted, as far as possible, into the native economic system. In this society, no one did anything for nothing. Equality was the ideal in reciprocal gift giving, but if there was a difference, prestige belonged to the person who gave the most. Quite early I began a pattern of distributing gifts on Sunday morning to those who had been particularly helpful to me during the week.
>
> —Hortense Powdermaker on her fieldwork in Lesu,
>   southwest Pacific, 1929–30

Reciprocity has always been an issue for anthropologists. Yet, for all their theoretical treatises, they tend to be less forthcoming about their own reciprocal relations in the field. As anthropologist Steve Lansing suggests, "[This] process is seldom mentioned because we tend to be a little ashamed of it, preferring to let it be thought that we are much loved by the people we study."[31] Few anthropologists admit to directly paying their "informants." Some acknowledge performing favors and giving small gifts in exchange for help. These can vary from emergency car rides to running interference with government officials and aid agencies. Hortense Powdermaker's Sunday morning gifts included knives, cloth, musical instruments, mirrors, and Christmas tinsel. As she says, "[T]he tinsel trimming was in much demand for ritual dancing, but unfortunately I didn't bring enough with me and my supply did not last long."[32]

Happily, the days of fitting into "the native economic system" by passing out Christmas tinsel are (in most places) long past. But there is still the question of reciprocity, and the relations of power and paternalism that it raises. Many anthropologists and filmmakers continue to work among peoples with value systems different from their own. Something that seemed almost negligible to Powdermaker came to be imbued with a ritualistic and symbolic value in Lesu. Likewise, many of the African art objects valued highly in Europe and North America are mundane, functional items in their original context, and were never considered "art" (or, for that matter, "African") by their makers. Culturally specific use- and exchange-values merge and diverge continually as previously incommensurable value systems rub shoulders in an ever more global economy. If you're filming in a cross-cultural context, you'll have to be creative in deciding what form reciprocity can best take. Should you give at all? What should you give? How should you give? To whom should you give? And what effect might it have on the community?

Of course, the power of the camera notwithstanding, documentary filmmakers are not always economically advantaged over their subjects. This may mean either that you're unable to reciprocate in any direct way or that it would simply be inappropriate to do so. You will have to weigh the situation for yourself. Still, filmmaking is usually a conspicuous activity, with an allure all its own. However, few documentaries break even, so the first thing you may have to do is disillusion your subjects about your resources. Additionally, in unscripted filming of unstaged behavior, there is a danger in compensating people at all, at least before the fact. Even if it does not exactly transform people's images into commodities, it implicitly draws your subjects' attention to the fact that they're providing a service to you. Rather than continuing to live their lives as they otherwise might, they begin to wonder what services you want—in other words, what they should be doing for you, how they should act, what kinds of images or scenes you may be after. As likely as not, this additional self-consciousness on their part will only interfere with what you came there for in the first place.

Thus, you may want to consider compensating people *only after the fact,* or being reciprocal in ways that are unlikely to be recognized as a return on a service. Paul Hockings describes how he and Mark McCarty decided to recompense individuals participating in *The Village:*

> We felt that as we expected to be in Dunquin for perhaps three
> months we did not want to, indeed could not, pay everybody
> for every word and gesture. Aside from emptying our budget, it
> would have led to much unnatural behaviour. The question of
> payment was complex, for evidently nearly everyone we dealt
> with was very poor, and every family in the village (bar one) was
> either receiving the pension or the dole (unemployment pay-
> ments) from the government. We found that a gracious, unos-
> tentatious but productive way of remunerating our friends was to

buy them drinks at the bar, something most of them could ill afford. In addition we gave people rides to Dingle town, ten miles away, or did shopping errands for them; for besides Kruger, the innkeeper, we were the only people in Dunquin to have a car at our disposal.[33]

Other ethnographic filmmakers have compensated subjects in different ways. Tim Asch, Patsy Asch, and Linda Connor, who made several films about Jero Tapakan, a Balinese healer, devised a plan for Jero to receive a share in the films' royalties. Rather than coming in biannual checks,

> [t]his money is given to her privately whenever someone we know and trust is going to Bali and can take her the cash. When emergencies have arisen . . . we have increased the amount to cover her debts. . . . Certainly this is a paternalistic decision, but given the financial difficulties of sending money to Indonesia, Jero's lack of understanding about things like royalties and percentages, and the tendency of the Balinese ritual cycle to absorb all known income, we felt this was the most equitable way to handle her royalties. These films are about Jero's life and she has the right to benefit, as should the subjects of most ethnographic films.[34]

As Tim Asch explains, they arrived at this decision with some difficulty:

> The dilemma resides in not what we, as filmmakers, can afford but in the effect that money can have on people who live in small, subsistence-based communities. If, as with the Jero films, the subject is a single person, the social relationships between that person and her neighbors can be altered radically if she is given a large sum of money. Is this desirable? If a film focuses on a group of people, to whom in the group should the money be given? . . . Are we justified in specifying that royalties be used for some purpose that we designate, such as education, health, or irrigation, rather than giving it to a local leader to spend at his discretion or to the regional government? Payment of royalties is a thorny moral question, but it is one that ethnographic filmmakers must consider.[35]

Some other ethnographic filmmakers, including Sarah Elder and Leonard Kamerling of the Alaska Native Heritage Film Project, share not only royalties but also copyright with their subjects. David and Judith MacDougall have made films with and for the community of Aurukun in Australia. Jean Rouch set up a film school in Niger to teach the trade. Tim Asch conducted video production workshops for Yanomamo in Venezuelan missions. Ever since consulting for a Disappearing World film on the Kayapo of Central Brazil, *The Kayapo* (1987), Terence Turner has been directly involved in the Kayapo use of video, both for their own intracultural dialogue and for resistance against national, even global, politics. John Marshall and Claire Ritchie established the Ju/'hoan Bushman Development Foundation, which has helped a number of !Kung establish farms. This was succeeded by the Nyae Nyae Development Foundation of Namibia, which has been active in helping the !Kung to get the water they need for their farms.[36]

Issues of reciprocity and remuneration are so complicated that one filmmaker, John Cohen, has even made a film in which compensation for local participation is in itself an integral part of the film. Cohen had made a number of films among the people of the Hautun Q'eros in the Peruvian Andes. One of the films had turned a small profit. So when he went to shoot *Carnival in Q'eros* (1990), he felt that it was important to compensate the community for their participation in his films. He arranged for a herd of alpacas to be shared among the five villages in Hautun Q'eros. The second part of the film is about the reciprocal gift of the alpacas. When Cohen first brings the issue up, one person asks why he doesn't just give them money. The reply is that the alpacas are a better gift, because they increase in number, and their price is going up. The community debates this for a while, before accepting the alpacas.

Funding community development projects raises a new set of problems, regardless of how carefully the donations are considered. Granada's Disappearing World series gives gifts and/or payments to the communities where they make their films, but will not directly pay people to appear in a film. Gifts are made "in close consultation"[37] with the anthropologist (who may then decide to hand out disbursements).[38] Mariane Ferme, the anthropologist for *The Mende,* tells us that the Kpuawala community, in Sierra Leone, was asked to set up a priority

FIGURE 7 *Carnival in Q'Eros* (1990), by John Cohen.

list of projects. From that list Granada and Ferme decided that building a school was the most feasible.

They planned the school project carefully, taking pains to ensure that the money went where it was supposed to. They purchased the construction materials themselves and put the village in charge of the building. By the time Ferme returned to the village a few years later, the school was up and running. But when Ferme went to test-teach a class, at the parents' request, she found that the students were not doing as well as they should have.

> One day I walked up to the school in the middle of the morning just like that. I went into the schoolroom and saw all the kids hanging out of windows. . . . The assistant teacher was lying down, snoozing on a bench. I woke him up and said, "Where's everyone else? Where's the teacher? Where's half the school?"

And he said, "Oh they're off gardening." . . . Sure enough, about ten of the school kids were working their butts off on the teacher's farm. . . . The parents didn't know this, or said they didn't know it. . . . [This project] set in motion all kinds of other power relations and potential exploitations that weren't there before.[39]

Ferme points out that the problem here is not what you might at first think: it's not that the school kids were doing the teacher's gardening *per se*. Physical labor is a component of institutional education and apprenticeship throughout West Africa, and in Sierra Leone it is fully expected that teachers supplement their irregular and inadequate salaries by having their pupils garden for them. Ferme's concern was, rather, that there was a high rate of absenteeism and that the teacher was not only poorly qualified but also from another area. Since the original impulse for the school was to reciprocate the Kpuawala community itself for its participation in the film, the fact that the teacher was rapidly becoming wealthy through the labor of his pupils and even their parents was problematic.[40]

Whether and how to compensate your subjects depends on a sensitive gauging of each situation. At the very least it is simple and *relatively* cheap (dubs still add up) to provide your characters with a video copy of the film. But even this gesture may be less benign and innocent than it seems. Certain visual representations may upset part or all of the community. Some Australian Aborigines have specifically requested that films of their rituals not be shown to other Aboriginal peoples, and that films of people who have recently died not be shown in their own community. Some Aborigines have objected also to the public screening of rituals of neighboring groups that are similar to their own, even though their neighbors have approved them being shown.[41] Tim Asch believes that had he shown some of his films to the Yanomamo, they might have become violent, assuming that, because he had taken their images, he was responsible for the deaths of everyone he'd filmed who had since died.[42]

An extraordinary example of the ethical implications of giving subjects a copy of your film is the collaboration between anthropologist Maurice Godelier and filmmaker Ian Dunlop in making films about the Baruya of Papua New Guinea. Together with the Baruya themselves, they arranged for a film print of all nine hours of footage to be stored in the Institute for Papua New Guinea Studies in the capital, Port Moresby. The Baruya signed a contract with the Institute restricting the films' distribution. As Godelier says,

> I can tell you the rules. It's a bit shocking for many people. No black woman is allowed to see the films and specially the Baruya black women, because [the films are about] male initiation ceremonies. All the male people with responsibilities, like teachers or missionaries, or ministers, are allowed to see the films. . . . All women [are] excluded in Papua New Guinea. But white women are allowed to see the films if they are in another country. . . . The Baruya have maintained the basic framework of their society.[43]

Here we are dealing, not just with a community that is internally differentiated (women and men, elders and youths, and so on), but with a case in which particular cultural values are projected universally onto the entire world, subsuming (or ignoring) moral frameworks very different from their own. In such a clash of values, you may find your own loyalties being divided.

An additional consideration is whether the people to whom you give a tape actually have the facilities to play it (in the proper standard). This may or may not matter, as the symbolic significance of the gift could supersede its functionality—especially if there's a photo of the community or individual on the tape's label. In any case, consider how your film may be used, particularly if it features several people. Be aware that the tape may be copied and recopied, even though it may be nominally protected by international copyright laws. We know that a number of "unauthorized" dubs of *In and Out of Africa* are circulating both in West Africa and among the Hausa community in New York, and it pleases us greatly. The MacDougalls have sometimes sent high-quality tapes of their films to Australian Aboriginal communities where they know nth-generation copies to be circulating.

Finally, remember that in making a film about people, you are not necessarily taking anything away from anybody at all. The innumerable travelers', missionaries', and anthropologists' reports of beliefs from all over the world about the camera's capacity to steal the soul are surely equally related to a peculiarly modern, and initially Western, culture of mimesis, fetishism, and image commodification. Depending on how your subjects perceive your filmmaking venture, it's perfectly possible that the mere act of filming (among) them may be reciprocity enough itself. This on no account means that you should be cavalier about additional forms of exchange, but you should make a sensitive judgment about the esteem in which your presence and filmmaking are held.

METHODOLOGY

In large part your methodology—*how* you make your film—will depend on what and where you're shooting and who you anticipate as your audience. While any game plan you devise in advance will be modified on location, there are some decisions you can make ahead of time.

A lot depends, obviously, on your time and your resources. The ideal situation would be to have enough of each to shoot what you want, and to have a little extra so you can go back and get "pickups"—images and sounds that either never occurred to you or for some reason you couldn't get at the time, but which you find yourself needing once you're in the editing room. Alas, few filmmakers find they have either enough time or enough resources. Would it be comforting to know that among the "classics" *The Ax Fight* was shot in a day (actually, a few hours)? The Disappearing World films are sometimes shot in a month, admittedly on a larger budget. On the other hand, the MacDougalls' Turkana Trilogy was shot primarily in the last three months of a fourteen-month fieldwork period. John Marshall's *The Hunters* was shot over the course of seven years.

FIELDWORK AND FILMING

Although one of the perks of independent work is that you're not subject to the tight deadlines of a television station, shooting ("production") typically takes the shortest time of any stage in filmmaking. The research ("preproduction") and editing ("postproduction") periods tend to take several times as long. However, these stages are not necessarily separate. Although the research period is where you lay most of the groundwork, shooting and editing are also processes of discovery. Shooting can begin at virtually any point, and can in itself be a part of the research or fieldwork process. Some filmmakers spend years in the field before shooting; others start soon after arriving on location. Your conception of the relationship between research and filming are part and parcel of the kind of films you make. As mentioned above, the MacDougalls usually undertake long-term research before beginning to film, carrying their equipment around with them all the time as an integral element of their identity. But they have occasionally started shooting almost immediately (for *Photo Wallahs* and *Tempus de baristas* [1993]). As David says, "One advantage in beginning to film immediately is that your initial response to a place and to a whole society can be quite important, but after a while you may begin to take things for granted. If you do begin to shoot right away, there may be a certain freshness to your shooting that will be useful to the film. It may capture some of the heightened awareness that you'll lose later on." [44]

The act of filming is often likened by anthropologists to the documentation or demonstration of research that precedes and determines it. It is seen to provide a record of intellectual work that, in essence, exists apart from it. This assumption misconceives the kind of interventions that take place when you film, and ignores differences between films and texts. Film images have an inextricable relationship to their object, and, while shooting, you're selecting and editorializing in ways that will be intrinsic to your final film. Once you recognize this, it's difficult to see research and filming as altogether separate stages. [45]

If documentary filming is itself considered a process of research, then being on location or undertaking fieldwork takes on a different hue. Although the gathering of data is always theory-laden, textual anthropologists can rest assured that they can do the bulk of their thinking and theorizing once they've returned from the field. However, during shooting, you're making decisions that ineradicably embody your theory. Fieldwork is thus a highly critical time for documentary. Some of the problems in anthropologist-filmmaker collaborations (discussed below) stem not only from different conceptions of the film but also from different notions of fieldwork.

One important methodological decision you'll have to make is whether to work with a crew, and if so, who to pick. The chances are that a crew of more than two wouldn't be able to stay on location for long, especially if you're paying for their time. This means that fieldwork and filming are likely to get separated out as two discrete processes, similar to the traditional distinction between preproduction and production. If you're filming close to home, this may still be a problem: you may be willing to invest several months in periodic filming, but your crew may not. You may find yourself having to use different crew members on different shoots, depending on who is available. The danger is that this may be slightly more disruptive to your subjects, who won't be able to feel a sense of continuity or build up rapport with the whole crew. Sticking with the same crew also has the advantage that everyone gets used to working together.

Much of the intimacy of observational films would be lost if they were shot with large television-style crews. Jean Rouch considers himself "violently opposed" to film crews, for several reasons:

> The sound engineer must fully understand the language of the people he is recording. It is thus indispensable that he belong to the ethnic group being filmed and that he also be trained in the minutiae of his job. Besides, with the present techniques used in Direct Cinema (synchronic sound), the filmmaker must be the cameraman. And the ethnologist alone, in my mind, is the one who knows when, where, and how to film, i.e., to do the production. Finally, and this is doubtless the decisive argument, the ethnologist should spend quite a long time in the field before undertaking the least bit of filmmaking. . . . [S]uch a stay is incompatible with the schedules and salaries of a team of technicians.[46]

With observational filmmaking, the director is often either the camera operator or the sound recordist. Ideally, there is an intimate interdependence between them as they respond to unforeseen clues and cues as the camera is rolling. It is often said of observational films that they make up in immediacy what they lack in appearance. Certainly, directors of a more controlled form of documentary usually insist on working with a separate camera operator and sound recordist, and perhaps also a camera assistant, a grip (a general jack-of-all-trades), a production manager, location managers, and so on—more in the manner of fictional features. (Some professional camera operators themselves understandably refuse to work without an assistant—finding it simply too demanding to prepare all the equipment before, and break it down after, every shoot.) This division of labor is likely to result in a more technically proficient and aesthetically polished (and more expensive) film, but, by the same token, what it gains in appearance it may lose in immediacy. In any case, the close relationship between director, camera operator, and sound recordist is less important when shooting in a controlled style, as the director can describe to the camera operator and recordist what to shoot and record before it happens.

Whether you're a lone filmmaker, a two-person team, or directing a crew, Rouch raises some important issues. What are the linguistic skills of your sound recordist and camera operator? What ethnicity, sex, class, and age should everyone be? As you navigate your fluid insider-outsider identity, there may be contexts or occasions when it helps to be "insiders" and others where you're best off being "outsiders." People reveal intimate secrets to strangers that they wouldn't dare tell close friends, but the opposite is equally true. In some situations, an all-women crew may be appropriate, in others, all-male. If you have a family and you're undertaking a long period of fieldwork-cum-filming, and bring your family along with you, your host community might sense more of a personal investment on your part than if you came in alone, and might act toward you and the film in a like manner. You may not think you'd get very far on a film about gay bathhouses with a straight crew, but you never know. Conversely, an openly gay crew might make a much more provocative and revealing film about a virulently homophobic individual than either a group of like-minded heterosexist males or a mixed crew divided along the lines of ethnicity, gender, and sexual orientation. Having someone from your host community in an important crew position will usually help with access, but it may also lead to added complications and torn loyalties on their part. Invariably, the most important factors are whether your crew members are competent technicians, easy-going, and all get along. Filming is always a stressful affair, requiring continual give-and-take, and any tensions within your crew will be communicated instantly to your subjects.

FIGURE 8 Director and cameraman Gary Kildea and sound recordist Rowena Katalingkasan during the filming of *Celso and Cora* (1983).

SUBSTANCE AND STYLE

In documentary filmmaking, style is not something that you should definitively decide on in advance. Filmmakers have individual techniques, to be sure, but your film style should also be a response to what you find in front of the camera. Nevertheless, it's helpful to keep a few ideas about style and method in the back of your mind as you film, including questions like these:

- *What is the subject or focus of your film?* Even if you don't want to be dogmatic or didactic, a film, in the end, has to be about something. What do you want to show or say? *How* do you want to show it? What shooting style will you employ? What kind of editing? What is your overall aesthetic? Uncontrolled or controlled? Unscripted or scripted? Unstaged or staged? Observational "fly-on-the-wall"? Participatory "fly-in-the-soup"? Reflexive "fly-in-the-I"? [47] Performative? Reconstructive?
- *How are you going to work with your subjects?* How far will you collaborate with them? How do you envisage compensating

them? What precautions will you take to make as ethical a film as you can?

- *How will the film "hang together"?* Will it span a long period of time or be a synchronous slice of life? Will it have a story line? Will it emerge naturally from your pro-filmic encounters and not distort events in order to cater to a foreign audience? How will you tell your story? Will you focus more on individuals, informal interaction, activities, events, or ideas? Will you use narration? How and why? Will you interview people? If so, how will you shoot and edit the interviews? Will you use archival materials? How and to what end?

- *What will the film actually* look *like?* Will you use a wide-angle lens to shoot long takes with great depth of field like observational filmmakers? Will you forego a tripod like Rouch? How will you edit your film? Will you retain the long takes or transform the picture and sound into short "montage elements" for a more associative effect? Will you shoot and edit for continuity, or not? Will you play with structure like Asch? Will you experiment with shooting like Trinh?

COLLABORATION

Collaboration, conscious or not, involves multiple authorship, acknowledged or not. Documentary filmmaking is by nature collaborative. Quite simply, it's impossible to make a film about other people completely on your own. Subjects and funders, anthropologists and filmmakers, may all have a role to play. Not all roles are equal nor are all collaborations easy. Collaboration entails complicated power plays and difficult negotiations.

COLLABORATION BETWEEN ANTHROPOLOGISTS AND FILMMAKERS

Anthropologists and filmmakers tend to bring different perspectives to bear in collaborations. Film is a quintessentially phenomenological medium, and it may have a different orientation to social life than anthropological monographs. It has a unique capacity to evoke human experience, what it feels like to actually be-in-the-world, while anthropological texts tend to be equally (although of course by no means exclusively) concerned with nonintuitive abstractions like social structure or population statistics. Life, as Keats said, involves "being in uncertainties, mysteries, doubts," and any film that attempts to evoke the experiences of its characters in all their fullness will have to respect their irreducible ambiguity—a respect that may be at odds with the theoretical and empirical closure toward which written anthropology typically tends. While some recent ethnographies have tried to operate with a cinematic imagination,[48] and while anthropologists are also concerned with embodied experience, collaborations between an anthropologist and a filmmaker are often fraught with tension because each may have different expectations of what a film can accomplish. Word-oriented anthropologists are often unaware of ways in which filmmakers editorialize through images and their juxtaposition, of how films implicitly formulate a theory about their subject matter. David MacDougall feels that many of the misunderstandings that arise in filmmaker-anthropologist collaborations stem from divergent notions of film's analytic potential:

> Anthropologists often don't trust a film to embody a theory about the subject, and to work it out in film terms. They want much more explicit kinds of statements than film is capable of providing, because film works by specific instances that can't necessarily be generalized. Film is very often ambiguous about things that writing would clarify, or that writing would take a single position on. So I think that often lies at the heart of the tensions. Also, just on the level of making records, there's a tendency for anthropologists to accumulate an encyclopaedic coverage of the subject rather than one structured by the needs of the film. . . . Film can certainly be precise in a descriptive way, but I think film still works intellectually through implication rather than through statement. . . . It is often difficult for people who express themselves through words to accept a form of communication that works so much through suggestion, implication, reference, ambiguity, and comparison without conclusion. It can be frustrating for them. And there's a tendency to try to push it in the direction of being more definitive. Therefore, there's always a demand for further contextualization, for narration.[49]

This is not to say that the differences between filmmakers and anthropologists are irreconcilable. What is important is that the differences complement and not contradict each other (unless the contradictions were to be incorporated creatively into the dramatic structure of the film). The essential questions a potential collaborative team should consider are: Why bother making a film? How can film work for an anthropologist? What can a film and/or a filmmaker's perspective add to an anthropologist's work? What can an anthropologist contribute to a filmmaker? Can the anthropologist adapt creatively to the cinematic medium?

These questions can be answered variously. Consider the number of successful anthropologist-filmmaker collaborations: *Dead Birds* (Karl Heider and Robert Gardner), the !Kung series (filmmaker John Marshall and a number of ethnographers, including his mother Lorna and sister Elizabeth), the Yanomamo films (of anthropologist Napoleon Chagnon and filmmaker Tim Asch), and the Indonesian films of Tim Asch and Patsy Asch (with anthropologists Linda Connor in Bali and Doug Lewis in Flores, eastern Indonesia). Granada Television's Disappearing World series regularly includes an anthropologist on the film team.

So what are the potential problems? Working as a team can be awkward, especially if you're used to working alone. Film crews, and all the equipment, are unwieldy and conspicuous. Maurice Godelier tells of filmmaker Ian Dunlop joining him to film a crowded and violent Baruya ceremony in Papua New Guinea. They were shooting in a *tchimia,* a large ceremonial house, when they noticed a ritual going on in one part of the room.

> Imagine a team of three people: cameraman, soundman, plus Ian Dunlop. Plus the master or two masters of the ritual. Plus me. There was no space. I said look, I don't see anything. I have to take pictures, he said. No, it's not possible. I am the anthropologist. I have to see what you are going to shoot. I have to be there, because I can understand things you will not understand. So piss off! There was a clash. There was an objective contradiction between the necessity for him to take pictures, close pictures, and for me to be there to see the same things—and to take a few notes. A ritual is warm and tough, and violent and smooth and

so on. Everything is important in some way. They don't repeat things. So you have to be there all the time and take a few notes.[50]

Godelier's dilemma raises issues of priority. The filmmakers were coming in on the back of the anthropologist, using him for access. Without Godelier the significance of what was being shot might have been lost on the filmmakers, and they may not have known what to concentrate on. Moreover, Godelier's loyalties were divided: he was conducting his own research, quite apart from his collaboration on the film. (It is also possible that well-shot close-up coverage would have served Godelier's own research after the fact, even if it interfered at the time.) In certain respects this is a worst-case scenario. Ideally, the first priority of both the filmmaker and the anthropologist in any collaborative team should be the making of the film itself. This may not always be possible, however, as a filmmaker and an anthropologist may not be able to free up the same extended length of time to devote exclusively to the film. If not, both partners should be very clear up front how far they're willing to commit to the project.

Research Footage or Finished Film?

Before electing to collaborate on a film, therefore, it's important for the anthropologist and filmmaker to discuss their conceptions of the end product. The task of the participants will vary according to whether you're shooting footage for research, for yourselves or other area specialists, or whether you're hoping to edit an actual film that will be of interest to a more general audience. Tim Asch suggests that if you shoot long takes of individual actions for research purposes, but also shoot "a few distant location shots and some cut-aways, as well as a few rolls of film related to a script, the footage should be equally valuable as a resource for editing film for instruction or for television."[51] But this may be overly optimistic. Even if it works for television (which is unlikely), it probably won't result in a great film, which has stylistic and structural requirements of its own.

Research footage does itself contain some interpretation: the filmmaker and/or anthropologist employ standards of significance in selecting when and what to shoot. (That does not mean that they can always articulate or even know exactly what those criteria are.) Nonetheless, the essential point of research footage is that it be as unselective and unstructured as possible—in other words, that it provide less *discourse about* social life than an *objective record* of it. As far as possible, the interpretation should come later and should focus, not on the filmic discourse, but on the reality of which it ostensibly provides a record. The camera is deployed as an impartial instrument in the service of science, fixing all that is fleeting for infinite future analysis.

This may sound like a neglect of the medium's potential. However, there are different kinds of filming, and "providing a record" is a valuable one. Paradoxically, shooting footage for later research embodies an idea that is at the core of documentary itself, that is indeed one of the features that distinguishes it from fiction and is prized by observational filmmakers. This is the hope that documentary images contain meaning in excess of the filmmaker's intentions; that such images admit, indeed maximize, uncoded detail.

How is it, then, that the best observational films are so different from the mass of research footage? It is because in its pursuit of objectivity, research filming tends to lack that engagement with human affairs that makes them, to their participants, real. The desire to be impartial tends to make the filming unselective, and so the footage may seem unstructured to anyone not already in the know. Research filming most certainly does have its place for anthropologists, psychologists and other human scientists. However, you cannot automatically shoot comprehensively for research purposes and expect also to be able at a later date to forge the result into a film that will interest others.

If you do collaborate to shoot footage for research, the filmmaker inevitably acts more as a technician than a director. It only makes sense that the anthropologist should assume a more commanding role. But if you collaborate to shoot a film with the expectation that it will be edited and shown to nonspecialists, and perhaps even nonacademics, the anthropologist will need to respect the filmmaker's expertise and experience in a language and medium that is new to them. Needless to say, it's vital for both partners to choose the other carefully.

Concerns of Anthropologists

Focusing a film is never easy, especially if the anthropologist and filmmaker bring different interests to bear. While filmmakers are trained to keep their audience in mind, anthropologists often have their subjects as their first concern. The differences will probably only be exacerbated if the film is to be a television production, made for a mass audience. Mariane Ferme has told us that she turned down Granada's requests to focus *The Mende* on women's secret societies and initiation because she was exasperated with the long-standing Western obsession with secret societies in the region.[52] As it happened, the film crew arrived during the Muslim period of Ramadan, and Ferme suggested that they concentrate instead on that.

> But the director just didn't want to do it. . . . [T]he implication was that he didn't think it was really African. He seemed to think that Islam was a foreign religion there and was not really Mende, so that went out of the window. I think the other reason for the film being less of a focused one was that it suffered from the conflict between myself and the director and our different interests, and our audiences in mind. . . . [H]e had to do something that Bert and Sophie in their living room would watch. With a commercial break and all that.[53]

Likewise, when anthropologist James Faris collaborated with the BBC on the film *Southeast Nuba* (1982), he objected to the extent of the film's criticisms of the Sudanese government and of Islam. He explained that "the film is principally to be shown in Europe and America, and the interview and commentary on the government and Islam seem to me to reinforce the all-too-ready European stereotypes of Islam and prejudices about the Third World and new nations."[54]

If you're an anthropologist who's been working in a field site for some time, you will have established a number of important relationships. Some of them may be quite delicate. It may be difficult to share those with an outsider, especially if it's someone who knows considerably less than you do about them. This can be compounded if the filmmaker does not know the language and is reliant on you to communicate. Obviously, it's important that filmmakers understand an anthropologist's relationship with the people they have chosen to study, often in a lifelong commitment. While filmmakers typically move onto other projects, anthropologists often maintain contacts with their field site, for both personal and professional reasons. If a filmmaker acts foolishly, the anthropologist may bear the brunt of the community's resentment.

Ideally, filmmakers may forge their own ties with the community. Learning the language helps, but as anthropologist Linda Connor points out, just having an open mind can work wonders. When she worked on the Jero Tapakan films with Tim Asch she noticed that "both Tim and Jero have an astonishing capacity to overcome communication barriers without a common language, and within a few days a mutually trusting and warm relationship was established, enhanced by my role as interpreter."[55] Nevertheless, Connor sometimes found it frustrating to act as a linguistic and cultural interpreter between Tim and the Balinese villagers they were filming. Moreover, she no longer was able to give her undivided attention to the villagers. "Just as Tim wanted to be filled in on any conversations I was having in Balinese, so did the villagers want me to tell them about what I was discussing with Tim, especially when we were laughing about something because they liked to share the joke."[56] Much of this tension was relieved when Patsy Asch joined them in the field to help film the sequels to the first Jero film. "The presence of two collaborators meant that they could talk to each other when I was occupied. Thus I did not feel I was consigning another person to silence every time I participated in a Balinese conversation. Moreover Patsy had learned some Indonesian and was able to have simple conversations. Rescuing her (and Tim) when they encountered linguistic difficulties became a source of amusement rather than frustration."[57]

There may also be advantages to the anthropologist by returning to the field with a filmmaking team in tow. The mere act of returning allows you to reestablish old ties. The presence of the camera and crew might also act as a catalyst for social behavior that is new to you: people may act differently and reveal previously hidden or unnoticed aspects of themselves. As Ferme readily admits, "The naive perspective of outsiders helped me see things that I hadn't seen. You sort of start looking anew with a fresh eye in a different way that you've lost with the long-term familiarity that you've had with a place. . . . I think that's one of the valuable things that can happen for collaborative projects of all kinds."[58] Finally, giving video copies of the finished film to friends in the field, or to the main characters of the film, might be a more mean-

FIGURE 9 Filmmaker Timothy Asch and anthropologist Linda Conner collaborating to film Balinese healer Jero Tapakan.

ingful form of reciprocity than presenting copies of your monographs, which your "informants" may not be able to read.

Concerns of Filmmakers

Professionalism is often an issue for filmmakers. Filmmakers and anthropologists alike complain about the difficulties of working with someone who consistently tries to do the other's job. It's best to agree on the division of labor ahead of time. As filmmaker Ellen Frankenstein puts it, some "anthropologists (and non-filmmakers in many fields, from bureaucrats to drug and alcohol counselors) . . . who are not familiar with the process, but have seen many films, have a tendency to be instant directors. . . . Sometimes they are very close to their work and have trouble standing back and thinking what would be good for the outsider/viewer." [59] (Of course it may be just as frustrating for anthropologists if filmmakers act as nouveaux ethnographers.)

But even experts make mistakes. Problems must be solved patiently, often more slowly than one would like. Equipment can break down.

Expensive footage can be wasted. One-time-only shots can be missed. It's all part of the game. Tim Asch recounts shooting a "large confusing ceremony" with anthropologist Doug Lewis in Flores, Indonesia:

> As it grew darker . . . I asked Lewis to go out and see which group was coming next. He came back shortly saying there was no way he could tell who was who among the hundreds milling around in the darkness and we would just have to sit and wait. I was furious, because I knew I could only film an entrance properly if I were prepared. . . . I stormed out to get the information myself but, although I did find the people I wanted, my anger interfered with filming and as a consequence I missed their entrance. The next day I realized I had put Lewis in an impossible situation. What I had perceived as the needs of filming interfered with our normal respect for one another and my emotional reaction became a real obstacle.[60]

Making the Film

How to make the film, what scenes to shoot, and what style to shoot them in should be of concern to the anthropologist as well as to the filmmaker. The more you discuss beforehand the better. Ironically, because anthropologists have traditionally been oriented more toward words than images, they may find it easier to collaborate with a television production than with an independent ethnographic filmmaker. Television programs tend likewise to rely heavily on words to get their message or story across. As David Turton has noted, "Being professionally committed to the view that culturally unfamiliar behavior needs to be contextualized if it is to be understood, [anthropologists] are likely to be much more sympathetic than ethnographic filmmakers to the typical television documentary's heavy use of commentary."[61] However, anthropologists may find the main storyline that most television programs construct to be superficial, and perhaps ethnocentric. Moreover, quite a few anthropologists have objected to the inquisitorial nature of interviews in television productions they've collaborated on. They would have preferred to have filmed more interactions between themselves and their subjects, and for the interviews to have taken place in more natural settings. In short, they would have been happier with a more observational style, one that rarely appeals to prime time programmers. Anthropologist Jean Lydall, who has collaborated with BBC filmmaker Joanna Head on several films about the Hamar of southern Ethiopia, describes their initial differences when making their first film together:

> I imagined the interviews taking place in typical Hamar scenes, such as while a woman was grinding grain or doing another woman's hair, so that they would also represent the typical busyness of Hamar women. . . . I imagined filming a typical fieldwork scene in which I would be seen in conversation with my Hamar friends. . . .
>
> Joanna, on the other hand, had different ideas about the interviews. She did not want the women to be engaged in any activities while being interviewed, not even to hold and breast-feed a baby, and she did not want me to appear in the interviews at all.

In the end, Lydall conceded to Head's wishes, rather than jeopardize the film. As she says, "In any case, I was very camera shy and quite relieved not to have to appear on film. What's more, I realized that, like Joanna, I was more interested in filming the Hamar women and letting them present themselves than I was in expressing the realities of fieldwork."[62]

Filming is demanding, and requires a degree of trust between anthropologists and filmmakers. Only the camera operator knows exactly what's being filmed, and the anthropologist has to have faith in their judgment about framing, duration, and focus. The anthropologist, however, probably understands the significance of actions and dialogue better than the filmmaker. To further complicate matters, both anthropology and film have their own jargon, ethics, and theoretical orientation. As visual anthropologist Allison Jablonko points out, "communicating 'the culture of anthropologists' to non-anthropologists takes a great deal of time and effort. Anthropologists have all gone through long periods of academic preparation and fieldwork. It is easy to forget that phrases and concepts that we anthropologists now take for granted may be quite unfamiliar to the general public."[63] By the same token, the jargon and shorthand of a film crew can be baffling to the anthropologist. Try to work out an efficient code of communication between yourselves. Few moments are more maladroit than a film crew suddenly arguing in front of subjects about what to shoot next.

Editing in Collaboration

The difficulties of collaboration don't end once the shooting is over. In certain respects, roles are reversed. Suddenly the filmmaker, who was so dependent on the anthropologist's expertise in the field, becomes the expert in the editing room. Though still needed as a translator and interpreter, the anthropologist may feel out of sorts amid the high-tech editing equipment. The length of time and repetitious work it takes to whip any footage into shape can exasperate even the most engaged anthropologist. Granada's solution for its Disappearing World series is to edit a two-hour rough cut before bringing the anthropologists into the editing room for comments.

Independent productions are likely to be more collaborative. Linda Connor worked with Tim and Patsy Asch intensively throughout postproduction. "From the beginning of editing, we decided to take all decisions collectively, even where individual competence varied. We wanted the final product to be one for which we all felt equally responsible."[64] Paul Hockings says of *The Village,* "[I]t was because the filmmaker and the anthropologist were always in the editing room together, arguing over the true meaning of every scene and the effect of every cut, that we were able to put into film the totality of our knowledge of this and other Irish communities."[65] Ellen Frankenstein proposes her own happy medium between the two extremes: "In my favorite collaboration . . . [the anthropologist] studied the footage, the logs and transcripts, brainstormed about the cuts, without ever going into the editing room. It was relaxed, fun, productive and we respected each other's talents and roles throughout the process."[66]

Successful Collaboration

Are there any surefire ways of ensuring compatibility? Not really, since a lot comes down to individual personalities. It is probably best for everyone if you can anticipate certain differences and smooth them out ahead of time. Tim Asch, who has collaborated with numerous anthropologists, suggests that a written contract be drawn up before filming begins. He points out that he advocates this "not so much to have a legally binding agreement . . . but because in writing a contract, in trying to reach agreement and plan for all contingencies, many problems become evident and some can be avoided. This can be a first step towards discovering whether a partnership is feasible." [67] He lists a number of salient points for such a contract (which we have expanded on in brackets):

a) a definition of the aims and goals of the project [including how the subjects of the film will be involved, methodology, possible structures and/or story lines];

b) an outline of the type of footage to be collected and its intended use [including what to do with and how to store outtakes; how the final product(s) will be distributed];

c) an outline of the responsibilities and duties of each member of the team during all phases of the project, including a commitment to complete all agreed-upon materials [for example, who will be responsible for such time-consuming activities as transcripts and study guides];

d) agreement on how much time each party will spend on each phase of the project: preparation, fieldwork, production [as well as fundraising, postproduction, and distribution];

e) clarification of ownership, copyright, and credits [including credits in festival programs, publicity, and distributors' catalogues];

f) clarification of financial responsibilities [and rights, including fundraising and royalties];

g) a clause outlining procedures for amending the contract or ending the collaboration. [68]

While this may seem excessive, the clearer you and your partners are on these issues, the more smoothly your film will be made.

COLLABORATING WITH AN ORGANIZATION

Collaborating with an organization can be both a help and a hindrance. Quite a number of documentaries have been sponsored by organizations: Flaherty's *Nanook of the North* was financed by Revillon Frères (a fur company), and his *Louisiana Story* by Humble Oil (which gave free copies to any theater that would show it). The World Bank has sponsored ethnographic filmmakers in Nepal and elsewhere. Organizational sponsorship need not be financial. Sometimes organizations provide in-kind support, such as equipment, housing, food, and, last but not least, essential introductions to the community. If you're considering organizational sponsorship in any form there are some issues to consider: Why might an organization want to support your film? (What's in it for them? What's their agenda? How will they use the film?) Who determines the final cut? Who owns or controls the finished film? Who owns or controls the outtakes? If the organization owns or controls everything, do you or your subjects have access to the material? If you control the film, what are your responsibilities to the organization? Will it be able to use your material? What kind of credits will everyone get? What if your sponsoring organization gets cold feet—do you have the alternative resources to complete the project without it? Do you have the legal or contractual right to do so?

A contract is essential in any collaboration with an institution. Their staff or objectives may change while you're in the middle of your project. Tim Asch recounts his disappointment when, after promising Pashtoon Afghani nomads that he was filming them for educational purposes, the film's sponsor gave away control of the footage. It was eventually turned into a film by the National Film Board of Canada, and finally re-edited by the BBC after the Soviet invasion of Afghanistan. "The narration implied that the people we had filmed, people named and located in the film, were part of the fiercest of Afghanistan resistance forces. Whether this was true or not, the new version of the film placed our subjects in grave danger. . . . We had been naive in accepting a verbal agreement for a contract that was never signed." [69]

COLLABORATING WITH SUBJECTS

Collaboration between filmmakers and subjects in documentary has aesthetic, ethical, and political consequences. The incentive to collaborate stems from the recognition that it is only reasonable that people should have some input into how they are represented. Moreover, if a film is about someone's subjective or emotional life, it will probably only be enriched by their active participation. The technology of film and video these days gives filmmakers almost unlimited freedom to

GETTING GOING

shape their subjects to appear however the filmmakers wish. Collaborative projects are an attempt to redress the balance.

Contemporary collaborations have precursors. While making *Nanook of the North,* Robert Flaherty solicited Nanook's criticism of the rushes and his suggestions about what to shoot next. In so doing, Flaherty hoped that the Itivimuit would "accept and understand what I was doing and work together with me as partners."[70] Other degrees and forms of collaboration can be found in Jean Rouch's work, particularly in *Jaguar* and *Chronicle of a Summer,* in the MacDougalls' participatory cinema in *Kenya Boran* and the Turkana Trilogy, and in the Alaska films of Sarah Elder and Leonard Kamerling. But in most of these examples, the filmmakers maintain ultimate control, and their own styles remain dominant.

Collaborations with Use-Value

There have been a number of projects in which filmmakers have collaborated with communities to make films that directly serve the communities' interests. The MacDougalls were employed by the Australian Institute of Aboriginal Studies to make a number of films with and for the community of Aurukun in the late 1970s and 1980s. The films have served a number of ends. According to David, "The making of film images and taping of spoken statements became a formal registration of rights which in the past had always been a matter of oral tradition. The Aurukun project also provided an opportunity of expressing community opposition to the encroachment of government and mining interests, particularly in *Takeover,* made in 1978."[71]

One of the most celebrated collaborations has been the National Film Board of Canada's Challenge for Change/Société Nouvelle Programme in the 1960s on Fogo Island, Newfoundland. The Canadian government was preparing to relocate the 5,000 Fogo Islanders. Over half of them were on welfare, and the community was divided by religious factionalism, geographical isolation, and a lack of communication.[72] The government dispatched filmmaker Colin Low with a crew to film it all. Rather than making a film about the Fogo Islanders, Low decided to make a film *for* them. As filmmaker Dorothy Henaut, who worked on later Challenge for Change projects, puts it, "The first concern was to improve communications on the island—to help people know and understand each other better."[73] Fogo Islanders were asked their permission before they were filmed. They were the first to view footage of themselves, and were given the opportunity to edit out anything they were not comfortable with. They were also asked to approve the final edit and were assured that nothing would be shown outside their community without their permission. This process encouraged an unusual spontaneity and self-confidence among its participants.

As the filmmakers edited the films, they screened them for the various villages on the island, following each screening with discussion sessions. Islanders realized that they shared common problems and a sense of community began to emerge. At this point, the films became an important communication channel between the islanders and the government. Footage conveying the islanders' concerns was shown to the Ministry of Fisheries, which responded, in turn, on film. Eventually face-to-face meetings took place, and the government helped the islanders set up a fishing cooperative. Another cooperative and a high school soon followed. According to Henaut, "The situation had turned around. Ten years later, Fogo Island was being cited as an example of successful community development."[74]

The Fogo Island project inspired a number of other collaborative enterprises, including Tim Kennedy's Sky River project in Alaska, VTR St. Jacques in Montreal, founded by Dorothy Henaut and Bonnie Klein, as well as further Challenge for Change projects. Henaut is quick to point out that her films did not work miracles on their own. Instead, they acted as a catalyst once other important elements were in place. All these projects demanded considerable devotion, time, and patience from the filmmakers and the community. Another important participant in many of these projects was a community development worker who stimulated discussion and generally acted as a community advocate. Crucial, too, was that the Canadian and American governments were willing to listen and to provide ongoing financial support for these projects.

Collaboration: A Fantasy?

Despite such success stories, we have to admit that collaboration is not only difficult in practice, it's also difficult in theory. Indeed, some critics charge that the very concept of collaboration is a chimera. They suggest that it's naive to suppose that all the perspectives of the various contributors can be combined into a kind of composite conglomerate, the singular perspective of the film. Certainly filmmakers and subjects have their own points of view, and we cannot assume that when they come together to collaborate on a project, these differences will suddenly disappear. The danger is that the filmmaker may remain the real author, with the participants simply being brought in to legitimate a collaborative rubber stamp.

Some collaborations work more smoothly than others, just as there is more real power-sharing in some cases than others. But there's still an element of truth to these charges. It would be sad if participants in collaborative projects were obliged to suppress their own interests in the service of a larger whole that never quite emerges. The answer, surely, is to reconceive the process of collaboration, not as a project by some imaginary univocal cooperative, but as a hybrid effort at polyvocal authorship, in which distinctions between the participants may be visibly (or aurally) retained in the finished film. This would allow collaborative films to contain contending points of view and even contending representations of reality. It would also acknowledge that the film embodies multiple sources and forms of authorship, each with their own distinct form of authority.

So before you commit to a collaborative venture, ask yourself the following: do all the viewpoints really coalesce into a unitary aggregate? If not, will any individuating marks of the various collaborators make it into the final film? Unless you're setting out to make a reflexive film precisely about the trials and tribulations of collaboration, how will you point to your respective differences in a way that doesn't seem fractious or narcissistic? Most importantly, will you all be able to get along?

Nuts and Bolts

PART TWO

3. Picture

This chapter discusses both the aesthetic and the technical side of image-making. First there is a brief description of composition, and how you can control it. Then there's an outline of different kinds of shots and camera moves, as well as transitions—ways you can connect shots in the editing room. Finally, there's a section on the technical side of film and video images—how to use the lens to create the kind of image you want, and how to respond to or adjust the lighting conditions to maximize picture quality. This last section, "The Camera's Eye," deals with familiar concepts, like focus and depth of field, but they will probably seem more complicated than you expect. Though this section takes a bit of work to wade through, it will repay the effort. For once you fully understand the concepts, you'll have much more control over your camerawork.

A word of caution in advance. A film's style tells you a lot about the relationship between the filmmaker, subjects, and spectators. The conventions of composition, and of shots, moves, and transitions are all laden with meanings of various kinds. It's up to you to ask yourself as you go along which style(s) are appropriate for the kind of film you want to make. Documentary tends to be a little looser about filmic rules and regulations than fiction, yet the way it constructs its visual universe is fairly similar. Although documentary is now made by people at all ends of the earth, it evolved initially in Europe and North America, and many of its conventions reflect cultural codes that were initially specific to that world. While style and substance are far from one and the same, they are deeply interwoven. Close-ups, to take a crude example, which cut subjects off at the shoulders, and are the stock-in-trade of broadcast news, are clearly related to modern—and still, to some degree, Western—notions of individuality and personhood. Cinematic conventions, in other words, come with cultural connotations built in, which you may not always be aware of. You can confirm them or you can contest them. In cross-cultural contexts, it's crucial to be as conscious of them as you can. Thus, it's important that if at any point you consider the codes of image-making outlined in the following pages to be unsuited to your project, you should feel free to abandon them. They're described here simply so you can start off knowing what they are.

◄ **FIGURE 10** *"Cannibal Tours"* (1988), by Dennis O'Rourke.

An image's composition is just as important to filmmakers as it is to still photographers and painters. But in film composition changes over time. Not only can objects or individuals in the frame move around, but the camera operator can move the frame (i.e., the camera and the lens) itself. Good cinematography involves responding creatively to changing composition.

Composition Rule of Thirds

In the final analysis, composition is subjective. If you feel that a composition suits your subject, you're better off shooting rather than stopping to wonder why. Still, composition is as subject to convention as any other aspect of film aesthetics. One of the most commonly reiterated codes is known as the "Rule of Thirds." Imagine your viewfinder, television, or cinema screen, divided into three vertical and horizontal bands:

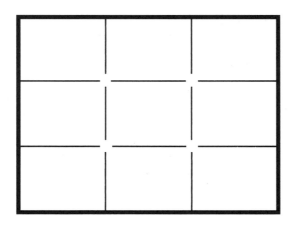

FIGURE 11 Composition Rule of Thirds. In conventional composition, the camera operator chooses an angle of view so that the centers of interest fall along imaginary vertical and horizontal lines splitting the frame into three in each dimension. In controlled situations, you can even try to place them at the points where the grid lines intersect.

FIGURE 12 In the left-hand image, where the Rule of Thirds is applied, the woman's face is located at an intersection of two of the imaginary grid lines, as is the boy's. In the right-hand image, where the Rule of Thirds is *not* applied, their faces are farther apart and do not fall along the grid lines.

Most filmmakers try to position their principal center(s) of interest slightly away from the center of the frame, in both dimensions—along the imaginary lines and especially at their points of intersection. So in a medium close-up of two people talking, most camera operators would position one to the left of center and the other to the right. Likewise, in a shot of two people walking, a camera operator might try and shoot from an angle that positions both people along the vertical lines.

It's usually best not to compose too symmetrically—in a shot of two people, try to position the camera so that the people don't occupy the same image size. The easiest way to do this is to shoot with one of them nearer the camera than the other. A shot of this kind is more subjective, more *perspectival,* than a shot of two people equidistant from the camera. The space seems more lived in, and the spectator feels more present, closer to being a participant than an outside observer.

Headroom

People's heads, and in close-ups their eyes, are usually positioned about a third of the way down the frame, to either the left or right of center. Too much "headroom" (the space between the top of someone's head and the top of the frame) looks awkward and amateurish to most viewers. Unless you're shooting a static interview, the headroom will change as your subject moves toward or away from the camera. Likewise, if you need to zoom in on or out from someone's face, try practicing first, as you may have to tilt the camera up or down (see "Movement of the Camera Head," below) to compensate for changing headroom.

FIGURE 13 Headroom. In a medium close-up, you usually place a person's face nearer the top than the bottom of the frame, allowing the viewers to see part of the shoulders (as in the left-hand image). By contrast, if you framed a face at the bottom, there would be empty space above the head, and the person might look decapitated (as in the right-hand image). On the other hand, there may be occasions when you want to place someone's face at the bottom of the frame—if, for example, there is something significant on the wall behind him, or if he's talking about someone behind his back in the distance.

Noseroom

"Noseroom" refers to the distance between the edge of the frame and the nose of a subject, who is at least partially in profile in a close-up shot. Typically, noseroom should be greater than the space on the other side of your subject's head. In other words, a subject facing screen right should be positioned on screen left, so that the screen right gives us an intimation of what they're looking at. This is particularly true if the person is moving toward screen right. If you positioned your subject on the right it would look as if they were butting up against the edge of the frame; they would look confined, hampered. (Of course, that might be just the desired effect—say, to show what's happening behind someone's back, unbeknownst to them.)

FIGURE 14 Noseroom. When shooting someone in (partial or complete) profile, the camera operator usually frames the shot with more image space in front of the person than behind, so that the subject's gaze seems to fill the frame (as in the left-hand image). When "noseroom" is applied, the spectators will thus assume that the subject is aware of whatever is in front of him/her. When "noseroom" is not applied (as in the right-hand image), background detail behind the person's shoulder may be felt to go against the grain of what the person is saying or what s/he represents.

Diagonals

Camera operators try to produce dynamic and arresting images through patterns and lines of composition. Diagonals in particular are conspicuous and vital; they tend to grab the viewer's attention the moment they form on-screen, and they emphasize activity, acting as a force line or a dividing line between different parts or planes (or tones or colors) of the image. "Dutch" shots or angles (when the frame is tilted off the horizontal axis) can also be effective, though they immediately change the aesthetic of a film. Diagonals of all kinds give more of a sense of three-dimensional space than horizontal or vertical lines. But be careful not to overdo them in long static shots, like formal interviews—for converging or coincident lines and planes can also distract from other aspects of an image. A stair banister (or telegraph pole) that looks as if it is jutting out of your interviewee's head could simply look ridiculous.

FIGURE 15 In this production still from Robert Gardner's *Forest of Bliss* (1985) of a boatman on the Ganges, numerous elements of the composition, including the side of the boat, the oar, the river, and the built-up bank, all converge on the subject. The subject himself, located at the lower right, symetrically balances the building on the upper left. Note also the extensive depth of field—even most of the background is in focus.

Depth

Unless you intend a particular flattening effect—a film about the significance of spectacle in today's world, for example, might obsessively depict nothing but surfaces—you should compose your shots in depth, emphasizing space to and from the camera, in what is called the "z" axis. Movement in the z axis, either toward or from the camera, is inherently spatializing and dynamic, especially in a close-up shot with a wide-angle lens.

A long shot of a distant landscape that also features objects in the foreground is more stimulating than one in which everything is equidistant from the camera. (It also helps the audience to judge scale.) Reflections, shadows, and mirrors all add depth to an image, as well as making it busier, more contrasty, and more interesting. Mirrors, in particular, allow you to play with sensations of depth, even deliberately confusing or surprising your viewers.

NUTS AND BOLTS

FIGURE 16 Yanomamo Series. The Dutch diagonal of the central roof beam in this wide-angle shot leads the viewer's eye to the subject's face, as do the parallel lines of his arms, continuing down his left calf. His right lower leg is also reflected in the vertical roof support. Dynamic, converging lines like these make for arresting composition.

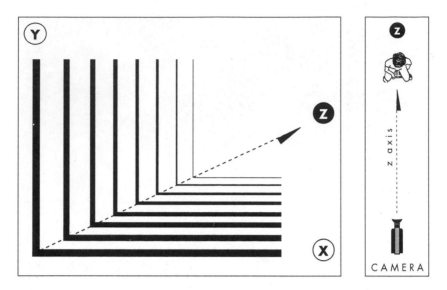

FIGURE 17 The X axis is the horizontal edge of the frame, and the Y axis is the vertical dimension. The Z axis extends out from the camera and adds a three-dimensional aspect to the image. Movement in the Z axis (by subjects or by the camera itself) makes the image come alive and the space seem lived in. The right-hand image shows the Z axis from above.

Center of Interest

Some filmmakers try to have only one real "center of interest" in each shot. If the screen is packed with important detail throughout, the spectators might not have enough time to see it all and understand its significance. But it is often difficult to have just one center of interest in documentary, as the center(s) of interest can both move and change during the course of a shot, depending on your framing as well as the action and dialogue. While most filmmakers try to frame their shots so that they don't cut people off at the edges (a rule generally worth following), it is sometimes unavoidable. And however "unacceptable" this is classically considered to be, it also reminds the viewers of everything that is taking place outside the frame, of how little is actually being represented on the screen. Moreover, many interesting documentaries do not so unequivocally sort out visual "signal" from visual "noise," and have multiple points of interest, constantly in flux. The result may be

FIGURE 18 In this shot of a Dani funeral from *Dead Birds* (1963), the sunlit arm immediately draws the viewer's eye to the visual point of interest, the face of the man in the center. If a shot like this is held for only a few seconds, the viewers do not have time to roam the image for digressive detail or other points of interest.

pleasantly dense to some viewers and merely distracting to others. In cross-cultural contexts, what is semiotic signal and what is noise is a dicey issue. In particular, were your subjects to watch your film, they would probably see a lot more significance at the edge of your frame than foreign audiences would. As you compose your shots around "centers of interest," it helps to imagine what they will mean to your prospective viewers, and how they might resonate differently for different audiences.

Camera Height

It's often said that a low camera looking up at a subject confers respect on them or accentuates their magnitude and grandeur, while an eye-level camera implies level-headed equanimity (the stereotypical composure of a mild-mannered journalist or demure ethnographer), and a camera looking down on someone insinuates that they are in some way or another inferior. There's some truth to this, but relative camera height has no hard-and-fast connotation, and the effect of a particular shot will probably derive more from the mood established in the images leading up to it than from its own camera position.

In Leni Riefenstahl's *Triumph of the Will* (1934), for instance, Hitler is initially shot from above. He has arrived in an airplane, and the camera gazes over his shoulder at the crowds that are lining the streets. The high camera angle in effect elevates Hitler's own status, looking down on the throngs of admirers before letting us clearly see Hitler himself. When we do get to see Hitler from the front, it is from a *low* camera angle, dramatizing his presence. But the camera angle on his admirers is also now from below. Rather than demeaning his followers, the effect is to transform them equally into almighty Aryan beings.[1] In this case, a high angle "over-the-shoulder" shot can have a similar significance to a low angle frontal shot.

Though you have considerable freedom in choosing your camera height, you should be cautious about shooting extreme low or extreme high shots. Particularly when accompanied by a wide camera angle, they tend to make subjects look so distorted and generally unfamiliar that the effect is more likely to be fantastic incongruity than it is condescension or submission. (This is why they are so common in horror movies.)

Screen Dominance

The larger someone's (or something's) image size, the more that image dominates the frame. If you have two or more people in a shot, the one who takes up more space on the screen will attract most of your viewers' attention—unless the other is brighter or in clearer focus. (Similarly, the person placed higher in the frame will also tend to dominate, as in Mesopotamian carvings.) In short shots this is particularly true, since viewers don't have time to roam the image in a search for detail and other points of interest. If the composition is changing as you're shooting, it's useful to stay attuned to who or what is dominating the screen.

Storyboarding

In order to visualize composition in advance, many fiction film directors "storyboard" their shots, making drawings for every shot of every scene.

FIGURE 19 Storyboarding helps you work out beforehand how you might shoot a scene. It is more useful in controlled than in uncontrolled situations, and can only be approximate. Whereas the storyboard makes each shot look still, there will also usually be movement within the shots. In this example, the sequence starts with an over-the-shoulder shot of a parishioner at the back of a church looking down the aisle to the priest behind the altar in the distance. The filmmaker then imagines shooting (or zooming in for) a medium frontal shot of the priest holding the eucharist bread and wine, followed by a long shot from the priest's perspective of the parishioner walking down the aisle. (In a documentary context, with a single camera and without any re-enactment, it would only be possible to shoot both Image 1 and Image 3 if the camera operator hurried down the aisle while the parishioner was standing still at the far end.) The filmmaker would then cut to Image 4, a frontal close-up of the bread and wine, representing the parishioner's point of view, before either cutting or else moving out and around to shoot a medium side shot of the priest (Image 5). From there, the film-maker would either cut, move the camera in, or zoom in to shoot Image 6, a close-up of the parishioner receiving communion. This style of filmmaking combines a multitude of different camera angles, and shots and reverse-shots.

The drawings may be schematic or highly detailed. In a practical sense, they can help you figure out what shots or camera angles you need to "cover" a scene satisfactorily. But storyboards are of mixed value in documentary. In part this is because a lot of the meaning and interest of documentaries derives from the content of the picture as it plays out over time, making composition—formal relationships between visual elements of a static frame—difficult to predict. The last thing you want is to find yourself trying to cover a scene unfolding differently from your expectations by confining it to a series of imaginary compositions that you had drawn up beforehand. If you find that storyboarding helps you visualize your subject without tying you to your preconceptions, it can be very helpful. If not, it's best to avoid it.

SHOTS AND MOVES

Filmmakers have their own jargon for various kinds of shots and moves. It provides a convenient shorthand used by the director, camera operator, and sound recordist on location, and the director and editor in the cutting room. The terms are also used in scripts and treatments to give people an idea of what possible scenes will look like.

SHOTS

Most documentary filmmakers try to combine a variety of different kinds of shots to maintain the viewers' interest—in particular, close-ups for detail and long shots for context. There are, in fact, six basic sizes that filmmakers and editors refer to (as well as infinite degrees in-between): "extreme close-up," "close-up," "medium close-up," "medium shot," "long shot," and "extreme long shot."

Extreme Close-Ups

An extreme ("big" or "tight") close-up could be someone's fidgeting finger, an ear, a big toe, or the stamen of a flower (perhaps shot with a special macro lens). The most common extreme close-up is of someone's eyes or, at a stretch, their eyes and nose. Because the object or body part is magnified, it can easily look ridiculously unnatural. Ex-

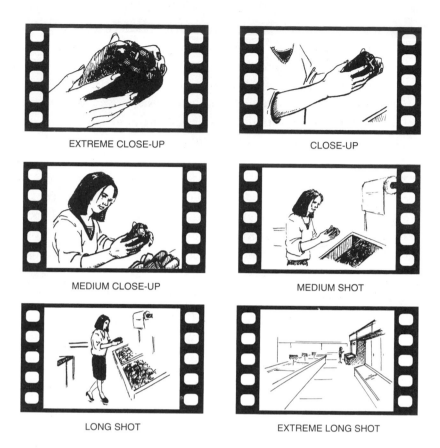

EXTREME CLOSE-UP

CLOSE-UP

MEDIUM CLOSE-UP

MEDIUM SHOT

LONG SHOT

EXTREME LONG SHOT

FIGURE 20 Shots classified by image magnification.

treme close-ups loom large in nature films but are quite rare in other documentaries. Exceptionally, Trinh T. Minh-ha uses extreme close-ups of body parts and architectural details in *Reassemblage* to introduce an aesthetic of fragmentation that is at odds with the holism and realism to which ethnographic films typically tend. If you like extreme close-ups, be sure to use them self-consciously, well aware that you may be defamiliarizing an object beyond all recognition. They can be quite effective at the beginning of a zoom out (see "Zoom," below), as the nature of the object will only be disclosed slowly over the course of the move, forcing your spectators to imagine and reimagine what it might be.

Close-Ups

Close-ups are common in both fiction and documentary. A "close-up" is a very dramatic, tight shot, often of someone's head, usually full-face, cut off anywhere from just above the chin to the shoulder line. A director might also ask for a close-up of an interviewee's twitching hands or of a picture above their head to use as a "cutaway" or "insert" shot during editing (see "Inserts or Cutaways," below).

It's important to shoot close-ups of your main characters, because one of the difficulties faced by documentary editors is making characters recognizable to the spectators—a problem particularly acute in the first few minutes of a film. Since documentary filmmakers have to shoot in wildly differing light conditions, on different days, often when their subjects are wearing different clothes, it's an uphill struggle to make main characters distinguishable from each other. Additionally, if your main distribution outlet is to be video or television, it's especially important to shoot close-ups, since a TV monitor is so much smaller than a cinema screen. (But remember that the final image, on a television or cinema screen, will probably cut off the outer edge of the frame visible in the viewfinder, so be sure to shoot tests first.)

In *The Good Woman of Bangkok* (1991), for instance, Dennis O'Rourke introduces his main character, Aoi (a Thai prostitute), through a series of close-ups. These are intercut with an on-camera interview with Aoi's aunt talking about her niece. First we see Aoi in close-up applying makeup in a mirror, then we see her hands dividing money, and finally there's a tilt down from her made-up face to her hands attaching a brooch to her bra, followed by another tilt back up to her face. Without yet hearing Aoi speak, these close-ups have already told us a lot about her, and we'll easily be able to recognize her throughout the rest of the film.

Because of the great magnification involved in close-ups and extreme close-ups, subject movement causes considerable screen displacement. Even the tiniest movement will be so accentuated that it may be difficult for you to keep the subject in the frame. This is not necessarily a problem: screen displacement, like magnitude generally, can be dramatic. You have two choices: you can zoom out or move away, or else you can simply let your subject go in and out of frame, deliberately creating a sense of off-screen space.

Medium Close-Ups

The standard medium close-up is a head-and-shoulders shot, and is probably the most common shot of all in television (though not in films). It's usually either a full-frontal picture or a three-quarter profile with your subject looking a little off-axis (say, to an interviewer to one side of the camera). It can also be a full 90° profile or even, more rarely, a shot of the back of someone's head. Unlike a close-up, it leaves some headroom above the subject and typically cuts off in the middle of the chest, above the elbow.

Medium Shots

Medium shots show most of the body, generally cutting off somewhere between the waist and the knee. They're often used when you're shooting interactions between two or three subjects. Usually the subjects fill the frame so that the spectators don't get much background, contextual information. The subjects are likely to be at least partially facing each other, rather than the camera (except in journalistic or mock-journalistic contexts).

Long and Extreme Long Shots

In long shots, subjects still fill most of the frame in the vertical dimension, whereas in extreme long shots, like panoramas, they will be relatively small in the frame. Facial detail (and so recognizability) will be minimal in long and extreme long shots; body size and bearing, clothes, and gait provide the main clues to character identification. Both kinds of shots are used to show a subject's relationship to their environment. (Long shots are sometimes called "wide" shots, which can be confusing since they aren't necessarily taken with a wide-angle lens.)

Both *Lorang's Way* and *N!ai, the Story of a !Kung Woman* open with revealing extreme long shots. *Lorang's Way* begins with an image of tiny men and then camels making their way across a vast East African plain in a dust storm. Though we can't see Lorang (or the features of any individual) we hear him speak of his life and know that the filmmakers are setting up a relationship between him and this harsh environment. By contrast, *N!ai* begins with a shot of indistinguishable individuals standing around in an ugly cement compound, part of the squalid environment in which the !Kung have been condemned to live.

Establishing Shots

"Establishing shots," often long or extreme long shots, introduce a setting in which a scene is being played out. Because they tend to contain a lot of detail, they need to be held longer than close-ups, which make their impact more immediately. An establishing shot lets viewers infer spatial relationships between a succeeding series of closer shots. Sometimes it's only in the editing room that you discover you're missing an establishing shot needed to keep your viewers oriented within a sequence of close shots. So it's best to shoot plenty of establishing shots on location, fully expecting that you won't end up using all of them.

When you get to the editing stage, it's important to bear in mind that a cut from an establishing extreme long shot to a close-up is likely to be too much of a jump for the audience to swallow, even if they recognize the character from the previous shot. Usually you have to cut first to a medium shot, and then to a close-up.

Slow Disclosure

Of course, filmmakers shoot and edit scenes in a variety of ways. Rather than beginning with an establishing shot, which sets the scene and lets the viewers navigate through the upcoming images, you can also begin a scene with close shots that don't disclose the whole space, and only gradually reveal the setting. This principle of slow disclosure is based on ambiguity as much as clarity. It's a way to introduce drama, or even suspense, as you oblige the viewers to make heads and tails out of the relationships between subjects, and between the subjects and their environment. Using this principle, you might begin a scene with a close-up, or medium close-up (perhaps with a short depth of field, which would leave the background out of focus), and work up to a long shot. While slow disclosure is constructed in the editing room, you can sometimes shoot a scene bearing it in mind. For instance, if you're shooting an activity observational-style, in a single take, you could start with an extreme close-up and after a while gradually pan across, tilt up, or move out to show the context. You will probably maintain the viewers' interest for far longer than if you immediately show them everything in a single long shot.

Robert Gardner, for instance, uses slow disclosure in introducing one of the main characters in *Dead Birds*. When we first meet Weyak, the "warrior," all we see are his hands twisting string. What is he doing? we wonder. Repairing a fence? Making a weapon? Next we see a close-up of his face, and after that his hands forming a woven band. He is weaving, the voice-over tells us, as all men do. But where is he? Finally, Gardner provides us with a long shot, showing Weyak sitting in a field. Perhaps this is where Weyak will fight, but we won't know this until later.

It's also common to move between different locations by cutting initially to a close-up of someone, which the audience may assume is set in the same space as the previous shot, and then cutting to a long shot of the same person engaged in the same action (say, walking or driving a car) in which, *retrospectively*, the viewers realize that they had already shifted settings in the previous shot.

Number of People

Another way filmmakers and editors describe shots is in relation to the number of people featured. "One-shot," "two-shot," "three-shot," "group-shot," and "crowd-shot" are the basic terms. In treatments and during production these terms are usually combined with others. Thus, a "medium two-shot" is a medium shot of two people, probably cutting them off just above the knee. If both subjects are the same distance from the camera, the camera couldn't go any closer than a medium shot without cutting their sides or shoulders out of the frame. But if the two subjects are shot in depth, with one closer to the camera than the other, you can also have a "close-up two-shot." In this case, the subject closer to the camera (and so larger on the screen) is said to be "favored."

Camera Height

Shots may also be referred to in terms of camera height—"high," "low," and "knee shots" are all common expressions. A "bird's-eye-view shot" is taken from overhead. Its perspective is unlike that of a human being's (except in rare conditions; for example, if you were looking over a cliff or off the roof of a building). It is usually read, not as a disinterested, objective shot (like a standard landscape or cityscape), but as indicating an abnormal subjective point of view—which is why it is more common in horror films than in documentaries.

Inserts or Cutaways

Another way of talking about kinds of shots is in terms of the use they serve in the editing room. Most filmmakers shoot "cutaways," also known as "insert" shots. These let you edit together two otherwise unbridgeable shots, as well as to manipulate the spectators' sense of time and space. Cutaways tend either to be close-ups of objects in the vicinity of the scene, often objects featured in the previous image or the hypothetical point of view of a subject (say, from a window), or else to be representations of an object or event that a subject mentions (say, a portrait of a loved one). If the cutaway is a close-up of an object in the previous image, it is usually shot from a slightly different angle. Both subject movement and the content of what someone says may be used to "motivate" or signal cutaways.

Observational filmmakers have launched a withering attack on cutaways, however, precisely on the ground that they're not really motivated at all by the material, that they dishonestly disguise an elision of time or a shift in space, and that they are used simply to join together two images that wouldn't cut together on their own. This is true of some cutaways, but not all. Almost all films are cut to some degree (how many twelve-minute single-take films or sixty-minute single-take videos have you seen?). Some images do cut together better than others. What observational filmmakers are right to protest against is a lazy use of cutaways to join together elements that don't really have any (pro-filmic or even extradiegetic) connection to each other.

Over-the-Shoulder and Reaction Shots

The easiest way of covering an interaction between two people is to frame them both in a medium or long two-shot. Another way is to shoot over-the-shoulder shots of each of them. You can do this either with close-ups of each person's face in turn or with medium close-ups that also show part of the nearer person's back or shoulder. Each shot is taken from over the other subject's shoulder. Some of them may be "reaction" shots of one subject responding silently but visibly to the other.

This way of shooting an interaction is more interesting and varied than a single, static two-shot, since it brings into being a more complicated relationship between (one subject) seeing and (the other subject)

FIGURE 21 Over-the-shoulder shots. In reverse-angle over-the-shoulder shots, the viewer shares the optical perspective of first one and then the other subject. They are usually taken from between 90° and 180° apart. In this example, they are taken from exactly 180° apart. Note that each person occupies the same position on the screen (i.e., the woman on the left in the first image is also on the left in the second image, even though she now has her back to the camera). This makes it easy for the audience to recognize the subjects across the cut.

seen. But since most documentaries are shot with only one camera, and since, in any case, a camera would be visible over the other subject's shoulder if the scene were actually shot in real time without any re-enactment, there is a logical limit to this angle–reverse-angle structure in documentary. It turns the viewer into an unseen mediator between the perspectives of the on-screen participants, stitching or "suturing" the two different camera angles into a seamless whole. Observational filmmakers in particular work against the grain of this "omniscient" camera-eye, and try to tie the camera to the actual optical perspective of the individual filmmaker, who can only be in one place at any one time.

Over-the-shoulder shots do not have to be of people interacting face-to-face. An over-the-shoulder shot of someone contemplating a land-scape will probably be interpreted as representing the person's subjective point of view. If you're shooting in an observational style, you can also shoot over someone's shoulder without then getting a reaction shot over someone else's shoulder.

MOVES

There are three kinds of camera movement—movement of the (zoom) lens, movement of the camera head (i.e., horizontally or vertically), and

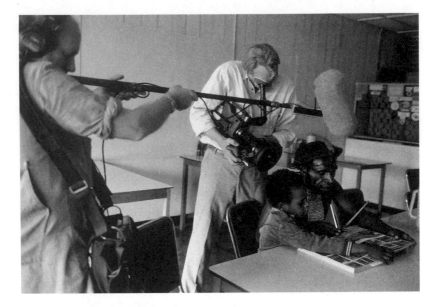

FIGURE 22 For *Roads End* (n.d.), Robert Gardner is shooting over the shoulder of Pua (of *Dead Birds*) looking at a photograph album (in Irian Jaya, 1989). This kind of shot is commonly used as a cutaway or insert shot in mainstream documentary.

movement of the camera in space, together with whatever it is mounted on (a shoulder, tripod, Steadicam™, or dolly). Much of the time you'll find yourself engaged in all three kinds of movement at the same time.

Zoom

A zoom lens is nowadays considered essential for documentary work, since it gives you much greater freedom than a series of fixed lenses. In the flash of an instant, you can zoom in to catch a piece of the action or a facial reaction that you'd miss if you had to move the camera physically. Tim Asch zooms in quickly, for instance, at the beginning of *The Ax Fight* as the fight breaks out, knowing full well that he doesn't have the time to run over there.

But a zoom should be used cautiously. Zooming alters the image size (the relative size of an object on the screen) rather than perspective itself. Thus, zooming into someone can never convey the same sensation as moving closer to the person. If you physically move up to someone, your whole perspective changes. Your audience will *feel* closer. But if you stay still and zoom into someone, your subject will simply end up occupying a larger image size and you will have a smaller angle of view. Your perspective on the person won't change. The move feels unnatural, and your spectators will sense (and share) your distance from the action. In effect, the zoom moves a scene closer to or farther from you and the audience, rather than moving you and the audience closer to or farther from it. This difference sounds subtle but it's not; it's immediately felt by the viewers. Thus, if you want to create the sensation of approaching or retreating from a subject, you have to move the camera itself, not just the lens. Fiction filmmakers "dolly" the camera along smooth "tracks" to mimic the perspective of a moving subject. Most documentary filmmakers just hold the camera on their shoulders as they walk in or away.

Be careful not to overuse the zoom. If you zoom too much, you may destroy the spectators' suspension of disbelief in what they're seeing. Zooming needs to be motivated, just like all other camera moves, since it changes the emphasis of a shot. It should reveal additional information or focus in on something that is germane to the scene. If you zoom, it's best *only* to zoom in or *only* to zoom out within a single shot. If you zoom in and zoom out within the same shot (or vice-versa), you distract from the scene itself, reminding the spectators that everything they see is mediated by your camera. (Of course, when you're shooting, you may want to zoom in and zoom out within the same shot, knowing that you'll probably cut out one of the moves in the editing room.)

It's also important not to zoom too abruptly. Very slow zooms, if well-executed, can pass unnoticed by spectators. Whenever possible, it's best to begin and end all camera moves, including zooms, on a static frame, which you should run for a few seconds before ending the shot. This is because it is easier to cut between two still shots than a moving and a still shot. Even if you end up choosing to cut into or out of the shot before the move is complete, you at least leave yourself the choice in editing. Additionally, all camera moves are at their most vulnerable (i.e., visible) at the beginning and end. Some editors throw out an otherwise smooth zoom shot just because it begins with a slight bump as the camera operator's finger touched the zoom control. There will be times when you have to zoom as fast as possible. These will be when you urgently need to change the field of view without missing any time. If you don't like the effect of a fast zoom, you can count on cutting out the move in the editing room.

Movement of the Camera Head

As well as moving the lens itself, you can also alter your image by moving the camera head. Horizontal movement of the camera head is called "panning," and the move, a "pan"—one that reveals a panorama. Vertical movement is "tilting," and the move, a "tilt." As with zooming, most filmmakers only move in one direction within a single shot, and they stop and start the move very smoothly. The exception is a "swish pan" (or more rarely a swish tilt)—a pan that moves extremely fast, but cuts out during the movement to a still shot, creating the impression that there was no cut at all and that the still shot is simply the end of the move. Another kind of swish pan cuts to a different image altogether, and signifies a different location.

Often you may want to pan and tilt at the same time—if, for example, you're following someone walking diagonally up a hill or an airplane coming in to land. Robert Gardner's *Dead Birds,* for instance, opens with a combined pan-and-tilt shot of a bird in flight. Though the camera is constantly moving, the shot is bordered at the beginning and end by large-lettered titles, making it unnecessary to start and stop on a still frame.

The timing of camera moves is crucial. In fiction films, moves often prefigure action—the camera might start panning right and the subject start walking right a second or two later. This can look odd in documentaries, as it implies that the camera operator knows what someone is going to do before they do it. In fact, documentary pans and tilts are often trying to catch up with action that has already begun, making it more difficult to perform them smoothly. Still, the earlier you anticipate a move, the smoother it'll be. Additionally, when panning along with a moving object, most camera operators leave more screen space in front of the object than behind it, so that we can see the space they're moving into before they get to it (and so the camera does not look like it's lagging behind).

If you expect that you might end up cutting from a pan of someone in motion (say, walking to screen right) to a still shot of the person at a later time, it's important to stop the pan at a certain point and let the subject leave the frame. Otherwise the cut will probably come across as a jump cut—one moment the person is walking, the next they'll be still.

Whenever possible (for example, with landscape shots), you should rehearse camera moves before performing them, because they're quite complicated. You need to position your body, especially your legs, so that you'll be comfortable throughout the move, and particularly at the end. This is true whether the camera is handheld or mounted on a tripod. If you want to shoot so wide a pan from a tripod that you'll have to cross one of the tripod legs during the move itself, you may need to rehearse it quite a few times before you can be sure you'll be able to follow it through smoothly all the way. If over the course of the move there is any radical alteration in lighting (say, you begin on a dark hole in the ground and tilt up to the sky), you may need to change the f-stop during the move (see "Aperture," below). Likewise, if there's any change in camera-to-subject distance, you may need to refocus. In either event, the move will be more difficult still, and if you're shooting (expensive) film, it's best to practice it until you get it right before actually shooting. If you can't rehearse a camera move beforehand, at least try to visualize it as precisely as possible before executing it.

Like zooms, pans and tilts need to be slower than you might suppose—otherwise the image will "strobe" (flicker) or "smear" (blur). If you're following an object in motion, this won't matter as much, since the spectators will be looking at the object, not the background, but if you're panning across a still landscape take special care. Try to allow at least six seconds for a small object to make it from one side of the frame to the other. If possible, practice pans of different speeds beforehand and, if you're shooting video, review them on a monitor to see how they look.

While cutting allows you to alter perceptions of time and space, and to set up relationships between the adjacent shots you juxtapose through editing, panning and tilting enable you to explore relationships *within* an image over time. You can lend editorial emphasis to contrasts in a way that is not possible with a simple, static shot.

Movement of the Camera Mount

Finally, you can move the whole camera through space during a shot, either by walking with it or by "dollying" (or "tracking" or "trucking") it. There's a memorable 2½-minute handheld walking shot at the beginning of *Celso and Cora* (1983), when Gary Kildea follows Celso and Cora through a poor neighborhood of Manila as they go to look at their new home. It's a shot that shows us far more about their environment than a succession of still shots would. New developments in independent camera suspension systems (such as Steadicam™), which partially remove the camera's center of gravity from the holder's body, allow experienced users to hold the camera steady while walking. There's a remarkable Steadicam shot in *Fronterilandia/Frontierland* that tracks past popular border personages standing around gnomically in a miniature architectural theme park in Tijuana, Mexico. The unreality of the Steadicam suspension and the slow motion of the film (as well as the fact that the model of the National Cathedral rotates) combine to create a fluid and lyrical nine-minute interlude initially devoid of any sense of scale in an otherwise very fast-paced and deliberately fragmentary film. (See chapter 5 for more on Steadicam suspension systems.)

A dolly is a mobile camera mount, the simplest dolly being a tripod on wheels. If a dolly can also move in the vertical axis during a shot, it's called a "crane" or "boom." These are expensive and more common in fiction films than in documentaries. You can improvise when it comes to dollies—rollerblades, skateboards, wheelchairs, bicycles, baby carriages, shopping carts, ski lifts, and cars are all regularly used by handholding camera operators.

TO USE OR NOT TO USE A TRIPOD?

The Russian filmmaker and theorist Dziga Vertov argued that the motion picture camera could see far more than our mere mortal, all-too-human eyes. He believed the camera could catch life "unawares" in a way that ordinary people, without a camera, never can. The camera, he insisted, could and would "render the ordinarily invisible visible to all."

FIGURE 23 Robert Flaherty setting up tripod-mounted shots for *Louisiana Story* (1948, together with Frances Flaherty, bottom right, and Richard Leacock, top left) and for *Elephant Boy* (1937).

I am kino-eye (cine-eye), I am a mechanical eye. I, a machine, show you the world as only I can see it.

Now and forever, I free myself from human ability, I am in constant motion, I draw near, then away from objects, I crawl under, I climb onto them. I move apace with the muzzle of a galloping horse, I plunge full speed into a crowd, I outstrip running soldiers, I fall on my back, I ascend with an airplane, I plunge and soar together with plunging and soaring bodies . . . free of the limits of time and space, I put together any given points in the universe, no matter where I've recorded them.

My path leads to the creation of a fresh perception of the world. I decipher in a new way unknown to you.[2]

Vertov's vision sounds exhilarating. Film cameras, together with telephoto and infrared lenses, slow and fast motion, can indeed show us aspects of reality that would ordinarily pass us by. However, a film or video camera is in fact, not more, but *far less* mobile than the human eye. The moment you put a camera on top of a tripod you're struck, not by the mobility and agility of the equipment, but by its colossal clumsiness.

Observational filmmakers responded to this predicament in the 1960s by taking the camera off the tripod, and holding it with their hands. As a result, an aesthetic of unsteady handheld imagery has come into being, appropriated by television commercials in the late 1980s and 1990s. Though it's no less arbitrary than the aesthetic of the steady, "professional" tripod-mounted shot, it has become one of the stylistic hallmarks of the documentary, connoting a lack of artifice and an authentic, intimate, and direct approach to one's subject. As Jean Rouch insists:

For me . . . the only way to film is to walk about with the camera . . . improvising a ballet in which the camera itself becomes just as much alive as the people it is filming. This would be the first synthesis between the theories of Vertov about the "cine-eye" and those of Flaherty about the "participant camera." I often compare this dynamic improvisation with that of the bullfighter before the bull. In both cases nothing is given in advance, and the smoothness of a *faena* (strategy of play) in bullfighting is analogous to the harmony of a traveling shot which is in perfect balance with the movement of the subjects.

Here again, it is a question of training, of the kind of mastery of the body that proper gymnastics might allow us to acquire. Then, instead of using the zoom, the cameraman-filmmaker can really get into his subject, can precede or follow a dancer, a priest, or a craftsman. He is no longer just himself but he is a "mechanical eye" accompanied by an "electronic ear." It is this bizarre state of transformation in the filmmaker that I have called, by analogy with phenomena of possession, the "cine-trance." [3]

Whether (or when) you choose to shoot with a tripod will depend on how you want your film to look. A tripod or other camera mount is almost essential for some shots. When shooting with a long focal length (see "Focal Length," below), you may not be able to keep the frame still without one. You may not even be able to keep your subject in the frame. Any shot with strong vertical or horizontal lines also accentuates camera movement. However, handholding the camera vastly increases your mobility. It's also objectively a lot less intrusive, and thus permits (but doesn't ensure) a more informal relationship with your subjects. If you want to film everyday life in an observational style, handholding your camera, at least much of the time, makes a lot of sense.

Smooth Handholding

When you handhold, you'll probably want to try to keep the frame as stable and balanced as possible. It's much easier to hold a wide-angle lens steady than it is a long focal length. Whenever possible, try to rest your arms or whole upper body on something—the top of a wall, a table, a car, or the ground. A blanket or any soft material like a cushion or a thick sweater will make your shot steadier still. If you can't rest your arms on anything, tuck your elbows into your chest. If you are standing, crouching, sitting, or kneeling, try also to lean your back against a wall, a tree, or other solid vertical surface. Position your feet apart and bend your knees a little. Most importantly of all, make sure you're comfortable. Palmcorders and other tiny handheld cameras are far more difficult to hold steady than models that can rest on your shoulder. You have to hold them tight to your forehead and push the viewfinder cup against your eye.

FIGURE 24 Jean Rouch, shooting a Dogon divination ceremony in Mali, West Africa. To keep the camera stable, he has his left lower leg resting on the ground, his right elbow resting on his other leg, and his left arm pulled into his chest.

Handholding the camera, particularly when you're walking, requires real discipline from your body, and lots of practice. Remember that your shoulders have a suspension system independent of your legs, and try not to let the camera bob up and down as much as your shoulders usually would. As ethnographic filmmaker John Bishop suggests, "You need to duck-walk, gliding along with bent legs, like Groucho Marx."[4]

TRANSITIONS: SHOOTING TO EDIT

> Not until you come to cut do you realise the importance of correct analysis during camerawork and the essential need for preliminary observation. For unless your material has been understood from the inside, you cannot hope to bring it alive. No amount of cutting, short or otherwise, will give movement to shots in which movement does not already exist. No skill of cross-reference will add poetic imagery to your sequence if you have been unaware of your images during shooting. Your film is given life on the cutting-bench, but you cannot create life unless the necessary raw stuff is to hand. Cutting is not confined to the cutting room alone. Cutting must be present all through the stages of production—script, photography and approach to natural material—finally to take concrete form as the sound is added.
>
> —Paul Rotha

Although shots are often considered the basic element of film, they're not the only unit. They are generally organized into "scenes"—series of shots set at the same place and the same time. Scenes, in turn, are sometimes said to be organized into "sequences," a collection of scenes related to each other, within the context of a larger story, and the film as a whole. Shots also cannot really be considered without taking into account what both join and separate them: "transitions." Most transitions are straight cuts, though there are other kinds described in chapter 8. While transitions are produced during editing, you also have to have them in mind when you're shooting.

Recently the tendency in mainstream documentary has been for shots to get shorter and shorter, thus making relationships established by cuts all the more important. Many of the strengths and possibilities

FIGURE 25 Screen axis. In this schematic bird's eye view, the axis follows the dotted line and passes through both people's heads. The trick is to try to keep the camera on one side or the other of the line within a single scene, or as long as you imagine you will want to maintain continuity.

of longer takes have thus been occluded. In Raul Ruiz's *Of Great Events and Ordinary People* (1979) there is a quiet moment in the middle of a relatively long take (a moment that television has accustomed us to consider "dead" or "empty"), at which point the voice-over narrator relieves the calm by remarking, "Now the narrator should say something to fill this space." The line could equally have been "Now the editor should splice in another shot to cut out this space."

SCREEN DIRECTION

The most common way filmmakers "shoot to edit" is with an eye to simulate a seamless continuity of space and time. Different shots, from different angles, taken originally at slightly (or very) different times, can be edited together to create the impression of ongoing real time. An essential element of continuity editing is maintaining *consistency of screen direction* (also known as the "axis," the "line," the "stageline," or the "180° rule"). The screen direction of a shot is easily grasped when you see it, although it may depend on a number of factors. The main factor is the direction in which the dominant screen subject is moving, facing, or looking. Imagine a hypothetical line dividing in two the three-dimensional space that extends out from the subject along their "sagittal plane"—through the front of their head and out the back. If there is no single dominant subject, imagine a line passing through the

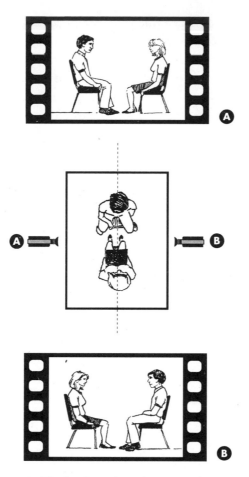

FIGURE 26 Screen axis. The first frame (at top) corresponds to camera position "A," and the second frame (at bottom) corresponds to camera position "B." If you cut between these two frames, the characters would suddenly change positions, and your audience might be disoriented. But if you cut between shots taken from the same side of the axis, the characters would maintain their positions on the screen, and the audience would be able to retain its bearings.

principal axis of action. The rule is to *stay on the same side of that line between any two shots if you wish to simulate continuity.*

For example, if you were shooting a two-shot of a conversation between a man and a woman, and the man was on screen left facing right and the woman on screen right facing left, and you cut to another shot of them, taken from the other side, they would seem to have all of a sudden switched positions and directions—the man would be on screen right facing left and the woman on screen left facing right. Your spectators would wonder how the two had gotten into each other's seats. Likewise, if you're shooting, say, a side shot of a train going to the screen left, and cut to a shot of the same train from another camera positioned on the other side of the tracks, the train would all of a sudden seem to be going in the opposite direction.

Editing in this discontinuous way (i.e., "jump cutting") is actually quite common, but it's used to indicate a break in space or time, rather than continuity. In other words, it tells the viewers that the two shots are separated by some period of time that has been left out of the film. In this example of the train, the cut could be read as signifying any number of things, depending on its context in the larger film—a contrast between the beginning and the end of the day, for example, or the endless back-and-forth drudgery for the driver. If a shot of a driver and car facing screen left were replaced by one of them facing screen right and that in turn by another of them facing screen left, it would probably be taken as implying that the driver was lost or that the journey was long, or futile. This kind of cutting is often used in high speed chases.

The trick, then, when you're shooting for continuity is to stay on one side or the other of the principal axis of action. This gives you an almost 180° angle to position the camera within. It is crucial to stay within this angle when shooting shot–reverse shots of two people talking—otherwise, when you edit the two shots together, it will look as if they are talking to different people or sitting in different spaces. Likewise, if you cut from a close-up of one of them on the screen left facing right to a close-up of the other, also on the screen left facing screen right, it would look as if they were both talking to a third party, or to different people altogether—in short, to anyone but each other. Try to stay on the same side of them. If you decide to shoot close-ups of each in turn rather than (or as well as) a single two-shot, frame one of them on screen left facing right and the other on screen right facing left, and you'll find they'll edit together perfectly. Similarly, if someone (or something) leaves from screen left, and you think you might want to cut to them at a later moment in the same action or journey, you may want to position the camera so that they enter from screen right. If possible, change their image size, too, so it doesn't look like a jump cut: if the first shot was a medium shot, consider cutting to a close-up or a long shot.

Of course, scenes often have more then one axis, which makes staying on one side more difficult. For example, if two people were walking down the road talking to each other, looking at each other half the time and at the road under their feet the rest of the time, there would be two axes—one along the length of the road, and another perpendicular to that, passing between the two subjects. Scenes with more than one axis give you more freedom in the editing room, because you can cross over one, but not the other, without disorienting the spectators too much. Most action scenes have two or more axis lines.

How to Cross the Axis

Often in the editing room, you'll want to cross over the axis—that is, to change the screen direction—and still maintain space-time continuity. How can you shoot so that you'll be able to do this? There are at least four ways. First, if you're shooting with a moving camera (i.e., on a dolly or handheld) you can simply move from one side of the axis to the other, *during the course of a shot, filming all the while.* Your spectators will then cross the line with you, and not be disoriented by the subjects' new screen positions. Once you've crossed the line, you've freed up your editor to cut to other camera angles from the new side of the line. A second way is to shoot from a neutral angle—one taken on the line itself (head-on, or directly from the back). If the editor cuts from a shot taken from one side of the line to a shot from a neutral angle, and then to one from the other side of the line, the audience can usually retain their bearings. Third, if your subjects are mobile, the line itself will change. So long as you follow how it changes, you can change with it, and you should be able to shoot to edit. A final way of letting the editor cross the axis is to shoot cutaways, such as close-ups of objects in the vicinity. This is easy, and perhaps lazy, but if you haven't crossed the axis with the camera rolling, or taken a shot from a neutral angle, it may be the only way your editor can integrate material shot from both sides of the axis and maintain continuity.

ADDITIONAL TIPS FOR CONTINUITY

Matching Action

Another convention of continuity is to shoot for an overlap of action. This lets you make a "match cut" between two different shots in the editing room, so that the action seems continuous. A medium shot of a woman walking up to a door could be followed by a close-up of her hand reaching for and turning the knob. Most viewers probably wouldn't even notice the cut, if it was done well, even though the two shots are very different.

In documentaries using only one camera, shooting for an overlap of action is literally impossible without reenactments. This is why documentaries are so often filled with cutaways. But if you shoot a continuous, repetitive action with a single camera, and especially if you change the camera angle from time to time, you can match cut by condensing the action. For example, if (like Robert Gardner) you were shooting Weyak weaving, you could shoot the whole process, with some long, some medium, and some close-up shots. If you had covered the weaving well, you'd be able to intercut between different moments, and make them seem continuous.

You can also match cut to a different but formally or compositionally similar action that won't be disconcerting to spectators. For example, an interior shot of a woman walking out through her front door and then the door closing behind her could be cut to the same woman opening her office door. Done well, the cut would not disconcert spectators, who would accept the elision of time. The cut would function pictorially like a match cut, even though we've been moved to another space and another time.

Camera Angle and Image Size

The "image size" is the relative area that something or someone occupies in the frame, the amount of space they take up on the screen. You can control image size in two ways—either by moving closer to or away from your center of interest, or by adjusting the focal length of your

FIGURE 27 Even though the action is not strictly the same, these two shots from *Dead Birds* (1963) are similar enough that if you cut between them, you could simulate rough space-time continuity. If you cut from the top shot at a point when the army on the left lurched forward, the result might even seem to be a match cut. The camera operator is much closer for the bottom shot, making the image come alive so that we viewers almost feel we're part of the action. (It was *not* taken with a long focal length—or zoom—lens from the same position as the top shot.)

lens (see "Focal Length," below). The "camera angle" is the relative position of your camera vis-à-vis the scene it's recording—for instance, whether it is to the left or right of your main subject. In other words, the camera angle is where you place your camera; it has nothing to do with the objective angle of view of the lens, which is a function of its focal length.

You'll make the editing a lot easier if you change the image size and camera angle between shots as you cover a scene. However, *changes in image size or in camera angle should be neither too small nor too large.* This sounds vague, but you'll soon develop a feel for what will work by trial and error. If the editor were to splice together two shots that had been taken from just a slightly different camera angle, the audience would wonder why the cut was necessary or useful. They would probably read it as a jump cut—a break in continuity. The same is often true for a cut that joins two shots of the same scene taken from vastly different camera angles.

Likewise, if the editor were to splice together two shots in which the subject occupies a similar image size, that too would seem unconvincing to viewers. For example, it's difficult to cut from a medium two-shot of two people to a medium two-shot of two other people. The editor would be better off cutting to a shot in which the second couple occupy a bigger or smaller image size. Similarly, if you're shooting two subjects engaged in an activity (e.g., dancing), and you want to match cut on action, any cut from a medium two-shot to another medium two-shot will probably come across as a jump cut. So if you shoot some medium close-ups and long shots, you'll provide the editor with the material to put together a scene. On the other hand, any vast change in image size, such as a cut from a long shot of a distant cityscape to a close-up of a facade, could be disconcerting unless the facade was recognizable from the previous image. Sometimes you'll find that you have to cut from a long shot to a medium shot before going to a close-up.

So, the point is to shoot different image sizes from various angles. Otherwise, you could shoot all your footage, head off to the editing room, and find it's uncuttable. The trick is to look through the viewfinder with the eyes of an editor. That said, largely because of increased exposure to observational and experimental films (as well as music videos), spectators are becoming more tolerant of, and less disoriented by, jump cuts.

All this talk about continuity cutting, different kinds of shots and moves, and composition is useless if you don't know how to shoot in the first place. Shooting is as much a technical as an aesthetic matter, and it is the technical side that is addressed in this section. You will find it easier to follow if you have a camera in front of you as you read it through.

As you shoot you're simultaneously dealing with various factors, among them the lens, the recording medium (film, video, or computer hard drive), and the lighting conditions. You'll want to control the focus, contrast, and exposure of what you shoot, but they in turn are affected by the kind of lens you use, the stock or format you record on, and the intensity and quality of light. So this section is divided into three parts, "The Lens and the Image," "The Medium and the Image," and "Lighting and the Image."

THE LENS AND THE IMAGE

The image registered by the camera is transmitted through the lens. By adjusting things like the focal length and aperture of the lens, you can control how much of your image is in focus. You also have some control over the perspective of the camera on the scene in front of it, as well as the mood of the scene itself.

Focus

Almost all camera lenses have a "focus ring" around the lens itself, which can be turned to make the image sharp—to "focus" it. Unless you're filming in strong sunlight, or filming a two-dimensional object that fills the frame, you have to choose what you most want to focus on. This is because there won't be enough light for you to have everything in focus at the same time. As you rotate the focus ring, you adjust the distance between the end of the lens and the plane that the lens is focusing the image on. The farther away the objects you're focusing on are, the closer the lens will be to the film plane within the camera. Most modern viewfinders go in and out of focus automatically as you rotate the focus ring, allowing you to focus relatively easily (except in low light conditions) with your own eyes.

You focus most accurately if you keep on rotating the ring, bringing your subject into ever greater focus, until the image begins to go out of focus, and then turn the ring back again. It's best to do this with the aperture wide open—this lets you see better and also minimizes the depth of the "field" that will be in focus. If you're using a zoom lens, you should set it on its longest focal length (i.e., the maximum zoom setting). Most lenses also have camera-to-focused subject distances engraved on the focus ring, which you can check (with a tape measure) to verify the accuracy of your viewfinder.

How then do you decide what to focus on? This depends on the depth of the spatial field that you can have in focus. Often you want to have as much of the image in focus as possible—the foreground and the background. But sometimes you may want only a little bit to be in focus. You might want to isolate someone from the environment— whether to emphasize the person's solitude or simply to draw the spectator's attention to that particular figure. For example, most of the shots of workers at the Renault factory in *Chronicle of a Summer* have a very short depth of field (see *Depth of Field*, below). Shot with a long focal length lens, in low available light, the workers are in focus, but what is in front and behind them often is not. The cinematography acts as an implicit commentary on the atomistic, alienating nature of their work when they are abstracted from their environment in this way. Alternatively, you might want to focus so that your subject in the foreground is blurred, allowing your viewers to see clearly only what that person's looking at in the background. With experience and a good camera, you have quite a bit of control over this kind of *selective* focusing.

If you're focusing on someone who moves nearer to or farther from the camera, you may have to change the focus (or "follow focus") as the person moves. A sudden change in focus between someone or thing in the foreground and someone in the background—as the one quickly comes into focus, the other just as quickly gets blurred—is called "rack focusing." You'll probably find yourself having to rack focus if you shoot in relative darkness a conversation between two people at different distances from the camera. The extent to which you'll need to do this will

—ERRATA—

Cross-Cultural Filmmaking: A Handbook for Making Documentary and Ethnographic Films and Videos
Ilisa Barbash and Lucien Taylor

On page 133, the legend to Figure 28 should read as follows:

Figure 28 Depth of field. In the top image, all the foreground and much of the background (if not the trees in the far distance) is in acceptable focus. This was taken with an f-16 aperture. The bottom image was taken in identical light conditions, but only the youngest child is perfectly in focus. This is because the photographer opened the aperture up to f-1.8. In the bottom image, the viewer's eye is drawn immediately to the two girls. In the top image, our eyes wander all over, searching out detail. (See "Depth of Field" and "Aperture," below, for an explanation of how this process works.)

On page 143, the legend to Figure 33 should read as follows:

Figure 33 Zeiss/Arriflex lens. The upper ring of numbers on this Carl Zeiss/Arriflex 16mm lens lists the T-stops. You adjust this to set your aperture. The lower ring of numbers lists the distances between the camera and the plane of exact focus. You adjust this to set your focus.

FIGURE 28 Depth of field. In the top image, all the foreground and much of the background (if not the trees in the far distance) is in acceptable focus. This was taken with a f-1.8 aperture. The bottom image was taken in identical light conditions, but only the youngest child is perfectly in focus. This is because the photographer closed the aperture down to f-16. In the bottom image, the viewer's eye is drawn immediately to the two girls. In the top image, our eyes wander all over, searching out detail. (See "Depth of Field" and "Aperture," below, for an explanation of how this process works.)

depend on your depth of field, and this is connected to focal length and relative aperture.

Focal Length

Lenses are usually classified first of all by their "focal length," normally measured in millimeters. Focal length has nothing directly to do with focus; rather, it determines the size of the image magnification. Strictly speaking, it refers to the distance from the lens's optical center (its "nodal point") to a plane, within the camera, where the image of an (hypothetical) object an infinite distance from the lens comes into focus (the "image plane"). The shorter the focal length, the more the lens has to bend light waves to have them resolve into a correctly focused image. The farther an object is from the lens, the closer behind the lens the rays converge, and the smaller the object appears in the frame. If you halve the focal length of your lens, the same object will be only half the original size in the film image (assuming your distance from it hasn't changed). If you double the focal length, it will be twice the size.

Angle of View. Focal length is directly related to the "angle of view": the longer the focal length, the narrower the angle. "Short" focal lengths have a wide angle of view, and long lengths have a narrow angle of view. So if your camera has a zoom lens and you zoom in on an object, the overall size of the object registered on the film increases while your angle of view decreases.

Zoom Lenses. Fixed focal length ("prime" or "hard") lenses have only a single focal length setting, while zoom lenses have a continuum of possible settings. This versatility is the main attraction of zooms— you don't have to spend time changing lenses and filters to get a different focal length. But zooms can be more troublesome than fixed focal length lenses. The mounting (or "seating") of a zoom on the camera is crucial, for if it's not well maintained or properly mounted you can find that your focused image has become blurred by the end of a zoom move. They tend also to be a little "slower" than fixed focal length lenses, that is, their aperture can't open up to the same degree, and so they're not as good in low light. Additionally, because they contain more glass elements, there's likely to be slightly more internal flare, and reduced image clarity. Still, they're almost indispensable for uncontrolled docu-

FIGURE 29 A short focal length shot from *Natives* (1991), by Jesse Lerner and Scott Sterling. This shot has an angle of view wide enough to feature one subject at screen right in the foreground and another at screen left in the background. The man and the woman are clearly located on different image planes, and the composition of the image sets up an ambiguous relation between them.

mentary work, and their advantages far outweigh any drawbacks. (For more on choosing zoom lenses, see chapter 5.)

Perspective. Because focal length establishes your angle of view, it also relates to perspective. Perspective is *the rate* at which the image size of your subject diminishes as it recedes from the camera. Focal length in itself doesn't alter the perspective. So long as you stand still, zooming into or out of a stationary object will not alter your perspective on it. *But when a change in focal length is combined with either a moving camera or a moving subject (i.e., a change in the camera-to-subject distance) it changes the perspective.* In other words, a short focal length shot or a long focal length shot of the same scene will have the same perspective on it, so long as the camera is in the same place—even though the short focal length shot will show you a lot of the scene and the long focal length shot just a little. But if you physically move your camera toward your subject, the foreground will become magnified at a faster rate than the background, changing the overall composition of the two-dimensional image. A wide-angle shot accentuates distance in the Z axis—the axis extending out from the lens away from the camera—and so also apparently increases the speed of movement to and from the camera, generally conveying the sensation of inhabited, deep space. By contrast, a long focal length shot seems to compress this distance. We have all seen a long focal length shot of bicyclists climbing up a hill toward the camera, wondering whether they will ever make it—their efforts seem so futile, their movement painfully slow. A wide-angle shot from up close creates the contrary impression—the bicyclists will whiz past you in a blur of movement. So if you want to make your foreground seem close to the background, you should use a long focal length; if you want to accentuate the distance between them, choose a short focal length.

The long and short of this for the documentary filmmaker is to get in close and keep the angle wide. That makes the scene seem more alive and real. If you stay back and shoot with a long lens, you flatten and deaden the space. Jean Rouch has aptly compared the effect of the zoom lens to the subject-position of a "voyeur who watches and notes details from atop a distant perch."[5] A long lens was very effective for the unforgettable images of waves exploding into white on the Aran Island coastline in Flaherty's *Man of Aran,* but it generally works against the impression of "being there," in all its immediacy. What John Bishop has said of video is true of documentary generally: "Video is very intimate, the camera gets uncomfortably close to people and the camera person has to break normal assumptions about staring at people unflinchingly."[6] Close-ups are the stuff of documentary. Initially, it takes a lot of confidence and courage to get in close, but your camera is your license. So, while taking care not to offend others' cultural norms, move in!

Natural Perspective.   Different focal length lenses can make a given space look either expanded or contracted. But what focal length lens approximates how the world normally feels to our eyes? That is, what focal length renders a "natural" perspective? This depends on a number of factors. On a 35mm still camera it's usually said to be a 50mm lens. On a 35mm motion picture camera, the equivalent is a 33mm lens. On a 16mm motion picture camera, a 25mm lens was long felt to result in a natural perspective. However, both the increased projection magnifi-

FIGURE 30 From Robert Flaherty's *Man of Aran* (1934). This shot was taken with a long focal length lens, which has the effect of compressing space. The figure in the foreground seems relatively close to the breaking waves in the distance. Had this shot been taken with a wide-angle lens, the scene would feel more three-dimensional, and the viewer might have been tempted to identify more with the figure contemplating the froth.

cation on the larger screens of modern cinemas, and the effect of television in cutting off the outer edge of the image means that a "normal" focal length producing a natural perspective has become shorter. For 16mm film, focal lengths of between 12 and 14mm are now felt to come close to the feel of the human eye, in terms of depth of field, angle of view, and perspective. Many documentary filmmakers work at 10mm or below—this lets you get close to your subjects while still having a wide angle of view, and it also makes movement on the Z axis seem slightly more dynamic.

On a video camera, normal perspective depends on the size of the image sensors, or CCDs (charge-coupled devices—see chapter 5). On a camera with ⅔-inch CCDs, focal length is around 12mm; on a camera with ½-inch CCDs, it's 9mm; with ⅓-inch CCDs, it's 6mm; and with

¼-inch CCDs, it's around 4.5mm. Be careful not to zoom out to focal lengths much shorter than these, especially when shooting head-on close-ups of people, since you'll distort their faces, and if they gesture in the direction of the camera at all, the movement will seem unnaturally fast.

Depth of Field

A lens can focus *exactly* only on a single plane a certain distance away from the camera: a plane of "critical focus." Any single point on this plane will be resolved as a point on the film. However, real-life space is not two- but three-dimensional, and so an image is said to have a depth of field. This refers to a zone, which extends either side of this plane (both toward and away from the camera), in which the focus, while not perfect, is nevertheless tolerably sharp to the human eye.

Depth of Field Rule of Thirds. The first way to gauge what will be in focus in a given scene is simply to look through the viewfinder—though most viewfinders, because they're so small, are far too generous. If you focus precisely on a certain plane (say, the bridge of someone's nose), the depth of field extends both in front of and behind it, but not equally. Of the total depth of field, about a third is in front of the plane of critical focus, and about two-thirds behind it. In other words, twice as much distance behind the plane is in focus as in front of it. So if you want to have two subjects in focus, at different distances from the camera, be sure to focus on a point between them that is slightly closer to the nearer one. For example, if in a well-lit daylight scene your closest subject is five feet from you and the farthest is twenty feet from you, you should focus on a plane about ten feet from the camera. (In low light, though, you may not have enough depth of field, and possibly neither of them would actually be in focus.)

Circle of Confusion. If you're shooting controlled documentary, or a static shot, there's another way you can determine the depth of field that corresponds to your aperture size and camera-to-subject distance. This is by referring to the "circle of confusion." This is the degree to which a point or plane can depart from perfect focus on the film plane (inside the camera) while still remaining acceptable. The circle of con-

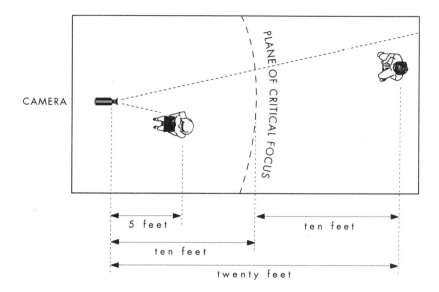

CAMERA

PLANE OF CRITICAL FOCUS

5 feet

ten feet

ten feet

twenty feet

FIGURE 31 Depth of Field Rule of Thirds. Regardless of your actual depth of field, roughly ⅔ of the zone that will be in acceptable focus extends back behind the point you focus on exactly (i.e., away from the camera), and only about ⅓ in front of it (i.e., toward the camera). So if you are shooting a two-shot, and your subjects are different distances from the camera, instead of rack focusing from one to the other, or having one subject always in focus and the other always blurred, you might want to focus on a point that is a third of the way between the two of them. This rule is useful when your subjects are stationary and when there is enough light to open up your aperture so that your depth of field is sufficient for both subjects to be in focus.

fusion for 16mm film has been estimated at between ¹⁄₁₀₀₀ and ¹⁄₂₀₀₀ of an inch, and widely available depth-of-field charts have been created on the basis of this measurement. (You can find them in the *American Cinematographer Manual*.)[7] Unfortunately, they're not absolutely accurate and don't always include the specifications for the widest apertures, so you should also consult the manufacturers' charts for all the lenses you're using. Even these don't take into account the size of the image screen, image contrast, or lighting conditions, all factors that affect the spectator's impression of sharpness. As a result, it's best to be conservative and estimate for a slightly shallower depth of field than the charts suggest.

Factors Affecting Depth of Field

A number of factors affect the depth of field—principally, the size of your aperture, the amount of light entering the lens, the distance between the camera and what you're focusing on, and the focal length of the lens.

Focal Length. The shorter the focal length, the greater the depth of field. So if you want to increase depth of field, choose a wider (or "shorter") lens or zoom out. A wide-angle lens in itself has hardly any greater depth of field *for a given image size* than a long lens, unless you set it at the "hyperfocal distance" (see below). But if you use a wide-angle lens to decrease the image size, you will increase the depth of field.

Camera-to-Subject Distance. Depth of field is also related to the distance between you and what you focus on (i.e., camera-to-subject distance). The farther your subject is from you, the greater the depth of field. If you're shooting a subject at close range, particularly if they're moving, focusing becomes especially crucial.

Light Intensity and Aperture Size. Another variable for depth of field is the intensity of light transmitted through the lens. You can control how much light *reaches* the lens and how much *passes through* it. If you decrease the size of your aperture, you increase the depth of field (see "Aperture," below). The more intense the incoming light, the more you need to "stop" the "iris" down (i.e., make the aperture smaller) to expose correctly. In sum, the depth of field will increase and decrease along with the intensity of incoming light.

Hyperfocal Distance. One way of maximizing depth of field in controlled situations is to set the lens at the "hyperfocal distance." The hyperfocal distance is the distance between the camera and the *closest* plane of *critical* focus for which the *far* limit of *acceptable* focus is infinity. In other words, you focus on the closest possible point to the camera itself which still keeps "infinity" (or the far horizon) in focus. Once you focus your camera on this hyperfocal distance, the *nearest* limit of *acceptable* focus will then be half that distance. So long as your subject doesn't break that limit, everything will look in focus, and you'll have maximized the depth of field.

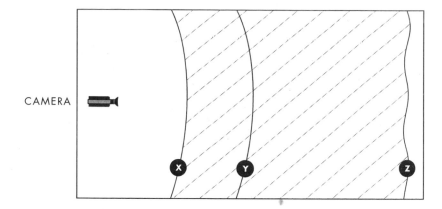

FIGURE 32 Hyperfocal Distance. The easiest way to set for hyperfocal distance is to focus first on the far horizon (Z), and then to turn the focus ring toward you until the horizon just begins to go out of focus. Then turn it back a little to find the last point at which the horizon was in focus. You have now set the camera to the hyperfocal distance (Y). Everything from *half* of that distance (X) all the way to the horizon should now be in focus (from X to Z). (Be aware, though, that not all viewfinders focus accurately and many are too generous.)

Hyperfocal distance varies according to aperture (f-stop) and focal length (as well as your estimation of the circle of confusion). The shorter the focal length and the smaller the aperture, the shorter the hyperfocal distance (i.e., the greater the depth of field). On very sunny days, with your aperture clamped down, setting the focus to the hyperfocal distance allows you to forget about focusing for all but the closest distances. The most accurate way of estimating hyperfocal distance is from the depth-of-field charts provided by the lens manufacturer. If your lens has a depth-of-field scale engraved on the outside, you can also select the hyperfocal distance by putting your desired aperture setting opposite the infinity setting of the focusing scale.

Depth of Focus. "Depth of focus" is a manufacturer's term that you see in technical specifications. It's confusing because though related to depth of field, it's different. Depth of focus is the distance on either side of the actual image focal plane *inside* the camera within which the film can pass through and still result in an "acceptably" focused image. It can be controlled only by technicians. All that filmmakers need to know is that depth of focus is inversely proportional to aperture size (i.e., the lower the f-stop, the shorter the depth of focus—see "F-Stops," below) but directly proportional to focal length. This makes depth of focus crucial on wide-angle lenses. Both zoom and wide-angle lenses have to be carefully mounted if they are to keep focus.

Aperture

Since lighting conditions vary from one documentary scene to another, you need to control the amount of light that enters the lens by adjusting the lens aperture (or "iris"). Lenses themselves work by reflecting light rays that bounce off the scene before them onto the film or video image sensors. Though you can control the apertures on many lenses, they still vary in their capacity to gather and admit light, and as a result, lenses have different "speeds." The apertures of some lenses open up more than the apertures of others. Fast lenses are best, as they admit the most light, and let you shoot in low light conditions that slow lenses can't accommodate.

Lens Speed. The "speed" of a lens is really its relative aperture. Relative aperture is measured in "f-stops," which is simply the ratio between a lens's focal length and the diameter of its iris diaphragm. Though you can change the focal length only on zoom lenses, you can control the iris diameter on almost all lenses (except for consumer camcorders) by turning the aperture ring to adjust the f-stop. This works the same way as the iris of your eye, which changes size in accordance with light conditions. If you're shooting in low light situations, therefore, you need to open the lens's iris up wide, and if you're shooting in sunlight, you'll probably need to shut it way down. The contrast between the light and dark areas of most real-life scenes is greater than can be handled by your camera (or, rather, by the film or video running through it). You can respond to this in a number of ways—by changing the lighting setup, choosing a suitable camera angle, selecting the appropriate film stock, adding a filter onto the end of your lens, and, above all, by adjusting the aperture.

F-Stops. In order to change the aperture, you select the f-stop you

FIGURE 33 Zeiss/Arriflex lens. The left-hand ring of numbers on this Carl Zeiss/Arriflex 16mm lens lists the T-stops. You adjust this to set your aperture. The right-hand ring of numbers lists the distances between the camera and the plane of exact focus. You adjust this to set your focus.

want on the aperture ring. Most ("reflex") viewfinders let you see how much light is passing through the lens by lightening and darkening accordingly. The standard sequence of f-stops is:

1, 1.4, 2, 2.8, 4, 5.6, 8, 11, 16, 22, 32, 45 . . .

Though not all lenses will have all these numbers written on the aperture ring, especially not those at either end of the sequence, and some will also mark half f-stops, the principle is always the same. Each full f-stop number is $\sqrt{2}$ times larger than the previous one. What is initially confusing is that, *as f-stop numbers mount, the aperture gets smaller*—the higher the f-stop, the less light is transmitted by the lens.

To be exact, each successive number admits half the amount of light of the previous number: f-2 results in half the exposure of f-1.4; f-2.8 results in a quarter of the exposure of f-1.4. Likewise, f-11 gives twice the exposure of f-16. By controlling f-stops on the aperture ring, you can control the exposure.

T-Stops. F-stops are the lens's focal length divided by the diameter of its iris. They're used for calculating depth of field. But they're not necessarily completely reliable when you're estimating exposure, since they make no allowance for the small amount of light that is lost when it passes through the lens. In fact, different lenses lose different degrees of light within their body—glass itself absorbs light and air-to-glass surfaces reflect and lose a little more still. In long zoom lenses, there can be as much as a whole stop difference from the f-stop selected. When you're calculating exposure, this would be crucial. As a result, in 1948 the Society of Motion Picture and Television Engineers (SMPTE) introduced T-stops (transmission stops), figures that adjust the f-stops to the characteristics of each particular lens. Most professional film lenses are marked in T-stops (and sometimes also in f-stops). For modern high quality prime lenses, the difference between an f- and a T-stop is often inconsequential, but with long zooms, it can be significant.

Sharper Images. A reminder: the most important effect that relative aperture has on the image is on the depth of field. The more you stop a lens down (raise the f-stop), the greater the depth of field. Similarly, almost all the aberrations inherent in lenses affect the picture quality less as you stop the lens down. This is bad news for documentary filmmakers who often have to shoot with their lenses as wide open as possible. Whether you're shooting wide open or stopped down, always try to keep the aperture at least two f-stops (minimally one) away from the limit at either end. Keeping the aperture between f-4 and f-11 will result in the sharpest images of all.

THE MEDIUM AND THE IMAGE

You can control the look of your images not only by adjusting certain variables of the lens but also by responding to the properties of your

FIGURE 34 In this cropped still from *The Nuer* (1970), the wall surrounding the opening serves as an additional frame, focusing our attention on the girl, whose body is aligned with the contours of the opening itself. However, the brightness range of the scene exceeds the contrast range of the film. The interior of the wall and everything outside is so under- or overexposed that all detail is lost. Usually you want to fit a scene's brightness range into your contrast range—by adjusting the composition and the lighting. But sometimes, for selective emphasis, you may want parts of the image to be technically over- or underexposed.

recording medium, be it film or video. In particular, if you are to expose your recording medium properly, you need to know how much (or little) light it can tolerate, and how to control the color of the light.

Exposure

The aperture not only affects image sharpness and depth of field; it also, most importantly, affects exposure. It controls how much light reaches the film. In the case of video, it determines the strength of the signal generated by electronic image sensors. Film and video differ in the way they are exposed (see chapter 5) and in how they register the image, but the properties of exposure hold for both media.

Brightness Range. When we look with our eyes at any scene, the objects in front of us reflect different degrees of light. On a sunny day, the light from the most reflective object may well be a thousand times more intense than that from the least reflective. Indeed, scenes with a "brightness" or "luminance" range of 1000:1 are common in everyday life. However, film and video are unable to reproduce such a broad scale, and you may have to compress the brightness range of a scene into something manageable by your medium. In documentary work, you have far less control over lighting conditions than in fiction filmmaking: you can't always compress a scene's brightness range enough to ensure that nothing in the frame is over- or underexposed. This means you may have to shoot knowing that part of the frame will be overexposed, "blown out" white.

Contrast Range. Different film and video stocks have more or less generous "contrast" or "exposure" ranges (sometimes incorrectly called "latitude")—black-and-white film more than color, negative color more than reversal color (see "Negative and Reversal" in the "Film" section of chapter 5), film more than video, Betacam more than VHS. Negative 16mm color film can tolerate a brightness range of around 100:1; it has an exposure range of around seven f-stops. When considering the relationship between a stock's contrast range and a scene's brightness range, you also have to think about the final viewing conditions you have in mind—whether, for example, your film will be projected in a dark theater or broadcast on a television screen. Current

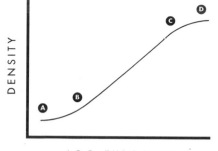

FIGURE 35 Characteristic Curve. The toe of the curve extends from A to B, and the shoulder from C to D. The trick is to try to expose as far as possible on the straight-line portion between B and C. Anything below B will be underexposed, and anything above C will be overexposed.

television and video technology can reproduce a brightness range of only around 30 or 40:1. This means that dark parts of films made for the big screen, like shadows that you can still see into, often become an impenetrable murk when they are broadcast on television.

Characteristic Curve

One way you can optimize exposure is by reference to a film stock's "characteristic curve." (The principles are similar for video, discussed in "Video Exposure," below.) Each film stock has its own curve, which plots the relationship between intensity of light and density of film emulsion. On reversal film, the more intense the exposure, the less the density. On negative film, the more intense the exposure, the greater the density. A typical (schematic) characteristic curve for a negative film would look something like the figure above.

Every characteristic curve is divided into three parts—a toe (A to B), a straight-line portion (B to C), and a shoulder (C to D). At some point between A and B an increase in exposure intensity starts to result in increased density in the film emulsion, which means that the light reflected to the camera will be registered on the film: this is the emulsion's threshold. Parts of the picture that fall between A and B on the curve make little impression on the film emulsion and, as such, show up as flat and muddy, or just plain black, on the final film. Similarly, parts of the picture that fall between C and D also make little difference to the emulsion density, and the film is unable to do justice to the differences in reflected light intensity in this area. Someone's face may end up looking as bright as their white shirt, or the cloudless sky behind them.

Optimum Exposure. Cinematographers usually try to expose as much as possible within the straight-line portion of the curve, resulting in an "optimum exposure," which makes maximal use of the contrast range of the film. You usually want to achieve the exposure that will reproduce as many tonal differences in your subject as faithfully as possible. An underexposed shot is thus one that falls in the toe area of the curve; an overexposed shot is one that falls within the shoulder. The laboratory that processes your film can lighten an underexposed scene and darken one that is overexposed, but the brightness or tonal range of the original scene will already have been overly compressed (by being over- or underexposed), resulting in a flatter, less contrasty, less lifelike image. Even on optimally exposed shots, however, shadows tend to fall within the curve's toe and highlights (or "hot spots" as they are known in video) within the shoulder. It's important to properly expose that part of your picture, say, a subject's face, for which you want maximal tonal separation, or highest contrast, knowing full well that your spectators won't be able to see any of the detail under the table and that the window will be wildly overexposed. The steeper the slope of a film stock's characteristic curve, the greater the contrast. Since the straight-line section is steeper than the toe or shoulder, you want to expose as much of the scene as possible within this area.

Gamma: Pushing and Pulling Film. The derivative (or "slope") of the straight-line section is known as its "gamma" (γ). Gamma is directly proportional to contrast or the separation of different tonalities. It is determined both by the emulsion (i.e., the film stock you choose) and by how (or how long) it is developed. If a roll of film is (deliberately or mistakenly) underexposed, you can ask the lab to "push" it when they develop it. This will lighten the film, as well as increase its graininess. Contrast variations in the lighter areas will also be increased. However, what was recorded as undifferentiated shadow (the toe of the curve) will remain such; blacks will look dull and foggy. You usually have to have a roll of film "pushed" if you want to shoot a scene but don't have enough light. For example, if you had 100 ASA film loaded, you could push it one f-stop by changing the camera dial to 200 ASA, and you would then be able to use a smaller (but probably still wide open) aperture and underexpose the film. So long as you tell the lab that you've underexposed the roll by one f-stop, they can correct for this when they process it. The advantage of a film stock with a low gamma, or a gentle slope, is that it accommodates a greater brightness range in the original scene. The opposite to "pushing," or raising the gamma of a given stock, is "pulling" or "flashing," which will result in higher contrast and greater detail *within the shadows,* but reduced overall contrast between the dark and light portions of the picture.

Although you usually push a film so that you can shoot with less light, you can also do so just to change the contrast of a scene. Fiction filmmakers often push their stock to imitate documentary. As a documentary filmmaker, you could push and pull film for various forms of synthesis and differentiation between different kinds of shots or scenes (though the predominance of realism in documentary has led to little experimentation in this regard).

Film Speed. The "faster" a film stock, the more sensitive it is to light; the "slower" a stock, the less sensitive it is to light. The speed is usually expressed as an ASA number (from the old American Standards Association) or in metric DIN (for Deutsche Industrie Norm). ASAs of 200 or above are considered high speed for 16mm film. A stock with half the ASA of another is half as sensitive to light. Film rated at 100 ASA, therefore, needs twice as much light as (one more f-stop than) film rated at 200 ASA.

Latitude. Film stocks have improved considerably in recent years, and all stocks have a higher exposure range (a longer straight-line section of their characteristic curve) than was imaginable two decades ago. They also have more "latitude"—that is, they are more tolerant of over- and underexposure than they used to be. Most 16mm color negative film has an exposure range of around seven f-stops, and can forgive up to two f-stops of overexposure and slightly over one f-stop of underexposure. This means that flashing and pushing film stocks is increasingly a special effect, rather than a process performed to ensure optimal contrast and exposure.

Video Exposure.   The principles of exposure are essentially the same for video as for film. If you overexpose video, the electronic image sensor will be overcome by the strength of the signal—it will be distorted above the full video "white level," and will lose detail and color accuracy. If you underexpose, the video level will be too low, and "noisy"—grainy and muddy. Because video has a much smaller contrast ratio than film, videographers have to take even more care about lighting conditions.

Most video cameras come with automatic iris control and a built-in light meter. Since the automatic iris and the light meter simply average out all the light reflected into the lens from the various parts of the frame, they make no allowance for the specific part of the frame you want to expose correctly. Some video viewfinders have another (optional) indicator of exposure, a series of black-and-white strips, known as a "zebra stripe," that appear over those parts of the frame exposed at or above maximum video level. Other cameras will also let you superimpose a waveform of the video level on the viewfinder image. Only professional video cameras give you any control over the brightness range they can assimilate.

Your ability to gauge exposure and contrast for yourself will increase with experience. How the image looks (once you know how to judge it) is more important than its objective video level. (For more on video formats and film stocks, see chapter 5.)

Controlling Brightness Range without Artificial Lighting

Responding to the brightness range of scenes often involves compromise. Unless you're setting up formal interviews or directing staged reenactments, you rarely have enough control over the action unfurling in front of your camera to compress its brightness range to the maximum contrast range of your film. If you're shooting video, which has a contrast range of between 30:1 and 40:1 (depending on your camera, format, and monitor), you have to be especially careful. The main way to manage brightness range lies in how you compose your shots. If you're shooting observational style, and don't want to interfere at all in what you're filming, you can control this only by choosing where you sit or stand with the camera.

Choosing What to Expose Optimally.   With some experience, you can tell whether or not the brightness range of your scene exceeds the contrast range of your film. Sometimes you simply have to accept a technically excessive brightness range. If you want to expose for a bright foreground—say, someone sitting in afternoon sun in front of a house shaded by a large tree—you may be well aware that all the background shades from middle gray to absolute black will be rendered alike as equally dark. Likewise, if you're shooting an interior scene of someone in front of a window that looks out onto the sunlit facade of a building across the street, and you try to expose for the facade, almost all the interior foreground will end up being rendered as undifferentiated silhouette and shadow. (This is a particular problem when shooting inside a car in daytime.) You would probably want to expose for the foreground, knowing full well that all the details outside the window will be lost in one big overexposed hot spot.

Pegging Key Tones.   When you shoot whole scenes—series of shots—it's important to peg the key tones, that is, to decide which ("key") tones you want to render optimally and to expose them consistently at the same level. In most documentaries, skin tones are the key ones, and you would try to expose them identically from shot to shot (within a scene set at a particular time). (See "Exposure: Incident and Reflected Light," below.)

Backlighting.   Backlighting is the most common cause of excessive contrast ranges. If you're shooting someone backlit close-up, you'll probably want to expose for the face, rendered slightly darker than normal, so that the image reflects the backlighting conditions, yet not so dark that the person is all shadow. But if you're shooting a long shot, with lots of background visible, you should probably stop down, so that the background is not "too" overexposed. This will slightly silhouette your subject, but in a long shot their facial features wouldn't be very clear anyway. If you expect to intercut between the two, it (oddly enough) looks more natural to expose them in this way at different settings than it does to have one image underexposed and the other over-exposed. But in very strong back-lit conditions—when you're shooting into the sun or against snow, sand, or sea on a bright day—you may end up with lens flare. If possible, recompose the shot, or block out the light with a shade, a piece of cardboard, or even a hand. Like landscape haze, flare overexposes (and fogs) film more than the high incoming light would anyway, so if you can't avoid it, stop down an extra half f-stop just to compensate for the flare. For high contrast scenes you can also attach a "low-con" (low contrast) filter to the end of your lens.

The Color of Light

White light, or hypothetically pure sunlight, is actually the sum of all additive colors, each with their own frequency. The visible spectrum extends from red, through orange, yellow, green, and blue, to violet. Black-and-white printing stock is only sensitive to violet and blue light. The three additive "primary" colors are red, green, and blue, and television screens are indeed composed of red, green, and blue phosphor dots. Color film, on the other hand, like oil paint, is composed of "subtractive" primaries that are complementary to the additive primaries: a layer of each of cyan, magenta, and yellow. In other words, if you take the red out of white light, you're left with blue and green, which together form cyan; and so on. Lens filters work in the same way, absorbing all colors except their own: a cyan filter will pass only red light, absorbing the blue and the green. Thus, color film actually has three characteristic curves, one for each color component of the visible spectrum—cyan on the bottom (sensitive for reds), magenta in the middle (sensitive for greens), and yellow on top (sensitive for blues).

Reds and Blues. Just as film and video cannot accommodate the vast brightness ranges that our eyes automatically compress, they cannot automatically make allowances for the different colors of the light coming through the lens. In the real world, light is always colored. Outdoor light, and everything it reflects on, has a bluish tinge, while most artificial indoor light, and everything it reflects on, is reddish. (Fluorescent tubes are greenish.) A person's face actually looks bluish outside and reddish indoors. Our brains are always making allowances for such changes in color frequency, so that we usually don't even notice them. But cameras, film stock, and video all have to be adjusted accordingly.

Color Temperature. The coloration of apparently white light is expressed as its "color temperature" and is measured in units called degrees kelvin (K). Color temperature really refers to the relative degree of red, green, and blue in a light source. If you heat a hypothetical substance physicists call a "black body," the color of light it radiates correlates with its temperature. The incandescent glow it emits will move from reddish toward blue as it heats up, until it becomes invisible to the human eye. Thus, light with a cool color temperature has a reddish tinge, and light with a hot color temperature is bluish. Unfortunately, camera operators (like most of the rest of us) describe scenes lit with reddish light (like a sunset) as *warm,* and those that are closer to blue as *cold*—so watch out.

Light emitted from a candle has a color temperature of around 2000K, about the same as deep red sunsets. Artificial interior light varies quite a bit: around 2000K for a standard tungsten lamp and shade, but 2800K or 2900K for *naked* tungsten bulbs; 3200K for stronger "photoflood" bulbs, often put in their place by documentary filmmakers to pump up the light intensity; and an equivalent figure of anywhere between 3500K and 4800K for fluorescent tubes ("equivalent," because they don't actually emit a continuous spectrum). Sunlight can vary from 4200K to 10,000K or above, depending on how close you are to the equator, the time of day and year, and the clouds, trees, or buildings in the way.

In practice, filmmakers reduce the spectrum of color temperatures to two standard varieties—3200K for indoors and 5500K for outdoors. Most color film is balanced to be exposed to colors at 3200K, and video television production operates on the same principle.

Correcting the Color Temperature. For interior scenes, fiction filmmakers can use special lights balanced to exactly 3200K. Documentary filmmakers usually have to adapt to the lighting situation as they find it. You have two choices: you can put a filter on your lens to bring the color temperature to 3200K or you can put a filter (or gel) on the light source itself, whether it's a bulb or a window. If you're shooting outside, it's clearly easier to filter the lens, since you can't exactly filter the whole sky. (A no. 85 filter converts 5500K to 3200K; see chapter 5.) If you're inside you may choose to filter the light source. Every filter has a "factor," which tells you how much you have to increase the exposure to make up for the light it blocks out.

Conflicting Color Temperatures. Problems arise when a single shot contains two or more different light sources that have different color temperatures. For example, you may need to shoot an interior scene lit not only by standard incandescent bulbs but also by light streaming in through a window. In a second example, you may want to follow a person moving from indoors to outside. As they open the door, the light color temperature will rise a couple of thousand degrees kelvin, and a reddish image would become tinged with blue. (Even if your field site has no electricity, and so the interior light is similar to the exterior, you cannot automatically average out the color temperature at around 5500K. For if you shoot near dawn or dusk, or if you want to shoot a night scene lit by candles only, your color could still be wildly off.)

You can resolve problems like this in various ways. In the first example, you could (1) turn off interior lights so that all illumination is coming through the window with the same color temperature; (2) put sheets of amber acetate gel (no. 85 or MT-2) up on the window, which will bring the color temperature of the window light down to 3200K; (3) put blue gel on the artificial lights; (4) filter your camera at an intermediate value and hope for the best. In the second example, you could (1) filter at 3200K when inside and switch to a 5500K filter on the move as you follow your subject outside (something easier said than done, the feasibility of which depends on the camera); or (2) cut the shot into two separate shots, an indoor one and an outdoor one, each balanced accordingly.

Film Stock Color Balance and Video White Balance

Motion picture film comes in two basic varieties: "Tungsten," which is made to be exposed at 3200K, and "Daylight," made to be exposed at 5500K. Whichever film stock you use, you have to color-correct the incoming light accordingly. Filmmakers tend to shoot most of their footage with Tungsten film (though on modern cameras it's possible to have two magazines loaded, each with a different kind of film, and to use the one you need). This is because whenever you add a filter to the camera you lose some light (and so set off a whole string of effects, changing the exposure, aperture, depth of field, and so on). Since sunlight is much more intense than interior lights, and you can afford to lose more of it, it makes sense to shoot with a film stock requiring outdoor, but not indoor, filtering. But if you're shooting a lot of interior scenes that aren't lit by electric lights, this won't apply.

Video operates on more or less the same principle as film. Most video cameras come with built-in filter wheels. Some consumer models may balance color automatically; others let you choose between "indoors" and "outdoors." Professional cameras incorporate a variety of filters, enabling you to reproduce a wide range of lighting conditions faithfully. The big difference between film and video is that there aren't different kinds of video tape stock balanced for different lighting conditions. Instead, video allows you to tell the camera what is "white light" for a particular location, and it will color balance accordingly. You hold a blank, white card in front of the camera (which, depending on the lighting setup, will reflect a particular ratio of red, green, and blue to the camera), zoom in and focus, and set the white-balance switch on the camera (you may also have to engage the appropriate filter). Now that the camera knows what "white" looks like it will reproduce all other colors faithfully—until you change the lighting conditions. When you do, you'll need to reset the white balance.

LIGHTING AND THE IMAGE

In addition to adjusting your lens and responding to the properties of your medium, there is a third way to control the nature of the image you record. You can control the intensity and quality of lighting. Film stocks, video formats, and even video cameras all require a certain minimum base illumination (given in the film stock and video camera specifications). Actual light intensity is usually expressed in "foot-candles" or "lux"—the intensity of light emitted by a hypothetical candle at a distance of one foot (foot-candle) or one meter (lux).

Exposure: Incident and Reflected Light

Because our eyes automatically compress vast brightness ranges, they're not the best guide to objective lighting conditions; you'll also want to rely on exposure meters. There are two basic kinds of handheld exposure meters: those that measure "incident light" and those that measure "reflective light."

Incident Light Meters. Incident light meters measure the intensity of light directed or reflected onto an object in the frame—how much light is actually falling on something or someone. If you were shooting a close-up of someone's face, you would put the incident meter next to their face, and point it toward the camera. Since the correct exposure of people's faces is generally crucial, an incident meter is often used to ensure accurate rendering of skin tones. You also use an incident meter to set your f-stop. Additionally, if you've composed a shot, you could take an incident reading of the lightest and darkest portions of the frame to see whether the scene's brightness range can be accommodated by the film's contrast range. If it can't, you could either recompose the shot, use artificial lights or a reflector to add light to darker parts of the frame, or else opt for a compromise exposure somewhere between the two readings, knowing that some parts of the picture will be overexposed and others underexposed.

However, incident readings do not provide an infallible measure of exposure, since different objects reflect different degrees of light back to the camera, depending on their size, shape, texture, and color. Also, while an incident meter is ideal if you want to take a reading for a close-up of someone's face, you can't use it to take a reading of a long focal length landscape shot or a view from a window.

Reflected Light Meters. Reflected light meters measure how much light is reflected from an object into the lens. Though more difficult to use properly, they tend to give more precise readings. You point them at your subject from the direction (if not actual position) of the camera. One specialized kind of reflected light meter often used in documentaries is called a "spot" meter. It can take a reflected light reading of a very small angle of view, enabling you to expose for a small subject area a long way from the camera. If, for example, you wanted a long

NUTS AND BOLTS

FIGURE 36 Incident and Reflected Light Meter Readings. In the top image, the holder is taking an incident reading, with the white spherical diffusion disc slid over the sensor. You hold the meter near the subject you want to expose optimally, and point it to the camera. The meter averages out all the light falling on the subject. You can also use it to point at individual light sources in order to estimate your lighting contrast ratio (see below). If you want to shoot at a particular f-stop (i.e., with a controlled depth of field), you can use the light meter to adjust the lights accordingly.

In the bottom image, the holder is taking a reflected reading (without the white diffusion disc). The meter measures the light that is reflected back to it from the subject. Different colors and surfaces reflect back different amounts of light. If you take a reflected reading off a neutral gray card, the calculated exposure should be the same as for an incident reading.

shot of a face in a crowd, only a spot meter (other than the light meter built into your camera, if it has one) would be able to give you a reading of it.

Despite the advantages of reflected and spot meters, incident meters are more common in documentary work. This is partly because camera or film-stock specifications tell you how much incident light they require, not how much reflected light. But it's also because reflected meters aim at an optimum exposure of "middle gray" (the median tone between black-and-white)—if you always shot uniform scenes and calculated exposure with reflected readings, everything would turn out middle gray. In general, however, you want to maximize tonal differentiation within the contrast range capacity of your medium. Camera operators develop a feel for the reflectance values of different objects and for the contrast range of their medium, and an incident meter gives them enough control in most conditions.

Skin Tone and the Gray Card. A "gray card" is a neutral gray piece of card that reflects back 18 percent of the light that falls on it, and is used as an approximation of an interior object of "average" reflectance. However, light skin can be twice as reflective as the gray card, and dark skin may be only half as reflective. Once you know (from experience) precisely what allowance to make for your subjects' complexions, you can expose for skin tones consistently just by taking incident readings. People with dark skin may need to be exposed at a whole f-stop below the gray card; people with light skin a whole f-stop above. The best way to determine how to expose consistently for someone's skin tone is to compare an incident with a reflected light reading of the person's face, taken in the same lighting conditions. The difference between the two readings is the difference from the incident (or reflected "gray card") reading by which you need to open up or stop down the iris.

In-Camera Light Meters. The light meters inside cameras take reflected readings. They can also double up as spot meters in the sense that their exposure adjusts according to angle of view and focal length. If you zoom into a face in a crowd and expose for that, you're in effect using your camera like a spot meter.

When you're shooting uncontrolled documentary, the automatic exposure calculated by the built-in light meter may be all you have time to use. The viewfinder on a professional videocamera is often good enough to let you set optimum exposure just by looking through it. However, most consumer videocameras come with an "automatic iris," which adjusts itself according to the lighting conditions. This is actually more of a liability than an asset (see chapter 5).

If you don't have time to take a handheld reading, you can zoom in on your center of interest (what you want to expose optimally), use the viewfinder to select the automatic exposure, open up or shut down the aperture as you think necessary, lock the exposure in place, then zoom out to the desired focal length to check that the rest of the frame is exposed as you would expect. If you want to see some detail in the shadows you'll have to open up the iris a little more. By the same token, if you want to see anything in the highlights you may have to stop down half an f-stop or more. If you set the exposure in this way, it will stay constant throughout the shot, indeed throughout a whole scene, regardless of any movement in the frame. The only thing to remember is that if lighting conditions change—say, dark clouds cover the sun—you may have to reset the exposure.

Almost all light meters—reflected and incident, digital and analog, new and secondhand—have scales or readouts that let you calculate your f-stop directly. Some reflected meters can be converted into incident, and vice-versa, with varying degrees of accuracy. Handheld reflected meters vary in their angle of acceptance, and take quite a bit of practice before they can be used accurately. If you're shooting video for the first time, you're probably best off sticking with the through-the-lens camera meter, since it's easier to use. Consumer cameras do not, in any case, give you any direct control over the f-stop.

Lighting Aesthetics

All documentary filmmakers exercise some control over the lighting—whether to compress or expand a scene's brightness range, or for aesthetic reasons such as modeling a subject's face. The extent to which you control lighting conditions obviously depends on your style of filmmaking. If you're scripting or staging scenes (like Errol Morris in *A Brief History of Time* [1992]) you may accord lighting as much importance as fiction filmmakers. If you're shooting in a more observational style, you may only be concerned to ensure that you have the minimum illumination to expose the image.

Lighting as a whole is as integral and as important to your visual image as composition, blocking and depth, movement within the frame, movement *of* the frame, or anything else. The intensity, quality, and directionality of light, as well as the interplay of light and shadow, affect not only the spectators' sensation of depth and realism but also the mood of a scene. In general, the more directional a light source (like direct sunlight), the harder, or more specular it is, and the cleaner and sharper the shadows. And the more unforgiving it is of people's complexions! Less directional light, as on a cloudy day, is softer, or more diffuse.

Four-Point Lighting. The classic lighting setup for fiction films and controlled documentaries employs four different light sources: a key, a fill, a back, and a kicker. Most filmmakers who use artificial lighting strive to make all the light seem "motivated." In other words, they try to make sure that all lights are true to the directionality the spectators would expect to see, whether from an overhead sun, a window in the wall, or a bedside candle.

Key. The "key" light is the brightest, and is usually hard and highly directional. It is positioned in the direction of the principal motivated light source, apparently naturalizing the lighting and often providing modeling on a subject's face. For this reason, it's usually placed above eye-level, a few feet off the camera-to-subject axis, so that the facial shadows it casts are visible to the camera but the larger shadows fall

▶ FIGURE 37 The conventional four-point lighting setup. In this arrangement, the main and most directional light is the key. The fill acts to partially "fill in" the shadows created by the key, which would otherwise be too strong. The kicker sets the subject apart from the background (often adding a glow to the edge of the subject's hair). An optional fourth light, the back, increases the visibility of the background. Though it is helpful to bear this classic arrangement in mind, it is more important to light by your own eye. If you want your lighting to be visually striking, you will need to experiment with the intensities of the different lights, or depart from this setup altogether.

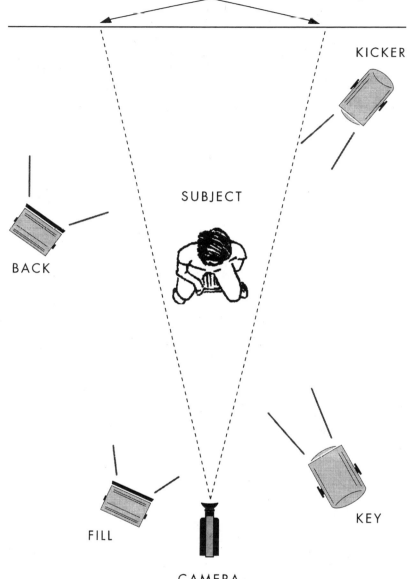

ANGLE OF CAMERA / FRAME

KICKER

SUBJECT

BACK

FILL

KEY

CAMERA

harmlessly on the floor rather than on walls visible in the picture. In documentary interviews, the key light is almost always on the same side of the camera axis as that toward which the subject is looking. If an interviewee is looking slightly to the left of the frame, the key will probably also be on the left. The farther off-axis the key, the more extreme the effect. Night scenes are more likely than day scenes to have the key set far off the axis.

Fill. The "fill" light is usually positioned near the camera but on the other side from the key, so that it partially fills in and tempers the shadows. It is placed near the camera-to-subject axis so that the shadows it generates will be as far as possible hidden from the camera. It is almost always more diffuse than the key. While the key source is often a direct "spotlight," the fill will either be a spot bounced off a wall, ceiling, or special reflector, or else a soft light.

Back. A "back" or "background" light is usually quite diffuse, and is added both to illuminate the background and to reduce the brightness range of the scene (not to be confused with overall brightness). Adding a back light can help accentuate a scene's depth. It's best to position it so that it doesn't just fall flat on the background. Try to light to accentuate the texture of physical objects—the grain of wood, the velvet of a sofa, the irregularities in a wall—and also to create shadows visible to the camera that emphasize the objects' solidity and reality. But if you want more diffuse light in the background, you can always bounce it off a ceiling, wall, or special reflector.

Kicker. The "kicker" (also occasionally called "hairlight," or, confusingly, "back") is typically positioned on the other side of your subject from the camera, out of frame and far enough from the camera axis so that it slightly illuminates the edges of your subject's head, hair, or shoulders without resulting in any flare. Usually a hard light, and often as strong as the key, a kicker distinguishes a subject from the background, focusing the spectators' attention, and adding three-dimensionality. It has a more theatrical than documentary look.

Documentary Conditions. Though this four-point lighting arrangement may be too complicated or simply inappropriate for many documentary situations (for example, when your subjects are highly mobile or you can't predict where they will move), the relationship between key, fill, and back lights is at least to some degree mirrored in many "natural" outdoor lighting situations—with the sun as key, the sky as fill, and reflections from background surfaces such as building facades (or a white reflector) as both fill and back. A simpler setup is to shoot your subject next to a window, and use a reflector to raise the illumination on the other side. It takes a little practice to position a reflector well. You have to catch the source light on it, and move it around until it reflects back on your subject. Then you can move it closer to or further from your subject to adjust the intensity of reflected light.

If you have only one or two lights, you can manipulate them to control both the brightness range and the mood and modeling of the scene. A light will often look more realistic if you bounce it off a reflector, a wall, or the ceiling. Again, if you're shooting in any kind of realist style, lights should appear to be motivated. If your viewers see a shot of an interior, lit only from a window on the left, in which there is nonetheless another unexplained light source from another angle, it will look staged and artificial. And if your viewers see more than one shadow cast by a single object, they will probably realize the scene has been "lit," and unrealistically at that.

Lighting Contrast Ratio: High-Key and Low-Key. As a rule, you want your shots to have areas of dark and areas of light, and to have them distributed over different planes to accentuate the sensation of depth. Variegated images are more arresting than flat, evenly illuminated and evenly exposed ones. The relationship between the intensity of the different lights in a shot is called the "lighting contrast ratio." Usually it expresses the ratio of the key and fill combined to the fill alone. A "low-key" lighting setup is one with a high contrast ratio, but which is quite dark overall. The *film noir* genre typically had a very low-key setup— such as the scenes at home and in the office at the end of *Double Indemnity* (1944). Documentaries (at least outdoor scenes and most set-up interviews) tend to be pretty "high-key"—low contrast and overall quite bright. *Roger and Me* (1989) is a case in point; *The Thin Blue Line* is an evident exception.

Since video has a lower contrast range than 16mm film, videomakers try to work with high-key, low contrast lighting ratios—often as low as 2:1. A 2:1 lighting ratio will seem flat and dull when you set it up, but it may be all your tape can manage, especially if you're using a consumer camera. As the quality of video improves in the future, so will its latitude and contrast range. Filmmakers using 16mm work with lighting contrast ratios of 4:1 or higher (i.e., two or more f-stops), measured as the ratio between incident readings of the shadowed and lit (by the key) sides of your subject's face in a close-up. Except in low-key night scenes, anything above a 4:1 contrast ratio will probably look unrealistic.

Controlling the Brightness Range. A scene's brightness range is more important than its lighting contrast ratio because it takes reflected light into account. If you're using artificial lights, you can control the brightness range in a number of ways, including the wattage of the lights and their relative proximity to your subject. Professional movie lights often come with "barn doors," flaps which allow you to control their spill—the angle of illumination they provide. "Flags" are boards or pieces of stretched, framed cloth that serve the same purpose. You can also hang specially prepared "diffusion" material in front of a lens to make it softer, and a "scrim" or screen to make it less intense. Outdoors, "butterflies" are large screens that filter out excessive sunlight in a small area. Reflectors can be used to lighten shadows, indoors and outdoors. Some reflectors are collapsible and portable, and some also have a hard white color on one side and silver or a softer gold on the other, and let you use whichever side you wish. If you're shooting in an area without electricity, a reflector will be invaluable.

Inverse Square Law. An important simplified rule that camera operators bear in mind is the "inverse square law." Clearly, as the distance from the light to the subject increases, the intensity of light falling on the subject decreases. For most lights, the change in intensity is roughly inversely proportional to the square of that distance: If a subject begins one foot from a light source and moves two feet from it (i.e., double the distance), the light intensity at the second position will only be a quarter as strong. If they move four feet away, it will be a sixteenth. If your main subject is quite a distance from the light source, moving a foot or two farther away won't affect your exposure much. But if a subject is very close to a light, even slight movement can make a big difference to the lighting ratio and exposure.

If you're filming outside, in sunlight, you won't have to worry at all about how far people are from the light source! Unless it's a very cloudy day, your main concern will probably be reducing a scene's brightness range—shooting your subject against a tree trunk or a building rather than the sky, or using a reflector to lighten their face, and in particular their eye sockets. Interviews conducted outdoors are quite often marred because the camera operator has exposed for the face, but left the eyes hidden in deep shadow.

Even if you're shooting an intimate scene in which any interference with existing lighting conditions, whether by adding lights or just using a reflector, would be too intrusive, it's still important to think about light and be on guard against excessive brightness ranges as you compose shots and choose camera angles. In the end, the most important rules are to shoot in lighting conditions that suit your subject and never to light by a preestablished method. Formulaic lighting will make your scene look like it was filmed in a cheap studio.

Lighting Equipment

Lights can be placed anywhere. They can be mounted on a camera or on a special stand. They can be stuck to a wall, window, or door. They can be hung from the ceiling or held by hand. Gaffer's tape and alligator clips can work wonders, attaching a light pretty much anywhere. But take care. If you use large lights, you'll need special stands. You shouldn't tape lights directly to the ceiling (it'll burn and they'll overheat). And if you use gaffer's tape to attach a light to wallpaper or a painted wall, it'll take the wallpaper or paint with it when you try to remove the light. Companies like Lowel and Arriflex (see appendix 3) make a whole series of versatile lights and accessories that let you position lights almost wherever you want them.

Fidelity to Light Source. As mentioned above, documentary filmmakers tend to enhance preexisting light conditions rather than recreate them anew. If an interior scene is lit only from a single window, you could put a reflector either just outside or just inside the window to gather more light. If you need to add a light, you could also place that next to the window, or, if there isn't enough room or if the light would be visible in the frame, you could put it just outside the window, with color-correcting gel in front.

Fluorescent Lights. Fluorescent lights have a color temperature that has to be filtered for both Daylight and Tungsten film and for video. If unfiltered, they give a nasty green tint to your image. They also cause flicker problems. (If you stick to a shutter speed of 1/60 second or below in the U.S., and 1/50 second in 50 Hz countries, you should be okay—see chapter 5 and appendix 2.) Because fluorescent lights are often attached to ceilings, they also tend to provide a particularly unattractive overhead light, resulting in deep and dark eye shadows. Additionally, not all fluorescent bulbs are the same color—some are bluer and some are greener, depending on the models the maintenance department had in stock when the last tubes blew. If you can, you may want to turn fluorescents off. If you need them, turn on as many as possible, *on as many separate electricity circuits as possible:* the dark period of some lights will then intersect with the light period of others, and minimize the flicker. You can also replace the fluorescent tubes with special tubes made for film and video work, balanced for Daylight or Tungsten.

Photo Bulbs. A very unobtrusive way of enhancing existing light is to put tungsten bulbs of higher wattage in existing sockets. "Photofloods" and "reflector floodlights" are bulbs especially color-balanced for Tungsten film, and fit right into household sockets. (There's also a model balanced for Daylight film.) A variety of wattages are available, including 250W, 500W, and 1000W. You can buy (or rent) special clamp-on ceramic sockets and position them wherever you can get a grip. Their disadvantage is that the bulbs only last a few hours, and their color temperature decreases as they burn—so be sure to bring plenty along to a distant shoot. (If you're shooting video, white balance as often as possible.) They also get very hot, so be sure the sockets you use are well ventilated, and remember that heat rises.

Quartz Lamps. Photo bulbs can only do so much to enhance existing light levels. John Bishop once used them successfully in lighting a whole church for the shoot of a wedding, and the congregation didn't even notice. But in many large interior spaces they won't be enough. A few "quartz" (tungsten-halogen) lights will also screw into regular household sockets and provide more illumination still. They're less fragile, last a lot longer, and their color temperature doesn't change over time. However, they're more expensive and become extremely hot. Quartz lights are used in documentary work more than any other kind of light. The brighter ones need special sockets of their own. Five hundred-watt and 750-watt lamps are the most common, though they go up to 10,000 watts! Some can be handheld; almost all can be mounted. Many come in small kits, with a stand and barn doors included.

Spots and Floods. There are various kinds of professional movie lights. Many "spotlights" are "focusable" in that you can control their specularity (the hardness of the shadows they cast). You can set them to a hard spotlight or a diffuse "floodlight," or somewhere in between. Unfocusable floodlights are also available, and are cheaper. Some spots let you control the width of the beam they emit, others don't. The wider the beam, the more diffuse the light. Many studio lights have a "fresnel" lens, which projects the light out in straight rays in front of the camera, sharply limiting its diffusion off the sides. Since a fresnel lens is heavy, it's not very useful for more uncontrolled documentary work.

Handheld, Battery Powered Lights. You may also want to consider battery-powered handheld lights, especially when shooting in a location without electricity. Not only do they allow you to shoot night scenes that might otherwise be unrecordable, but they can also double as regular (if low wattage) key or fill lights in interior scenes and as fill lights in exterior scenes. They let you control modeling on close-ups. With experience you can hold one still enough that viewers won't be able to tell it's handheld. Cine-60 in New York (see appendix 3) pioneered the "Sun-Gun" system—a trademark that's become a generic term—which is a handheld or camera-mountable, soft, wide-angle focusing light (from 70W to 350W), powered either by a small battery pack or a battery belt that wraps around your waist.

FIGURE 38 Lowel™ Omni-light (with barndoors, upper left; in hand, upper right; with Frame-up, lower left; on door mount, lower right). This tungsten halogen light can be mounted on a stand, attached to a camera, clamped to just about anything, or held by hand. You can use it as a key or a kicker, or, with diffusion or an umbrella, as a fill source. Barn doors, scrims, flags, and gels are all attachable.

Courtesy Lowel-Light Manufacturing Inc.

On-Camera Lamp.   An on-camera lamp is useful if you're filming solo in low light. But they tend to be specular and to make your footage look journalistic, since news reporters often use them. If it's the only light you have, see if you can get hold of a bracket that will raise it above the camera. The light source will still look to your viewers as if it's mounted on the camera, especially if there are any camera movements, but it will result in a slightly less flat image and introduce some modeling.

Electricity.   It's important not to overload the electricity system you plug into. You don't want to blow a fuse in the middle of filming. If you're filming in any public service facility, like a hospital or a computerized office, this could have dire consequences, quite apart from ruining your shot. In order to calculate your electricity needs, remember that

watts = amps × volts.

When you're location-scouting, check how many amps the circuit you'll be plugging into is rated for. The rating should be written on the circuit breaker or the fuse box, or else on the fuses themselves. Household current in the U.S. is usually fused at around 15 amps, and is almost always 100/110V, 60 Hz AC. In Europe and much of the rest of the world, current is 240V, 50 Hz AC (see appendix 2 for particular countries). Before plugging anything in, make sure that all your equipment is compatible with the frequency of the alternating current.

If the circuit is 110V and is rated for 15 amps, it would deliver 1,650W. It's best to consider this as 1,500W to be absolutely safe. You could power three 500W lamps off it (so long as nothing else is plugged in—you may need to turn off fridges, freezers, and so on). Since the fuse rating reflects the wiring system, never replace a fuse by one of higher amps. This could make the system catch on fire.

If you want more wattage than can be supplied by a single circuit, you need to determine which electrical outlets hook into which circuits. A single household room in the U.S. (but not in most of the world) will probably have one or two circuits in it, not more. If no one knows, you'll have to find out by trial and error, by plugging something (say, a light, or portable radio) into all the various outlets and removing the fuses or turning off the circuit breakers one at a time (be sure to turn off the circuit breaker before touching a fuse). Even if all your power requirements can be accommodated by a single circuit, you should, whenever possible, run your camera and video deck off an on-camera battery so it won't be affected by power surges or failures.

Bring along plenty of (heavy-duty) long extension cables, as you may well have to plug into other rooms, or even other buildings—although long cables, like overloading the system generally, can cause the voltage to lower, and this will change the color temperature of the lights. Since people can easily trip on them, try to tape them down, and cover them with rubber mats. Bring extra fuses, gaffer's tape, a gaffer grip to hold a stray light, three-to-two prong adapters, and insulated gloves to change blown bulbs. Be sure that you always ground your lighting equipment, that your lights are mounted very securely, that their sockets won't overheat, and that you never touch quartz lights with your fingers, as the grease from your hands may make the lights explode when they heat up.

Finally, a word of caution. In much of the world, domestic (and even industrial) electricity circuits are not subject to stringent safety regulations, and you would be well advised to hire a local electrician who knows how things work. If you don't trust the electricity, or don't have any, you can still power lamps from a generator, a car battery, or special lithium batteries.

Now you should be ready to go out and shoot your picture. But first read the next chapter so that you're also prepared to record sound.

4. Sound

Picture and track, to a certain degree,
have a composition of their own but
when combined they form a new
entity. Thus the track becomes not
only an harmonious complement but
an integral part of the picture as well.
Picture and track are so fused that each
one functions through the other. There
is no separation of *I see* in the image
and *I hear* on the track. There is
instead the *I feel, I experience,* through
the grand-total of picture and track
combined.

—Helen van Dongen, editor of Robert
Flaherty's *Louisiana Story*

The visual often takes pride of place among filmmakers and in cinema schools, with sound firmly relegated to a subsidiary position. The very word "film" conjures up a visual image; "video" likewise makes no mention of audio. But the cinematic or televisual experience is as sensuous aurally as it is visually. Just as the picture transforms the spectators' experience of the sound, the sound transforms the spectators' experience of the picture. Recording the sound is both a technical and aesthetic endeavor. Generally, your first concern is to record the original "live" sound as faithfully as possible. Later you can play with it in the editing room.

This chapter is divided into four sections. The first, "The Culture of Film Sound," briefly outlines how filmmakers create sound tracks. "The Nature of Film Sound" then delves into the physics of it all, and describes what you should have an ear for when recording. The third section, "Sound Recording Equipment," discusses how to choose and use sound recorders (including how to record sync sound), microphones, and other accessories. (Information about specific makes and models can be found in appendix 4.) Finally, "Recording Tips" contains some practical hints on how to record the best quality sound.

THE CULTURE OF FILM SOUND

SOUND RECORDING

Sound, like picture, has perspective built in to it. The codes for sound continuity are similar to those of picture. To put it crudely: if spectators hear a continuous noise, they will suppose they're in the same space; if they hear a different noise, they will suppose they're in a different space. But the codes for sound and picture continuity are not absolutely analogous. If the editor makes a visual cut from a wide shot of an interviewee to a close shot, that would not normally be matched by a corresponding shift in perspective in the sound track. Usually the microphone ("mike") corresponds *roughly* to the camera position, but doesn't change drastically when the camera operator changes focal length (zooming in or zooming out).

◄ FIGURE 39 *Nanook of the North* (1922), by Robert Flaherty.

Whenever you change the distance between mike and sound source, you alter the perspective of the recording, and there will be a corresponding shift in the relative ratio of direct (unreflected) and indirect (reflected) sound. This can make continuity sound editing difficult. If you're recording someone who is stationary, there's no problem since the mike position will stay fixed. But if the camera moves to follow action, the sound recordist usually moves the mike with it. And if the scene is set in an interior space, the sound will probably change quite a bit as the subject moves around. When it comes to editing the scene, any differences in the sound track are disguised during the mix by adding "atmosphere" (see "Ambience," under "Recording Tips," below) and using multiple tracks.

SOUND EDITING

In fiction filmmaking, sounds are classified into three basic types: Dialogue, Music, and Effects. During postproduction, numerous sound tracks may be "premixed" together in preparation for a final sound mix, where they will be reduced to a single- (mono) or two-track (stereo) master. Documentary sound is at once simpler and messier than this. You have far fewer tracks, and they're much more unruly. Your location sound track(s) might contain Dialogue and Music, as well as sounds that fictional filmmakers would simulate as Effects. Still, even if your sound is quite simple, you could need four tracks in the mix. Two would be for the sync tracks of location sound, including dialogue. If you intend to add music at all, you'll need a track, or part of a track, for that. A fourth track might be for sound effects—anything from a bird song to a freeway roar. Observational filmmakers try to use only their location sound, but other documentary filmmakers often embellish their tracks in the mix.

THE NATURE OF FILM SOUND

The nature of sound is so complex that sound recordists usually know something about the physics of it. If you'll be shooting with a professional video camera or on 16mm film, you have a lot of control in recording the sound, and knowing how sound works helps you to produce a high-quality recording. But if you'll be using a consumer video camera or other recorder with no controls, your control over the sound will be limited to your choice of mike and where you point it. In that case, you may want to read "Microphones" first, and come back to this section later.

Sound is propagated through the vibration of molecules—not through any net movement, but through the disturbance, or oscillation, of adjacent molecules. The speed at which sound moves depends on the medium: the denser the medium, the faster the sound. That's why railroad tracks start ringing before you hear an approaching locomotive through the air, and a swimmer in the ocean would hear a boat's motor before a sunbather on the shore. Sound moves through air at around 1130 feet per second, though its exact speed depends on temperature and humidity. Since light moves a lot faster than sound, the sound track on film generally precedes the picture by a frame. This gives the sound a head start so that it will be in sync with the picture when perceived by the spectators. (Video hasn't yet compensated for this difference, because it's still rarely projected before a large audience.) In a cinema, the row with "absolute sync" is thus 47 feet in front of the screen (1130 ft./ sec. comes out at 47 feet per frame, at 24 frames per second), and certain cinephiles always try to sit in the right row. The difference between the speed of sound and of light also affects how some films are made. For example, theatrical films with extreme long shots of battle scenes tend to move the gunshot blasts to the point just after you see the smoke coming out, because audiences wouldn't believe that it could take so long to hear what they see. They find the real-time recording unrealistic!

AMPLITUDE AND LOUDNESS

When recording and editing sound, you have to be able to measure the strength of the signal. While you might call this loudness, it is actually referred to as the signal's "amplitude" or "intensity." Sound recorders and professional video cameras come with a meter that measures this. Loudness is in fact the subjective correlate of intensity; it's what you actually hear. But intensity and loudness are not directly proportional. Roughly speaking, as amplitude (or stimulus) increases geometrically, loudness (or sensation) only rises arithmetically. The more intense a sound, the less sensitive your ear: a sound that is twice as intense as another is actually only *heard* as about a quarter again as loud. Since you hear loudness, but your recorder registers amplitude, the difference between them is important. Someone's voice might sound only a little bit louder to you than that of another person. But if you set the recording level by the quieter person's voice, the recording could overmodulate and end up distorting.

Decibels

The relative intensity of sound is measured in units of "decibels," or dB, on a logarithmic scale. Decibels are units used in all sound recording equipment. A sound ten times as *intense* as another is represented as 10 dB higher, though it would only be *heard* as a little more than twice as loud; 100 times as intense would be 20 dB higher. However, some "dB" specifications are confusing, so beware. While a true dB scale only tells *proportional* sound intensity, and so has no reference point, many "dB" meters are actually "dBSPL" meters, for "sound pressure level." (The problem is that SPL is rarely printed on the meter or in the specifications.) On the dBSPL scale, 0 dB is the threshold of human hearing; 120–130 dB is the threshold of pain. A soft whisper in a film would be around 25 or 30 dB, and regular movie dialogue is around 75 dB, about twice as loud as (i.e., 10 dB higher than) it is in real life.

Dynamic Range

The "dynamic range" of a sound is the range between its softest and loudest moment. Like the contrast ranges of film and video, the dynamic ranges tolerated by sound recorders and recording media vary. Sound recorders allow for a much smaller dynamic range (also called "signal-to-noise" or "s/n" ratio) than the 120 dB accommodated by our ears. At the low end, quiet sounds get lost behind the electronic noise inherent in the recorder and the tape, and at the high end, sounds become distorted. Thus, just as creative camerawork involves compressing the broad range of lights and darks in the real world into a range that can be registered by the film or video, creative sound recording similarly involves squeezing all the different sounds we hear every day into the narrower scope of the recording medium. This means amplifying quiet sounds above the system noise and tape hiss and reducing loud noises below the level of distortion.

FREQUENCY AND PITCH

Hertz

The next most significant aspect of sound for filmmakers is its frequency. Sound consists of alternating waves of high and low pressure, or "compressions" and "rarefactions." The frequency of these sound waves is measured in "hertz," or Hz, which are simply cycles per second (cps). Audible sounds are anywhere from 20 Hz to 20,000 Hz, and their wavelengths are anywhere from ¾ inch to 56 feet. (Theatrical films also use infrasonic bassy sounds of around 12 Hz to unsettle the spectators.) If you double the frequency of a musical note, you raise the note an octave.

Phons

The frequency of a sound is heard subjectively as its "pitch." It takes a lot more intensity to hear a low-frequency sound than it does a high one, which is why low-frequency noises sound quieter than mid-range ones. It's also why many hi-fi music systems have a "loudness" switch. Another unit you'll come across in technical specifications is the "phon": phons measure subjective "loudness-cum-frequency." For example, 40 phons loudness may be either 40 dBSPL at 1 kHz frequency or 90 dBSPL at 20 Hz.

Fundamentals and Harmonics

Most of the sounds that we hear (and record) are actually composed of numerous sound waves interfering with each other. If the constituent sounds were exactly "in phase" they would combine to create a more intense sound, while if they were precisely "out of phase" they would cancel each other out. In reality, most interfering sounds partly cancel each other out, some of the time, and partly reinforce each other the rest of the time. But, in theory, all complex sounds can be broken down into any number of "pure" tones, which are known as sine waves. A tuning fork discharges such a single frequency. A musical note, on the other hand, consists of a "fundamental" note and any number of "over-tones" (also called "harmonics"), which are multiples of the frequency of the fundamental. The richer and fuller a sound, the greater number of audible harmonics it has. Thus, the more a recording captures the overtones of the original, the better its quality.

REFLECTIONS

Sounds in Their Environment

The sounds that we hear and record not only interfere with each other because of their *original* pattern of radiation, they also interact with their environment. They're both *absorbed* and *reflected* by the objects they encounter along their path. Even the atmosphere absorbs sound, especially high frequencies. Sponges, curtains, and carpets are all extremely absorbent, while smooth and hard surfaces like glass windows and cement walls tend to be highly reflective. The way sound is reflected depends both on the absorbency of the objects it hits and on their shape. Flat planes and spheres, for instance, reflect sound at different angles. Reflections can always be added artificially during postproduction, if really necessary, but they can almost never be gotten rid of once you've recorded them.

Diminishing Reflections

Most of the time you have to work hard to diminish reflections, especially in interior scenes, simply so that the speech you record will be intelligible. Sound recordists often bring along special cloth blankets to drape over reflective surfaces like mirrors and windows. But in documentary, you may not want to interfere too much with the shooting environment. In any case, it would be impossible to get rid of all reflections. Moreover, sound tells your audience a lot about the size and kind of space a scene is set in. It helps them "visualize" the space they see on the screen. For example, we learn as much about the living conditions of *Celso and Cora* from the street sounds audible inside their new apartment as from the appearance of the apartment interior itself. Sounds originating outside the frame fill in the off-screen space, and provide clues to what is going on there. Since much of the sound that we hear in real life is reflected, totally direct (i.e., nonreflected) sound would seem unrealistic, spaceless. (When the location sound isn't good enough, feature filmmakers often use nonreflective "foley rooms" to simulate sync sound "effects," and then add reflections to it later to make it realistic.)

Reverberations

Sound recordists distinguish between "first reflections," which take effect within 35 milliseconds of "direct" sound (i.e., sound that is unmediated in its travel from source to listener), and "later reflections." These later, overlapping reflections are often called "reverberations," and extremely strong and late reverberations (60 milliseconds or more after the original sound) are called "echoes." Though first reflections help spatialize a scene, reverberations tend to interfere with the clarity of sound, particularly speech. Since sound recordists often have to filter out quite a bit of ambient or background noise, the last thing you generally want are reverberations too. You can, however, use reverberation to special effect, as with the wizard's voice in *The Wizard of Oz* (1939).

Cocktail Party Effect

Sound recordists have a concept for the difficulties they have recording conversations in a crowded, reverberant space. They call it the "cocktail party effect." The idea is that if you're at a real life "cocktail party"—any noisy, crowded, especially interior, space—you can usually understand a lot of what people are saying by a process of selective concentration whereby your mind ignores all the noises it deems irrelevant. Most of the time we're not even aware of how exclusive our brains are. This doesn't work when you're recording. Although some mikes are highly "directional," and can exclude sounds that originate from anywhere other than on a very small axis, they aren't as agile as human hearing. Try as the recordist might, much party or crowd dialogue in documentary situations is unintelligible when recorded. So bear in mind that if you're shooting a conversation between a number of people, not all the speech may be understood by your spectators, especially if several people are speaking at the same time (a characteristic, of course, of some cultures, and some people, more than others). As soon as you start monitoring the sound with headphones, you'll hear the high level of background noise that your brain subconsciously filters out. You'll probably find that you have to get closer to your subjects than you're used to, and even comfortable doing, if your audience is to understand them.

That said, in uncontrolled documentary situations, you have to go with the flow. If you ask people to speak more slowly or one at a time, you'll destroy the spontaneity and naturalness of their interaction, which is what you're there to film. It's better to control the sound simply through the choice and placement of the mike.

Finally, a cautionary word about cross-cultural perception. Auditory experience is as mediated as visual experience: there is a cultural component to hearing just as there is to sight. Moreover, the relationship *between* the different senses is itself culturally variable. Though the cocktail party effect is a technical, not a social, phenomenon, the fact remains that what some people may isolate as "signal" may be "noise" to others. Thus, conceiving of a cocktail party effect in a cross-cultural context is an equivocal enterprise. Indeed, in settings where the collectivity is privileged over the individual, the significance of sound might precisely be *the lack of differentiation between separate speakers.* To concentrate on certain speakers at the expense of others may be to misconstrue the meaning of the event altogether. Needless to say, this is part of a larger problem of translation that cuts to the core of cross-cultural documentary itself. Unfortunately, there is no solution except to be as sensitive as possible to what a particular experience means to the actual people who live it.

Boomy Interiors

A particularly bothersome kind of reverberation happens when a wavelength of a sound you're recording fits exactly in the space you're recording in (e.g., a 20 Hz tone in a 56 foot room) and causes a variation in pressure. A boomy sound results, making speech difficult to understand. If you're recording dialogue in a small, contained space, be on your guard against this. If you have a mixer, you may be able to cut out or reduce the offending frequency; many mixers and some mikes contain "low cut" filters which can also help get rid of the boomy noise characteristic of some larger rooms. Lacking a mixer, you may want to move elsewhere.

Diffraction

Reflections are also often accompanied by "diffraction," that is, by sounds that are reflected around corners. Most of the sound we hear in everyday life contains diffracted components. As with reflections, diffracted sound helps your spectators spatialize the image on the screen. It can also allow them to hear off-screen dialogue or action while following the screen action visually. But diffracted sounds, like all reflections, impede intelligibility, and you usually have to try and cut them out— by closing doors and windows, and so on.

Refraction

Finally, the atmosphere may not simply *reflect* and *absorb* sound, it can also *refract* it. As sound waves hit warmer air, they speed up, and if they hit it at an angle, the leading part of each wave hits it first, and so speeds up before its tail follows suit. This bends the waves, and sends them off in a different direction, within the warmer air. However, if the angle at which the waves hit the warmer layer is sufficiently slight, they won't be able to penetrate it, and will be reflected back. In most documentary situations, this is unlikely to make that big a difference, though you should be aware of this refractive effect if you're recording sound across a body of water. Generally, atmospheric refraction near water will be greatest in the early morning and will decrease during the day as the sun warms the air that the water had kept cool. (In this case refraction may result in sounds traveling farther at ground or water level.)

Water or no water, if you're returning to a location for "pickups" (i.e., to film something that you forgot at an earlier shoot), always try to do this at the same time of day as your original shoot, in similar climactic conditions. Otherwise, sounds from the two shoots might not cut seamlessly together.

SOUND RECORDING EQUIPMENT

SOUND RECORDERS

Single-System and Double-System Sound

Regardless of how much you know about the nature of sound, the quality of your recording will always be limited by your recorder and

FIGURE 40 John Terry (sound) and John Bishop (camera) using double-system sound to shoot *Muharum,* a film about Islamic observance transposed from India to Trinidad. The sound recordist is using a fishpole boom and pistol-grip windscreen to hold the mike just above the camera frame line—as close as possible to the sound source (the modeler's hands) without intruding into the picture. This maximizes the ratio of direct-to-reflective sound recorded on the sound track.

the recording process you choose. Two main ways have been developed to record sound—"single-system" and "double-system." With single-system sound, the sound and picture are recorded on the same medium; with double-system sound, they are recorded separately and only later reconnected. For a long time, news programs used to be recorded on single-system 16mm magnetic film. This was always rather crude and cumbersome. For while the film picture moves *intermittently,* with each frame in turn being placed and exposed in front of the aperture, the sound is recorded *constantly.* Additionally, single-system film recording is impractical when it comes to editing, as any picture cut also makes a break in the sound. All 16mm film sound today is "double-system," with the audio signal being recorded most often on either an open-reel (also called "reel-to-reel") ¼-inch tape deck or else on an ⅛-inch cassette recorder. Though the sound is initially recorded on tape, it is later dubbed onto "fullcoat" magnetic film (usually just called "mag") for syncing up with the picture during editing. Single-system sound would now be obsolete if it weren't for the invention of video, and especially TV news production, which records the sound and picture information side by side on the same piece of tape.

Video Sound

If you're shooting video, you'll probably want to record your sync sound with a mike plugged into the camcorder, either directly or routed via a mixer. Most video formats record audio and video separately—on the same tape, but on different tracks, using different camera "heads." Some systems only have one video track and one audio track, but the majority let you record on at least two separate audio channels at the same time. If your deck has two audio channels, you can plug an exterior mike into one and the on-camera mike into the other. When we shoot video, we tend to use a high-quality exterior mike for our main sound (say, someone speaking), and the on-camera mike as a back-up (or for voices or sound sources at different angles, or close to the camera, such as our own). When we come to edit the sound tracks we find we rely almost exclusively on the track that was recorded with the exterior mike.

Until recently, sound has been recorded linearly, or "longitudinally," with one or two stationary audio heads. But increasingly sound is recorded, like the picture, with "rotary" heads—heads that rotate in order to maximize tape-to-head speed and hence audio quality. On smaller video formats (like Hi-8 and Super-VHS), a single rotary head may record both the audio and the video information; the high-end formats have a dedicated head for each (see chapter 5).

Even if you plan on working in video, a separate tape recorder can also come in handy. You may not want to record video every time you need some audio, especially if you're recording voice-over narration. If you have to interview someone for their words, not their image, they may be more relaxed speaking into a small tape recorder. Having an additional track may also help in the editing room, and audio tape tends to be cheaper than video tape. Moreover, high-quality tape recorders give you more control over your sound recording than most video cameras. If you're considering this option, a digital recorder will be much easier to sync up to the video than an analog model (see "Analog or Digital?" below).

Open-Reel and Cassette Recorders

Until recently, almost all sound recorders used in film production have used open-reel ¼-inch tape. But in the last few years, as quality has increased, ⅛-inch cassette recorders (the standard consumer format) have become more popular. They're light, small, and relatively cheap. Most ¼-inch sound recorders will record a single track of "mono" sound across the whole width of the tape; ⅛-inch cassette recorders will typically be able to record two-channel stereo sound that spans only half the tape width, enabling you to turn the cassette over and record on the other side. Most documentary sound is mono, and unless you intend to build up a complex sound track or record with multiple microphones, a single-channel recorder will be all you will need. In the U.S., the Public Broadcasting System now requires all masters to have stereo tracks. Although you can get a waiver for mono productions, there will be increasing pressure to mix (but not necessarily to record) in stereo.

The Mechanism of Recording

Sound recording works in essentially the same way in all (analog) recorders, regardless of format: it involves storing sound waves as magnetic fields on a tape composed of an acetate or polyester base and an emulsion of either ferrous oxide, chromium dioxide ("CrO_2"), or a so-called "metal" formulation. The mike transmits a signal which is amplified by the recorder and then transferred to the tape by a head, a two-part C-shaped electromagnet with a field coil wrapped around each half. The "gap" between the two arms of the "C" is crossed by the tape, which thereby completes an electromagnetic circuit. As the tape moves across the gap, the tape's particles take on magnetism, and this is your audio information. (Digital recorders often come equipped with a rotary scanner containing four heads, two for recording and two for playback.)

Bias

Unfortunately, the tape emulsion's ferrous oxide particles don't react proportionally to the magnetism. In order for the sound to be recorded

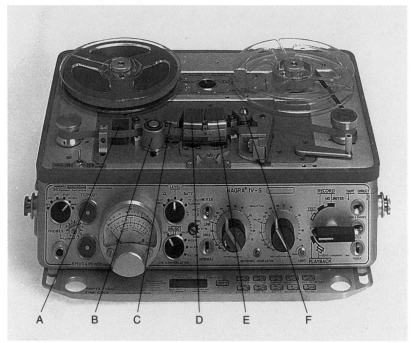

FIGURE 41 Nagra IV-S recorder. This is the stereo model in the portable, battery-powered Nagra tape recorder series. In passing from the spindle on the left onto the spindle on the right, the tape moves in turn past a full-track erase head, which makes sure that the tape is clean (A); a stroboscope roller (50 Hz or 60 Hz), which verifies that the machine is running at the right speed (B); a two-channel recording head, which transmits the input audio information onto the tape (C); a center track FM pilot or time-code head, used for synchronization during recording and playback (D); a two-channel playback head, which lets you listen to what you've recorded (E); and finally the capstan shaft, which moves the tape past the heads at a virtually constant speed (F).

(and played back) in a linear way, a further high-frequency charge has to be applied to the recording head simultaneously: this is known as "bias." Many tape recorders have various bias settings, enabling them to accommodate tapes with different settings; others need to be adjusted by a technician. As a rule, the higher the bias strength, the lower the "noise," and the less distortion and "drop-out" (momentary recording losses). High-frequency response is reduced, and low-frequency response is increased.

Generally, you want to maximize your bias. But it's more important to ensure that your recorder setting is compatible with your tape setting.

Tape Heads

When the tape is replayed it passes over either the same head as the one that recorded the sound, or else (on more expensive models like the Nagra pictured above) a separate "replay" or "playback" head. This playback head has a slightly smaller gap than the record head, so that the recorder can read the shortest wavelengths, which wouldn't be picked up by the same head. As the tape passes over the playback head the ensuing currents in the coils surrounding either half of the head are then re-amplified and sent to a loudspeaker to produce sound. (A speaker is really just an inverted moving coil dynamic mike; see "Microphones," below.) Another advantage of a separate playback head is that it lets you monitor your recording while you're making it (an "A/B test"). Tape recorders that combine the playback and record heads into one only let you monitor the sound just *before* it is recorded, rather than the recording itself, and so you can never be sure of the quality of the signal. If your heads are dirty or worn out, this can be disastrous. Thus, when recording on a deck with separate playback and record heads, it's advisable to listen to the playback head, so you can keep tabs on the actual recording quality and (even if it's too late) on whether the tape's run out!

Most professional tape recorders, particularly the larger ¼-inch open-reel models (including the Nagra pictured above), also have a separate erase head, which ensures that there is no signal on the tape before it reaches the record head. (As a safeguard, many sound recordists also use a bulk eraser or degausser to demagnetize their tape reels before using them; this also helps reduce tape hiss.) After the heads, there's a rubber "pinch wheel"; this keeps the tape in contact with a "capstan," which moves the tape past the head at, as far as possible, a constant speed.

Variations in Tape Speed

No tape recorders run at an absolutely constant speed, and this introduces two problems. There are speed variations that repeat themselves less than ten times a second, which are called "wow," and there are speed variations that repeat more than ten times per second, which are called "flutter." All professional tape recorders include specifications for wow and flutter. An important rule of thumb when choosing a recorder is to make sure that the combined wow and flutter figure does not exceed 0.1 percent of the tape speed.

In all tape recorders, except for digital models, there are longer-term tape speed variations. These are caused by tape elasticity, slippage at the capstan, and the changing amounts and weight of tape on the feed and take-up reels. The result is that the audio recording can be synced up with the picture during the editing only if there is a record of its speed variations and a means of adjusting them. This is the function of a regular "pilot" tone, which is usually recorded onto the tape by a separate pilot head. (See "Sync Sound," below, for different kinds of sound-picture syncing.)

Volume Unit and Peak Program Meters

Probably the most important control for you on the recorder will be a VU meter or PPM. The meter lets you see the signal strength, and a control or "potentiometer" lets you control the recording level. (Some meters, such as the "modulometer" on ¼-inch Nagra recorders, also double as battery-level indicators.) VU (volume unit) meters are older and slower to respond. PPMs (peak program meters) are more expensive and more accurate; they're also more fragile. Because of the VU meter's relatively slow response, it is actually a better measurement of loudness than of intensity, especially for short, sharp sounds, which stop before the indicator has a chance to reach the full level. But only a PPM allows you accurately to gauge during recording whether a short sound will distort on playback. Both VU meters and PPMs may use either a moving needle or a series of lights called LEDs (light-emitting diodes), or a combination of the two, to measure the signal. Their high-tech appearance notwithstanding, LEDs are not necessarily better.

Setting the Recording Level.　Most VU meters extend from around −20 dB to +3 dB, and signal the difference between plus and minus with a change in color. As a rule, you should record your signal as loud as possible without distorting it. (Distortion is the result of a tape being

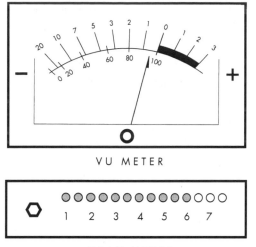

VU METER

PEAK METER

FIGURE 42 VU and Peak Program Meters. These meters let you monitor the strength of incoming sound. PPMs provide a better estimate of a signal's (objective) intensity, and VU meters correspond more to (subjective) loudness. Either kind of meter may use a moving needle or a series of LEDs. Generally, you want the meter to hover just under 0 dB on a VU meter. On a PPM, the line-up level is normally set at 4, and the indicators hover between 4 and 6. Anything above 6 results in distortion.

so saturated with magnetism that it overmodulates.) That way you maximize your signal-to-noise ratio, and you can always reduce the level during editing. (The quieter the background noise, the more important this is, as the tape noise is correspondingly more audible.) Consequently, *you usually want the meter to hover just under 0 dB.* However, you'll have to make allowances for the slow response of VU meters. If you're recording impulsive percussive sounds ("transients"), like hammering, millet-pounding, or much music, and were to turn the level up so that they registered at around 0 dB, they would actually be wildly overmodulating. Likewise, if you're recording dialogue, you'll generally want it set it at around −8 dB on a VU meter, assuming that on average it will actually be peaking about 8 dB higher.

Whatever kind of meter you use, the most important test is your own ear and your own experience. The more practice you can get recording and playing back before starting production the better. Even if you're working with video, and recording sound with your camera directly onto the video tape, the principles are the same. However, many low-end video cameras boast a feature called "automatic gain control." They try, with only some success, to average out the recording level to somewhere above the system noise but below distortion. The feature is often inaccurate and leaves you with no control over the level at all. If you're working alone, and recording only with the single (usually low-quality) on-camera mike, you may need the simplicity that automatic gain control offers. But the quality of sound recording is likely to suffer.

Other Features

Many tape recorders include a number of other switches and settings that you can adjust, including the following:

Equalization. An equalization switch gives you some control over the relative strengths of the different parts of the frequency spectrum. Most recorders "pre-equalize" their signal during recording and "post-equalize" it during playback, in order to bring out high-frequency sounds faithfully, and to ensure a flat frequency response overall. Some recorders have switches to adjust equalization according to tape stock and the desired speed; others will change equalization automatically as you select the speed.

Tape Speed Choices. Most ¼-inch open-reel decks let you choose between three speeds: 15, 7½ and 3¾ inches per second (ips). In general, faster tape speed means a higher quality recording, lower wow and flutter, and easier sound editing. Since more tape is allotted for the same signal there is more distance on the tape between different sounds. The setting favored by most documentary sound recordists is 7½ ips. The standard speed for ⅛-inch cassette recorders is only 1⅞ ips, which, until recently, has resulted in much lower recording quality. Some cassette recorders have a switch that lets you double the speed to 3¾ ips: your tape will disappear faster, but the recording quality will be higher. One problem to bear in mind, though, is that not all editing equipment can play back at atypical tape speeds.

Noise Reduction. A final feature of most cassette recorders and some ¼-inch tape recorders is a "noise reduction" switch, which reduces unwanted tape noise. Noise reduction increases high frequencies during recording and reduces them during playback. This leaves them unchanged overall while reducing the high-frequency tape hiss, and increasing the signal-to-noise ratio, or "headroom" (the number of decibels above reference level before distortion). Most noise reduction units are made by Dolby, of which Dolby B is the most common (a simplified, lower-end version of Dolby A, Dolby's first professional system; Dolby SR and S are more professional systems now in use). Dolby B improves the signal-to-noise ratio by about 10 dB. Because of the slow speed and relatively high noise level of cassette recorders, it's advisable to select noise reduction when using them. But, here again, the most important rule is to edit (and play back) *with the same kind of noise reduction you used during recording.* So, if you don't use noise reduction when recording you shouldn't use it during playback, or you'll end up losing high frequencies.

Sync Sound

While most video sound is single-system, almost all 16mm film sound is double-system: the picture is shot on film, and the sound recorded on magnetic tape. Double-system sound recording is more complicated, but it can also be liberating because the camera and mike don't need to be connected by a cable.

For sync sound recording (so that the picture and sound will be able to be synchronized exactly with each other during editing), the respective speeds of the camera and recorder have to be controlled. Film has sprocket holes along the edge to ensure it runs at a constant speed, but ¼- and ⅛-inch magnetic tape does not, and is subject to uncontrollable slip and shrinkage. Nowadays, the most common means of syncing is called "crystal sync," which does away with the need for a cable between the camera and recorder. A crystal motor in a 16mm camera ensures it runs at exactly twenty-four frames per second (sound speed), and a "pilot" or "pilotone" in the recorder lays down 60 pulses per second in models bought in 60 Hz countries, like the U.S., or 50 pulses per second in models bought in 50 Hz countries like most of Europe (see appendix 2). Many tape recorders do this with a dedicated "pilot head" positioned between the record and replay heads: recording a pilot signal either over the full width of the track with a head rotated 90° from the record head, or in two thin tracks down the center of the tape that are out of phase with each other, and thereby cancel each other out, preventing the replay head from playing them back. (The miniature Nagra SN records a 10 Hz signal along with the audio itself, which is filtered out on playback.) Pilote (Maihak), Perfectone, Ampex (Fairchild), and Rangertone are older sync pulse systems that were replaced by the "Neopilotton" system. You will only find them on secondhand machines. On all crystal-sync systems, when the audio tape is played back, a motor ensures that the tape moves at the right number of pulses per second. During postproduction it will be transferred to sprocketed mag film, which can then be lined (synced) up with the picture.

Slating. In order to be able to put the picture and the sound in sync, you need to line up a recognizable point on both the picture and sound track: once this is done, the rest of the shot (before and after) can also be put in sync. To this end, filmmakers "slate" each take. A slate is any short, sharp signal that can operate as a cue in both the picture and sound track. In fiction filmmaking and controlled documentary, the most common slate is a clapper board, a slate or plank on which information about the take is chalked or penned, with a hinged slat of wood on top that makes a sharp noise when it is slapped down onto the slate.

One problem with a clapper board is that it can make the scene before the camera feel like a set, and your subjects like actors. If you prefer to use a less obtrusive slate, you can consider one of the following systems: (1) a special slate light attached to the tape recorder, which emits a sound and must be shot by the camera; (2) simply tapping the mike within the frame while the camera is running (and then saying "slate" or giving other contextual information orally into the mike immediately afterward); or (3) using a radio transmitter that simultaneously sends an audio signal to the recorder and fogs a few frames of film in the camera ("blooping"). Additionally, some crystal sync 16mm cameras permit time code to be printed on the edge of the film and recorded on the tape, allowing them to be automatically synced up on a special editing

FIGURE 43 Lorrain Luke, assistant to cinematographer Nina Kellgren (right), holds up a standard clapper board during the production of Isaac Julien's *Frantz Fanon: Black Skin, White Mask.*

table later. (Most applications of film time code, however, are in emerging nonlinear or video postproduction, particularly in the Telecine transfer to video "prints"; see chapter 8.)

Typically filmmakers try to slate at the "head," or beginning, of a shot. But in documentary, you're often trying to catch up with unexpected action and don't have time for this. In such cases, unless your camera and recorder automatically print time code, you have to "tail slate" at the end of shots. Tail slates also have the advantage of being less obtrusive and noticeable to your subjects than head slates.

But there are some filmmakers who find slating to be a waste of time or an unnecessary intrusion. Dennis O'Rourke, who films alone, recording sound and shooting picture all by himself, is one of them. As he says, "I *never* slate! What a stupid thing to do! Okay, sometimes, at the end of a camera roll, if it hasn't run out and there is nothing more happening, I will snap my fingers in front of the lens or tap the mike in the frame, or just say, 'Camera running out now,' so that the recorder will pick it up. Before anyone accuses me of selfish and 'unprofessional' practices, I should add that I sync up my own rushes (and I enjoy it)." [1] If you choose not to slate, you have to search your footage for real-life "substitute" slates to sync up the rushes. Usually you'll look for any "moment" in a take that makes a short, sharp sound and visual imprint—a cup being placed on a saucer, a foot hitting the ground, a door being closed. If you're shooting dialogue, you may have to "lip sync"— match up the sound track to someone's lip movements—which is a little more difficult. Bear in mind that if you don't slate, it will probably take quite a bit longer to sync up your rushes, and sometimes you may not be able to find exact sync points at all.

Analog or Digital?

Most tape recorders simply record the audio signal as an analog waveform. But digital recorders convert the analog audio signal from the mike into a series of binary pulses, which collectively map out the amplitude of the waveform. These DAT (digital audio tape) machines have some advantages over analog recorders. They don't degrade in quality over "generations" of copies; they have virtually no tape hiss, undetectable wow and flutter, and hence a much higher signal-to-noise ratio; and they have a flat frequency response across the entire audio range. (The fact that information stored digitally doesn't degrade over generations means that you can transfer your sound directly from a DAT recorder to a computer hard-drive in a digital postproduction facility without any loss of quality.) With total harmonic distortion of less than 0.0008 percent, most DATs can reproduce audio frequencies between 10 Hz and 22 kHz. Unlike analog recorders, digital models can also check for drop-out and other errors in the tape, and even conceal the gaps.

Portable DATs (sometimes called RDATs) use helical scan (rotating) heads like video recorders, allowing them to store information more densely than analog recorders. For most documentary purposes, this means that neither the width nor higher speeds of ¼-inch decks are necessary (although the best DATs are still ¼ inch). You can record high quality sound on a much smaller and lighter ⅛-inch machine.

Many DATs come with built-in TCGs (time code generators), and the capacity to lock into incoming SMPTE and other film time codes, which can make syncing up a lot easier. However, because DAT recorders run at an almost constant speed (in effect self-resolving to their own sync pulse), they make time code unnecessary for most documentary purposes. For they will stay in "lip sync" with the picture, give or take a few frames, over an eleven-minute film roll or fifteen- to twenty-minute video take. This enables you to bypass all the systems that have been developed to keep the film and the sound track in sync.

When we helped John Bishop shoot *The Fandango Project* (1993), a video about Veracruz musicians interacting with young people in Richmond, California, the sound was recorded through a single-point stereo mike onto a DAT recorder, and later synced to visual tracks from three separate camcorders, all of which had been running at the same time. Since VCRs and DATs both have virtually consistent time base (i.e., move at an almost constant speed) in playback, DATs are very useful for double-system sound, recording two (or four) tracks of their own, which can be combined with the camera-point-of-view sound from an on-camera mike during the editing.

The crucial link in the chain for DAT recorders is the conversion from analog to digital, and it is here where there is most room for error. As the technology develops, most of the improvements will probably be in the "sampling," "quantizing," and "coding" of data. You should check these specifications before splurging on a particular model. At the current time, most domestic digital equipment (such as CD players) sample the waveform only at a 44.1 kHz rate, while the professional rate is 48 kHz. Check what a portable DAT recorder can do before committing yourself to it. It's important that the sampling rate (the frequency with which samples are taken of the analog waveform) be at least twice that of the highest frequency, for otherwise additional spurious frequencies will appear at each harmonic of the sampling rate. To prevent this "aliasing," as it's called, most digital recorders now "oversample." The more they oversample, the better.

Though the film world is moving toward DAT, there are a number of drawbacks you should consider. A few models are built to withstand the rigors of location recording, but all DATs are more fragile and more affected by humidity than analog machines. Because their circuitry is very intricate, there are relatively few DAT service centers, and if a DAT recorder breaks down in the field, it may be unrepairable. DAT recorders also use far more current than analog machines, and if you're shooting in a location without continuous or reliable electricity this may also be an issue. (How many batteries will you need to bring? How quick and effective is your solar recharger?) A final peculiarity is that DATs have a very "hard ceiling": when you overload a digital recording chain, the sound just goes totally silent, while an analog chain would distort. If you're not monitoring the sound carefully, or if you're recording music that varies widely in loudness, you might end up with no sound at all! However, since DATs have such a wide dynamic range (more than 90 dB) and high signal-to-noise ratio (more than 85 dB), this shouldn't be a problem, so long as you keep the gain down and monitor the meters closely.

MICROPHONES

Microphones are a lot simpler to understand than tape recorders. Like ears, mikes are sound-transducing diaphragms, transforming acoustical into electrical energy. Mikes differ from each other in terms of their frequency response, polar pattern, impedance, sensitivity, and strength, all of which are important to take into account in making a selection. For documentary, the most important characteristic of a mike is its "directionality" or "pickup pattern"—its angle of reception, or how selective it is.

Directionality

You'll probably want to use an "omnidirectional" (or "omni") mike for general action scenes, which have little or no dialogue, or else when lots of people are speaking from different directions. Omnis are sensitive to sound from all angles (though there's always a little acoustical interference from the mike body itself). "Bidirectional" mikes are sensitive in the front and back, and relatively insensitive at the sides; they're less common in documentary. In recording dialogue, you're generally best off with a "unidirectional" (or "uni") mike. Unis are sensitive in front, and relatively insensitive at the sides and the back, which means that they have a high incident-to-ambient (or direct-to-reflected) pickup ratio. They're either "cardioid" or "supercardioid" (ultradirectional). Supercardioid mikes are also called "shotguns" because they're long and thin. Some mikes even come with a parabolic reflector attached, when hyperdirectionality is needed, but these are used more in natural history or sports films than in most documentaries—in part because most parabolic reflectors are about a meter across, making them extremely unwieldy, and in part because they only capture frequencies whose wavelengths are shorter than the reflector is.

Unis have more off-axis frequency miscoloration than omnis (i.e., high frequencies reaching the mike at an angle to the direction the mike is pointing in, which will not be accurately reproduced). Suppose you point a uni at a person talking, and someone else sitting off to the side says something. If the mike picks up this second person's voice at all, not only will the volume be low, but the frequency will also be a bit off. Unis are also more susceptible to wind noise. However, the higher direct-to-reverberant input ratio of unis and their selective directionality more than compensate for their drawbacks when you're recording dialogue. They're also an advantage if you ever record a public orator speaking through a PA system, allowing you to discriminate against the loudspeakers and record more of the speaker's voice directly. (Though whenever possible you should also plug into the PA system itself.) Additionally, their narrow-angle response makes them easier to keep out of the frame.

When we were shooting the garment factory scenes for *Made in USA* (1990), we used an omni for the general ambient sound of all the sewing machines working away, but a uni to isolate specific machines or movements. By contrast, *In and Out of Africa* was shot exclusively with a supercardioid shotgun. The film's sound quality, particularly in the crowd scenes, would undoubtedly have been better if we'd also had an omni.

Transducing Mechanism

When choosing mikes, you also have to consider *how* they transduce sound waves into electrical energy. Different mikes are better in different conditions. "Dynamic" mikes are probably the most common type used in documentary, at least until recently, because they're robust and inexpensive. A diaphragm is attached to a moving coil of wire and this in turn is attached to a magnet; incoming sound moves the diaphragm, which moves the coil, which then changes the magnetic field, resulting in an electrical audio signal. Dynamic mikes tend to have good frequency response and may be omni- or unidirectional. Their moving coil mechanism is also used in some clip-on mikes (see "Lavalier, Clip-On, or Neck Mikes," below). However, they tend not to be very sensitive to high frequency sounds, and while this may not be a problem in most documentary situations, it is something you should bear in mind, especially if you will be recording music, or if you can afford only one mike.

"Condenser" mikes are usually high quality and are extremely sensitive to all sound, even at high frequencies. True condensers work through a polarizing voltage produced by the diaphragm and a backplate acting as a variable capacitor. "Electret" (also called "fixed charge," "permanently polarized," or "ENG shotgun") condensers work though a continuous electric charge. There's a big difference in quality between the true, full-fledged "electrostatic" condensers and the moderately-priced electret condensers. True condensers offer superior sensitivity and reach. Both types are used in supercardioid shotgun mikes and clip-on mikes. By contrast, most on-camera mikes are electret condensers.

The disadvantage of all condensers is that they're relatively fragile (though electrets are less so), generally expensive, and require a power source. On electret condensers this might be a small battery (1.5V or 5.6V) included within the mike body or else a "phantom" power supply through the mike cable. This allows them to be plugged into the low-impedance mike input (sometimes labeled "dynamic") on recorders and mixers. But true condensers require an external power supply of 12V or 48V (from a battery, a Nagra equipped with a pre-amp, or even AC mains).

Condenser or Dynamic? Both true electrostatic and electret condensers produce much higher quality recordings than most dynamic mikes and are desirable for *most* documentary situations. But if you're shooting in rough conditions, a dynamic mike may make sense— they're more rugged, more resistant to intemperate climates, are insensitive to RF (radio frequency) and electromagnetic interference, and don't need to be powered. They also tend to have poor reach, which, if you are trying to isolate a voice from the background, can actually be an asset. In other words, they capture less of the background noise that can interfere with speech intelligibility. Moreover, they automatically compress unexpected loud noises, which would otherwise distort the system, in a way that condensers cannot.

Frequency Response

You need also to consider a mike's "frequency response"—the spectrum of frequencies it can faithfully reproduce. No mike can accurately reproduce all frequencies, and you'll need to choose one that suits your needs. Mikes made expressly for voice pickup will reproduce well the middle-range frequencies characteristic of speech (of most people, most of the time, in most cultures); they'll do less well with the high frequencies of much music. Mikes with a wide frequency response are quite a bit more expensive than those with a narrower pattern, and are correspondingly more likely to pick up the highs and the lows. When you decide on a mike, check the manufacturers' specifications, and ask the dealer, rental house, or technical facility for advice. The frequency response of high-quality models extends over a 20 Hz to 20 kHz spectrum, without varying more than $\pm 2-3$ dB, on *or off* the axis.

Impedance Level

Another significant mike specification is "impedance level"—that is, the degree of resistance the mike offers to electrical energy. Impedance is expressed in ohms (Ω). There are two basic categories: high and low. High impedance (or "high Z") means that the mike has an impedance of above 600 Ω; anything below that is referred to as "low Z." Low Z equipment can send a signal over a long cable with minimal quality loss. High-quality mikes tend to be low Z, with an impedance of around 150 Ω. You'd be ill-advised to use a high Z mike. Dynamic mikes which don't incorporate a step-up transformer may be rated as low as 30 Ω, which is fine. If you're considering a dynamic mike, make sure its impedance doesn't increase with frequency, because if it does, it will need to be connected to an amp with an impedance a lot higher that its own to ensure a flat frequency response. Whatever your mike, be sure to maintain continuity; if you have a low Z output, be sure to connect it to a low Z input.

Handholding

The most important quality of a mike is how it feels and sounds when you use it. If at all possible, try out different mikes (with headphones if you can't make a recording) before settling on a particular model. Most documentary work uses handheld mikes. Check that you can attach a pistol grip to the mike, which will minimize barrel and other handling noise.

When trying a mike out, ask yourself the following questions: Does the wire at the back stay away from your hand and arm, and not rustle when you move the mike or your hand? Is the tube long enough to keep the sound entry ports along the side of the casing from being accidently blocked by your fingers? Can you move the mike through the air without any or much wind noise? Sound recordists often loop a little bit of cable in the hand that's holding the mike, so that they don't tug on the connector and introduce interference. If possible, only use a mike that's "shock-mounted," that is, specially designed to prevent handholding noise. Some mikes explicitly designed for rough handholding incorporate two transducers—one for your source (or "signal") and one for you and all the impact noise your handholding introduces. This second transducer produces an antiphase output when it is combined with the other, and thus is canceled out. Finally, for any exterior recording, you'll need to enclose the mike in a special windscreen—check which screens are compatible with your mike and listen with headphones to see if they add any more noise (or cut out too much sound).

Wind Noise

The most common problem when shooting outdoors is wind noise. The slightest breath or draft can ruin your recording. Be sure to use a windscreen with your mike, even if the mike incorporates a double breath screen. (This is because if the mike is close to a speaker's mouth, certain consonants, especially *b*s and *p*s, are particularly explosive and will result in "popping.") Good windscreens cut down drastically on wind interference and hardly affect sound quality. There are various kinds, varying from a plastic foam shaped to fit tightly over the mike to a large cloth or foam "zeppelin" model suspended at a distance from the mike itself, stilling the air within. These latter tend to be more effective at counteracting wind: generally, the bigger the better. Sometimes you also have to add an extra outer layer, a "windjammer," around the windscreen to further reduce wind whistling. Unfortunately, the bigger the more obtrusive, so you'll have to strike a balance at some point. If worst comes to worst, and you find yourself without a screen at all, try covering your mike in some foam, a stocking, or even a sock. (If you have a zeppelin windscreen, a stocking wrapped around it can double as a windjammer.)

Mike Mounts

The most useful mike mount is a "fishpole" or a small "boom." A fishpole is a lightweight aluminum or fiberglass rod that telescopes up to lengths of around fourteen feet. It lets you (or the sound recordist) place the mike near the source and stay out of the picture. A fishpole acts as an extension of your hands, enabling you to record dialogue from individual members within a crowd, or to hold the mike high above your head or down at your toes without bending.

A fishpole provides a lot more flexibility than handholding, but it's more obtrusive and requires a dedicated sound recordist, apart from the camera operator. Additionally, you usually position it just above the picture frame, which is tiring and requires some practice. Nonetheless, for typical documentary applications, most sound recordists swear by a fishpole that extends three or four feet. If you do use one, make sure it has a shock mount attached to the mike end, to isolate it from your handling noise. You don't have to use a fishpole every time you record— if you're shooting observational-style, it may be too awkward—but it's a good idea to have one available.

Sometimes you won't want to handhold the mike. Plasticine-like substances (such as "Blue-Tack") can be useful for temporarily attaching a mike to a wall or other surface. Rubber bands let you attach a mike to any number of objects with a minimum of fuss. You can also use thin string or nylon line to suspend a mike anywhere on a line between two points.

Short "desk" or longer "floor" stands are mike mounts that eliminate all handholding interference (so long as you don't have to move them).

You may want to use them in controlled interview situations, or for musical or other public performances.

Lavalier, Clip-On, or Neck Mikes

Another useful mike for documentary is a lavalier, or clip-on mike. This is a tiny mike that you can hang around someone's neck, or attach to their clothing. If you hide it in their clothing, it'll be invisible to the camera. And if you combine it with a miniature wireless transmitter, you'll free the person up to move and turn around, recording continuous sound all the while. Jean Rouch and Edgar Morin used lavaliers in *Chronicle of a Summer* as did Gary Kildea in *Celso and Cora*. Dennis O'Rourke has used them in almost all his films. Lavaliers are liberating, and your subjects are more likely to forget about them than if they're always gazing down the barrel of a handheld mike.

Lavaliers have a lot going for them, but there are a few things to watch out for. Dialogue always sounds close when recorded with a lavalier, and this may be at odds with the camera position. (It can also make speech sound meditative, almost like interior or subjective speech.) Since a lavalier is attached below rather than in line with someone's mouth, it tends to make speech bassy and nasal, deprived of its sibilant consonants. Additionally, if your subjects are wearing clothes, they may well rub against the mike, producing rustling or even distortion. This is especially likely if you use a lavalier on someone who is walking or running. Wind noise may also be a problem when you use a lavalier on an exterior shoot. Moreover, the pickup pattern varies widely according to how your subject moves his or her head (however, because lavaliers are commonly used in TV news, many viewers are now used to making allowances for this).

If you want to attach the lavalier to a miniature wireless transmitter (a "bodypack"), you have to decide where to put it—typically in your subject's pocket or a pouch, as Barbara Kopple did in *Harlan County, USA* (1976). As a rule, you should try to position the aerial as close as possible to your signal source, and to have the receiver as close as possible to the transmitter. It's also essential to scout a location beforehand to check that there will be no interference from nearby transmitters: anything from a police or fire station to a synthesizer to neon lights can cause electrical interference in your own RF signal. Any metal on your subject's body can also interfere with the signal. Make sure that the receiver and not just the transmitter can be powered by batteries.

Sound recorded through a lavalier can also be combined with sound recorded from another mike, which will introduce more ambience to the overall recording. On a Nagra this can be easily done, mixing the two sound sources live, with the lavalier fed through a wireless "line" (amplified) input. Lavaliers are also often used with Betacam video production—where the sound recordist, monitoring the sound with headphones, has a boom and a small mixer that feeds the transmitter, and the deck is fed a line level from the receiver. The signal is recorded onto the video tape, but you have all the advantages of double-system sound.

Most lavaliers are omni-electret condensers, though dynamic and condenser models are also available. Dynamic lavaliers are cheaper, stronger, and need no head amp or power supply, while electret condensers are usually smaller and better quality.

Other Mike Characteristics

Some mikes come with a built-in double breath screen (or "close-talking" shield), protecting against excessive breath noise. Like gusts of wind, sharp exhalations of breath are recorded by mikes as loud, low rumbling noises, which will be rendered as distortion. To some people they sound like thunder; to others as if someone is hitting the mike itself. Again the best test is not the specifications but your ear: try speaking into the mike at very close range while listening with headphones.

Some mikes also come with a "base cut" switch, which reduces the bass frequency response in order to increase speech intelligibility. (In close quarters, mikes are more sensitive to low frequencies.) But many modern mikes have small enough diaphragms that they don't need additional bass reduction. If you're considering a model with a bass cut switch, listen to it with headphones first, as many cut out too much bass, making speech sound weightless.

ACCESSORIES

Mixers

If you're shooting double-system sound for film, you can easily control the intensity of the incoming signal by riding the level on the recorder.

But with single-system video, the controls are on the camera itself, which means that the sound recordist would have to walk over to the camera to change the level. Just touching the camera could upset the shot. To avoid this, you can plug in a mixer between the mike and the camera. The sound recordist can hold the mixer and monitor the level on its VU meter or PPM without having to check the camera controls. Whenever we've shot video, we've found using a mixer to be almost essential.

Mixers are actually meant to combine multiple channels (usually at least four) into a single output channel, but with single-mike mono documentary work, you use a mixer just to monitor the level and filter out undesirable frequencies. You should make sure that your mixer is "active" (i.e., allows you to control the amplification) and is equipped with a VU meter or PPM. If you know you'll only be using one mike, all you need is a master VU meter or PPM for the output to the recorder; but in case you ever want to mix signals, it's best to make sure there are meters for all incoming channels too. Most mixers allow you to choose whether to send the signal at a "mic" or "line" level—it doesn't matter very much which you choose so long as you remember to put the recorder (or camera) on the same setting.

Even if you're recording with only one mike, you still want two separate level controls on the mixer—one for the incoming mike channel and one for the output channel. As a rule, recordists set the master level lower than that of the incoming channels. You'd usually set input controls to 7 or 8 (on a scale of 1 to 10) and the master to 3 or 4. (A higher master setting will add needless system noise.)

Try to make sure your mixer has a built-in 1K "tone oscillator" or "tone generator": this will allow you to set the master gain level and to coordinate it with the VU meter or PPM monitoring the incoming signal on the camera itself, setting them both to zero. If they're not properly lined up, your audio will all be over- or under-recorded. If your mixer doesn't have a tone generator, you have two choices. You can plug in an external tone generator. Or you can eyeball the levels with some "wild" sound—any sound, preferably continuing for at least a few seconds at a constant volume, long enough for you to get the camera and mixer meters to the same level. (But remember that consumer camcorders boasting "Automatic Recording Level" have no level for you to adjust, which means that a mixer is useless in controlling the input intensity; see chapter 5.)

Most portable mike mixers also come with frequency controls, at least bass cut filters enabling you to block out some unwanted background noises. There's a strong temptation to use the mixer to equalize sound as it is being recorded, reducing ambient noise or any undesirable frequencies. This may be a mistake, both because it can make editing the sound tracks difficult (a person's voice will not match if you've equalized it differently on separate shoots), and because it can always be done during postproduction. Some mixers also provide phantom power for condenser mikes; whether you need this will depend on what mike you go with.

If you only intend to use a mixer to control the sound recording level for video, you can probably get away with using a pre-amplifier instead. Check that it has a VU meter or PPM that lets you set the level, and make sure it's cheaper than a basic mixer (many aren't).

Cables and Connectors

Audio cables may carry either balanced or unbalanced lines: the former are more professional and expensive, the latter cheaper and more susceptible to electrical interference. The world is becoming increasingly urban and increasingly electrified: most people today live their lives surrounded by powerful magnetic fields. Occasionally we hear the hum of power pilons or are unlucky enough to get a shock, but most of the time we're oblivious to them. However, since the electrical signal recorded by a mike is very weak, it tends to pick up other electricity circulating in the vicinity. As a result, mikes and their cables should ideally be "shielded" from the electricity around them by another magnetic conductor, which will prevent outside interference from reaching the lines carrying the audio signal itself. Usually this is a metal mesh around the wires.

Unbalanced cables are fine for headphones and earphones, but they are a liability when they carry your recording signal. While an unbalanced ten to twenty-foot mike cable is short enough that it will rarely be subject to interference, you should ideally only use cables that carry *balanced* lines—these contain three wires, two for the signal and one as a ground against interference. Bear in mind that all your cables must be balanced if the signal is to be protected. The easiest way to tell whether a cable is balanced is by looking at its connectors: they should be three-pronged Cannon "XLR"s. All other cable types and connectors are unbalanced: these include "phone" plugs (often used on headphones), "RCA" plugs, and "miniplugs" (typically used for earphones, and some mikes).

Headphones

VU meters and PPMs only tell you about the strength of the signal you're recording, and nothing about the quality. Headphones (or, as a last resort, an earphone) are essential to monitor sound quality. Without headphones, our brains write off many sounds as irrelevant, and they never even come to consciousness. Headphones let you hear the background noise for what it is and also let you in on important sounds being picked up by the mike that you might not have noticed. Cushy ear pads that envelop your ears are more comfortable and block off more outside noise than small pads that lodge in your ear (and are essential if you're recording music), but they also tend to be more distracting to your subjects.

Tape

Audio tape has an emulsion of either ferrous oxide, chromium dioxide ("CrO_2"), or "metal." Metal and CrO_2 tapes tend to have a higher dynamic range than ferrous oxide tapes, and so are less likely to distort. On a ⅛-inch analog cassette recorder, you would be advised to go with either CrO_2 or metal. Metal tape runs the battery down about 30 percent faster than other kinds of tape; it also is liable to oxidize before CrO_2, which makes the latter more popular among filmmakers.

For reel-to-reel recorders, ¼-inch open-reel tape is made at thicknesses of both 1.0 mil and 1.5 mil. The standard reel size is 5 inches; threaded with 1.0 mil tape, a reel will last 24 minutes, and threaded with 1.5 mil tape it will last 16 minutes. Even though it doesn't last as long, 1.5 mil tape is preferable because it is less subject to "print-through" (sound transferring to the next layer of tape on the reel). Additionally, tape made with a polyester base is preferable to tape with an acetate base, because it is stronger and more reliable.

MINI MALE

RCA MALE

1/4" MALE PHONE

FEMALE XLR

FIGURE 44 Connectors. Minis, RCAs, ¼-inch phones, and XLRs are the most common connectors for recorders and mikes. Only the XLR can carry a balanced line that shields the signal from outside electrical interference.

Additional Tools

If you expect to be shooting for any extended period far from a repair shop, you may want to invest in some extra tools. A set of small screwdrivers is always useful; at least one should be a tiny "jeweler's" model. Pliers or wire cutters can cut cables and other wires and, if necessary, can be used to change connectors or cut out a short circuit. Grips let you hold the cables. A battery-run (or lighter fluid-powered) soldering iron allows you to make a new connection. (Always heat up the wire before melting the solder.) A "solder sucker" sucks out old solder. An "inverter" that fits into an automobile lighter adapter will transform a DC input into 110V AC, allowing you to recharge batteries in your car. If your tape recorder or mixer contains one or more fuses, you should have some spares on hand. You should also have a spare AC adapter as well as spare (if possible, alkaline) batteries. Finally, a tiny portable voltage meter (preferably with a continuity tester) lets you verify connections and currents.

RECORDING TIPS

Recording Preparations

Like your film or video camera, your sound recorder needs to be maintained and to be prepared specially for a shoot. Before you rent a recorder and before you go out on a shoot, you should check that the heads are clean, demagnetized, and in good condition. As heads wear, their gap gets larger, and they begin to under-record high frequencies. They should be cleaned regularly (but gently) to remove tape particles with either clean cotton swabs or special audio swabs soaked in rubbing (isopropyl) alcohol or a professional head cleaning liquid. (On DAT or video heads, you should only use special swabs, never regular cotton swabs, holding them still as you rotate the head.)

Many sound recordists demagnetize their heads every 20 hours or so with a hand degausser; others use a "magnetometer" to see if they need it, and some even wait until the recording quality noticeably suffers. (You shouldn't try demagnetizing your heads until an experienced technician has shown you how.) Heads also need to be perfectly positioned so that the gap is at an angle of exactly 90° from the tape path; they should be checked regularly by a technician for realignment. Check also that the capstan and rollers are clean (otherwise you'll have extra wow and flutter). If you're going to be shooting sync sound, try to verify that the sync pilot level is recording. Some recorders have a filter setting that will let you hear it; on others, you need to add an additional "resolver." Most importantly, *do a test recording,* making sure that you can adjust the recording control and move around without introducing any static.

Reducing Reflections and Background Noise

As you record you have to respond to the acoustics of the space you're in. Sound is much less easily controlled than light, but is just as important. The standard rule of thumb for documentary sound is to *record it as cleanly and clearly as possible.* (You can make the sound track as complex and multivocal as you like in the editing room.) If you're filming set-up interviews, you'll want to choose a space with as few shiny, reflective surfaces as possible—unless, that is, you deliberately intend the reflections to be part of the sound track, to convey a certain effect. If you can't choose the space yourself, you may want to cover reflective surfaces with absorbent material. Common ways to reduce reflections include draping blankets, underfelt, or even your clothes over doors, walls, and tables, and sometimes even windows (though that may cut out your main light source, and alter the color temperature too). You may even need to stuff up the gaps around the doors or windows of the room you're in.

If you're shooting observational-style, and know you'll be filming in a highly reflective space, consider going with a lavalier rather than a handheld mike. If you can't move your subject(s) away from reflective surfaces, you should position yourself so that you're not picking up most of the reflections: try to move near the reflective surfaces and point the mike away, rather than having the mike point directly at them.

Likewise, try to place the mike at an angle that minimizes the background noise. If, for example, you can't avoid shooting a conversation near a road, you can reduce the background automobile noise in at least three ways: (1) You could try to filter it out with a mixer, either when recording it or (preferably) in postproduction; (2) You could position the sound recordist's back to the road, thereby blocking sounds from reaching the mike; (3) You could lavalier-mike your subject, and shoot them with *their* back to the road, their body blocking sounds from reaching the mike.

Generally you want to place the mike close enough to your sound source so that you maximize the ratio of direct-to-reflective (and incident-to-ambient) sound, but not so close that it distorts. If you get extremely close, there will be a "proximity effect," as the base frequencies will be heightened. This sounds intimate and subjective, but is generally unrealistic. If you're keeping the mike out of the frame, this won't be a problem.

If you attach a lavalier to someone's clothes, the clothes may rub against the mike. You can use an antistatic spray to reduce the electric discharge, and simply dampen stiff or starched clothing with water. The closer you position the lavalier to your subject's mouth, the less nasal and bassy it will sound. Remember, too, to keep the aerial as close as you can to the signal source, and the receiver as close as you can to the transmitter.

Consistent Level

Try to stick to a single recording level for each location or scene. Having a variety of levels makes it more difficult to edit. If you foresee a drastic change in volume (e.g., a speaker raising his or her voice), try to adjust slowly and imperceptibly, so that you're prepared. If you're recording any rehearsed performance or event, you can prepare for changes in volume by also recording (or listening through headphones to) the rehearsals. Often you'll find yourself having to compromise between louder and softer sounds—for example, between two different speakers—adjusting the level and their position accordingly. You may also sometimes need to let one sound overmodulate (certain musical instruments and audience applause are common offenders) in order to record another at an acceptable level.

When trying to maintain a consistent level, bear in mind the "inverse square law," according to which the intensity of sound (like light) falls off approximately at a rate of the square of the distance between source and recorder: if you were 3 feet from your subject and move to 12 feet, the new level will only be 1/16 what it was. If you need a stronger signal, it's a much better idea to get closer to your source than to use the recorder control to increase the level setting.

Reference Tone and Recording Data

If you're shooting film, you should record ten seconds or so of "reference tone" (generated by your recorder) at the beginning of each reel or cassette. This helps set the levels when you transfer to mag in postproduction. If you're shooting video, you should record thirty or (preferably) sixty seconds of color bars and reference tone (generated by the camera) at the beginning of every tape: these too are helpful when editing and dubbing. Immediately before or after this, it's useful to log in such details as the film title, the date, the tone level recorded (0 dB, −8 dB, or otherwise), and the sound reel or cassette (and, if relevant, film roll) numbers. The more detail you can give just after a scene has been recorded about the events that were filmed, the easier it will be to sync up and log later. If the camera operator shoots something without sound, you should still record a note to that effect—otherwise you can spend countless hours searching for the nonexistent audio later. Likewise, if you record wild sound when the camera isn't rolling, you should say so, at the beginning or end of the recording.

Ambience

Before leaving a shoot, you should record a minute or so of "ambience" (also called "presence," "atmosphere," "atmo," or "room tone"). Each space, inside and out, has its own aural characteristics, and whether you notice them or not, your tape will pick them up. Sound editing can be difficult if you don't have an ambience track to smooth over cuts: however quiet a location, it will never sound like blank tape. If you notice that the background noise changes in the middle of a shot or scene—a fridge turns itself on, say, or a boiler goes off—you should try and record ambience before and after the change. Likewise, if you happen to be shooting near a railroad track and a train goes by, you may want to hang around until another one passes through and record its sound, for use in editing the first one. The same goes for airplanes and any other intermittent sound sources.

If you can control the sound conditions of your location, you should lower the ambient noise as far as possible. It helps to turn fridges, heaters, clocks, and air conditioners off, and to cover obvious reflective surfaces before beginning recording.

Recording Music

When recording music, it's especially important to maximize the ratio of direct-to-reflective sound you are recording. This means that you need to place the mike close to the sound source. If you're using a single mike to record more than one instrument, you need to find the right balance. If you're recording a rehearsed performance, you can find the optimum mike placement by trial and error by moving the mike around during a rehearsal, monitoring with headphones. (You should also check whether the musicians will be in the same positions during the live performance, and always be prepared for them not to be.)

The advantage of recording with two mikes is you can use an omni for the overall sound, and a uni to isolate a prominent instrument or voice. However, in order to avoid phase cancellation between two or more mikes (when one's highs cancel out the other's lows), place them so that they are facing away from each other. If possible, make sure that they are at least three times as far away from each other as each mike is from its sound source. Ideally you should feed each mike to a separate track rather than mixing them onto a mono recording. You can wait to mix them in postproduction.

If your camera or recorder will let you, switch off any "automatic gain control" feature, and try to ride the recording level(s) as little as possible. That way you will record the level evenly, and be able to cut between different sections without a change in the ambient sound. It should, after all, be the music, not you, that determines the relative intensity of the sound.

As a rule you should place the mike(s) closer to the softer than to the louder instruments, for otherwise they will be drowned out. Generally, the mikes should be slightly above the sound sources. Most brass instruments are highly directional, which means you're best off placing a mike some way *off* their axis (otherwise the sound intensity and quality will vary as the musician moves the instrument). Strings are best recorded by placing the mike at 90° to their face. For woodwind instruments, the results will be best if the mike is at least six feet away. (However, special close-up mikes are available for flutes.) Piano lids should be opened. Whenever you record electronically amplified music, you should mike the speakers or PA system. This way you will catch the distortion and other elements that are integral to the live performance. Additionally, if you want to give a sense of the acoustics of the space in which the performance is being staged, you will also need to have a mike at a considerable distance from the sound sources so as to pick up the reflected sound.

Finally, you may also want to consider shooting with more than one camera. This will be a big help in the editing room, as musical performances are notoriously difficult to cut for continuity. The more, and more varied, footage you have of the musicians, instruments, and (if relevant) audience, the easier a time you will have editing it.

Staying Alert

Since in many documentary contexts you don't know what's going to happen in advance, you should always be ready to record sound. Unlike film, audio tape (and video tape) costs very little: a scene can often be salvaged if its beginning was caught on audio even if it wasn't shot on film. So don't hesitate to start recording if you have any reason to think something interesting may be about to happen. (Just be sure to say "no shot" into the mike if it doesn't pan out.) Also, nothing is worse than running out of tape in the middle of a crucial shot. So, if you're shooting film, you may want to change reels every camera roll or two (even if there's some tape left), while the camera operator is changing magazines.

Dialogue that sounds unintelligible through your headphones as you record it will probably turn out to be unusable on playback, so don't hesitate to let the camera operator know before a whole roll is wasted on a useless take. Stay in close communication with (and eyesight of) the camera operator, so that each of you knows whether and what the other is recording. Try to stay away from the blind side of the camera whenever possible.

Finally, one of the best ways to practice with your equipment is to record either with your eyes closed or in the dark. Ideally, you should know the equipment well enough to shoot at night.

Monitoring Recording Quality

A reminder: although the VU meter or PPM on your camera, sound recorder, or mixer gives you a reasonably accurate indication of the intensity of the incoming sound, it tells you next to nothing about what it is you're actually recording. You should always monitor the sound with headphones. They alert you to excessive background noise and to electrical or radio frequency interference. If headphones are off-putting to your subjects, they can be slung around your neck, and you can check the recording occasionally by bringing them up to your ears.

Solo Shooting

Finally, if you're planning on filming alone, you should consider shooting video rather than film, since it's single-system and simpler. That said, solo shooting with film is doable. Dennis O'Rourke filmed and recorded *"Cannibal Tours," The Good Woman of Bangkok*, and (most of) *The Sharkcallers of Kontu* (1982) by himself. If you do decide to shoot film, recording sound may be easier if you use a crystal-converted Walkman Pro, a small DAT, or an older Nagra SN (see appendix 4). Whether you're shooting film or video, you may want to use either an on-camera mike, despite the drop in sound quality, or else a lavalier. If possible, don't rely only on an in-built mike, but attach a directional mike to the camera (either on a special mount or with tape). A wireless lavalier frees you from your subject, and can record higher quality sound. Solo shooting is the one time when it makes sense to use some kind of automatic recording level on your recorder. Alternatively, you can set the recording level at the beginning of the scene and then leave it alone, taking care to stay roughly the same distance from the sound source. If the intensity varies a lot, you may have to reset the level.

Whether you want to film alone or with a crew of ten, all this airy talk of technology will seem much more concrete once you get your hands on the equipment itself. What you have to decide now is whether you want to shoot video or film.

5. Film or Video?

Medium, Format, and Equipment

One of the first decisions you have to make as you put your project together is whether you want to shoot in film, which is more than a century old, or video, which in portable form has been around only since the mid-1960s. Part of that decision involves choosing which film gauge or video format you would work in and what equipment you would use. The first section in this chapter lists the main differences between film and video. Depending on which you choose, you can then either move to the next section, "Video," or skip to the following one, "Film." "Video" discusses the various video formats and the features to look for in a video camera. "Film" describes the different film gauges, what to look for in a film camera, and which film stock to use. The final section in the chapter lists various film and video accessories you may need. (Information about particular makes and models is given in appendix 4.)

FILM OR VIDEO?

Film and video each have many things going for them. Choosing between them is not a cut-and-dried matter. Some projects may look better in film, and others are better suited to video. Which you choose will depend on an array of factors—what you're used to, your budget, the equipment you have access to, the climactic and geographic conditions you'll be shooting in, your preferred image aesthetics, your final distribution outlet, and so on. The following paragraphs discuss the most salient differences between the two.

Medium

Whereas film exists in three-dimensional space, video is nothing other than pure voltage: its medium is not really space at all but time. Film used to be made from a flammable substance called cellulose nitrate (which is what allowed most of the first version of Flaherty's *Nanook of*

◀ **FIGURE 45** (*preceding page*) For *The Land Where the Blues Began* (1978), John Bishop films R. L. Burnside singing a corn song while he ploughs a cotton field. Bishop is shooting ¾-inch video with an Ikegami HL-77 broadcast-quality camera.

the North to catch on fire from cigarette ash), but it's now made out of cellulose acetate. By contrast, video makes no use of photographic emulsion, and is simply *stored* on a physical medium: either a tape with a polyester base and a surface of ferric oxide, chromium dioxide, or metal particles, or else a nonlinear "hard" or optical disk.

Film cameras transmit light through the lens onto the unexposed film strip itself, making a photochemical impression. Video uses camera image sensors (which, increasingly, are solid-state semiconductors known as "charge-coupled devices") to convert or "transduce" light into an electronic signal.

Development and Playback

Because film uses photographic emulsion, it has to be processed after it is exposed. Developing a roll of film takes at least a few hours, and usually a day or more. Although Flaherty developed his own footage in the Arctic while making *Nanook,* most filmmakers have their footage developed in a professional laboratory, and then have a workprint (also known as "rushes" or "dailies") sent to them to check for technical quality. But if you're shooting in a location so inaccessible that this is not feasible, there are a number of risks to choosing film over video. There could be a problem with the original stock—it may have been X-rayed unbeknownst to you, or left to overheat on an airport runway; you may have inadvertently exposed some film to light; your camera may be running at the wrong speed, its claw (or "shuttle") not properly advancing the film in front of the aperture; your light meter may be inaccurate; and so on. However, since express courier services now deliver to most of the world, this is only rarely an issue today.

Unlike film, recorded video can be played back instantly on a VCR, or videocassette recorder (also called a VTR, or video tape recorder), and you don't have to wait till you get your rushes back from a lab before checking them. If you have a monitor, you can also show your footage to your subjects—something that allows you to gauge (and even record) how they respond to your material.

Picture and Sound

Because video records both picture and sound side by side on the same piece of tape (or computer disc), they always (in theory) stay in sync with one another. With film, however, only the picture is actually re-corded on the film strip, and the sound needs to be recorded on a sepa-rate medium (audio tape). These are synced up later before they merge again in a final optical release print. (For high-quality recording, video sound can also be recorded on a separate medium like DAT, but it doesn't have to be.) If you're going to be a one-person team, video will probably be your only practical medium. As mentioned in chapter 4, only a few documentary *film*makers (such as Dennis O'Rourke) manage to record both picture and sound by themselves.

Ease of Use

If you haven't shot film or video before, you'll find video easier to use, at least to begin with. You don't have to protect video tape from the light, develop it, wind it through a special "magazine" or through the camera, or sync up the sound and picture later.

Consumer video cameras and some Super-8 film cameras let you just point and shoot. Most documentary filmmakers, however, find they want a higher quality image and need more control than these allow. With a little practice, 16mm film cameras are in certain respects easier to use than professional video cameras (see "Video Cameras" and "Film Cameras," below). They have far fewer buttons to press!

Portability

Video comes in different formats. The older semi-professional ¾-inch format has now been almost completely replaced by three smaller for-mats, "Super-VHS," "Hi-8," and "DV" (Digital Video). Both the tapes and the cameras for these formats are much lighter and more portable than the ¾-inch models. Some video cameras weigh as little as one pound, a lot less than the fifteen pounds or so of your average 16mm film camera. Videocassettes are also a lot lighter and smaller than rolls of 16mm film. However, higher-end (or "prosumer") Super-VHS, Hi-8, and DV cameras, as well as professional "Betacam-SP" cameras, weigh as much as 16mm film cameras.

Expense

Video tape is cheaper than film stock. In the U.S., a top-quality one-hour Hi-8 tape costs between $6 and $10, and a DV tape about twice that. Eleven minutes of 16mm color negative film stock (400 feet) costs around $100. (Color reversal costs about ⅘ the price of color negative, and black-and-white negative or reversal about ½.) Film developing costs at least $50, and a workprint (which you need in editing) costs another $100. (You can also choose to shoot on film and edit on video; in this case, you would need a "video workprint" which costs about $30.) All in all, ¾-inch video tape costs about one-tenth of *processed* 16mm color film.

Because video tape is so much cheaper, you can shoot a lot more of it. If you're shooting in uncontrolled conditions, or a lot of dialogue, video will thus let you cover a lot more than you'd be likely to if you were shooting film. (It will allow a higher "shooting ratio.") On the other hand, the high cost of film makes camera operators more selective, more careful about what they shoot. This process of structuring and editing with the film camera can actually be helpful, making you focus your project early on in a way that video doesn't.

Video cameras are also generally cheaper than film cameras. Consumer VHS or 8mm models start at around $500; semi-professional Hi-8, Super-VHS, and DV at around $1,000 continuing up to $10,000 or more; and professional Betacams from $15,000 to $50,000. A new high-end 16mm film camera will cost you between $60,000 and $90,000, depending on the options you choose. That said, you can happen upon secondhand 16mm cameras for as little as a couple of hundred dollars. A secondhand Arri BL, an excellent camera that, equipped with a good lens, will produce images of as high quality as a new $90,000 camera, can be picked up for around $4,000.

Editing Technology and Costs

At the editing stage, video is not necessarily cheaper than film. Video editing has traditionally been divided into two stages: a lengthy "off-line" period where all the creative decisions are made on copies (or "dubs") of your original "master" tapes, and a brief "on-line" session where all these decisions are executed by a qualified on-line technician-editor from your original masters (see chapter 8 for information about nonlinear editing). On-line editing is very expensive indeed, especially if you're working in a fully professional video format. If you have to rent off-line editing equipment, that too can add up over time. There are too many variables involved to generalize about whether film or video postproduction will be the more costly. The higher quality you want your video, the more expensive its postproduction, and so the more likely the overall cost will approach that of film. But the cost of video editing is going down, and rates for basic Betacam-SP on-line editing facilities are now almost as low as those for the older ¾-inch format.

Sixteen-mm film editing is also divided into two stages: you make rough cuts on a copy of your negative, and once you've made all your decisions you have your negative cut and have a fine cut printed. A lot of the expense is in the making of the copy of your negative. This work-print is a low quality positive copy of the processed negative, which can later be matched frame for frame with the original when the time comes to cut the negative and make a release print. As a result, many filmmakers are now shooting on film, developing the negative only, then transferring to video for the off-line editing, before finally cutting the negative (see "Film," below).

Camera Maintenance and Climate Control

Video cameras are more fragile and difficult to maintain than film cameras, although the new CCD video cameras are much more reliable than the older tube models. If something goes wrong, it is usually an electronic problem, and you may have to take your camera to a qualified technician to get it repaired. Problems with film cameras are more likely to be mechanical, and so are more easily repaired by yourself. Video technology is also less able to withstand extremes of temperature and humidity than film.

Sixteen-mm film cameras are rugged and built to last. Many film camera operators use cameras that are twenty or thirty years old. Developments in film technology are mostly in the film stock itself, not in the cameras, while much of the improvement in video is in the cameras and recorders. This means that with the rapid evolution of video technology, you're more likely to have to change your video camera than your film camera.

Longevity

If 16mm film is stored properly, it can last a very long time indeed: certainly many decades. If not, it will deteriorate quickly. So long as one master print or the negative is stored carefully, any number of prints can be struck from it over time. Video tape deteriorates much faster and so is not really an archival medium at all. Broadcast engineers see a loss of quality and resolution within a year, even under optimum conditions, though they will play back tapes for around ten years. On the other hand, as John Bishop says, "Some claim that home cassettes, which are less critical, can be expected to last 50 years if played two or three times a year. This is probably optimistic, but certainly home video longevity surpasses the 10 years typical of Super-8 Ektachrome film."[1]

With the optical disc drives, video discs, and digital video that are emerging, it is now possible to have digital masters of videos that theoretically are not subject to any deterioration at all (other than that inherent in the coding and uncoding of information). It is possible to strike any number of copies without the loss of quality involved in going down generations in analog media.

Video disc systems have the added advantage of allowing very nearly instantaneous access to video and audio (and even textual) information stored anywhere on the disc. Nonlinear "desktop video" (DTV) has transformed the process of editing, but it's not yet a portable recording medium for shooting. It also still takes an extraordinary amount of computer "memory" to store moving images, and if you're worried about the longevity of your record, you may still decide that 16mm film is worth the extra expense. All magnetic tape loses coercivity over time, and because digital tape is so energetically packed, it starts losing its signal faster than reel-to-reel audio tape.

International Standards

When shooting abroad you have to be aware that international standards may differ from your home country. The world standard for sound film is 24 frames per second (fps). (Silent film runs at 18 fps.) In Europe and countries where the electricity current oscillates at 50 Hz, film *shot expressly for broadcast television* sometimes runs at 25 fps. This is generally not a problem, since the difference is not really noticeable on projection.

With video the image is reproduced by an electronic beam. In 60 Hz countries (including much of the Americas and Japan), the image is reproduced 60 times a second. That means there are 60 "fields" per second, each with 262.5 lines of electronic information, which in turn form 30 "frames" per second, of 525 lines each. In 50 Hz countries (including China and Europe), there are 25 frames per second, and 625 lines per field. Thus, when film is transferred to video in Europe there is a 1:1 frame correspondence, 25 frames of film and 25 frames of video. In the U.S., film shot at 24 fps can be transferred to the 60 fps of video only by favoring some film frames over others: whereas each odd-numbered film frame is projected onto two video fields, each even-numbered frame is projected onto three. (As a result, if you are shooting film for television only, you may want to shoot at 30 fps.)

When video was black-and-white, it was relatively easy to convert between the 60 fields per second in the U.S. and the 50 fields per second of the U.K.—it was just a matter of modifying the receiver. Color complicated matters. The U.S. standard, NTSC (for the National Television Systems Committee), was developed early in the 1950s, and enabled the black-and-white television sets then in existence to receive color. Unfortunately, it's now the world's worst standard, because the intensity and hue of the color signal are not consistent, so that television sets have to come with such controls as "color" and "tint" or "saturation" and "hue." (Some people call it "Never Twice the Same Color.") Germany and Britain improved on NTSC with a PAL (Phase Alternating Line) system, which not only has higher resolution but also reverses the phase of successive lines, thereby doing away with the need for a tint control. France developed a system that is altogether incompatible with black-and-white, SECAM (Système Électronique pour Couleur avec Mémoire), in which lines alternate between green plus blue and green plus red, and which has no need of any color or tint controls. This system produces the highest quality of the three.

Divergences in these international video color standards complicate the shooting of videos abroad. If you rent, borrow, or purchase equipment in the country where you'll be shooting, it may be incompatible with the editing and playback system in your country(ies) of distribution. By the same token, if you're shooting with your own equipment in a country with a different standard and want to be able to play back your footage and screen it for your subjects (not just through your silent 1-inch monotone viewfinder), you may have to bring a compatible monitor with you. Relatively inexpensive three-inch LCD (liquid crystal display) monitors are available for this purpose, though their resolution is poor and you will probably need a separate sound system (unless you use earphones for one viewer at a time). Small television monitors, some of which operate from batteries as well as electricity mains, are also available. Generally speaking, PAL is the norm in Western Europe, anglophone Africa, and the Middle East; SECAM in France, Russia, Eastern Europe, and francophone Africa; and NTSC in North and Central America, and areas of the Far East (see appendix 2). However, "multisystem" VCRs and monitors, which can play back all three standards, are becoming increasingly popular, especially outside Europe and North America.

Technical Quality and Distribution Outlets

If you hope to have your work shown in cinemas, you're better off sticking to 16mm film. *Hoop Dreams* (1994) is one of very few videos (later blown up to film) to be released in cinemas. Many of the more prestigious festivals only accept films. If you want your work to be broadcast on national television, you should also consider shooting on either film, Betacam SP, or digital video. At 30 fps, video is closer than film to our real life perception of continuous movement, but (except for digital Betacam) it cannot compete with film in terms of image sharpness, depth, contrast ratio, and color reproduction quality. Even so, most of television is shot on video, and station engineers are getting more lenient about formats like Super-VHS and Hi-8, especially for dedicated documentary slots.

If you have academic distribution first in mind, film has almost entirely given way to video. Film prints are expensive and easily damaged. Universities have very few qualified personnel to project 16mm film, and many do not maintain their 16mm projectors adequately. Since many teachers know how to use a VCR, but not a film projector, they often prefer to show a video.

Aesthetics and Social Relations

Small consumer video cameras have one major advantage: a single operator can record image and sound and hardly even be noticed. High-end video and film productions usually require a crew of at least two, preferably three, and are more intrusive. If you want to make an intimate portrait of informal life, you may find it easier to work alone, or with someone from the community, using a small camcorder. You can teach someone to take sound in a matter of minutes (as we saw in the last chapter, this doesn't mean taking good sound is easy). Camcorders have penetrated all over the world, and though even they usually represent a provocation to the social fabric, they are a lot less alien than a large foreign film crew.

Ethnographic film- and videomaker John Bishop sums up the difference between the media and formats in these terms:

> You see differently through different media. The gestalt of observing in 16mm film is different from looking at the world in Betacam video, and small format video (Hi-8, Super-VHS, DV) is a different language entirely. It has to do with the texture of the recorded image, the quality of the viewfinder, the ergonomics of the camera, how technically forgiving the medium is, and how social space is affected by the camera.
>
> The 16mm film camera is hefty and well-engineered for hand-holding, so I can move with confidence. The through-the-lens viewfinder shows more than the frame, which gives a warning of what is happening immediately off-screen, and it looks natural, so I can use color contrast to judge composition. Film frequently interprets color and tonal gradation in ways that make the footage more beautiful than the reality, even if I don't hit the exposure exactly. And there is considerable range for color and density correction in both printing and telecine transfer to video. Film says that the subject was, is, and will continue to be important. This encourages reaching for bold compositions.
>
> Broadcast-quality video feels electric; the image sparkles. Video says that the subject is exciting right now. The viewfinder is usually black-and-white, with contrast peaked to facilitate focusing, so I use tonality to judge composition. The net effect is a psychological distance from the subject and a greater intimacy

with the video image itself. As with film, the color playback is often more beautiful than what I shot.

In general, it is much easier to shoot well in 16mm (with an Aaton or Arri) or with a good Betacam than it is to shoot consumer video, but personal video cameras see a different world. Because they are very light, and the viewfinders are at the back, most do not sit easily on the shoulder for conventional hand-held shooting. However, mounted on a Steadicam JR [a hand-held stabilization system] with its off-the-eye viewing screen, a small camcorder can move with a range and freedom that a film or broadcast camera can't approach. I have made 18 minute single takes moving through a rehearsal room of dancers, moving the camera from above my head to my ankles, all seamlessly. If not using the JR, I design my coverage with more static shots, and anticipate editing out awkward moves. The viewfinders are difficult to focus, so I tend to zone focus. The lenses do not have the high contrast and acutance of cine/broadcast lenses, and the recording chain does not have the contouring of broadcast electronics. This means that scenes with busy detail and high contrast do not record well, so I concentrate on finding scenes and compositions that the camera will render gracefully. I find myself pre-visualizing and moving the camera into the desired configuration rather than searching through the camera. This makes me more aware of the context in which I am working. The great advantage of the consumer camera is that it does not attract attention, it falls into the informality of family pictures. This allows access where professional gear would be excluded, and the easy-going intimacy of a friend taking pictures of a friend instead of a subject and a crew. I have found this liberating. The end result is footage that feels like ordinary life.[2]

While the best observational *film*makers have managed to portray daily life as evocatively and intimately as most people using personal video cameras, Bishop's point should be borne in mind. Even if the image quality of consumer camcorders does not yet appeal to television engineers, the new technology opens up the possibility of representing the personal and domestic domain of human life with a degree of informality that is hard to come by with a film camera and crew.

If you've decided to shoot video, you first need to decide what format you want to work in. This decision also affects what kind of camera and editing equipment you'll use.

VIDEO FORMATS

The actual camera part of a video camera (the lens and image sensors) used to be separate from the recorder. The two were joined by a camera cable. But increasingly the two components are combined into a "camcorder." Lower-end camcorders are often a single, indissoluble unit. Higher-end models tend to feature a separate camera and recorder, literally joined ("docked") together for the shooting. When the camera and recording deck are separate components (whether joined by a cable or physically docked together), you can choose a camera without having to commit yourself once and for all to a video format. You can use the same camera with different recorders for the different formats. But if you choose a unified camcorder, you're also choosing a format that you'll have to stick with.

Video technicians actually talk about three different kinds of tape use—acquisition (production, whether in the field or a studio), post-production (editing), and distribution. These stages are interconnected. If you choose a low-quality tape to shoot on, you can never improve on the original in the editing or distribution stages. When you rent a movie from your local home video store, it'll almost certainly be a VHS cassette (even if it originated on 35mm film), just as almost all home VCRs in the U.S. are VHS. However, only home consumers shoot using VHS and 8mm video tape. Their resolution and color are not really adequate for broadcast, or even for educational distributors.

At the other end of the spectrum, high definition television (or HDTV) currently combines a wide aspect ratio (its height-to-width ratio is 9:16, while the ratio of the conventional TV screen is 3:4) with over 1,100 horizontal scanning lines. Its resolution quality approaches that of 35mm film. But for various technological and financial reasons, it hasn't yet taken off. In the meantime, you will have to choose between the following formats: Hi-8, Super-VHS, DV, ¾-inch U-Matic, Beta-cam SP, M-II, and various other emerging digital formats. The high-end formats use metal tapes with a dense coat of high quality recording particles—resulting in better picture resolution and color as well as better audio. When deciding on a format, here are a few factors to bear in mind.

Hi-8

Introduced in 1989, Hi-8 is small, light, and highly portable. It is still principally a consumer medium, though it is used by some documentary videomakers and news producers. It has better color and resolution than regular 8mm tape. It also lets you record two hi-fi (AFM, or Audio Frequency Modulation) and two digital (PCM, or Pulse Code Modulation) audio tracks at the same time. Both Sony and Fuji produce high-quality metal particle and evaporated Hi-8 cassettes, and these have more dynamic range than most hi-fi music cassettes.

Half-inch VHS and ¾-inch U-Matic and U-Matic SP record a "composite" signal. This means that each video track contains not only the sync details (for picture and sound) but also the luminance (Y) and chrominance (C) information. By contrast, Hi-8 and Super-VHS use what is called "Y/C signal processing." Although Hi-8 and Super-VHS don't actually record Y and C channels on different tracks, as do true "component" formats like DV and Betacam SP, they process and output the luminance and chrominance information as separate signals, resulting in higher image resolution and color quality. This makes Hi-8 and Super-VHS technically superior to the older ¾-inch video.

Hi-8 can also record "time code," which is a numerical system of identifying every individual video frame. Time code is almost essential when it comes to editing. There are two different kinds of Hi-8 time code—"RC" (rewritable consumer) on consumer cameras and "8mm time code" on more professional models. Bear in mind that these two systems are incompatible, not only with each other, but also with the standard SMPTE (Society of Motion Picture and Television Engineers) time code, which is the norm for video editing the world over. The professional 8mm time code functions similarly to SMPTE in that it can be transferred from one tape format to another, and can be either recorded during field production or added later to prerecorded tapes. But you need an additional accessory interface to convert it to SMPTE if you're going to edit in another format.

Desktop Hi-8 editing systems have been slower to develop than Hi-8 cameras, and many Hi-8 users transfer to another format for editing, not even bothering with the 8mm time code. This way you lose a generation in the dubbing, but so long as you transfer to a higher quality format, such as Betacam SP or a computer hard drive, the deterioration should be minimal.

If you're set on Hi-8, and want to couple it with a Steadicam JR stabilization system (see "Stabilization Systems" in "Film and Video Accessories," below), your camera needs to weigh less than four pounds.

Super-VHS

Super-VHS (or S-VHS) was introduced to the market in 1987, and with the recent development of high-quality dockable camcorders, has become a very popular "prosumer" documentary format. Like Hi-8, it can provide 400 or more lines of resolution and employs separate Y/C signal processing. Better Super-VHS models offer four audio channels: two longitudinal and two hi-fi (the hi-fi information is squeezed into the video tracks, using the rotary video head).

Super-VHS tapes are about four times as big as Hi-8 (they're the same size as ½-inch VHS), but Super-VHS cameras are not necessarily any bigger than their Hi-8 counterparts. Unless you're really pushed for space, however, tape size is not a crucial difference.

Super-VHS does offer two advantages over Hi-8, for the time being. Some Super-VHS cameras let you record real-time SMPTE time code, and your Super-VHS editing deck will be able to read it, so you won't have to lose a generation in the editing. Also, users report that "dropout"—a loss of oxide coating, so that some of the video and/or audio information disappears (occasionally clogging tape heads)—is less of a problem for Super-VHS tape than for Hi-8. The main drawback of Super-VHS (and VHS), in comparison to Hi-8, is their poorer color quality. Super-VHS looks so much better than VHS simply because its luminance has been extended—it has better black-and-white resolution, and the eye is much more sensitive to this than to color.

As with Hi-8, if you want to couple a Super-VHS camcorder with a

FIGURE 46 Time Code on Video Frame. SMPTE time code is a standardized numerical system that lets you keep picture and sound in sync during editing. The video equivalent of edge numbers in film, SMPTE time code identifies every frame of your footage. It is a digital form of reference that in itself is invisible. During off-line video editing, however, you can "burn in" time code onto your dubs, so that it is visible at the bottom of the screen, as in this image. This lets you quickly and easily mark down the entry and exit points of every shot in your final rough cut, enabling you to begin your on-line edit with a frame-accurate edit decision list (EDL).

This 01:12:53:13 figure burnt into a video frame from Melemchi, Nepal, corresponds to (01) hours: (12) minutes: (53) seconds: (13) frames. SMPTE time code continues counting frames up to the maximum figure of 23:59:59:29. If you shoot more than 24 hours of footage, the next figure would revert to zero (actually 00:00:00:01 for the first frame) and continue from there. See "Time Code Generator" in the "Video Cameras" section below.

Steadicam JR stabilization system, your camera needs to weigh less than four pounds. Consider using a Super-VHS-C camera, which uses a minicassette. (But check first whether the editing suite you expect to use has an adapter for Super-VHS-C.)

¾-Inch U-Matic and ¾-Inch U-Matic SP

If you're going to buy or rent a camera, it's best to avoid the ¾-inch format, the first one widely used by television stations for field production. It's gradually giving way to DV, Super-VHS, and Hi-8. Because the ¾-inch format requires a cable to join camera and recorder, you really need two people to operate them: a sound recordist and a camera operator. However, in their favor, cameras and recorders using ¾ inch are very rugged and durable, and many are still in use today. Schools in particular have been reluctant to upgrade. If you do shoot on ¾ inch, try to use U-Matic SP (Superior Performance) tapes. They're slightly more expensive, but record a better image.

Betacam SP

Betacam SP is the broadcast standard. It is a ½-inch recording format, the same size as VHS, but it's a component system, recording the luminance and chrominance signals separately. Like Super-VHS, it offers up to four audio tracks: two longitudinal and two hi-fi. (The lower-end industrial models only offer two longitudinal tracks, which is all you really need anyway.) Though it's expensive, it's getting less so all the time. Industrial Betacam SP camcorders are almost as cheap as high-end Hi-8 and Super-VHS models (although all three are giving way to DV). In addition, Betacam SP is an excellent editing format, even if you shot your original footage on Hi-8 or Super-VHS.

M-II

M-II (and the earlier M) is an almost identical format to Betacam SP (and Betacam), the main difference being that it was developed by Matsushita, not Sony. It's cheaper but less common, and so editing facilities are harder to find. And while Betacam SP is wholly compatible with the earlier Betacam, M-II is incompatible with M. Betacam (SP) and M (II) are mutually incompatible, so you have to decide between them, for shooting *and* editing, before you start.

Digital Formats

"Digital Video," or DV (initially called DVC), is an early warning death knell to the other small formats. Nominally a "consumer" format, using tiny ¼-inch (6.35 mm) tape, the recording quality of DV is far superior to Hi-8 and Super-VHS. With its true component recording (of luminance and chrominance separately), 500 or more lines of horizontal resolution and signal-to-noise ratio of at least 54 dB (see below), DV is in fact more or less equivalent in quality to Betacam SP, the analog professional leader. Along with the video information, it is also able to record either two (48 kHz, 16-bit) or four (32 kHz, 12-bit) tracks of audio, as well as SMPTE time code. Moreover, since it is digital (and all the data on the tape is compressed at a ratio of 5 : 1), it can be transferred with minimal quality loss onto a computer for editing (often at four times real-time speed).

However, while the recording end of DV is Betacam SP quality, the front end is frequently just a consumer camera, and the technical quality of low-end DV cameras (especially their lenses) is not always sufficient to allow you to profit from the potential of the format. As a result, high-end industrial camcorders, with interchangeable lenses (such as DVCAM and DVCPRO) have been developed from DV (although they are not always compatible with it). So although DV is a very promising medium, choosing the right camera is equally important (see appendix 4).

While consumer DV was introduced only in 1995, various professional digital formats had been around for some time earlier. D-1 and D-2 are both high-quality editing (rather than production) formats using 19mm tape (around ¾-inch). D-1 records a component signal on oxide tape, D-2 a composite signal on metal particle tape. Portable camcorders are nominally available for the later D-3 (composite) and D-5 (component) formats, though these too are used mainly in postproduction. All these formats record uncompressed full-band video, unlike DV, which compresses its signal at a 5 : 1 ratio (and loses some quality in the process). The top of the line portable digital format, for which professional camcorders are available, is Digital Betacam. It has only a 2 : 1 compression ratio, and samples the chrominance signal more frequently than DV. In terms of color and image resolution (and cost), Digital Betacam gives 16mm film a run for its money.

When deciding on a camera, try to talk to a video technician about your needs and the latest technical developments. Most institutions with video facilities will have someone on staff who can answer your questions. To get an idea of the latest features and prices, talk to a professional vendor or a video supply store like B & H Photo-Video in New York City (see appendix 3). (Ask them for a copy of their latest "Professional Video Sourcebook," which contains information and prices for a wide range of video equipment—desktop editing, audio, tripods, lighting, power, and monitors as well as cameras.)

Most video cameras fall into three main ranges of cost. The top end consists of fully professional Digital Betacam and Betacam SP cameras. The purchase price of industrial cameras (Betacam SP or digital video), which also record a broadcast-quality image, is less than half as much. Hi-8, Super-VHS, and DV are the main formats at the lower end of the price range, even though the quality of DV can equal Betacam SP.

If you're interested in investing in the consumer or prosumer rung, you should take what consumer video store shop assistants say with a grain of salt. The video market, like the home electronics market as a whole, is saturated with hype, and it's very difficult to make sense of all the apparently earth-shattering features boasted by the latest releases. Some of the "features" may be as much a hindrance as a help. The following is a rough-and-ready guide to help you sort the wheat from the chaff.

Standard Features

Almost all consumer camcorders nowadays come with an array of attributes (under various names), which you can probably take for granted. They usually include:

- automatic focus capability
- automatic iris (exposure) capability
- automatic white balance (color temperature) capability
- automatic audio record level capability
- automatic shutoff (saves the battery)

- flying erase head (an erase head, in front of the video record head, allowing you to perform elementary "insert" editing)
- stereo recording capability (your eventual master and distribution cassettes will probably be mono, but this means you can record at least two channels of audio)
- rechargeable battery (you will need to buy extras)
- playback capability on external monitor and/or television (RF, or radio frequency, output)
- in-camera record review
- automatic backspace editing (ensures continuous synchronization and clean cuts between recorded shots)

On top of these standard features, most models will be advertised with an array of others.

Editing Features

Some features, such as "video dub" (also called "video add" or "video insert"), "audio dub," and "sound on sound" could conceivably be of use. "Video dub" lets you add video or audio over prerecorded segments without erasing the previous recording, and "sound-on-sound" lets you add another sound track, at a higher level, to the one already there, so you can combine, say, narration and ambience. But these features and others like them (such as the capacity to fade to or from black or white) are really just consumer simulations of a professional editing console, and since you will almost certainly be going into postproduction, you won't need them. Also, since they are performed on your original tape (your "master") their effects are ineradicable. Finally, a built-in digital "time base corrector" will make no difference to recording quality at all, and unless you use your camera as a playback deck during editing, it's as good as useless.

CCDs, Pixels, and Horizontal Resolution

Video can record an image in various ways. Older cameras used "vacuum pickup" tubes, and contemporary models use "charge-coupled devices" or CCDs. If possible avoid pickup-tube cameras: they're very fragile, their tubes need constant maintenance to ensure they're aligned or registered, and they can be ruined by being exposed to overly bright light ("burn in").

CCD cameras are sturdier and show a lot less "lag": either a smeared retention of the previous image caused by camera or subject movement or the "comet tail" effect caused by panning or tilting across too bright a light source. However, CCD cameras can suffer from a different kind of image distortion called "smear"—a vertical band above and below an overly bright light source in the image. Smear is related to the number and quality of "pixels" in the CCDs; it is measured in dB (like audio level) and will be specified for professional cameras. Try to use a camera with a reduced smear level.

Generally, the more CCDs (or "chips") the better. Three-chip cameras have the best color reproduction and image resolution, as one chip is allocated for each of video's prime colors (red, green, and blue). Cameras with two chips (a chip for green and another for red and blue combined) are better than those with only one.

There are different kinds of CCDs. Diagonally, they may be ⅔ inch, ½ inch, ⅓ inch, or ¼ inch across. They also contain different numbers of "pixels" (short for "picture elements," which are metal oxide conducting points or silicon semiconductors which transform light to an electronic signal). At press time, chips with over 300,000 pixels are considered to be of reasonable quality, although prosumer and professional cameras have at least 400,000, and often 600,000.

Information about lines of resolution can be confusing. All NTSC cameras will produce images with the standard 525 (625 on PAL and SECAM) *vertical* scanning lines per frame. This is defined by the format. The *horizontal* lines of resolution have to do with the number of pixels; the more the better. There may be 750 horizontal lines or more *in the camera,* 500 or so on Betacam or DV tape, and fewer still on Super-VHS and Hi-8.

Automatic and Manual Focus

Automatic focus systems are improving all the time. Most of them focus on whatever is in the center of the frame. Some are slow and inaccurate, moving from being out of focus (focusing in front of your subject) through being momentarily in focus to being out of focus again (focusing behind your subject), before finally recognizing the need to recorrect. All search continually for perfect focus, but rarely find it. If you're shooting a moving subject, an automatically focusing camera may be out of focus quite a bit of the time. Moreover, even with a still subject, autofocus does not work well in low light.

So, if you have the choice, use a camera that also lets you focus manually. Try the camera out to see whether you can do this easily, whether it is obvious from the viewfinder if the image is in focus or not (see if you can hook it up to a monitor in the store or rental house), whether you can change focus and aperture at the same time, and whether you can keep the camera still while you focus. The larger the focus ring the easier it will be to use.

Automatic Iris and Gain Control

In many consumer cameras, the iris, or aperture, is controlled automatically. The video "gain" is adjusted electronically in accordance to the brightness and contrast of the image on the chips. This too may be controlled automatically. If so, the camera regulates the overall signal in accordance with a standard video white level. But because most brightness ranges exceed video's contrast range, many shots may end up partly over- and partly underexposed. You, not the camera, need to be able to choose which part of the frame you wish to expose optimally. Additionally, you don't want the exposure to change drastically if a dark or light object crosses the frame. A manual override switch allows you to adjust the iris yourself, at your own speed.

Try out different models to see whether they are easy to operate, whether you can change the exposure smoothly as well as suddenly, and whether you can comfortably alter focus and iris at the same time. Don't mistake a manual iris with a "video gain" or "gain boost" switch, which is used in low light. Some models come with extra switches that are intermediate between auto and manual iris. A "backlight" control can compensate when shooting a subject against the sky or sun or any other light background, but it's not equivalent to a manual iris. One useful switch is a momentary auto-iris, which will correct exposure for your current conditions (say, an interior room), and then hold the iris at that setting till you reset it—thus allowing you to pan across an open window without the iris wildly oscillating. "Over" and "under" switches are also becoming common—switches that offset the iris setting either over or under by half an f-stop, in case you find yourself continually over- or underexposing a particular subject.

Automatic Audio Record Level and Audio Gain Control

All cameras have headphone sockets, so you can monitor the sound as you record it. But many consumer models adjust the audio recording level automatically according to the strength of the incoming signal. The problem with this is that the camera corrects "overmodulations," and overcorrects them at that, only *after* the damage is done. As it adjusts its level to the median sound volume it picks up, it also turns up the gain when things get quiet—if someone who is talking starts whispering, for example, or moves or turns away from the camera. This changes the ambient level, magnifies the hum and hiss of the system, and generally makes it hard to edit.

If possible, use a camera with an override of the "Automatic Audio Record Level" (or one without automatic leveling at all). Other mystifying terms for this override include "Manual Audio Input Control" and "Manual Gain Control Circuitry." Try also to use a model with an audio level potentiometer, either a VU meter or a PPM (see chapter 4). Additionally, an audio peak "limiter" switch can keep short, sharp percussive sounds from distorting.

Some models come with an in-built monitor speaker, which lets the camera operator overhear the recorded sound being monitored on headphones by a sound recordist. Some cameras will even beep to you through this speaker if there are certain problems. But check to see if you can control the volume of the speaker, or even turn it off altogether, for if you're using the on-camera mike, you might pick up the speaker sound, which can also cause feedback.

External Mike Input(s) and Mount

Most consumer camcorders come with a built-in electret condenser mike. Its audio signal is converted into a line level by a pre-amplifier within the camera (since unamplified mic-level signals are feeble). On-camera mikes tend to be of low quality and to record camera zoom and other handling noise. You have little control over them, and they are often farther from the sound source than they should be. Even "zoom" on-camera mikes, which adjust their degree of directionality in rough accordance with the camera lens, are generally not of high quality. So you'll probably want to use an external mike for better sound recording quality. High-end cameras often have a special mount where you can attach an additional mike. Try to make sure your camera has two external audio inputs, each destined for a separate audio channel. This lets you record one channel with a mike mounted on the camera, and a second channel with a separate mike (handheld, lavalier, or mounted). Make sure that external audio sources can override the camera mike.

Audio Track Position

All tape-based formats and cameras that allow for two (or more) channels of audio to be recorded will position one track along the inside of the video tape and the other along the outside. Ideally, you should find out from the camera manufacturer, vendor, or rental house which channel is recorded on the inside, as this is the "safe" track (it is better protected), and plug your main mike into that. If you are also using a second backup mike, you can plug that into the outer track.

"Video Gain" or "Video Boost"

For low-light shooting, many cameras incorporate a switch that can boost the video gain level. This lets you catch color that would otherwise be lost. The side effect is that you'll see a loss in the overall quality of the image. So you will want to have the switch on only when you really need it. Some portable video cameras now have settings of up to +30 dB of gain (dBs are used to measure video as well as audio). This may be called "hyper gain," "lolux," or the like. Try to use a camera that allows you to have as much gain as possible; even +18 dB can be very helpful.

Some consumer cameras can now operate when there is as little as one or two lux illumination (see "Lighting and the Image" in chapter 3). Single-chip camcorders are in fact often better in low light than two- or three-chip models—for as light is transmitted through a prism it loses some of its intensity. As a result, the 18 dB and 30 dB switches are more likely to be found on professional three-chip camcorders than on consumer single-chip models—because they're needed more.

One of the most important tests when choosing a camcorder is to point it into an area of low light and see what the image is like. Check skin tones particularly. If possible, hook different models up to *the same* monitor and compare their images. For applications in extremely low light—say, an important night scene—there are specialized cameras available (see "Video Cameras" in appendix 4).

Shutter-Speed Control

CCD cameras come with an electronic shutter. Most models let you adjust the shutter's frequency. Normally you won't need to change the shutter speed, but there are times when you might—in particular, if you're shooting high-speed movement or if you're shooting under artificial indoor light (or if you want to shoot a computer monitor or television screen). Camera shutters that can be increased to $1/1000$ or $1/2000$ of a second eliminate most of the blurring of high-speed movement. (Many camcorder shutters now go up to $1/10,000$ of a second.) Incandescent lights do not flicker badly, since their filaments stay hot as the power fluctuates, but fluorescents do, unless the tubes have been coated to retain luminescence. If you see flicker in the viewfinder, try experimenting with different shutter speeds. NTSC cameras often come with a special 100 Hz setting for flicker reduction when shooting with fluorescents in 50 Hz countries.

Lens Quality, Zoom Ratio, Zoom Speed, Wide Angle, and Macro

While most dockable cameras let you mount whatever lens you want, consumer camcorders come with an incorporated zoom lens. There are a few things to look out for in a lens. First, ask what its "zoom ratio" is—that is, the ratio of its longest focal length to its shortest. It would be a mistake to have a minimum zoom ratio of less than 10:1 (or 10X). Many filmmakers like a ratio of around 17:1 (17X). Second, find out what is the widest-angle setting of the lens, and what is the diagonal measurement of the pickup tube or CCD image sensors. If a video camera has ⅔-inch CCDs, make sure its widest angle setting is below 12mm (12mm gives a "natural perspective" like a 50mm lens on a 35mm still camera). For ½-inch CCDs, natural perspective is 9mm (and its widest angle setting should be less), for ⅓-inch CCDs, natural perspective is 6mm, and for ¼-inch CCDs, natural perspective is around 4.5mm (see "Focal Length," in chapter 3).

Beware of extraordinary claims for "digital zooming," which might extend a normal 8:1 zoom ratio to something like 80:1. Digital zooming simply magnifies the pixels in the CCD(s), so the more you zoom the more fragmented the image. On the other hand, this digitized mosaic special effect might be something you would occasionally want.

Another factor to look for on your lens is a "macro" switch or lever that lets you convert the lens itself to a "macro lens," which is used for extreme close-ups, usually of details or small objects. Check also for the closest focal distance of a lens—how close an object can be to the camera and remain in focus, without going over to macro. It should be at least as close as two or three feet.

Check the speed of the zoom feature itself. Some consumer camera zooms operate at only one speed: whether you press the "zoom in" or the "zoom out" button you'll zoom in or out at a constant speed. But this speed is rarely the one you'll want to be moving at; it will also probably stop and start too abruptly. If possible, make sure your camera has a "continuously variable" zoom, sometimes called a "zoom rocker." This gives you total control of the zoom speed—from a slow crawl to a quick glide—and lets you keep the zoom movement smooth. A zoom with several different set speeds is no substitute. Always try out a zoom before deciding on a lens: experiment with its fastest and slowest speeds and the smoothness of the movement, especially as you start and stop. Listen also to how much noise the zoom motor makes (the on-camera mike may pick it up).

If possible, use a camera that also lets you zoom manually (in fact many camera operators only zoom manually). If you need to move more or less instantly from a long to a short lens, a manual zoom will be the only way of doing it. How smooth is the manual zoom? How easy is it to use? Can you change focal length, focus, and iris, all at the same time?

One of the main drawbacks of consumer cameras is that their lenses and heads are not as high-quality as Hi-8, Super-VHS, and DV tape itself. This means they don't give you the high resolution and image quality that the formats are capable of. Unfortunately, a fully professional video lens costs as much as a high-quality 16mm zoom lens: $5,000 to $10,000. (For exceptions, see "Video Cameras" in appendix 4.)

Image Stabilization

Prosumer camcorders come with a cushioned shoulder mount and are precisely weighted to rest evenly on your shoulder. In contrast, some consumer camcorders have become so compact that they simply rest in your palm. Their viewfinders tend to be at the back rather than halfway down the side.

Camera manufacturers have introduced various forms of optical and electronic image stabilization to counter the inherent instability of these "palmcorders," or camcorders that are too small to be balanced on your shoulder. In theory such stabilizing systems let you record a smooth image when you're handholding, and even when you're walking or moving around. The ones that work well free you from your tripod, and produce a remarkably stable image. Some are better than others, however, so beware.

Certain models work by gauging camera movement from movement in the subject. This means that if you shoot a close-up of a flickering candle light, the camera might try and correct the flickering! Some don't work when you're zooming. Some work poorly in low light. Some sacrifice image resolution or alter image size. And a few hardly have any effect at all (see appendix 4 for more information).

Viewfinder Size and Color

Optical viewfinders, which show you a full-color image from light reflected through the lens, are being replaced by electronic viewfinders, which are really tiny TV screens coupled with an adjustable diopter (two-part, focusing) lens. Although you see less clearly through electronic viewfinders, they let you monitor the camera's actual focus and image quality more easily, since you're seeing exactly what the image sensors have registered. On professional cameras, viewfinders are usually 1½ inches in diagonal; on consumer models they tend to be a much less workable ½ inch. Check that you can adjust contrast and brightness, quickly and easily. (Some consumer models require Phillips screwdrivers to make the adjustments, and you may not have time for that in the field.) If an NTSC camera has a color liquid crystal display (LCD) viewfinder, check that you can adjust color, brightness, and hue (or "tint").

Viewfinders may be black-and-white or color. Black-and-white view-finders use cathode ray tubes (CRTs) and a phosphor coating. They're easier to focus and cheaper than color viewfinders, which are active-matrix LCD. In choosing between them, you should bear a few things in mind. Most professional camcorders still have CRTs, which have higher resolution, a higher contrast ratio, and less smear and lag. It's also easier to judge the contrast and tone of a scene on a black-and-white viewfinder. But color is an important component of an image, and it helps to be able to see it as you record. Additionally, so long as you've set the LCD hue correctly (on most current models you can only guess at it), a color viewfinder lets you monitor color temperature. Larger LCD viewfinders of four inches across or more allow camera warnings, otherwise communicated through the viewfinder in codes or (often not very intuitive) icons, to be stated in plain English: you might see "The tape ends soon" rather than a flashing rectangle.

There are other qualities you should look for in a viewfinder. Can it replay the last scene you have recorded? Is it "overscan"—that is, does it show the edge of the image that TV monitors or receivers tend to cut off? And if so, does it superimpose "safety zones" so that you can tell which part of the image will make it onto the monitor? Can the view-finder be tilted and rotated in a number of directions, so it won't ob-struct camera moves when mounted on a tripod, and so you can shoot from the hip or with the camera at arm's length? Can the viewfinder rotate or be mounted on either side of the camera (this is especially important if you are "left-eyed")? Can the (CRT) diopter and view-finder eyecup be flipped back, so you can look at the image from a distance? Is the viewfinder detachable altogether and watchable at a dis-tance? This frees the camera from your eye, so that you can raise it above your head or lower it to your feet. Some viewfinders now even come as "virtual" goggles with stereo earplugs. (In 1986, ethnographic film-maker John Bishop wrote, "I foresee the day when the camera will be a flat disc that you glue to your forehead like a Hindu *tika* mark. A hair-sized fiber optic will feed the signal to an ultra-miniature solid-state memory behind your ear, and whenever you are feeling particularly good, the recording system will turn on automatically."[3] This cyborgian future may not be far off.)

FIGURE 47 Detachable Viewfinder. Some camcorders let you look through a view-finder that is separate from the camera, so that people might not even know you're filming.

"Confidence" Heads

The viewfinder on most camcorders shows you only what the CCDs register, not what is actually being recorded on the tape. A few camcorders feature "confidence heads," video heads placed after the recording heads, which allow you to verify the images just after they are recorded. They sound snazzy, but really aren't necessary.

Color Temperature and White Balance Controls

Consumer camcorders have at least two basic settings, or internal filters, with which to respond to the color temperature of incoming light: "indoor" and "outdoor." All professional and some prosumer cameras now come with a combination of filters (on a "filter wheel") and with a *separate* white-balance switch. Standard filter settings are 3000K, 3200K, and 5600K; "3200K + ND," "5600K + ¼ND," and "5600K + ¹⁄₁₆ND" are others. "ND" refers to a "Neutral Density" factor incorporated into the filter. This doesn't alter the temperature of incoming light; it just reduces its intensity when it's too high. For bright exterior scenes you'll often want to use an ND filter. (You can also engage the filter just to push open the camera aperture, and reduce the depth of field.)

A separate white-balance switch helps to record colors faithfully, since it lets you adjust the relative intensity of red, blue, and green. (Some companies now refer to the different filters as "white-balance settings" or "auto white balance," but don't be taken in!) If possible, make sure your model has a white-balance switch that lets you set white balance both "automatically" and "manually." You white balance automatically by zooming into a white object and setting that as your standard white for those conditions. You white balance manually also by zooming into something white, but then you adjust the setting by hand. (You should have an absolutely white or a gray card with no color tint expressly for this purpose.) Some cameras can recall the last white-balance setting, which means you don't have to reset the camera every time you turn it off (as long as the lighting stays the same).

White-balance switches are often combined with or next to a "color bar switch," which can be used to record the standard NTSC color bars (white, yellow, cyan, green, magenta, red, and blue) onto the head of all your tapes before you start recording. This helps you standardize colors during editing. Some models also boast a "black balance" or "auto black" switch, which sets the black level, but this isn't essential.

When choosing a camera, check to see how easily and quickly you can change the white-balance setting. Often in documentary you'll find yourself filming people going in and out of doors, and you may have to deal with massive color temperature changes within a single shot. Some cameras can adjust the white balance automatically in response to changing conditions. This feature is sometimes called "Auto Tracing White Balance." Check to see how well it actually works.

Time Code Generator

Time code is necessary on video for frame-accurate editing. A numerical counter on the camera, including a "real-time frame" counter, is *not* a time code counter. Only a time code counter reads the actual time code numbers that have been assigned to each frame of video, which means that it won't matter if you accidentally hit the reset button. Unless you're going to shoot *and edit* on Hi-8, RC and 8mm time code won't be much use, and you'll have to record SMPTE time code onto your tapes. For that you can wait till you prepare your tapes for editing.

High-end camcorders often either have built-in time code generators or allow for portable ones to be attached. There are two basic kinds of generators: longitudinal (LTC) and vertical interval (VITC). VITC is smuggled into a video track, and so leaves both audio channels open for audio itself. LTC needs a special cue or address track, but not all camcorders or VCRs have this facility. Many camcorders record LTC in one of the audio channels, leaving only one channel for your audio. You want to have as much freedom in recording sound as possible, so if LTC is specified for a camera, you should ask expressly whether this will take up one of the audio channels. (Also, find out if your editing facility can read both kinds of time code. Equally, if you want to wait till postproduction before recording or "striping on" time code, as many people do, check what system is available at your editing house and whether it will take up one of the audio channels.)

FILM

If you've decided to shoot film, your first decision is which gauge to go with. In movie theaters, film is normally projected at 35mm, which is the most common gauge for all stages of theatrical filming. Edison's first films in the 1890s were shot on 35mm, and it's still the trade norm today. But 35mm film is out of the price range of most documentary filmmakers. And although there is a 35mm Aaton that weighs only about a pound more than 16mm cameras, it holds only 4 ½ minutes of film, in comparison to the 11 minutes of 16mm cameras.

DOCUMENTARY FILM FORMATS

Most documentaries are shot on 16mm, which was introduced in the 1920s and has an image which is a quarter the size of 35mm. Film stocks have improved dramatically in recent years, although when 16mm is projected onto a large screen it still looks grainier and fuzzier than 35mm. A few documentaries are shot on Super-8, which was introduced by Kodak in 1965 as an improvement on the regular (double)

8mm film, which dates back to 1932. Music videos and commercials are sometimes shot on Super-8 and then transferred to Betacam or digital video. Super-8's image size is a third of 16mm's, and runs at 72 frames a foot as compared to the 40 frames of 16mm. They both run at 24 fps for sound film and at 18 fps for the older silent film.

Aspect Ratio

Video, Super-8, and 16mm all have the same "aspect ratio" (ratio of frame width to height) of 1.33:1, which is the same as most TV screens. This was the full-screen aperture for silent film selected by Dickson and Edison, created to allow for an optical sound track running along the side and a wider aperture than the 1:1 square which came about with the introduction of sound around 1927. Nowadays it is usually called "Academy Aperture." Contemporary mainstream theatrical projection, however, is 1.85:1 in the U.S., and 1.66:1 in Europe. Since full-frame 35mm sound film also has an aspect ratio of 1.33:1, it must be either cropped at the top and bottom or else "squeezed" and "unsqueezed" with anamorphic lenses if it is to be projected at the right aspect ratio.

Negative and Reversal

Film stock may be either "reversal" (like, until recently, Super-8) or "negative" (like 35mm and most of 16mm since the 1970s). Film consists of a cellulose acetate base with a layer of emulsion of silver halide crystals on one side, and anti-halation backing on the other (to prevent light rays reflected back from reexposing the emulsion). The silver halide is exposed to light and later developed into a metallic silver image. With negative film, the unexposed silver halide is then washed away by a "fixer," leaving an image of reversed tonalities (light as dark and dark as light). With reversal film, bleach is used to wash away the metallic silver, leaving only unexposed silver halide, which is then reexposed to a uniform light, developed again, and finally fixed—as a positive image with the original tonalities intact. Reversal film is thus a bit like still-camera "slides" or transparencies. At this stage it's ready for viewing, even projecting, while negative film still needs to have a negative copy made of it, and then a final positive viewing print from that.

The main advantage of negative film is that you can strike any number of copies from it. Copies of reversal prints show more grain, more contrast, and less overall definition. Reversal also can accommodate less contrast in a scene than negative. (Black-and-white reversal film, however, tend to show less grain than color reversal, because of peculiarities of the development process; this is one reason to shoot in black-and-white.) Copies from a reversal print are also expensive.

Here's a quick guide to the different documentary formats.

Super-8

Super-8 film costs somewhere between a third and a half of 16mm, but it is still quite a bit more expensive than low-end video. Its advantage over (anything but Digital Betacam) video is simply that it looks better—it can accommodate a wider brightness range and produces a deeper, more lifelike image. Most commercial Super-8 film distribution has given way to video, however, and it is no longer much used as a distribution medium. Super-8 labs are now few and far between, but you can save money by shooting on Super-8 and then blowing it up to 16mm for distribution (though it won't look like it was shot on 16mm).

Super-8 cameras are available secondhand, often for a few hundred dollars or less. They are easy to use, light, and portable, as well as being more rugged and durable than video cameras. They also accept light-protected cartridges, rather than the spools or rolls of 16mm, so you don't need any specialized knowledge or experience to "thread" them. However, there's a down side to this: generally the cartridges are only 50 feet long. This comes out at 2½ minutes if you're recording sound, or 3½ minutes at silent speed. Only a few cameras also accept 200-foot cartridges. Having to stop filming to change cartridges every 2½ minutes can be infuriating. By comparison, the standard 16mm film roll is 400 feet, and it runs for about 11 minutes at sound speed (36 ft. per minute).

Sound.   The sound quality on Super-8 is not as high as on 16mm, because the film travels more slowly and the cameras are noisier. Super-8 sound is most often single-system, in that it is recorded within the camera on a magnetic stripe track running down one side of the film. This makes it easy for a single operator to record picture and sound, whereas 16mm generally needs two, one on the camera and one with a tape recorder. But it's extremely arduous to edit single-system sound. Whenever you want to cut the picture you have also to cut the sound. Likewise, any cut in the sound means a cut in the picture. And because the sound head on Super 8 projectors is located eighteen frames ahead of the film gate, on the film itself it is also recorded eighteen frames ahead of the frame with which it is synchronized. This means that every picture cut—in fact every end and beginning of every shot as they are recorded—contains eighteen frames of the "wrong" sound. To some degree, you can shoot bearing this in mind, but it's still difficult to run a sound track over a picture recorded at a different point. Many Super-8 users find they need to use a separate tape recorder. If you can afford or have access to one, you can also use a "displacement recorder," which puts sound and picture in spatial sync—that is, it moves the sound eighteen frames back. When it comes to projection, you can then use it to move the sound eighteen frames forward again. Of course, if you're not shooting sync, these inconveniences of single-system sound don't matter so much.

Editing and Processing. Super-8 is difficult to edit. Sixteen–mm film has "edge numbers" printed along it, which lets you match your workprint (a cheap copy you make all your editing decisions on) to the original, frame for frame. But Super-8 doesn't come with edge numbers, so the process of "conforming" can only be done by eye, which is particularly tedious since Super-8 is so small that it's very difficult to *see*. As a result, some Super-8 filmmakers edit only minimally, and project the original film, splices and all. Finally, many of the ways to fine-tune the image quality that are habitually used for 16mm when release prints are being prepared (such as color correction) are unavailable for Super-8.

Distribution. The possibilities for theatrical distribution of Super-8 are limited, for the image can only be projected up to a size of around 2 meters across before it begins to deteriorate to an unacceptable degree (in most people's eyes). However, if your final distribution medium is going to be 16mm or video, you could shoot on Super-8 and edit on video, thus retaining some of the realism, color, and depth of Super-8. A company called "Super-8 Sound" sells and processes Super-8 film, and also deals with specialized video houses that will transfer it via a Rank "telecine" to video. In addition, this company now offers

Super-8 negative film, which it packages itself from Kodak stock. (It even sells an adapter letting you use a Beaulieu 7008 Super-8 camera on a Steadicam JR; see "Equipment and Services" in appendix 3.)

16mm

Sixteen-mm film is no longer the distribution medium it once was. Schools, universities, community centers, nonprofit organizations and religious institutions have mostly shifted to video. But 16mm film is still the preferred medium of most documentary filmmakers. Connie Field, Barbara Kopple, Jean Rouch, Trinh Minh-ha, Carma Hinton and Richard Gordon, Susan Todd, and Andrew Young have all worked almost exclusively in 16mm film. Technical advances in film emulsion, camera precision, and lens quality have made it a fully professional medium and format, and even if you anticipate that your main release format will be video, or television, there's a lot to be said for shooting in 16mm. You have a wide variety of cameras, lenses, film stocks, and editing equipment at your disposal, as well as the possibility of optical effects and invisible-splice film printing that are unavailable in Super-8.

Sound. Other than the cheapest models, modern 16mm cameras run almost silently (though you should still cover, or "blimp," the camera if the mike is nearby). Since the sound can be recorded in sync with the picture on separate audio tape, you have more freedom in recording and ease in editing than you do with single-system Super-8 (or with the few single-system 16mm cameras that are available). Sixteen-mm double-system sound is usually edited by transferring the audio tape recording onto 16mm magnetic oxide film with the same kind of sprocket holes as the 16mm picture film itself. With a "synchronizer" or an editing table, the picture and sound can be kept in sync, sprocket to sprocket. The editor then creates a number of audio tracks on separate magnetic strips. The simplest synchronizers play one strip at a time, so the editor has to imagine what it will sound like with the others added. More sophisticated editing tables will play two or three sound tracks as well as the picture and keep them all in sync.

Once all the editing decisions are made, the sound tracks are mixed onto a single track, and the film is sent to a negative cutter and processed by a lab. The lab corrects for color and brightness from shot to shot, and typically transfers the mixed magnetic sound onto an optical track that will run along the side of the film. Although optical sound is of lower quality than mag sound, if you want to strike a few prints of the same film, it will be cheaper.

Ease of Use. Working in 16mm film requires time, ability, dedication, and resources. Sixteen-mm film does not come in easy-to-use cartridges like Super-8. It comes either on spools, which you can thread in daylight ("daylight spools"), or in rolls, which have to be threaded in total darkness. The standard 400-foot rolls (11 minutes at 24 fps) are generally loaded into "magazines" in a lightproof changing bag, so that they are ready to be attached to the camera as soon as you want to shoot. (A few cameras, however, accept exclusively 100-foot daylight spools, which only last for 2¾ minutes.) The film then has to be threaded carefully into the camera, and exposed with considerable precision. Because the sound is double-system, you will almost certainly need a crew of two, probably three. In short, the whole 16mm filmmaking process demands quite a bit more technical know-how and practice than Super-8 and low-end video.

Shooting for Video Postproduction. Sixteen-mm filmmakers are increasingly opting to edit on video, whether they intend to release only on video or whether they plan to return to film to make a final print. Video editing used to be more cumbersome and time-consuming than film editing. If you change a cut in (linear) video, you have to rerecord (in real time) everything that comes after it—that could mean an hour or more of waiting. With film you simply splice in the shot of the length and in the position you want it, and everything that succeeds it is automatically repositioned. Film, in this sense is "nonlinear," while video has traditionally been "linear." However, it can be cost-effective to transfer film to video and then edit, because you avoid having to print a film workprint. Since many universities are expanding their video stock, they may no longer maintain their film editing machines, so it's possible you could borrow or rent a 16mm camera for the filming, and use an editing room at the university for ½-inch VHS "off-line" editing. Additionally, with recent advances in random-access digital video, nonlinear video editing is now even quicker and easier than film (see "Nonlinear Video Editing" in chapter 8).[4]

Sixteen-mm film is usually shot at 24 fps, but if you will be editing on video, with video or TV as your distribution/broadcast outlet, you may want to shoot at 30 fps (or 29.97). It will be more expensive, since you'll shoot more stock, but the result may look more lifelike, because the camera fps speed will match the NTSC video speed exactly.

Super-16

Few commercial theaters other than specialized art houses have 16mm projectors. For full theatrical release, films shot on 16mm have to be blown up to 35mm. If you're set on a theatrical release, you should consider shooting on Super-16 instead. Though it's not a distribution gauge, if you will be blowing it up to 35mm it has certain advantages over originating in 16mm.

Super-16 produces a larger, less grainy image than 16mm. It has an aspect ratio of around 1.66:1, and so is much closer to the 1.85:1 of the standard U.S. theatrical wide-screen format than 16mm. It is also closer to the aspect ratio of HDTV, and the picture quality of Super-16 transferred to HDTV is, well, super. Super-16 film stock costs only a little more than 16mm, and if you transfer to video for editing, the whole process can be *relatively* inexpensive.

However, there are a few drawbacks. If your distribution turns out to be only 16mm after all, you'll have to crop off some of the sides. New 16mm cameras from Aaton and Arri come with special mounts that can accept Super-16 film as is, but most older models have to be modified to be able to run it (including having the lens centered and the aperture widened). Some models can be modified more easily and cheaply than others. Finally, not all lenses are compatible with Super-16.

FILM CAMERAS

The Mechanics of a Film Camera

How does a film camera actually work? A strip of unexposed film is fed from a supply reel into the camera body. It then passes behind the lens, and through the "film gate." Once in the film gate, the film is squeezed between two plates—an "aperture plate," which lets light through from the lens, and a "pressure plate," which keeps the film in position. As the film passes through the gate, a "claw" extends into one of the film's

FIGURE 48 Arri SR Camera. The matte box attached to the end of the lens helps block out glare from the sun and can hold special filters. Tripods are very helpful when shooting landscapes, cityscapes, and still lifes.

perforations, and pulls it down one frame at a time, holding the frame still while it's exposed. The claw moves intermittently, to stop and start each frame in its turn. Because it moves intermittently while the supply and take-up reels move continuously, there has to be some slack in the film on either side of the film gate. The size of these slack "loops" is crucial, enough so that the film doesn't pull on the claw (and ruin the exposure), but not so much that it scratches on the camera casing. A few 16mm cameras, including the Canon Scoopic and some Bolex models, form their own loops, but on most models loops must be put in place by the operator. If you don't make a proper loop, you may ruin a whole roll of film.

Before one film frame is moved away from the aperture by the claw, and another frame exposed, the camera "shutter" closes to stop the frame from blurring as it moves. Many camera shutters are 180°. The angle of the shutter, as well as camera speed (fps), determines the exposure time (i.e., the speed of the shutter). As a rule, the slower the shutter speed, the higher quality the image. At slow shutter speeds, motion is "frozen" or "stilled" more successfully onto each successive frame, and is less likely to result in "strobing," which happens when the image displacement in adjacent frames caused by either camera or subject movement causes the eye to see continuous movement as discontinuous. (Strobing—also called "skipping"—often happens on camera pans.) If your camera has a 180° shutter, and you're running the film at 24 fps, your shutter speed is $\frac{1}{48}$ of a second (generally written as $\frac{1}{50}$). The slower the shutter speed, the longer the exposure. Hence a slow shutter speed will let you work in lower light than a fast one. (Shutter speeds faster than $\frac{1}{60}$ of a second can also flicker if you are shooting with fluorescent light. Most filmmakers use a 144° shutter when shooting a TV monitor.)

Once the film has passed in front of the gate, and been exposed to the light coming through the lens, it is then spooled on a take-up reel or stored in a cartridge. It has to be shielded from all light until it's developed.

The Film Laboratory and the Postproduction Process

Either during production or when you come back from the field, you have to send your exposed footage to a lab to get it developed. Sixteen-mm labs are getting fewer and farther between. If you're based in the U.S., you may want to send your film to New York or Los Angeles, where there are still reputable, high-volume labs.

If you're going to edit on film, you'll want a film workprint. While the lab is processing your film and making a positive workprint for you, it (or a separate sound house) will also resolve your location audio tracks to 16mm mag. When they give these back to you, you or your editor will sit down in front of a flatbed or upright editing table, sync the dailies up with the mag sound, and then start editing. Once you've edited the workprint and sound just as you want them (days, months, or even years later, depending on your budget and schedule), you'll have a special sound mix for the audio tracks and have your negative cut for film printing. The section "Film" in chapter 8 explains the process in greater depth and provides details on how to prepare your film for the lab.

Super-8 Cameras

Super-8 cameras are usually lightweight, relatively inexpensive, and easy to use. They accept quick-loading lightproof film cartridges, which means you don't have the same problems of 16mm—forming a loop of the right length and protecting the film from light. Whereas most Super-8 cameras use 50-foot cartridges, a few will accept 200-foot ones, which makes shooting in an uninterrupted observational-style more practicable. A 50-foot cartridge lasts for 3½ minutes at silent speed and just over 2½ minutes at sound speed, while a 200-foot cartridge will run for 14 minutes at silent speed and 10 minutes at sound speed. Some cameras will not record sound, which means that it has to be recorded double-system, with all the attendant problems of synchronization (and potential for higher quality). Others will record sound within the camera on the film itself, single-system.

Rather like consumer camcorders, Super-8 cameras often offer a dazzling array of features that are rarely found on their professional 16mm cousins. Some of these are gimmicks that are usually reserved for postproduction, but since postproduction facilities are limited in Super-8, they can be a real boon. Recommended features include the capacity to fade and dissolve, animation effects, time-lapse exposure, multiple running speeds, through-the-lens viewfinders, built-in or attachable zoom lenses, electronic zoom control, and automatic exposure. (For these last two features, try to choose a model that can also override them.)

Most Super-8 camera models are now only available secondhand, although there is one "professional" model still being manufactured today. For details, see "Film Cameras" in appendix 4.

16mm Cameras

Here is a brief list of features to look out for when selecting a 16mm camera:

Handholding Ease. Since so much documentary filming is done with a handheld camera, the weight, balance, and ease of use of your camera are essential. Check how well different models are balanced by trying them out. How much pressure do you need to apply to keep a camera from falling off your shoulder? How comfortable and stable is the handle? Is there a pistol grip? (Aaton cameras, for instance, are beautifully crafted for handheld sync-sound documentary work.) You're probably best off having a shoulder-mounted camera. Body braces, forehead braces, shoulder pads, and shoulder pad-and-belt systems are also available for some models, both new and secondhand. Because they make the camera more comfortable, they tire you out less and improve your shooting.

Sync Sound and Camera Noise. Cameras designed before the advent of portable sync sound are often difficult to adapt to sync-sound shooting, mainly because they're so noisy that you can hear them on the audio. For sync-sound shooting you really need a silent-running ("self-blimped") camera which makes less than 30 dB noise. But even self-blimped cameras can sometimes make quite a bit of noise, enough to be audible on the sound track. The only way to know for sure what a camera sounds like is to try it out, in a very quiet interior space. Cameras and magazines tend to make more noise as they age. You could also consider getting a "barney," an insulated soft camera cover, which blocks out still more noise while allowing you access to the controls. A barney can also double as camera insulation on cold weather shoots; some even have battery-operated heaters built in.

Camera Viewfinder. Contemporary cameras have TTL (through-the-lens) or "reflex" viewfinders. Some of the light entering the lens is diverted into the viewfinder, so you see the exact image the camera records. Light is deflected into the viewfinder in one of two ways. Some models use a "beam splitter" prism, located either in the camera body or in a zoom lens. This is a mirror that reflects a little of the incoming light away from the film. Others use a "mirror shutter," which alternately directs the light to the film and (when the shutter closes) to the viewfinder. The mirror shutter is more popular, since the beam splitter prevents anywhere from a third of an f-stop to a whole f-stop of light from exposing the film, making it difficult to use in low light. (Consequently, secondhand beam-splitter cameras are a lot cheaper than mirror-shutter cameras.) Still, mirror-shutter systems also have their downside: because the viewfinder receives light only some of the time, the image you see flickers. Generally this should not be a great problem—but because the images fed to the viewfinder are *precisely not* those reaching the film, what you're seeing is not what you'll get, and countering flicker (say, from lights, or computer or TV monitors) becomes more difficult.

Beam splitters and mirror shutters typically employ different focusing systems. Most beam-splitter systems let you adjust focus only in the center of the screen (with either a microprism or split-image range finder, as in 35mm still cameras). There are two problems with this. First, the subject you want to focus on may not be in the center of your frame. Second, they do not give you an accurate impression of your depth of field.

Mirror shutters use either full-ground glass or fiber optics to focus. Both of these let you focus easily, and both show depth of field—though only up to a point. Because the viewfinder image is so tiny compared to the size of the image when projected or even shown on a TV monitor, the viewfinder tends to amplify your depth of field. Fiber-optic screens have the advantage of being brighter and so provide more visibility in low light. Since you tend to have your camera aperture wide open in low light, with a correspondingly short depth of field, focus is all the more crucial. If your budget permits, a fiber-optic screen is well worth the investment.

Some viewfinders (often fiber-optic ones) can be detached from the camera body. Connected only by a cable to your viewfinder, the camera is free to assume a multitude of positions—from shooting someone's steps with the camera right next to the ground to an overhead crowd shot. Short of a detachable viewfinder, try to get an "orientable," or "dovetail" one that can rotate for viewing in various positions, so that you can shoot from your knee or your waist. If you'll be doing a lot of handheld work, the viewfinder should be as close as possible to the film plane itself: a "zero finder." For tripod work it should extend to the back of the camera. If you expect to be doing a lot of both, you may want to have interchangeable viewfinders.

One problem with reflex viewfinders (particularly beam-splitters) is that light can enter through the eyepiece and fog the film. If your eye is up against the eyecup when you're shooting, this will cut out all stray light, but sometimes you may want to move your head back in the middle of a shot to see what's going on outside the frame, and it's possible that light can return through the viewfinder. Some viewfinders come with an automatic light trap, which opens when you're looking through it and closes when you stand back.

Other things to look for in a viewfinder include various boxes or frames etched onto the screen, indicating the safe viewing area, TV safe action area, and even projector aperture (the camera aperture is in fact 1.37:1, while the projector is 1.33:1). If you know in advance that you'll be blowing 16mm (or Super-16) up to 35mm for theatrical distribution, you'll want an indication of the wide-screen area. "Safe viewing area" markings also let you see the mike boom before it enters the image, and reframe (or communicate to the sound recordist) accordingly. Since the markings let you see some off-screen action, you can also prepare for a camera move—a pan, say, as someone enters the frame—before it's too late. Some viewfinders display such useful information as exposure and even sound recording level, as well as warning you when you've lost your sync or that your film is about to run out.

Try to get a viewfinder that lets you focus the eyepiece diopter easily. If you're a crew of two or more and are taking turns at shooting and sound recording, this is important, for the eyepiece needs to be refocused for each new user. Some eyepieces come with a switch that can be locked into a position until you reset it.

Early cameras with viewfinders located on the side with their own lens (separate from the main camera lens) are still bought and sold secondhand today. These "nonreflex" viewfinders are generally ill-advised, because of their parallactic effect. The image you see through the viewfinder never coincides exactly with what the lens is recording. For long shots, this doesn't matter much, but for close-ups it can be a big problem. Also, most cameras with nonreflex viewfinders can only be focused by estimating or measuring the distance, and few can support zoom or long lenses.

Camera Motor. There are a few hand-cranked 16mm cameras still around, including the famous Bell and Howells with spring-wound motors. Their advantage is that they are extremely sturdy and can be used in arctic conditions; their disadvantage is that they have to be wound by hand and generally only shoot for thirty seconds before having to be rewound. They thereby limit shot length to thirty seconds or less, creating a distinctive aesthetic—evident, for instance, in Rouch's film about Hauka possession in the Gold Coast, *Mad Masters* (*Les maîtres fous*) (1953–54). Sync sound cameras use electric motors, powered by batteries or electricity. However, some motors (all "wild" motors and most "governor" motors) are not regular enough for sync sound recording. Sync motors generate their signal from either the 60 or 50Hz of AC mains (these are not portable), from tuning forks, or from DC crystal oscillators.

For slow motion effects you need a camera that will run at least up to 64 fps; many will run up to 75 fps. For faster speeds you'll need a higher-speed motor (up to 128 fps, or occasionally more) or else a special high-speed camera (up to 10,000 fps or more). Except for very special applications, you won't need to shoot faster than 72 fps, which will stretch out one second of recorded "real-time" time into three on projection.

Film Magazines. For most documentary work, it's best to have a camera that accepts 400-foot (11-minute) mags. Two-hundred-foot and 1200-foot mags are also widely available. Some older cameras *only* accept 100-foot daylight spools, which last for only 2¾ minutes. But not all magazines accept daylight spools. You should always have an extra black bag so that you can save your "short ends" (the ends of rolls that haven't been exposed). "Quick change" magazines are heavier and bigger (and more costly) than regular mags, but they can be changed over in just a few seconds. You should have at least two mags, preferably three. (They should generally all be loaded before starting a day's shooting.) Magazines are very delicate and need a lot of care for proper maintenance.

Lens Shade and Matte Box. You'll want to shade your camera lens so that stray light doesn't flash or fog the film. You can do this with a "lens shade," preferably in rubber. Or else, if your camera will accept it, you can attach a more obtrusive matte box. This attaches to the front of the lens, and doubles as a sunscreen and a (glass and gelatin) filter holder. If you might ever use filters, such as polarizers, split-field diopters, and graduated NDs, that have to be oriented in a certain way, then

FIGURE 49 Aaton Camera Body and Two Magazines. The camera body (center) contains the camera motor, optics, film aperture, gate, and pull down claw (which, on this model, doubles as a registration pin). The mag on the left shows the take-up side. The gears that pull the film strip through are inside the mag. You can see the film loop (which is inside the mag when the mag is loaded onto the camera), and the silver pressure plate. The mag on the right shows a full load of film on the feed side. In practice, you load the film onto the feed side in the dark (i.e., in a changing bag) and close the door. The rest of the threading takes place in normal light. When a mag runs out, or if the lighting conditions alter, you can change it for another loaded mag in about ten seconds.

it's easier to use a camera that either has a *nonrotating* front element or else comes with a matte box. With both lens shades and matte boxes, make sure they don't impinge on the picture when you're using your zoom or wide-angle lens.

Registration Pin. Almost all cameras use a claw (or "shuttle") to hold the film frames still in front of the aperture while they are exposed. However, the film is never completely motionless, and some superior cameras (such as the Arri SR) also have a "registration pin" which catches a perforation, to further increase the stillness of the film. This tends to result in a higher quality, sharper image.

Lens Mount. Most modern cameras have their own lens mounts and, as a rule, won't accept other kinds of mount. The Arri steel bayonet mount is better than their earlier standard model. The earliest C screw mounts are the weakest of all. If you want to use a zoom lens, you should avoid them. Adapters allow some lenses to be fitted on cameras with different mounts, though you always run the danger of making the lens out of focus. Adapters are also available for mounting 35mm still camera lenses on some 16mm motion picture cameras.

Video Assist. Manufacturers are increasingly emphasizing the quality and versatility of the "video tap" possibilities of their cameras. Modern Aatons and Arris allow a monitor or recorder to tap into their viewfinder, for quality control and other purposes. Although a video image gives you little idea about the quality of the film you've just exposed, you can use it to compare different takes, decide which ones to print, and so on. In field sites where you can't watch your dailies before returning from the field, a video assist can be a big help. In highly controlled documentaries, it can even be used for continuity: seeing the last shot can help you set up the next.

Pre-Shoot Tests. Before choosing a particular camera, you should shoot some film with it. By processing and projecting the film, you can check the image quality for yourself. How the actual image looks is far more important than an enumeration of a camera's features. Standard tests performed on cameras are described in "16mm Camera Tests," below.

16mm Lenses

When picking lenses, you need to decide whether you want a zoom lens, prime lenses of fixed focal lengths, or both. Many older 16mm cameras featured built-in "turrets" that accept two or three lenses permanently mounted on the camera. New cameras come with a stable single-lens mount, allowing you to select one or more lenses ranging from 1.99mm to more than 1000mm! Some documentary filmmakers

FIGURE 50 Trinh Minh-ha shooting *Naked Spaces:Living Is Round* (1985) in West Africa. This Beaulieu R16 camera comes with a permanent revolving "turret" with three prime lenses of different focal lengths. You swivel the lens you want in front of the aperture. Most modern 16mm cameras have only a single-lens mount, to which you can attach prime or zoom lenses.

shoot with a combination of prime lenses—typically a 9mm or 10mm lens, a 25mm lens, and a 75mm long lens. It's difficult to handhold lenses longer than 50mm (and certainly 75mm) absolutely still. If you expect to be shooting from a car, plane, train, or any unsteady location, your shaky hands will be a lot less evident with a lens of around 9mm. Most documentary filmmakers nowadays use a zoom, allowing them to choose whatever focal lengths they like within the limits of the lens. The new higher-end zooms approach the quality of the best primes. Be sure to check both the ratio of a zoom, and its widest angle. It's advisable to use a zoom that has a wide-angle setting of at least 12.5. Few film zoom lenses have a ratio much higher than 10:1. As a rule, the longer the zoom, the more it costs, and certainly the more it weighs.

When choosing lenses you need to see how closely they can focus, how fast they are (i.e., how much light they admit), and whether they change f-stop over the range of the zoom. Many zooms can't focus any closer than five feet without a close-up (or "plus") diopter attachment. A few can focus at two feet or closer.

With zoom lenses there's a trade-off between speed and ease of use. Long zooms are more conspicuous and more difficult to balance. When you try out a camera, be sure to balance it on your shoulder *with the zoom lens you'll be using.* On the other hand, longer lenses tend to be faster at long focal lengths than slightly shorter lenses at similar focal lengths. If you expect to shoot mostly at the wide-angle end of the lens, this won't matter, and you'll be better off with a shorter zoom.

Zoom lenses are generally slower than primes. An f-2 is considered to be fast, and for documentary work the faster the better. Most lenses are calibrated in f- and T-stops (which are always slightly higher). If you'll be using a number of prime lenses, you need to go by T-stops to ensure that you expose consistently. Likewise, if you use a zoom, make sure that T-stops are indicated on one side of the iris diaphragm ring. Don't judge a zoom's widest aperture by its f-stop: there can be ⅔ of a stop difference between f- and T-stop (such as a lens with f-2 and T2.5). Zooms are now made as low as T1.3, though T1.9 and T2 are more common.

Watch out for zooms that change f-stop over the course of their range. Some lenses only have their widest aperture setting (the lowest f-stop) at wide angle. The idea behind these is to maximize lens speed, if only at wide angle. If a zoom changes more than a quarter of an f-stop during the course of its zoom, the loss of exposure will be noticeable. Some lenses with a shifting minimum f-stop prevent you from zooming over a range that would alter the aperture setting.

Zooming can either be automatic or manual. Sixteen-mm zoom drives are external to the lens itself: check how many zoom speeds there are, whether they're variable, and how easy and smooth the zoom is to use. Most documentary camera operators zoom manually. Zooms with rods or cranks are awkward for handheld shooting; if possible use a zoom with a short joystick or just use the zoom ring on the lens. Also try to choose a zoom for which you can adjust the resistance. To make slow, imperceptible zoom movements, you'll need a tight control.

Another characteristic of zooms is that though all their respective focal lengths are color-matched to each other, they vary considerably in how they transmit color overall. It's a good idea to test a number of zoom lenses for their color rendition before committing yourself to one. If you'll be combining a zoom with prime lenses, try to stick with prime lenses that are color-matched to each other. For this reason, it's best to stay with lenses made by the same manufacturer.

If you'll only be using a zoom, you may want to get a close-up ("plus") diopter that can be screwed onto its front, as well as a "retro-zoom" attachment that will give you wider camera angles. (There are also retrofocus primes, which are wide-angle lenses with greater "back focus" distance—making them less likely to show vignetting or reduced exposure at the edge of the frame.) As with video, an assortment of macro lenses are also available. Additionally, "split-field" diopters allow half the frame to be focused in the distance and the other half up close. Bear in mind that any rear-mounted attachment (i.e., between the lens and the camera) will reduce both the lens speed and the relative aperture.

Generally, the more elements in a lens, the more subject it is to unwanted flare. Zooms are thus especially susceptible. Try to use only lenses whose elements have "high-efficiency" antireflective coatings. These minimize both flare and light loss. You should also check manufacturers' data for lens diffraction, and for the lowest f-stop at which a lens is "diffraction-limited" (aberrant-free other than inherent diffraction). For the best primes (and even the Angénieux 10–120mm T2 zoom) this can be as low as f-4.

Finally, image sharpness is a combination of factors, among them resolution and contrast, and is often measured as "acutance." MTF, or "Modulation Transfer Function," is a system that has been developed to measure the combined sharpness (and so mutual compatibility) of a camera lens and a film stock. Some lens manufacturers have even designed their lenses to work optimally with Kodak's color negative film. Lenses, like film stocks, may come with data sheets specifying their MTF curves for different f-stops. If possible, use a lens and film stock whose MTF values match.

(For more information, see "16mm Lens Tests," below, and "16mm Lenses," in appendix 4.)

Black-and-White or Color?

The first decision is obviously whether to shoot in black-and-white or color, or to combine them. Black-and-white offers its own aesthetic—which is greater realism or greater abstraction, depending on your point of view. It has a higher contrast ratio, and is much cheaper. (Between purchasing the raw stock and processing the exposed footage, it ends up between ⅓ and ½ the price of color.) But now that high-speed emulsions enable color film to be shot in available light situations, most documentaries are shot in color. Additionally, not all 16mm labs process black-and-white.

Negative or Reversal?

Shooting reversal film is cheaper than negative, for the simple reason that you can project it without having to make a print. But if you decide to strike a workprint and then finished prints from a reversal original, it will end up being more expensive than if you had started off with negative. Reversal prints also tend to be contrasty and grainy. Negative has a higher contrast ratio than reversal, and is better able to manage light sources with conflicting color temperatures within any single scene. Titles and subtitles are cheaper in reversal film, since they can be burnt onto the print directly. Additionally, subtitling negative can sometimes involve going down an extra generation, with a corresponding loss of quality.

Speed (ASA)

You also have to choose the speed of your film. High speed offers a lot more freedom. It lets you film in lower light, choose a higher f-stop, and gives you greater depth of field. But it also produces a grainier and duller image. It's preferable to go to the field with a fast stock and a slow stock, which can be loaded into different magazines—one for indoor use, the other for outdoors.

Film speed—its sensitivity to light—is measured in either ASA numbers or in DIN. The ISO number (International Standards Organization) specifies the ASA/DIN. ASA 100 is generally considered medium speed. ASAs of 200 or more are high, and ASAs of 40 or less are low. A film with an ASA of 100 needs twice the exposure of (i.e., one more f-stop than) a film with an ASA of 200. Remember that if you're stuck on a shoot with film stock that's too slow, you can shoot with it, exposing it *as if* it were faster (say, ASA 50 as if it were 100), and then get the lab to "push" or "force process" it. The result will be grainier and more contrasty than ASA 100 film, but it will be properly exposed, and you'll have been able to shoot a low-light scene that otherwise you'd have missed. ASA 500 color film can nowadays be pushed to ASA 1,000 or even 2,000, letting you shoot in extremely low light. Be sure to change the ASA setting between rolls, not in the middle of one.

Color-Balancing

Color film can be balanced either for Tungsten or Daylight. If you have Daylight film loaded and want to shoot a lit interior, or have Tungsten film loaded and want to get an exterior shot, you need to use filters. If you want to use only one stock, and will be shooting in daylight as well as artificial light, you should buy Tungsten-balanced film. Daylight film is very sensitive to ultraviolet light, and you should use a UV or skylight filter with it (see "Filters," below). (If you're shooting Tungsten film outside, remember that the 85 filter already has an in-built UV filter.) But for interiors with no artificial lighting, you should stick with Daylight film, so you don't have to lose any stops. If you're shooting Tungsten high-speed film in low daylight, you can also use a Tiffen LL-D filter. This cuts out some of the blue light without diminishing transmission. Another possibility is simply to use no filter at all, and to ask your lab to "time out" the blue cast when it makes the prints.

Ordering Film

When you order raw stock from a manufacturer, you need to quote the stock name and catalogue number, and specify "rolls" or "footage." It's best to make sure that all your stock has the same emulsion number, as this ensures it will all be the same (batches vary from one to another), and (with 16mm) that it has "key" or "latent edge" numbers every twenty frames (you will need them later when conforming the original to the edited workprint). Generally, you should arrange for film stock to arrive not much more than a week before you take off for the field or start shooting.

Storing Film

Try to keep all film away from heat and humidity. If your film will be stored in a humid area (above 70%) before shooting, watch out that the cans don't rust and that all the moisture-proof tape seals remain intact. If you're storing it in a freezer or refrigerator, put it in airtight freezer bags, and, to avoid condensation, allow *at least* 1½ hours for the film to come up to environmental temperature before breaking the seal. In humid areas, you'll need to allow more time. Once you've opened a can, expose the film as soon as you can (color dyes fade quite fast, and as film ages it becomes increasingly insensitive to light), and process it as soon as possible after that (a delay can cause the latent image quality to deteriorate). Exposed film should be kept in an icebox or refrigerator until you get it to a lab. If you're affiliated with or can arrange access to an institution with its own lab, check to see which stocks it can process. It will generally be cheaper than a professional lab. Whichever lab you choose, be sure to ask other filmmakers their opinions first.

Kodak, Fuji, and Agfa are the leading film manufacturers (see appendix 3 for addresses and appendix 4 for specific stock numbers). Other companies buy and sell unused unexposed stock and short ends at considerably reduced prices. You can save a lot of money with these companies, but since you never know where the film you buy from them has been, you should shoot test each batch very carefully.

16MM CAMERA TESTS

Whether you borrow, rent, or buy a camera, it's vital to run camera tests with each magazine and lens before you set out for the field. A camera's quality can really only be judged by testing it—in particular for the registration of the image it produces, film scratching, the focus system, and whether there are any light leaks. The following are among the camera tests that you should undertake before each shoot (or at least each project).

Registration Test

A camera is registered if the film in it is properly aligned as it's exposed. If it's poorly registered, the processed images will look unsteady. The best cameras have a registration pin as well as a claw to minimize jiggle.

But there's really no way of knowing how strong a camera's registration is without testing it, and since registration can deteriorate over time, try and test your camera before every long shoot. You can do this quite easily. The simplest way is to project some film you've just shot with the camera, and adjust the frame line so that it's completely visible: the more it appears to change in width, the worse the registration. If the image as a whole (not just the frame line) seems to move in and out of focus, then either there's a problem with the projector or the camera pressure plate needs to be tightened. If the image is completely blurred, apparently smeared up and down the screen, then your camera (or the projector) has lost its loop. If it's partly smeared in the vertical direction, then your shutter and claw are out of sync. If you notice only excessive jiggle between the frame line and the screen edge, it's almost certainly the projector that's at fault.

A more careful test is to thread the camera with reversal film. Remove the lens and use a permanent marker pen to mark on the film the outline of the frame of film in the gate. Then remove the magazine and punch a hole in the marked frame of film. Replace the lens and magazine, put the camera on a tripod and shoot a stationary grid pattern at about ten or twenty feet. Taking care not to move the camera at all, remove the magazine and, in a black bag, rewind the film until you feel the hole punch. Then replace the magazine on the camera and remove the lens again. Line up the hole punch in the gate exactly. Replace the lens and shoot the same grid. If your camera is properly registered, the two grid patterns, processed and projected, should appear to be just one. This test also tells you if the viewfinder frame line is the actual frame line. If you mark the frame line on the grid with colored tape, this should be the border of the image when projected back full frame.[5]

Scratch Test

If the film isn't loaded properly, or if the camera isn't functioning perfectly, the film can be scratched as it runs through the camera. This can ruin your footage. Ideally, you should check for scratches at the beginning of every roll. After running the film for a few seconds, examine the film in the take-up reel by holding it in front of a light. If necessary, rethread the film, or try to locate the camera problem. This waste of a few feet is well worth the added security. Likewise, projectors can easily scratch projection prints if they are not threaded properly, and they too should be tested at the beginning of every reel.

Viewfinder Test

The standard test for viewfinder accuracy uses a chart of nested rectangles with 1.33:1 aspect ratio, usually numbered consecutively. You adjust focal length for different rectangles, shooting each in turn, and then check your developed footage. (See also the test for registration, above.)

Light Leak Test

Light leaks are one of the most common problems with 16mm cameras, particularly at the point where the magazine meets the camera. You should always run camera tape around the magazine lid and camera cover. Even if you're using daylight-loaded film, take care to load it in low light—in the shade or inside. Before taking off on a shoot, you should run a test by loading the camera with film, exposing the frame in front of the aperture, and moving a strong light all round the camera, lens, and mag. Once the film is developed check to see if there are any streaks or fogging on the film strip *outside* the image frames themselves. If so, you have a light leak.

Checking the Aperture Gate, Film Gate, and Pressure Plate

If possible, the aperture gate, film gate, and pressure plate should be cleaned before and after every roll of film you shoot. (Carry a small flashlight with you so you can see them.) Otherwise any dirt ("hairs") lodged in the aperture can both scratch the film and become part of the picture, exposed as silhouettes at its edges. Film emulsion from its light-sensitive side also tends to build up in this area. Quick-change mags with their own pressure plates can be checked easily. Some cameras are more accessible than others; some attract more dirt than others. You should use toothpicks or cotton swabs to clean the edges of the aperture (take care that none of the cotton stays behind). If you can't get rid of the emulsion, you may have to use acetone (though this can also dissolve the paint). The shutter itself is very fragile and easily damaged.

Lens Tests

Your lens is the most precious link in the whole chain. It has to be correctly "seated" or it won't focus properly at infinity; in fact its focusing could be off altogether. The seating of a zoom is especially crucial, since it might correctly focus at certain focal lengths and be wildly out of whack at others. If you find that, when you focus on an object at the telephoto end of the zoom, and then zoom out, the viewfinder image goes out of focus, you know that your lens is "out of collimation." Technicians use a "collimator" to check a lens's seating; they can also check and, if necessary, recalibrate the lens itself. If lenses are not properly "centered," some parts of the image will have more detailed resolution than others.

Should your zoom go out of collimation during a shoot, you can still use it, though not really as a zoom. You can pretend it consists of an (infinite) number of prime lenses, each needing focusing at its own position. In other words, so long as you change focal length between shots, rather than within them, everything should stay in focus. With reflex focusing systems, it's more difficult to tell if a zoom is out of collimation—you're really best off testing by processing and projecting some trial zooms to see whether they stay in focus throughout the move.

Image Aberration. Problems of seating and zooming aside, all lenses contain various kinds of inherent image aberration. Different color rays are bent at different angles as they pass through the lens; likewise, rays entering the edge of the lens are bent differently from those entering at the center. Lenses are also "astigmatic" in that horizontal and vertical lines focus on different planes.

Some of the cheaper wide-angle lenses are afflicted by "vignetting," whereby more light reaches the center of the frame than the edges; this results in underexposed image edges. Vignetting is at its worst in wide-angle lenses that are wide open. Diffraction, on the other hand, may occur at f-stops of 16 or above, resulting in a less sharp image. It, too, is more pronounced in wide-angle lenses. Bear in mind also that a zoom lens's T-stop (as opposed to its rated f-stop) changes over time, and that you should get your zooms recalibrated every couple of years.

The best judge of a lens is whether you like what it does with light. If at all possible, perform a test with a zoom lens before deciding on it.

If you want to purchase a lens, see if the store or seller will let you take it to a lens technician, so you can have it checked for aberrations and overall image quality.

FILM AND VIDEO ACCESSORIES

Just as it's hard to tell whether all the features boasted by consumer camcorders are helpful or harmful, it's also difficult to make head or tail out of all the accessories they may be advertised with. What follows is a discussion of accessories that you should consider, for either video or film.

Filters

Cameras that accept add-on devices give you more control over the incoming light than those that don't. If you can attach add-on devices to your camera, you may want to use some of the following filters.

"Neutral Density" (ND) filters reduce the intensity of incoming light, let you control depth of field, and help you keep the lens f-stop between f-4 and f-11, where the image quality is at its greatest.

A special kind of ND filter is called a "polarizing" filter, or a "polarizer." Polarizers can be used to increase the color saturation of your image as well as to remove reflections from shiny surfaces. They significantly deepen the color of sky, water, and the (green) environment. Because polarizers determine the direction of polarized light, the effect depends on how the filter is screwed on to your lens as well as on the direction of the camera. The effect will change during any camera move (even during focusing, as this shifts the lens). This means that a polarizer can't easily be used on a camera that has a rotating lens front, for you wouldn't be able to focus once you'd rotated the polarizer to the optimal point. If it has a dot on the side, the dot should be kept at the top of the lens. Rotate the polarizer as you look through the lens until the sky is as dark as you want it or the reflection has gone.

"Fog" or "diffusion" filters are used to change the mood of an image by reducing its clarity and sharpness. They're more common in porn movies than documentaries. "Color" filters change the color of the whole image. (Make sure you color-correct or set the white balance *before* adding them; otherwise the effect will be lost.) A sepia filter will apparently age the image without removing all the color, though you can best achieve this effect in postproduction. "Color correction" filters should be unnecessary on video if you use your camera's white balancing technology. "Graded" filters will introduce an effect or a color over half the image, and leave the other half as is. You can use them, for example, to enhance the sea or the sky, while leaving the rest of the frame untouched. "Center-stop" filters either diffuse, colorize, or underexpose the edges of the frame, but do not affect the center. "Break-up" or "multiprism" filters can multiply, disfigure, and refigure the image in any number of permutations. Finally, a "star" or "starburst" is an etching engraved on the filter itself, and is used to distort light sources into patterns of your choosing. A star filter can be used on a film or a CCD video camera, but should not be used on a tube video camera (it can blow the tube).

If you're shooting film, NDs and color filters can be mounted behind or on the front of the lens; special-effect filters generally have to go on the front. You may need an adapter ring to mount a glass filter (and a retainer ring for two). Make sure that your glass filters (especially the clear, or 1A skylight filter most people use to protect their lens) are of as high quality as the lens itself. Before buying any filters (they can be very expensive), remember that different lenses need different sizes. An alternative is plastic gelatin filters ("gels"), which are cheaper and can go either behind the lens (if your camera has a slot for them) or in a matte box. Be aware that if you mount them behind the lens you change the focal plane; since you'll probably be using a wide-angle lens, this could make your image go out of focus, and you should get a technician to adjust the flange focal distance. (This then commits you to using a clear gel when you have no need for a filter.) Gels scratch and generally wear easily, so keep them dust-free; handle them with care, and only at the edges.

If you're shooting color film, the filters you most often need are "conversion filters"—red or yellow filters (the 85 series) that let you shoot Tungsten film, balanced at 3200K, outdoors (or indoors with daylight); and blue filters (the 80 series) that let you shoot Daylight film, balanced around 5600K, under tungsten lights. An 80A filter adjusts to the standard 3200K, and an 80B to 3400K, which is the color temperature of photofloods (see "Lighting Equipment" in chapter 3). An 81A filter lets you use film balanced for 3200K at 3400K. Remember that not all daylight actually has a color temperature of 5600K—sunrise and sunset are around 2000K, and a midday summer sky can be 20,000K or higher. Moreover, whenever you add filters, you block out light: 85 series filters cut out ⅔ of an f-stop and 80 series filters cut out 2 whole f-stops. The amount of light a filter blocks out is called the "filter factor": you need to open up the iris by one f-stop each time the filter factor doubles. The high filter factor involved in shooting Daylight film under tungsten often results in poor color reproduction. If you end up not having the right filter with you, or forget to add it, the lab can usually make the color corrections (so long as you're not shooting reversal) when they process it—but be sure to mark on the can exactly what you've done. Filters and film stocks also come with data sheets. If possible, you should get a color temperature meter and chart that tells you the degrees Kelvin of the light source and even what filter you need to balance the color. For more details on filters and light sources, see the *American Cinematographer Manual.*[6]

Color filters can be used when shooting in black-and-white too. A red filter will lighten all red in the image and darken its complementary color, cyan (blue-green). You can use it to darken the sea, the sky, a field, or foliage. Red filters also diminish atmospheric haze (ultraviolet light) on landscape shots. An orange filter is not as radical as the red (and cuts out a little less light), but still intensifies skies. UV and 1A filters, unlike color filters, do not need any exposure compensation.

Gels can also be attached to lights, and even (in large rolls) taped over entire windows. When your lighting arrangement includes a variety of color temperatures, some color correction is preferable (if, in documentary, not always possible).

Retrofocus Lens Attachments, Range Extenders and Reducers

You can increase or decrease a lens's effective focal length by attaching a wide-angle retrofocus attachment or else a rear-mounted range extender or reducer. Since the wide-angle limit of a lens, particularly on many consumer camcorders, isn't really a wide-angle at all, you may want to add a "wide-angle spreader" to increase its angle of view. Extreme wide angles, however, will distort the image's perspective and create a special "fish-eye" effect. Rear-mounted range extenders affect the lens's aperture and speed, and you have to adjust the exposure accordingly; front-mounted extenders and retrofocus attachments generally do not.

Split-Field Diopters

There is an accessory for the lens's matte box (or a lens in itself) you can use to increase your depth of field, though it will only make sense in certain controlled conditions. It's called a "split field diopter" and lets you focus a portion of the frame on the background and a portion on the foreground. The problem is that everything between the near plane and the far plane will be more or less out of focus—unless it's either very sunny and your aperture's closed way down or it's very dark and your spectators can't see whether the middle ground is in focus or not. These lenses can only be used for set-up shots with no camera moves.

Lens Care Material

You should clean your lens(es) before every shoot with nonabrasive photographic cleaning tissue moistened with a professional lens-cleaning solution. "Luminex" microfilter cloth will remove fingerprints, but check that there's no dust on the cloth before using it. Dust on the lens can be removed by blowing on it (either yourself or with a can of compressed air) or with a special hair brush. Never use regular tissue paper to clean a lens.

Batteries

Most film and video camera batteries are rechargeable and may be either internal or external to the camera itself. External batteries usually clip onto the camera or slip into a special compartment. Internal batteries tend not to last as long as clip-ons—one to two hours instead of three to four. Most cameras use "NiCad" (nickel-cadmium) batteries, which generate a "memory" over time. This means that unless they're discharged all the way every time they are used (or almost all the way—a complete discharge would kill them), they last for shorter and shorter periods. To maximize their performance and life, try to use a recharger with the capacity to "dump" the residual charge of a battery before recharging it, as this will preserve their memory much longer. Some cameras use rechargeable lithium-ion batteries, which have more capacity per size than NiCad batteries and don't suffer from an ever-decreasing memory. (Avoid lead-acid batteries at all costs, as they are unreliable.)

You should have a number of spare batteries, *of as large a capacity as possible,* even though they seem very expensive. Nothing is more infuriating than a flat battery when you're shooting. Consider also equipping yourself with a battery belt or two (sometimes called "expedition belts"), which may be worn around your midriff (see "Accessories" in appendix 4). They can, for instance, power up to 13,000 feet of 16mm footage (more than six hours at sound speed) before needing to be recharged.

Special disposable lithium-based batteries may be useful for remote or harsh conditions (see "Accessories" in appendix 4). First tried out by Timothy Asch and Napoleon Chagnon in 1977 when shooting their Yanomamo films, they have been used since on the summit of Mt. Everest, on the South Pole, and in the Persian Gulf. They have a long shelf life and can power video or film cameras as well as lights and tape recorders. They offer between 7.5 and 15.8 volts, 8,000 and 16,000 mAH (milli-amp hours), 60 and 240 watt-hours, and weigh between 12 and 48 ounces. They are relatively expensive and so make the most sense in cold conditions or if you have no access to electricity and cannot rely on strong enough sunshine to recharge NiCad batteries with a solar recharger. Lithium batteries are poisonous and should always be carried out of the field. Some airlines restrict their transport.

Batteries are less efficient in the cold; in severe conditions they may discharge in a matter of minutes. Try to keep them warm before you start shooting. If you're shooting in icy conditions, you may even want to use a heated camera case—which will protect the camera, the battery, and your hands. Such cases are heavily insulated and can double as a camera carrying bag (see "Accessories" in appendix 4). One advantage of battery belts is that you can wear them under a coat and warm them with your body heat.

If you plan to shoot in different parts of the world, you should try to acquire a battery recharger that will transform both 220–250V and 100–120V AC to the 12V or 24V DC that video and film cameras use. Otherwise you'll need an extra transformer, and transformers are heavy, expensive, and often overheat and break down. In some parts of the world, where AC current is unreliable, you may need at least a surge protector. (Standard U.S. surge protectors, designed for 110V circuitry, will blow the moment you plug them into 240V.) If you expect to use AC to power your camera during shooting, and not just to recharge the batteries, it's also best to have a voltage regulator on hand.

Solar and Car Cigarette Lighter Rechargers

If you are shooting where there's no electricity, you may want to equip yourself with a solar recharger. A less expensive option is to buy a solar panel (of around 1 sq. ft.) and attach it to a car or (cheaper still, and less heavy) a motorcycle battery. You can trickle charge the vehicle battery all day, and use that to recharge your NiCad batteries at night. Solar panels can be found at recreation vehicle stores.[7] Alternatively, you can purchase prefabricated solar rechargers from specialized outlets.

If you will have a vehicle on location that has a socket for a cigarette lighter, consider also investing in a 12V charger. You plug it into the cigarette lighter socket and attach the wires at the other end to your batteries.

Tripods

The most common way to stabilize your camera as you shoot is to mount it on a tripod. Tripods have three legs and a head. On motion picture tripods, the legs and head are separate. Companies like Miller Fluid Heads manufacture a wide variety (see "Equipment and Services" in appendix 3). They're also available at rental houses. If you expect to have any camera moves at all (pans or tilts), it's important to use a fluid (not friction) head tripod. Fluid heads incorporate a hydraulic mechanism that introduces a very steady resistance to your moves, giving you considerable control over them. (Gear-driven assemblies are also available but are much bulkier.) Make sure you can control the degree of resistance, since you will want to make both fast and slow camera moves. (Sometimes fluid-head tripods are called "multistep pan and tilt fluid drag systems.") Be sure also to use a quick release camera platform, which is a small plate that attaches to the bottom of the camera and is clasped by the tripod. This allows you to take the camera off (or put it on) the tripod instantly, and to move between handheld and mounted shooting almost without a pause. Additionally, make sure that the tripod has an easy-to-use and accurate leveling device, such as a spirit level and a ball-in-socket head. Otherwise your shots may be lopsided. Finally, with anything other than a light camcorder, you should place the tripod feet in a "spreader," so it will be steady and can be placed on floors without damaging them.

Stabilization Systems

There are various other kinds of stabilization systems you can use. If you're shooting with a video camcorder, a high-quality internal image stabilization feature may be sufficient. If you feel you need something more, do not have internal image stabilization, or are shooting film, you can make your own shoulder braces or back harness. Or you could use specially designed, commercially available mounting equipment, like the Steadicam, which stabilizes the camera even while you move around. Through a deceptively simple system of weights and balances, it takes the camera's center of gravity partially away from your own body, and its gravitational independence allows you to walk up steps, run through fields, and jump across ditches, all the while maintaining a stable image. (You can easily pan and boom; it's much more difficult to tilt.) Shooting with a Steadicam can transform the look of your video, bringing you shots gracefully sailing around any space. Since you hold it away from your eye, you can end up having a lot more eye contact with your subject(s) than you would otherwise. It can also be transformed in a split second into a shoulder mount. But it takes some time to learn how to use the Steadicam with ease, and it's a relatively heavy and expensive piece of equipment.

There are different Steadicam models for different kinds of cameras (see appendix 4). Rather than buying or renting a Steadicam yourself, it may be easier to hire a Steadicam operator, with his or her own equipment, for a day's or an hour's shooting. After all, you may only need one Steadicam shot in a whole film.

Monitors

Even the best viewfinder isn't a match for a separate video monitor. If you're shooting video (or will be screening video dailies in the field from a film original), you may need to take along a monitor. A monitor lets

FIGURE 51 Camera Stabilization System. This Steadicam JR is supporting a Hi-8 camcorder, and partially removes the camera's center of gravity from your own, so that you can shoot smoothly as you walk around. Because you can see the image on a separate monitor, your eye is away from the camera eyepiece, and you can be more directly in contact with the world you're filming. On the other hand, in most contexts a stabilization system draws additional attention to yourself and the act of filming.

you check the quality of your recording and also screen footage for your subjects. If you're shooting in a controlled style, you can also use a monitor to visualize shots or camera moves before performing them.

When choosing a portable monitor bear in mind that the cheaper LCD models do not have very fine resolution, may be difficult to watch outdoors, may be too small for a large group of people to gather around, and may not have any audio output. Portable cathode ray tube monitors can have screens as small as five inches in diagonal, and have higher resolution. Ideally, a monitor should accept 110 and 240V AC, as well as battery DC current. It should have an internal speaker and/or a speaker and headphone jack. Unless your camera can output an RF-modulated signal (i.e., picture and sound mixed together), you'll need a "monitor" or combination "monitor-receiver," not just a television receiver.

If you want to use a monitor to play back footage to your subject(s) and to record their response, make sure that your recording mike isn't too close to the monitor speaker, or else you'll hear high-pitched audio feedback.

Color Temperature Meter

Most camera operators shooting film estimate a scene's color temperature by eye. Color negative film also allows a lot of color corrections to be made when it comes to printing. But it's more accurate to use a color temperature meter (a "kelvinometer"), especially when you have a number of light sources in a scene, with divergent color temperatures. If you only have to balance tungsten and daylight, a "two-color" meter (red and blue) will do the job; if fluorescents are present, you'll need a "three-color" meter (red, green, and blue).

Changing Bag

If you're shooting 16mm film (or if you will be loading film into Super-8 cartridges yourself) you need a changing bag. If you use a secondhand changing bag, check that there are no tears in it and that it really is lightproof. You should try to use a changing bag only in the shade or inside. Small rips can be covered in an emergency with gaffer's tape. The bag should have a double zipper, and sleeves to cover your arms beyond your elbows. Practice loading and unloading film in the bag before setting off for the field. And, finally, don't pull on the end of a loose-wound reel to tighten it.

Sound Recorders, Microphones, and Lights

A separate sound recorder is essential for 16mm sound recording and can also be used with video to record additional tracks (see "Sound Recorders" in chapter 4). For mike accessories, see "Microphones" in chapter 4; for lighting accessories, see "Lighting Equipment" in chapter 3.

Stages of Filmmaking

PART THREE

6. Preproduction

Documentary filming tends to be both incredibly fulfilling and supremely frustrating. Fulfilling when, out of the blue, you suddenly find yourself confronted with one of those rare revelatory moments in people's lives, and manage to catch something of it on film. Frustrating always, because in the endless hurry-up-and-wait of filmmaking, you're forever scrambling to keep up with life unfolding pell-mell before you. Some of this scramble can be eased with careful preproduction. While you can't predict exactly what's going to happen, you can still think through the possibilities ahead of time and organize your shoots accordingly. Even if you want to shoot in a purely observational style, the end result will probably be a lot more interesting if you're well prepared, practically and intellectually.

Preproduction refers to the tremendous bulk of work you do before you start shooting. It can take anywhere from a few days to a few years. The tasks include undertaking research and/or fieldwork, choosing your subject matter, getting to know the people you'll be filming, developing a treatment (or script) and a budget, fund-raising, location scouting, gathering a crew, and assembling your equipment. The intellectual side of preproduction—focusing in on a theme or topic, the aesthetics and ethics of working out your approach and style—is addressed in chapter 2. This chapter will discuss the practical side: how to write a treatment, raise funds, compose a realistic budget, schedule shoots, and organize travel. It ends with some "Preproduction Tips." If you're lucky enough to have a rich patron, be working on a sponsored student project, or for any other reason already have your funding taken care of, you may want to read the "Treatments" section first and then skip ahead to "Schedule."

TREATMENTS

To raise the funds for a film it's becoming increasingly necessary to know what you want to say or find out about your subject, often before you encounter it firsthand. You may therefore find yourself in something of a double-bind, having to write a "treatment" or even a "script"

◀ FIGURE 52 Lorna Marshall interviewing !Kung San men, 1959.

before you start filming. In some ways this is antithetical to the spirit of documentary. If we know how we will represent our subject before we experience it, then do we not do an injustice to the very concept of documentary? If you're to sidestep this conundrum, it's important to be clear about different kinds of treatments. Treatments can serve at least five different purposes: (1) they are almost indispensable for fundraising; (2) they may need to be shown to officials to secure permission to film; (3) they can be used to attract crew members; (4) they may be of interest to your potential subjects (whose reactions may be of interest to you); and (5) they can help you approach your upcoming filming with some discrimination. So long as you keep the treatments you write for yourself separate in your mind from those you send to sponsors, and don't feel bound to the letter of either (and especially the latter), all should be well.

TREATMENTS FOR YOURSELF

Writing treatments for yourself is probably the best way of forcing yourself to *visualize* your film—not so much to reiterate what you might want the film to say, but to imagine what scenes and shots the film might show. Many documentary filmmakers revise treatments of this kind not only during preproduction but even while they are shooting. Writing up the day's events, whether you're location scouting or in the thick of production, and relating them to your conception of the film as a whole, helps clarify what you have and haven't caught on film. (You'll find that the distinction between what you anticipate filming and what you actually film begins to blur the moment you meet your subjects.) Often it is only by externalizing your thoughts in this way that you realize that you haven't really caught someone's true character on film, or that the film is going to be about something quite different from your initial expectations. Preproduction, production, and postproduction are all processes of progressive restructuring and refining, and rewriting your treatments helps you to keep abreast of the footage's evolving shape and to become aware of scenes you still want to shoot.

A treatment generally conveys on paper *what* you're going to show or say in your film, and *how* you're going to show it. You need to convince your prospective sponsors (and perhaps collaborators) that you know something about the topic, and that you can, indeed must, present your interpretation visually, in video or film (rather than in a monograph). The amount of research you have to undertake for a treatment depends on how much you've already completed. If you haven't yet done extensive archival and field research, a review of available films and literature on the topic and area would be helpful, not only for contextual information, but also to get an idea of the different approaches others have already taken to the subject (both theoretically and visually). In your fund-raising treatment, you may want to mention any number of these, emphasizing how your work will depart from them (and thus make an important new contribution). If possible, undertake some preliminary fieldwork, whether with interviews or participant observation. Your treatment should express your understanding of the subject or people you hope to feature. Whenever possible, mention people by name, describing what makes them compelling or intriguing characters. Some filmmakers even include a list of interview questions in their proposals. If yours is to be an interview-based film, this is a good way to convince prospective sponsors you know what you're talking about.

The exact content and tone of your treatment will probably depend on who you're going to show it to. You may need several versions—perhaps one for film-oriented funders (which would be significantly more visual, and possibly more story- or narrative-based than you expect your piece to be); one for scientific, educational, or anthropological funders (which would be more theoretical, and discuss ethical and methodological issues as well); and one for business-oriented sponsors (which would develop the story line, stress the film's originality and potential commercial value, etc.). As long as you're not making anything up out of the blue, there's little harm in emphasizing certain features over others according to a potential sponsor's interests.

How you organize your treatment will probably also depend on who it's for. You may want to give it (and your film) a catchy or descriptive title. (As a film critic for *The New Yorker* declared, "Beware of baggy titles. . . . As a rule, the longer the title, the more firmly it should be understood as shorthand for 'Look Out, Here Comes a Complete Stinker.'"[1] Remember: this is a film you're making, not a journal article, replete with subtitle, indigenous proverb, and all.) It's a good idea to start with a two- or three-paragraph synopsis of the project, making it sound as visual and vivid as you can. You can follow that with a detailed, expanded version in which you address the elements below:

Facts

Identify the individuals or population you want to work with. Discuss their history, and the specific situation that intrigues you.

Structure or Story

Describe how you will make your project cinematic (keeping in mind that some topics that are effective on paper do not translate easily to film). What will the film look like? How might you structure the film? Vividly describe any specific events or people you'll focus on. If your film will revolve around one or two protagonists, sketch their characters (and relationships), and suggest how they embody the themes at the heart of the film.

One of the most popular ethnographic and documentary film structures is, simply, to tell a story. No wonder, since film has conventionally been used as a narrative medium, and a well-told tale appeals to audiences and funders alike. If you want to make a narrative-based film and discern a story in your early research you'd do well to outline it in the treatment. As mentioned above, a surprising number of documentary and ethnographic films rely on rather conventional narrative patterns. Typically they begin with a contextual overview, an introduction to the characters and their (cultural) setting. The story usually involves a line of action, an interpersonal conflict, or a problem of some kind. This comes to a head in a climax, when the dramatic tension is at its height, before being resolved at the end.

The classic tale of "the journey," or a hero's or heroine's quest, recurs in many films. John Marshall's *The Hunters* follows four !Kung men out on a hunt. The climax comes as they stalk and finally kill a giraffe. They bring the food back home, and share the meat with others of their community—creating a sense of closure. Jean Rouch's *Jaguar* follows three young Nigerien men out to seek their fortune in the distant Gold Coast. We transposed Rouch's transnational tale into a transcontinental one in *In and Out of Africa,* which follows the Hausa art trader Gabai Baaré from the Ivory Coast to the U.S. The film arrives at a climax toward the end when Baaré sells several thousand dollars worth of objects to Long Island gallery owner Wendy Engel.

Some films are framed by time: *Nanook of the North* comes across as an abstract "day in the life." Although it's clear that the events take place over a longer period of time (and there's even another night in the middle of it), it begins with shots of the arctic, with the sun peeking over a hill and ends with Nanook, his family, and dogs bedding down for the night in an arctic storm. *The Village,* which was filmed over the course of a summer, becomes the chronicle of a weekend. Paul Hockings explains why: "In lieu of a story—for we had never shot to the requirements of a script and were not about to write a narration that would impose a story on the visuals—we had decided to order shots in the film to represent the events of a typical summer weekend, beginning with the milking early on Saturday morning, and continuing on through to the Sunday afternoon boat-race and its muted conclusion." [2] Gary Kildea's *Valencia Diary* (1992) takes time more literally as the filmmaker provides a chronicle of the days preceding presidential elections in the Philippines, set out in a diary-like format.

Other films may be structured around a single event, as are many of the Marshall sequence films about the !Kung, Asch and Chagnon's *The Ax Fight* and other films in the Yanomamo series, and Asch, Asch, and Connor's *A Balinese Trance Seance* (1979). Tim Asch argues that such structures are more faithful to reality. This is why, together with Karl Heider, he advocates shooting "whole events" in order to "provide a more complete and objective relationship than can be achieved through edited and spliced short takes. What is more, the participants in the event rather than the film editor, provide the chronology and action of the event." [3] However, as we've hinted earlier, one could argue that the starting and stopping points of such events are quite arbitrary, and are still constructed by the filmmaker. The origins of the skirmish in *The Ax Fight,* as we are told in narration, can be traced back for years through personal disputes and village fissions. One could have started filming *The Ax Fight* years before Chagnon and Asch ever met the Yanomamo. Most films, of course, take advantage of cinema's capacity to manipulate the spectators' sense of time and space, and only rarely shows events either "wholly" or chronologically.

Other popular story lines are personal biographies or portraits. *N!ai, the Story of a !Kung Woman* features footage of N!ai at various stages as a young girl growing up, and finally as a woman. Jorge Preloran's *Imaginero* (1969), the MacDougalls' Turkana Trilogy, and Gary Kildea's *Celso and Cora* are other personal profiles. Direct Cinema filmmakers also produced a great number of portrait films including *Jane* (Fonda) (1962), *Meet Marlon Brando* (1965), and *Don't Look Back,* about Bob Dylan. Many documentaries, though not literally portraits, focus on one or several characters as windows onto their culture and worldview.

If you do want to "tell a story" in some way, you should think carefully about what kind of story you want to tell and why. Ask yourself also if it is your story, or your subjects' story? Are you "finding" a story out there, in the midst of people's messy lives? Are you telling one manifestly of your own? Or are you imposing an apparently realistic story onto events to create a neat, self-contained structure with a sense of closure that stems more from your imagination than from the turn of events? What investment do you have in telling the story?

Clearly, all stories are subjective—this is part of what makes them stories. The characters in your film would probably tell stories altogether different from yours. In fact, they may not even recognize your story as a "story" at all. The greater the cultural difference between filmmaker(s) and subjects the more likely this will be. Indeed, their and your narrative traditions may be incommensurable, or at least at odds with each other. Moreover, it's likely that the collaboration of your characters in the filmmaking as well as the film itself will become the source and subject of numerous stories in the local community.

One response to these sorts of considerations is to try and make a film that tells several stories, from various points of view, that embodies the perspectives of a number of the participants. Although in most cases the filmmaker retains ultimate control of the film, no documentary is the construction of the filmmaker alone. It is an exciting challenge to make films that reflect in their form not only your own personal and professional biases but also the contributions of your subjects—their desires and their narrative styles. This is easier said than done, and every case is different. It may mean playing loose with the more hackneyed narrative patterns and conventions of realism, experimenting with both structure and style.

Audience

Identify your intended audience(s). Describe how you will reach them and why they'll be interested in your film. Outline any distribution strategies you may have in place.

The traditional audience for documentaries has been pretty much anyone who wants to watch them and who can get to see them. Ethnographic films have been seen almost exclusively by a much smaller group of anthropology students and an inner circle of aficionados. But since academic as well as global demographics are fast changing, new and transformed audiences for these films are also coming into being. Although *Nanook* is an early example of (partial) collaboration, it is only recently that most ethnographic and documentary filmmakers have come to conceive of their subjects as one of their audiences. Filmmakers and their subjects often both turn up at festivals where their films are featured. *In and Out of Africa,* for instance, is circulating not only in and out of anthropology, art history, and African studies classrooms in Europe and the U.S., but also within the francophone African community in New York and among Hausa art traders in the Ivory Coast.

As the subjects chosen by documentary filmmakers have become more various, inevitably their audiences have too. Trying to imagine who your possible audiences will be, and what the prospective film might mean to them, is all part of preproduction. While it is almost always restrictive to "target" a specified audience, it reassures potential sponsors if you show that you have a grasp of who your viewers might be, and how they will get to see your film.

Point of View

Some agencies may be interested in your motivation for being attracted to the subject. Emphasize all the qualifications and personal interest you have. While you don't want to give the impression that you're out to create a piece of propaganda, it doesn't ring true to pretend that you have no point of view on your topic. After all, why do you want to make the film in the first place?

How do you clarify your point of view both to yourself and your potential funders? You can start by writing down your take on your subject—what you want to show and why you want to show it. Then imagine *how* this might be communicated to your audience—visually and aurally. Remember, in making a film you're not writing an essay; you have nothing but moving images and sounds at your disposal. (The images and sounds may include words, of course, whether in dialogue or narration, but they aren't reducible to them.) How can you justify having people watch your imagined film? Why will they want to sit through it? What will they get out of it?

At this point you might want to screen some other documentary and ethnographic films to see how their makers position themselves. There may be voice-over narration, in either the first-, second-, or third-person. Sometimes it may be in one voice, at other times in another. The filmmaker's presence may or may not be explicitly acknowledged on the screen or in the sound track. The film may be strung together through interview segments, "talking heads." Or the film may apparently efface the filmmaker altogether, leaving the viewers to interpret the images passing before them "for themselves." Whatever the style, the filmmaker is there with a point of view, from beginning to end.

Methodology

Describe and justify your methodology and anticipated aesthetic. Will it be first-person and provocative or third-person and observational? Intimate and affective or calm and collected? Participatory and/or performative? Realist and/or reflexive? Will you blur styles? If so, to what end? Will the film include formal or informal interviews? Will you use archival footage or photographs? How will you incorporate them into the body of the film as a whole? Will you use narration? Whose? Why? Will your style be singular and seamless or multiple and disjunctive? Why? To what extent will you involve the subjects of your film in its production? Why? How will you portray your subjects in a manner of which they'll approve? (Will you at all?) How can you be sure that their consent really is "informed"?

Need for the Film

Why are you producing your film *now?* When fund-raising, it's usually to your advantage to make your film sound timely, or even urgent. Emphasize, too, the project's feasibility, describing how you (and especially you) will be able to pull this off. What kind of an "in" do *you* have? Describe all your valuable contacts.

Finally, a reminder: it's crucial to regard all treatments as conditional. As long as grant-givers want to fund only pre-scripted documentaries, you may find yourself having to be more articulate, and more knowledgeable about your subject than you feel comfortable with. Never allow yourself to feel constrained by the treatment(s) you wrote when raising the funds. Try, whenever possible, to be upfront with potential producers about the liberties you may need to take. Remember that *all* treatments, including those written for yourself, will fall by the wayside once you begin filming. The last thing you want to do is to try to manipulate the events you find unfolding before you to accord with your preconceived notions of what the film will be about. When shooting, go with the flow, and revise your treatment (in your mind, at least) every night, as you imagine the kinds of scenes you may want to shoot in the upcoming days.

FUND-RAISING

The best advice for fund-raising is simply to be creative. Finding the money to make a film can be tormenting and time-consuming. Even seasoned documentary filmmakers like Barbara Kopple have trouble raising money for their projects, and that *after* winning her first academy award for *Harlan County, USA.* But as a filmmaker-friend of ours puts it, ask yourself, "What would life be like without my film?" Successful fund-raising is a matter of convincing folks that your project absolutely must happen, will happen, and that supporting it is the best thing they can do.

Fund-raising often works piecemeal, as the chances of securing all the backing for a film from a single source are slim. Most filmmakers have to apply to a number of different kinds of sponsors, rewriting their grant proposals in order to fit each potential funder's criteria. Securing the first grant is usually the highest hurdle, for once other funders know that there is some funding in place, they're more likely to contribute. The downside is that the whole process can take years, which means documentary filmmakers usually have to give themselves considerable lead time to raise money before they can start shooting. They also tend to have lots of projects simmering on the back burner at the same time.

The positive side of putting together your own funding is that the film usually remains your own. We've seen a number of filmmakers lose control over their projects when they've clashed with funders over content. Even if this doesn't happen, whenever a film is to be owned by someone else there will always be constraints on how it's made. This is almost unavoidable, no matter how many concessions you win on your contract, and no matter who you are. Many of the films by John Grierson and his associates were sponsored by such apparently unlikely bureaucratic sources as the British Empire Marketing Board, the Ceylon Tea Propaganda Board, and the General Post Office. As Arthur Calder Marshall once quipped, "Mr. Grierson is not paid to tell the truth but to make more people use the parcel post." Robert Flaherty's *Louisiana Story* was funded by Standard Oil. The company gave Flaherty carte blanche to make the film as he liked, as well as full ownership. It didn't even demand any acknowledgment in the credits. Nevertheless, despite its distinct Flahertian style—*Louisiana Story* is a beautiful portrait of nature and man's struggle to control it—the film also contains an implicit message about the virtues (or at least environmental innocuousness) of the oil industry. No wonder it was distributed free to any theater that would show it.

Funding sources for documentary are various. They include governments and nongovernmental organizations (NGOs), corporations and other businesses, foundations, private donors, television stations, distributors and self-funding. Some sponsors may demand a "Producer" credit, and may also own or have rights to the film itself (outtakes and all). More often filmmakers seek outright "grants," which give them quite a bit of leeway on the content, as well as ownership of the product. But you'd be surprised at how many early productions are funded on nothing more than the producer's credit cards. Frederick Wiseman says that when he made his first film, *Titicut Follies,* he had to get a loan from the bank to buy film stock, borrow equipment, and get credit from the film lab.[4] If you do end up funding your own film, don't count on turning much of a profit. As wonderful as they are, many documentaries fail to make their money back.

Government Sources

Government agencies have historically supported a variety of media arts and other programs for which you may be eligible to apply for support. For the time being, the National Endowment for the Humanities in the U.S. funds both the development and the production of media projects. In addition, every state has councils for the arts and for the humanities, which may fund media projects. The National Endowment for the Arts might also be a source of funding (call for guidelines; see appendix 3). Other sources of governmental funding include several different Fulbright fellowship programs, including a fellowship in Film and Television based in the United Kingdom. Contact the Fulbright office at the Council for International Exchange of Scholars in Washington D.C. for details (see appendix 3). When you contact these agencies tell them you are interested in both media and research grants, so that they send you as much funding information as possible. And ask to be added to their mailing lists, so that in subsequent years you'll be sent application materials directly.

Foundations

A good way to find out about foundation funding in the U.S. is to contact an affiliate of the Foundation Center. The Foundation Center is a national organization established by charitable foundations to provide information about all kinds of private "philanthropic" sponsorship. They publish several useful publications and maintain up-to-date information about over 30,000 private and community foundations. There are several principal centers located in large metropolitan areas, including New York, Washington, Cleveland, Atlanta, and San Francisco. In addition, there are over 200 cooperating collections located around the country. By calling their free customer service number (see appendix 3) you can order publications and find out about local cooperating collections. To attract foundation support, you should shape your project as closely as possible to the interests and goals of particular foundations—which means undertaking extensive research about a foundation before applying to it. The Ford Foundation, the John Simon Guggenheim Memorial Foundation, the Rockefeller Foundation, and the John D. and Catherine T. MacArthur Foundation are among the larger foundations that have supported media projects in the past (see appendix 3).

There are also a number of local and national film and video organizations that may disburse grants, and should be able to give you an idea of who else does. Some of them publish serials listing funding deadlines and information. Among these are the Association of Independent Video and Filmmaker's *Independent,* Film Arts Foundation's *Release Print,* Visual Studies Workshop's *Afterimage,* and International Documentary Association's *International Documentary* (see appendix 3). You should also check the bulletin boards of your local film organizations, museums, libraries, and universities (particularly around the art and media departments).

Anthropologists

If you're an anthropologist, or you're working with an anthropologist, you may have additional funding possibilities in the U.S. Anthropologists have procured grants for filmmaking from various private and government sources, including the National Science Foundation. Although technically some of these might not fund films, if a scholar can convince the agency that making a film is integral to his or her research, funding might just come through. It's worth checking with the various benefactors of anthropological and scientific research. It's also advantageous to have (or to be) an anthropologist on the production team when applying to the National Endowment for the Humanities or state councils for the humanities, as these may require extensively researched proposals and demand that filmmakers consult with a number of scholars specializing in the film's subject matter.

Special Interest Groups

You should also look up special interest groups. For example, when we made *Made in USA,* a film about sweatshops and homework in the Los

Angeles garment industry, we approached garment workers' unions and various immigrant support groups for information and funding. For our documentary about the trade in African art, we appealed to museums, African affairs organizations, and local art collectors' clubs. Even if the interest groups you contact don't pan out as funding sources, they could prove valuable contacts in other ways. They might write letters of support that you could show to other potential funders. They will probably be useful sources of information and resource materials. And certainly when it's time to distribute your film, they'll be interested in seeing it and may even sponsor a screening.

Nonprofit Productions

A stipulation of many sponsors is that they will only fund nonprofit productions, or films produced by a nonprofit agency. (This way they get a tax deduction.) You could form your own nonprofit, but it takes time and is not strictly necessary. If you're affiliated with a university or another nonprofit organization, like a museum or a religious institution, see if you can filter the grant through them. (Be careful with universities since they notoriously take huge percentages of grants as administration fees. If your grant is to be administered by your university, try to arrange that they receive a reduced percentage. And secure whatever promises they make in writing.) Alternatively, there are nonprofit film and video organizations offering what are called "fiscal sponsorship programs." If one of these takes on you and your project, it will be able to accept your grants and turn the proceeds over to you, usually for an administrative fee of 5 to 10 percent of your total grant. This fee is quite normal; if you're lucky the organization will provide additional services, including some accounting, advice, and perhaps even photocopying. Read the fine print of any agreement you sign with them carefully. They may want certain rights to your film or demand additional hidden fees.

Television

A number of established documentary filmmakers have had their projects funded in advance by television stations. These have included Channel Four, the ITV Network Center, and the BBC in England, La

Sept/ARTE in France/Germany, CBC in Canada, individual PBS stations in the U.S., and the SBS in Australia. The Corporation for Public Broadcasting in the U.S. also accepts proposals. In addition, the U.S. Congress has recently established ITVS (Independent Television Service), an agency to fund production and promotion of independently produced programs for the public broadcasting markets. ITVS has an annual open call for programs, as well as calls for specific series (for addresses, see appendix 3).

Though U.S. network television rarely funds outsiders' work, cable companies (such as the Discovery Channel) may offer other possibilities. All of these opportunities are competitive, even for filmmakers with long track records. On the other hand, you might have an inside take on the hottest issue at the moment, and the funds will flow in. National Geographic Explorer has recently been seeking anthropologists to take video cameras into the field with them. Even if a station won't fund you, they may say they'll consider airing your project when it's complete. Ask them to put that in writing and add it to your grant proposal package.

Begging, Borrowing, and Bartering

Many of the potential funders described above routinely offer in-kind donations, in addition to or instead of direct contributions. Film- and videomakers have persuaded postproduction facilities, labs, airlines, and film archives to give discounts, restaurants and food companies to donate food for the crew, and manufacturers and stores to pitch in video tape or film. These are the obvious items. Just about anyone can help out with something. When fund-raising for *Harlan County, USA,* Barbara Kopple would "go into banks and say, 'Hey, you want to invest in a film on coal mining?' They would think I was crazy. Then I'd say, 'O.K. Well, can I use your Xerox machine? Can I use your stamp machine?' And I'd sit there and I'd Xerox 117 proposals and then stamp them all. Collate them all over the bank's floor. This continued for the entire four years of filmmaking." [5] Many of these donors will ask for a credit at the end of your production.

Filmmaker Ellen Frankenstein describes other kinds of exchanges she contrived while making *A Matter of Respect* (1992): "We got transportation of a car, equipment, the director/camera operator and sound person on the four-day ferry ride from Washington to Southeast Alaska, by saying we'd give the ferry companies 10 VHS copies of the video (one for each ferry); we got housing in a place where it is scarce and expensive, by living in married student housing over the summer on a college campus and producing an eight-minute admissions promo. . . . I bought a camera . . . right out of grad school and bartered the use of [it] for editing time."[6] In other words, fund-raising is as creative as you care to make it. Why not throw a big party and charge admission?

Applying for Grants

Once you've identified your potential funders, how do you get the grants? Independent filmmaker Jesse Lerner thinks a lot turns on luck and timing:

> Unfortunately, issues tend to become "hot" for about fifteen minutes—until something else comes along. One moment it's rain forests, the next day it's race relations, after that it will be something else. I think part of the secret of getting funded . . . is having a project that's perceived as being "timely." Of course every foundation or panel has its own agenda. Sometimes that is stated very explicitly on the application. The Paul Robeson Fund, for example, will tell you up front that they want politically progressive, grass-roots, activist projects. Other times, especially when the foundation's agenda is defined less narrowly, I believe it depends more on the particular individuals that make up the evaluations committee. . . . With grants like the Western States Fellowship or ITVS, which are relatively easy to apply for, the numbers are really working against you. You can complete a Regional Media Arts Fellowship application in less than a day, which means that they must get a huge number of projects submitted. In contrast, when [we] applied for an NEH grant, we had to write the equivalent of a small book. That alone discourages most people who would want to apply.[7]

As Lerner says, one of the secrets to getting funded is to find out what the funder is looking for. Some funders state their areas of interest clearly on their application package. If they don't, you can figure them out with a little background research at a library or the Foundation Center, or by asking other filmmakers and the funder itself. Many foundations have personnel whose job is to work with grant seekers. Get to know these people, and pick their brains. Keep in touch with them so you can ask about the status of your grant, and get constructive feedback if your proposal is rejected.

Most agencies require you to submit a written proposal. A film or video funder will likely have a typed form with strict categories for you to complete. For a private donor or special interest foundation the form may be much freer. A large part of the determination (not only of your eligibility but of your project's value in their eyes) may even be done over the phone. Most funders require a treatment, a budget, and a schedule. Many funders ask for sample works, which they use to evaluate your filmmaking "ability," and to have an idea what you will do with their money if they give it to you. If you have a good sample, go ahead and send it. If you don't think your sample is representative of your true talents, it might be better to send still photographs, or a sample from someone in an important "creative" position on your crew. Because many funders often only look at about ten minutes of a sample, make sure you cue your piece up to the best ten-minute segment on the tape or film. If possible, find out first exactly how long a section they will view. It also might be helpful to see examples of successful proposals and treatments. Ask other filmmakers for copies of theirs or look in the libraries of your nearest film or video organizations.

Funders frequently ask you how you're going to distribute your film. Typically, they want to be assured that it will reach a relatively broad audience. This doesn't mean that you should just write "general PBS audience" in the distribution box on the application. Try to show that you have a good game plan. It may be useful for you to meet with a distributor before you even get started, so you can establish contacts and gauge the marketplace. They'll know better than anyone if your idea has been covered too often, and they may have ideas about a fresh approach. And again, letters of support from distributors, specific television channels, scholarly consultants, and special interest groups should all go into your proposal package.

If rejections start rolling in, don't give up. Everyone gets them, throughout their careers. Some of the organizations that turn you down may be able to give you advice about improving your proposal. Some may have suggestions about other organizations to contact. Try calling the foundations back, if they don't include written review comments. Any unsuccessful source may lead to a successful one. Barbara Kopple's strategy is to be relentless: "I would also apply year after year to the same foundation. So some of them, after three years, would finally give me a grant. As to the ones that did reject me, I'd call them up and ask why. Then I'd invite them over to see footage and then ask them for a list of other people who they thought might help. So I started becoming somewhat of an expert on foundations."[8]

BUDGET

Filmmaking costs have a way of escalating, and you don't want any nasty surprises. Before you get too far along you'll want to write a budget. Indeed, most sponsors require a budget from you. They want to know what percentage of the funding would come from them, and whether you have any other funders on board. So do you make your budget low to convince the funder that you can get it all done for little? Or do you make your budget high, to cover your bases comfortably? The answer is probably to make it realistic, but to keep each sponsor's resources in mind. Some have a specific limit; others prefer to fund an entire project. Find out how much each usually gives (if it's a nonprofit foundation this is public information). Your budget should include all salaries, living expenses, materials, equipment rental and purchase, and any bureaucratic costs. A comprehensive budget also includes at least a small contingency fund for when the unforeseen happens. As you start to run up expenses, don't forget to check them against your budget as you go along. Should your production change significantly, revise your budget accordingly.

How do you go about writing a budget? You'll have a better chance of remembering everything you'll need if you start with a standard form and fill in all of the applicable categories with the market rate for each line item. This will take some research on your part. Ask all acquaintances for advice on where to get the things you need. Then call around—rental houses for equipment; manufacturers and film and video supply shops for stock; travel agents; and so on. Rates vary, so try to get a few quotes. Unless you're going to shoot right away, you may want to fill in the average rate for an item, since prices could well go up within a year. (But keep your notes on any good deals.)

No matter how much research you do, your budget will seem exorbitant. But once you begin production there may be ways to cut corners. You should be able to solicit some goods and services for free or at a significant discount . . . if you ask nicely, plead poverty, and offer your potential benefactors a mention in the film credits. If you're affiliated with a university or a similar institution, you may be able to use offices, fax machines, phones, or mailing services. Look around to see if there is any equipment you can use for free or for a deferred rate. Though it may be hard to come by a camera that you can take to the desert, you'd be amazed at the different university departments that have off-line video editing systems that you might be able to use at off hours when you get back. A few have old 16mm editing flatbeds lying around too. Scout out departments of Architecture, Art, Art History, Earth Sciences, Ethnic Studies, Film, Geography, and Sociology, as well as Anthropology. Many institutions also have a centralized Media Services department.

Consider approaching the companies that manufacture film and video equipment and stock. Some of them may have in place specific lending programs for independent filmmakers or students. (Kodak, for example, has the Educational Allowance Program for film students and an Independent Filmmakers' Program, both of which offer significant discounts.) If you can't get the name of a specific contact in a company, call or write to their public relations department. Someone may be interested in your project and want to help you out. Allow plenty of time for these requests to be processed, and never count on anything until it's in hand.

The budget reproduced on the following pages is a standard format, and is followed by commentary on each section of the form. You can adapt the format to your own needs. If your production is relatively modest, some of the items may not be pertinent. But even so, the simple act of itemizing all your possible expenses in a standardized way will help you keep abreast of your costs as they mount (often unbeknownst to you).

WORKING FILM TITLE

BUDGET PROPOSAL
Director/Producer (or Contact Person):

Name
Address
Phone/ Fax

BUDGET SUMMARY

		Cost
1.	Project development or preproduction	_____
2.	Producing staff	_____
3.	Rights and permissions	_____
4.	Participants	_____
5.	Production expenses	_____
6.	Postproduction	_____
7.	Production administration	_____
8.	Distribution	_____
9.	Insurance	_____
10.	Legal fees	_____
11.	Contingency	_____
	COSTS TOTAL	_____

1. PROJECT DEVELOPMENT/ PREPRODUCTION

	Cost
Director/ producer's salary	_____
Consultant/ anthropologist's salary	_____
Additional research materials and fees	_____
Office rental	
Phone, fax, photocopying, postage, etc.	_____

(for preliminary interviews)

Tape recorder and tapes	_____
Transcripts	_____

(for location scout)

Round trip air fares	_____
Lodging	_____
Food	_____
Local transportation & expenses	_____
SUBTOTAL	_____

2. PRODUCTION PERSONNEL

Director/ producer	_____
Consultant/ anthropologist	_____
Associate producer	_____
Production manager	_____
Production assistant(s)	_____
SUBTOTAL	_____

3. RIGHTS & PERMISSIONS
    Music: search, rights, & reproduction   _____
    Photos: search, rights, & reproduction   _____
    Archival footage: search, rights, &
        reproduction   _____
    Location fees   _____

    SUBTOTAL   _____

4. PARTICIPANTS (TALENT)
    Honoraria   _____
    Narrator(s)   _____

    SUBTOTAL   _____

5. PRODUCTION EXPENSES
Travel/ Lodging/ Food
    Round trip air fares   _____
    Local transportation   _____
    Lodging
    Food   _____
Equipment rental/ purchase
    Camera package   _____
    Sound equipment   _____
    Lighting   _____
    Grip   _____
    Batteries   _____
    Still camera, film & processing   _____
Crew
    Camera operator   _____
    Sound recordist   _____
    Assistant camera operator   _____
    Gaffer (lighting technician)   _____
    Production assistant(s)   _____
Stock
    Film stock or videotape   _____
    Sound stock (if shooting double-system)   _____

    SUBTOTAL   _____

6. POSTPRODUCTION
(for film)
    Dailies processing (workprint)   _____
    Sound transfers   _____
    Mag sound stock   _____
    Edge coding   _____
    Rough cut editing equipment rental   _____
    Rough cut editing suite   _____
    Negative cutting   _____
    Answer print   _____
    Corrected answer prints   _____
    CRI   _____
    Release prints   _____

(for video)
Stock for window dubs _____
Transfers _____
Off-line editing equipment rental _____
Off-line editing suite _____
On-line editing _____
Master tape stock (for film & video) _____
Titles, subtitles, intertitles, effects, graphics _____
Sound mix _____
Fullcoat purchase/ rental for mix _____
Original music _____
Narration, voiceover recording _____
Editorial supplies _____
Transcription tapes _____
Transcription services _____
Postproduction staff
Director/ producer _____
Editor _____
Consultant/ anthropologist _____
Assistant editor _____
Administrative staff _____

SUBTOTAL _____

7. PRODUCTION AND POSTPRODUCTION ADMINISTRATION
Office rental _____
Office expenses: postage, phone, fax,
   photocopying _____
Carnets _____
Shipping _____
Accounting _____

SUBTOTAL _____

8. DISTRIBUTION
Director/ producer's salary _____
Festival fees _____
Preview tapes _____
Broadcast/ festival copies _____
Closed captioning (for PBS) _____
Publicity stills _____
Postage, packaging, photocopying, etc. _____

SUBTOTAL _____

9. INSURANCE _____

10. LEGAL FEES _____

11. CONTINGENCY (5% – 10% BUDGET) _____

Project Development or Preproduction

This covers what you need to do to set everything up so that you can actually start filming. The amount of money you'll require can vary wildly. If you're an anthropologist who has already undertaken fieldwork in an area, or if you're working with an anthropologist who has, most of the preparatory research may already be complete, and you may be ready to write a treatment and set up the project. But if you're starting from scratch and are undertaking your own research, you'll need to budget in research expenses. These might include books, library fees, preliminary interviews and transcripts, location scouting and research trips (including transportation, lodging, food and local expenses), and your salary for doing all this.

After you've finished your research, setting up the project involves a host of creative and organizational decisions. If you don't expect to need an actual office (and most documentary projects do), at the very least you'll want a system to orchestrate all the administrative and logistical tasks ahead of you. These include securing the appropriate permissions to shoot, finding subjects, hiring crew, procuring equipment, buying stock, devising travel and accommodation arrangements, and reserving postproduction facilities. Your budget items may thus range from office rentals to postage, telephone calls, faxes, photocopying, secretarial help, messengers, and so on. (Of course you may not get all this done before you start shooting, but the more you do, the better.)

Production Personnel

This line includes a salary for filmmakers, anthropologists, researchers or consultants, and any assistants who will be on-board for at least two stages of the three-stage project—preproduction, production, and postproduction. These could include associate producer, production manager, and production assistants. If you're submitting your proposal to foundations oriented toward film, you should probably give both the filmmakers and anthropologists titles such as director, producer, associate producer, or film consultant. If you're submitting it to a more academic funder, it makes sense to stress the credentials of the anthropologist.

If you pay the principal filmmakers and anthropologists a reasonable salary for every week they actually work, the overall sum will probably seem high compared to the rest of the budget. This is particularly true if you're working on a low budget, making deals, cutting corners, and soliciting in-kind donations. When we pointed this out to one funding agency, its representative said to go ahead and put in fair salaries, but she also admitted that these are the first things to go when an independent filmmaker needs to pare down the budget. There are no easy answers. One solution is to underestimate (only on the version of the budget you send out) the number of weeks for certain tasks (such as preproduction). Another is to list every job you perform separately. For example, if you were both the director and the camera operator, you could list the two titles separately, paying yourself as a director during pre- and postproduction, but paying yourself only as a camera operator during the production itself.

Rights and Permissions

If you envisage any kind of distribution (educational, broadcast, or otherwise), you'll need written permission for all the copyrighted material you feature in your film. This includes music, film or video footage, photographs, and news clippings. Even a recognizable tune playing on a radio in the background should be cleared through the proper channels. Many owners of these materials charge for permission, so you should emphasize that yours is an "educational," "academic," "nonprofit," or "student" production. Fees vary according to both the length of the copyrighted excerpt, and your distribution plans (worldwide broadcast rights, for example, cost much more than local cable rights). So be clear about what you are asking for, and read contracts carefully before signing. As British independent filmmaker Alrick Riley says, "Research the material you think you'll need before putting it in the final draft of the script. Don't always take no for an answer and try and develop a library of archive sources or better still get a professional researcher who, if they're good, will know their way around the archive market."[9] Remember also to budget not only for permissions but also for search and reproduction fees. (For more on this, see "Archival Materials" in chapter 7.)

Large-scale productions often obtain location releases, giving them permission to shoot in particular places. If they shoot on government property (and even, in many countries, on the street), they need to get some kind of municipal permit. Some private establishments charge location fees to cover their wear and tear, security, and so on. Even if your crew is tiny, you'll need all sorts of permissions if you shoot out of the country (see "Travel," below). You should make sure you have money in your budget to cover these location fees, as well as the office expenditures in obtaining them.

Participants (also known as "Talent")

This budget line is where you list any fees or other compensation you've decided to give your participants, including narrators. (See "Reciprocity" in chapter 2.) At press time, the voice-over narration honorarium required by SAG (the Screen Actor's Guild) for educational distribution alone is $322 for the first hour and $94 for each half hour after that. PBS rates can be about 20 percent lower. A professional narrator will usually be able to give a satisfactory reading in only a couple of takes.

Many television stations, production companies, and universities require that producers have their subjects sign personal release forms for themselves and their dependents. (See "Responsibility to Subjects" in chapter 2 for a discussion of the ethics of release forms.) These rather intimidating forms give you, the producer, permission to use what you shoot of that person in pretty much any way you want. You have to decide whether to get your subjects to sign a release form before or after shooting them. Which decision is better is a crap shoot—if you ask an interviewee to sign after the interview, you risk their refusal, and the whole shoot will have been wasted. If you ask someone before, and they sign, they may then be more guarded during the interview than if you had waited till afterward. You might want to mention the release in beginning, and have your subjects sign afterward. That way there are usually no nasty surprises for anyone (see appendix 1 for examples of release forms).

Production Expenses

Travel / Lodging / Food. This should include round-trip air fares, local transportation (car rentals, drivers, taxis), and lodging expenses.

The line for food should be based on three meals a day and snacks for your crew. Some companies give the crew a per diem instead of or in addition to meals.

Equipment. You may want to divide this line into equipment owned, purchased, and rented. If you're using your own, you can write typical rental figures in the numbers column. Many filmmakers try to pay for their own equipment by spreading out the cost over several productions. If you're planning to shoot a number of films it may make sense to buy at least some items, especially if the rental cost over your time frame approaches the purchase price. If you're renting equipment, you should know there's usually a discount on long-term rentals. And if you're renting locally, you can reduce costs by shooting on a weekend (many places charge a one-day rental for this). Rental houses usually require that you insure the equipment and/or leave a large security deposit, so include these in your budget as well.

Crew. This is the line item for technical production personnel: camera operators, sound recordists, lighting, grip and construction people, and local production assistants. If you're hiring additional crew, choose them carefully, especially if you will be traveling with them (see "Film Crews" in chapter 2). If you'll be employing union personnel you should discuss rates with the appropriate union. Most crew members work for a daily rate, but many will negotiate. Some will even work for deferred payment. They may ask for points (a percentage of the profits), they may just want the experience because they like the project, or they may be happy with a free trip. Any deals you make should be in writing and should include details about payment, specific tasks, overall time to be spent, daily hours, provisions for overtime, days off, food, lodging, transportation, and insurance if they don't have it. If you're traveling abroad, make sure your crew's passports are in order, and that they're in good health!

Stock and Ratio. The amount of stock you'll need will depend on your style of shooting. If your film is carefully scripted, your shooting ratio (hours shot in relation to hours used in the final film) might be 10:1, meaning you shoot ten hours for a one-hour program. Tim Asch edited John Marshall's footage of the !Kung into numerous "sequence films" which had at times a 3:1 and even 2:1 ratio. *The Ax Fight* had, according to Asch, a 1:3 ratio, since much of the footage was used more than once.[10] But if you're shooting in an observational style, or if you're shooting video, your ratio will probably be much higher. Barbara Kopple shot 50 hours of film for *Harlan County, USA* (which was less than 2 hours long).[11] Of course you want to make sure you've got everything covered. As filmmaker Ellen Frankenstein puts it, "You can't create a cutaway, a reaction shot, an establishing shot in the editing room, perhaps thousands of miles away."[12] But bear in mind that the more you shoot the more it will cost in terms of master stock, transfer stock, processing and transfer time, and your or the editor's valuable time.

Finally, you may be able to get a manufacturer's discount on stock. There are also discount shops that sell preowned stock and stock that's due to expire soon. (Both are risky so be sure to shoot and process tests before you leave town.)

Postproduction

Note: The process of postproduction is described in detail in chapter 8, where many of the terms used here are explained.

First, you should choose the most efficient and cost-effective methods of editing both the rough cut (with video, off-line) and the fine cut (with video, on-line). If you're shooting and editing on film, you have to debate the relative merits and prices of flatbed and upright editing machines. If you're editing on video, ¾ inch is more accurate for rough cuts but VHS stock and equipment is cheaper and more compact. If you have the space, you can sometimes rent a VHS editing system or a 16mm flatbed in the privacy of your home, saving money on an editing room. Video editing is becoming increasingly computerized. Although nonlinear video editing equipment is still relatively expensive, it can save you so much time in the long run that you may end up saving money. Renting equipment for large chunks of time is cheaper than paying by the hour. And if you hire an editor or editing assistant, it's best to negotiate a rate for the job, based on a reasonable assessment of the time it will take.

For the fine cut, be sure to use the best negative cutter or on-line system you can afford. Some on-line houses will offer you a discount if you work at odd hours (nighttime or weekends). You can save time and money if you put all video titles and superimpositions on your character generator before you start on-line editing.

Always be very specific with your instructions for transfers and processing. Find out if you can save money by doing two transfers at once. For example, try to make audio cassettes for your transcriber at the same time you make window dubs, or transfer ¼-inch audio tape to mag, and so on.

If you're shooting video, you also need to include additional stock here, for your rough cuts. You can save money by purchasing degaussed secondhand tapes for window dubs and rough cuts. Try to anticipate all your needs so you can buy at a bulk discount.

You should probably include a fee for transcriptions. If you decide to hire someone else to transcribe your tapes then negotiate a precise rate of pay. Some professional transcribers charge an hourly rate, others by the page. Paying by the hour is risky because transcribers' speeds vary. You're best off negotiating per job, or hiring a local production assistant with some transcribing experience (especially if you're working in a foreign language).

Finally, don't forget editorial supplies: pens, pads, tape, and so on. If you buy everything in large quantities at the beginning of production, you can salvage a few cents.

Production and Postproduction Administration

This is where you list administrative and office expenses for the production and postproduction stages. In addition to repeating the items mentioned in the project development/preproduction line, you should add production shipping and customs charges (including carnets—see the "Travel" section) and accounting.

Distribution

Even if you plan to hand your film over to an outside distributor right away, you should keep a line in the budget for distribution. You may wish to enter festivals, send dubs to participants and crew, add subtitles or closed captions for broadcast, and pay yourself for your time in doing all this. If you choose to self-distribute, this line item should be quite extensive.

Insurance

Doesn't it seem as if every time you have good insurance you don't need it, but whenever you don't something terrible happens? Filmmakers purchase all kinds of insurance. Some are more useful than others. Rates vary significantly, so you should shop around for a policy, and go with a reliable broker. Some film organizations have arranged for special insurance discounts for their members, so approach them first for a recommendation. It's usually cheaper to buy a year-long equipment and liability insurance policy than to insure two different shoots in the same year. So if you're using an organization's equipment, you may wish to share the costs of an annual policy with them.

Equipment. The most important insurance is for equipment theft and damage. You can take out a policy that covers both your rental and your own equipment. Make sure it includes replacement costs, rather than a particular item's (depreciated) market value. Check whether the policy includes accidental breaking. Prices for policies will depend on where you're shooting. Some companies have been known to offer "global" coverage that in the fine print turns out to exclude large portions of the world! And many will not cover you in event of war, popular uprisings or extreme civil unrest, or governmental (military or police) confiscation.

General Liability. This protects you against claims for bodily injuries or property damage caused by your production. Many private property owners and municipal governments require that you show proof of such insurance before allowing you to shoot on their property (including city streets). If you want this protection on shoots outside the U.S. and Canada, ask your insurance company to arrange for foreign liability coverage.

Third-Party Property Damage. This covers damage to property (other than equipment) in your care, control, or custody—such as furniture and other property on a shooting location.

Faulty Camera, Stock, and Processing; and Negative Film and Video Tape Insurance. These are two different policies, usually issued together, that will reimburse the cost of reshooting due to loss or damage to film or tape that you've already shot. Consult a broker for the specific details.

Worker's Compensation. This covers medical costs and disability payments for uninsured employees injured while working for you. Before hiring anyone as an independent contractor, ask them for proof of their own health and worker's compensation insurance. If they don't have these, you may need this policy.

Errors and Omissions (E & O). Broadcasters and distributors typically ask that producers indemnify them from lawsuits over a film's contents. They may even require that you buy an errors and omissions policy to back this up. Before issuing this policy, an insurance company will demand that you secure the appropriate rights, permissions, and releases for your project in writing.

Extra Expense Coverage. This covers any expenses you incur if damage to or destruction of any property used in connection with your production (such as a location) causes a delay in any way.

Weather. Well, yes, you can insure your production against inclement weather, but it's very expensive. Besides, if you're trying to film "reality," isn't a little rain just part of life?

Legal

You may need to consult a lawyer at least once during the overall production. Lawyers can help you compose release forms and location permits, look over crew deal memos, examine permissions for archival materials, and negotiate distribution contracts. If you're planning an extensive production and don't already have a lawyer, you should look for one with some experience in documentary film, or at least entertainment and the arts. There are over forty Volunteer Lawyers for the Arts organizations throughout the U.S. and Canada providing free or discounted legal services for artists (see "Legal" in appendix 3).

Contingency and the Bottom Line

At this point, your budget will look phenomenally high. So how do you reduce it? Start by trimming the fat. Go through each line and ask yourself if every expenditure will be absolutely necessary. You may also now want to incorporate any special discounts you've negotiated. Look at salaries. Can you defer or reduce any of them? Do you need to have everyone on board for as long as you first thought? Don't trim it all too much, however. Remember, too, that you should earmark a certain amount of contingency (usually between 5 and 10 percent of the rest of the budget) for when the unexpected happens.

SCHEDULE

There's no formula for scheduling. Sometimes filmmakers are constrained by a time frame: you may have a provisional broadcast date from a television station, you may have a sabbatical or summer free that is only so long, and if you're a student engaged in a class project, you probably have a semester or less. But many independent filmmakers grind to a halt when they feel their film is finished, they've run out of money, or simply can no longer bear to look at their footage. When scheduling, think in terms of the three-stage process: preproduction, production, and postproduction. Though production tends to take the shortest time, the other two stages are usually scheduled around it. For if there are specific events or people you will be filming, you'll need to plan your shoots around them. Once you've decided when you're shooting, you need to backtrack (if possible, at least a few months) to start your preproduction and then schedule (preferably, several months of) postproduction on the other side. The amount of time for postproduction can vary widely, depending on how long you want your finished product to be, whether you edit full- or part-time, how many people are editing, and how clear an idea you initially had of what you wanted.

For example, *In and Out of Africa* took 2½ months of preproduction, one month of principal photography in the Ivory Coast, two months of intermittent additional photography and principal interviews in the

U.S., roughly one month of transferring and transcribing, three months of editing before a first rough cut, four more months of rough cuts, and then one month on the fine cut and mixing (about nine months of postproduction, in all). On the other hand, *Harlan County, USA* took about three years to film fifty hours of material, and a year to edit. Some of Tim and Patsy Asch's films have been edited years after shooting was completed. Some of Orson Welles's footage was edited after he was dead! There's no one way to do it. ·

Here are a few hints about scheduling your shoots: Start by determining when important events are occurring and when people are available. Presumably you'll have little or no control over their timing, so you'll need to work around them. If you will be shooting in more than one location, you should try to shoot everything you need in each location before moving on to the next. Don't be alarmed if this means you have to shoot things in a different order from how you intend them to appear in the final film. Most documentaries are shot "out of sequence." Another point to bear in mind is that if you or your crew is new to the subject or to each other, you're better off initially filming less important sequences, since it takes time for everyone to adapt.

Your schedule should also contain contingency plans for inclement weather or if someone falls sick or is suddenly unavailable. Each morning or evening, before starting the next shoot, you should think through the whole production: What have you gotten so far? What do you need to do today? What kinds of scenes and shots would embody the themes or ideas or personalities you're hoping to convey? Write daily (but flexible) schedules, as well as back-up contingency plans. Make sure you schedule in ample time for travel, setup, and break-down, since these always take much longer than you'd imagine. Finally, don't forget to give yourself, your crew, and participants a rest. Allow time for meals, breaks, and days off.

TRAVEL

If you've ever packed your bags and realized you had more than you wanted to carry, the general rule is to reduce it by half and depart happily on your trip. Alas, you won't be able to do that if you want to film abroad. Unfortunately, the better prepared you are, the more stuff you have. The trick is to reduce your equipment to the bare essentials, while remaining prepared for the most unusual accidents.

Before You Go

If you're traveling abroad, your first step is to make sure your and your crew's passports are up-to-date, and to secure the various visas and permits you officially need to enter and film in the countries you'll be visiting. (Even if you're shooting only in your home country, you should probably carry your identity card with you, and you may need to apply for various filming permits.) Though the nearest consulate will normally be able to issue you a visa, it may not be able to give you permission to film. Some countries have a ministry of information, an international film commission, or a similar body that handles film permits. The surest way to avoid trouble is to go through official channels, though they may demand certain concessions—that you hire local assistants, be accompanied by a ministry official, or submit a detailed shooting schedule in advance. Many such regulations have been devised for big budget feature filmmaking, and are inappropriate for small documentary productions, so you might want to emphasize the educational nature and tiny budget of your project.

Secure all of your permissions in writing. Procuring one permission may be contingent on your having another. Find out whether local permits will be required and if you'll need to renew your visa once you arrive. Ask about the costs, and for the local address where you can obtain permits. In many countries you can renew visas only in the capital. The municipal authorities of provincial towns may require that you officially check in with the local police. Expect that the requirements on the ground may be slightly different from what you were told by the consulate. A few years ago when we went to Mali, the consulate told us that photo permits in certain areas were no longer required. When we went to the tourist office in the capital we were told that this was indeed true, but not all of the local authorities were aware of the change, so we should come back the next day and pay a huge fee for a document stating we didn't need a permit. Needless to say, bribing can be dubious and dangerous; only you can judge whether in a particular instance it might be effective or expected.

In much of the world, it is helpful to have official letters on hand to show local authorities. Generally, the more "official" they look, the more effective. Make several copies in case one is confiscated. If you're attached to a university or similar institution, try to procure a letter with an official stamp (signed by someone with a title) describing your project and its academic significance, and vouching for your integrity. When filming abroad, a letter from a government agency (your own or the host country's) may help even more.

Business cards convey an aura of importance, especially if you're a student. They also may be the only way people will remember your name. Various authorities may be intrigued to see your treatment or proposal; you have to decide whether it would help or hinder to have copies on hand.

Assess the political situation before you leave. If there's unrest in the area you're traveling to, make sure you can actually reach the places you want to film. You may need to reorient the film accordingly. We've shot in cities when curfews were in effect, and missed exterior establishing shots that we felt we needed. Check governmental and other public travelers' advisories before leaving.

Talk to everyone you know who may have traveled or worked where you're going. Ask all the standard questions about where to stay, to eat, to obtain emergency medical care, and, if you're going abroad, to change currency. Do they know anyone who lives locally who could help you? The saying goes that in this ever-contracting world there are six degrees of separation between any two individuals.

You may need to hire someone local to assist you, even a "location manager." (Some countries require this.) At worst, you could have a costly assistant who gets in your way. At best, you might have a helpful guide, interpreter, and production assistant. If you arrange it ahead of time, you could ask the person to pick you up at the airport, and even to help you through customs. You may need to hire someone with an insured car. Although local cabs and buses can move you around most capital cities, outside large cities you could be on your own. Renting a car abroad can be very expensive and, if you're not familiar with your surroundings, dangerous. (You should still take along an international driver's license to keep your options open.)

Before leaving, be sure to check your equipment carefully. If need be, have equipment serviced. You should shoot tests before you leave. Make sure you bring along all the tools and accessories you need to keep the equipment in working order. Stow your equipment in hard cases with padded interiors. If you're traveling to a climate that is especially hot, cold, or wet, pack accordingly. Be sure to bring rain protection, silica gel, dust-off, head cleaner, lens cleaners, and sealing tape. If you can afford it, bring extras of everything or figure out a way to get hold of a back-up camera and sound recording system should an emergency arise.

Another important consideration is how you'll supply power to your equipment. Even if you choose not to take lights, you'll need to charge your camera batteries. And in order to plug into AC mains, you'll need to know the local voltage (see appendix 2). You should bring a high-quality, heavy-duty adapter in case the voltage differs from the input demands of your equipment. If you'll be far from AC mains, you'll need to consider other options. Some filmmakers bring generators or charged car batteries on location. Filmmaker John Cohen has been using disposable lithium batteries for years, to run his camera, tape recorder, and even lights. Although lithium batteries are very expensive, they're long-lasting and hold up well in cold weather. Another option is to use solar panels to recharge your batteries, though some are unreliable when it's not actually sunny. We've found that a few models need consistently strong sunlight to fall on *all* the solar panels if they're to recharge the batteries at all.

Keeping stock and equipment safe and sound is always a dilemma when you travel. If you don't want to take out insurance for your whole production, at least consider it for your equipment. Make sure you list all items, along with serial numbers and replacement costs, and keep a copy of your inventory with you. Prices and restrictions vary from country to country. We bring all sorts of locks and chains with us, to attach the camera and other equipment to whatever is on hand. We also have with us any papers that establish the provenance of our equipment—rental agreements and sales receipts. Some border officials may try to confiscate cameras, recorders, and accessories if you can't prove that you're the rightful owner. The papers, together with an ATA carnet (discussed below), should also exempt you from local taxes.

Additionally, as with all travel, having local currency on hand when you arrive lets you pay for porters, telephones, and taxis. If you arrive on a weekend or unforeseen holiday, you could find it difficult to change money. Bring plenty of traveler's checks and a little of your own country's cash (in some countries, you may get a better rate of exchange in the "informal economy"). Though the electronic culture of plastic credit cards seems to be increasingly global in extent, some countries have adopted electronic verification systems that don't accept foreign cards (even if they say they do).

Finally, if you are filming abroad, embassies and consulates will inform you of the immunizations countries demand. Consider also contacting the World Health Organization for the latest local information. In the U.S., the Atlanta-based Centers for Disease Control and Prevention (see "Travel" in appendix 3) provides recorded information about disease outbreaks around the world. They'll even fax information should you request it. A university health service should have an immunization or advice nurse who will provide information and inoculations. Most antimalarial medicines need to be taken for some time both before and after you travel. Some immunizations need to be given over a period of time. The service that provides you with your shots should furnish you with an International Certificates of Vaccination booklet, which you'll need to enter certain countries. Hold on to it for future trips, because some inoculations are good for as many as ten years. Before leaving you should also get emergency contact numbers, including your local embassy and, if possible, local doctors and hospitals. You may also want to take out an international health insurance policy, if you have no coverage abroad. Some policies offer options that would pay for air transportation should you need to be evacuated for medical reasons.

Getting There by Air

Although airlines provide special services for television networks and large productions, they're less likely to give much of a break to independent filmmakers. But it's worth a try. Even if you can't wangle a free ticket, you may be able to arrange other bonuses, such as upgrading your seats, skipping long lines, or waiving surplus baggage charges, in exchange for a mention in your credits. (Make sure beforehand they'll even accept surplus baggage.) Sometimes you can cut your baggage fees on domestic flights by paying a porter a little extra at curbside check-ins. Try to ensure that any deal you arrange will apply on your return trip as well. Charter flights are a slightly risky option for filmmakers: they tend to be cheap, but may be crowded, run late, and have a more restrictive baggage allowance. Be sure to ask about their refund policy. Try to avoid paying in cash and check your ticket carefully to make sure it's valid. You may wish to call the airline and hotels to verify that you really have reservations. Finally, be sure to arrive at the airport early so you can try to upgrade your seat, board comfortably, and stow your carry-on luggage.

Try to fly with everything you need. If need be, you can send equipment by air freight, but there can be delays, packages can arrive at different times, and customs officials can make it difficult (and expensive) for you to retrieve it. If you're flying internationally and have a lot of equipment, you might consider obtaining an ATA carnet (ATA stands for "Admission Temporaire / Temporary Admission"). These are administered worldwide by the International Chamber of Commerce, and in the U.S. by the U.S. Council for International Business. (There are regional offices in New York, Los Angeles, Houston, and San Francisco, among others.) The carnet is an international customs document in which you preregister all your equipment, thus facilitating its transportation in and out of the 45-plus countries that participate in the carnet system. It's a guarantee that you won't sell any of your equipment abroad and will thus leave each country with everything you brought in. A carnet will probably help you to avoid customs delays and duties; it's also proof on your return that you didn't purchase the equipment abroad (and thus owe duty on it). Large productions use carnets as a matter of course. They cost between $120 and $250, depending on the value of your equipment, and require that you post a refundable security of at least 40 percent of the total equipment value. You must apply for them in advance; allow at least five days for processing. Whatever you decide, make sure that you understand the restrictions of your own country, those that you'll be visiting, and the airline.

When traveling, try to take your camera and most expensive equipment as "hand luggage." Be prepared to carry these off the plane during stopovers. And try to insist on hand inspection of equipment and accessories. Film, especially, can be damaged by X-rays; you may want to wrap it in lead shielding, and demand hand inspections of film you

STAGES OF FILMMAKING

carry on with you. In theory, if your film's ISO or ASA is 400 or less, and if you're traveling only in well-maintained FAA-regulated airports, X-ray machines should not hurt your film. Even though the effects of X-rays are cumulative, tests have shown that 200 ISO film is barely affected by 16 rounds through an X-ray machine. Similarly, a study done by the EG & G Astrophysics Research Corporation asserts that Linescan Systems and metal detectors will not hurt video or audio tapes or any magnetic memory devices.[13] But why take a chance, especially if you're traveling in countries with outdated security systems and older X-ray equipment?

Arriving

Arriving at an airport with film or video equipment in tow can be quite hectic. This is the moment when letters of authorization and a certain amount of patience will come into their own. Keep an eye on your passport and equipment; some of the people offering to help you may not be proper officials, and not all of the officials may be proper. Arranging for a local contact to meet you could help cut through red tape, especially if the person has diplomatic credentials.

Being There

You will want to shoot tests right away, to make sure equipment and stock have not been damaged in transport. Even well-packed equipment may have been left in the sun on the runway or in another climatically extreme place at some point, and been damaged. If you're shooting video, be careful not to replay the tapes so much that they become worn.

If you're shooting film and want an idea of what you're getting, you're going to have to send some of your footage to a lab. You should make arrangements for this in advance. Short of sending your film off with a trusted individual, you might try to use a courier company or diplomatic pouch (we know one filmmaker on a Fulbright who managed to do this). Otherwise you'll have to send it air freight. Picnic coolers can come in handy for this purpose. The MacDougalls fill theirs with film, seal it with strapping tape, and add an address label to the outside. (They also use coolers to carry miscellaneous equipment, and even as tables and chairs.)

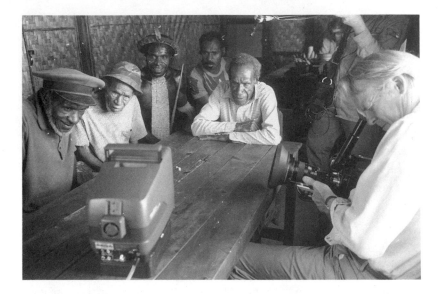

FIGURE 53 Robert Gardner filming Weyak, Kurelu, Pua, and Wali in Irian Jaya watching *Dead Birds* (1963) twenty-five years after it was shot. A monitor on location enables you to check the technical quality of your video footage (or video dailies, if you're shooting film), and shows you what you have actually shot as opposed to what you suppose you've shot. It also lets you screen the footage for your subjects, making the filmmaking process potentially more participatory.

Screening Your Footage. Whether you're shooting video or film, screening your material as you shoot serves more than a technical purpose. It gives you an idea of what your footage really looks like, which may be a far cry from what you had in mind when you shot it. Since the footage itself is what counts, not your intentions, it's important to view it with as disinterested an eye as possible. A scene that seemed very rich and resonant as you witnessed it may not come alive at all on the screen. You may also spot people who seem stimulating on-screen who hadn't really caught your attention before, and want to shape your future filming more around them. Additionally, you may want to show your footage to your subjects. It will give them an idea what kind of film you're making, and their responses to the material will almost always be interesting. You may even want to record (aurally or visually) their responses.

Thus, if you're shooting video, or will be screening video rushes made from your film, you will need access to a video monitor, and perhaps a player. If you're editing on film, and will be on location for some time, you should try to project your rushes. Check that the projector is clean and in working order before threading it. And stop and look for scratches after a few frames before screening a whole reel.

Official Contacts. If you're shooting abroad, you may or may not want to check in with your country's embassy when you arrive. Some embassies may exchange your traveler's checks, and charge a lower commission than banks. If you're going to be in the country for a while you could even offer to give a slide lecture or talk, or to donate a copy of your film to their library. On the other hand, you may not want to build too strong a tie to official diplomatic agencies, especially if you're not to capitalize on their authority or be taken for a representative of your government.

Going Home

As you pack to return home consider leaving behind some of your unused items. Batteries, mosquito nets, and still film are prohibitively expensive in much of the world and would in certain contexts be welcome recompense for someone's invaluable help. However, if you used a carnet, be sure to take with you all of the equipment you listed. Be sure also to write down everyone's names and addresses so you can send thank you letters, royalties, and copies of your final film. You might even want to make preliminary arrangements for a formal screening once the film is complete.

PREPRODUCTION TIPS

Production Notebook

Whether you're filming at home or abroad, it's helpful to keep all production paperwork in one place so that it's accessible when needed. (But if you can, retain extra copies of everything separately.) Your notebook might contain the treatments; a contact sheet (with phone numbers and addresses of your crew, subjects, locations, emergency contacts, and places or people you can go to for replacement equipment if yours breaks down); any necessary release forms; your budget; shot lists; interview questions; and tape logs. It should also contain an equipment checklist.

Equipment Checklist

Equipment can be easily lost in the fray of production. It's a good idea to write out an equipment checklist before leaving for your location, and to verify you still have everything at the end of every shoot. A standard checklist would include the items listed on the following page.

Bring Extras

On each shoot, you should bring extra charged batteries and a battery charger, extra film or video tape, an extra light meter, an ASC manual, and even snack food. You can use a 35mm still camera to take production stills, which your distributor and festival programmers will want later. Some documentary filmmakers use an instamatic Polaroid™ camera for continuity. As a gesture of reciprocity it may or may not be appropriate to give your subjects photos of themselves.

Location Scouting

If possible, check locations *before* you shoot in them so that you can anticipate noise or logistical problems. Try to scout locations at the same time of day (and, if possible, week) that you plan to film. Otherwise someone you had anticipated being present may be absent, or a space may be closed that you had relied on being open. Find out who else might be using the location. There may be a loud soccer match, for example, or an occasional itinerant market next to a spot where you intended to shoot an intimate interview. Consider the following questions in scouting locations.

Access. Will all the relevant spaces and buildings be open and accessible? Your subjects may not know all the entry and safety restrictions. What kinds of permissions do you need? Could you be subject to interference from local law enforcement officers, whether acting with the sanction of the state or on their own authority? What degree of civil

EQUIPMENT CHECK LIST

For Film and Video:
Camera
Lenses
Filter kit
Exposure meter
Color temperature meter (optional)
Camera supports:
    Tripod
    Fluid tilt head
    Harness
    Spreader
    Portable stabilization system
Power supplies:
    Batteries
    Battery belt
    Battery charger

For Video:
Video recorder (if not built-in)
Monitor w/ AC adapter
Camera cable extension

For Film:
Magazines
Changing bag
Slate system
Barney

Audio
Sound recorder (especially for film)
Mixer (especially for video)
Mikes:
    Omni(s)
    Shotgun(s)
    (Radio) Lavalier(s)
    Mike pistol grip
    Mike boom
    Mike windscreen
    Connectors, adapters, and
      cables
    Headphones
    Extra batteries

Lighting
Lights
Light stands and attachments
Extra bulbs
Bulbs for location lights
Sun gun
Barn doors, scrims, filters
Gels
Reflectors
Extension cords
Tie-in cables
Adapters (including 2-prong to 3-
    prong, or vice-versa)

Stock
Videotape
Film (Tungsten- and Daylight-
    balanced (for color film), high-
    and slow-speed)
Audio stock (plus spare take-up
    reel for ¼″ tape)

And
Repair kit, including jeweller's
    screwdrivers
Tool kit
Cleaning materials
Compressed air
Head demagnetizer
Small flashlight (to check film gate)
Gaffer's tape
Camera tape
Pens
Pencils
Rubber bands
Ear syringe
Tweezers
Log sheets
Penknife

(dis)order is there in the area, and what kind of response might your film equipment and crew provoke? If you're shooting indoors, will there be anyone there to answer questions about electricity or to let you into locked rooms? If you're shooting outdoors, will you need or want to close off a space from curious but potentially noisy onlookers? (Or might you actually want to encourage them, as in the street scene at the end of the MacDougalls' *Photo Wallahs?*) How many crew members can you bring along? How many will you need? Can you add more if necessary? How safe and easy will it be to unload your equipment and shoot? Are there ramps or a sidewalk for unloading?

Aesthetics. Where do you want to shoot? What might be the mise-en-scène? Can you predict how people might move around? What angles could you use? Is there room for you to place the camera and mike everywhere you want? Will it be easy for you to move around, both as you shoot and between shots?

Lighting. How does the sun affect your location? What time of day will you shoot and from what angle will the sun be coming? Are there fluorescents? How many sources with divergent color temperatures will you have to juggle? How can you control light if necessary?

Power. Will you need it? Is there enough? What's the voltage and frequency? How many circuits are there? How many lights will they power? Where's the fuse box? Can you charge your batteries? Will you need extension cords? Can they be laid down safely, away from public thoroughfares, and secured with tape to prevent tripping?

Sound. Where's the ambient sound coming from (traffic, construction, machinery, animals, music, air-conditioning, plumbing)? Is it steady or intermittent? Can you or do you want to control it in some way? Are there any sound problems you can anticipate?

Other Logistics. If you'll be arriving in a vehicle, how close can you park? Will you need to guard it? If it rains, could you get stuck in mud? Is there a telephone? Food? Toilets? Will you need to have crowd control? Are there potential safety hazards? Is there anything that can be damaged, and thus should be protected?

The following items might be useful when you scout: a director's viewer, tape measure, checklist, Polaroid camera, electrical outlet tester, notebook, pens, location permits, money.

If you're shooting observational-style, these kinds of constraints and problems tend to be last minute, rather than foreseeable long in advance. But you still have to be ready to think about them, to evaluate quickly what a location has to offer.

Protecting Equipment and Stock

You may need to work out beforehand how you will keep your equipment and stock cool and dry on location. The degree of relative humidity and temperature is less important than *variations* in either—try to avoid going in and out of air conditioning in the humid tropics, or in and out of heated cars in the freezing cold.

Most video camera manufacturers claim that modern cameras can be stored between $-4°F$ and $140°F$ ($-20°C$ and $60°C$) and will operate between $32°F$ and $104°F$ ($0°C$ and $40°C$). (Some models will function at more extreme temperatures.) They are often equipped with moisture sensors and automatically stop functioning if moisture condenses inside the camera or on the tape, in order to prevent the tape from sticking to the head drum. Some documentary film- and videomakers keep their lenses dehumidified by storing them with silica gel in hermetically sealed boxes. Videomaker Ellen Frankenstein suggests the following for humid climates: "If you're in a wet place (tropical or temperate) and moisture freaks out your camera or deck, try an electric blanket. [In Sitka, Alaska, I] went over to a bed-and-breakfast run by a Tlingit-Greek couple and volunteered to make beds while my deck napped in their bed. It worked!" [14]

Most film camera manufacturers claim their cameras can function between $-4°F$ and $122°F$ ($-20°C$ and $50°C$). However, film itself becomes brittle at low temperatures, and can even break. The time code on modern film cameras is only accurate between $32°F$ and $122°F$ ($0°C$ and $50°C$). If you'll be shooting film or video in a very cold climate, you may want to bring along a heated camera case.

Try also to keep your film or video stock dry and dust-free. If possible, keep black-and-white film below $80°F$, and color film below $50°F$.

Though you should try to order film stock to arrive just before your shoots, in some circumstances you may have to store it for a period beforehand. Unexposed film stock stored between 50°F and 65°F should be fine for at least six months. (Most refrigerators keep the temperature at around 50°F.) Kept in a freezer, it should be good for years. You should always seal your raw-stock cans with moisture-proof tape, which will protect the film from condensation and spotting so long as the relative humidity remains under 70 percent.

Whenever you have to move your film or video stock or camera between extremes of temperature, try placing them in sealed plastic bags, so they can adjust to the new temperature gradually. Video tape should be kept away from magnets, sun, and smoke, and maintained at a temperature and humidity in which you feel comfortable. If possible, store the tapes on end, side by side.

Of course, not all of the above considerations may be relevant for you. You may have a minuscule budget or an unlimited time frame. Still, bear in mind that the better prepared you are during preproduction, the smoother your production will be.

7. Production

Ideally, a chapter on production might tell you *how* to shoot a documentary. But there are various documentary styles, and so much of filming is spontaneous and serendipitous. Many of your decisions about filming will have to be made on the spot, depending on your style of filmmaking, your vision of your film, your rapport with your subjects, what happens in their lives, and your access to locations and events. This chapter can only help you prepare for decisions you'll have to make for yourself.

This chapter is divided into sections on actualities, interviews, and archival materials. But there's much less of a distinction between these film elements than there might seem. The very division between actuality and interview makes no sense within certain documentary genres. "Actualities" implies action footage: people going about their lives. Interviews are often conducted as a mode apart, functioning as a slightly distanced reflection or commentary on actualities or historical footage. Archival materials, including film footage, photographs, and sound recordings, connote history, or at least memory—actualities or interviews from the past. But these divisions are continually fractured by filmmakers (and sometimes film subjects). As you're filming, say, two bakers taking the morning bread out of the oven, they might all of a sudden begin talking about various doughs and the temperatures at which they rise. And if the dialogue was in any way (wittingly or unwittingly) provoked by the camera, then it is in fact as close to being an interview as it is to unadulterated "actuality." Likewise, you could use archival footage not to illustrate the historical past *per se* but as a counterpoint to reminiscence set in the present. So as you read this chapter, don't think of actualities, interviews, and archival materials as radically different in kind. They're divided into separate sections here for the sake of simplicity, but in your filmmaking style you could call into question the very distinctions between them. You could do this either by parodying them by pushing them to their limits, or, like observational filmmakers, by shooting in such a style that your footage does not fit neatly into any of these categories.

◀ FIGURE 54 The Flahertys on location at Avery Island during the production of *Louisiana Story* (1948).

When you're shooting pictures of events, it's like playing ping pong. . . .
[Y]ou're thinking about where you are; what you're getting and what you're
missing, constantly. . . . You're in the middle of an event; you're half part of
it and you're half observing it.

—John Marshall

VISUALIZING YOUR FILM

Before you begin shooting actuality footage, it helps to have a conception of what you want your film to show or to say. Even if you want to
shoot in the most observational of styles, you have to be selective about
when and where to roll the camera, so it's important to think through
your vision of your project beforehand. During the course of production, you'll be asking yourself constantly what realities you want to depict, or ideas to impart, and what kinds of scenes might convey them.
What scenes are pivotal to the lives of your subjects, and what larger
themes might these reveal? Implicitly or explicitly, you'll have to share
your developing vision with your subjects, your crew (if you have one),
and, when the time comes, your viewers.

Shot Lists

Though few documentary filmmakers storyboard their productions as
rigorously as fiction filmmakers, it may help to compose lists of hypothetical shots (see "Storyboarding" in chapter 3). This helps you visualize different possibilities. Documentary is a constant process of revision and improvisation as life always exceeds your expectations. As soon
as you shoot one scene, you have to imagine others that could come
together around it, whether contextualizing it or developing it further.
So long as you treat your shot (or sequence) lists as revisable, they'll
facilitate your ongoing reconceptualization of your film's structure. If
you have a shot list for a specific location, be sure to revise it the morning of your shoot—the weather may be different, the people you'd anticipated being there may not all have turned up, and so on. If you're
working with a separate camera operator, it's best to compose the shot
list together.

Crew Dynamics and Communication

Filming with a crew is very different from going it alone. If you have a crew, you need to be alert to group dynamics. Film production is stressful, and conflict within the crew common. Consider showing the crew your treatments, as you'll get the benefit of their feedback, and the whole venture will be more collaborative. Solicit their suggestions for shots and scenes. Production meetings, and screening and evaluating dailies together in the evening, can also maintain the coherence of the team, and ultimately of the film. Encouragement, of course, is usually more constructive than criticism.

Before you start shooting, you should develop a system of signals for communicating with each other. Most directors, camera operators, and sound recordists have a series of subtle hand or facial signals to say "Roll film," "Are you shooting?" "Cut," "Move in," "Pan right," "Zoom out," "There's a sound/image/technical problem," and so on. The more experience you have working together, the more codified and automatic this will become. If possible, have the camera operator and sound recordist practice recording together beforehand. If the director is not the camera operator, they too will need to be in tune with each other. The best partnerships occur when the director and camera operator have a similar aesthetic sense: the director can then ask the camera operator to shoot certain *kinds* of shots (in terms of content and form), and not have to specify each one, or always look through the viewfinder him- or herself.

NOT DIRECTING YOUR SUBJECTS: ACTION AND REACTION

If you're shooting in a loose observational style, you will want your subjects to direct themselves, so to speak, rather than to be directed by you. But how exactly should you present yourself to your subjects in order to ensure that this will be so? It can be difficult to translate what your film is about, even if you're fluent in their language. Often it will only become clear to you (as well as your subjects) as you go along. Screening rushes usually tells your subjects more than anything else, though it may also make some people more self-conscious than they already were. And screening rushes doesn't help you explain your presence to people at the outset. If you say that you're there to make a film about, say, their "neighborhood," their "lives," or even something as specific as an upcoming wedding ceremony or a day in the life of a bartender, won't your subjects start to reflect on themselves and their lives in a way that they otherwise wouldn't? The answer is yes: if people realize they're being filmed, they become, willy-nilly, actors and accomplices.

What then, in the name of naturalism, can you say to your subjects? Many documentary textbooks and film school instructors urge you to tell them not to look into the camera. Your first inclination might be to suggest they just be themselves, do what they ordinarily do, or simply "act natural!" The problem with this is that few scenes looks more *un-natural* than nonprofessional actors acting as if they were not acting. How many people spend their days in front of a film crew desperately trying to act normally (wondering what *is* normal, and what would *seem* normal to you), or pretending that there isn't a camera and camera operator two feet from their face? In fact, as soon as you suggest to your subjects that they do anything at all (or, equally, that they *not* do something), they'll start tailoring their behavior for the camera. A remark as apparently innocuous as "Hang on a moment before walking down that alley, the camera's not rolling yet" may have a profound if subtle effect, reorienting your subjects *to turn to you to direct their lives*. Once people start looking to you for what to do next, it may be too late to revert to a non-interventionist style. Clearly, then, you need to be circumspect about this from the outset.

Documentaries in which subjects *never* acknowledge the camera are suspect: the intimacy they convey is likely to be false. While they're actually shooting, some hard-line observational filmmakers try to insinuate themselves into a position of insignificance or indifference: they try to get their subjects to forget that they're there. But there are few situations where this is likely to happen absolutely of its own accord. Oddly enough, this attempt not to intervene allies "pure" observational films with the classic documentaries they were reacting against, where the incriminating frames when the camera was acknowledged were consigned to the cutting room floor. Very different as they are, both styles seek to deny the effects of the camera in the scenes it records. Vérité takes a more open approach. It recognizes that the camera acts in part as a catalyst of the action it's recording. But even so, as a spectator it's almost impossible to tell precisely how the camera changed things. Even with Vérité, a lot of circumstances happen both outside the frame and before and after the camera is rolling. Sometimes a scene was staged and you just can't tell; other times a scene seems staged that wasn't.

The fact is, then, that you *are* there, and why should your encounter with your subjects be hidden from the film when it's actually at its core? Bringing yourself into your film need not be obtrusive or narcissistic. If you're not deliberately directing your subjects' actions, the chances are that, much of the time, they really will forget about you. After all, they have their lives to get on with, and your novelty value will soon wear off. You need to think about this carefully: what kind of interaction do you wish to have with your subjects? And how will you hide it or show it in the film? Some filmmakers (like the MacDougalls and Gary Kildea) tend to draw attention to their presence at the outset of their films, and then allow the camera to be a focal point of the action only occasionally—when invited by the subjects, or when the filmmakers want to ask a question.

Of course most films want to depict something more, or other, than an isolable and all-consuming filmmaker-subject encounter. There's a difference between having people pretend that your camera isn't there and giving them enough time to become comfortable with it. In fact, subjects usually take their cue from filmmakers: if you act as if what you're doing is no big deal, your subjects will probably follow suit and forget about you. If your method is largely non-interventionist, it helps to let prospective participants get used to you and your equipment before starting shooting. Allan King had his cinematographer carry around an empty camera for weeks in a school for emotionally disturbed children in Toronto before shooting *Warrendale* (1966). This kind of preparation is common among observational filmmakers, for whom the equipment may be produced as an integral part of their identity.

You'll also find that people are less self-conscious about the camera when they're doing something that's more exciting than you are. As philosopher-filmmaker Edgar Morin has noted (just a little optimistically), "Whenever there is a pole of interest or feeling stronger than the camera, the latter ceases to disturb the phenomenon."[1] It's much easier to shoot a crowd scene or a communal, ceremonial ritual without bringing all action to a grinding (or giggling) halt than it is to film a couple

STAGES OF FILMMAKING

talking quietly in a café. "Just be natural" is hardly likely to have the desired effect on the couple in question. The intrusiveness of our presence, just like the intensity or sociality of human behavior, extends over a continuum, and it's disingenuous for us to pretend otherwise in our films.

DIRECTING YOUR SUBJECTS:
REENACTMENT AND AUTHENTICITY

At the other end of the spectrum, some filmmakers choose to stage part or all of their films. They do this for both formal and material reasons—to foreground the ineluctable fictionalizing of filming or to portray events that would be inaccessible to a documentary camera. Directors of docudramas usually justify their reconstructions on one of two grounds. In intimate or secret settings, they may feel that a camera would be so alien an intrusion that filming would destroy the nature of what they were seeking to record. Or else they may suppose that the subject itself is inherently out-of-bounds to documentary—being set in the past or in an area of civil unrest.

Staging is not a cut-and-dried matter. Accepting the subjectivity of filming doesn't mean that you have to shrug your shoulders, give up on documentary, and embrace fiction. (The *docu-* of docudrama, after all, makes a claim for its firm foundation in fact.) But it does mean that, as we make our films, we should be sensitive to the flow between fact and fiction. Some staging is inevitable: as noted above, you affect events by your very presence. Staging is also multiform: events can be set up in many different ways, and to different degrees. You can ask someone to repeat a crucial line at the end of the day because it wasn't quite intelligible when you recorded it earlier. You can introduce two people who might otherwise never have met, and film what happens. Or you can spend weeks staging an entire scene of a docudrama.

Thus there's no need to outlaw, or even minimize, staging. Some filmmakers feel strongly that the observational "gaze" is unreciprocal and objectifying, and only feel comfortable filming human subjects if they can transform them into self-conscious filmic actors—and shoot them in a style that obviously shows them to be such in the film itself. Whether these newfound actors are, in the end, any more self-conscious about their own role in your film, and whether they are any more empowered than people who are filmed unawares or who are confidently nonchalant about the camera, remains a moot point. Whatever your position, it is a challenge to leave the nature of your interactions with your subjects implicitly visible in the film itself. In other words, to reveal, to the best of your knowledge, how events and scenes have been contrived, converted, and changed for the camera. How you might do this will depend on your own aesthetics and ethics.

Many of the problems of staging lie in how it is done. It usually works worst when filmmakers try to disguise it. When we arrived in the Ivory Coast to shoot *In and Out of Africa,* we hoped to film Gabai Baaré as he bought art objects in the rural hinterland. But we found to our dismay that he'd already done most of his buying. As he put it, he wanted to be free for our filming! Since we wanted to shoot his bargaining techniques, we asked him to buy a few more things. This request resulted in what are probably the most leaden and artificial scenes in the entire documentary. To a sensitive viewer, the scenes of Baaré going through the motions of buying are seemingly self-conscious, but we neglected to acknowledge them as such in the film itself.

Reenactments tend to be more successful when their status is not disavowed in the film. Asen Balikci's acclaimed *Netsilik Eskimo* (1967– 68) series reconstructed the lives of Eskimo from the Pelly Bay region of the Canadian Arctic. Shot between 1963 and 1965, the series was set in 1919, before European acculturation. The distributors' blurb seeks to downplay the mediations of the films: "These films *reveal* the *live reality* of *traditional* Eskimo life. . . . A *minimum* of cultural reconstruction was required. . . . [T]he Netsilik families *readily* agreed to live in the old way once more. . . . All videos are in *color,* with the *natural* sounds of the region." [2] The wording hints that the filmmakers feel ambivalent about the authenticity of reconstruction: they admit that they did it, but seem to wish that they didn't have to, that they had original footage from 1919. Despite this ambivalence, the films do an extraordinary job of humanizing the Eskimo to an exotic North American and European audience, in large part due to the sensitive cinematography of Robert Young.

Rather than feeling embarrassed about moments of staging and whole scenes of reenactment, you can also draw attention to them or set them off stylistically from the rest of film. David Achkar's *Allah Tantou*

STAGES OF FILMMAKING

(1991) is a documentary hybrid about his father, who was imprisoned and secretly executed by his Guinean government in 1971. The film combines newsreels and home movies with dramatized prison scenes (over which we hear letters written at the time but never received). The dramatizations are never disguised, and far from evoking the full extent of his prison experience, call attention to its filmic *absence,* its virtual unrepresentability.

Reenactments do pose problems of their own. As much as observational footage set in the present, reenactments can distort and mislead. The more stylized they are, the more ambiguous they're liable to be. Is an actress reciting the actual words of an historical subject, or do her words represent the filmmaker's ironic commentary? Or is she switching between different voices from one phrase to the next? It may be difficult to know. Indeed, the filmmaker may not want you to be able to tell: the confusion may be part of the point. Just as a viewer of a Vérité film has no sure way of knowing exactly how things were influenced by the camera, a viewer of a dramatized reenactment has no insider knowledge of the status of its different filmic elements.

You may even want to play with prevailing codes of authenticity in order to challenge viewer assumptions about veracity. For instance, the interviews in Trinh Minh-ha's *Surname Viet Given Name Nam* (1989) and the reenactments in Errol Morris's *The Thin Blue Line* are both highly stylized, clearly drawing attention to their orchestration by the filmmaker. But it is only some way into *Surname Viet* that it becomes clear that Trinh's interviewees, who've spent as much time on the edge of and outside the frame as they have within it, are Vietnamese women in the U.S., standing in for indigenous Vietnamese in Vietnam. *The Thin Blue Line* overlays multiple and conflicting testimonials with multiple, conflicting, and highly "unrealistic" reenactments.[3] Reenactment is used here, not to recreate an original that never was, but to highlight its uncertainty.

Reenactments, then, raise issues of both style and substance. Whether you intend to maximize or to minimize your own directorial role in the act of filmmaking, if you choose to reveal your provocations, interventions, and reenactments for what they are, you can do so in subtle as well as stylized ways. You can leave your questions in the sound track, you can appear on frame, you can allow people to talk among themselves about the effects of your presence, you can leave a shot in the film even though someone glances at the camera, you can even ask someone to gaze at the camera so openly that they couldn't be seen as being anything but self-conscious, and so on. None of these ways solves the problems of subjectivity and objectivity once and for all, but they're all efforts at disclosing the nature of the encounter between yourself and your subjects. And for that, they're valuable.

WHEN AND WHAT TO SHOOT

> The salesman would knock on the door, and I would have to make a judgement then and there whether to start filming at that moment—which I did sometimes—or whether to put the camera down. Then maybe he would start chatting, and I would be filming. Then, not so long after that, Paul or Raymond [one of the salesmen] would introduce us by name and we would usually explain why we were there.
>
> —Albert Maysles, on shooting the Direct Cinema film *Salesman*

Whether you have a strict shooting schedule structured around key events, or are hoping to film more informally, it's difficult to be sure when and what to shoot. After all, you can't shoot everything. It's too expensive; what's more, you'll go crazy in the editing room if you have too much footage. And if you don't want your film to be a series of unmotivated images strung together by a voice-over, you'll have to think hard about what kinds of behavior reveal the personalities of the participants and how they do so.

Often your decision about what actions or interactions are significant must be made on the spot. So it's important to stay on the ball even when your camera's off. Hart Perry, the cameraman of *Harlan County, USA*, says that he "watched behavior, nuances of behavior, and tried to be aware of scenes as they developed."[4] Learning to look is an art in itself. Even if you end up *not* shooting something, spending time informally with your subjects can solidify your relationship and otherwise be illuminating.

Comprehensive Coverage

Whatever your shooting style, you'll be continually making judgments about relevance and expressiveness as you shoot: should the camera stay

FIGURE 55 John Marshall stands on a tree in the Kalahari (1955), to shoot from the closest thing to a bird's eye view.

with one group of people or pan over to another? Should you rack focus onto someone's bored or attentive face or else tilt down to your subject's feet? Should you move the camera to someone entering the room whom you notice only after they're already through the door or should you keep the camera on an intimate conversation in the far corner? Should you shoot through an open window or the branches of a tree? The choices are limitless and continuous.

Where to place the camera and mike as action unfolds are perhaps your most important decisions—not only so that you can "cover" the action as comprehensively as possible, but also because these decisions say a lot to your audience about your relationship with your subjects. Are you above them or below them, close or far away? If you shoot long takes of "whole bodies and whole people in whole acts," you will show more of the spatial relationships, but what you gain in context you may lose in detail and selectivity. What John Bishop says of filming Cambodian court dancing is true of documentary in general: "Long wide shots don't work—too much is going on in the fingers and the eyes. You need close ups. At the same time, you also need to convey the total body and the group choreography. The trick (and even truth is a sleight of hand)

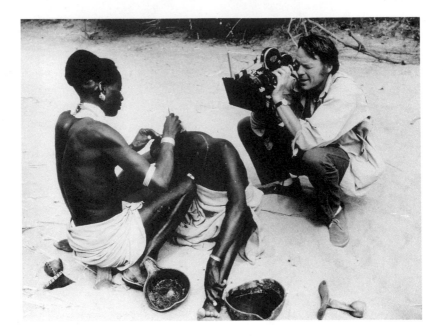

FIGURE 56 For his film *Rivers of Sand* (1974), Robert Gardner gets in close to film one Hamar man dressing the hair of another. Note that he is resting both his elbows on his knees for balance.

is to shoot so that the artistry and aesthetic is that of the dancers and not the gambit of the filmmaker."[5]

Getting in close may be embarrassing, especially for a shy and retiring anthropologist who has spent years cultivating fragile relationships, but it's almost essential if your images are to come alive. David Wason, series producer for Granada's Disappearing World, has this to say:

> Many anthropologists squirm (at first) when they see our cameramen getting *in* there, but they normally like the results! So, anthropology aside, if a group of people is dancing, film them from without, sure, but get in there too, and don't be afraid of looking a fool. Squat down and film their ankles as they dance towards you. Climb a tree for a top shot. I've personally never known the subjects of our films to be offended by our techniques, although it may well be that it is because they know we are "doing our job," and I suppose they may feel differently if the person they have known as an anthropologist starts doing it.[6]

A handheld mobile ("first-person") camera usually does a better job at combining both close-ups and contextual shots than a ("third-person") camera mounted on a tripod, so long as you can hold it still enough. As a rule, keep zooming to a minimum (Wason recommends pumping glue into your zoom control!) and work toward the wide-angle end of your lens—the picture will be more alive, and your unstable holding will be a lot less evident. Practice treating your shoulders as an autonomous suspension system. (If you're using a small camcorder, David MacDougall suggests simply taping a brick to it to help with the balance.)

Cinematic Conventions

Almost all documentaries, even the most experimental of them, follow some of the norms of continuity editing, so you need to remind yourself what they are. As we emphasized in chapter 3, you will probably want to shoot so that the editor can maintain a consistent screen direction (i.e., by not crossing the axis in a disorienting manner, or by getting a shot along the axis that will allow the editor to cross over it in the cutting room). Likewise, whenever it makes sense, let your subject enter or leave the frame: this provides immediate editing possibilities, and eliminates the need for so many cutaways. If someone leaves the frame and you cut to the same character elsewhere, many audiences will read that as a time lapse, not as a jump cut. If your film comes together around a main character (or two), you may want to shoot them closer, so that they'll be more recognizable to your audience. This is especially important if you're not controlling or directing their actions, and you're shooting them over a number of days, as they probably won't always be wearing the same clothes (making them harder to identify on-screen). Be sure to change the image size whenever appropriate: an audience may read a close-up of someone followed by another close-up of the same person as a jump cut, but will accept either a cut to a close-up of someone else or a cut to a long shot of the same person. Remember that movement within the frame, especially to and from the camera, adds a sensation of depth and space to your two-dimensional screen.

It's a good idea to shoot long. This ensures you don't shut down before a poignant ending. You can cut the beginning and end off a shot in the editing room, but you can't re-create them. Shooting long may also help you cut on movement, overlapping action from one shot to the next. In unstaged documentary, you need to be constantly on the lookout for possible transitions, for ways of condensing real-time action, and for how you can match spatial relationships between adjacent shots. As you shoot, consider the following: What shots might work well together? How could one motivate the next? Are your camera movements motivated by the content of the images? What do moving shots tell us that still shots don't? If you envisage employing parallel editing (cross-cutting between different scenes) at all, you should shoot accordingly: it could be too late if you wait till the cutting room. But will parallel action be consistent with the style of the rest of the film? Do you want it to be?

Most documentary uses establishing shots, master shots, close-up re-action shots and cutaways to some degree. Be sure to shoot as many of them as you need. But don't let this prevent you from concentrating on the actions and interactions that seem to you most significant. If you feel you need an establishing shot, for instance, you may be able to shoot it after having shot the heart of a scene. Cutaways too should be motivated in some way, and if you shoot them beforehand you may find they're irrelevant to a scene once you come to edit it.

Most importantly of all, don't shoot *only* with the editing room in mind. As far as possible, shoot in a way that embodies your instinctive response to your subject. As Direct Cinema filmmaker Albert Maysles says:

> I don't think in terms of actions and reactions. I don't think in technical terms at all, but rather of what I really want to get, and what I really want to get is a front head-on look at the person who is talking at the time. I'm not thinking of an artistic shot or an artistic composition of shots, though that's important. I suppose that approach makes the editing more difficult, but I feel that it is one of the reasons why the human content of the film [*Salesman*] is so strong and so totally convincing, because my concentration is on what I feel I have to get of the person rather than some artistic thing I have to prove.[7]

Finally, don't forget that even at the end of the globalizing twentieth century, cinematic conventions, continuity-cutting included, are still culturally relative. A scene that may seem amateurish in its camerawork or sound recording to one community (say, to mainstream "Western" cinemagoers) may set off quite a different series of resonances for another (say, its subjects). Figuring out who your audiences are and filming accordingly is an elaborate endeavor in any cross-cultural context. Writing from the vantage point of an outsider, Eric Michaels gives the example of *Coniston Story,* a video made by the Warlpiri-Australian, Francis Jupurrurla, in 1985. The video records an oral narrative by an old man about a massacre of Warlpiri by Australian police that he witnessed in 1939. When watching the video, says Michaels,

> one is struck by the recurrent camera movement, the subtle shifts in focus and attention during the otherwise even, long pans across the landscape. The superficial conclusion is that we are seeing the effects of "naive" camerawork: the preference for landscape is a preference for things that don't move, and are easily photographed: the shifts in focus and direction seem evidence of a simple lack of mechanical skills. Jupurrurla denies this. When asked, he provided a rationale suggesting a meaning in everything his camerawork does. The pans do not follow the movement of the eye, but movements of unseen characters—both of the Dreamtime and historical—which converge on this landscape: "This is where the police trackers came over the hill," "that is the direction the ancestors come in from. . . . " Shifts in focus and interruptions in panning pick out important places and things in the landscape, like a tree where spirits live or a flower with symbolic value. The camera adopts technical codes to serve a predetermined system of signification.[8]

The point here is not really that the pans, and other aspects of filmic style, "do not follow the movement of the eye," but that they follow the movement of *some* eyes—Jupurrurla's, perhaps the old Japangardi narrator's, or even, at a stretch, the Warlpiris'—but not of *others*—those of non-Warlpiris. This example shows that as you develop your own style, you implicitly position yourself in relation to both your subjects and your spectators, and demand more or less (insiders') contextual knowledge to make sense of your mise-en-scène. You have to ask yourself what and whom you are making your film for. How restrictive you want or need to be in your style is up to you.

Practically speaking, the sound recordist tries to do two things during production: (1) record as high quality (clean and comprehensible) a sync sound track as possible; and (2) record plenty of wild ambience and possible "effects" in order to disguise cuts and improve imperfections. With video in particular, where the two tracks are often just tweaked in the on-line edit, getting good sound is crucial. Here are some guidelines.

Try to record sync sound for all actions that you shoot. It's difficult and time-consuming to reconstruct sound during the editing. With cross-cultural films this is especially important as the significance of many sounds may partly elude you. As Allison Jablonko found out when editing a film about the Maring of New Guinea, "There are some Maring activities in which the coordination of sound and movement is so totally different from anything in our own culture, that there is no way of constructing verisimilitude."[9]

As mentioned in chapter 4, the recorded sound typically duplicates as far as possible the perspective of the camera. This requires a degree of coordination between the camera operator and sound recordist. A good sound recordist always has an eye on the focal length of the lens. Normally the sound recordist follows the camera operator's cue, although if the recordist is also the director the roles may be reversed. This doesn't mean that you need to stand on top of each other. In order to get the cleanest possible sound, the recordist stands close to the action, just outside the frame.

If you're shooting video it can be critical for the camera operator to follow the cue of the sound recordist. This is because whenever the camera stops, the sound track will be cut too. Whenever you need continuous sound (from musical performances to interviews), the camera should keep on recording, even if the camera operator is sure that the visuals won't make it beyond the editing room. (This could be a good time to shoot cutaways.)

Remember also to record wild sound. This should include a variety of sounds for each activity and location, not only while shooting but also at other times of the day. Record also at least a minute of "ambience" (see "Ambience" in chapter 4) in every space at every shoot, as well as any unusual noise that suddenly intrudes. If you're shooting film, the sound person can get wild sound on their own. If you're shooting video, you'll need to keep the camera running in order to record the sound on tape.

INTERVIEWS

Documentary dialogue ranges from scrupulously staged and scripted interviews to the impromptu prattle of daily life. The degree of formality, of remove from ordinary conversation, will depend on your filmmaking style. This section addresses structured interviews; the filming of more informal speech is considered below in the section "Informal Dialogue." Each puts into play a different relationship between filmmaker and subjects, and produces a different viewing experience. So it's important to read both sections before deciding on your own approach.

When many filmmakers think of interviews they think of talking heads. And what, they suppose, could be duller than that? Interviews can no doubt communicate complicated verbal information without resorting to voice-over narration, but isn't such information more textual and conceptual than it is cinematic? As French film historian Gabriel Marcel argued, "Let us imagine that I would make a professor of philosophy at the Sorbonne appear in a film. Of course, nothing will prevent me from having him discuss the doctrine of Kant. From the viewpoint of the aesthetics of film, however, this would be a ridiculous misuse. Why? Because the spectator does not go to the movies to listen to explications."[10]

Still, interviews do allow your subjects to communicate their thoughts, if not in their own way exactly, at least more or less in their own words. Interviews can also be used in sophisticated ways to question the meaning of the interviewees' memories and pronouncements. Employed judiciously, they can enrich a documentary. As even Marcel in the end had to admit (if in something of a behaviorist vein), "Most assuredly a historian of philosophy can be a film character, but [only] under [certain] conditions or under a very strictly controlled aspect.

What must be accentuated and thrown into full relief is his comportment in a behaviorist sense, his manner of walking, of sitting down, and with regard to speech, his intonations and perhaps his facial contractions." [11]

SETTING UP THE INTERVIEW

Filming an interview is something like sharing the driver's seat of a car. While you'll want to let your subject speak openly and freely, you'll occasionally feel the need to interject, to alter the direction of the conversation—just as you would in everyday life or in ethnographic inquiry. Most people like to talk about themselves and are flattered to have a captive audience. The key is usually to act like an attentive listener and to ask questions that are meaningful for *both* your subject and your spectators.

Pre-interviewing

Much of the creativity of interviewing happens before you film the interview itself. You may want to "pre-interview" possible subjects. This lets you select your interviewees and prepare questions that you know they'll be able to answer. It also helps you establish rapport with your subjects, to enable them to be relaxed enough to talk personally about themselves. When making *The Life and Times of Rosie the Riveter* (1980), Connie Field undertook extensive pre-interviews: "Seven hundred women were interviewed over the phone, two hundred in person on audio tape; thirty-five were video taped; and we filmed five. We interviewed so many for two reasons. First, the response to our press releases was overwhelming. Second, the oral histories were a crucial part of the original research necessary for the film." [12]

There is, however, a danger to pre-interviewing that you should consider. It may make subjects feel jaded and the interview sound (over)rehearsed. It tends also to set the filmed interview further apart from the flux of life than it would already be. And it can as easily make interviewees *not* want to relive traumatic memories as it can prepare them to do so. Any pre-interviewing we've done has usually been very informal, just enough to gauge whether someone would be effective on film and has an interesting perspective on the subject at hand.

Interviewer: On Camera or Off?

One of the first decisions you'll have to make is whether the interviewer should appear on camera. If you're shooting a formal interview, and want the interviewer to be on-screen, whether in the same image as the interviewee or in reverse–angle shots, you'll probably need to shoot re-action shots—of interviewer and interviewee alike, each listening to the other. If you only have one camera, you may even need to shoot the interviewer asking the questions, all over again, once the interview is over. You can also shoot a two-shot of interviewer and interviewee on the same axis, whether hovering around a mike or sitting on a sofa with hidden lavaliers, but this looks too much like a location news report or a sitcom for most documentary filmmakers. If you don't want the inter-viewer to be on-camera, you need to decide whether you want to hear the questions. The questions provide a context to your subjects' an-swers, but some filmmakers feel they detract from the immediacy and sense of presence they're trying to establish for the interviewees themselves.

Choosing the Interviewer

Who do you want to conduct the interview? The interviewer-interviewee rapport will be a function of many factors—among them their culture and ethnicity, their sex and sexual orientation, their age and class, and most importantly of all, their personalities. Usually as a filmmaker-interviewer you try to get close to your subjects, to win their trust so that they'll speak about matters that are intimate to them. But there are some interview styles, and questions, in which it helps to be an outsider. If you're a film crew going in on the back of an ethnogra-pher, he or she may already have established a personal relationship with the subjects. But ethnographers have different ways of gathering data, and some don't like to ask structured questions. If the ethnographer has a phlegmatic temperament, you may not get a spirited enough interview to hold an audience's attention. Many ethnographers collaborating with a film crew will simply assume that interviewing is their vocation, and will be irritated if someone else is appointed. One way of resolving such potential conflict is for the filmmaker and ethnographer to collaborate in writing out the questions beforehand.

Single or Multiple Interviewees?

Do you want to interview people individually or in company? One woman may be effusive alone but stultified by her spouse—do you want to hear what she has to say, uninterrupted, or are you after their inter-action, which may be revealing in itself? Someone else may be taciturn when isolated in front of your camera and a garrulous buffoon among his friends—which do you want to show? Interaction and conflict are the stuff of many documentaries.

Tripod or Handheld?

Will you shoot with a tripod? If you can shoot close to your subject, with a wide-angle lens, you may be able to hold the camera still enough not to draw attention to itself (particularly if you don't have any horizontal or vertical lines near the edges of the frame). Equally, if you actually want to draw attention to yourself as you interact with your interviewee, handholding your camera makes sense. Your subject may also be more at ease and willing to open up if you don't use a tripod—it's an impressive piece of equipment, and tends to alter the social dynamics. If you're planning on interviewing someone walking around (which can seem dynamic or artificial, depending on how you shoot it) a tripod will be restraining. On the other hand, you may want the camera to seem more of an objective observer than a participating player. In which case, a tripod would be a big help. If you want the viewers to be able to concentrate on your interviewees, and forget about the whole interview setup, you should use a tripod. If you want to keep people as well as equipment to a minimum, you could even mount the mike on a light stand facing your subject, and have the sound recordist ride the mixer or recorder levels some distance from the interview.

Location Choice

Where do you want to shoot your interviews? You'll need to choose locations beforehand. Whenever possible you should have backup locations too. Backgrounds can reveal a lot about interviewees (at times against the grain of what they're saying), so you may want to interview people in their own environment. For example, if you're about to interview a football player, his locker room may make a better location than a bland studio. Your viewers would probably learn more from listening to a sugarcane cutter talk about her work if they see her in a field. The danger is that this "constructed authenticity" can look to your viewers as just that—constructed. It's a good idea to discuss any choices with your interviewees, and decide together on which background would be a more faithful representation of their life. For example, if you were going to interview a seamstress who sews at home, you would probably want to schedule a day when there were plenty of garments around the house. The seamstress's inclination, however, might be to clean up. After all, there's a film crew coming and the apartment should look its best. Your own conception of gritty realism may not dovetail with your subject's public persona.

Try to film interviews at a location where you and your subject can control the immediate surroundings. If you're shooting in an interior space with windows, the slanted rays of early morning or late afternoon light will probably be the most visually striking. But since the angle of the rays changes the fastest at this time, the interview could end up being difficult to edit—for example, you may want to cut together a shot in which a shadow falls across your subject's leg with one in which it falls on her arm! You might even have to add artificial lighting at some point, changing the color temperature of the scene. The longer the interview lasts, the more of a problem this will be.

Interview to Edit

Be sure to cover everything you'd hoped for in the interview. It's difficult to maintain continuity if you have to return to ask some more questions another day. This means that you have to think of your questions all at once. You'll also have to be ready to reformulate them as the interview goes along. If you do have to return to ask a few more questions, or just get some pickups, you'll probably want to try to duplicate the previous situation in every way: same place, same time of day (for lighting), same background noises, same equipment. On the other hand, if you want the different times to be legible as such in the final film, or if the passage of time is itself significant, this won't apply.

Since most interviews are edited down for the final film, the ambient sound and visual background should generally remain consistent. For example, if you're interviewing a mother with a child on her knee, and the child leaves the frame at some point during the interview, it will be almost impossible to edit the two segments together without a jump cut. Even bridging the segments by a cutaway is unlikely to disguise your phony synthesis.

Consider also your interviewees' clothes. They may want to dress up; you might need them to look like they've been working all day. Clothes with red or white colors, as well as patterns of parallel lines or small squares, tend to get very fuzzy as you go down video generations. Some documentary filmmakers ask their subjects to wear the same clothes throughout shooting, since dress is one of the most basic cues enabling the audience to identify a character on-screen.

Setup Time

Allow plenty of time to set up interviews. It always takes longer than you expect to arrange your gear and resolve any technical problems. It can be disconcerting to an interviewee to watch a crew fumbling with equipment. Also, it may take a while for some interviewees to unwind, and be psychologically prepared to answer your questions.

INTERVIEW PICTURE

Eyeline

Where do you want your subject's eyeline to be? As we mentioned in chapter 3, an eye-level camera is often said to position the viewer and the subject on the same social as well as physical plane, on an equal footing. An above eye-level camera is said to look down on, and a below eye-level camera to look up at your subject. Do you want to conform to these conventions or play with them? Most TV interviews are conducted at eye-level in an attempt to be neutral. Cross-cultural interviews are complicated, because different cultures have different associations between height and authority, and the values of your subjects may differ from those of your spectators.

If you ask your interviewees to stare directly into the camera, they may look like a newscaster. Most filmmakers have the subject look slightly off camera, though filmmaker Errol Morris designed an apparatus (which he's dubbed an "Interrotron") enabling his subjects to look directly at him and the camera (and so his audience) at one and the same time. You can control your interviewee's gaze by where you place yourself (or the interviewer) in relation to the camera. If you think you might intercut two interviews as a counterpoint to each other, you may want to play with their position (if you've placed a wife toward the right-hand side of the screen, consider having her husband on the left).

Framing

Most formal interviews are framed pretty conventionally (something mimicked famously by Jean-Luc Godard and mocked recently by Trinh Minh-ha). Bearing in mind the "composition rule of thirds" (see chapter 3), subjects are typically positioned to one side or the other of center. If an interviewee is looking to screen left, s/he will probably be placed on the right side of the screen, so that her/his gaze appears to fill the frame, creating a diagonal from right to left. The side of the face near the center of the screen tends to be lit more than the side near the image edge. If someone looks or gestures to one side of the frame, you may want to pan in that direction, either just enough to keep the subject properly positioned, or all the way across to the source of interest itself.

Usually interviewees are framed with their heads near the top of the image. The headroom (see "Headroom" in chapter 3) is greater with longer shots. So if you zoom into or out of your interviewees, you'll have to tilt the camera in the process: you probably don't want them to look either as if they're stuck to the top of the frame or about to sink out of view.

By changing the contrast and content of the frame, you can control distractions like a bright light or a startling picture hanging on the wall that might have nothing to do with the interview. Remember, too, that if you shoot someone head-on during the daytime in an interior space with a window behind them, they'll probably be silhouetted. Likewise, if you shoot an interview with someone outside and there's bustling activity behind them, it may be distracting (it could also add another layer of meaning). Some documentary filmmakers have quite a lot of input into interview settings, rearranging the furniture, even bringing in props specially.

You will add vitality to your interviews if you compose them *in depth*—with a fore-, middle-, and background. Likewise, it's always a good idea to shoot three-dimensional objects (buildings, chairs, people, or anything else) from an angle where you can see more than one side or see them "in the round."

Focal Length, Image Size, and Camera Angle

When shooting the interview, you may want to vary the shot between a medium and a close-up. This increases your options in editing. Some people only zoom, or change focal length or camera angle while a question is being asked, not while the interviewee is talking. It's also common to zoom in slowly when someone gets personal, seems vulnerable, or says something that resonates within the film as a whole (e.g., as a counterpoint to what someone else may have said or done). The zoom focuses the attention and lends significance to what the interviewee is saying, but the move is now so common as to be a cliché.

Cutaways

If you're going to shoot cutaways, you should probably get them just after the interview. Even if you're not sure you can use them in the final film, it's important to shoot them at this time: things will look different later, and it may be difficult or impossible to return to the location. You should make a mental list of possible cutaways during the interview itself. (If it's not distracting, it may help to jot down notes as you go along.) Cutaways can be almost anything—a wide shot of the interviewees' environment, a detail of their hand movements, or a shot representing whatever they're talking about, be it an object, a place, an event, a person, or a dream. (Depending on your editing style, you may be able to cut in a shot of anything with the right significance—something with a symbolic rather than literal or physical relationship to what the subject is saying.) At the time of the interview, consider shooting some of the objects or outlooks your subject has mentioned, gestured toward, or glanced at. Shots of different parts of the room (photos and paintings, clocks and cracks, bugs and banisters) as well as a window view are all common inserts. If you're interviewing two or more people, the facial and bodily reactions of the people listening can add a lot.

As always, if you pan or tilt, be sure to complete the movements and begin and end on a static frame—even if you don't think you'll use it all. If your interviewee is doing something else while talking, you may want to zoom in or shoot close-ups of what they're doing. Some film-

STAGES OF FILMMAKING

makers ask subjects to repeat actions specially for the camera after the interview itself. It will probably look more natural if instead you ask some "throwaway" questions, and then zoom in on their hand movements, and whatever else you might want as a cutaway. If the action is intrinsically unrepeatable or the appearance of an object is being irreversibly altered (say, your subject is sculpting as she talks to you), you'll have to shoot close-ups of her hands during the interview itself if you shoot them at all.

INTERVIEW SOUND

In most interview settings, you'll want to reduce background sound as much as possible. It interferes with intelligibility more than you imagine when you're there at the time. It can also make editing difficult. If there's a loud noise like a lawn mower or even a droning refrigerator during part of the interview, and you try to edit to and from a quiet part, you'll hear every cut. If you can't block out a continuous background noise, record at least a minute of it. If it's variable but repeating, you should record more, preferably a complete cycle. This allows you to introduce it as an extra track in editing and conceal the audio cuts. Unless you have a particular reason for it, you should never do an interview with any audible music in the background (or foreground!): *every* cut will contain an aural discontinuity. Remember, too, when you record ambience after an interview to keep the mike and people in the same position, and the recorder set at the same level.

Outdoors is usually noisier than indoors. A passing airplane, especially, can make sound recording frustrating. If you're in the middle of an interview, you may wish to stop and let it go by. When you interview indoors, try to turn off phones, refrigerators, air conditioners, clocks, heaters, and other appliances. Fidgeting—someone tapping on a table, thumbing through sheets of paper, or simply wringing their hands—is far noisier than you would suppose without the headphones on. Young children are often unable to stay quiet, even if beseeched to. On the other hand, it would be completely unnatural to film in many cultures without there being children around.

You may need to cover hard and shiny surfaces with blankets (or clothes) to reduce audio reflections. Walls made from earth and most woods are much more absorbent than concrete, brick, or steel. If possible, position the mike and interviewee so as to cut out further reflections and ambient noise: try to make sure that your subject is never placed between a handheld mike and a background noise. Remember that it's much easier to add ambience and reverb than it is to cut them out. Some mikes and recorders let you filter out bothersome low-frequency sounds. But be careful not to roll off too much; you can attenuate the bass later but you can't easily restore it. Unless the background level is very low, you're probably best off using a cardioid mike, close enough to maximize the ratio of direct-to-reflective sound, but not so close that you get the "proximity effect." (For more on mike choice and placement, and on how to reduce reflections and the ambience level, see "Microphones" and "Recording Tips" in chapter 4.)

PERFORMING THE INTERVIEW

Interviewer's Persona

It's up to you to create your own persona as an interviewer. Some filmmakers with strong personalities—such as Michael Moore, Skip Blumberg, Ross McElwee, and Nick Broomfield—make a point of highlighting themselves in their filmic encounters. If you're not going to edit out your questions, the interview may be all the more engaging and interactive if you freely express your own character. Of course, the danger is that your own presence will color the interview at the expense of your subject's. A more obviously ethnographic approach (one familiar to all fieldworkers in foreign places) is to act as innocent and ignorant as possible without appearing ridiculous. This naïveté may seem endearing to some viewers and condescending to others. (False naïveté always runs the risk of disguising your own authority.) Ethnographic filmmaker Melissa Llewelyn-Davies asks the questions only an outsider could get away with in her films on the Maasai (e.g., *The Women's Olamal* [1984], *Memories and Dreams* [1993]), encouraging her subjects to reflect on their lives in a way that people wholly caught up in them rarely would. Some interviewers are so timid that they won't probe beyond the surface of a subject's remarks; a few are so laconic that they hardly interact at all. We have found presenting alternative perspectives (whether attributed to others or ourselves), and presenting them solicitously rather than belligerently, to be a stimulus that elicits new information and often a more considered response. Whatever your interviewing style, the more you get to know your interviewees beforehand, the more sensitive you will be to their own (direct or indirect) manner of talking, their sense of humor, and taboo subjects of conversation.

Preparing Your Subjects

It's up to you to put your interviewees at ease (assuming that's what you want), both by being relaxed yourself, and also by listening intently to what they say. Maintaining eye contact, smiling encouragingly, occasionally nodding and raising your eyebrows (or whatever the culturally appropriate gestures may be) are the easiest ways of conveying approval, if not assent. These are all nonverbal cues, which means that your own voice doesn't interject on the sound track. Errol Morris finds that giving cues like this takes up so much attention that he can't concentrate on what people are saying! Still, he finds it worthwhile. As he says of his film *The Thin Blue Line,* "Listening to what people were saying wasn't even important. But it was important to *look* as if you were listening to what people were saying. Actually, listening to what people are saying, to me, interferes with looking as if you were listening to what people were saying." [13]

Interrupting can be off-putting, but you may need to if you're to keep the interview focused. You should warn your subjects that if you do interrupt them it doesn't mean that anything's wrong. On the other hand, the conversational (and even interviewing) style of many cultures involves continual interruptions and sudden shifts in topic, and it may be not only unnatural but positively off-putting if you refuse to reciprocate and *don't* interrupt your subjects constantly. You'll soon realize if this is the case, and adapt accordingly. Either way, it helps to explain that you'll be shooting far more footage than you'll actually use, and that you can easily edit out moments when interviewees are confused or imprecise. Most people are wary in front of the camera for the first time, and if you need to redirect their replies, do so gingerly, reassuring them that nothing's wrong. But be careful that your comments (complimentary or otherwise) don't lead your subjects to start tailoring their words to your desires. Even when your questions are specific, try not to make them at all leading.

Regardless of how you phrase your questions, interviewees are still likely to reply at least some of the time in incomplete sentences that would only make sense if your viewers were to hear your questions. But many filmmakers cut the questions out in the editing room—the audience hears the answers, which sound like statements in their own right, but they don't hear the questions that provoked them. This leaves the answers open to misinterpretation, as they can be taken out of context. Problematic as omitting your questions may be, it continues to be the norm. If you ask your subjects to incorporate the question into their reply, and begin with a complete sentence, they'll usually be able to do so. You should explain why you need this from them—it's not at all obvious unless you're a hardened filmmaker. If you feel that guidance of this kind will interrupt your interviewees' flow and reinforce your role as director, you'll just have to go with what you can get. Try rephrasing the question in other ways, until you elicit a response that you can use.

People often realize when they are becoming inarticulate, and may panic. Allow them to pause (and even, if they insist, turn the camera off) while they recollect themselves. Let them try to say something again and again, until you're both happy with it. If someone seems to be rambling, it's usually preferable to let them finish: you'd be surprised how often people move on to an unexpected and interesting topic. If someone strays completely off the subject you can ask a more specific question, phrased differently, to get back on track.

Formulating Questions

For more formal interviews, it's advisable to draw up a list of questions in advance, starting off with the more general and impersonal and working up to the emotional, intimate, or controversial. This lets you develop a rapport and solve any technical problems before reaching the thick of things. But try not to consult your list too often—it interrupts the flow and prevents you from really listening. Often the process of writing out the topics or questions beforehand will commit them to memory.

Try to introduce emotion and feeling into your interviews—when people reveal their desires and fears, their fondest memories and most frightful nightmares, they're usually at their most captivating. But they're also at their most vulnerable. Only you can decide how far to press with delicate or painful questions, how far you feel justified invading someone's privacy. "The public's right to know" has a pretty hollow ring to it in most cases. Remember, too, that representation *is* intervention in documentary filmmaking—and that it can change someone's life, irrevocably.

Most interviewers tell their subjects in general terms what they're interested in having them discuss—in fact it would be difficult to set up an interview with someone without doing this. It may be an idea to repeat the larger themes you want them to address at the outset. If, for example, you were interviewing N!ai (of John Marshall's *N!ai, the Story of a !Kung Woman*), you might start with saying something like "Okay, as I said earlier, I want to know how you feel the lives of the !Kung have changed over the years. It's important for me to know how *you* feel, how *your* life has changed." Because film is such a sensory medium, it's generally more effective if your interviewees discuss their own ("emic") feelings rather than pontificate in an abstract ("etic") manner about the state of the world—unless of course you want to highlight your subject's particular manner of pontificating, which may be interesting in itself. A question along the lines of "To kick off, N!ai, could you tell us about the effects of cultural change upon the !Kung" might force her to speak in an impersonal third-person voice, adopt an unfamiliar discourse, and perhaps ignore her own experiences altogether.

As a rule, it's best to ask descriptive questions that are likely to elicit more than a yes, no, or other one word answer. If you're going to cut out your questions, an answer like "yes" is unusable—none of your viewers will know what the question was. For example, if you were interviewing a Mexican immigrant laborer (as we did in *Made in USA*), you wouldn't want to ask questions like "Do you come from Mexico?" ("Yes") or even "Where do you come from?" ("Jalisco"). Try to create a kind of conversation, in which the subject can explore his or her own memory: "*Tell me about* where you're from." Or "*Describe* your early childhood." ("Well, I grew up on a farm in Jalisco in Mexico, and . . .") Or even "*What experiences* did you have immigrating to the U.S.?" Not all your questions need be that particular. A question like "Give me an example of what happens on a typical workday" could also elicit an interesting reply.

Another reason to ask descriptive questions is that they provoke subjects to *relive* their past experiences as they remember them and evoke them now for the camera—making the experiences come alive for us as they do for them. The more you let people describe their own experiences, feelings, and views in their own terms, with their own images, metaphors, and circumlocutions, the richer they will be. The process of remembering may make them forget about composing themselves, and what they are saying, especially for the camera. One memory often leads subjects to other memories, and to make connections that may be as surprising and revelatory to themselves as they are to you.

Listen very closely to the language and idioms your interviewees use. One way to convince people to speak in their everyday language, and to describe detail that they might otherwise think is inconsequential (to you), is to incorporate local idiomatic rhetoric into your own questions. For example: "N!ai, tell me about when you used to eat =ubee root and n=a." The more specific you can get people to be, the more vivid they'll be to your spectators; the more you enable them to speak in their own "authentic" discourse, the more your audience will learn about their worldview and values. Imagine what kinds of questions your subjects might ask each other. Suppose you want N!ai to tell you about !Kung medicine. You could approach /Gunda, N!ai's husband. If you see him treating a baby, listen to the questions people ask him as he works. Another technique is to ask people point-blank for interesting questions they might have for each another. You could ask N!ai, "What would be a good question to ask /Gunda so we can learn about his medicine?" You could even invent a hypothetical scenario, and ask, "N!ai, if you wanted to become a healer what kinds of questions would you ask /Gunda?"

Silences in interviews resonate. For the viewers, they let enough time pass for a personal or shocking revelation to sink in. They also allow interviewees to go further into their reveries or prod them to probe more deeply into what they've just said. Many of the most interesting admissions and reflections come after a (seemingly interminable) pause. Often you'll sense that someone has more to say. If you keep quiet, the person may feel obliged to carry on. And if not, pauses can always be cut out in the editing room.

When you feel you've exhausted all your questions, or interviewees seem to be lagging, it's always a good idea to ask them if they would like to add anything. This gives them a chance to come up with their own angles. If the content of an interview has tended toward the abstract or the informational, this more personal perspective may well be the most compelling. Subjects also loosen up at the end of an interview (unless you've enraged them with your questions!). As you shut down your camera, they tend to let down their guard, and if there has been any discrepancy between what they've been telling the camera and what they *really* feel, they may let you in on it. Consider allowing the interview to "close," and make motions of disassembling your equipment; when they regain their normal composure (and so long as they don't object) start up again. What they have to say may be more spontaneous, more idiomatic, and more revelatory than anything they've said in the previous two hours. (Pretending that you are not shooting, however, would be unethical.) [14]

INFORMAL DIALOGUE

Observational filmmakers forego the kind of formal interviewing described above because they're more interested in filming people actually living their experiences rather than filming them talking about them. They claim that the interview, setup and set-apart, inflicts a kind of violence on lived experience. Like interrogation and confession, interviewing is coercive in its own way. Moreover, interviews can contain lies and distortions, for what people say they do is often very different from what they actually do. As Direct Cinema filmmaker Ricky Leacock has put it, "I want to discover something about people. When you interview someone they always tell you what they want you to know about them. . . . What I want to see is what happens when they are not doing this." [15]

There is much truth to this. Informal dialogue often has a density lacking in interviews, and is imbued with the ambiguity of life itself.

Rather than setting up formal interviews, you may prefer to film dialogue in informal contexts, where your own presence is less of a determining factor. And instead of leaving a tripod-mounted camera on your subject's face throughout an interview and shooting cutaways after the fact, you may want to handhold your camera and move it as your subject is talking. You could follow what they're doing with their hands, and where they're looking; you could explore their surroundings, zooming in on other people nearby, and watching what *they're* doing. If you have a good mike (or two), and your sound recordist is on the ball, the "offstage" comments of people in the vicinity can also add a complex counterpoint to what your main subject is saying (if there's a "main subject" at all). This tends to result in an interplay between the picture and the sound that is richer and more revealing than talking heads typically are. The trick is to *let the camera itself roam, discover, and reveal, even as you are listening to someone speak.* A mobile camera tends to mark conversational scenes with an immediacy, an authorial presence, and a trace of the encounter that are often absent in interviews.

Of course, no matter how impromptu dialogue may be, it is always "enacted," never utterly unself-conscious. So, if you film in an observational style, you still face the challenge of leaving your own provocations legible in the finished film. The status of someone like Paul, the unsuccessful bible salesman in *Salesman,* delivering what is virtually a monologue to no one in particular is dubious.[16] (As sound designer Tomlinson Holman once said, only crazy people and people in documentaries talk to themselves.)[17]

As with images generally, you can hint at the status of the speech you record in myriad ways. If you're filming an apparently extemporaneous conversation among a group of people, in which you or your camera nonetheless gets an occasional mention, you can deliberately leave this recognition in the final scene. Likewise, if someone looks at the camera, having clearly forgotten about it, but now reminded of or even disturbed by its presence—you can leave that image in too. If you've arranged for two people to talk who otherwise might not meet, or for two friends to gossip, in their own way and according to their own dynamic, about a subject of your suggestion, you (or they) could acknowledge your instigation in the sound track, in intertitles, or even in the visuals.

Sometimes it may be too difficult to make your effects on the dialogue you record obvious in the film. For if speech seems "unnatural" to spectators, even you may not know why! It may not be that you deliberately directed the conversation in more ways than the film reveals. It could equally be that, despite your very best attempts to record only uncontrolled, unprovoked dialogue, unbeknownst to you, your subjects were still made awkward, and their words constrained, by your presence or the camera. In cross-cultural films, the "unnatural" feel may also be due to unknown or imperfectly understood cultural differences between the subjects and the spectators. Often a combination of these factors will be at play.

There's no sure way out of this conundrum, for it's inherent in the nature of documentary. The challenge is the same as that faced by the ethnographer. It is to be as attentive as possible to ways you transform the world in the act of recording it, and to hint at these ways (diegetically or, if it is your style, extradiegetically) in the body of the film itself.

ARCHIVAL MATERIALS: ART WORKS, FOOTAGE, PHOTOGRAPHS, AND MUSIC

Observational style has been criticized for providing only a fragmentary and synchronic picture of the present. How then can you represent the past or introduce an historical context? One way is through reenactments. Another way (actually as common in observational as in interview-based films) is to feature people talking about the past, remembering their experiences. A third is to incorporate archival materials. Archival materials may be anything that wasn't originally produced for your film, such as found footage, photographs, art works, musical recordings, and written materials, such as diaries or letters. You can find them in attics as well as museum libraries.

As a way of bringing the past to life visually and aurally, archival materials have no equal: they are actual records from the time. They may be combined with actuality footage, with interviews or reenactments, and with music or ambient sounds, to create a multidimensional film. Ken Burns's documentary series *Baseball* and *The Civil War* integrate photos, music, "expert" interviews, and old footage—all used as authoritative historical testimonials.

One problem with archival materials is that they offer only *signs* of the past, not a living embodiment. The truth of historical documentaries is rarely challenged unless they have overt political implications for the present. If archival materials are overlaid with eyewitness or expert testimony, they may be being used to validate what's being said. But someone talking about the past is recounting a story, *their* story. And just because archival materials may be evocative doesn't mean they're historically accurate or representative.

Archival images are inherently open-ended. You'll find that you have as much freedom with them as with all the other elements of your film. They may be contextualized and interpreted in any number of ways. They need not even be specially selected or edited to do so. For instance, in the U.S. government-sponsored *Why We Fight* series (1942–45) Robert Capra used footage straight out of Nazi propaganda films to promote a clearly opposed ideology.[18] Rather than being presented as "the past," archival footage can also stress the uses to which the past is put in the present: how it is remembered, by whom, and why. Some films (like Connie Field's *The Life and Times of Rosie the Riveter* or John Akomfrah's *Handsworth Songs* [1986]) deliberately *re*contextualize found footage, precisely to draw attention to its partial quality.

Even if you don't intend to recontextualize archival materials in a stylized manner—by, say, slowing them down, speeding them up, or changing their contrast—you should still be alert to their "overdetermination." The meanings of images and sounds inevitably change over time, and if they have been featured before in another context, will contain other connotations still, at least for certain audiences. If, for example, you wanted to use the Zapruder footage of the assassination of John F. Kennedy, you'd have to anticipate the assumptions of untold numbers of young viewers who saw those images for the first time in Oliver Stone's 1991 feature film *JFK*. What was originally shot as a home movie of sorts became tragic news footage, and then dramatic evidence, supporting critics of the Warren Commission and finally Kevin Costner's (Oliver Stone's and Jim Garrison's) conspiracy theory.

Though archival materials can be used in sophisticated and evocative ways to introduce an historical consciousness to otherwise predominantly present-oriented material, they will mean different things to different people. Take care, then, to imagine all the possible connotations of your found footage before selecting it.

Among the more general questions you should ask yourself when choosing archival materials are the following: To what purpose are you using them? What kinds of assumptions might an audience make about them, and about the film as a result of your incorporating them? What were the original and/or intended implications of the materials? How have these materials been used in different contexts in the past? What kind of responses (emotional and intellectual) would they have elicited, and how will they differ for your audience(s) today? (It's a good idea to show the materials to friends and filmmakers to see how they react.) How will you contextualize your images? How will you juxtapose your various archival elements? Remember that they have visual and aural rhythms of their own.

Consider also the relationship between picture and sound. Would music add a counterpoint? The laying of period music over archival images to extend their evocative quality—as if culturally and historically "appropriate" music somehow authenticates them—is perhaps the most popular and most manipulative use of all, frequently camouflaging an otherwise incoherent sequence of unmotivated editing. But music can be used self-consciously too. Would the sound of a projector, say, evoke the archival images' materiality, emphasizing their age (and even authenticity), or might it in fact draw attention to their mediation, their status as filmed representations? Might a voice-over add another layer of expressiveness? If the materials are ambiguous, will you need a narrator to forestall incorrect interpretations, or do you want to leave their meaning open?

When selecting stock footage think about whether and how to set it off from the rest of the film. Sometimes archival images are so different from the rest of the production that you can immediately tell them apart. In *Trobriand Cricket: An Ingenious Response to Colonialism* (1976), Gary Kildea and Jerry Leach's film about the hybridization of the British game of cricket in the Trobriand Islands, much of the stock footage is in black-and-white, while the rest of the film is in color. Likewise, in *Night and Fog,* Alain Resnais intercuts black-and-white archival footage of World War II concentration camps with contemporary color footage of an empty former camp, now a tourist site. Some old stock footage will run faster than production footage, or will be silent. (Remember, though, that silent movies generally had live musical accompaniments.) Since a dissolve usually indicates a telescoping of time or a shift in place, it can easily indicate another era. But most archival images are so obviously such that a simple cut will do the trick. On the other hand, you might want to draw attention to the way people in the present remember the past, or to ways that the past lives on in the present unbeknownst to us. In these cases, you may prefer to disguise the status of your stock footage, or to incorporate it seamlessly into your film up to a certain revelatory point.

Still photographs pose their own set of considerations. Since they're static, they're formally at odds with your moving images. If you want to preserve the original nature of the photographs you use—in particular their detachment and stillness—you're best off shooting them whole, and shooting them long. That way you preserve the original frame, and allow your viewers time to really look at them. On the other hand, just by incorporating photographs into your film you are transforming their nature (your spectators can't move on to the next image till you let them), and you may want to hybridize the form further by shooting parts of photos or with a moving frame.

You have a number of options in shooting still images, depending on your budget and the facilities at your postproduction house. You can always stick images up on a stand and shoot them from a camera on a tripod. "Animation stands" can be programmed to perform zooms, pans, and tilts while the camera records. Some postproduction facilities can add borders to highlight or cut off parts of the image. All this can be expensive, and will look it too. Polished moves have a very different aesthetic from observational footage; they look more of a piece in a historical reconstruction film like *Ishi, the Last Yahi* (1992). If you shoot still images yourself, first try out various moves, and in both directions (if you're shooting video, you can run the camera). Since you'll need a little extra at the head and tail for editing, shoot a good ten seconds of video and two seconds of film at the start and finish of each move. And you should always record still shots of each image in case you end up not wanting the moves at all.

SOURCES

Finding the elements you need is like going on a treasure hunt: they could be in archives, museums, public libraries, television networks and stations, movie studios, newspapers and magazines, personal photo albums, private collections, published books, and records. Film, video, and audio libraries can be found in the large cities throughout the world; they'll sell you film footage, video tape, musical recordings, and special effects. Different sources may charge different prices for the same or similar material. Often a private collector will charge a reproduction fee for something that is in the public domain (i.e., is not or is no longer copyrighted) and is also housed in public archives (like the National Archives in Washington, D.C.). If you're working in the U.S. and aren't sure exactly what you want, the National Archives is a wonderful place to begin, containing literally miles of old newsreel and government film footage. If the material is in the public domain, the Archives will make a copy for you and only charge for lab or transfer costs.

COPYRIGHT

In principle, all original artworks are subject to copyright. Copyright laws are evolving constantly, and differ from country to country. Currently, the copyright for film, television, and radio productions in the U.S. and Great Britain lasts fifty years from the first broadcast or public screening. Educational institutions are granted some exemptions. Unless copyright is renewed, most materials enter the public domain after fifty years. Copyright breach is common in the film and television world, but it's illegal. You're obligated to receive permission from the holder to reproduce any copyrighted image or sound. If the copyright holder isn't obvious—and often it isn't—you'll need to do a search before you can assume something is in the public domain. In the U.S. this means contacting the Library of Congress Copyright Office (see appendix 3). Though you're welcome to do your own search, they can do it for you within a few months. At press time, the current rate is $20 an hour, payable by check in advance, along with a written request. (You can telephone a bibliographer to get an estimate of how long a specific search might take.)

Established archives, movie studios, and television networks usually provide their own release forms or contracts. Check these documents carefully to see whether they exempt you from obtaining additional permissions (from people appearing in the photos or footage, and even the musicians who originally performed the background music). If they don't, then you're liable for obtaining them yourself. As a document published by Washington Area Lawyers for the Arts states, "To avoid violating privacy rights, filmmakers should obtain permission from all individuals depicted, mentioned, or otherwise identified in their works. This applies to actors, people interviewed, or the subject of a biography." [19] If someone signs a release form allowing you to reproduce his or her image, that in itself doesn't allow you to reproduce objects the person owns or has created. (We know of one filmmaker who is embroiled in a legal dispute over her reproduction of some artists' paintings in a film about the same artists.) Whenever we've filmed someone's artwork or photographs, we've simply added a clause to a personal release form stating that we have permission to reproduce them in our film. But as with all permission forms, it's safest to check exact wording with a lawyer.

Musical recordings and performances are both subject to copyright law, and the recordings can themselves have multiple copyright owners. If you want the right to reproduce a segment of a published recording (e.g., on a CD, record, or cassette), you'll need "synchronization rights" from the record company *and* the publisher. A lot of classical music is in the public domain, though even here, unless you hire and record your own musicians, you'll need permission from the record company, and possibly from the musicians or their union.

Most archives and commercial music libraries charge a permissions or reproduction rights fee (i.e., with copyright clearance). Rates depend both on how you will use material and how much you will use, and on the nature of your production—whether it's educational or commercial, for profit or not-for-profit, and so on. Worldwide broadcast rights to a segment of film may be as much as $4,000 per minute, while permission may be granted freely to a nonprofit student or educational filmmaker for nontheatrical, nonbroadcast distribution. The fact that you may be a student or researcher gives you no inherent rights or exemptions. "Fair use" laws allow people to reproduce short excerpts of material without clearing the copyright, but you should check with a lawyer about your own case. If you don't have clearances for all copyright material in your film, you probably won't be able to get it broadcast, and it may even be rejected by some festivals and distributors.

REPRODUCTIONS

Most archives will charge you for a reproduction, and will not loan you an original (film negative, photographic image, or audio recording). Even if you intend to alter the footage in any (optical or aural) way, you'll want to start out with a copy that's as close to the original as possible. If you're reproducing footage, you should generally request a copy in the format you'll be editing in. With video you should specify the standard (NTSC, PAL, SECAM) and the time code mode (drop or nondrop, and even what numbers you want to have). With film be sure to specify the millimeter gauge (8, 16, S-16, 35), frames per second, and desired contrast. Editing will be a lot simpler if all your materials are uniform. You may need to time code or edge code your material in a special way that marks it as archival material. Finally, when ordering footage, always remember to allow a few additional seconds on each side of the shots you want, so that you'll have enough material for editing.

PRODUCTION TIPS

Much of your time during production will be taken up with problem solving. Though you should always hope for the best for every shoot, be prepared for the worst.

Be Systematic

Charge all your batteries the night before you shoot. (Make sure you discharge them before recharging them, since most batteries develop an ever-shorter memory.) As you shoot, label each tape or film roll with a number and brief description, including the date and location of the shoot. If you're shooting film, try to slate the head of each roll of film and audio tape with the same information. Take the necessary safety precautions to preserve what you've shot immediately: if it's video- or audiocassette, slide the tabs across or pop them out; if it's film, tape the can up carefully. Before you wrap up at a location, always remember to record ambience, wild sound, and cutaways. If you've written out a shot list, check that you've got everything you'd hoped for.

Be sure also to write down people's names, titles and addresses. If your subjects are literate, ask them to sign their releases when you film them, as they may not be there if and when you go back. (If they're not literate, and you feel you need releases for them, you'll need some other signature identification system. You could ask them to say who they are and that they give permission to be filmed, etc., on film.) By recording an interviewee saying their own name, you'll also know how to pronounce it (you may want to refer to them in narration).

If you have the time, it's advisable to start your transcriptions as you shoot, since this allows you to clarify any confusion you might have about someone's words on the spot. Moreover, the act of transcribing helps you focus in on what exactly people have and have not said, and thus on what you might still want to ask them in a later scene or interview. Transcribing and translating is especially important if you're not fluent in your subjects' language. Whenever possible, have all the dialogue (informal and interview) translated—whether by one of your subjects, a local assistant, or an anthropologist—before leaving a location. (Anthropologists collaborating with Granada Television's Disappearing World series generally dictate their translations of all dialogue at the end of each day's shooting, and a member of the production team then transcribes it.)

Finally, don't forget to thank everyone!

Be Comprehensive

It's important to shoot everything you need while you're on location. Even if you're sure you'll be returning, either during editing or soon after, you never know what will come up to prevent you, or how things may change in the meantime. While shooting *In and Out of Africa*, we made the mistake of putting off most of our interviews with our main protagonist, Gabai Baaré, until we returned to the U.S. We had almost run out of video tape, and were sure that he'd be on the plane after ours. Six weeks later he still hadn't showed up. We started filming a lot of extra interviews with other people involved in the African art trade to cover the sections we had planned for Baaré's voice-over. Finally he arrived, and we were able to make the video more or less as we wanted. But it was a painful and expensive lesson.

Be Flexible

Always have backup plans, locations, and if possible, subjects. Be willing to shoot out of sequence and to revise your treatment and schedule. Don't let your preconceived vision of the film interfere with what happens in front of the camera.

Be Inventive

No matter how prepared we are, we always find we lack something vital on every shoot. Here's a list of some makeshift items.

Lighting.   Just about anything white or shiny can be used as a reflector, to maximize available light. We've used aluminum foil and white notebook paper. David MacDougall has carried around a white umbrella, which doubled as a reflector and a rain protector for his camera. A white bedsheet also makes an excellent reflector, and is compact and almost indestructible. The night scenes in John Cohen's *Carnival in Q'eros* were lit by a movie projector bulb attached to a lithium battery, alligator clips, and a little diffusion paper. We've been desperate enough to use portable flashlights on night shoots.

Camera Support.   Perhaps the most useful makeshift items we've heard of are David MacDougall's two camera harnesses, one set up to support an Aaton or Arriflex and the other an Eclair ACL. They are modifications of a prototype made by the cameraman Haskell Wexler. As MacDougall describes them,

> The brace fits on an old-fashioned pack-frame, or H-frame. A metal arm comes over the shoulder and is adjustable for height and forward movement. It is attached to the top of the camera

FIGURE 57 David MacDougall filming at Collum Collum Station, northern New South Wales, Australia, 1983. MacDougall's harnesses are designed for different film cameras. You could just as easily adapt a harness for a video camera.

(using different methods depending on the type of the camera), so that the camera is in effect suspended in front of your face. It is supported by your whole body. You can have both hands free if you want to, so you are able to zoom and change focus simultaneously, or change focus and f-stop simultaneously. But I think the most important thing is that the brace allows you to keep the camera in a filming position all day long if you want to. Not only that, it means you are not always picking the camera up and signaling every time you're about to make a shot. As far as your subjects are concerned, you're potentially always filming. And the brace gives you quite a bit of stability in hand-holding as well.[20]

Rain Protection.   If a white umbrella is too bulky, pack a white plastic sheet. And if you forget that, try to find a garbage bag at your field site: if you poke a hole in it, you and the camera can stay dry while you shoot.

Climate Control.   Remember that if you're filming in a hot or very humid climate, you need to keep your film stock cool. So long as you seal your cans well, you can store them in a fridge. If there's no electricity, see if you can borrow or rent a kerosene fridge. Failing that, bring along a "picnic" cooler chest. If you have no way of freezing self-contained chemical "freeze packs," you may be able to buy sealed bags of ice to cool the chest down. At the very least, if you keep the chest closed during the day and open at night, the chillier night air will remain locked inside. If you'll be on location for quite a while, and will be sending your film to a lab back home, you can even follow the MacDougalls' example and send it packed inside a cooler chest. Until then, the chest can double as a chair or a table.

Be Determined

Access is always an issue, whether it's to people, places, or information. Varying degrees of flattery, general cajoling, and gall can work wonders. But remember, ethical responsibility rests with you: access may be of the essence, but the ends don't always justify the means. If you're filming in a foreign culture, you're less equipped to estimate when you're in the breach. Wherever you are, if you violate any legal, religious, or social codes, you will (or should) be answerable for your actions and their repercussions. Here are two examples of resourcefulness:

While filming *The Village,* Paul Hockings sensed that the parish priest wouldn't let them film in the church: "Accordingly, McCarty and I dressed in our Sunday best, made a social call on the parish priest to explain our next step . . . and then I sprang it on him: 'You wouldn't want us to portray these villagers as being without religion, would you? Everything else out of their lives is shown in the film.' The ploy worked, and within minutes we had permission to wire the church for light and sound and film the next Mass." [21]

Throughout the production of *Harlan County, USA,* Barbara Kopple continually countered obstacles to filming in public locations:

> In the courtroom? Well, I used to use a radio mike whenever I thought I couldn't be somewhere where I wanted to be, and I wanted to tape it and know what was happening. So I put the wireless mike on a defendant in the courtroom. There was a ter-

rific amount of commotion and confusion. . . . Everyone was getting up and saying different things to the judge. Hart [the cameraman] saw all this confusion, opened up the back door to the courtroom (not being inside), filmed and pushed the film two stops. In other words he filmed from the outside.

In the jail we just walked right in. We followed the people who were going to jail, smiled nicely at the jailer and just walked right through and did it. At the stockholders' meeting they would only let one of us in. Because I didn't think they would let either Hart or myself in I had already miked a miner. So we looked sorry and said, "Oh, all right, we'll just have the camera go in." So I stayed outside, Hart went inside, and we got the sound from the miner.[22]

Keep Things in Perspective

Documentary production is physically and mentally demanding. Unlike writing, an answer is never only a penstroke away, and many filmmakers go all out to cover their bases. This can mean abusing your subjects (intruding into their personal lives, willfully misrepresenting or harming them), abusing your crew (asking camera operators to hang upside down from a balcony by their feet), and abusing yourself (going without sleep for days on end). And far from always shielding you from civil disturbance, your camera may even incite it. The cine-trance evoked by Jean Rouch may magically put you at one with your subjects, but it can equally allow you to confound your film with life itself. So, remember that the world will go on, film or no film.

8. Postproduction

In a sense the whole act of filmmaking is one long process of editing. It begins the moment you start considering a theme, a subject, or a character. It continues with your imagining possible images and sequences, carries through your actual recording of the picture and sound, and winds up when you reorganize all the footage in the cutting room. "Postproduction" is this last stage of editing, but it comes on the back of all the work you've done before. Dziga Vertov, the pioneer Russian filmmaker of the 1920s and 1930s, stressed this foundational role of editing in "organizing the visible world." Conceiving of each film as an experiment in the observing and recording of "life caught unawares," Vertov made a useful distinction between six stages of editing:

1. *Editing during observation*—orienting the unaided eye at any place, any time.
2. *Editing after observation*—mentally organizing what has been seen, according to the characteristic features.
3. *Editing during filming*—orienting the aided eye of the movie camera in the place inspected in step 1. Adjusting for the somewhat changed conditions of filming.
4. *Editing after filming*—roughly organizing the footage according to characteristic features. Looking for the montage fragments that are lacking.
5. *Gauging by sight (hunting for montage fragments)*—instantaneous orienting in any visual environment so as to capture the essential link shots. Exceptional attentiveness . . .
6. *The final editing*—revealing minor, concealed themes together with the major ones. Reorganizing all the footage into the best sequence. Bringing out the core of the film-object.[1]

The first three kinds of editing, which occur during preproduction and production, are more important for documentary than they are for scripted fiction films. With an observational style, which tries to do away with scripting, rehearsing, and reenacting altogether, *editing during filming* assumes additional importance. As Jean Rouch puts it, contrasting a filmmaker to an ethnographer, "Instead of waiting until he

◀ FIGURE 58 Helen Van Dongen and Robert Flaherty editing *Louisiana Story* (1948).

has returned from the field to elaborate upon his notes, [the filmmaker] must try, under threat of failure, to synthesize them at the very moment he observes particular events."[2]

Editing, whether in your head, the camera, or a cutting room, involves intervening in space and time. In postproduction, sequences shot in real time are chopped up and reassembled into a new cinematic reality. You have to ask yourself what you want this specifically cinematic reality to be and what kind of relation you want it to have both to the real world it represents and to the spectators who will watch it. This chapter first discusses various theories of editing in the abstract, then describes the actual principles and practices of editors, and ends with brief technical guides to editing on video and film.

EDITING THEORIES

Since editing involves manipulating space and time, it's not surprising that different people over the years have come up with different ideas about how exactly it does this. Some of the ideas are prescriptive—they say how editing *ought* to be done—and others are simply descriptive, saying how editing actually is done. You don't have to affiliate yourself with any one of the ideas, but it helps to know what they are. They all bear witness to the awesome power you have in the editing room to craft images to say what you want. Since in documentary you're representing historical reality, often dealing in images of actual human beings whose lives you may affect irreversibly, it's important to be aware of this, and to take precautions accordingly.

V. I. Pudovkin and L. Kuleshov

The great Russian filmmakers and early film theorists of the 1920s and 1930s, Vsevolod Pudovkin and Lev Kuleshov, felt that editing was crucial to filmmaking. They noted that a camera recording a long shot at some distance from a scene is quite a passive instrument. It can have a more dynamic storytelling role if is moved around and brought closer to the action. But whereas D. W. Griffith (*Birth of a Nation* [1915]) would shoot a scene in one long master shot, and then shoot close-ups that he would later insert to heighten the dramatic intensity, Pudovkin felt that a sequence should be constructed out of *nothing but* close-ups, each in turn revealing another significant detail. In other words, he thought that films should be composed of only so many fragments, the individual shot being the fundamental film fragment. That, he said, is how narrative works: each additional shot must tell us something new.

Of course, few documentaries are shot in this way. (How many have you seen that are composed only of close-ups?) However Pudovkin's insistence that every shot should reveal something that the previous shots don't is important to bear in mind in the editing room. If, say, you're making a one-hour film out of forty hours of footage, you're going to have to throw out 97.5 percent of your footage! That said, few documentaries tell a single story as tightly as fiction films do. In an attempt to catch something of the gist of real life, documentaries may at moments be deliberately digressive. This means that when judging the suitability of a shot, and wondering what it adds to the shots you've assembled before it, you have to take other matters into consideration than simply whether it furthers a single narrative. Shots can be revealing—about character, relationship, and experience—in other ways too.

Pudovkin and Kuleshov noticed that the meanings of individual shots are affected by the shots they're next to. They conducted an experiment to prove their point. Pudovkin shot a close-up of a famous actor, Mosjoukhin, with a deadpan expression on his face. In one sequence they intercut the close-up of Mosjoukhin with a shot of a bowl of soup on a table. In another, they intercut the same close-up with a shot of a woman lying dead in her coffin. And in a third, they intercut it with a shot of a young girl playing with a teddy-bear. When they projected the sequences, the spectators had an interesting reaction. First of all, they felt that Mosjoukhin was himself *looking at* the soup, the dead woman, and the child. In other words, they thought that the shots were spatially related. Secondly, the spectators felt that Mosjoukhin's acting was simply fantastic; they were astonished at the variety of his expressions. How pensively he stared at the soup bowl, how sorrowful he was when looking at the dead woman in her coffin, how happily he smiled while watching the girl playing with her teddy-bear!

In a similar experiment, Kuleshov intercut a shot of a gun with two different shots of Mosjoukhin, one when he was smiling and another of him frowning. In the first sequence, we see Mosjoukhin smiling, then we see the gun, then we see him frowning. In a second sequence, we see Mosjoukhin frowning, then the gun, then him smiling. Again the audience praised his performance—how fearful he looked in the first sequence, but how brave in the second!

What do these experiments tell us that we need to bear in mind when we're editing? First of all, that the meaning of shots is colored by those you put them next to. Second, that their meaning depends on the order in which they're assembled. And third, that the cinematic reality created by the succession of shots is somehow greater than the sum of its parts. The shots come together into a whole, a sequence that cannot be reduced to its individual components. Indeed the "shot–insert shot–reaction shot" sequence—a shot of someone turning their head or looking off screen, followed by a shot of what they're supposed to be looking at, and then back to a reaction shot of how they're responding to it—may be the most common way that films render screen space subjective.

Sergei Eisenstein

Another Russian filmmaker and theorist of this period, Sergei Eisenstein, turned Griffith and Pudovkin on their heads. Eisenstein argued that close-ups, parallel action, flashbacks, and so on, far from being inherently cinematic, are no more than translations of originally literary (Dickensian, said Eisenstein!) figures. Contrary to Pudovkin, he felt that the point of editing should not be to assemble a sequence of so many fragmented details into a smooth and apparently continuous sequence. Rather, cutting should create conflicts. It should stimulate a series of shocks, startling the spectators out of their stupor. He called this effect "montage." As he put it, "If montage is to be compared with something, then a phalanx of montage pieces, of shots, should be compared to the series of explosions of an internal combustion engine, driving forward its automobile or tractor: for, similarly, the dynamics of montage serves as impulses driving forward the total film."[3]

The fundamental filmic unit, Eisenstein believed, is not the shot, but, rather, what emerges out of their *collision*. By being edited together, adjacent shots generate something new, and a viewing experience of multisensory synesthesia—the putting into play of different senses at the same time. Shots, he felt, are like "cells." They contain stimuli that need to be animated in editing, through the collision of such "attractions" as masses, depths, scale, shades, screen direction, depth of field, and focal length. Each shot contains many such attractions, one of which, in Eisenstein's view, will be dominant—whatever immediately makes the most impression on the spectators. It could be a novel revelation in the plot—the person you thought was dead you now see alive—but it might equally be something quite unrelated to the narrative—an abstract pattern of fluctuating light and dark formed by leaves fluttering in the wind. For a truly cinematic viewing experience, a cut from, say, a long shot to a close-up should not only further the story, or show us a detail, but also change the composition, the lighting, or other visual stimuli. For this reason, Eisenstein felt that long takes—so dear to observational filmmakers a generation later—were boring and unintelligent. Far from evoking the sensation of lived reality in spectators, long takes were to his mind antithetical to true cinema, which makes its points and counterpoints in montage.

André Bazin

Whereas Eisenstein felt that long takes displayed a deficiency of meaning, economy, and intelligence, in the 1950s French theorist André Bazin urged to the contrary that films try to retain the uncertainty of meaning that is part of life itself, and that they do so with long takes, shot with a long depth of field. Diametrically opposed to Eisenstein on the subject of editing, but just as dogmatic in spirit, Bazin decreed, "When the essence of the event is dependent on the simultaneous presence of two or more factors in the action, cutting is forbidden."[4] Eisenstein had celebrated a "unity of meaning" as a potential of cinematic montage. But Bazin argued that this is a truncated, reduced meaning. In its place he proposed a renewed realist cinema. Cinema, he said, "attains its fullness in being the art of the real."[5]

At the heart of Bazin's criticism of classical cinema was an important distinction between "psychological" and "technical" realism. The most common legitimation of editing as a means of reproducing reality is that it mimics our own mental processes. The argument goes like this. Film, unlike still photography, shows us *what* we see (and hear) as it unfolds in time: it is lifelike because it reproduces the sensation of movement. And film editing is lifelike because it reproduces *how* we see (and hear).

STAGES OF FILMMAKING

If a long shot is followed by a close-up, revealing detail that would otherwise be invisible, that is because our own consciousness and attention work in a similar way. When we walk into a room, we take a general look around before our eyes catch on a particular detail, say a (close-up of a) person's face. Our field of vision doesn't objectively change as our attention is drawn to their face, but our concentration becomes selective in an analogous manner. But what kind of editing are we talking about here?

Bazin argued that classical Hollywood cinema is based on a kind of "psychological realism" that is very convincing but in fact false. It claims to model the mind of the spectator (or the characters), fragmenting events in a way that reproduces the shifts in our attention as if we really were present. The standard shot–reverse-shot structure of editing, for instance, lets us identify first with one character's perspective and then with another's, just as we might if we were watching two people have a conversation in real life. As such, when classical editing is at its best, it is invisible, naturalized. Cuts pass before us unnoticed, as we are carried along with the flow of the film. Space is dissected and reassembled by the editor; it is elided and expanded to conform to the logic of a narrative.

However, said Bazin, this illusion of witnessing real events unraveling before us as if in real life conceals a sleight of hand. For reality actually exists in continuous space, not in the succession of fragments that we see on the screen. Psychological editing according to the logic of a narrative is flawed because it supposes that reality has a singular meaning, that it can disclose this unambiguously to us, and that the meaning is determined exclusively by the narrative. For example, if a long shot of a room of people is followed by a close-up of the face of someone in the room, the film gives the spectators no choice but to look where the filmmaker directs us to look. Some spectators might instead, had they been making the film, have cut to close-ups of other people, others to a two-shot of a conversation, and others still to a tapestry hanging on the wall, to the view from the window, or to something that isn't even in the room. In real life, in short, nature does not dictate its meaning to us. If it did, we would know everything! Actual experience involves a free interpretive interplay with the outside world. We all have some freedom to interpret the world as we witness it. Outside the cinema, we are active agents, not passive viewers. Thus, Bazin felt that a truly realist cinema would transform us back into active agents as we try to decipher the scenes passing before us.

Bazin argued that long takes, shot in depth (i.e., with a long depth of field), are more realistic than montage because they go further to preserve the autonomy of objects within a continuous space. The sensation of space and time created through montage is, he pointed out, synthetic and abstract. By contrast, long takes allow action to develop on its own over an extended period of time. They reproduce the true spatial relationships between objects. (He loved Flaherty's shot of Nanook tugging against the seal under the ice in *Nanook of the North*.) Though editing creates relationships *between* shots, Bazin noted that long takes can display relationships *within* shots, and on different planes (close to the camera and far from it). They are more faithful to the homogeneity of real space, and they empower the spectator accordingly. Multiple and shifting meanings vie for the audience's attention. By contrast, said Bazin, the "unity of meaning" sought for by the advocates of montage is really an attenuated meaning.

So What About Documentary?

Although these theorists imagined they were opposed to each other, documentary filmmakers have found value in all of their positions. Observational films would seem closest to Bazin's realist "cinema of duration," since they employ an aesthetic favoring long takes, synchronous speech, a tempo faithful to pro-filmic real life, and accordingly discourage cutting, directing, reenacting, and interviewing. Much of the montage of observational cinema takes place *within the frame*. As Belgian anthropologist Luc de Heusch puts it, "The documentary cinema . . . recovers something of the ancient prestige of the Lumière cinematograph: it reintroduces real time into the metamorphosed time created by editing, at certain key moments when the picture tends to reidentify itself completely with reality."[6] Most observational films have a "technical realism" that is distinct from the "psychological" montage of classical narrative. On the other hand, because they do away with the direct address of expository documentaries, they are oddly enough allied with classic fiction films.[7] Whereas expository filmmaking typically uses images to illustrate or support an argument elaborated in the voice-over, observational filmmaking generally constructs scenes that are internally spatiotemporally continuous. Observational films borrow from fiction films some of the codes of continuity cutting in the fabrication of their diegesis—a credible spatial and temporal world. They also force viewers to make sense of the images for themselves, just as we have to when watching fiction films. However, while observational films use far longer *takes* than most conventional fiction films, they tend to use more close-ups and fewer long *shots*. And insofar as observational films tell stories, the stories tend to be more partial, loose, multiple, and open-ended than those of fiction films.

By contrast, much expository (and even impressionistic) documentary—that is, most of the mainstream—is closer to a montage-based film style, in that its editing makes little effort to fabricate a world of homogeneous space and time. The images can leap all over the place, with little regard for formal continuity, because they are being led, and held in tow, by the narration. The images are edited to accompany an exposition, to illustrate a rhetorical argument, or evoke a sensibility articulated in the voice-over, rather than to tell a story in themselves. But mainstream documentaries tend to be a far cry from the "intellectual" montage envisaged by Eisenstein. Eisenstein was excited by the possibilities offered by sound (it was just being developed in his day), but he insisted that it be used as a "new montage element," as a distinct counterpoint to the picture. By contrast, mainstream documentary typically uses disembodied voice-over to direct the images, to dictate their order and meaning, and thereby reduce them to a subordinate position.

Most ethnographic and documentary films lie somewhere in the continuum between Bazin's cinema of duration and Eisensteinian intellectual montage. One style is not inherently superior to another. (Both Bazin and Eisenstein had an almost Brechtian conviction that spectators should have to work out what a film is about for themselves and not be spoon-fed its meaning. *That* is in contrast to the dominant style of television documentary.) It is up to you to choose an editing style, as early in the filmmaking process as possible, that you feel suits your subject.

CHOOSING AN EDITOR

Some documentary filmmakers, like Frederick Wiseman, Mike Rubbo, Dennis O'Rourke, and (most of the time) the MacDougalls, edit their own films. Others, such as Jean Rouch and the Maysleses, prefer to work with an "outside" editor, someone who wasn't present during the filming itself. There is a case to be made for both arrangements. You, the director, with memories of the process of filming and ideas about what the film should be about, will likely find it hard to look at your footage with the unknowing eye of a spectator, to distinguish between what the images really show and what you want them to show. An outside editor can bring a fresh approach. He or she has an impartiality and a degree of objectivity that you can never have. You may be set on making a film about three people, but a different editor might notice that you just don't have the footage to bring all of them alive, to turn them into fully fleshed-out characters. The chances are that when you first show your footage to an outside editor, their response will be different from yours. The editor may be surprised by things you take for granted or hadn't even noticed—for example, finding someone you'd envisaged as a charismatic central character to be indifferent or unsympathetic. This is why Rouch argues that the editor "must never participate in the filming, but be the second 'cine-eye' [the camera operator being the first]; not being acquainted with the context he only sees and hears what has actually been recorded (whatever the intentions of the filmmaker might have been)."[8]

But even outside editors get sucked into the images, losing their fresh perspective, during postproduction. By the time the images have been assembled into a preliminary "rough cut," the editor will probably be making assumptions about the images, their resonances and relationships, that would not be picked up by a first-time viewer. At the same time, there are some directors who, through a force of mind, are able to look at their footage with a fresh eye, to see it as others would. Another consideration is that, although the director will tend to "read into" the images resonances that won't be discernible to outsiders, it's also true that precisely because the director is aware of a multiplicity of latent meanings that would pass over an outside editor, the director is in a better position to keep working on the footage until the implications become evident. So if you do work with a separate editor, be sure to keep pointing out the nuances that you feel are significant, until they finally emerge in the cut. At some point early on, it's a good idea for the director and editor to show a cut to someone who's never seen the footage to see how they respond.

SEARCHING FOR STRUCTURE

Narrative

The art of filmmaking is often said to be storytelling, and many documentaries do tell stories of one kind or another. But, thinking back to all the documentaries you've seen in the past, you may remember some of their stories more as the filmmakers' (mis)perceptions than as honest and open inquiries into the lives of their subjects. A few films may have story lines that seem organic, as if they were the only stories the footage could have told. Fewer still avoid narrating a story at all.

Narrative is usually defined as the recounting of events, connecting them in a story. It typically has a temporal dimension: the events occur over time. And its temporality lends itself to linear, causal associations. Narrative often involves a sense of wholeness and closure, as well as orientation toward a goal. In this sense, many documentaries have only a slight narrative structure—they're more open-ended than a single story would strictly permit. They often recount multiple incomplete narratives that are not exactly, or obviously, related to each other. In part this is a response to the fact that reality itself does not submit to the conclusive closure that a strong narrative structure would demand: life is messy and in flux, and it goes on after the film is finished. The conventions of classic narrative—the focus on central characters, a conflict-and-resolution structure, a point of view and pattern of agency that is frequently male and culturally dominant ("Western"), and mechanisms of closure—seem too limiting to many documentary filmmakers. They try instead to make films that in their structural complexity mirror the social complexity of real life.

So although a documentary will be tighter (and for some people more exciting) if it stays closely focused on its main story, its main characters, or main themes, it will probably be a lot less reductive if it gives them some breathing room. Including digressive scenes helps create a balance between exposition, description, humor, and reflection, and can make a film more elaborate and heterogeneous. For example, at one point in *Celso and Cora,* Gary Kildea's film about a poor Filipino family, Cora tells a long story about a trained pig they once had. The tale is funny and poignant, but hardly central to the story of Celso and Cora at that point. But it not only provides a little comic relief, it also is an ironic counterpoint to their present predicament (one presumably intended by the filmmaker but not by Cora): once upon a time Celso and Cora had the money to feed their pig, but now they can barely afford to buy milk formula for their two children.

Frederick Wiseman's films (e.g., *Titicut Follies, High School* [1969], *Hospital, Welfare* [1975]) focus on institutions, like schools, hospitals, mental asylums, and zoos, and typically follow a number of individuals in different contexts, not necessarily chronologically. His films tend to contain lots of snippets of different stories involving different protagonists. Dramatically speaking, one character tends to get substituted for another as the film goes along. Their structure has been described by film critic Bill Nichols as being a "mosaic" as a whole, but narrative in its parts, each part with its own internal diegetic unity. As Nichols suggests, this multi-stranded organization is one documentary response to the fact that social events invariably have numerous causes and may be seen as patterns of overlapping influences.[9]

Many documentaries concentrate on relationships between people. Though the relationships are necessarily played out over time, they are rarely constrained into a single story. Ellen Hovde co-edited and -directed *Grey Gardens* (1975), the Maysles brothers' film about Edith and Edie, an eccentric and reclusive mother and daughter living together. She describes her philosophy of editing in these terms: "I was always, I guess, looking for relationships. I think we were pushing in film terms towards a novel of sensibility rather than a novel of plot. . . . The main themes that Muffie (my co-editor) and I decided to go with were the questions 'Why were the mother and daughter together?' 'Was it possible that little Edie was there to take care of her mother, and it was the demanding mother who took care that her daughter wouldn't

FIGURE 59 Production still from *Celso and Cora* (1983), by Gary Kildea.

leave?' and 'Was the relationship really a symbiotic one?'"[10] While observational films tend only to have a slight narrative structure, most share with narrative films a sense of sequential ordering and at least some indication of opening and closure (i.e., framing): a beginning, a middle, and an end.

Sequence

Some films adopt a straightforward, chronological approach—editing events in the order that they were filmed. Others rearrange them to make them more classically dramatic. Most try to build suspense by "rising" to some kind of climax. The felling of the giraffe in *The Hunters,* the killing of the young boy in *Dead Birds,* and the moment when Michael Moore finally confronts the elusive Roger Smith in *Roger and Me* are all clear climaxes to which the films have been heading.

Many cinematic climaxes involve a revelation or conflict. This is usually between individuals (or groups), though it may also be thematic (or "intellectual"). Tension is typically generated by wondering if and how the conflict will be resolved. In *The Women's Olamal* the desires of Maasai women to stage an *olamal,* a fertility ritual, conflict with the men's insistence on controlling events. The film builds up suspense by showing how much the ritual means to the women. At the point at which the men begin to assert themselves, the spectators have been led to identify with the women to such an extent that they are completely caught up in finding out whether or not the women will hold their *olamal.*

The so-called crisis structure of much Direct Cinema in the 1960s is a clear documentary adaptation of this standard fictional structure. Although you can still play around with time within the crisis structure (you don't have to make it strictly chronological), most such films come with an obvious sequence built in. Direct Cinema filmmaker Robert Drew explains what he would look for: "What makes us different from other reporting, and from other documentary filmmaking, is that in each of these stories there is a time when a man comes against moments of tension, and pressure, and revelation, and decision. It's these moments that interest us most."[11] This approach affected not only how the films were edited but also the very topics chosen for filming. For example, one Direct Cinema film depicted a presidential primary between John Kennedy and Hubert Humphrey (*Primary*), another the Indianapolis 500 (*On the Pole* [1960]), and another Paul Crump's death row appeal (*The Chair* [1962]). The idea behind the structure of these films is that personal crises strip away people's public personae, and leave them bare and exposed, revealed before the camera, and perhaps even ready to confess. The crisis structure often makes for gripping drama. However, since most people's lives are not perpetually ridden with crises, one wouldn't want all documentaries to be made in this way. There's also an inherent danger in setting out to make a film structured around a crisis, which is that it may not materialize. As a result a whole genre of "Waiting for . . . " films has come into being (e.g., Michael Rubbo's *Waiting for Fidel* [1974], Charlie Nairn's *The Kawelka—Ongka's Big Moka,* and Nick Broomfield's *The Leader, his Driver, and the Driver's Wife* [1991])—films that try to generate suspense in leading up to an encounter, event, or moment that never "satisfactorily" takes place. Such films evoke the state of anticipation—what it feels like to wait— for its own sake, and tend also to throw into relief some of the more hackneyed conventions of narrative, such as the orientation to conflict and resolution, and the movement (as Kenneth Burke put it) from purpose to passion to perception.

STAGES OF FILMMAKING

Beginning and End

Since life doesn't turn out as neatly as films do, deciding on an opening and closing can take quite a bit of work. Most openings are designed to hook their audience. Many made-for-television documentaries begin and end in ways that independent filmmakers find clichéd and unnecessary. On the other hand, independent filmmakers are not competing with . . . 56 other channels for the audience's attention.

One common opening is to convey information that sets the stage or provides a context for the rest of the film. This often takes the form of third-person expository voice-over, something that many viewers find uninteresting and even alienating. But voice-over, like the opening images, can also be poetic or provocative, cryptic or enigmatic. Trinh Minh-ha's *Reassemblage* opens with these words over a drum beat:

> Scarcely twenty years were enough to make two billion people
>   define themselves as underdeveloped.
> I do not intend to speak about
> Just speak near by
> The Casmance
> Sun and palms
> The part of Senegal where tourist settlements flourish
> A film about what? my friends ask.
> A film about Senegal; but what in Senegal . . .

Rather than trying to explain everything clearly at the outset, you may want to plunge the viewers *in medias res*—right in the thick of it. That way you get viewers immediately involved in trying to figure out what's going on, what the film's about, and where it will lead. This tends to make for a more dramatic opening. *Lorang's Way* opens in a dust storm. When *The Ax Fight* begins, the fight itself is already well under way. *Paris is Burning* (1990) starts with shots of New York by night, moving into a gaudy fashion show within a couple of minutes.

Reflexive openings, or arrival scenes, are also quite common. Gary Kildea's *Valencia Diary*, Diane Kitchen's *Before We Knew Nothing* (1988), and the MacDougalls' *A Wife among Wives* all begin with black-and-white stills of the filmmakers intercut with color actuality footage. *A Wife among Wives* opens on the Turkana landscape, intercut not only with stills of the filmmakers but also with close-ups of the covers and pages of their notebooks. The viewers hear the filmmakers describing the conditions of their stay and their interest in getting started filming. In effect this tactic places the viewers with the filmmakers, in the present tense at the outset of the filmmaking process itself.

Many filmmakers (and audiences) like their endings to bring a tidy sense of resolution. The Maasai women finally manage to hold their ritual in *The Women's Olamal.* Nanook, his family, and dogs bed down for the night in *Nanook of the North.* The !Kung hunters return home with enough meat to feed all of their group in *The Hunters.* But other films are more open-ended. Even if some issues have been resolved or events have come full circle, they seem to want to tell us that, for better or worse, life goes on. Although Cora returns to her husband after a brief separation at the end of *Celso and Cora,* it's clear that they won't be breaking out of their cycle of poverty in the near future. *Lorang's Way* ends with a metaphysical meditation by Lorang as he surveys his cattle and wonders out loud, "What then is life? It's animals . . . or what?" *Madame L'Eau,* Jean Rouch's whimsical film about building low-tech sustainable windmills to irrigate the banks of the River Niger, ends with his voice-over, which is at once hesitant and poetic: "And, in this country where, in the course of time, man has become used to the passage from starvation to plenty, and plenty to starvation, what will become of these windmills, so robust and so fragile? The engineers need three years to come to a final conclusion. Three years to work, but also three years to dream."

Casting

As you edit, you need to reevaluate whether you're telling the right story(ies) and developing the right character(s). If your documentary was tightly scripted around a particular story or character, this may not be much of an issue; besides, your footage may not allow any alternative arrangement. But if you were shooting in a more observational style, you'll probably go through a process of casting and recasting in the editing room. The Maysles brothers' film *Salesman* is a case in point. As the editor Charlotte Zwerin says: "David and I started structuring a story about four salesmen, very much in the order the thing was filmed. . . . [I]t took a long time because we started off in the wrong direction. We spent about four months trying to make a story about four people and we didn't have the material. Gradually we realized we were dealing with a story about Paul, and that these other people were minor characters in the story. . . . The first thing was to concentrate on Paul, and go to the scenes that had a lot to say about Paul. So that automatically eliminated a great deal of the other stuff."[12] Often when viewing your footage you find that the individuals you'd imagined would be your main characters don't have the strength of personality you'd sensed in them when you were filming. This can mean radically revising your film. Ask yourself if your characters have the same appeal on the screen as they do in real life. Dramatically, it's difficult to develop more than two or three characters in a documentary (whatever the length) in a well-rounded way. As you flesh out your characters into recognizable human beings, be aware that viewers tend to take individuals as somehow representative of a group or culture. Of course the notion is ludicrous—no single person ever exemplifies a culture—but you may find that is how they are being interpreted. The more you develop characters as individuals, with distinguishing or idiosyncratic features of their own, the less likely this is to happen.

Editing for Your Subjects

As you restructure and pare down your film in the editing, you need to think about how faithful it remains to your subjects, and whether your editing style is consonant with their cultural style. In particular, do your narrative conventions synchronize with their own, and if not, or if not entirely, are there ways you can hint at this within the film? Even documentaries that are not strictly structured around a crisis tend to use or create conflict in order to generate drama. But some societies and some people may not express conflict in ways overt enough to be easily represented on film. For instance, when David and Judith MacDougall began filming in Australian Aboriginal cultures, they found that the Aborigines' undemonstrative "styles of public demeanor made the representation of character, and identification *with* characters . . . difficult. Direct confrontations were often avoided, or acknowledged only in symbolic behaviour. Real tests of power could run beneath the surface for years before erupting suddenly and, for an observer, inexplicably. Personal success and tests of achievement, as in the stages of initiation, were matters of public reserve or secrecy."[13] In response to this reticence, the MacDougalls tried to bring their subjects alive for a non-Aboriginal audience by using various forms of "interior commentary"—voice-over reflections by central characters, often improvised as they were looking at the footage in the editing room. David considers this only a partial solution, and advocates experimenting radically with cinematic conventions whenever the encounter between filmmaker and subjects is intercultural.

Due to the absence of portable sync sound, Rouch had had a similar problem with *Jaguar*. A fabulous, playful commentary was made up by Damoré and Lam, two main characters, as they watched themselves on screen in Accra in 1957. In fact, since the introduction of mag sound in the 1960s, "interior commentary" has become a mainstay of standard documentaries, which lay their characters' voices non-synchronously over other images. In doing so you put into play a new relation between their words and the images you lay the words over. If your characters' commentary was provoked by their looking at your rushes or a rough cut then that *might* be apparent in their word choice and inflection. But you should be very careful whenever you lay someone's words, recorded on location, over images they've never seen. For in so juxtaposing them, you're creating links and implications that are not of your subjects' own making. In sum, whatever editing strategies you choose, you need to be constantly on your toes about the relationship between the *style* and the *subjects* of your film.

Finally, if you are editing not only *for* but *with* your subjects, you will have to be alert to the power dynamics and vested interests of all the involved parties. Collaborative editing is one way to bring into being a more participatory form of filmmaking. However, you should also think carefully about whether your various perspectives coalesce into a single point of view, or whether you want to try and craft a film that embodies a number of different perspectives. (For more on issues of collaboration, see "Contextualization" and "Collaboration" in chapter 2.)

Editing for Your Spectators

As well as editing in a way that is faithful to your subjects, it's also important to edit with an eye to your audience(s). You'll need to make a number of difficult decisions about how much you need to explain to them, and how much you can allow them to discover for themselves. As ethnographic filmmaker Allison Jablonko argues,

> [P]eople in our culture (including most anthropology students) have minimal time or ability to just watch anything in an open-ended way. Any scene is immediately either "domesticated" by being naively explained as analogous to something in our own culture, or it is dramatized and appears as a projection of unconscious or suppressed elements of our own culture. People only "see" what they already have in mind. To change what people have in mind, so that they can begin to see things previously unfamiliar to them, is a great challenge.[14]

One could also argue that if "people only 'see' what they already have in mind" then that's partly the fault of the film. The best films always get us to see things in ways that were previously unfamiliar to us. Surprisingly, films that are most successful at this are those that do not go out of their way to explain, or to foreclose certain readings—that is, films that deliberately leave their meanings somewhat open. It's more respectful to viewers to let them come to their own conclusions, and make of the images what they will. Anthropologist Paul Hockings says that his goal in making *The Village*

> was to immerse the viewer in an alien culture and leave him perplexed, even shaken, and also eager for the answers to a hundred different questions.
>
> We have, in fact, tried to eliminate the distance between the viewer and an alien subject. The viewer experiences much the same culture shock as would an anthropologist arriving in the field. He finds himself alone among strangers in a kitchen, a peat bog, a pub, a boat, even a church. No one guides him, tells what is going on, or even translates everything said. The viewer must try to put the pieces together himself as he returns again and again to the same places, the same people. Soon, like an anthropologist in the field, he finds himself almost unconsciously beginning to understand, to see patterns.[15]

Although editing is a creative act it is also a restrictive one. You are excluding side stories, cutting out parts of people's personalities, foreclosing certain readings. It is important not to try and make things *too comprehensible* to your audience. As editor Dai Vaughan notes,

There can be few editors who have not been disturbed by the ability of their medium to suggest that a subject has been exhausted. The mere act of cutting a sequence into a coherent shape, the craftsman's compulsion to resolve irresolution and tidy up mess, contributes to a tradition whereby the viewer sails under sealed orders: and the very structure of the film conspires with the well-turned commentary to rob it of that penumbra of incomprehensibility which would preserve its link with reality and encourage the viewer to grant it further thought. Comprehensibility has a way of implying comprehensiveness: and anything that can be told comprehensively in an hour can only be a lie.[16]

PACE

Much of the way spectators respond to a film stems from its pace. The pace sets the energy level, and to some degree the mood, of the film as a whole. The Turkana and Jie films of the MacDougalls, for example, tend to unfold slowly, almost cautiously, giving the audience the impression not only of the intimate and respectful regard the filmmakers have for their subjects but also for the unhurried pace of life in these pastoral societies. By contrast, the lively pace of Jean Rouch's *Jaguar* (conveyed through short takes and the buoyant collaborative voice-over of the filmmaker and the subjects) seems to reflect the jubilance of happy-go-lucky young men out to discover a different part of the world. Thirty years later, Rouch's *Madame L'Eau*, which features two of the same subjects, conveys a similar exuberance, toned down just a little, perhaps because of new technology (sync sound cameras that can shoot longer takes), and perhaps also because of the maturity of the collaborators. One can only wonder to what extent the different pacing of the MacDougalls' and Rouch's films has to do with the personalities of the filmmakers themselves.

As a filmmaker you affect the pace both by how you shoot and by how you edit. The behavior you cover, the camera angles and focal lengths you choose to film it with, as well as the length of takes and the way they are linked together—all these affect pacing. Documentary (and especially ethnographic) films are occasionally criticized for having a slow pace, and certainly they don't move along at the speed of news

STAGES OF FILMMAKING

stories and many narrative feature films. But slowness is relative, and it may be a virtue rather than a flaw. Generally, the content of documentary films is complex, often containing information that may be new to those members of an audience who are unfamiliar with the subject or culture portrayed. Thus, it's important that these films unfold at a more subtle, perhaps even "realistic" rate. One of the most crucial aspects of editing is settling on a pace that will engage the audience, present enough exposition, and be faithful to the rhythms inherent in the events on the screen.

Pacing can be controlled from shot to shot, scene to scene, and through the overall shape of the film. Even if you have a fascinating story or theme, it won't be very stimulating unless you tell it in an interesting way. Usually you want to keep your film moving forward, revealing new information, or at least new ways of looking at old information. (If you tell your audience everything in the first two minutes, why would they bother to sit through the rest?) A film holds the interest of a viewer in a somewhat similar fashion to the way a novel holds its reader's attention. The plot is disclosed gradually, anecdotally in a sense, over the course of the whole work. The excitement of reading or viewing is in piecing it all together. In contrast, many social science monographs adumbrate their thesis at the outset, and then spend two hundred pages fleshing it out.

Pacing is especially difficult in cross-cultural filmmaking, where foreign viewers don't come to the film with the same cultural knowledge as insiders. When Allison Jablonko was making a film about the Maring of New Guinea, she disagreed with her editor about how much of their footage they could cut out. The editor wanted to eliminate a lot of "repetition," believing that viewers would quickly become bored if they were made to watch "the same thing" twice. But Jablonko was sure that foreigners wouldn't learn much about Maring culture if they weren't allowed to see anything more than once. As she said, "From my own experience in the field, I knew that by seeing a scene once, one can do no more than understand it in terms of the 'already familiar' of one's own life and culture." Moreover, she insisted, repetition is culturally relative. "The editor was not able to distinguish small variations in the behavior of people from another culture . . . although he was highly attuned to slight variations of Western behavior in essentially repetitive scripts."[17] In a way, the editor and Jablonko each have a point. The narrative structure of most Western Hollywood-style films is highly formulaic. The "small variations in . . . behavior" are where all the action is, the nuances of personal specificity and cultural resonance. If some ethnographic films seem needlessly repetitive, the answer may not be that this is because they are presenting culturally unfamiliar material to exotic audiences. It may be that they are shot and edited in such a homogeneous, distant, unilluminating style that they don't bring their subject matter alive, or impart empathy in their subjects. If you do end up shooting apparently repetitive action, it's always a good idea to shoot it from various angles, often getting in close to reveal the emotions and feelings of the participants, and then editing the sequences in a different order, or at a different pace.

Cutting at a constant rate can cause the tempo of a film to be predictable and monotonous, and it's advisable to adjust the pacing by varying the lengths of shots and scenes. The impression of fast or slow pace has more to do with the relative degree to which you accelerate or decelerate the pace than the absolute speed. However, pacing is not simply a formal matter, that you can measure without considering the content of the shots. For instance, a shot revealing a new detail or space will need to stay on the screen for longer than a shot of a space the audience has already seen. Whenever you consciously vary the rate of cutting, you should take into account the content of both the picture and the sound track—sync sound as well as music and narration, if you have them. Long takes and slow-moving scenes can be extremely engaging, just as fast-cutting will not in itself make a boring scene any more exciting. It all depends on what we're watching.

CONTINUITY CUTTING

Time and space are articulated cinematically through the conventions of continuity cutting. While some documentary filmmakers try to resist these conventions, most of us still use them, if a little carelessly, much of the time. But what exactly are these codes of continuity? The section "Transitions: Shooting to Edit" in chapter 3 gave some hints about how to shoot in ways that will make it easier to edit later on. Now that you're at the editing stage, what should you be on the look out for?

- *Watch out for potential jump cuts.* Jump cuts are failed continuity cuts— rather than hiding a cut, they draw attention to it. They often occur when a shot looks either too much or too little like the preceding shot. They tend to make it look as if something is missing between the two shots. For example, if someone is dancing in one shot, and at rest in the next (and doesn't leave the frame in the first shot), it will probably look like a jump cut, and your audience will wonder what happened in between.

- *Try to overlap action from shot to shot.* It is normally easier to disguise a cut if it takes place on movement, and not between two still frames. In order to match movement from one shot to the next, the movement may need to be in the same direction, and at roughly the same speed.

- *Try to splice together images that were shot from significantly different camera angles.* If you cut from a long shot of two dancers to another long shot of the same dancers taken from a *slightly* different angle, the chances are it'll look like a jump cut. The images would look too much alike, and there would be no obvious reason to the spectators why you had cut. Remember that cuts should add new information. A cut from a long shot to a medium shot taken from another angle will give your audience a fresh perspective on the dancers' movements. On the other hand, a cut from an extreme long shot to a close-up of something within the same frame may look strange. In any case, the audience may not be able to make the connection between the two shots.

- *Be wary about cutting together shots taken with substantially different focal lengths.* One of the ways that filmmakers maintain the illusionistic realism of the cinema is *not* to vary focal length much, for the corresponding changes in spatial perspective will be evident to the viewers. Vast variations in focal length should preferably be motivated in some way. If, for instance, you cut from a short focal length close-up of someone's back as they looked over a landscape to a long focal length shot of part of the landscape itself, the audience would probably accept the second shot as corresponding credibly to the person's angle or concentration of vision. A more experimental variation of focal length (too experimental for most documentary directors) might, say, employ a short lens for one person's point of view and a long lens for another's.

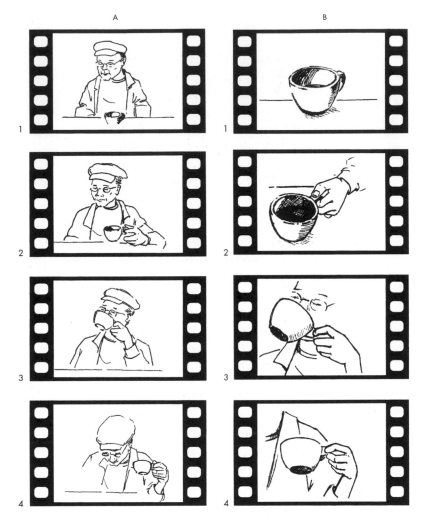

FIGURE 60 (above and opposite) Cutting on Action. Editors often try to cut on action, to make the editing both more dynamic and more invisible. In this schematic example (where each image represents a number of frames), the editor has two different shots of the same man drinking a cup of tea—one a medium close-up of the man (A), the other an extreme close-up of the cup (B). The editor could combine these shots by intercutting them (A + B, see facing page)—taking certain frames from each. In this case, the editor starts off with the medium close-up as the man raises his cup (A1 and A2), then cuts in a brief extreme close-up of the man drinking (B3), and, finally, returns to the medium close-up of the man as he puts the cup down (A4). Well-executed, match-cutting on action passes unnoticed by most spectators.

A + B

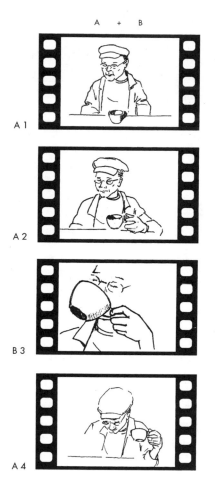

A 1

A 2

B 3

A 4

FIGURE 61 Conventional Continuity. In this example, it would be possible to cut from frame 1 to any of 2, 3, 4, or 5, because each of these additional frames either provides a different emphasis or image size (2, 3, and 5) or else reveals new information altogether (4). On a still subject, a cut from 1 to 2, 3, or 5 might jar, because they are all taken from roughly the same camera angle, but since the subjects are moving here, it could pass unnoticed. Conventions of continuity dictate that a cut from 1 directly to 6 would be a jump cut, since they are too similar in camera angle and image size. It would, however, be normal to cut from any of 2, 3, 4, or 5 to 6.

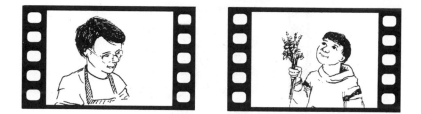

FIGURE 62 Eyeline. Eyelines follow people's gazes, whether they're looking at an object or another person. The cut between these two images makes sense spatially because the woman in the first frame is looking down right and the child in the second frame is looking up left. It is also made easier because the woman was shot slightly to the left of the center of the frame, and the child slightly to the right.

- *Try to match spatial relationships, screen position, and eyeline from shot to shot.* In other words, when you cut between shots featuring the same people or objects, take care that they stay in the same spatial relationships to each other. If you're editing an interaction between two people, make sure that their eyes are looking in the right direction.
- *Try to match lighting conditions.* If you cut from a sunny and bright shot to one that is overcast and dark (and they're supposed to be the same scene), your audience will notice, even if you shot both in the same place within a few seconds of each other. It would jar still more if you cut back to another sunny shot, or to a continuation of the first sunny shot.
- *When intercutting between two shots of the same subject(s), you should try to sustain the energy level.* If someone is animated one moment and weary in the next shot, your audience will wonder what's happened.
- *Try to maintain a consistent screen direction.* In a static scene, this usually means staying within a 180° arc, or else cutting to a shot from a neutral angle before crossing the axis (see "Screen Direction" in chapter 3). If a scene is moving, the axis will move with it, which may free you up in the editing room. The same is true if the camera is moving.
- *Try to cut in on camera movements (like pans and tilts) before they start, and wait till they've stopped before cutting out of them.* Also, you should let objects and people leave the frame before cutting to a still shot of them.

FIGURE 63 Cutting: Leaving the Frame. Most editors allow a subject to leave the frame (whether in a tracking, pan, or still shot) before cutting to a shot of the person at rest. In this case the editor holds a long shot of a bicyclist riding along until he leaves the frame, and then cuts to a shot of him resting. An alternative is to have the subject enter the frame in the new shot or else to cut first to another shot altogether, and then to a shot of the subject at rest. This "rule" of continuity is, however, one of the most frequently breached.

- *Resort to cutaways to avoid a jump cut, if need be.* "Cutaway" was a dirty word in the heady days of Direct Cinema in the 1960s, but you may find them almost unavoidable. If you do insert cutaways, try to choose images that are germane to the scene in question. An unmotivated cutaway will call attention to a cut rather than smooth it over. For example, an obvious way to bridge two shots of dancers that wouldn't otherwise cut together would be to intercut a close-up of one of them, or a shot of a musician, or perhaps even a shot of someone in the audience. Whether these would work will depend on the overall context of this scene in the film as a whole—what docs a shot of a musician or spectator reveal to your audience that they don't already know?

- *Last but not least, don't follow these prescriptions to the letter!* Formulaic editing, like formulaic anything, always looks as dead as mutton.

Selecting Shots

Usually you choose shots because of their content: they reveal information or further action at the right moment. But there are a few principles worth bearing in mind. Unless you want to stick with a particular kind of shot for stylistic reasons, varying shots between close-up, medium, and long shots helps give an idea of a scene's spatial setting. If you cut to a new scene, the audience may wonder where they are. A long, or establishing, shot lets them get their bearings. But if it's not interesting in its own right, or if it doesn't further the story, an establishing shot can be dull. Starting a scene with close-ups may be more suspenseful (spectators must figure out the relation between shots, the topography of it all), but can also be confusing. Typically, when you introduce a new character, the audience will want a close-up of the person's face as soon as possible.

When to Cut

Cuts can be used either to elide or extend time, or else to juxtapose two shots that clearly belong to different times or places. Whether you're trying to condense time within a scene or just get out of one shot and into the next, you have many possible motivations (or excuses) to cut. Cues to cut may be visual or aural, graphic or narrative. A telephone ringing, a car horn blowing, someone raising an eyebrow or looking off-screen, a farmer turning his head to look at the clouds overhead—these are all obvious cues deriving realistically from a film's diegesis. Indeed, spectators have become so habituated to certain cues for a cut that they may be surprised if you don't—which can make *not* cutting very effective. For example, if you were shooting an interior shot of two people arguing, and one got up in a huff and slammed the door, the audience might well expect a close-up of the other person looking at the closed door just after it was slammed. (A fiction film would as likely cut to the person walking away outside.) Just letting the camera run with a long shot of the closed door might be much more effective.

Transitions

There are various possible transitions between shots. The simplest is a cut—a straight and immediate shift from one shot to the next. Two frames from different shots are joined right together, front to back. Good continuity cuts appear to move the story along, uninterrupted, and often go unnoticed.

Dissolves (also called "lapses," laps," or "mixes") are gradual transitions between two shots that momentarily overlap on the screen, as the new shot is superimposed over the old. Short dissolves (of less than a second) are sometimes used in continuity cutting to mask a bad cut. More often, dissolves (of up to three seconds or more) are used to indicate the passage of time—of anywhere from a few seconds to many years. You can also use them to imply a shift in space, as with cross-cutting on parallel action. Unlike straight cuts, dissolves interrupt a scene, hinting at a discontinuity of some kind. They set off sequences of shots, or scenes, from each other. Dissolves are sometimes used to set off dreams, "analeptic" flashbacks, and "proleptic" flashforwards, from the rest of the film (the cinematic present). A flashback takes the audience back in time to an earlier, historical or imaginary moment. A flashforward prefigures the action, either by showing what will actually happen, or what a character imagines (or dreams) might happen.

You can also "fade" to black (or to any other color). Like dissolves, fades tend to set off scenes from each other, but are more emphatic. Fades usually express a more substantial rupture (of space, time, theme, or plot) than other transitions. You can fade out to black and then fade into another shot, or else you can fade out and then cut in, or cut out and then fade in. Cutting to and from black has a similar effect, but is slightly harsher still.

Yet another kind of transition is a "wipe." Wipes used to be quite common in early films to indicate a change in place. One shot is progressively replaced by another, which seems actually to wipe the first one off the screen, either from top to bottom, right to left, or vice-versa. You might recall the whirling bat images from the television series *Bat-*

man which wiped one image off and another onto the screen. A "flip-over" wipe looks like the pages of a book turning. With digital video, you can theoretically make wipes of any kind.

BEYOND CONTINUITY CUTTING

Some viewers find that cuts in observational films often jar. This may be because the filmmaker is transgressing continuity codes—deliberately *not* disguising the fact that the images reflect his or her limited perspective at a particular time. *Lorang's Way*, for instance, is striking for the relative absence of cutaways. Many of the obvious cues—when someone looks off-screen, gestures to something in the distance, leaves the frame, or starts talking about something or someone else—are ignored. The filmmakers are scrupulous about staying with what is in front of them. Initially, because we are so used to the shot-insert-reaction shot style of most films, taken from a camera roaming all over the place with unearthly ease, this may seem constricting, even stifling. However, it can also be felt as liberating, for continuity codes in documentary have a very different significance from their application in fiction.

If a fiction filmmaker shoots a long shot of an actor going through a door and cuts from this to a close-up of a hand on a door knob, and if the editor does a good job in matching the action, the audience won't even notice the cut. The two images would have been shot at different times (at least a few minutes apart), and perhaps even in different spaces (the long shot on location, the door knob in the studio), but when they're joined together on the screen we accept them as a recording of continuous time in the same space. In a fiction film there is no problem here, but used in a documentary such conventions of space-time continuity are more problematic. For example, in Allison Jablonko's Maring series (1963–1980), there's a scene set at Simbai airstrip. But the filmmakers had forgotten to shoot the airstrip itself, so they cut in another one from the Eastern Highlands. Unless you had been to both airstrips you wouldn't notice.[18] This example may seem minor, and most documentaries do this kind of thing to different degrees. But what is going on here is actually quite important. The film's diegesis pretends to represent the real pro-filmic world, but in fact does not: it assembles fragments from all over the place in telling a story that is rather more fictional and synthetic than it seems. In the example above, two separate actions (someone approaching a door, and a hand holding the knob) are transformed by the film into one. In Jablonko's case, two spaces are transformed into one. As documentary editor Dai Vaughan puts it, continuity cutting in documentary tends to efface the pro-filmic "in the projection of a hermetic reality, a closed diegetic world defined only by the narrative which it calls into being to inhabit it and, though masquerading as everybody's world, intelligible only from the standpoint of its narrator."[19]

You can be aboveboard about gaps in continuity in various ways. You can incorporate jump cuts or largely dispense with cutaways. You can also, like Gary Kildea in *Celso and Cora,* splice gray leader between shots. Dai Vaughan once heard an anthropologist-filmmaker being raked over the coals by a colleague for having intercut images of a market stall-holder and a buyer that were shot on different days—making them look as if they were of the same scene at the same time. Vaughan proposes a number of possible ways to highlight the various statuses of different documentary images, and the tensions between cinematic conventions like continuity cutting and the connotation of documentary as a record of a particular pro-filmic reality:

> One [approach] . . . might consist in pushing the received conventions to the point of parody so that, whilst still functioning to articulate the material, they would be perceived in their arbitrariness. Another would be to employ methods of jump-cutting whereby one theme—the logic of an argument, perhaps, or the local narrative of one character's actions—would be articulated as a continuity whilst the remainder respected the discontinuity of the pro-filmic. Where commentary must be used, it might take the form of two voices disagreeing as to the proper interpretation of the evidence. If cutaways are needed, perhaps they should be graded differently or wear different clothing from synchronous shots of people listening, as a mark of their different grammatical status.[20]

On the other hand, it's also true, as Vaughan notes, that once the spectators are confident they're watching a documentary and not a fiction film—in other words, once they trust that there's an indexical relation between the film's diegesis and the pro-filmic world it records—then "a continuity-cut which in fiction would certainly signify a single action may take on the force of a jump-cut signifying two."[21] In many observational films this is precisely what happens: edited loosely in accordance with the norms of continuity cutting, they can nonetheless be read as indicating breaks between neatly adjoining cuts. Certainly this is the case with Edgar Morin and Jean Rouch's *Chronicle of a Summer,* whose editing is otherwise quite conventional. Indeed, once a responsive audience decides that a film is an unstaged documentary, and seems to have been filmed with only one camera, continuity cuts can *only* be read as discontinuous—as cutting out a stretch of time. When this occurs, the codes of continuity have literally been turned on their head.

If anyone ever doubted that continuity codes were culturally as well as historically variable, their suspicions were definitively put to rest in the summer of 1966 by an experiment visual anthropologists Sol Worth and John Adair conducted in the American Southwest. Curious whether the Navajo might have a film grammar unique to themselves, one related to their culture and even their language, they handed out Bell and Howell triple-turret 16mm cameras. They found that the neophyte Navajo filmmakers were most idiosyncratic in their editing:

> The Navajos frequently cut in ways that had people jumping around the screen as if by magic. A boy who was walking toward a tree from the left would suddenly jump to the right side of the screen on the other side of the tree, or a man kneeling would suddenly appear walking. When asked whether these sequences looked "funny" or had "something wrong" in them, the Navajos were at a loss to answer, even though they knew they had made a "mistake," and they wanted to give the right answer. Finally, we had to ask point-blank, "Doesn't it look funny to have Sam suddenly go from kneeling to walking?" The filmmakers answered, "Oh—of course not! Everyone knows that if he is walking, he must have got up." Or in the case of the boy and the tree, when we asked a similar question, they replied, "No, it's not funny—that's not wrong— you see, why should I show him behind the tree? Everyone knows that if he's here and then there, he got there. When he's behind the tree, you can't see him walking anyway."[22]

Evidently these Navajo had been no more inculcated into the dominant (Euro-American) rules of filmic realism than any other first-time filmmakers. Equally evidently—thanks in part to the Navajo, the French new wave, Cinéma Vérité, MTV, and much else besides—the rest of the world has since caught up. Formerly disorienting breaches of cinematic custom have since been incorporated into the mainstream. The challenge, in short, is to use and abuse codes of continuity, not for its own formal sake, but in such a way that your style reflects on itself as at once a presentation and a *re*presentation of reality—hinting at the relationship between image and referent. This can be done in a myriad of implicit and explicit ways.

EXTRADIEGETIC CUTTING

Much of editing involves selecting shots for aesthetic and intellectual reasons that have little if anything to do with the film's diegesis: they are not directly part of the plot. Some documentary styles are more concerned with aesthetic form and editorial comment than others, but none are entirely indifferent to such considerations. Many cuts involve a formal or compositional likeness between dominant visual elements in the shots they adjoin. This could be anything from a realistic resemblance—between, say, a human face and a gargoyle—to an abstract analogy—as in the dissolve between the ceiling fan and helicopter blades at the beginning of *Apocalypse Now* (1979). In *Rivers of Sand,* a film about the subjective effects of patriarchy among the Ethiopian Hamar, Bob Gardner cuts between a girl's neck iron and the branding of a cow's neck. The relationship between the two images has less to do with similarity of form (the neck iron doesn't really look like the brand) than it does with similarity of content (two bodies, one human and one animal; two necks; two forms of marking). But the principal relationship established by the cut is more than one of content. It's metaphorical and editorial: the cut "says" that wearing, or being made to wear a neck iron, is in some way like being branded. (Of course, it doesn't say *how* the two are similar, or whether any Hamar would make the same connection.)

Cutting can thus be conceptual—as for instance when it suggests an ironic juxtaposition that may not have been entertained by the characters themselves. Such cuts are ten to a dozen in Eisenstein's films (for example, in his first film *Strike* [1925] he juxtaposes a fox with a man's face). *Deep Throat* (1972) cuts from the protagonist's orgasm to the launching of a rocket ship. In *Fury* (1936) Fritz Lang cuts from gossipy housewives to a barnyard full of hens. Conceptual edits like these make a metaphorical association between images.

Filmmaker Vsevolod Pudovkin argued that as a form of "psychological guidance" of the spectators, editing could work in a number of ways. He distinguished between contrast, parallelism, symbolism, and leitmotif.[23]

Contrast

Contrasts are a very common form of editing, and because they lend themselves to editorial moralizing, are easily overused. If you cut between the living conditions of a poor person and those of a rich person, you set up a contrast. (The exact nature of the comparison will depend on the film's point of view as you've established it up to that moment.) You can also edit so as to suggest contrasts of a more subtle nature, allowing the audience to make the connections for themselves. Rouch's *Madame L'Eau* is structured around a whole series of contrasts— between white and black, North and South, Holland and Niger, industria and agraria, submarine drainage and desert irrigation, science and superstition, and so on. Yet these are strung together by way of the principal narrative of the film, a journey from Africa to Europe in search of windmill technology for use in farming the banks of the River Niger, in such a way that they assume much more force and subtlety than a mere enumeration of binary oppositions would ever suggest.

Parallelism

Parallelism, or the use of parallel action, involves cutting back and forth between two different scenes or actions. It's more common in fiction than in documentaries shot with a single camera, because it involves intercutting two scenes, set in different locations, that are hypothetically taking place at the same time (sometimes also using form cuts between the two scenes). It is often used to indicate an ironic contrast or to introduce suspense—we see a person stuck in a traffic jam trying to reach a friend's house before the friend leaves, whom we also see preparing to go. Documentaries often use a looser form of cross-cutting, again to set up a contrast, between scenes that took place at different times. One scene may be used to prefigure another; or it may be used retrospectively to reinterpret an earlier event. Rather uncharacteristically, Fred Wiseman uses parallelism in *Titicut Follies,* when he cuts back and forth between a mental patient being force-fed through a tube with later shots of the same patient being prepared to be buried. Although Wiseman has said that he tries "to make a more abstract, general statement about the issues, not through the use of a narrator, but through the relationship of events to each other through editing,"[24] he is usually more subtle than he was in this scene.

Symbolism

Symbolism is an attempt to introduce an abstract concept to the spectators without the use of a textual intertitle. Robert Gardner's *Dead Birds* is framed by references to birds as a symbol of human mortality. The film begins with an image of a bird in flight. Gardner's voice-over narration tells us: "There is a fable told by a mountain people living in the ancient highlands of New Guinea about a race between a snake and a bird. It tells of a contest which decided if men would be like birds and die or be like snakes, which shed their skin and have eternal life. The bird won and from that time, all men, like birds, must die." Gardner attempts to root the symbolism in the mythology of the Dani themselves. Bird imagery reappears at various moments in the film: in the feathers the Dani men wear when they go to war; in the bird that a young boy, Pua, cooks and eats; and at the end of the film, when the commentary tells us that men "kill to save their souls, and perhaps to ease the burden of knowing what birds will never know, and what they, as men who have forever killed each other, cannot forget."

But some symbolism can be quite a stretch. In observational films, in which the images are presented as unsullied diegesis, editorializing kinds of symbolism would seem out of place. Symbolism like Eisenstein's in *Strike*—for example, his intercutting of workers being shot down with a bull being slaughtered in a stockyard—subordinates the diegetic action to the heavy-handed commentary of the filmmaker. On the other hand, there is no reason why symbolism of this kind should be out of bounds in documentary but acceptable in fiction. (Observational films are, after all, narrated too.) It's just that you have to be careful when you combine different stylistic repertoires.

Leitmotif

Editing around a leitmotif involves reiterating a theme, or returning to an image that evokes a certain theme. This is quite a widespread way of editorializing that also lends itself to moralizing. Used judiciously, however, it can be very effective. In John Marshall's *N!ai, the Story of a !Kung Woman,* for instance, N!ai picks up a stringed instrument and begins to sing. From then on the film returns intermittently to N!ai as she sings the same tragic song: "Don't come to me now. Don't look at my face. Death is dancing with me now."[25] Because this leitmotif recurs throughout the film and is juxtaposed with various events in the lives of the !Kung, it seems not only to refer to N!ai's own tuberculosis, but also to function as a commentary on the tragic circumstances in which many of the !Kung found themselves after being forced to move to a small reservation.

POSTPRODUCTION SOUND

Sound often takes a back seat in postproduction. With the exception of dialogue, it's usually edited, "sweetened," and mixed after the "real work" of editing the visuals is complete. Yet the power of sound to convey atmosphere, mood and essential information shouldn't be underestimated. Take the sound of the blustering wind at the beginning of *Lorang's Way:* this, almost more than the images of people and animals struggling in the dust storm, evokes a sense of what it must be like to live in this harsh climate. In *The Good Woman of Bangkok* there is an abrupt contrast between the peaceful, bucolic sounds of rural Thailand where Aoi comes from and the incessant blaring of traffic penetrating the hotel room in Bangkok where she works as a prostitute (and film subject/actress). But here the meanings are more complicated: her rural family drives Aoi to her work in the city, and both environments seem so cruel that each alternatively becomes a refuge from the other. Thus, sound can be used both as a complement and as a counterpoint to image.

Continuity Sound

There's a practical reason why you'll have to look at sound and picture separately during the editing. If you cut your sound track whenever you cut the picture, the sound would seem different from one shot to the next. Continuity cutting of the sound track involves masking these cuts. You can do this in a number of ways. You can fade or dissolve (rather than cut) from one sound to another. Or you can extend the sound from one shot over another. Sometimes you have to extend the sound from one shot over both the image(s) before it and the image(s) after it. Some documentary filmmakers even find themselves occasionally having to lay an apparently sync sound track over some shots that were shot at a different time and place altogether. Finally, you can mask a sound cut either by adding music or voice-over, or even a distracting sound immediately on either side of the cut (whether or not there ever actually was one).

Building the Sound Track

When editing sound, it's important to bear in mind that our perception of sound differs from that of images. While we see only what is in front of us, and in our peripheral vision, we can hear sounds from sources that are not immediately visible. This may confuse an audience if there are noises that are never identified (such as people speaking off-screen), but it can also add another level of reality. For example, we often hear things before we see them. In *Celso and Cora* we see a crowd milling around some railroad tracks as a train approaches. We hear the train long before we see it—which is only logical since that is also the perception of the crowd. While some documentary purists insist on only using the sound that was literally recorded in sync with their images, other filmmakers embellish their sound tracks—either to make them sound fully realistic (location sound is often poor quality) or even to make them surreal in some way. The seemingly straightforward drilling scene from Flaherty's *Louisiana Story* is a good example of the kind of creative control you have over the sound track. As the editor Helen van Dongen notes,

STAGES OF FILMMAKING

while the image shows one detail, the track may:

1) sound the same detail,
2) sound the same detail plus (in the mixed track) sound another detail happening simultaneously, or
3) occupy itself exclusively with another, off-screen detail.

Usually when close-up sounds are heard in this sequence, another, more general noise is heard simultaneously, representing the total effect of noise heard on a derrick in operation. Sometimes this general and other secondary noises are pushed quite far into the background. In this way one sound standing out in the middle of sudden silence is more ear-shattering than the combined din of many noises. (See for instance the clattering of the chain around the pipes.) This brake applied to the quantity of sound during increased activity on the screen intensifies the emotional impact.[26]

Sound as a Montage Element

You can also use sound contrapuntally—to editorialize, explicitly or implicitly. Sound can be diegetic, extradiegetic, or somewhere in-between. Cora's story of the trained pig in *Celso and Cora* is told in sync, so it is fully part of the film's diegesis. But, however accidental, it would seem at the same time to be an implicit comment by the filmmaker about the family's poverty and humanity. The most obvious way to use sound contrapuntally is to introduce elements in the track that contrast in some way with the picture. Eisenstein felt that the realistic or naturalistic use of sound was antithetical to the culture of montage he was proposing, but he also thought sound had a lot of potential as a separate montage "element" that would collide with the image. Basil Wright's classic *Song of Ceylon* is a good example of this. Wright deliberately brought together "completely incongruous" elements in picture and sound to show that the impact of Western industrialization on Ceylon (now Sri Lanka) was only superficial and not necessarily beneficial. The picture shows scenes of everyday Ceylonese life while the sound track features the sounds of the Europeans who were doing their best to control it. As Wright puts it, at one point in a section called "Voices of Commerce" there's a dissolve to a long shot of a boy "coming through a coconut grove towards the camera; we hear three different voices, inter-cut rapidly with each other, all dictating business letters. These are so timed that when the boy gets to the foot of the tree he is just about to climb and raises his hands in prayer to the god of the tree, the three voices repeat, one after the other, 'Yours faithfully.' "[27]

Sound and Silence

Just as many filmmakers hesitate to go to black in the middle of a film, even more assiduously avoid silence. Most films have a continuous soundtrack running throughout, and even if the track *seems* quiet it actually contains at least an ambience track. Silence, on the other hand, is the absolute absence of sound, and it is quite startling. Trinh Minh-ha explains why she used silence in *Reassemblage:*

> In many films the sound begins as soon as the titles appear on the screen and is typically used to get an audience into a certain mood. My film begins with silence over the titles and only later introduces music and mood. Silence is an important part of the work; it makes it breathe. I am aware that silence can also be dis-quieting and disorienting; whenever it occurs in the film, I can see by the reaction of the audience that some people are made uncomfortable. Good friends of mine have asked why I don't use natural sound as background instead of cutting off all the sounds and just leaving silence. But I do think that silence has more to offer than just being disquieting and disorienting. It suspends ex-pectation (music usually tells you what to expect) and is neces-sary as a moment of restfulness or pause, just like the black spaces in the film. The rhythm of *Reassemblage* is very quick but it would lack dynamism and could become monotonous without the silences and the occasional darkness.[28]

Of course there are many film styles in which the sound track wouldn't call attention to itself so explicitly. Observational filmmakers share Trinh's disdain for certain uses of extradiegetic music, but they would never use silences as she does. For them the sound should as far as pos-sible be a sync track. You can build your sound track as you like, but you should try and make it of a piece with the aesthetic of your film as a whole.

Dialogue

Documentary dialogue poses a special problem. Unlike the crystal-clear speech in mainstream fiction films, dialogue in non-fiction films is not always audible or comprehensible. In part this is because sound recorded on location is subject to lots of unwanted "noise" that interferes with clarity and which can be cut out in a sound studio or under controlled conditions. But it's also because people in fiction films don't really speak like we do in real life. Not only do their accents and inflections vary a lot less, they also don't all speak at the same time—which, in real life, in many cultures, is exactly what we do. What's an editor to do with people who slur their language, tread on each other's words, speak at vastly different volumes, and at times in an accent barely intelligible to someone outside their subculture?

In short, there's not a lot you can do about dialogue except ensure that the sound recordist gets the cleanest possible recording. When you edit dialogue you almost always have to make compromises. Even if a line is not strictly audible, the context or lip movements may provide a clue. In the mix you may be able to raise the volume of quieter voices and lower those that are too loud (or simply unimportant to the scene). If someone is particularly difficult to understand, you can always resort to subtitles (but see "Subtitles," below). As a last resort, you should know that even observational filmmakers have asked their subjects to repeat especially important lines. As editor Ellen Hovde says of *Grey Gardens:*

> One of the . . . problems with the cutting was that these women talked on top of each other all the time, and there was almost no room tone—no silences. As one conversation finished and you wanted to say, bam that's the end of a scene, the other voice would begin. . . . So we said, "Go back and get Edie to repeat this sentence." Edie was a pro. She could hear the original recording and then repeat it with the same emotional tone. We never asked her to say something she had not said, but both she and her mother were able to give you a new line that was clean.[29]

If you rerecord lines of dialogue, try to preserve the rhythms and energy level of the original speech, and to record them in the same space, with the same background noise, and at the same volume.

Voice-Over Narration

Disembodied off-screen narration—i.e. voice-over—is quite common in a wide variety of documentary styles. The old omniscient "Voice of God"—usually white, Western, and male—prefiguring and explaining more or less redundant images, is still alive and well on television. Vaughan's sarcastic summary of the state of television in the early seventies is scarcely less true today:

> Commentary . . . is being used, not simply to clarify points in the narrative that would not reveal their full significance without it, but to supply wall-to-wall reassurance for the audience, who are held, despite the example of the commercials, to find film language too demanding. The doctrine of "signposting," initially seen as an irreproachable attempt to point up the architecture of a film and to minimize confusion, has now swollen into a grotesque insistence that everything should be explained. The viewer must be told what a talking head is about to say, for fear he may presume to draw his own inferences from what is said.[30]

In contrast to mainstream television practice, voice-over was out of favor between the 1960s and the 1980s in independent documentary. Emile de Antonio went so far as to call it fascistic! However, voice-over has enjoyed a resurgence in documentary since the 1980s: it is often diaristic rather than essayistic; first and second person rather than third; incongruous and ironic rather than sober and straightforward; multiple and contrary rather than singular and monolithic; and personal, questioning, and interpretive rather than impersonal, didactic, and dogmatic.

Quite a few documentary filmmakers narrate their films themselves, often in the first person. The voice-over may acknowledge not only the filmmakers' presence but also their position as "outsiders" in some way. Among the ethnographic filmmakers using first-person narration are the MacDougalls (particularly in the Turkana Trilogy), Diane Kitchen in *Before We Knew Nothing,* and even some of the Granada Disappearing World anthropologists. Documentary filmmakers like Jean-Pierre Gorin (*Poto and Cabengo*), Ross McElwee (*Sherman's March*), Marilu Mallet (*Unfinished Diary*), and Tony Bubba (*Lightning over Braddock*

[1988]) have perhaps been more inventive still with their first-person voice-overs.

Trinh Minh-ha's *Naked Spaces: Living Is Round* is an innovative example of the filmmaker-as-narrator approach. Trinh wrote out a commentary that is read over the film by herself and two other women—three voices each with their own pitch and timbre, cultural and "racial" inflections, and discursive styles. "In their statements," says Trinh, "these voices constitute three ways of releasing information and of undermining the dominant documentary mode of informing."[31] The deepest voice, "the only one that can sound assertive, quotes the villagers' sayings and statements, as well as African writers' works. The high-range voice . . . informs according to Western logic and mainly cites Western thinkers. The medium-range voice . . . speaks in the first person and relates personal feelings and observations."[32]

Some filmmakers opt to share the voice-over with the subjects of their films, thus sharing authorship if not actual authority. In *N!ai,* both Marshall and N!ai act as narrators. Most of the narration is spoken by (an English-language singer representing) N!ai. Marshall interjects, as he puts it, "when I know something that nobody else in the film is aware of."[33] (Not surprisingly, N!ai tends to talk very personally about her own experience while Marshall provides an historical and statistical overview.) In making quite a few of his films, Rouch has projected the (edited) footage to his subjects in order to elicit from them a voice-over for the final film. The MacDougalls' experiments in "interior commentary" in their films about contemporary Aboriginal Australians (e.g., *Goodbye, Old Man* [1977], *The House Opening* [1980], *Takeover, Three Horsemen* [1982], *Familiar Places* [1980]) offer other examples of this (usually the narrators looked at some of the unedited, as well as edited, footage). In *Three Horsemen,* which is about the relationships between three generations of stockmen—a boy, his father, and his great uncle—all three are featured on the sound track. In *Takeover,* a commentator from the community both addresses the camera on-screen, and is featured off-screen in the voice-over.

When you consider narration, then, ask yourself not only who the narrator(s) should be, but how many there should be. Should the rhetoric be first, second, or third person (or a combination)? First person

("I," "We") evokes the narrator's subjectivity. Second person ("You") implicates the viewers directly in the address. Third person tends to sound either impartial and objective, or else a parody of the very rhetoric of impartiality. In short, what perspectives do you want the narrator(s) to represent, and what tone do you want to adopt?

As the filmmakers above would surely admit, just as interviewees are often used as surrogates for the hidden filmmaker's point of view, so, too, multiple narrators can stand in for the real narrator: the filmmaker him- or herself. Dispersing narration in this way represents a novel response to problems of authorship and representation, but it does not resolve questions of authority and power. Investing the sound track with the subjectivities of your characters, and giving voice to various points of view, can be invigorating and stimulating. But it's important not to pretend that you can hide your own viewpoint on your subject behind theirs.

Quite often filmmakers don't decide whether to use narration until they're in postproduction. Usually this is because they find they cannot convey what they want without a little boost from narration, which can provide historical and other background information very economically. (Historical films as stylistically different as *The Sorrow and The Pity* [1970] and *Ishi, the Last Yahi* would not really hang together without their narration.) But if you find yourself all of a sudden relying on narration to explain almost everything, then you may wish to reconsider what you're trying to say. Rescreening your footage (rather than the rough cut) with as much psychological distance as you can muster, you may find other themes latent in the images. Alternatively you might find you need to go back and shoot some more footage, and that this would enable you to tell your tale cinematically, rather than as a kind of moving slide show or an illustrated lecture.

On-Screen Narrator

An on-screen narrator is rare in ethnographic and documentary films, largely because it so obviously represents the voice of authority and is such a mainstay of television journalism. But since the advent of the political New York– and San Francisco–based filmmaking group Newsreel in 1968 (e.g., *Garbage* [1968], *Black Panther* [1968], *The Woman's Film* [1971]) and with the contemporary vogue for reflexive films featuring the filmmaker on-screen, it has enjoyed a revival of sorts—but with a twist. Rather than the earlier "unmarked" white male on-screen narrator, recent films are featuring woman and members of "minorities" as narrators (television news has since caught up); some films feature multiple narrators, at times even contradicting each other's testimony; and a few films deliberately and provocatively blur the distinction between narrator and character, or between filmmaker and subject. There is still a lot of room for experimentation with on-screen narration.

EDITING INTERVIEWS

One alternative to telling your story with narration is to tell it through interviews. (You can also combine the two.) Interviews have a number of advantages. As mentioned above, classic disembodied voice-over turns the usual cinematic image-sound hierarchy on its head. Although interviews are also sound- and word-based, they seem to restore the image track to its pride of place. Certainly they don't separate out the sound and picture in the way that narration can. Whereas your garden-variety voice-over seems to stand apart from the rest of the film, outside its internal diegesis, interviews come across as very much part and parcel of the film as a whole. Interviews allow your subjects to reflect on their lives, tell their stories, and offer their perspective on the world with an immediacy and clarity that is rare, even in observational films.

But interviews pose problems of their own. Because interviews work through direct address (to either the audience or an interviewer, who may be on- or off-screen), the viewing experience is very different from that of the typically indirect address of a more observational style. It's often difficult to integrate "actuality" footage and interview segments without subordinating the actualities to the interviews, which then seem to comment on and explain the action. Moreover, although interviews may seem to disperse authority in a way that narration-based exposition doesn't, in fact they offer an easy way to editorialize without appearing to at all. The filmmaker simply hides behind the voices of the interviewees. After all, it's the filmmaker who chooses whom to interview, how to interview them, and, above all, how to cut and paste the interviews during the editing.

That said, interviews have been used in original and provocative ways by quite a few contemporary filmmakers. Emile de Antonio made word-based collage-like films (e.g., *Point of Order* [1963], *Rush to Judgment* [1966], *In the Year of the Pig* [1969]) with a strong political point of view by juxtaposing manifold interview segments both with each other and with fragments of archival footage. In so doing he constructed a dialectic between the present of the interview and the past of the historical fragment. Each seems to comment on and destabilize the other, making it seem strange and unfamiliar, making us look at and listen to it again. Although de Antonio's films eschew voice-over commentary, and only rarely include his own voice in any way, his authorial presence is so conspicuous in the editing as to be perceptible throughout. Far from hiding behind the voices of his interviewees, he clearly marshals them to an argument of his own making.

Errol Morris's *The Thin Blue Line* also foregoes narration for interviews, and it too has a pronounced authorial presence. The film counterposes interview segments with highly stylized dramatic reenactments ostensibly illustrative of the stories the interviewees relate. But as each reenactment is weighed as "evidence" for each person's version of events, it becomes clear that many of the stories conflict or are simply implausible. Rather than supporting the interview testimony, the dramatizations reveal how partial and problematic it can be. The testimony of three surprise "eye witnesses" becomes not entirely credible. The conventions of both interviewing and reenactment are brought into question.

Even if your interviews are less stylized and directed than these examples, you're still faced with the question of editing them. People tend to be both digressive and repetitive when they're interviewed, and you may want to cut out large chunks of what they say. However, as much as anything else, interviews have a rhythm of their own, and in cutting them up into pithy sound bites you may lose some of their original effect. Pausing or hemming and hawing can be just as expressive and informative as what someone goes on to say. Errol Morris is a master editor of interviews (see, e.g., *Vernon, Florida* [1988] and *A Brief History of Time*). Just as you begin to wonder if one of his subjects is rambling, they come out with a gem.

As you come to edit your own interviews, these are some of the questions you'll need to consider.

- *Do you want to include your questions or not?* If so, are they audible? If not, you have a number of choices. If your interviewees' words make sense on their own, and the audience doesn't need to hear your questions to understand them, then you can simply cut out the frames when you're asking your questions. But if you think it's important for the audience to hear what you asked, you can either recapitulate your questions in a voice-over track or you can interject in written form by using title cards.

- *How will you bridge cuts you make within an interview?* Do you have a visual cutaway? If you don't feel the need to disguise your cuts, you can simply cut or dissolve between two interview segments. It will "technically" be a jump cut, but this is becoming quite common and accepted. You can also cut or fade to black between them.

- *How do you want to identify your interviewees?* Standard contemporary documentary practice is to superimpose a textual identifying tag (a "chest caption" as it's known in television-speak) when a subject first appears on screen. One question you have to ask yourself is what it is about an interviewee's identity you consider to be crucial. Superimposing someone's name when they first appear on the screen has the merit of presenting them as a named individual. Listing their occupation tells you more, but it may not be applicable or relevant. You may want to include their self-representation, or describe (in a word or two) their relationship to other people in your film. *The Village,* for instance, opens by showing the main characters at work, identifying each in turn by name and occupation in a supertitle. As Paul Hockings says,

> after seeing these opening sequences the audience begins to recognize the same people in other roles: the boat men are now at the bar, and the car-owner (there was only one) turns out to be the innkeeper. . . . Later we see yet more of these people in other social and religious contexts, till the recognition of their various roles cumulates to a sense of the social structure in the mind of the viewer. It was, I believe, an editing strategy which allowed us to complete the film without resorting to a commentary to hold it together.[34]

If you want to identify your subjects by name, but don't like supertitles because they impinge on the original image, you can identify them in either narration or intertitles (see below). However, if culturally and, above all, existentially, you feel your interviewees express their identities adequately in the interview itself, then you may not need a supertitle at all. Errol Morris, for instance, tends not to identify his interviewees until the end titles.

Occasionally you may be asked to preserve the anonymity of a subject. This is a perfectly valid request, but it presents a few problems. Certainly if anyone has reservations about appearing on camera, these should be honored. However, a lot of the information about and intimacy with a character is lost if we can't see the person's face. If someone is happy to be in the film but insistent that you disguise their identity, you can digitally "mosaic" or blot out their face in (video) postproduction. For legal reasons, this technique is common on broadcast news. It has the advantage that the original (non-mosaicked) footage exists. If, through changes in circumstances or just a change of heart, the person later decides against anonymity, the possibility is still open to you. On the other hand, backlighting someone so that they appear as a silhouette, or underexposing the image as a whole, may result in a visually more striking image, but has the disadvantage of being irreversible. Backlighting also requires controlled conditions and a static shot, whereas a video mosaic can be applied to any part of any frame, allowing you to move around as you shoot, and allowing the audience to see everything in the image that you don't blob out.

MUSIC

> Music envelops one, can put one to sleep, lets bad cuts pass unnoticed, or gives artificial rhythm to images which have no rhythm and never will have any. In brief, it is the opium of the cinema and, unfortunately, television has exploited the mediocrity of this process.

> —Jean Rouch

Jean Rouch's position is the standard one in the ethnographic filmmaking community. Rather like expository voice-over, music is thought to impart significance to images that, taken alone, wouldn't really hang together. It is sometimes said that extradiegetic music violates the purity or authenticity of an ethnographic film. In his 1976 book, *Ethnographic Film*, Karl Heider expresses the common opinion:

> Music is inevitably a distraction except when it is sound which was actually happening when the visuals were shot, or, like the wild sound of the orchestra in [Margaret Mead and Gregory Bateson's] *Trance and Dance in Bali* [1952], is very appropriate to the visuals. The most common sort of music in ethnographic films is folksongs or instrumental music from the particular culture, but usually appearing in quite inappropriate contexts. . . .
>
> It may seem somewhat harsh to criticize such music, because it is undeniably pleasant, audiences enjoy it, and it fills in those silences which cinematic convention has declared to be abominable. But the main criterion for ethnographic films should not be the quantity of information and impressions and sensory enjoyment they can convey, but rather how successfully they convey information. The primary criterion for a sound track should be that it reinforces the visuals by providing information which is very complementary, or that it at least be neutrally silent and not work in opposition to the visuals by introducing vastly new information.[35]

Of course this conception of "appropriate" and "inappropriate" uses of music is rather blurry. After all, even apparently synchronous diegetic music, if cut according to the rules of continuity, will disguise a few cuts here and there. Heider's strictures have been deliberately flouted by filmmakers like Trinh Minh-ha, who, in *Naked Spaces: Living Is Round*, goes out of her way to lay music from one culture over images of another.

Extradiegetic Music

Extradiegetic music of the kind that is anathema to ethnographic filmmakers is still alive and well in the mainstream documentary world and of course in fiction films. Even in the early days of silent movies, organ music provided an affective dimension that wasn't always apparent on the screen alone. It conveyed the fear, sadness, suspense, and happiness of the characters and induced similar feelings in the audience. It's no accident that music is such an essential part of so many films. As philosopher Suzanne K. Langer has argued,

The tonal structures we call "music" bear a close logical similarity to the forms of human feeling—forms of growth and of attenuation, flowing and slowing, conflict and resolution, speed, arrest, terrific excitement, calm or subtle activation or dreamy lapses—not joy and sorrow perhaps, but the poignancy of both —the greatness and brevity and eternal passing of everything vitally felt. Such is the pattern, or logical form, of sentience; and the pattern of music is that same form worked out in pure measures, sound and silence. Music is a tonal analogue of emotive life.[36]

And that, of course, is exactly the problem. Music imparts emotional qualities to images that, by themselves, might not evoke the same response. Moreover, if music is an analog to emotive life, then clearly (since human emotions vary from culture to culture) there are no transcultural, transhistorical principles of music. A particular sequence or song might evoke one sensation in one person and quite another feeling in someone else. If the song was popular at an earlier point in their lives, it will probably also evoke different memories for each of them. This is equally true at the level of cultures.

For documentaries that don't cross cultural boundaries, and that aren't tied to an observational style, this is less of a problem. *The Thin Blue Line,* for instance, features the distinctive music of Philip Glass. It gives the film, as Errol Morris says, "an underlying feeling of inexorability, of inevitability, which is part of the film noir aspect of the story. . . . No matter what Randall Adams did, he got further entangled. This feeling of doom and desperation is underlined by Glass' music."[37] Because of the way the film is stylized, the stirring and unsettling music is of a piece with the film as a whole. But over a different kind of documentary, it would seem manipulative and melodramatic. If it were added to *N!ai,* over the images of !Kung quarreling in a camp, or even to *Dead Birds,* over the Dani funeral, it would likely seem to trivialize the emotions of the films' subjects rather than express them.

If you're not tied to an observational style, then you may want to consider using extradiegetic music as an editorial counterpoint to your images. Dennis O'Rourke uses music by Mozart at various points in *"Cannibal Tours"* to express a sense of irony at Western tourists' encounters with Papua New Guinean villagers. Jean Rouch's *Moi, un noir* features a whimsical version of the romantic French song about the Ivory Coast city of Abidjan to underscore the impact of colonialism on the city. You could also consider commissioning a musical score. Original music has the advantage that spectators won't bring their past associations along with them. It also allows you to avoid copyright problems.

Original Scores

Quite a few recent documentaries boast original music scores of "intercultural" blends. Depending on the subject, and how the music is used, such scores can add a further conceptual dimension to the film. In Allison Jablonko's documentary series on the Maring, a composer was commissioned to (as Jablonko puts it) "acculturate" Maring sounds by synthesizing them. As she says, "I finally gave my consent, thinking that the Maring themselves would be pleased to see their music accorded the same 'respect' as Western music rather than being treated as a museum piece. I thought they would appreciate this opportunity for their own music to 'go modern.'"[38] Though it's not clear whether Jablonko actually asked any Maring how they felt about this use of their music, after one screening a Western woman told her that it "created a familiar bridge for viewers between their own culture and the 'visual foreignness' of Maring culture."[39] (Of course the sensation may equally be illusory and the feeling of connection one-sided.)

Aboriginal Australian television producer Frances Peters composed her own music for her *Oceans Apart* (1990), a documentary about three contemporary urban Aboriginal women who do not "look" stereotypically Aboriginal. Rather than using "traditional" Aboriginal music, her music more accurately reflects the lives of her subjects. She says that she "wrote the music deliberately to be very commercial sounding, like a pop song. . . . What I did was listen to scales in the music style of Aboriginal traditional music—scales that you don't find in European music—and I adapted that into a pop music style."[40] For *In and Out of Africa* we laid a syncretic Afropop tune (which we'd had composed) over the scene of Baaré's arrival at JFK airport. The music was meant to emphasize the transcultural fluidity of people and objects as it plays over images of arriving airline passengers: Americans wearing African clothing, an African wearing an American flag T-shirt, Hassidic Jews coming from Israel, and Baaré and other Muslim traders disembarking from a flight from Nigeria. Though we intended it as extradiegetic (our own commentary on the scene), we also used it to cover up discontinuities in the location sound tracks. In fact the tune is so schmaltzy that most spectators seem to assume it's the genuine article: sync-sound airport music.

Between Diegetic and Extradiegetic

The opposite process can also happen. Sync music can at times express a resonance or irony that seems too good to be true, and that smacks of an editorial hand. The filmmaker may or may not have been aware of it during the act of filming and editing. Depending on the context and the assurance of the filmmaking, it will be felt to be either a profoundly revealing coincidence or a cheap commentary. For instance, there's a scene in the documentary series *An American Family* where the mother, Pat Loud, is lounging at the pool after kicking her husband out of the house. Her daughter Delilah is in her bedroom listening to Carole King's "Will You Love Me Tomorrow?" and the sounds carry out to the pool. As documentary critic and filmmaker Jeff Ruoff has said of this scene, "Although documentary filmmakers often imply in interviews that such incidents simply happen and are just happy coincidences, their use clearly demonstrates an intention on the part of the makers, a sense of aesthetic and thematic unity, and an implicit point of view. The music comments on the action, providing an editorial perspective for interpreting the images."[41]

TRANSLATION

> Translation . . . implies questions of language, power, and meaning.
>
> —Trinh Minh-ha

In a sense anthropology is all about translation, rendering aspects of one culture intelligible to another. Cross-cultural *filmmaking* is also an act of translating in a further respect. Myth, ritual, kinship, politics, the economy, and so on are conceived by many anthropologists as structures for the articulation of sociocultural meanings. In a cross-cultural documentary, not only must these structures be made comprehensible to outsiders, they have also to be transformed into a discourse and a medium of another kind altogether: cinema. Thus, anthropologists and filmmakers are both brokers of meaning, and cross-cultural filmmakers are doubly so. Whether in subtitling or dubbing, shooting style or editing, cross-cultural films are engaged in every respect with translating. As Trinh Minh-ha notes, "Whether you translate one language into another language, whether you narrate in your own words what you have understood from the other person, or whether you use this person directly on screen as a piece of 'oral testimony' to serve the direction of your film, you are dealing with cultural translation."[42]

Translation is an act both of interpretation and of negotiation. It invariably requires compromise. If we truly believe in the reality of cultural difference, then we have to admit that there are respects in which social meanings remain *untranslatable* across cultural boundaries. Translation is an ideological and potentially reductive process that can only ever be approximate. As cross-cultural filmmakers, we have to ask ourselves: How much do we feel compelled to translate, allowing that some meaning will always be lost? How can we fill in the gaps of understanding? And how, if at all, can we reveal to the spectators our role in translation and interpretation for what it is?

You have a number of practical options if you want to translate people's words. Subtitles, intertitles, dubbed voice-over (or combinations of each) are all commonly used. You can also opt *not* to provide verbal translations, and simply allow the images to communicate for themselves, as Robert Gardner did in *Forest of Bliss,* his controversial film about death in Benares. You should choose the option that best enables you to communicate what you think is important, and that integrates best with the rest of your film. Each method has its pros and cons and none is inherently superior to the others.

Subtitles

In 1972 the audience at the Venice Anthropological Film Festival were astonished to be able to understand African pastoralists speaking, in their own voices in sync sound, on the big screen. In *To Live with Herds* David and Judith MacDougall rejected the familiar technique of voice-over in favor of a combination of subtitles and intertitles to translate the

Jie's words and to explain on-screen events. Tim Asch and John Marshall had experimented with subtitles in some sequence films made with the !Kung San in the Kalahari during the early 1960s, but *To Live with Herds* was the first ethnographic film to have a wide-ranging effect and to impel others to follow suit.

Subtitles are most often used to provide a (more or less simultaneous) written translation of someone's spoken words. Usually they appear at the bottom of the screen. They're just as subjective and selective as a dubbed voice-over translation, but they have the advantage of letting the audience actually hear people speaking in their own voices. They don't obliterate the auditory and musical qualities of what people say. Many viewers feel subtitles let them get closer to screen subjects than dubbing does. Idiosyncratic nuances of voice and speech are part of what define people as individuals, and it conveys a sense of respect for them by allowing the audience to hear their own words. Though the filmmaker-anthropologist still has to translate idiomatic and vernacular expressions from one language (the spoken one) into another (that of the subtitles), it may be less offensive than doing so with voice-over. (Subtitles, unlike dubbing, don't have to find analogs for particular accents.)

If you choose to subtitle dialogue, you'll soon find how selective you have to be. Should you translate every word, and translate them literally, your audience would probably have to spend more time reading the text than looking at the images. Even so, you'd find that often you don't have the time to translate a line fully before someone else starts talking or before you cut to another shot. Most speech, especially overlapping dialogue, has to be condensed. Usually, you'll want to choose the most succinct translation you can think of that conveys a sense of what is being said. But in many cases literal translations of metaphors may be confusing or even incomprehensible to viewers foreign to the culture. Indeed, however familiar you are with the culture and language yourself, there may be cases when you're not exactly sure what someone meant by something. In short, although subtitles were introduced to allow screen subjects to communicate in their own words, you'll soon notice how much editorial discretion you have to exercise just to produce them.

What are the more obvious dangers of subtitles? At a practical level,

FIGURE 64 Lorang speaking, subtitled, in *Lorang's Way* (1979), by David and Judith MacDougall.

they may limit your audience. Most television programmers (especially in the U.S. and Germany) currently prefer dubbing to subtitling. Although the best documentaries rarely cater to the lowest common denominator, it is true that the physical imprint of subtitles on a screen is intrusive and distracting. And while film is as much an aural as a visual medium, reading (subtitled text) is a different cognitive process from listening and watching (moving photographic images), demanding a different kind of concentration.

Subtitles also raise sticky ethical questions. If your subjects speak the language of your target audience, should you subtitle those among them who are difficult to understand, because of their dialect, accent, slang, or even a speech impediment? English is the dominant language in the world today, but it's often spoken in ways that are more or less incomprehensible to an unmarked Euro-American audience. By subtitling speech that is, by the norms of your intended audience, ungrammatical, you may be seen implicitly to be pointing a patronizing finger at it. In the past, we've opted to subtitle a few key words and completely obscure phrases rather than whole speeches. We've done this in an attempt to allow the audience to have some idea what's being said, but also to make them struggle a little as they attempt to make sense of grammar and accents with which they're unfamiliar. A recent video by Stephen Olson and Maria Luiza Abolm about a visual anthropologist, *John Collier, Jr.: A Visual Journey* (1993), uses subtitles to help clarify Collier's words (although he spoke in English, a childhood accident had affected his speech). *The Harder They Come* (1975), a fiction film about Jamaican music, starts off by subtitling the dialogue but progressively drops subtitles as it goes along and the (potentially North American) audience becomes used to the Jamaican accents.

There are other intellectual problems with subtitles. They highlight what is said at the expense of the other activity on the screen. As such they privilege dialogue over other forms of nonverbal interaction. Moreover, real life dialogue is inherently indeterminate as we constantly try to figure out what people *really mean* from what they say. But because of the esteem accorded to the written and especially printed word, subtitles tend to allow and underwrite a single, attenuated interpretation of what people might mean. Further, by authorizing this translation, and making it seem a natural and unmediated rendition of what someone is saying, the intimacy with characters that subtitles enable viewers to feel may be quite illusory. As David MacDougall cautions, "Subtitles may induce in viewers a false sense of cultural affinity, since they so unobtrusively and efficiently overcome the difficulties of translation. They may reinforce the impression that it is possible to know others without effort—that the whole world is inherently knowable and accessible."[43] Trinh Minh-ha's *Surname Viet Given Name Nam* plays with subtitling conventions to make precisely this point. Going against the grain of subtitles' habitual realist transparency, Trinh occasionally substitutes other words for the actual (English language) ones that are spoken. It comes as a shock to the viewer to realize the lack of concordance between the written and the spoken.

Dubbing

Many television programmers and some educators prefer dubbed to subtitled films. That is, they would rather you added a voice-over track that translates sync dialogue. Dubbing has certain things to be said for it. The viewing experience remains one of looking and listening, while subtitles also make people read. Dubbing also has a practical advantage over subtitles. In real life, people often speak at the same time. If this happens in a documentary, even if the dialogue is in your own language, it can occasionally be hard to hear everything and to figure out who said what. If the dialogue is in a foreign language and is subtitled, your audience may at times have no idea whose line is on the screen at any one moment. Even if one person's subtitles are italicized, another person's capitalized, and so on, it can still be difficult to stay on top of who's speaking. By contrast, if your characters' voices are dubbed, and if you make the voices different enough from each other, it's pretty easy for the viewers to figure out who's talking.

But there are problems too, as the "Subtitling" section indicates. Dubbing your subjects' voices virtually annihilates the rhythms, inflections, and nuances of their speech. You can try and mimic them in the dubbing, but it's difficult to do it well. And in so doing, you open up a Pandora's box of translation problems. Obviously you need to translate your subjects' words as accurately as you would if you were subtitling them, and to write simply and clearly if they're to be understood. But there are further problems, for finding analogs in one language for differences of dialogue, accent, and vernacular in another is impossible. The way someone speaks English, for example, tells you a lot about who they are—details of nationality, region, class, education, ethnicity, and so on—which will never correspond very well to internal differences of a foreign tongue, especially of non-Western cultures. As David Mac-Dougall has noted, "Informalities of speech are introduced, including slang, and people speak English with foreign accents, as though to suggest that this is how the original speakers would speak English if they could. . . . One Kenyan woman was so gifted at doing this sort of work that her voice was used for films made in several different parts of Africa."[44] Clearly problems of authenticity abound.

To write your dubbing script you'll be faced with many of the same challenges as with subtitling: you'll want to render a faithful but comprehensible translation of the speech you're dubbing. But, because the spoken word can be understood faster than the written, you may be able to have a longer dubbed translation than you would with subtitles. Moreover, you can add your own culturally relative inflections to the dubbed speech in order to enhance meaning. Nevertheless, you still have to be aware that certain idioms and metaphors may be difficult to translate, and you may find yourself having to compromise between preserving a language's natural poetry and clarity.

It's important to consider whose voice(s) you want to feature in your dubbing, and how. *N!ai, the Story of a !Kung Woman* uses a combination of subtitles and English voice-over for N!ai's words. When N!ai appears on camera, she is subtitled, and when she is speaking as voice-over, her words are dubbed by the South African singer, Letta Mbulu. This works surprisingly well, although some spectators are confused about who the dubbed voice belongs to. Alternatively, Argentinean filmmaker Jorge Preloran partially sidesteps problems of translation by often using a voice that is identifiably his own to dub his subjects (e.g., *Imaginero, Cochengo Miranda* [1974], and *Zerda's Children* [1978]). There is also no reason why films could not be as playfully self-reflexive about dubbing as *Surname Viet Given Name Nam* is about subtitles—choosing manifestly or ambiguously nonanalogous dubbing voices to represent the originals (upper class for lower class, American for British, Nuorican for Chicano), changing the dubbing voices in the middle of a film, and so on. This would be more experimental than your regular realist fare, but you may want to consider it.

Intertitles

Intertitles, those wonderful written cards that popped up as commentary in old silent films (such as *Nanook of the North*), also have their uses. They can translate dialogue, provide background or historical context, clarify the story when the images aren't clear, or comment editorially in another way.

In Tim Asch and Napoleon Chagnon's *The Feast* (1970) intertitles appear in a lengthy prologue describing the action to come. The titles are superimposed over frozen images from the film, so by the time the film rolls at full speed, the audience has a pretty clear idea of what's happening. In *Valencia Diary*, Gary Kildea uses intertitles not only to orient the viewer, by describing the area and its economic situation, but also in a diaristic way to give the date and so mark the passing of time. In *The Good Woman of Bangkok*, Dennis O'Rourke uses them to set the

FIGURE 65 Director Dennis O'Rourke and his actress and subject, the prostitute Aoi, in *The Good Woman of Bangkok* (1991), a story about "the impossibility of being good in a bad world."

stage and introduce his characters (including himself). The titles induce an almost confessional sense of intimacy in the viewers and, in combining past and conditional tenses, prefigure an ambiguous revelation that comes at the end, that what we have just seen is a "documentary fiction." The film begins thus:

> The filmmaker was forty-three
> and his marriage had ended.
>
> He was trying to understand
> how love could be so banal
> and also profound.
>
> He came to Bangkok,
> the mecca for western men
> with fantasies of exotic sex
> and love without pain.
>
> He would meet a Thai prostitute
> and make a film about that.

In the Turkana Trilogy, David and Judith MacDougall use intertitles for various rhetorical effects. In *Lorang's Way*, for instance, intertitles function as geographical and temporal locators ["Turkana District/ Northwestern Kenya/1973–4"], as chapter headings and narrative pointers to the filmmakers' subjectivity ["Part 1: Making Up for Lost Time"], as identifiers of characters and speakers ["Naingiro, Lorang's wife's sister"], and, combining the active and passive voice, as summaries of the filmmakers' actions and words ["We put the following to Lorang," and "Ngimare, a close friend/ of Lorang visits/ the filmmakers.// He is asked if he/ will talk about/ Lorang's past."]. Despite the apparent preponderance of text, the intertitles are not very intrusive. They appear at a leisurely pace, at times over black and at times over images, generally in a matter-of-fact, unassuming tone. They mildly mock the connotations of narrative omniscience that intertitles still carry with them from the days of silent films. Rather than furnishing an authoritative explanation of events portrayed in the images, they foreground the tentativeness of the MacDougalls' attempts to establish relations with their subjects, and propel us into the present of the filming in all its contingency.

You can also use intertitles to stand in for your own questions—either because they didn't come across clearly on the sync sound track and you don't want to rerecord them, or simply because you don't want the audience to hear them at all. Of course, intertitles don't let the viewers hear the sound of your voice. Nor, unless you use them to give a literal word-for-word transcription of your questions, do they let the viewers know exactly how you phrased them (and even if they were a word-for-word translation, viewers would still have to take it on faith). However, intertitles have the merit of mimicking visually the interruptive, interlocutory quality of the questions themselves.

The intertitles in Jean-Pierre Gorin's *Poto and Cabengo* are reflexive and rhetorical. The story of American twins who communicate only in their own private, invented language had fascinated news reporters and linguists alike. Gorin tells a tale about the twins, their parents, the outside attention they had received, and his own interest in all of this. He uses intertitles (as well as his own first-person voice-over) not only to mimic and mock the words of the journalists and scientists, but also to interpolate himself as an authorial character (and yet another investigator) into the fabric of the film itself.

Not *Translating*

You may not want to use subtitles or intertitles, dubbing or voice-over at all. You could choose to leave all foreign dialogue untranslated. This would certainly be a controversial decision, and leave you open to charges of self-indulgence, ethnocentrism, abusing your subjects, even "orientalism." On the other hand, ethnographic and documentary films tend to be dialogue-heavy, and you may wish to struggle against the partial representation of people and cultures that privileging dialogue entails. Robert Gardner and Trinh Minh-ha have both at times chosen not to translate what people are saying. The viewing experience becomes much more visual as we attend to what is shown as opposed to what is said. Although a filmed depiction of human experience that doesn't allow us to understand what people have to say might seem absurd, we are also freed up to look for expressions of experience that would never find their way into words anyway: people's physiognomies, non-verbal forms of interaction, and much other visual and aural detail besides. Moreover, we can listen to people's words in a different way. Trinh has this to say about *Reassemblage:*

> What interests me is the way certain rhythms came back to me while I was traveling and filming across Senegal, and how the intonation and inflection of each of the diverse local languages inform me of where I was. For example, the film brought out the musical quality of the Sereer language through untranslated snatches of a conversation among villagers and the varying repetition of certain sentences. Each language has its own music and its practice need not be reduced to the mere function of communicating meaning.[45]

EDITING PRACTICES

Most films take time to emerge. Even if you meticulously scripted yours in advance, the chances are that it will go through multiple revisions in the editing room. Practically speaking, editing tends to be a three-part process. First of all, you put together an "assembly." Usually a series of bulky sequences, joined together quite loosely and sometimes awkwardly, it will be too long by far, but it's the first step in discounting footage that doesn't fit. As you go on to refine this assembly, casting aside more footage, and refining what you have, you can go through any number of "rough cuts." The end of the road, when you've arrived at the version you'll stick with, is called the "fine cut." You return to your original "master" materials and execute all the editing decisions you've made.

THE ASSEMBLY

Master List

First, you should number each film reel or video tape and make a master list of what's on each—a sentence or two will probably be enough to enable you to recall its contents. (You can get a head start if you do this systematically during production itself.)

Transcriptions

Accurate transcriptions of all important dialogue are invaluable for editing. It's preferable to make audiocassette copies of your masters, and to transcribe from these. This will save wear and tear on your originals (even professional transcribers need to start and stop the tapes frequently). If possible, transcribe onto a word processor as the text will be much easier to work with when you start editing. Once you've completed your transcripts, make several copies, because you may be cutting and pasting them.

Screen and Log Your Footage

Most filmmakers and editors screen all of their material at least once *before* beginning to edit. The challenge is to put aside all your assumptions of what the film's about, and to look objectively at the footage that you actually have with fresh eyes. As you screen the footage for the first time, try to record your initial, intuitive impressions (speaking into a tape recorder or writing notes). Be particularly attentive to subjects, scenes, and even shots that surprise you in some way, even if you can't tell why. Which characters stand out? Which are less emotionally engaging? Which scenes seem well-covered and which not? Note your reaction to dialogue on your copy of the transcripts: how people say something is often more important than what they say.

If possible, you should wait to log your footage till the second time you screen it. Logging can be done in various ways. Some people use separate notebooks for each element (shot log, interview transcripts, and, if relevant, photo log, archival footage log, music and sound effects log). Others use log sheets, putting them into one big notebook or folder with sections. The idea is to identify each element you'll be working with so as to be able to find it at a moment's notice. Your shot log should have notes on each new scene or shot. Note any significant cutaways and wild sound. Note also, if you can at this point, what shots you'll probably want and which ones you're sure you'll throw away. Similarly, you should go through your transcripts and highlight the parts you might want to include.

If you're working in video, note the time code numbers for the beginning and end of each scene, shot, or section of dialogue. If you have a VCR at home, you can use a counter number or stopwatch to time more or less where each shot is on your tapes (but remember that counters can vary from VCR to VCR). If you're working in film, you should note the camera roll number, machine edge code number, and "latent edge" (or "key") number of each element.

Once you've screened and logged everything, you're ready to start assembling your footage. Some filmmakers prefer to make their first assembly on paper only; others like to get right to work on their footage.

Paper Assembly

Paper assemblies are particularly useful if you have limited access to editing equipment. As long as you have accurate logs and transcripts, you can do a surprising amount of thinking outside the editing room. The idea is to organize on paper (or notecards, or a word processor) your material into a loose structure or story in an outline form. Include the scenes, shots, and dialogue you want, in the order you *think* you want them (by the end of the process you'll almost certainly change this order). If you use notecards, consider color-coding them—for different themes of the film, or for different elements (actuality footage, interviews, etc.). Even after you've begun editing the footage itself, it can be useful to revise your paper assembly as you go along.

Edited Assembly

If you have a high shooting ratio, you may initially want to transfer onto dedicated tapes or reels the footage that you're considering incorporating into the film. That way you might cut down, say, forty hours of original footage to ten hours. This makes it easier to work with, though it only makes sense if you're *sure* that there's a lot of your footage you won't want to use. (At the same time, you have to be as liberal as possible in jettisoning footage if your film is ever to get edited.) Label each new reel and make a log of them. Try to limit your reels to a half hour or less; anything longer will take too much time to shuttle through.

The next stage is to piece together your first assembly. Having watched the footage at least once, you should examine your logs and transcripts, conceiving of possible structures the film may assume or stories it could tell. You will probably want to review parts of the footage. Once you feel you're in a position to mould the footage into some kind of (invariably flabby) shape, start editing scenes loosely, and order them into a sequence. Imposing a sequence on your footage allows you to start conceiving of your film as a finite whole, with all the concomitant structural requirements that demands. Don't worry too much at this stage about redundancy or repetition; the fine tuning of details comes later.

THE ROUGH CUT

Beginnings and endings have a habit of changing during editing, so you may want to start editing the scenes that are the clearest in your mind. Before editing a scene, it's a good idea to screen all the relevant footage again, taking even more detailed notes. You will probably edit some scenes that won't end up in the final film, but it's too early to tell which they'll be.

As you edit your scenes and place them in a sequence, you'll finally see your film taking shape. Though you may feel like you've finished, few documentaries are edited that quickly. You'll almost certainly need to keep refining your cut for some time, and may even have to restructure the entire film at some point.

Restructuring

Restructuring does not mean that you have to throw out all of the hard work you've done so far. The realization that you need to add or eliminate entire scenes is integral to the editing process, and the more complicated your film, the more likely this will be. But restructuring may often be more a matter of rearranging sequences (possibly including the beginning or ending) and shortening or extending certain scenes. This was all necessary, for instance, when the MacDougalls edited their Turkana Trilogy. As David explained it:

> The editing of the films has been a slow process. . . . *The Wedding Camels* was edited first, because it represented the most straightforward narrative line. It is about an event, a marriage and the negotiations that precede it, and its immediate aftermath. But *Lorang's Way* is about a person, and it developed much more slowly. At various times the film was completely taken apart and recast. At one early stage it involved the filmmakers much more directly in the film, with snapshots and extracts from their letters and journals; but this emphasis on self, and how they met Lorang and became fascinated by him, threatened to capsize the film and divert attention and understanding from Lorang. Similarly, the themes of the film took time to develop—and the notion of how these various glimpses of Lorang with family and associates, and the testimony of others would combine to make a portrait.[46]

Test Screenings

After working with the same footage for weeks or even months on end, even the most experienced editors begin to feel a little jaded and to lose perspective on the film. One of the best ways to find out how well your film is working is to hold test screenings of your rough cuts. Screen them for select audiences, especially people who are unfamiliar with your project. It's best not to say much beforehand about the film, so you can gauge how people respond to the film itself, rather than your description of it. Find out from them what they think it's about. Ask how they reacted to your main characters, who they identified with, which parts they found too long, too slow, or just confusing. A common struggle of editing is trying to establish the main characters early on. You may find that some people started to recognize your characters before others. Remember to write down (or record) everybody's comments, otherwise you'll forget them later.

Bear in mind that test screening rough cuts is often a grueling experience. You can never make a film that will satisfy everyone, and some viewers may respond by telling you about the film that they would have made, not the one you're trying to make. Don't be discouraged by negative responses in the early stages. At the same time don't merely dismiss them. Even when some people's suggestions for improvements seem ridiculous, confused, or inarticulate, they may well have put their finger on a problem area.

APPROACHING THE FINE CUT

You need to prepare all of your film's elements before going into the fine cut stage. This includes having not only a "locked-down" (more or less final) rough cut but also recordings of any narration, dubbing, and music, and prototypes of subtitles and intertitles.

Composing Narration

Using narration involves certain aesthetic and practical choices. The whole experience of watching the images is very different once narration is laid over them. Their pacing will seem different, and you'll have less time to look at them. (Also, words that land on cuts tend to be emphasized.) If the images are to have time to breath, you may need to edit at a slower pace than if you were going only with a sync track. If you write your narration late in the editing stage—after you've edited the picture but before you've locked all your decisions into place—your film will be more visually-driven, and you'll still have time to fine tune some shots and even sequences if you need to. However, don't be surprised if you find yourself having to completely re-edit some sequences where you introduce narration. Laying the narration over the picture at the beginning of the editing stage circumvents this problem, but you may then subordinate the picture to the voice-over.

If this is the first time you're composing narration for a film, you'll be amazed at how time flies, at how little commentary the film can accommodate. Remember that the spectators are also going to be concentrating on the picture, and that the narration won't have their undivided attention. In general, it's clearer to make short statements with the verb near the beginning of the sentence. The active voice is more comprehensible than the passive. You may wish to sacrifice grammar for the sake of clarity.

Although you want to keep the narration to a minimum, you also need to time it out carefully. Narration introduces a pacing of its own. If you start it off wall-to-wall, it'll be difficult to let up, since your spectators will come to expect it. Try using it only at judiciously timed moments. You will probably want your words to correspond precisely to particular shots, in which case you may need to time the shots before writing the narration.

Once you've composed the narration, you'll want to see how well it fits with your film. In particular, you'll want to critically evaluate its tone and content and to check your timings. The best way to do this is to record it on a scratch track—a rough version on another medium (say, an audiocassette). If you're editing on video you can record this onto an audio track of a dub of your rough cut. Alternatively, but with less precision, you can have your recorder play along with your entire video or film. Bear in mind that if your final narrator is not the same as the one you used for your scratch track, both the tone and the timings will certainly change.

When you record your final narration, and unless you need any special background noises or special effects (which can probably be added in the mix anyway), you should choose a quiet room, with minimal reverberation. Experiment with different distances from the mike, for this affects the direct-to-reflective ratio and so the tone of the narration. You can achieve an almost surreally subjective effect by having your narrator speak into the mike at *very* close range, as close as physically possible. If you have the time, you should do a few different takes of the narration, perhaps changing the pacing or speaking with another inflection. Pay close attention both to the narrator's energy level and the sound recording, and try to keep them constant. Any slight variation in the animation of the narration will be very noticeable when the final film is screened (the sounds are amplified more than you expect). If you can set it up, you may want to play your rough cut against the narration from time to time, to see how they feel together. Finally, before you leave, record a minute or two of ambience, leaving everything as it was when you recorded the narration. This will be *essential* for editing, to fill in the silences.

Subtitling

The general rule in writing subtitles is to begin with as literal a translation as you can manage. Then try to imagine how much of the language needs further translation to be properly understood by your target audience. Having revised the subtitles accordingly, you need to time them out against the image and whittle them down so that they'll fit and can easily be read. At this point you'll have to consider how long you want them to stay up on the screen. Since subtitles are visual, they transform the screen, and have a pacing of their own. Try to be consistent in how long you leave them on the screen (unless you intend a deliberately unsettling effect). Short exclamations don't need to stay up for as long as whole sentences. But if the image is dense, busy, or moving, you may need to leave the subtitles up longer to allow the audience enough time to read them. At times you may also want to extend the duration of a subtitle to distract attention from a bad cut.

Generally an individual subtitle should not be more than two lines long. (If you are identifying someone with a superimposed title at the same time, this is especially important.) As a rule, each line should contain no more than thirty-six characters *and* spaces (forty as an absolute limit). Subtitles usually appear sixteen frames clear of a cut. You should hold them on the screen at least for one (film) frame per character or space, plus eight frames per line. That allows the eye to register the presence of the title and, if need be, to travel to the beginning of the second line. David Wason, the series producer of Granada's Disappearing World series, suggests starting each subtitle on the first modulation of dialogue and, if the picture cutting permits, leaving them up for as long as the relevant dialogue lasts (i.e., not removing them at the minimum frame count just for the sake of it).[47]

Almost all editing arrangements give you some control over the appearance of your subtitles. Choose a color, typeface, and font size that is easily legible and able to withstand going down several video generations (i.e., for video release copies). Adding an outline or drop shadow to the subtitle characters may help increase their visibility against the background. The subtitles in the Disappearing World films are set against a grayish but semitransparent box that adjusts to the length of the subtitle lines.

Video subtitles are usually fabricated during the on-line edit with an electronic character generator. You will have to decide whether or not to subtitle your master directly. This will probably turn on the quality of your original recording. If you subtitle the master, that means you will have no copy of your video without subtitles. Will all of your target audiences need or want subtitles? If you subtitle your master in English, you won't be able to make a master in another language without returning to your original tapes and going through the on-line process all over again—an expensive and time-consuming procedure. The only disadvantage of not subtitling your main master, and instead subtitling copies of your master (each in turn becoming your "English language master," "Spanish language master," etc.) is that you'll have gone down an extra generation. Rather than your release dubs being copies of the main master, they're copies of copies. If you're editing digitally, this won't matter; if not, you will probably see a degradation in quality. If the quality of your original will permit this degradation, you'll save a lot of money and time. On the other hand, if you're absolutely sure that you only need one release version, you can subtitle the master directly.

If you're editing on 16mm film, subtitles are usually burnt into an "intermediate" or CRI (color reversal intermediate) copy once the original negative has been "conformed" to the workprint. This then allows you to subtitle a number of intermediates in different languages, and to duplicate these intermediates for your release prints. If you shot on color negative film you can make optically printed CRIs of the original, and subtitle these. If you shot on reversal, it's probably best to make an internegative of the original and subtitle that.

Dubbing

Recording a dub track is similar to recording narration. When laying down dubbing, the sound mixer can either completely cut out the original voice, or leave it in but turn down the volume, so that you hear it in the background. It's quite common to begin with a character's own voice at full volume, and then dip it down after a few seconds, as you start the dubbed, translated voice-over. This can easily be done in the audio mix.

Intertitling

As with subtitles, and dub and narration scripts, you'll want to compose your intertitles judiciously, without overloading your film with unnecessary text. You have many options in fashioning intertitles, depending on your medium, your budget, and personal taste. You can lay them over a black, white, or colored background, or else you can superimpose them over either frozen or moving images from the film or any other photographs or artwork. If you're editing in video, you can use a character generator (or a PC or Mac equipped with the right software) and video switcher in an on-line editing suite. If you don't have access to a character generator, you can always write, draw, paint, or print your own titles, shoot them off the wall or floor, and then edit them in as you would any other stretch of video. They may look less "professional," but you'll have more flexibility in making them as you wish.

If you're editing on film, you will probably have your intertitles, along with your beginning and end titles, made at a professional optical house. If you choose to shoot them yourself, you should, as with video, first write, draw, paint, or print them all out. Try to make sure that the letters are at least ⅟₂₀ as high as the screen, or else they may be illegible, and that the lines are well composed within the "safe title area" of the frame. Certain ornate typefaces are too finicky and will "bleed" when you shoot them. Make them as high contrast as possible—typically white or off-white over a totally opaque, pitch black background. (If they are to be superimposed over another image, this is essential.) Shoot them with as high contrast (Hi Con) a film stock as you can find. If you print them out on film as clear lettering on an opaque background, you get a better result by lighting them from behind (having filled in any specks with a special marker pen). If you have to light them from the front, use an incident light meter to ensure that they are evenly illuminated on both sides and on the top and bottom. Place lights on both sides of the camera at some angle from its axis (to minimize glare). Place the camera on a stable tripod. Be sure to shoot the titles long. Once they're processed, and you come to splice them in, a standard rule of thumb is to leave titles on the screen long enough for a slowish reader to read them aloud twice.

This said, all rules are made to be broken, and you can make inter-titles any which way you want. For *Eze Nwata—The Small King* (1982), ethnographic filmmaker Sabine Jell-Bahlsen didn't like dubbing and couldn't afford subtitles, so she superimposed titles translating Ibo dialogue over transparencies (slides). She mounted the back-lit trans-parencies and her Bolex camera on a special horizontal titling stand. Then she filmed each transparency for a certain number of frames, re-wound the camera and shot white text with a black background over the same stretch of film. Finally she spliced in these intertitles with her actuality footage.[48]

As with subtitles, you may want to leave intertitles off your master, cutting them in as you make each foreign-language version. (Alterna-tively, you can translate intertitles with foreign-language subtitles.)

Using Music

Music transforms the pacing of the images it accompanies, and will thus affect how you edit them. If you intend to feature extradiegetic music in your film, start thinking about it as early as possible in the editing process. You need to allow time to find the appropriate music or to have it composed. It may also take a while to secure the necessary contracts or permissions. If you use prerecorded music, be aware of the potential associations it may have for your viewers. There really is no such thing as generic music. The closest you can get is to license a piece from a stock-music house. For a hundred dollars or so, you can have a record-ing or two, plus the rights to use it. Be careful, though, because the same pieces of music are sold again and again and you may find yourself using the same composition someone else just bought for a television commercial.

If you choose to have music composed, look for someone who un-derstands your film and with whom you can communicate well. Show the composer a rough cut and discuss what you're after: Where in the film do you want music? What purpose should it serve? What tempo and mood are appropriate? The composer may have already produced music that will fit, or might need to compose anew. If you have trouble describing the kind of music you imagine, try playing for the composer examples of the sort of thing you have in mind.

When you come to cut the music, you'll need to time it out precisely. You may find you want certain notes to correspond with particular images or cuts. If you know where you want it to end, you'll need to back time it. If the beginning then hits at an awkward point, you can either adjust the picture or cut or extend the music in some way (or have it recomposed). Should you need to cut the music, be sure to follow the rhythm by cutting on the beat, or at the end of a section or measure. If you need to extend it, you can repeat a section or so, still taking care not to disrupt the rhythm. To some extent you may be able to mask such cuts with voice-over or sync sound.

Editing and Mixing Sound

The sound track in most films and videos consists of various simultaneous layers of sound, carefully mixed together for an overall effect. For example, if you wanted to introduce narration over, say, a scene of a midnight Mass, you'd probably want to keep the sync sound from the church running under the narration, lowering it a little so that your audience can hear both the voice-over and the church sounds at the same time. If you wanted to add the sound of church bells at the beginning of the scene, you'd need to balance that with the sound of the Mass. And if one of the shots in the scene is of a child shuffling in his seat, you may need to add the sound that he makes in an extra track. Typically, you would place these four different sounds—the sync sound from the church, the bells, the child, and the narration—each on a separate sound track during editing, and then blend and balance them during a sound mix.

Even if you only imagine using sync sound, you may still want to play around with your sound tracks in the mix. Just to maintain continuity within a scene you will almost certainly need to extend, shorten, or eliminate some of your sync sound. For example, if in your scene of the midnight Mass you cut together shots that were recorded a few moments apart, or from various camera angles, your audio track would sound very choppy if you cut sound every time you cut picture. Supposing that the focus of the scene was the sermon, but that you also wanted to include close-ups of parishioners listening, you'd probably leave the sound of the sermon running continuously under the shots of the congregation. Otherwise the sound track would jump all over the place.

If you were then to cut to a scene of people leaving the church, you'd have other choices about the sound. If you wanted an abrupt transition, you could simply cut the sound as and when you cut the picture. Or you could either "cross-fade" or "segue" the sound from the church to the exterior. (In a cross-fade, one sound gradually gives way to another; in a segue, the first sound fades out completely before the second fades in.) The easiest way to do this in the mix would be to place the interior and exterior sound on two different tracks. In the mix you would choose the speed and duration of the fade. A fade would make for a smoother transition than a straight cut. Both are effective; choosing between them just depends on your taste and the effect you hope to achieve.

The number of tracks you need depends on how many elements you want to have playing at once and whether or not you're planning a mix. Films are almost always mixed by a professional mixer, but videos are often simply "sweetened" in the on-line edit. Although both film and video editors generally cut the sync sound roughly together with the picture as they go along, they do so in quite different ways. A film editor may work with one or two audio mag tracks as they edit the picture (one track is easier, but two gives a better idea of what the finished film will sound like). At picture lock (when all your picture-editing decisions have between pinned down), sync sound is typically split between two tracks. Effects are usually just added to the sync tracks, although ambience sometimes needs to be laid on a track of its own; music and narration almost always require their own dedicated tracks. In a sound mix, all the sound tracks are interlocked to run in sync with the picture and then are mixed back (in mono 16mm) to a single track. The mix is where all your sounds are blended together and "fixed" with equalization, volume level control, filtering, and compression. With this in mind, you usually want to lay sounds needing similar equalization onto the same track so that the mixer has to fiddle with the EQ less during the mix, and thus avoid unnecessary, and expensive, stopping and starting. The final mixed track can then be transformed into an optical track running down the edge of the film for your release prints.

With video, the process is slightly different. Typically you lay two sync audio tracks down along with the video as you edit the rough cut. In the final on-line edit, you mix your sync tracks, together with other sound sources (e.g., music and narration), which have themselves usually been transferred onto separate (and otherwise blank) video tapes. If your budget permits, you may also be able to afford a separate sound mix, which happens after the on-line video edit. This involves dubbing all your sound sources onto (usually) a multitrack tape, mixing them together, and then dubbing the mixed track(s) onto your video master. Often in documentary, this is unnecessary and the final audio is edited at the same time as the video in the on-line edit. (For more detail, see "Audio" in the "Linear Video" section below.)

EDITING TECHNOLOGIES

Film and video editing use different technologies. Video editing is electronic and film is mechanical. Both processes usually involve progressing through a number of (increasingly short) rough cuts using a *copy* of the master video tapes or film negative. Once you have the exact cut you want, you go back to your originals. If you're working in film, you have your negative cut and strike prints. If you're editing in video, you make a final edited master from your original tapes.

NONLINEAR VIDEO

Whether you shot on film or video, you have the choice of editing on nonlinear video. If you choose a high-quality system, you will probably save a lot of time, and might even save money. But what does "nonlinear" mean?

Traditional video editing is "linear" in that you have to edit in sequence. For example, if your rough cut is one-hour long, and you want to make a change in the first minute (by adding, say, a cutaway), you'll have to re-record the fifty-nine minutes that follow it in order for the cut to be executed. Otherwise, if you simply inserted an extra cutaway, it would cover whatever shot was underneath it. Film editing in this sense is nonlinear. In order to add in the same cutaway, you'd simply remove the splice between the two images and splice in your cutaway between the two of them. The following fifty-nine minutes would be automatically reordered, and the whole change may have taken you two minutes to put into effect.

Nonlinear video editing also allows you to make out-of-sequence changes, more or less instantly. Whereas linear video tape has all the information locked into space (its location on the tape), nonlinear video information exists in time. Every shot is determined by two pieces of data: "source in" and "source out." Most modern nonlinear video systems store all the electronic audio and video information, not on tape, but on digital computer "hard-drives." This allows random access to all the information they contain. So, you start off with an analog recording medium (video tape), transfer the information (or the sequences you may need) onto a hard disc, make all your editing decisions, and only at the end (if at all) do you return to video tape. "Digital capture" cameras are now being made by companies like Ikegami and Avid, which store the information directly in digital form on a disc; it's possible that video tape may soon be a medium of the past.

The main problem that nonlinear video editing systems are facing is that moving pictures require a tremendous amount of electronic storage space. Most of today's research and development focuses on increasing computer processing power and allowing for greater digital compression of information. (The storage requirement of uncompressed film and video varies between 1MB and 40MB per frame,[49] so you can imagine how much space twenty hours of original footage, shot at twenty-four film or thirty video frames per second, would take up.) As digital technology replaces analog and the capacities of digital compression and storage increase (and their costs decrease), old-fashioned linear video editing is fast giving way to nonlinear. Companies like Media 100, Avid, and ImMIX (see "Equipment and Services" in appendix 3) have developed fully professional broadcast-quality nonlinear video editing systems—on-line and off-line. However, while they save time and labor, they're expensive and require training to operate.

A cheaper alternative for the off-line stage is to use software specially developed for personal computers. Working with Adobe Premiere, Avid Cinema, or Media 100's Vincent on a Mac might well be cheaper than

FIGURE 66 The nonlinear "VideoCube" digital video workstation, from ImMIX.

renting a ¾-inch or VHS off-line editing system (and will offer a whole array of special effects to boot). You need to price the alternative when you reach the postproduction stage. If you're not familiar with Adobe Premiere, Vincent, or other software possibilities, or don't have access to a computer or aren't computer-literate, you may still prefer to edit in the conventional linear way.

LINEAR VIDEO

On-Line and Off-Line

There are two stages to linear video editing: "off-line" and "on-line." As you put together your rough cuts, you're working from dubs of your original tapes. During this off-line stage you make almost all of your creative decisions. You select every shot and sound, and put them in sequence. Every video and audio element has an "in" point and an "out" point. This whole process is performed on inexpensive equipment, typically either VHS, Super-VHS, or ¾ inch. The better off-line editing systems use frame-accurate SMPTE time-code; while this is helpful at the off-line stage, it is not strictly necessary. Once you've made all your creative decisions, and written or printed them out in an edit decision list (EDL), you're ready to return to your original tapes, and edit from them onto a master tape. At this point, you have an on-line edit, for which you need the machinery to be as accurate as possible. If you can afford or have access to a facility, you should perform your on-line edit in a professional editing suite, using SMPTE time code. If not, never fear. Computer-controlled editing systems typically used at the off-line stage are becoming increasingly accurate, and this may be all you need. In fact, even if you have access only to an elementary VHS off-line system, you can still make a final video of high technical quality. It may not satisfy the strictures of national television engineers, but cable television companies, film festivals, and art houses have all been known to program videos that were shot on VHS or 8mm and edited on the simplest system of all.

Editing Setup

Video used to be edited like film—cut up and physically reassembled in another order. But even on two-inch tape, it was hard to be sure where one frame stopped and another started. On today's smaller formats it's impossible, and video is now edited electronically. At its simplest an editing system consists of two VCRs, a control unit, and one or two monitors (with speakers inside them). One of the VCRs is a record or edit deck; it contains the cassette you're recording your rough cut on. The other VCR is the source or playback deck: you put in it the cassettes (one at a time) that you want to record *from*. The separate control unit allows you to decide what stretch of video (or audio) you want to record from the cassette in the source deck onto the cassette in the record deck. It has remote controls for both decks, "in" and "out" point controls, and (ideally) a search dial that lets you move at variable speeds through the footage.

You edit by selecting three edit points: an "in" *and* an "out" point on one deck, and *either* an "in" *or* an "out" on the other deck. The control unit will then automatically calculate the fourth edit point. (You can get by with only selecting "in" points on both decks, but then you'll have to select your "out" on the fly.) You rehearse and execute all edits from the control unit. The decks will rewind or fast forward to locate the edit "in" points, then back up for about five seconds, and . . . roll. When the recording deck cassette reaches its edit "in" point, the monitor above will suddenly cut to the new shot, coming in from the source deck. This lets you visualize the edit before performing it. It can take a long time to get a cut absolutely right.

A slightly more sophisticated editing setup has not one, but two source decks. This ("A/B roll") system gives you greater control over the audio, and also lets you dissolve between shots (so long as the two shots in question are on the two different source decks) as well as some other special effects.

Assemble and Insert Editing

There are two basic types of linear video editing: assemble and insert. Assemble editing involves editing sound and picture together as you go along. Insert editing involves initially laying down "video [or crystal] black": literally, a black color appears on your tape. This black creates a "control track," which is a constant video signal of sync pulses. The control track allows for more flexible editing than is possible with assemble. It also lets you separate your two audio tracks from each other,

FIGURE 67 In this off-line VHS editing setup, the two video decks are on the left, and the control unit is on the small table in front of the operator. This arrangement features a single monitor, which displays the video from whatever deck is playing. When you rehearse or perform an edit, it displays the video from the record deck (i.e., the previous shot and the one you're now adding to it).

and from the video. Thus, when insert editing you edit over the black and control track as you go along. It's important never to break your control track because it cannot be repaired by anything other than re-recording the whole control track from that point onward. So before editing you'll need some "blacked" tapes and to make sure that your control panel has the "Insert" icon illuminated.

Window Dubs

Unless you're on a shoestring budget, one of your first steps will be to make editing dubs and transcription dubs (or audio copies) of your master tapes. The editing dubs should be in the same format as your off-line editing system. Although VHS is the least accurate, the tapes and equipment rental rates are cheaper, and the tapes can be played in a home VCR. If you'll be using time code in the on-line edit, then you should specify that your editing dubs be "window dubs." This means that they will feature a visual time code burnt into the picture that corresponds to an electronic time code on the original tapes. This enables you to read off the frame-accurate "in" and "out" points from the rough cut when the time comes to return to your originals in the on-line edit. If you will also be using time code in your off-line edit, be sure the time code from your original tapes is duplicated *electronically* onto your dubs (in addition to the "window").

If your original tapes are in a format for which you don't have access to satisfactory editing equipment, you may want to transfer them to Beta SP (making these your new masters), and make VHS or ¾-inch SP window dubs all in one pass. You should generate new SMPTE time code, taking care to change the hour with each tape. (It's much easier to work with tapes that are no more than one hour long.) Time code only goes up to twenty-four hours, so you may have to start over at 00:00:00:01 at some point (either with the twenty-fifth tape, or, if you think it's simpler, at the twenty-first).

Off-Line Editing

During the assembly and rough cutting it's best to keep video and audio generally in sync, because you'll be able to adjust the sound continuity later on. When you make your first rough cut you'll be recording segments from your assembly reels or masters onto a new tape. If you don't yet have a beginning or an end, don't worry: just leave ten minutes or so of blank space at each end of the tape so there's room to add them on. (Nonlinear editing makes this a lot simpler.) As you make each new rough cut, try to use your previous cut(s) as your source tapes. (Never record over earlier rough cuts; you may need to refer back to them.) If the picture and sound become too indistinct as you go down generations, you'll need to return to your assembly reel.

Preparing for the On-Line Edit

Once your video is just how you want it, you should prepare for on-line editing by taking the following three steps:

1. *Create an edit decision list* (EDL). You need to have an edit decision list describing on paper or disk each shot and sound you're going to use, in the order you're using them. You might want to use a script, with all

dialogue and narration written out. Go through the rough cut shot by shot, writing down the source tape and time code numbers for the "in" and "out" points of each shot and sound. Your initial edit logs should help you find them on your original master tapes. (If you've been editing on a computer, it can generate an EDL for you. Just be sure to check it over carefully to make sure nothing is omitted, and that all the edit points are clear.)

2. *Collect all your materials together.* For the on-line edit, you'll need your script and edit decision list, the final rough cut and your master tapes, and any other sound elements (e.g., music, narration) you're using. Make sure that all your sound elements are transferred onto video tapes compatible with the editing setup. (If possible, the video tapes should have visible time code burnt in, so if you're fiddling around with "in" and "out" points, you'll be able to see them represented on the screen. Even if your editing facility allows you to pass directly from a CD or cassette to your master, it's easier to find exact edit points on a video tape.) Make a careful log of all these new tapes.

3. *Prepare your subtitles, titles and credits.* As with your subtitles, you should type up a list of titles and credits ahead of time, in the order they'll appear on the screen. It's an expensive waste of time to do this in the editing room. Check the spelling of everyone's name, and try not to forget anyone. Be sure to use a typeface and color that can be read easily on a small screen and that the titles all fit within the TV safety zone. Try to keep supertitles down to two lines, otherwise you may conceal someone's face.

On-Line Editing

During the on-line edit, you have to proceed in a strictly linear manner from the beginning to the end. Be sure to edit onto the highest quality tape in the best format within your budget, since this will become your master. First of all, you need to lay video black on it. You should then perform certain steps in the following order:

1. *Lay down slate,* including producers, title, running time, and audio description (Audio 1 and 2, Mix, Dolby, etc.). You should leave about three minutes before the slate, in case you need to add something later, like a disclaimer, or a distributor's logo.

2. *Lay down bars and tone* (thirty seconds to one minute). Every time you turn the equipment on, check the color bars against the waveform monitor and the tone level against the VU meter or PPM on the record deck. Tone should always register at zero. You'll need to use these standards later on when you make dubs. You should have at least one high quality monitor, which you should adjust with the color bars, since colors vary from (NTSC) monitor to monitor.

3. *Lay down black and countdown* (optional), which stops at two, leaving two seconds of black before the start of the film. Put your titles in as you go along, or leave precisely measured spaces (to the frame) for them. If you're fading in and out, take care not to cut into the "reading time."

4. *Edit your video,* remembering to

- *check the color, contrast, and brightness of every shot.* You may need to make minute adjustments to a shot using a waveform monitor, but be sure to return it to the default setting afterward.

- *rehearse every edit to make sure that it's exactly how you want it.* Even computerized time code editing machines can slip, so you may not be able to redo each edit perfectly. Try to minimize changes from your rough cut. Drastic modifications made at the last minute are rarely the magical solution they seem.

- *verify each edit after you perform it.* Check off your EDL as you verify that every frame has been filled. (Sometimes an unwanted frame of black may have slipped in.)

5. *Edit your audio,* remembering to

- *smooth out transitions.* If you wish to cross-fade your audio from one scene or shot to the next, put the outgoing and incoming sound on the two different tracks and extend the audio edits beyond the picture edits. (When mixing, fade your incoming sound up and the outgoing sound down.) If you have only two tracks, mix as you go along.

- *ensure your sound levels are consistent from shot to shot.* A general rule is to allow normal speech to range between −5 and −20 on a VU meter. Background should be between −10 and −20. The loudest sounds should peak between zero and −3.

- *smooth out sound within scenes.* Add ambient sound where needed to cover cuts, or extend it from one shot to the next to create the illusion that they're set in the same space.

- *clean up your tracks for maximum intelligibility.* Use the equalizer to roll off low frequencies, such as traffic and tape noise. (Don't forget to turn the equalizer back to normal once you've completed the shot or scene.)

- *add any masking, "foley," sound effects, or reverberation you want.* Masking involves adding a loud noise at the head of a cut in order to hide it. (A telephone ringing or a door slamming can help but also be distracting, so mask judiciously.) Foley involves recreating and adding sounds that should have been recorded in sync but weren't.

- *fade audio in or out during a dissolve at the same rate as the accompanying picture.*

- *back time music, if necessary.*

6. *Lay down your credits.* If yours are to roll upward from the bottom of the screen, make sure the roll is slow enough that they can be read.

Audio

If you're editing without time code, you will have to rely on a control track editor and won't be able to have a true sync mix. In this case, it's best to mix (or sweeten) your sound as you "on-line" onto the two audio tracks of your master. If you want to play two sound sources at the same time (like voice-over and ambience) you should lay them on separate audio tracks. When organizing your source tracks, the general rule is to keep sounds that are different in intensity or quality on different tracks. Ensure that the relative levels are how you want them. You will probably need to dip the level of the sync track when you introduce narration or music. If you want to hear three or more elements simultaneously, and you're not using an edit system that allows simultaneous control of multiple tapes by SMPTE time code, you should premix two of them onto a track on another (blacked) video tape and then edit that to one audio track of the master. This will mean losing an audio generation, and you won't be in perfect sync with the picture. So be sure to choose for this premix two elements that don't need to be in exact sync, such as voice-over and music—not location sync sound.

If you're on-line editing with time code, you will be able to keep all your sound elements in perfect sync. First, you should decide how many tracks you'll need. The general rule is to allot two for sync sound (and effects), and one for each of the other elements. So if your video is to feature narration, dubbed voice-over and music, as well as sync sound, you'd have at least five tracks. You can premix your tracks in any order, though it always makes sense to leave the sync dialogue tracks to last, as they're the most important to keep intelligible. Music and effects are often premixed together. If your sync tracks also need premixing, you can do that. (Keep them separate from music and effects until the final mix, because if you sell your video abroad to foreign-language television, they may want to dub over your dialogue.)

A fully professional sound mix can come in any number of shapes and sizes. In one standard method, the video on-line edit is performed first, usually with sync laid onto the two audio tracks. You then make video-only copies of this new, edited master, and lay down two audio tracks per tape (music, narration, effects, etc.). As you build your tracks, you should note all the audio "in" and "out" points on special cue sheets. You then take all these tapes, together with a (usually ¾-inch) video-only window dub, to a professional mix studio. They will "strip" (in real time) all of your audio onto tracks of either two-inch fullcoat mag or DAT. As you watch your video window dub, the mixer will then mix all of your tracks (under your guidance) onto another track (or two tracks) on the fullcoat, and, finally, record the mixed fullcoat track(s) back onto your video master.

Once your on-line edit and mix are over, you'll be more than ready to move into distribution.

The first thing to do after you've shot your film is to pack it up and send it off to a lab for development. You should put each roll of exposed film in a black bag and, preferably, in the same can it came in. If you have to put it in another can, make sure the can doesn't have any different raw stock data on it. Tape the can carefully, so that no light can enter where the top and bottom halves join.

Processing

On every can of exposed film you should write the following information with an indelible marker pen:

- "Exposed"
- Your name
- The title of your project
- Footage
- Stock type
- Roll number
- Processing instructions
- Film or video dailies

The processing instructions include whether you want the film to be developed normally, or push or pull processed. Labs can also perform "neutral flashing" to lower the contrast, or "color flashing" to create special moods or effects. If you have shot under fluorescent lights without color filter correction, the lab can also compensate for the green tint—without affecting the film's exposure index. If you're not sure how the film should be processed, you should ask for the lab to perform a "head" or "tail" test. They will develop about fifteen feet at either the beginning or the end of the roll before doing the rest. You (or the lab) can then look at that fifteen feet and see if it needs any correction. Tail tests are easier, because the lab won't have to rewind the roll. It's important to choose a section that's representative of the lighting conditions for the roll as a whole.

If you've decided to edit on video, you'll need to request "video dailies," of which there are two main kinds. A "video matchback" is a video transfer that will only be used as a workprint (when you want to return to the film negative itself, either because you'll be ending up with film prints or because you'll be using the negative for video mastering). "Video completion" means that you transfer to a video master (and so you end up on video tape only). The technician in charge of the film-to-tape transfer (a "colorist") will ask you lots of questions about time code, frames per second, sync, color, and so on. You should discuss very carefully what you want. (You should also be able to supervise the transfer yourself if you like.) Once you have your video transfer, you're ready to begin editing (see the guides to video editing above).

Workprint

If you're editing on film, you'll probably want to do this on a "workprint" (the "dailies" or "rushes"). It's only really possible to edit directly on the original if you shot in reversal, and only then if you can't afford a workprint. An untimed workprint is the cheapest, but you can also request a "timed" or "color-balanced" print, which will be corrected for exposure and color-balance from shot to shot. An untimed print looks worse, but has the advantage that it lets you see variations in the negative for what they are. The important corrections are made in your final answer print in any case. When ordering a workprint, you should specify that the lab print the latent edge numbers along the edge of the film. You will need them later when you "conform" your edited workprint with the original.

Once you get your workprint back from the lab, you should screen it with a clean and functioning projector, as some camera problems of flicker will not be visible on your editing table. If you notice excessive flicker, or other problems, you may need to reshoot.

Editing Machines

Depending on the equipment you have access to, you'll be working on either an upright or a flatbed editing machine. Both of these let you sync up picture and sound and watch them in sync. However, upright Moviolas are much more difficult to use than flatbeds as they require a separate editing bench with a special synchronizer. They also tend to damage sprocket holes. If you have the choice, select a flatbed. A flatbed (such as the Steenbeck model) with eight "plates" is preferable to one

FIGURE 68 Six-Plate Steenbeck flatbed editing table, model 1900. Filmmaker David MacDougall and Thomas Woody Minipini, an Australian Aboriginal collaborator, working on *Goodbye Old Man* (1977).

with only six, but they're less common. An eight plate has two sound heads and two picture heads, while a six plate has two sound heads and one picture head.

Sound Transfer

Before beginning the editing, you need to transfer your ⅛-inch or ¼-inch sound to sprocketed "fullcoat" magnetic film, using a special magnetic film recorder. You may be able to do this yourself if your institution has one; otherwise, you'll have to pay for the service at a special sound house. Unlike audio tape, "mag" does not stretch and shrink, so you'll be able to run it in perfect sync with the picture. Your sync sound needs to be "resolved" when it is transferred to mag—that is, the original needs to be sped up or slowed down according to the pilot pulses laid down by the crystal. When you buy your mag, make sure that it's demagnetized before you do the transfer. Professional sound houses should do this for you (but make sure they do); if you're having the transfer done at a university or other institution, you'll need to do this yourself using a special magnet. Always handle your mag sound with great care, since it will be the source material for the mix.

Syncing Up

The next step is to sync up your sound with the picture. Most filmmakers record more sound than picture—typically before and after the camera starts rolling. That means that your mag sound will be longer than your workprint. You can either cut the non-sync sound out and spool it on dedicated rolls, or you can leave (all or some of) it as is, and add in "blank" leader to the picture track to make up for the difference. Whenever you make a cut in either the sound or picture tracks (whether it's to add or cut out a shot), you need to "splice" the two parts together. For this you use a special "splicer." The older cement splices have largely given way to tape ("mylar") splices—clear for picture, white for sound. Whenever you make a splice in the sound be sure to splice the base side of the mag to the emulsion side of the leader (otherwise the leader emulsion will harm the sound head).

Most of your footage shot with sync sound will have a slate, either at the beginning or the end. You should match each visual slate up to the identical point on the mag. You need to be very accurate, otherwise the offset between picture and sound may be noticeable when projected on the big screen. For sync shots that you didn't slate, you need to find substitute sync points—any sharp sound that has an equally precise corresponding point in the picture track. If all you have is a close-up of someone speaking, you'll have to sync up very carefully to the movements of their lips. If your crystal sync was malfunctional, or if for any reason you recorded picture and sound at the same time without a sync mechanism, you can still put them in sync with a little extra work. The trick again is to find substitute sync points in your footage. Because the sound wasn't resolved in the transfer to mag it will soon drift out of sync, and you'll have to cut out a few frames. Since it's easier to cut out a short stretch of sound without anyone noticing than it is to cut out a few frames of picture, it's a good idea to run the sound a tiny bit slowly in the transfer. (Ask for professional advice if this is your first time.) This means you'll end up occasionally cutting out a stretch of mag rather than having to add to it or cut out picture.

Edge Coding

When all your footage has been synced up, you should have it professionally "edge-coded." This has nothing to do with the latent edge numbers printed on the film. Edge-coding involves having the same "rubber numbers" printed between the sprocket holes on the film and the mag. It lets you easily find the corresponding stretch of sound to any shot, and vice-versa.

Editing

Initially, you'll be cutting out large chunks of your footage. These "outtakes" should either be hung in order in a special "trim" bin or (if you're sure you won't need them) "reconstituted" on their original rolls (keeping them in order and sync as you do so, with the help of the edge-code numbers). As you cut down your film, you'll have more and more outtakes. Be sure to include them in order on the original rolls, otherwise you may never find them again. (You may decide that a scene that you had discarded will work, after all.) You should also have a dedicated trim bin for the shots you're working on to build up scenes. Shots of less than twenty frames might not have any (latent) edge numbers printed on them. Be sure to write edge numbers on these with a grease pencil before you cut them; otherwise you won't be able to find where they belong when you have the negative cut.

Whenever you make a cut, you should count on losing at least a frame from each adjoining shot. This is because when the original negative is conformed to the edited workprint, the splices are made with "cement," not tape, and one frame has its emulsion scraped off before being glued to another. For fades or dissolves, you will need every frame that will overlap with another one. That means you have to start the dissolve *before* the shot ends (by however many frames you want it to be); you cannot wait till it ends and then expect to have a dissolve.

You need to add blank leader to the beginning and end of every roll of picture and mag. As you start creating outtakes, it's best to put leader at the beginning and end of them too. You can also use leader as a "picture slug" if you don't have the footage yet, or if a section of the film is damaged. Secondhand prints can also be used as slug, and are cheaper. (You cut them into your assembly upside down so you don't confuse them with your own film.) If you find them too distracting, you'll need to use leader.

As you edit the sound, you build up tracks. As mentioned above, most flatbeds let you listen to two tracks in sync at any one time: you can thread whichever two tracks you want to listen to. A single track saves time (and splices), but gives you less of an idea of the final sound track. If you eventually combine dialogue and effects on a single track, you may be able to get away with two tracks in total. Probably you'll need three or four: two for sync, and the others for narration, effects, or music. Once the editing is over, you will have a professional sound mix, which will synthesize all your tracks into one.

If this is the first time you're editing film, you'll need assistance in preparing the tracks for the mix. Briefly, in order to maintain sync, you use an editing table and synchronizer to add an equal length of leader (with sync marks and beeps) at the head and tail of every track, and intersperse the mag tracks with nonmagnetic filler (or slug) wherever there is no sound on them. (The synchronizer ensures this is accurate to the frame.) You may wish to splice together or purchase prefabricated "loops" of effects like ambience, bird songs, traffic, and so on, since these will help fill in holes in your tracks. You then write out cue sheets, specifying which sounds are where on what tracks, their relative volumes, and whether they are to be cross-faded, faded, or brought in abruptly. Finally, be sure to choose a studio and mixer who come well recommended, because a professional mix can be very expensive.

Conforming to the Original

Once you have your film edited as you'd like it, it has to be conformed to the original. If you shot on negative film, this means cutting (or "matching") the negative. It's a long and tedious process. Many filmmakers do it once, at the start of their careers, and thereafter pay a professional to do it for them. The matcher will usually organize the negative into two separate rolls: A and B rolls. One shot will be on the A roll with nothing but black leader on the same stretch of the B roll (which lets through no extra light). The next shot would be on the B roll, with nothing but black leader on the A roll. This way of cutting the negative hides the cement splices behind the black leader, so you don't see them on the release prints. It also lets you dissolve between or superimpose two images by positioning one on the A roll and the other at the same point on the B roll. At this time you also need to prepare your beginning and end titles—either by shooting them yourself, or paying an optical house to do them for you.

Printing the Original

Once the original is conformed (i.e., the negative cut), you need to have it printed. You can make a "release print" directly, but (especially if you want more than one release print, or if you have subtitles or other optical effects) usually you'll need to go to an intermediate and have release prints struck from that. There are a number of different technologies of printing. "Full immersion wet gate contact" printing minimizes scratches and grain and generally maximizes image quality. The print will be timed from shot to shot, and corrected accordingly. Some labs can perform their own optical effects (like freeze frames), but if you have any elaborate effects, you may need to go to a separate optical house. The first print the lab will make for you will be an "answer print." It will be timed and color corrected, but may not be perfect. Once you've viewed this, and either given your okay or asked for further corrections, the lab may make a "Corrected First Answer Print" for you. (Since all the information is stored in a computer, you can keep ordering new prints until it's as good as it will get.) You can then have an intermediate and your release prints made. Your mixed magnetic sound track will become either a magnetic-striped track or an optical track alongside the film frames. Optical tracks are the norm, even though they're worse quality (lower frequency response and higher noise level), because if you're going to run off a number of prints, they're a lot cheaper. If possible, have your film lab also make your optical master. The lab will tell you how you should prepare the mixed magnetic track for them. Finally, when ordering your release prints, you'll need to specify whether you want the prints to be balanced for tungsten (3200K) or xenon (5400K) projection. (Larger cinemas tend to have xenon projectors.)

At this point, you're more than ready for distribution.

9. Distribution

Independent filmmaking . . . [involves]
a radical difference in understanding
filmmaking. . . . Once your film is released you may have to travel with it and
the direct contact you have with the
public . . . impact[s] the way you'll be
making your next film. . . . [Y]ou [and
the public] challenge each other in
your assumptions and expectations. . . .
[T]his mutual challenge between the
work and the film public, or between
the creative gesture and the cinematic
apparatus is precisely what keeps
independent filmmaking alive.

—Trinh Minh-ha

Now that your film's finished, you probably feel some combination of exhaustion and exhilaration. Many filmmakers experience a wealth of conflicting emotions as they prepare to release their film to scores of unseen spectators. Since the moment you complete your film marks the beginning of its (social) life, you'll want to think carefully about how and who you want to distribute it.[1]

"Distribution" is the process of letting your film loose on the world. It is the crucial link between artists and audiences, and production and exhibition. Far from washing your hands of your film, you now have the chance to enter the fray with it—to observe it being viewed, discussed, evaluated, reviewed, and regurgitated. As Trinh suggests in the epigraph above, this experience will probably be both rewarding and enlightening for you. After all, you really don't know what your film's about until you see how people (and communities) respond to it. Moreover, distributing your film permits a *relatively* democratic firsthand encounter between you and your viewers that is all too rare in an age of home videos and multimillion dollar Hollywood box office hits. That is, your presence at festivals and other screenings should be equally enriching for your film's viewers.

It's hard to believe, but an effective distribution strategy is as important as any other aspect of filmmaking, and can be as absorbing (and costly) as the production itself. But if you really want people to see your film, it's worth the effort. The first question is what you want to do with your film. Would you like it to be watched by as many people as possible? Have you targeted specific audiences, interest groups, or markets? (Archival/academic research only? Educational or theatrical? The film festival circuit? Local community cable channels? Broadcast television? Home video? Domestic? International?) You also need to consider how much control you want to have over distribution and marketing. How much money and time can you spare? And how much do you expect to make (or recoup) from it?

Some filmmakers prefer to distribute their film themselves or in filmmakers' cooperatives. Others develop long-standing relationships with

◄ **FIGURE 69** A group of Mursi watching *The Mursi* (1974) during the making of *The Migrants (1985)*, by Leslie Woodhead, Mursiland, Ethiopia.

a trusty distributor. Others again choose a combination of distributors, depending on the market. We've tried it both ways, self-distributing and handing everything over to an educational distributor. This final chapter discusses in turn self-distribution, professional distribution, broadcast television, theatrical distribution, and film festivals. At the very least, if you envisage doing no more with your film than entering a few film festivals, you should read the next three paragraphs and the section on festivals at the end. But you'd be surprised at how many people out there would be interested in what you've made. If you have time, consider distributing your film yourself. If not, why not approach a few outside distributors to see if they're interested in taking it on (they'll do all the work for you)? After all the time and effort you've invested in making your film, isn't it worth a little more to make sure people actually have a chance to see it?

SELF-DISTRIBUTION

Why consider self-distribution? Among the most important qualities you want in a distributor is a keen interest in and understanding of your film. You also want a strong commitment to it. And who could be more committed than you? It can be a tremendous pleasure to follow your creation closely as it makes its way out into the world. If you do your own distribution you'll be the one to receive all the phone calls and letters about it—and hence have an additional level of contact with your audiences over and above your exposure on the festival circuit or in your own classroom. Then there's the pecuniary factor: after all you've invested in the film, you may need to get something back. While educational distributors in the U.S. currently offer around 25 percent of the selling price as royalties, if you self-distribute you'll pocket 100 percent of the net proceeds. The flip side, of course, is that self-distribution can be extremely time-consuming and expensive: striking prints, dubbing tapes, and putting together and mailing brochures, flyers, posters, and other forms of publicity all take a lot of work and money. But don't let this put you off. As veteran self-distributor Ayoka Chenzira (*Hair Piece: A Film for Nappyheaded People*, 1985) testifies,

Before you begin lashing yourself with thoughts of all the money you've spent to get a good mix, how you fought with the timer at the lab who accused you of being too picky, and all the graveyard hours and money you spent at the on-line session, know that anything can be rented and sold in this country [the U.S.]. Anything! Somewhere there is an audience for your work. You may need help in identifying them, you may stumble on them by accident, but they are out there. Also know that you have advantages over traditional distributors. For you there is a tremendous opportunity to explore and create new markets and to effect social change through what people see as well as what they expect to see. You already have information about your potential audiences simply because you've gone through production and have met key people in the process.[2]

GETTING STARTED

The first challenge in self-distribution is to get the word out, hyperbolically: you've got a great new film that people simply must see. One way to start is to submit it to festivals. If you envisage a mass audience, the theatrical market can be a satisfying but difficult one to crack. You can also approach television stations. But for most independent documentary and ethnographic films, your best bet is the educational market. Most universities, libraries, museums, and even high schools all have budgets for audiovisual materials, including films and videos.

Publicity

So how do you go about it? First of all, you'll probably want to have a brochure or a flyer made. At the very least, it's inexpensive to make photocopies of a one-page information sheet you've composed yourself on a computer. Although many filmmakers have their publicity professionally designed and printed, since you can now incorporate digitized images in computer files, it's quick and easy to put together passable-looking publicity yourself. (This also lets you revise your flyer every time your film receives an award or has a noteworthy exhibition.) Film flyers typically feature a provocative production photograph, a snappy summary of the content (you'll need to make this much more racy than run-of-the-mill academic prose if you want to entice anyone's interest), a list of awards and prestigious screenings, and the name, address, and phone number of the distributor (you, in this case). You may also want to include a few laudatory comments—whether from other filmmakers, film critics, anthropologists (if relevant), or anyone else. (Getting blurbs is not as difficult as you might suppose. If a scholar or critic expresses appreciation for your work, why not ask them to give you a few sentences in writing? If there's someone whose support you think would be particularly meaningful, why not send them a VHS dub of your film, and ask if they would consider commenting on it? Many people are flattered to be solicited.) Finally, if you'd like to be considered for speaking engagements, along with your screening, you should include that information too.

Direct Mailing

Once you have your flyer or brochure, you're ready for a direct mailing. Even if you think your film will appeal to everyone, you'll save yourself some trouble if you concentrate on certain constituencies. Libraries, universities, and museums are good bets, especially for ethnographic films. Consider also contacting curators of film programs and traveling series at "nonprofit showcases" or "art houses," at home and abroad (see "Theatrical Distribution," below). If a curator is very enthusiastic about your film, he or she will probably generate further exposure to it, directly and indirectly. Like film librarians and professors, curators may persuade their organizations to buy or rent your work. Many of them sit on the boards and juries of film festivals and programs. In addition, a fair number write critical articles and books—and a mention in print would also contribute to the general awareness of your work.

When you pitch to universities, be creative about which departments your film might appeal to. Certainly anthropology departments are a good place to start for ethnographic films, but what about others related to your topic? While we were self-distributing *In and Out of Africa*, it was bought by departments of African-American studies, African studies, art history, cinema studies, communications, museum studies, political science, sociology, world cultures, *and* anthropology. We probably should have tried business schools too (the film is about international trade) but never got around to it. Independent filmmaker Julia Reichert recommends getting hold of college catalogues to see what kinds of departments exist these days.[3] It helps to send your publicity to named individuals—department heads, librarians, and professors interested in the themes addressed in your film. Although the costs of mailing will add up, you may get a substantial discount by buying a bulk rate permit from your local post office.

It's helpful to have a few good mailing lists. For many academic disciplines there are professional umbrella organizations that publish membership directories. The directory for the American Anthropological Association (AAA) lists professors' areas of specialty. You can buy this from the AAA in Washington, D.C., or find it in your local library or in any anthropology department. The AAA also has an annual conference at which they screen ethnographic films. They don't pay a rental fee but do give out awards. The meetings are attended by anthropologists from around the world, as well as by a few distributors, so you may receive interesting and informed feedback (and perhaps even a distribution offer). The AAA also publishes a monthly newsletter in which conferences of affiliated organizations are listed, often as early as a year in advance. Other professional, academic, and cultural organizations also hold conferences that occasionally include film and video screenings. If you write to the organizers well ahead of time, enclosing a flyer, they just might show your film.

Another useful organization is the National Alliance for Media Arts and Culture (NAMAC) in Oakland, California (see "Media Organizations" in appendix 3). It publishes an up-to-date directory of media organizations in the U.S., many of which show documentaries. In addition, they put out a monthly newsletter, *Media Information Network* (MAIN), in which you and your work can be listed under the following categories: touring media artists, touring programs, and new works. The newsletter is consulted regularly by media curators looking for additions to their programs.

You can also get the word out through reviews and press coverage. If your film is to be screened somewhere, whether as part of a festival or another event, you may want to send flyers to local newspapers and magazines, including university publications. If you're lucky, some of them may review your film. Many reviewers, particularly those of an academic stripe, will want to see your film more than once, so make a number of review copies and don't expect to get them back for a while, if ever. If interest is strong at this point you should consider assembling a press kit. This would include an eye-catching folder containing your brochure, perhaps a longer summary, a "press release" describing the making of the film, filmmakers' and subjects' biographical statements, extra blurbs, and publicity photos (usually black-and-white), both of the subjects of the film and of the filmmakers "in action." Make sure you label all your tapes (even if you made a film, you will probably want to send out VHS dubs initially) and photos clearly with the film title, and the name and address they should be returned to. Mark the running time on the cassette, as well. If you're feeling creative, you might want to put some thought into how you package the tape itself. To protect the tapes, you should only mail them in a hard plastic case. Some cases feature a transparent window pocket in which you can insert a photo-copy or print of a production still. You can also add the title to the spine. Putting this together will not be cheap but if it gets you reviewed, that may be worth considerably more than the cost of the kit and cassette.

Another way to elicit interest in your film is to send publicity mate-rial to film and video, anthropology, and sociology journals, as well as any periodicals geared toward your specific subject. You may want to consider *Cinéaste, Afterimage, The Independent, Anthropology Today,* and *Visual Anthropology Review* (see "Publications" in appendix 3). *Release Print* and other film publications may not review your film, but if you're a member of the organization that publishes them, they might list de-tails about awards your film wins and upcoming screenings. You could also send publicity material to serials that are thematically related to the subject of your film: if, say, you've made a film about sweatshops, you could contact serials published by labor organizations. Additionally, there are a number of independent catalogues and databases that list films and videos, also organized thematically—anything from the Pro-gram for Art on Film's *Art on Film* to the Television Trust for the En-vironment's *Moving Pictures Bulletin* to the Media Network's *Guide to Anti-Poverty Media.*

If you're not systematic about it off the bat, dealing with the business end of distributing your film can become the bane of your existence. You'll need to decide on a purchase and rental price. Get a hold of a few distribution catalogues so you can see how films are marketed and what might be reasonable fees. Generally, films are priced by format (film or tape, ¾ inch or ½ inch) and by length. You might want to set one purchase rate for institutions and another for individuals. Some distributors have sliding fees so they can offer a reduced rate to nonprofit groups that can't afford the regular rate. You should add a separate packaging and shipping cost on top of the sales or rental fee (domestic, international, and rush). Some distributors include pricing and purchasing information directly on their brochure; others create a separate price sheet, which they mail out along with the brochure.

As a rule, you shouldn't send a print or tape out until you receive a purchase order, purchase order number, or a written request specifying the date the institution will screen it, and the format they want (16mm, VHS or ¾ inch). If you don't create a paper trail, you'll probably have a hard time getting paid. Thus you'll need to compose separate rental and sales agreements, outlining specific conditions for each. Consider whether or not you want people to sign these before you send them your film. At the very least, you should include the conditions on the invoice. On both rental and sales agreements and on the invoice you should specify price, conditions of payment (e.g., thirty days), to whom the check should be made out, and where to send it. (Some distributors allow people who initially rent the film to apply the rental cost toward purchase, within a specified time period—say, sixty days.) You should also stipulate that the tape is protected under (in the U.S., federal) copyright law and cannot be duplicated for any purpose, and that if it is not purchased, it should be returned the day after the screening, insured for its purchase price. And mention also that the customer should *not* use fiber-filled envelopes, since they damage video tapes and VCRs, and that the customer is responsible for all damage to the tape or print. Finally, be sure to inspect every tape or print for damage after it's returned.

However careful you may be, the chances are you'll run into occasional problems. Some potential purchasers insist on previewing a film before buying it (and you've got to admit that buying a film sight unseen is fairly ludicrous). You can try to persuade them to rent it, but if they refuse, you may want to accept a preview request in writing, and charge only for shipping and handling so long as the film is returned in good condition within a week or two. In our experience, nine times out of ten people buy the film after seeing it. While most distributors don't send previews out to rental customers, if you have a dub available, you may want to send it out under the same conditions as a purchase preview.

Unfortunately, piracy (illegal copying) is an endemic problem—especially for videos. While it's difficult to protect yourself against it, there are a few measures you can take. You can ask your dubbing house to have a supertitle, along the lines of "Preview Copy" or "Not For Classroom Use," pop up at odd intervals in the tape. There is also an invisible "Copyguard" that many dubbing houses can add to your tapes, which theoretically deforms the signal if it is copied. But any semi-savvy technician can bypass it, so it is no more than partly effective. On the other hand, institutional buyers may occasionally ask your permission to duplicate a tape they have purchased from you, to allow them to circulate one copy and always have a good one "in the vault." If you do give them written permission to do so, you may want to specify that the dub(s) be used only at the institution itself. Alternatively, you could charge institutions a considerably lower price for a replacement copy (so long as they return the broken or worn out original). Finally, you should know that a few universities may insist on having the right to rent your film out to other individuals and institutions around the country. Be aware that a number of state institutions may intend to rent out your film without telling you (unless you ask expressly), which would cut into your profits since they won't give you a royalty. You don't have to sell to them under these conditions, and you may be able to negotiate certain restrictions. (We've always stipulated that they rent it out only within their own state.)

You'll need to devise a detailed logging system to keep track of the following: (1) how many tapes or prints you have available (if you number each one you can monitor how many times they go out); (2) who needs which tape or print and when; and (3) which tapes and prints are out, when they were sent, when they're due back, and whether or not they've been paid for. You should also create a careful invoicing system for rentals and sales. If you're in the U.S., consider consulting an accountant about handling sales tax. You'll need to develop a computer file or use a carbon-form package of first invoices, second invoices, third invoices, and reminders, since people may not pay you within the time you request. And if regular reminders don't get you paid, Julia Reichert says that enclosing copies of all previous correspondence along with an explanatory "letter of last resort" to the head of the organization that owes you money is guaranteed to "get results!"[4] To keep tabs on everything, you should photocopy every check you receive and attach the copy to the purchase order and other correspondence from that client. You may soon find that you need a dedicated bank account. Remember to keep very careful track of all expenditures (tapes/prints, postage, photocopies, etc.) as well as any income. You'll have to reckon with it all come tax filing time.

Some institutions may ask if you're available for speaking engagements. They will usually pay you a lecture fee, and reimburse your travel expenses. Appearing in person is a wonderful way to receive direct feedback on your film, and engage in a dialogue with your spectators. For her film about a first generation African-American concert dancer, Ayoka Chenzira would give a "slide/lecture presentation on other women in dance, entertain a question and answer session, and, to top it off, teach a master dance class!" For two years she traveled from university to university—"until I could no longer bear to get on a plane, face another faculty luncheon or answer questions as though I had not heard them before."[5] If you're feeling entrepreneurial, you can use appearances as an opportunity for more marketing. We've seen filmmaker Les Blank arrive at a classroom screening with a duffel bag full of tapes, books, and even T-shirts. Of course there may come a point (as there did for Ayoka Chenzira) when you'll have made so many appearances that the questions and discussion become repetitive, and you decide it's time to stop taking engagements. On the other hand, you can pick and choose your venues, and there are always the occasional comments and questions that add a new twist to your understanding of the film, and may even turn your own notions on their head.

Self-distribution can be all-consuming, but if it seems overwhelming, it needn't be. Some funding organizations give grants specifically for distribution. You can apply for grants to help you with any or all of these tasks. There are shipping houses that can send out your tapes and prints. Publicists and press agents can handle your publicity. An accountant can set up a billing system for you. A distribution cooperative (composed of filmmakers like yourself; see "Distributors" in appendix 3) can also take on much of this. On the other hand, an outside distributor, with a little help and guidance from you, can do just about all of it.

OUTSIDE DISTRIBUTORS

Of course it's much less time-consuming to have a professional distributor do most of this work for you. Distributors take a large percentage of the gross from the sales (normally 70 to 80 percent in the educational market), but if they're savvy and competent, they'll send literature about your work all over the country, and perhaps internationally. They often have comprehensive mailing lists, and established contacts in libraries, school systems, museums, television stations, and festivals. Of course not all distributors are equally proficient, and some have better connections in a particular market than in others. Educational distributors, for instance, rarely have extensive affiliations in the television world—and besides, even if you strike a deal for 25 percent of the gross of educational sales, you may find in the fine print that the distributor will receive 90 percent of the proceeds from a TV sale. Some distributors will take on both domestic and international distribution, but unless they have an established international track record, you might want a separate foreign distributor for overseas (although documentaries sell and rent for considerably less outside the U.S.). All of this, in principle, is negotiable.

How do you find a distributor? Get recommendations. Start by asking other filmmakers whose work is similar to your own. Look through festival catalogues, and the "Distributors" section in appendix 3. The Association of Independent Video and Filmmakers has also put out the excellent *AIVF Guide to Film and Video Distributors*. Peruse distributors' catalogues and flyers to see what kind of films they distribute, and whether yours would fit. If your film overlaps thematically with others, a distributor might include it in a special "theme" brochure. Once you identify distributors you're interested in, ask them how they would promote your film, and which markets they can reach. Will they give your film its own flyer or brochure? Will they provide you with flyers to pass around yourself? Will they enter your film into festivals? Which ones? Who pays the entry fees? Who pockets the financial awards?

Personality is also important. Do you like the people you'll be working with? After all, you'll probably be signing a contract granting them rights for as long as five years, or even longer. How efficient and courteous are they? (If they don't return your phone calls or letters, they may treat your prospective customers in the same way.) Do they like and understand your film? If you want to be involved in designing flyers and other marketing tactics, will they be receptive to your suggestions? If you don't want to be involved, are they competent and creative enough to market your film themselves?

Remember, however, that a distributor has to choose you, too. They'll do this primarily on the basis of a screening of your film, which you should send them (probably on VHS), along with a press packet detailing awards, screenings, blurbs, and reviews you may have accumulated up until that point. If you receive an offer from one distributor, you should politely let any others you are interested in know that. It could help you negotiate a more favorable contract. If you don't receive any immediate offers, you may wish to hold off approaching a distributor until your film has been in a festival or two. But don't despair, there are a number of potential distributors out there (including you), and, as distributor Debra Zimmerman points out, sometimes the smaller ones will give you the special attention a large distributor cannot.[6]

DISTRIBUTION CONTRACTS

If a distributor makes you an offer, they'll probably issue you a "standard contract." Even though this looks official, nothing is standard, and there may be quite a bit to negotiate (though the deal also has to be worthwhile for the distributor). At this point, you may want to hire a lawyer to look it over and decipher the legal jargon. This is an added expense, but most filmmakers feel they've worked too hard to throw away their proceeds because of some oversight.

Here are a few questions to bear in mind as you negotiate a contract.

Rights

Which "markets" do you want your distributor(s) to handle? Which markets do you want to target yourself or give to another distributor? Do you want to grant "sole and exclusive rights" for certain markets, or do you want to share them? Some (not all) distributors will insist on having exclusive rights, at least within the educational sphere. Either way you should be very clear about what exactly is involved. What happens if people contact you directly—can you sell or rent them a copy or are you obliged to refer them to your distributor? What territory does your agreement cover—international and/or domestic? If you're in the U.S., does "domestic" include all of North America? If the distributor does not cover international distribution, does it have relations with or recommendations for foreign distributors? And, if your agreement is only domestic, will the distributor pass on to you any inquiries that they receive from abroad? What period is covered by the contract?

Royalties

Royalties are a percentage paid to you based on a calculation of rentals and sales. There's no standard for this percentage. It could be based on either net or gross profits—terms that should be carefully defined within the contract. We have a contract with an educational film distributor that provides us with 25 percent of the combined fees of all educational sales and rentals. The distributor pockets the other 75 percent, out of which it pays the distribution expenses. Some educational distributors offer 60/40 or 50/50 deals if you're willing to share expenses. Other contracts, particularly for noneducational markets, will be different. You should find out how often you will receive royalties and whether royalty reports include details about who is renting and purchasing your film. Some distributors, like book publishers, may offer an advance against royalties. Lawyer Robert Freedman suggests that filmmakers also insist on the right to audit (at their own expense), so they can check up on their distributor if they ever suspect any accounting errors.[7]

Pricing

What will the distributor charge for the sale or rental of your film? Will discounts be offered to particular groups? (Distributors may, for example, extend significant discounts to public libraries.) Will they give a discount to groups representing your special causes? If your film is about a certain community or interest group, what kinds of rights (to viewing, to distribution, and to royalties) will they have? Can you arrange free screenings or benefits? Is there a separate home video price? Will the film be sold to university libraries that rent out copies? If so, do you get a percentage of those rentals? (Probably not.) Can all (or some) of the pricing details be tied down in the contract?

Your Responsibilities

What do you need to provide to the distributor? Usually the distributor will request a master tape or "CRI" from which they can strike copies (do not give up your negative or original master, however, as you may need it in the future). They'll also want publicity photos, reviews, and blurbs for the flyers. The costs quickly add up. Try to negotiate who pays for them.

If you want to write a study guide to accompany the film—something that may make it a more enticing teaching tool for some academics—ask the distributor if they're open to it. If so, will they help you produce it? Our distributor has warned us that study guides do not automatically increase sales. (Study guides, by "framing" viewings with your own interpretation of your film, pose the danger of foreclosing alternative ways of viewing it. On the other hand, the additional contextual information contained in a study guide may outweigh its possible disadvantages.)

Prints, Dubs, and Reviews

Will the distributor provide you with copies of your film at "cost" price? How much will that be? (Because distributors often order large quantities of tapes or prints, the cost may be far less than if you were to have a dub made yourself, should you suddenly need another one.) If you need a copy, who orders it and how fast can you get it? Usually distributors won't let you deal with their postproduction or duplication house, but may well have prints or tapes on hand, and can send you some at short notice. You should also stipulate that if your agreement ends you have the right to buy back all remaining copies at cost.

Additionally, you should ask the distributor to provide you with copies of any reviews or mentions they receive about your film.

Cutting and Citing

You should be explicit about what the distributor can and cannot do to your film. Some standard contracts say that the distributor can make cuts in it, or sell excerpts of it. Be aware that they will probably put their logo at the head of your tapes or prints. Make sure they don't cut into the beginning of your program, particularly if it starts in black: check their video dubs before they start sending them out. When you deliver your master you should write out very clear instructions about where your program begins.

Jumping Ship

Finally, you should have a clause in your contract that reverts distribution rights back to you if you think your distributor is not keeping their end up. This might include their violating the contract, not promoting your film, or not responding properly to customers or reviewers. Distributor Mitchell Block has pointed out, however, that creating a market for some documentaries can take time. Even if someone wants to purchase a copy, it may take a year before they have the funds in their budget to do so.[8] So allow your film and distributor time to gather momentum.

TELEVISION

A national television broadcast will probably expose your film to a thousandfold more viewers than any other form of distribution. It is also the best way for you to recoup your expenses (or even turn a profit). Obviously not all filmmakers want their films to be broadcast—the subject may be unsuitable, or the material too "dangerous," too open to misinterpretation, or too controversial. You may even have made a film not only *with* but also exclusively *for* your subjects. But if it is your goal to have your film televised, you have a number of avenues to explore.

In the U.S., your best option is Public Broadcasting (PBS), since the networks only occasionally broadcast independent work. The national PBS series "POV" ("Point of View") has an open call for programs once a year. "Frontline" (based at WGBH in Boston) is a prestigious independent series for productions closer to journalism (especially exposés) than your regular ethnographic fare. If you can't secure a national broadcast, many local public television channels also have series, with varying life spans. The Corporation for Public Broadcasting publishes a *Public Broadcasting Directory,* which contains useful names and addresses in the area of television broadcasting. Often individual public television stations would rather buy films from affiliate stations than directly from independent producers. Many stations don't want the hassle of dealing with independents, preferring to acquire prepackaged, preapproved programming (at a lower rate). Therefore, if you can persuade one public television station to buy your film, consider allowing it to sell the film to others. You'll receive a smaller share of the pie, but it may be the only way to go. And you may end up with much greater exposure than if you went it alone.

Cable television (carrying, for example, the Discovery Channel in the U.S.) and other private production companies (such as National Geographic Explorer) are also options. If you don't care about being paid and your goal is simply to have your program seen, there are a number of community access organizations and university stations on cable television looking for programming. You can find out about these through your city government and local universities, or you can contact the National Academy of Cable Programming in Washington, D.C., for their *Producers' Source Book: A Guide to Cable TV Program Buyers* (see "Television" in appendix 3). Another more lucrative educational possibility is Instructional Television (ITV), which "narrowcasts" in participating classrooms around the U.S.[9]

There are also quite a few international television options you might want to try: Great Britain has the British Broadcasting Corporation (BBC), regional independent television (ITV) stations, and Channel

Four. The latter has a reputation for being a little more politically *engagé*, multicultural, and aesthetically experimental than the others; but they all regularly broadcast documentaries. Australia's Special Broadcasting Service (SBS) and Australian Broadcasting Corporation (ABC) and Canada's Canadian Broadcasting Corporation (CBC) might also be interested in your work. Since 1992, France and Germany have shared a dedicated "cultural" channel called La Sept/ARTE (a collaboration between the French La Sept and the German ZDF and ARD), which funds documentaries as well as broadcasting them. FR3 (France 3) shows quite a few documentaries, and Germany has a new "alternative" station in Berlin, FAB (Fernsehen aus Berlin), which shows documentaries and experimental videos. Japan has NHK, Belgium RTBF, and Switzerland RTSR. Your chances are not necessarily going to be better in larger countries—smaller (or at least poorer) countries have tighter production budgets, and therefore need to purchase more outside programming.

Independent filmmaker Karen Thorsen suggests that foreign sales are determined by six factors: "(1) The person you've chosen to make the sale [i.e., yourself or an agent]; (2) the kind of film or video you're trying to sell; (3) the festivals that have screened your work; (4) the country you're trying to sell to; (5) the release format you've chosen for that particular country; and (6) the effort you put into your sales pitch." [10] As with domestic distribution, careful timing is of the essence. Foreign television sales are typically both easier to secure and more lucrative than international box office revenues or educational royalties, and so you may want to concentrate on them. The main way to get in touch with a potential foreign purchaser is through the festival circuit—both internationally and at the more prestigious festivals at home, which are regularly attended by foreign buyers. If you are intent on a theatrical release in a particular country, it's advisable to set that up before selling broadcast rights—few cinemas want to screen a film that's already aired on national television. When deciding whom to sell broadcast rights to, it's best to sell to national stations and networks before satellite stations, since the broadcast range ("footprint") of the latter may extend over several countries. With the "unification" of Europe and the probable proliferation of transnational channels around the world in the coming years, you should be especially cautious. Likewise, if you're set on selling to local cable companies as well as a national station, check first that neither interferes with the stipulations of the other. And if you're negotiating both educational and broadcast rights within a single country, there's sense in signing with an educational distributor first because university and school librarians may otherwise tape your program off the air.[11]

Regardless of whom you sell to, the revenue you receive from licensing fees will probably be less than the cost of producing the film itself. Therefore, if you're intent on foreign sales, you should try to tap a number of markets. You might well want to have your film broadcast in the country in which it was shot: if the film is uncontroversial and presents no danger to your subjects, this may be an appreciated form of reciprocity. Even if the financial dividends are insignificant, it provides a local airing and should provoke public discussion of the issues, events, or people represented in your film. Likewise, if your film has regional or diasporic significance or, indeed, in any way transcends the interests of its originating country, there could be numerous television outlets. Many New World countries, for instance, especially those in the Caribbean, are as interested in broadcasting films about Africa as are African countries themselves. Finally, in order to sell to international television it's almost imperative to have a clean (non-subtitled, unmixed) version of your film so that foreign broadcasters can add a sound track or subtitles in their own language.

A word about dealing with television stations: unless there's an open call or you're just aiming for local cable, your chances of being broadcast as an unknown are slim (but not impossible). You might prefer to have a distributor approach television stations for you, especially in foreign markets. Although you'll have to share your profit, stations tend to take distributors more seriously. Bear in mind that broadcasters usually have strict technical standards, and some may stick their noses up at the less expensive production formats, such as Hi-8. Some will broadcast ¾-inch video while others will insist on a 1-inch or Betacam master. Stations will usually need the master to be in whatever broadcast standard they use (NTSC, PAL, or SECAM). Remember too that 16mm film runs at 24 fps in the U.S., and at 25 fps in Europe. You should also be aware that the ideal length of a program may vary from one country to the next, and in some cases you may be asked to shorten your film.

Since both editing and transferring are expensive, try to get the station to pay for them. Television stations invariably require documentation of releases and permissions (or they will ask you to sign a contract indemnifying them from lawsuits). The contract will also include the territory and licensing period, as well as the number of times the station may broadcast your program. They may insist on premieres or exclusive rights within certain areas. You and a lawyer should look the contract over carefully before you sign it.

THEATRICAL DISTRIBUTION

Documentaries rarely receive an extensive theatrical release, and ethnographic films more rarely still. But it does happen from time to time. Witness the success of such recent films as *Roger and Me, Paris Is Burning,* and *Hoop Dreams.* At least part of the popularity of such films has to do with their controversial subject matter. While these films played in theaters all over the U.S., the best most documentary filmmakers hope for is a limited release in selected art houses and nonprofit showcases. These are small movie theaters, often in college towns, or tucked away in corners of large cities. (See "Art Theaters" in appendix 3.) Curators form quite a closely-knit network, often sharing information about new works, and co-planning traveling series and guest-curated evenings. Since curators are cultural brokers, they excel at helping you reach appreciative audiences.

Drawing the attention of art houses is not always easy. One film archivist friend recommends sending a whole press package, including reviews, lists of previous screenings, and, if you can afford it, a tape of your film directly to a theater's programmers (not simply to the theater itself). If you don't get a response after a couple of months you should then contact the programmers by phone; even if they're not interested in screening your film, they may have suggestions for other venues. Another way that your film may be brought to the attention of art house programmers is through important festivals showcasing new independent work, such as Sundance or New Directors/New Films (at New York's Museum of Modern Art and the Film Society of Lincoln Center).

If you're feeling competitive, the Independent Feature Market is also a good (albeit expensive) place to show your film and to find a theatrical distributor (see "Festivals" in appendix 3).

Another possibility is to "four wall" a theater, also known as staging your own preview. This involves renting a theater or other exhibition space for one or several screenings, doing your own publicity, and collecting the proceeds (if there are any left!). This gives you the opportunity to screen the film for distributors, reviewers, and the general public in a "proper setting"—on a large screen, with an audience. Screenings are sometimes packaged as benefits, whether for a cause related to the film's subject matter or to raise completion money for the film itself. It does, however, require considerable resources (or persuasion) to line up a theater, and a tremendous amount of publicity.[12]

FILM FESTIVALS

Film festivals are fine venues in which to show your work, especially if you manage to go in person, since they provide you with a chance to interact with your audience, watch an array of other films, and meet like-minded filmmakers. Some offer prizes, more often certificates than cash. A few also pay a rental fee. Awards and even screenings may help you find funding for your next project. Still, there are countless festivals, and you'll probably have to choose between them. A few have been in existence for decades, and have consecrated international reputations. Others have started more recently or may last for only a few years. Some run like clockwork and others will leave you exasperated at their lack of organization; some are cynically cool and professional and others are intimate and personal. Festivals are run by a variety of organizations, including film societies, museums, arts centers, universities, and religious or political organizations. Because of the expense involved in entering them—everything from entry fees, postage, packaging, and copies of reviews, to dubs or prints, and production stills—you should try for festivals you have a realistic chance of at least participating in (and then maybe a few long shots if you can afford it). Finally, keeping on top of the festivals is a lot of work in itself, so you may want to keep a detailed up-to-date computer log with the name of festivals, entry dead-lines, fees, when and how you sent out entries, their current status, which copy you sent, and when the screenings or award announcements are.

Finding Festivals

Many of the major American film and video organizations publish periodicals, which they send to their members. These often contain festival information and other useful listings. The Film Arts Foundation (based in San Francisco) sends its members *Release Print,* a monthly newsletter with festival listings in the back. *The Independent* is sent to members of AIVF (based in New York City) and is available at a few news vendors. The AIVF has also published a comprehensive guide to film festivals (see "Outside Distributors," above). Other useful books are Alan Gadney's *How to Enter and Win Film Contests* (n.d.) and *The International Film Guide* (n.d.) (Festival Publications, P.O. Box 10180, Glendale, CA 91209, USA).

Choosing Festivals

If you entered every festival you're eligible for, you'd do nothing but . . . enter festivals. There are literally hundreds. It's also expensive to pay entry fees, postage, packaging. First off, you should determine whether you're eligible. Check the medium and format(s) they require: many of the more mainstream festivals will only show films (although some will accept video-to-film transfers). Almost all festivals accept VHS dubs for preview, though quite a few festivals that accept videos will only show ¾ inch or Betacam. The larger international festivals may require a world or at least a national premiere. You may wish to choose your premiere accordingly. (But be careful playing around with dates, since festivals tend to accept for competition only those films made within the previous year.) Double check the subject matter of the festival. Some festivals are geared toward special topics. Student festivals are iffy. They tend to be conservative, especially in the documentary section. Some seem to prefer more polished, narrative-style films, and student ethnographic filmmakers will be competing with graduate students from film schools.

Entering Festivals

Be sure to read the rules carefully, and check the deadline. Does the tape have to be received or just postmarked by a given date? Alan Gadney advises filmmakers to send tapes ahead of the deadline, in case the judges are reviewing films on an ongoing basis (you'll have a better chance of their actually watching yours).[13] Usually late entries are disqualified, but you should call and check since festivals occasionally extend deadlines if they don't receive enough high-quality entries. Sending a tape by regular mail is the cheapest option but there's no saying when it'll arrive and if it gets lost, it'll be impossible to trace. Independent courier companies tend to be more reliable. Rates vary depending on the speed of the service, the tracking options you choose, and whether you purchase their insurance. (One curator we know recommends taking out insurance with your chosen carrier. This is especially important when sending out expensive film prints.)

If you are sending tapes or prints internationally, be sure to follow the mailing instructions on the entry form carefully to avoid having your project stuck in customs. If it's left up to you to figure out how to ship your work, it may be easiest to pay your carrier to do the customs work for you. Alternatively, a professional customs broker can provide the service for a fee. To avoid paying unnecessary duty, be sure to stipulate that your work is being sent for noncommercial use and will be returned to its country of origin.

Film festivals often have different juries for different categories. Your film may fit within more than one category so think carefully about which one you want to enter. This can make the difference between reaching a responsive audience, and even winning a prize, and not. Even such luminaries as Lynn Hershman and Trinh Minh-ha have had trouble with this. As Trinh says, "Festival categories have always posed problems for me; I have to decide quite arbitrarily what kind of jury I want for the films and in most cases the decision does not turn out to be a good one. Fact-oriented eyes do not like experiments and vice versa, as if science and experimentation can ever do away with each other."[14] Many festivals feature "local filmmaker" and "student" categories, often with lower entry fees. However, juries for these categories may also be more conservative, so your chances of an award are not necessarily any higher.

Other considerations to bear in mind when entering festivals include the following:

- Some festivals will ask on their form for the right to excerpt clips for festival publicity. You may want to insist on choosing and providing these excerpts yourself. You should also check on the length of the excerpts (one festival that showed one of our films redefined the term "excerpt" by playing it in its entirety on cable television without consulting us).

- Send a high-quality, clean (i.e., drop-out free) dub. (*Never* submit your original—films and tapes often get lost or damaged in this process.) Clearly label cans, containers, and cassettes. If the technical quality of a preview tape looks sloppy, the festival will wonder about the quality of the master.

- Be sure to have a supply of VHS dubs on hand. You may want to order them from a professional duplication house. The more copies you have made at any one time, the cheaper the cost per tape.

- If you're asked to provide a summary, try to alert the judges to any surprises you might have at the end, because often they will watch only the first ten minutes or first third of a tape before making up their minds.

- Some festivals will return a video tape to you only if you ask them in writing and if you send a stamped self-addressed envelope. Make sure you follow all their instructions or you'll never see your tape again.

- Send all publicity materials the festival requires: photographs, brochures, news clippings (if you have them). If your work is selected, your photographs may be reproduced in the program. You might want to put together a press folder. Don't count on getting these materials back.

- Package your film or tape carefully to prevent damage. You should use hard cases for the tapes, and boxes or bubble (fiber-free) envelopes.

- Check that your film or tape arrives. Many festivals ask you to include a self-addressed postcard that they will return to you. Make sure you put the name of the festival on the card (some festivals just stick the card in the mail without marking anything on it).

- Festivals are generally understaffed and underfunded; if your film is not selected you may not hear from them for a long time, occasionally not until well after the festival is over. If you're included in the festival, they will *probably* call you. You may need to send them a screening copy or print immediately. If it's a big festival they might pay your way. Some festivals offer accommodations, and almost all a free pass to the screenings. Since distributors and broadcasters often attend festivals, they provide an opportunity for you to seek out wider distribution. And if you do go, bring plenty of posters, flyers, and video dubs. You may want to spread the word about your individual screening, get names and addresses of people interested in your work, and follow up on their inquiries later.

- If your film is accepted at a festival but the programmers make no mention of paying your way there, it does no harm to ask if they could help out. Although festivals that fly filmmakers in and put them up generally advertise the fact up front, there are always exceptions, and having your film screened at a festival will be more rewarding all around if you can be there in person.

You may feel that in its attention to the practical and economic nitty-gritty of distribution this last chapter has sounded a disquieting note. Don't be put off by it. The sense of curiosity and engagement you and the viewers of your films can experience as you interact with each other, both firsthand and at one remove, will far outweigh the banality of such businesslike considerations. Moreover, as film critic B. Ruby Rich has noted, the disdain in which distribution is often held is unjustified, as if "the service of linking filmmakers to their audiences, users to their desired works of art, is somehow inherently less noble than serving filmmakers and the public in the various other sanctioned, but equally mediated, methods."[15] By undertaking to put and keep your films in distribution you're providing a service both to yourself and to the viewing public.

Finally, there is one additional service you can provide us all. That is to go out and make another film. Real life may always exceed the reach of our representations, but, as we said at the beginning of this handbook, the challenge is to keep on after it.

Appendix One
RELEASE FORMS

Here are three prototype release forms, differing in length, amount of legalese, and overall fearsomeness, which you may adapt as you wish. None of them involves any payment. In the U.S., a $1 honorarium (or "consideration" fee) is often drafted into the form, to make it (more) legally binding. Remember though that even a signed release form—with or without an exchange of money—is no guarantee against lawsuit, and you should check with a lawyer before writing up your own.

STANDARD PERSONAL RELEASE FORM, MODEL 1
(Letter Form, No Payment)
Date
   Dear *Name,*
   We are very grateful that you have agreed to participate in our film/video, provisionally titled *Title,* that you agree to the recording of your image and voice, and that you cede all the necessary rights for the reproduction, exhibition, broadcast, and sale of the recording, with no temporal or geographical limits, by all means and on all media (whether available today or invented in the future), and without any obligations on our part to you.
   We have the right to edit your recording/interview according to our needs, and are not obliged to include any or all of it in any resulting program.
   With many thanks for your contribution;
   Yours sincerely,
      Filmmaker's or Filmmaker's Representative's Signature
      For *Production Company Name*
      Address
Read and Approved:
      Signature of Subject

STANDARD PERSONAL RELEASE FORM, MODEL 2
(Short, No Payment)

Participant's Name
Program Title
Production Date(s)
Location

    I authorize *Producer/Production Company* to record and edit into the Program described above, my name, likeness, image, voice, interview, and performance. *Producer/Production Company* may use and authorize others to use all or parts of the Program. *Producer/Production Company* shall own all rights, title, and interest in and to the Program, including the recordings, to be used and disposed of without limitation as *Producer/Production Company* shall in its sole discretion determine.

Participant's Signature
Date
Address

ADDITION FOR MINORS

    I represent that I am the parent and/or guardian of the minor who has signed above or is the participant in the Program. I agree that we both shall be bound by this agreement.

Parent's/Guardian's Signature
Date

STANDARD PERSONAL RELEASE FORM, MODEL 3
(Long, No Payment)

Participant's Name
Program Title
Production Date(s)
Location

   In consideration of my appearance in the above Program, I hereby authorize *Producer/Production Company* to record my name, likeness, image, voice, and performance on film, tape, or otherwise for use in the above Program or parts thereof. I agree that the Program may be edited as desired and used in whole or in part for any and all broadcasting, audio/visual, and/or exhibition purposes in any manner or media, in perpetuity throughout the world. I understand that I have no rights to the Program or any benefits derived therefrom.

   I consent to the use of my name, likeness, image, voice, and biographical material about me in connection with the promotion of the Program.

   I represent that I have the right to enter into this Agreement and that my performance and the rights I have granted in this Agreement will not conflict with or violate any commitment or understanding I have with any other person or entity.

   I agree to indemnify and hold harmless *Producer/Production Company* from and against all claims, losses, expenses, and liabilities of every kind, including reasonable attorney's fees, rising out of the inaccuracy or breach of any provisions of this Agreement. I expressly release *Producer* from any and all claims arising out of the use of the Program.

   This Agreement represents the entire understanding of the parties and may not be amended unless mutually agreed to by both parties in writing.

Participant's Signature
Date
Address

ADDITION FOR MINORS

   I represent that I am the parent and/or guardian of the minor who has signed above or is the participant in the Program. I agree that we both shall be bound by this agreement.

Parent's/Guardian's Signature
Date

Appendix Two

INTERNATIONAL TELEVISION STANDARDS
AND ELECTRICITY CURRENTS

The specifications below are true to the best of the authors' knowledge at press time. However, for locations where more than one video standard, voltage, or frequency is listed, and wherever there is a gap in the table, you should check beforehand with the relevant embassies for the exact regions where you will be filming.*

Location	Video Standard	Voltage (V)	Frequency (Hz)
Abu Dhabi	PAL, SECAM	220	50
Afghanistan	PAL, SECAM	220	50
Albania	PAL	220	50
Algeria	PAL	127, 220	50
Angola	PAL	220	50
Antigua	NTSC	110, 220	60
Argentina	PAL	220	50
Armenia	SECAM	220	50
Australia	PAL	240	50
Austria	PAL	220	50
Azores	PAL	220	50
Bahamas	NTSC	120	60
Bahrain	PAL	220	50
Bangladesh	PAL		
Barbados	NTSC	120	50
Barbuda	NTSC	110, 220	60
Belgium	PAL	127, 220	50
Belize	NTSC	110, 220	

Benin	SECAM	220	50
Bermuda	NTSC	120	60
Bolivia	NTSC	115, 230	50
Botswana	SECAM	240	60
Brazil	PAL	220	60
Brunei	PAL	220	50
Bulgaria	SECAM	220	50
Burkina Faso	SECAM	220	50
Burma (Myanmar)	NTSC		60
Burundi	SECAM	220	50
Cambodia	PAL	220	50
Cameroon	PAL	127, 220	50
Canada	NTSC	110, 240	60
Canary Islands	PAL	127	50
Cayman Islands	NTSC		60
Central African Republic	SECAM	220	50
Chad	SECAM	220	50
Channel Islands	PAL	127, 220	50
Chile	NTSC	220	50
China (People's Republic)	PAL	220	50
Columbia	NTSC	110, 220	60
Congo (People's Republic)	SECAM	220	50
Costa Rica	NTSC	110	60
Cuba	NTSC	120	60
Curacao	NTSC	120	60
Cyprus	PAL	220	50
Czech Republic	SECAM	220	50
Denmark	PAL	220	50
Diego Garcia	NTSC	110	60
Djibouti	SECAM	220	50
Dominica	NTSC	220	50
Dominican Republic	NTSC	110	60
Dubai	SECAM (H)		
Ecuador	NTSC	120	60
Egypt	PAL	220	50
El Salvador	NTSC	110	60

Equatorial Guinea	SECAM	220	50
Ethiopia	PAL	127	50
Fiji	NTSC		
Finland	PAL	220	50
France**	SECAM	230	50
Gabon	SECAM	127, 220	50
Gambia	PAL	220	50
Germany	PAL***	220	50
Ghana	PAL	230	50
Gibraltar	PAL	230	50
Great Britain	PAL	220	50
Greece	SECAM	220	50
Greenland	PAL	220	50
Grenada	NTSC	110, 220	50
Guam	NTSC	110	60
Guatemala	NTSC	110, 220	60
Guinea	PAL	127, 220	50
Guyana	NTSC		
Haiti	NTSC	115, 220	50
Hawaii	NTSC	117	60
Honduras	NTSC	110, 220	60
Hong Kong	PAL	220	50
Hungary	PAL	220	50
Iceland	PAL	220	50
India	PAL	230	50
Indonesia	PAL	220	50
Iran	SECAM	220	50
Iraq	SECAM	220	50
Ireland	PAL	220	50
Israel	PAL	230	50
Italy	PAL	127, 220	50
Ivory Coast	SECAM	220	50
Jamaica	NTSC	110	50, 60
Japan	NTSC	100, 200	50, 60
Johnston Island	NTSC	110	60
Jordan	PAL	220	50

Kenya	PAL	240	50
Kuwait	PAL	240	50
Laos	PAL	240	50
Lebanon	SECAM	110, 190	50
Liberia	PAL	120	60
Libya	PAL	120	50
Luxembourg	PAL, SECAM	120, 208	50
Macau	PAL	220	50
Macedonia	PAL		
Madagascar	SECAM	127, 220	50
Madeira	PAL	220–240	50
Malawi	PAL	220	50
Malaysia	PAL	240	50
Mali	SECAM	125, 240	50
Malta	PAL	240	50
Mauritius	SECAM	220	50
Mauritania	SECAM	220	50
Mexico	NTSC	127, 220	50, 60
Micronesia	NTSC	110, 220	60
Monaco	PAL, SECAM	125	50
Montserrat	NTSC	220	60
Morocco	SECAM	115	50
Mozambique	PAL	220	50
Namibia	PAL		
Nepal	PAL	230	50
Netherlands	PAL	220	50
Netherlands Antilles	NTSC	120, 220	50, 60
New Zealand	PAL	230	50
Nicaragua	NTSC	117	60
Niger	SECAM	220	50
Nigeria	PAL	220	50
North Korea	PAL, NTSC		
Norway	PAL	230	50
Oman	PAL	220	50
Pakistan	PAL	220	50
Palau	NTSC		

Panama	NTSC	110	60
Papua New Guinea	PAL		
Paraguay	PAL	220	50
Peru	NTSC	220	60
Philippines	NTSC	115	60
Poland	PAL	220	50
Portugal	PAL	110, 220	50
Puerto Rico	NTSC	120	60
Qatar	PAL	220–240	50
Romania	PAL	220	50
Rwanda	SECAM	220	50
Samoa (American)	NTSC	120	60
Samoa (Western)	PAL	220	50
Sao Tome e Principe	PAL		
Saudi Arabia	PAL, SECAM	120, 230	50, 60
Senegal	SECAM	220	50
Seychelles	PAL		
Sierra Leone	PAL	230	50
Singapore	PAL	220	50
Slovakia	SECAM	220	50
Somalia	PAL	220	50
South Africa	PAL	220	50
South Korea	NTSC	100	60
Spain	PAL	127, 220	50
Sri Lanka	PAL	220	50
St. Kitts & Nevis	NTSC	220–230	60
St. Lucia	NTSC	220	50
St. Vincent & Grenadines	NTSC	220–240	50
Sudan	PAL	220	50
Surinam	NTSC	115–127	50, 60
Swaziland	PAL	220	50
Sweden	PAL	220	50
Switzerland	PAL	220	50
Syria	PAL	115, 220	50
Taiwan	NTSC	100	60
Tanzania	PAL	230	50

Thailand	PAL	220	50
Tibet	PAL	220–240	50
Togo	SECAM	220–240	50
Tonga	NTSC		
Trinidad & Tobago	NTSC	117	60
Tunisia	SECAM	117, 220	50
Turkey	PAL	110, 220	50
Uganda	PAL	220	50
United Arab Emirates	PAL	220	50
Uruguay	PAL	220	50
U.S.A.	NTSC	110	60
Former U.S.S.R.	PAL, SECAM	220	50
Venezuela	NTSC	110, 220	60
Vietnam	PAL	220	50
Virgin Islands (U.S. & U.K.)	NTSC	110, 220	
Yemen	PAL, NTSC	220	50
Former Yugoslavia	PAL	220	50
Zaire	SECAM	220–240	50
Zambia	PAL	230	50
Zimbabwe	PAL	220	50

*Thanks to Devlin Videoservice, Four Media Company, John Bishop, and Bob Templer for their help in preparing this table.

**These figures hold for metropolitan France as well as the overseas remnants of empire (Guadeloupe, French Guiana, Martinique, Réunion, French Polynesia, Wallis and Fortuna, New Caledonia, St. Pierre and Miquelon, and Mayotte).

***The standard for East Germany was SECAM.

Appendix Three
NAMES AND ADDRESSES

This appendix contains the various names and addresses that are scattered throughout the book. It is divided up into the following sections: (1) Media Organizations; (2) Publications; (3) Funding; (4) Legal; (5) Equipment and Services; (6) Travel; (7) Archival Materials; (8) Festivals; (9) Art Theaters; (10) Distributors; and (11) Television.

MEDIA ORGANIZATIONS

Many of the organizations listed here provide special services for members, hold film festivals, and produce serial publications.

Academy of Motion Pictures Arts
   and Sciences
8949 Wilshire Boulevard
Beverly Hills, CA 90211 – 1972
Tel. 310 247 3000
Fax. 310 859 9619

American Film Institute
2021 N. Western Avenue
Los Angeles, CA 90027 – 1625
Tel. 213 856 7787, 856 7707
Fax. 213 462 4049

Association of Independent Video
   and Filmmakers (AIVF/FIVF)
304 Hudson Street, 6th floor
New York, NY 10013
Tel. 212 807 1400
Fax. 212 463 8519

The Documentary Center
   at Columbia University
2875 Broadway, 2nd floor
New York, NY 10025
Tel. 212 854 9578

Film Arts Foundation
346 Ninth Street, 2nd Floor
San Francisco, CA 94103
Tel. 415 552 8760
Fax. 415 552 0882

International Documentary
   Association
1551 South Robertson Boulevard,
   Suite 201
Los Angeles, CA 90035 – 4233
Tel. 310 284 8422
Fax. 310 785 9334

National Alliance for Media Arts and
    Culture (NAMAC)
1212 Broadway, Suite 816
Oakland, CA 94612
Tel. 510 451 2717
Fax. 510 451 2715

National Black Programming
    Consortium
929 Harrison Avenue, Suite 104
Columbus, OH 43215
Tel. 614 299 5355
Fax. 614 299 4761

Society for Visual Anthropology
American Anthropology Association
4350 North Fairfax Drive, Suite 640
Arlington, VA 22203
Tel. 703 528 1902
Fax. 703 528 3546

Visual Studies Workshop
31 Prince Street
Rochester, NY 14607
Tel. 716 442 8676
Fax. 716 442 1992

Women in Film
6464 Sunset Boulevard, Suite 900
Los Angeles, CA 90028
Tel. 213 463 6040
Fax. 213 463 0963

PUBLICATIONS

These publications may list information about funding, festivals, upcoming
screenings, employment, equipment for sale, television calls for films, and
other opportunities.

AfterImage
(See Visual Studies Workshop, in
    "Media Organizations," above.)

Anthropology Today
Royal Anthropological Institute
50 Fitzroy Street
London, W1P 5HS
Great Britain
Tel. (44) 1713870455
Fax. (44) 1713834235

Art on Film
Art on Film Database
Program for Art on Film
c/o Pratt SILS
200 Willoughby Avenue
Brooklyn, NY 11205
Tel. 718 399 4206
Fax. 718 399 4207

Cinéaste
200 Park Avenue South, Suite 1601
New York, NY 10003
Tel. & Fax. 212 982 1241

The Independent
(See Association of Independent
    Video and Filmmakers, in "Me-
    dia Organizations," above.)

International Documentary
(See International Documentary As-
    sociation, in "Media Organiza-
    tions," above.)

Moving Pictures Bulletin
Television Trust for the Environment
TVE Centre for Environmental
    Communications
Prince Albert Road
London, NW1 4RZ
Great Britain
Tel. (44) 1715865526
Fax. (44) 1715864866

Release Print
(See Film Arts Foundation, in "Me-
    dia Organizations," above.)

TAKE ONE
(See National Black Programming
    Consortium, in "Media Organi-
    zations," above.)

Visual Anthropology Review
(See Society for Visual Anthropol-
    ogy, in "Media Organizations,"
    above.)

FUNDING

The institutions listed here can provide information about possible funding
sources, sometimes including themselves.

The Foundation Center
79 Fifth Avenue
New York, NY 10003–3076
Tel. 212 620 4230; 800 424 9836
Fax. 212 807 3677

The Ford Foundation
320 East 43rd Street
New York, NY 10017
Tel. 212 573 5000
Fax. 212 599 4584

Fulbright Scholar Program
c/o Council for International
    Exchange of Scholars
3007 Tilden Street, NW, Suite 5M
Washington, DC 20008–3009
Tel. 202 686 4000
Fax. 202 362 3442

Funding Exchange
Paul Robeson Fund for
Independent Media
666 Broadway, # 500
New York, NY 10012
Tel. 212 529 5300
Fax. 212 982 9272

John Simon Guggenheim Memorial
Foundation
90 Park Avenue
New York, NY 10016
Tel. 212 687 4470
Fax. 212 697 3248

Independent Television Service
(ITVS)
190 Fifth Street East, Suite 200
St. Paul, MN 55101
Tel. 612 225 9035
Fax. 612 225 9102

The John D. and Catherine T.
MacArthur Foundation
140 S. Dearborn Street
Chicago, IL 60603
Tel. 312 726 8000
Fax. 312 917 0334

National Assembly of Local Arts
Agencies
927 15th Street, NW, 12th floor
Washington, DC 20005
Tel. 202 371 2830
Fax. 202 371 0424

National Assembly of State Arts
Agencies
1010 Vermont Avenue, NW,
Suite 920
Washington, DC 20005
Tel. 202 347 6325
Fax. 202 737 0526

National Endowment for the Arts
Media Arts Program
The Nancy Hanks Center
1100 Pennsylvania Avenue, NW
Washington, DC 20506
Tel. 202 682 5452
Fax. 202 682 5721

National Endowment for the
Humanities
Division of Public Programs
Humanities Projects in Media,
Room 420
1100 Pennsylvania Avenue, NW
Washington, DC 20506
Tel. 202 606 8278
Fax. 202 606 8557

The Rockefeller Foundation
420 Fifth Avenue
New York, NY 10018
Tel. 212 869 8500
Fax. 212 398 1858

LEGAL

California Lawyers for the Arts
Fort Mason Center
Bldg. C, Room 255
San Francisco, CA 94123
Tel. 415 775 7200
Fax. 415 775 1143

Library of Congress
Copyright Office
Washington, DC 20559–6000
Tel. 202 707 3000
Fax. 202 707 2371

Volunteer Lawyers for the Arts
1 East 53rd Street, 6th floor
New York, NY 10022
Tel. 212 319 2910 (hotline)
Fax. 212 752 6575

Washington Area Lawyers
  for the Arts
1325 G Street, NW, Lower Level
Washington, DC 20005
Tel. 202 393 2826
Fax. 202 393 4444

EQUIPMENT AND SERVICES

Film and Video Accessories

Aaton Des Autres (West Coast)
4110 W. Magnolia Boulevard
Burbank, CA 91505
Tel. 818 972 9078
Fax. 818 972 2673
or:
ABEL CINE TECH (East Coast)
66 Willow Avenue
Staten Island, NY 10305
Tel. 718 273 8108
Fax. 718 273 8137
or:
AATON
2, Rue de la Paix
38001 Grenoble
France
Tel. (33) 76426409
Fax. (33) 76513491

Arriflex Corporation
617 Route 303
Blauvelt, NY 10913–1123
Tel. 914 353 1400
Fax. 914 425 1250
or:
Arriflex Corporation
600 N. Victory Boulevard
Burbank, CA 91502–1639
Tel. 818 841 7070
Fax. 818 848 4128

Audio Services Corporation
10639 Riverside Drive
N. Hollywood, CA 91602
Tel. 818 980 9891; 800 228 4429
Fax. 818 980 9911
or:
Audio Services Corporation
32 Punch Street
Artarmon, NSW 2064
Australia
Tel. (61) 29014455

Automated Media Systems
  (for lithium batteries)
Attn. Stuart Cody
8 Holton Street
Allston, MA 02134–1377
Tel. 617 787 4313
Fax. 617 787 4438

B & H Photo-Video
119 West 17th Street
New York, NY 10011
Tel. 212 444 6601; 800 947 9901
Fax. 800 947 9003

Cine 60 Incorporated
Film Center Bldg.
630 Ninth Avenue
New York, NY 10036
Tel. 212 586 8782
Fax. 212 459 9556

Cinema Products Corporation
(for stabilization systems)
3211 S. La Cienaga Boulevard
Los Angeles, CA 90016
Tel. 310 836 7991; 800 955 5025
Fax. 310 836 9512

The Film Group (for crystal sync
conversions)
Attn. George Odell
500-B Silas Deane Highway
Weathersfield, CT 06109
Tel. & Fax. 860 529 1877

K & H Products Ltd.
PO Box 246
North Bennington, VT 05257
Tel. 802 442 8171
Fax. 802 442 9118

Lowel-Light Manufacturing, Inc.
140 58th Street
Brooklyn, NY 11220
Tel. 718 921 0600; 800 334 3426
Fax. 718 921 0303

Miller Fluid Heads (USA) Inc.
410 Garibaldi Avenue
Lodi, NJ 07644
Tel. 201 473 9592
Fax. 201 473 9693
or:
Miller Fluid Heads
30 Hotham Parade
Artarmon 2064
Sydney
Australia
Tel. (61) 24396377
Fax. (61) 24382819

Nagra Tape Recorders
Kudelski SA
Route de Genève 22
CH-1033 Cheseaux
Switzerland
Tel. (41) 217320101
Fax. (41) 217320100

Schoeps Microphones
c/o Posthorn Recordings
142 West 26th Street
New York, NY 10001
Tel. 212 242 3737
Fax. 212 924 1243

Sennheiser Electronic Corporation
PO Box 987
6 Vista Drive
Old Lyme, CT 06371
Tel. 203 434 9190
Fax. 203 434 9022

Super-8 Sound
2805 W. Magnolia Boulevard
Los Angeles, CA 91505
Tel. 818 848 5522
Fax. 818 848 5956
or:
Super-8 Sound
95 Harvey Street
Cambridge, MA 02140
Tel. 617 876 5876
Fax. 617 497 0151

Swiss Professional Movie Equipment
Ltd. (Bolex)
38 West 32nd Street, Room 1206
New York, NY 10001
Tel. 212 594 6340.
Fax. 212 714 0719
or:
Bolex International SA
15 Route de Lausanne
CH-1401 Yverdon-les-Bains

Switzerland
Tel. (41) 24216021
Fax. (41) 24216871

Film Stock

AGFA Information Center:
Tel. 800 568 1378

Fuji Professional Motion Picture
    Products
Sales and Marketing
6200 Phyllis Drive
Cyprus, CA 90630
Tel. 714 372 4200; 800 326 0800
Fax. 714 894 6018

KODAK Information Center:
Tel. 800 242 2424

KODAK Distribution Centers:
New York City Region:
360 West 31st Street
New York, NY 10001
Tel. 212 631 3450; 800 621 3456
Fax. 800 755 1816
Hollywood (Western Region):
6700 Santa Monica Boulevard
Hollywood, CA 90038
Tel. 213 464 6131; 800 621 3456
Fax. 213 468 1567; 800 648 9805

Super-8 Sound
(See "Film and Video Accessories,"
    above.)

Film Laboratories

DuArt Film and Video
245 West 55th Street
New York, NY 10019
Tel. 212 757 4580
Fax. 212 977 7448

Fotokem / Foto-Tronics
2800 West Olive Avenue
Burbank, CA 91505
Tel. 818 846 3101, 846 3102
Fax. 818 841 2130

Four Media Company (also performs
    video-to-film and film-to-video
    transfers)
2901 West Alameda Avenue
Burbank, CA 91505–4455
Tel. 818 840 7000; 800 840 7000
Fax. 818 840 7249

Nonlinear Video

Avid Technology, Inc.
Metropolitan Technology Park
One Park West
Tewksbury, MA 01876
Tel. 508 640 3326; 800 949 AVID
    (ext. 3326)
Fax. 508 640 0063

ImMIX
644 E. Fort Avenue, Suite 207
Baltimore, MD 21230
Tel. 410 783 0600
Fax. 410 783 0606

or:
ImMIX
PO Box 2980
Grass Valley, CA 95945
Tel. 916 272 9800
Fax. 916 272 9801

Media 100
Multimedia Group
Data Translation
100 Locke Drive
Marlboro, MA 01752
Tel. 508 460 1600, 800 832 8188
Fax. 508 481 8627

TRAVEL

United States Council for International Business, Inc. (for carnet information)
39 Broadway, Suite 1915
New York, NY 10006
Tel. 212 747 1800
Fax. 212 747 1948

Centers for Disease Control and Prevention
Atlanta, GA
Tel. 404 639 2572

ARCHIVAL MATERIALS

Library of Congress
(See "Legal," above)

Museum of Modern Art Film/Stills Archive
11 West 53rd Street
New York, NY 10019–5498
Tel. 212 708 9530
Fax. 212 708 9889

National Archives at College Park
Motion Picture, Sound, and Video Branch
8601 Adelphi Road
College Park, MD 20740–6001
Tel. 301 713 7060
Fax. 301 713 6904

UCLA
Arts Special Collections
22478 University Library
University of California
Los Angeles, CA 90024
Tel. 310 825 7253
Fax. 310 825 1210

FESTIVALS

United States

Ann Arbor Film Festival
PO Box 8232
Ann Arbor, MI 48107
Tel. 313 995 5356
Fax. 313 995 5396

Chicago International Film Festival
415 N. Dearborn Street
Chicago, IL 60610–9990
Tel. 312 644 3400
Fax. 312 644 0784

CINE (selects films and videos for
    representation in international
    festivals and disburses awards)
1001 Connecticut Avenue, NW,
    #1016
Washington, DC 20036
Tel. 202 785 1136
Fax. 202 785 4114

City Lore Festival of Film and Video
72 East First Street
New York, NY 10003
Tel. 212 529 1955
Fax. 212 529 5062

Human Rights Watch International
    Film Festival
485 Fifth Avenue, 3rd floor
New York, NY 10017
Tel. 212 972 8400
Fax. 212 972 0905

Independent Feature Market
c/o Independent Feature Project
104 West 29th Street, 12th floor
New York, NY 10001
Tel. 212 465 8200
Fax. 212 465 8525

International Documentary Associa-
    tion Congress
(See "Media Organizations," above.)

International Robert Flaherty Film
    Seminar
305 West 21st Street
New York, NY 10011
Tel. 212 727 7262
Fax. 212 727 7276

Margaret Mead Film and Video
    Festival
American Museum of Natural
    History
Central Park West at 79th Street
New York, NY 10024–5192
Tel. 212 769 5305
Fax. 212 769 5329

National Educational Media
    Competition
655 13th Street
Oakland, CA 94612
Tel. 510 465 6885
Fax. 510 465 2835

New Directors/New Films (MoMA)
Film Society of Lincoln Center
70 Lincoln Center Plaza
New York, NY 10023–6595
Tel. 212 875 5610
Fax. 212 875 5636

New York Film Festival
Film Society of Lincoln Center
140 West 65th Street
New York, NY 10023
Tel. 212 877 1800
Fax. 212 724 2813

San Francisco International Film
Festival/Golden Gate Awards
1521 Eddy Street
San Francisco, CA 94115–4102
Tel. 415 567 4294
Fax. 415 921 5032

Society for Visual Anthropology
Film Screenings
Attn.: Joan Swayze Williams
523 Garcia Street
Santa Fe, NM 87501
Tel. 505 988 5782
or contact:

American Anthropological
Association
1703 New Hampshire Avenue, NW
Washington, DC 20009
Tel. 202 232 8800
Fax. 202 667 5345

Sundance Film Festival
225 Santa Monica Boulevard,
8th floor
Santa Monica, CA 90401
Tel. 310 394 4662
Fax. 310 394 8353

International

Amsterdam International Documen-
tary Film Festival
Kleine-Gartmanplantsoen 10
1017 rr Amsterdam
Netherlands
Tel. (31) 206273329
Fax. (31) 206385388

Berlin International Film Festival/
Internationale Filmfestspiele Berlin
Budapester Strasse 50, D-10787
Berlin
Germany
Tel. (49) 30254890
Fax. (49) 3025489249

Bilan du Film Ethnographique
Musée de l'Homme
Palais de Chaillot
17 Place du Trocadero
75116 Paris
France
Tel. (33) 147043820
Fax. (33) 145535282

Bilbao International Festival of
Documentary and Short Films
Colon de Larreategui, # 37
PO Box 579
37–4 Dcha
488009 Bilbao
Spain
Tel. (34) 44245507
Fax. (34) 44245624

Cinéma du Réel
Bibliotheque Publique d'Information
Centre Georges Pompidou
19, Rue Beaubourg
75197 Paris Cedex 04
France
Tel. (33) 142771233
Fax. (33) 142777241

Dreamspeakers Festival
9914 76th Avenue
Edmonton, Alberta, T6E 1K7
Canada
Tel. 403 439 3456
Fax. 403 439 2066

Edinburgh International Film
  Festival
88 Lothian Road
Edinburgh, EH3 9B7
Scotland
Great Britain
Tel. (44) 1312284051
Fax. (44) 1312295501

Festival Dei Popoli
Via dei Castellani 8
50122 Firenze
Italy
Tel. (39) 55294353
Fax. (39) 55213698

Gottingen International Ethno-
  graphic Film Festival
c/o Institut für den Wissenschaft-
  lichen Film
Nonnenstieg 72
D-37075 Gottingen
Germany
Tel. (49) 5515024160
Fax. (49) 5515024400

Leipzig International Documentary
  Film Festival /
Internationales Leipziger Festival für
  Dokumenton-und Animations
  film
Postfach 940
04009 Leipzig
Germany
Tel. (49) 307828702
Fax. (49) 307829740

London International Film Festival
South Bank
London, SE1 8XT
Great Britain
Tel. (44) 1718151322
Fax. (44) 1716330786

Nyon International Documentary
  Cinema Festival
POB 2320
CH-1260 Nyon
Switzerland
Tel. (41) 223616060
Fax. (41) 223617071

Royal Anthropological Institute In-
  ternational Festival of Ethno-
  graphic Film
c/o Granada Center for Visual
  Anthropology
Coupland 2
University of Manchester
Manchester M13 9PL
Great Britain
Tel. (44) 1612753999
Fax. (44) 1612752529

Sunny Side of the Doc
Doc Services
3 Square Stalingrad
13001 Marseilles
France
Tel. (33) 91084315
Fax. (33) 91843834

Sydney Film Festival
Box 25
Glebe, NSW 2037
Australia
Tel. (61) 26603844
Fax. (61) 26928793

Toronto Festival of Festivals
69 Yorkville Avenue, # 205
Toronto, Ontario MR5 1RB
Canada
Tel. 416 967 7371
Fax. 416 967 9477

Venice International Film Festival
Ca. Giustinian, San Marco
30124 Venice
Italy
Tel. (39) 415230852
Fax. (39) 415204163

Yamagata International Film Festival
Kitagawa Bldg 4f
6–42 Kagurazaka
Shinjuku-ku
Tokyo 162
Japan
Tel. (81) 332669704
Fax. (81) 332669700

ART THEATERS AND ALTERNATIVE EXHIBITION SITES (U.S.)

911 Media Arts Center
117 Yale Avenue, N
Seattle, WA 98109
Tel. 206 682 6552
Fax. 206 682 7422

Anthology Film Archives
32–34 2nd Avenue
New York, NY 10013
Tel. 212 505 5181
Fax. 212 477 2714

Art Institute of Chicago/Film Center
Columbus Drive at Jackson
   Boulevard
Chicago, IL 60603
Tel. 312 443 3735
Fax. 312 263 0141

Boston Museum of Fine Arts
Education Dept.
465 Huntington Avenue
Boston, MA 02115
Tel. 617 267 9300 (ext. 305)
Fax. 617 267 9328

Center for Contemporary Arts
   Cinematheque
PO Box 148
Santa Fe, NM 87504
Tel. 505 982 1338
Fax. 505 982 9854

Chicago Filmmakers
1543 West Division
Chicago, IL 60622
Tel. 312 384 5533
Fax. 312 384 5532

Cleveland Museum of Art
11150 East Boulevard
Cleveland, OH 44106
Tel. 216 421 7450
Fax. 216 421 7438

Exploratorium
3601 Lyon Street
San Francisco, CA 94123
Tel. 415 563 7337
Fax. 415 561 0344

Facets Multimedia Inc.
1517 W. Fullerton
Chicago, IL 60614
Tel. 312 281 9075
Fax. 312 929 5437

Film Forum
209 West Houston Street
New York, NY 10014
Tel. 212 627 2035
Fax. 212 627 2471

Hallwalls
2495 Main Street, Suite 425
Buffalo, NY 14214
Tel. 716 835 7362
Fax. 716 835 7364

Harvard Film Archive
Carpenter Center for the Arts
19 Prescott Street
Cambridge, MA 02138
Tel. 617 495 4700
Fax. 617 495 8197

Legacy Productions
The Center for Contemporary Arts
PO Box 775333
St. Louis, MO 63177
Tel. 314 534 2291
Fax. 314 726 6904

Museum of Fine Arts
1001 Bissonnet
Houston, TX 77005
Tel. 713 639 7530
Fax. 713 639 7595

Museum of Modern Art
What's Happening? Film Program
11 West 53rd Street
New York, NY 10019
Tel. 212 708 9530, 708 9610
Fax. 212 708 9531

Neighborhood Film and Video
    Project
3701 Chestnut Street
Philadelphia, PA 19104
Tel. 215 387 5125
Fax. 215 895 6542

Northwest Film and Study Center
1219 S.W. Park
Portland, OR 97205
Tel. 503 221 1156
Fax. 503 226 4842

Pacific Film Archive
2625 Durant Avenue
Berkeley, CA 94720
Tel. 510 642 1413
Fax. 510 642 4889

Pittsburgh Filmmakers
3712 Forbes Avenue, 2nd floor
Pittsburgh, PA 15213
Tel. 412 681 5449
Fax. 412 681 5503

San Francisco Cinemateque
480 Potrero Avenue
San Francisco, CA 94110
Tel. 415 558 8129
Fax. 415 749 4590

Wexner Center for the Arts
Film and Video Program
Ohio State University
North High Street at 15th Avenue
Columbus, OH 43210–1393
Tel. 614 292 0330
Fax. 614 292 3369

UCLA Film Archive
1438 Melnitz Hall
Department of Theater Arts
405 Hilgard
Los Angeles, CA 90024
Tel. 310 825 8263
Fax. 310 206 3129

DISTRIBUTORS

U.S. Distributors

Arthur Cantor Films, Inc.
2112 Broadway, Suite 400
New York, NY 10023
Tel. 212 664 1290
Fax. 212 496 5718

Budget Films
4590 Santa Monica Boulevard
Los Angeles, CA 90029
Tel. 213 660 0187
Fax. 213 660 5571

California Newsreel
149 Ninth Street, Suite 420
San Francisco, CA 94103
Tel. 415 621 6196
Fax. 415 621 6522

The Cinema Guild
1697 Broadway
New York, NY 10019
Tel. 212 246 5522
Fax. 212 246 5525

Corinth Films
34 Gansevoort Street
New York, NY 10014
Tel. 800 221 4720; 212 463 0305
Fax. 212 929 0010

Direct Cinema Limited
PO Box 10003
Santa Monica, CA 90410–9003
Tel. 310 396 4774
Fax. 310 396 3233

Documentary Educational Resources
101 Morse Street
Watertown, MA 02172

Tel. 617 926 0492
Fax. 617 926 9519

Drew Associates
19 Butler Hill
Somers, NY 10589
Tel. 212 391 8380
Fax. 914 277 5567

Facets Multimedia Inc.
1517 W. Fullerton Avenue
Chicago, IL 60614
Tel. 312 281 9075; 800 331 6192
Fax. 312 929 5437

Filmmakers' Library
124 East 40th Street, Suite 901
New York, NY 10016
Tel. 212 808 4980
Fax. 212 808 4983

Films Incorporated, Video
5547 North Ravenswood Avenue
Chicago, IL 60640–1199
Tel. 800 323 4222
Fax. 312 878 8648

First Run/Icarus Films
153 Waverly Place, 6th floor
New York, NY 10014
Tel. 212 727 1711; 800 876 1710
Fax. 212 989 7649

Flaherty Study Center
Claremont School of Theology
Claremont, CA 91711
Tel. 909 626 3521
Fax. 909 626 7062

Frameline
PO Box 14792
San Francisco, CA 94114
Tel. 415 861 5245
Fax. 415 861 1404

Interama
301 West 53rd Street, Suite 19E
New York, NY 10019
Tel. 212 977 4830
Fax. 212 581 6582

Jorge Preloran
4834 Maytime
Culver City, CA 90230
Tel. & Fax. 310 837 9916

Kino International Pictures
333 West 39th Street, Suite 503
New York, NY 10018
Tel. 212 629 6880
Fax. 212 714 0871

Kit Parker Films
1245 10th Street
Monterey, CA 93040–3692
Tel. 800 538 5838
Fax. 408 393 0304

Lafayette Films
152 Wadsworth
Santa Monica, CA 90405
Tel. 310 587 9200
Fax. 310 452 1698

Maysles Films, Inc.
250 West 54th Street
New York, NY 10019
Tel. 212 582 6050
Fax. 212 586 2057

Movies Unlimited
6736 Castor Avenue
Philadelphia, PA 19149
Tel. 215 722 8398
Fax. 215 725 3683

Museum of Modern Art (MoMA)
Circulating Film and Video Library
11 West 53rd Street
New York, NY 10019
Tel. 212 708 9530
Fax. 212 708 9531

National Film Board of Canada
1251 Avenue of the Americas
New York, NY 10020
Tel. 212 586 5131
Fax. 212 246 7404

New Yorker Films
16 West 61st Street
New York, NY 10023
Tel. 212 247 6110
Fax. 212 307 7855

Ogbuide Ltd.
487 Broadway
New York, NY 10013
Tel. 212 226 7854

PBS Video Finders
4401 Sunset Boulevard
Los Angeles, CA 90027
Tel. 800 343 4727
Fax. 818 637 5291

Pennsylvania State University
Audio-Visual Services
Special Services Building
1127 Fox Hill Road
University Park, PA 16802
Tel. 814 865 6314; 800 826 0132
Fax. 814 863 2574

Pennebaker Associates
262 West 91st Street
New York, NY 10024
Tel. 212 496 9195
Fax. 212 496 8195

Phoenix Films Inc.
2349 Chaffee Drive
St. Louis, MO 63146
Tel. 800 221 1274
Fax. 314 569 2834

Swank
201 S. Jefferson Avenue
St. Louis, MO 63103
Tel. 314 534 6300; 800 876 5577
Fax. 314 289 2192

Third World Newsreel
335 West 38th Street, 5th floor
New York, NY 10018
Tel. 212 947 9277
Fax. 212 594 6417

University of California Extension
    Center for Media and Indepen-
    dent Learning
2000 Center Street, Suite 400
Berkeley, CA 94704
Tel. 510 642 0460
Fax. 510 643 9271

Video Verité Library
22-D Hollywood Avenue
Hohokus, NJ 07423
Tel. 201 652 1989
Fax. 201 652 1973

Women Make Movies
225 Lafayette Street
New York, NY 10012
Tel. 212 925 0606
Fax. 212 925 2052

Zeitgeist Films
247 Center Street, 2nd floor
New York, NY 10013
Tel. 212 274 1989
Fax. 212 274 1644

Zipporah Films
1 Richdale Avenue, Unit #4
Cambridge, MA 02140
Tel. 617 576 3604
Fax. 617 864 8006

U.S. Cooperatives

Canyon Cinema Inc.
2325 Third Street, Suite 338
San Francisco, CA 94107
Tel. & Fax. 415 626 2255

New Day Films
121 West 27th Street, Suite 902
New York, NY 10001
Tel. 212 645 8210
Fax. 212 645 8652

International

Argos Films
6 Rue Edouard Nortier
92200 Neuilly
France
Tel. (33) 47229126
Fax. (33) 46400205

Australian Institute of Aboriginal
    and Torres Strait Islander Studies
PO Box 553
Canberra
ACT 2601
Australia
Tel. (61) 62461111

Black Audio Film Collective
7–12 Greenland Street
Camden
London, NW1 OND
Great Britain
Tel. (44) 1712670846
Fax. (44) 1712670845

BBC Video Education and Training
Room A 2090, Woodlands
80 Wood Lane
London, W12 OTT
Great Britain
Tel. (44) 1815762541
Fax. (44) 1815762916

British Film Institute
21 Stephen Street
London, W1P 1PL
Great Britain
Tel. (44) 1712551444
Fax. (44) 1714367950

Film Australia
Eton Road
Lindfield
NSW 2070
Australia

Films de la Pléiade
Comité du Film Ethnographique
Musée de l'Homme
Palais de Chaillot
17 Place du Trocadéro
75116 Paris
France
Tel. (33) 147043820
Fax. (33) 145535282

Granada Television International Ltd
BRITE, London Television Centre,
    Upper Ground
London, SE1 9LT
Great Britain
Tel. (44) 1717378602
Fax. (44) 1719288476

Istituto Superiore Regionale
    Etnografico
Via A. Mereu 56
08100 Nuoro
Italy
Fax. (39) 78437484

Jane Balfour Films Ltd.
163 Gloucester Avenue
London, NW1
Great Britain
Tel. (44) 1715863443, 1717225050
Fax. (44) 1712674241

Les Films de Jeudi
17 Rue Mesnil
75016 Paris
France
Tel. (33) 147042620
Fax. (33) 147042784

NFI Productions
Netherlands Film Institute
PO Box 515
1200 AM Hilversum
Netherlands

O'Rourke & Associates—
    Filmmakers
GPO Box 199, Canberra
ACT 2601
Australia

Royal Anthropological Institute
(See "Publications," above.)

Ronin Films
PO Box 1005
Civic Square
ACT 2608
Australia
Tel. (61) 62480851
Fax. (61) 62491640

Sankofa Film/Video Collective
Unit K
32–34 Gordon House Road
London, NW5 1LP
Great Britain
Tel. (44) 1714850848
Fax. (44) 1714852869

TELEVISION

United States

Corporation for Public Broadcasting
111 16th Street, NW
Washington, DC 20036
Tel. 202 879 9737
Fax. 202 783 1019

Discovery Channel
7700 Wisconsin Avenue
Bethesda, MD 20814–3522
Tel. 301 986 0444
Fax. 301 986 4628

Frontline
WGBH
125 Western Avenue
Boston, MA 02134
Tel. 617 492 2777
Fax. 617 254 0243

National Academy of Cable
    Programming
1724 Massachusetts Avenue, NW
Washington, DC 20036
Tel. 202 775 3611

National Geographic
1145 17th Street
Washington, DC 20036
Tel. 202 857 7680
Fax. 202 775 6590

POV
220 West 19th Street, 11th floor
New York, NY 10011
Tel. 212 989 8121
Fax. 212 989 8230

International

AUSTRALIA

Australian Broadcasting Corporation
GPO Box 9994
Sydney NSW 2001
Australia
Tel. (61) 29503177
Fax. (61) 29503169

Special Broadcasting Service
4 Cliff Street
Wilsons Point
N.S.W.
Australia
Tel. (61) 29642828
Fax. (61) 29573571 & 29565393

BELGIUM

Radio-Télévison Belge de la Com-
munauté Française (RTBF)
Boulevard August Reyers 52
B-1040 Brussels
Belgium
Tel. (32) 27372111

CANADA

Canadian Broadcasting Corporation
(CBC)
1500 Bronson Avenue
PO Box 8478
Ottawa, Ontario K1G 3J5
Canada
Tel. 617 724 1200

FRANCE

France 3 (FR3)
116 Avenue du Président Kennedy
75790 Paris, Cedex 16
Tel. (33) 142302222
Fax. (33) 146479294

ARTE
2a Rue de la Fonderie
F-67000, Strasbourg
France
Tel. (33) 88522222, 88522311
Fax. (33) 88522200
or:
La Sept/ARTE
35 Quai André Citreon
75015 Paris
France
Tel. (33) 140593977
Fax. (33)145780927

GERMANY

Zweites Deutsches Fernsehen (ZDF)
Ezzedheimer Landstrasse
Postfach 4040
6500 Mainz
Germany
Tel. (49) 6131702450
Fax. (49) 6131702452, 6131702157

Arbeitsgemeinschaft der Öffentlich-
rechtlichen Rundfunkanstalten
der Bundesrepublik Deutschland
(ARD)
Bertramstr 8
600 Frankfurt/Main
Germany
Tel. (49) 69590607
Fax. (49) 691552075

Fernsehen aus Berlin (FAB)
Fernsehen International
Europa TV-Ideas, News and Pictures
D-1000 Berlin 27
Germany
Tel. (49) 304335000
Fax. (49) 304335000

GREAT BRITAIN

British Broadcasting Corporation
   (BBC)
Television Centre
Wood Lane
London W12 7JR
Great Britain
Tel. (44) 1817438000, 1815761371
Fax. (44) 1815768806

Channel Four Television
Documentaries
60 Charlotte Street
London WIP 2AX
Great Britain
Tel. (44) 1716314444
Fax. (44) 1714362059

The ITV Network Centre
200 Gray's Inn Road
London, WC1X 8HF
Great Britain
Tel. (44) 1718438110
Fax. (44) 1718438157

JAPAN

Nippon Hoso Kyokai (NHK)
NHK Building
2–2–1 Jinnan
Shibuyaku
Tokyo 150
Tel. (81) 34651111
Fax. (81) 34864712

SWITZERLAND

Radiotelevisione Della Svizzera
   Italiana (RTSI)
Direzione Radio e Télévision,
   Télévisione
Case Postale, CH-6903
Lugano-Besso
Switzerland
Tel. (41) 91581661

MAKES AND MODELS

TAPE RECORDERS

Whether you should record sound with a ¼-inch open-reel tape recorder or an ⅛-inch cassette recorder, or an analog or a DAT machine, will probably depend on a range of contingent factors such as your budget, the climatic conditions of your location, or the models that are available from the institution with which you're affiliated or your local rental house.

There are four standard analog ⅛-inch cassette recorders used in documentary, and they currently run from around $350 to $600. Three of them are made by Sony, the TC-D5 Pro 2, the TC-D5M, and the smaller "Walkman Pro," the WM-D6C. One is made by Marantz, the PMD-430. These are all two-channel stereo models, which means that they can undergo crystal conversion for sync sound recording (at a cost of around $375 to $425). The Walkman Pro is the smallest, lightest, and cheapest, but is more fragile, has small connectors and controls, no VU meter, and no speaker. The differences between the two sturdier models, the TC-D5M and the TC-D5 Pro 2, are slight: the 5M ¼-inch has phono plugs and the Pro 2 has XLR connectors (see "Cables and Connectors," chapter 4), while the 5M but not the Pro 2 has a "metal tape" setting. The only company that performs crystal sync conversions on these recorders (as well as selling them already converted) is The Film Group in Connecticut (see "Equipment and Services" in appendix 3).

Most documentary filmmakers with the resources still choose to use ¼-inch tape recorders, almost all of them high quality models manufactured by Nagra (see "Equipment and Services" in appendix 3)—such as the 4-S, the 4.2, the 3, the E, the IS, the SN, the 4-S, and the D. The two-track stereo ¼-inch Nagra 4-S can come with either its own FM-modulated Pilot system (at around $10,000) or equipped with internal SMPTE time code (at around $12,000). In most documentary applications you're unlikely to need stereo sound. The rugged and flexible mono Nagra 4.2 is the standard documentary model, selling new for around $8,500. You can rent or buy secondhand the older Nagra 3 for *much* less—and, for documentary purposes, it is almost as good. The E and the discontinued IS, developed for reporters in the field, are both smaller and lighter, and also use ¼-inch tape. The considerably smaller and less obtrusive SN uses ⅛-inch open tape, and is also only available secondhand. It comes with a "compression" rather than VU meter: you simply increase the recording level until the limiter cuts in, and it peaks only occasionally. All of these analog models may be adjusted for sync sound recording, and can be operated in temperatures from $-4°$ to $160°F$ ($-20°$ to $70°C$).

For digital sound, the 4-channel ¼-inch digital Nagra-D sells for approximately $21,000 without time code, and $23,000 with internal SMPTE time code. Other high-end portable DATs, equipped with mike pre-amplifiers like the Nagras, and made by Fostex, StellaDAT and Portadat, cost between $6,000 and $15,000. On top of its professional PCM-2000 PAC, Sony makes two lower-end portable DAT recorders, the TCD-D10 Pro 2 and the very inexpensive TCD-D7 ($600 or less). To sort the wheat from the chaff, you may want to contact a company such as Audio Services Corporation (in the United States and Australia), which will send you a copy of their "Sound Catalogue" on request (see "Equipment and Services" in appendix 3). This explains how the latest audio equipment works and which models are good for what.

MICROPHONES

Sound recordists tend to have several mikes on hand and to use them in different circumstances. The first choice if you're using a Nagra for film production will probably be a true condenser mike manufactured by Schoeps or Sennheiser, attached to the end of a "fishpole." (For addresses, see "Equipment and Services" in appendix 3.) Schoeps offers the most sensitive and subtle of all mikes, boasting extended bass, extremely flat response, and minimal off-axis miscoloration. Their mikes are "pressure gradient" condensers, which means that they don't pick up nearly as many of the reflections generated in small interiors that plague shotgun mikes. They also work as a capsule module system, which means that the transducer head is separate from the amplifier module (with phantom powering)—so you can buy a single module and any number of attachable heads, each with its own pickup pattern. The heads offered by Schoeps include an omni, a cardioid, a "hypercardioid" (i.e., supercardioid), a bidirectional, and even a single switchable cardioid, omni-, and bidirectional head (the MK6). Schoeps also manufactures a filter that cuts out distortion from wind and rumble *before* it passes through the amplifier. But the sensitivity of Schoeps mikes makes them subject to wind and handling noise, and they require delicate handling. In documentary conditions with high background noise, they also tend to pick up a lot of ambience.

The Sennheiser MKH series of RF condenser mikes (particularly the 416 and 816) are competitive with Schoeps in terms of quality and price, though they're not available as a capsule module system. They also display slightly more off-axis miscoloration, and catch more of the boominess of hard-walled interiors. Both the Schoeps and the Sennheiser MKH series should be used with a very quiet shock mount and a professional blimp windscreen.

Sennheiser also manufactures an electret condenser modular system that is a good choice if you're on a tighter budget. This is the K6 (formerly K3) series. Omni, cardioid, supercardioid and lavalier capsules are all available, and should be used with blimp windscreens. The K6 system is both cheaper than true condensers and less sensitive to faint ambient sounds, which means that dialogue may be clearer but that the recording can sound thinner overall.

Finally, there are two excellent lavaliers, both with minimal off-axis drop-off: the Sennheiser MKE 2 and the Sony ECM-77.

FILM CAMERAS

16mm

There are two great sync-sound 16mm cameras being manufactured today: the XTRplus (or XTRprod) from Aaton and the SR-3 from Arriflex (see "Equipment and Services" in appendix 3). They both cost around $50,000 just for the camera body, but closer to $90,000 once you have all the accessories you need (magazines, lenses, power supply, etc.). A new 11–110mm Zeiss zoom lens alone costs between $13,000 and $15,000. If you're going on a short shoot, it'll be much cheaper to rent a sync-sound camera (and perhaps even hire an operator) than to buy one.

Quite a few documentary filmmakers shoot with older cameras, many of which they pick up secondhand at quite reasonable prices. Arri SR-1 and SR-2 packages, as well as earlier Aatons, sell for $10,000–$15,000 in the U.S. A serviced Arri BL, when combined with a high-quality lens, produces results comparable in image quality to an Aaton or an Arri SR, and can be found for as little as $4,000. Other cameras available secondhand that also have very stable film movements include Eclair NPRs and ACL, although they are a little more difficult to maintain. Arri-Ss, Bolexes, Cinema Products (CP) cameras (16A and 16R), and Canon Scoopics (which come with a permanently mounted single zoom lens) are also readily available, and cheaper, but have less stable camera movements, so the frame may wobble a bit when the film is projected. Bolex, Bell and Howell, Beaulieu, Canon, and the Arri 16S and SB models are among the non-sync cameras still circulating quite widely. The Bolexes are spring-wound, freeing you from any need for a power supply but limiting you to about 30 seconds per shot before you have to wind them up again. One factor to bear in mind when choosing a camera and lens(es) is that film emulsions have improved so much recently that they often exceed in quality the resolving power of older lenses.

Super-8

Super-8 cameras have been manufactured by countless companies over the years. Numerous models can be picked up secondhand from around $20 and up—less still, if you find one at a garage sale. The one "professional" model being manufactured today is the Beaulieu 7008 Pro 2. It is crystal-controlled and, therefore, easy to sync up with sound recorded by a portable DAT or crystal-synced cassette recorder. It can run at a variety of speeds and accepts interchangeable lenses. (Available zoom lenses include an Angénieux 6–90 mm, a Schneider 6–70 mm, and a Beaulieu 7–56 mm.) It can also be equipped with video assist. With a light lens attached, it may be mounted on the Steadicam JR. Complete kits, including a lens, are available from around $8,000 from Super-8 Sound (see "Equipment and Services" in appendix 3).

16MM LENSES

Documentary camera operators tend to shoot most of the time with a zoom lens. The Angénieux 12–240mm zoom has an extraordinary range (20:1), although the Angénieux 12–120mm lens (10:1) is more commonly used. Secondhand Angénieux and Zeiss 12.5–75mm zooms are widely available, as is the heavier Angénieux 9.5–95mm lens. Canon manufactures an 8–64mm (T 2.3) zoom and an 11.1–138mm (T 2.5) zoom, and Zeiss an 11–110mm model—all of which cost around $15,000 when new. One advantage of Canon's 8–64mm zoom is that it can focus as close as 2½ feet, whereas most zooms will focus no closer than around 5 feet.

An excellent prime lens for wide-angle, low-light shooting is the 9.5mm T1.3 Zeiss-Distagon Super-Speed lens.

VIDEO CAMERAS

The emergence of consumer DV and industrial DVCAM and DVCPRO, together with the descending cost of industrial Betacam SP camcorders (such as Sony's PVW-637), will probably kill off the high-end 3-CCD Hi-8 and Super-VHS camcorders (which sell for around $5,000–$11,000). In terms of cost, there are now three major rungs of video cameras: "professional" Digital Betacam ($40,000–$90,000); "industrial" DVCAM, DVCPRO, and Betacam SP ($10,000–$15,000); and "consumer" (and "prosumer") DV, Hi-8, and Super-VHS ($700–$5,000). Cameras at all levels are made by companies like Canon, Hitachi, Ikegami, JVC, Panasonic, Sony, and Toshiba.

The drawback of most DV, Hi-8, and Super-VHS cameras is the lens, which rarely provides the same image resolution as the video tape itself. Notable exceptions are the 3-CCD Panasonic AG-3 and the 1-CCD Canon A1, L1, and L2 cameras. Many Canon cameras (including the L1 and L2) have the advantage of allowing you to interchange lenses. The L2 features a ½-inch CCD with 410,000 pixels, and a choice of fixed and zoom lenses (from 5mm to 250-plus mm).

Most DV, Hi-8, and Super-VHS camcorders also boast various kinds of optical or electronic image stabilization. Some mechanisms of stabilization actually result in the image looking worse rather than better. (If you're shooting a flickering candle, they might try to "correct" the moving flame!) By contrast, the electronic ("Steadyshot") stabilization developed by Sony, for their TR101 Hi-8 camcorder and incorporated into subsequent Hi-8 and DV models (as "Super Steadyshot"), has received good consumer report ratings. Canon's optical stabilization, which it has extended even into its broadcast-quality lenses, has also been acclaimed.

The first DV cameras to be released were Sony's 3-CCD DCR-VX1000 and their cheaper 1-CCD DCR-VX700, followed by Panasonic's DVC-Pro. A protocol for connecting different digital devices called "Fire Wire (#1394)" can be connected to Sony cameras and allows you to dump your digital data directly onto a nonlinear hard drive. Sony's industrial DSR-130 camcorder (which consists of the DXC-D30 DSP camera docked to the DSR-1 DVCAM recording deck) features a system called "ClipLink" that allows you to upload to the hard drive only those scenes you select *in the camera,* thereby potentially saving valuable editing time. If you're after the tiniest DV camera on the market (some the size of a Walkman), look at JVC's GR-DV1u or Sony's line; if you like a large LCD viewfinder, check out Sharp's, Sony's and Matsushita's cameras. DV products are exploding onto the market all the time; be sure to stay abreast of consumer reports.

Finally, for specialized applications in low light, you may want to consider renting either a Silicon Intensifier Target (SIT) tube camera, or else the 3-CCD Ikegami HL-87M, which has about 2,000 times the sensitivity of a conventional portable camera. The HL-87M requires a minimum illumination of only 0.02 lux, has a signal-to-noise ratio of 57 dB, and produces images with much less time lag than the SIT cameras. Since this camera is designed for only "ultra super low light," you shouldn't use it for scenes with normal lighting.

CAMERA SUSPENSION SYSTEMS

The Steadicam "JR" is for camcorders (and some Super-8 cameras) weighing under 4 lbs. It comes complete with a 3½-inch LCD monitor (which frees your eye from the viewfinder), and a 3200K Obie light, weighs approximately 2 lbs, and costs anywhere between $300 and $500. The other models are heavier and more expensive. The Steadicam "SK" is for video cameras weighing between 8 and 17 lbs. In theory the SK doesn't require any professional instruction, but you should try to spend at least a day with an experienced user if you can. The Steadicam "EFP" is for film and video cameras up to 24 lbs, and the "3A" for film and video cameras up to 40 lbs. Both of these require professional instruction. Steadicams are manufactured by Cinema Products Corporation, who will provide further information and locate a dealer near you (see "Equipment and Services" in appendix 3). And look out for stabilization systems that are beginning to be made by other companies, often selling at competitive prices.

FILM STOCK AND VIDEO TAPE

Kodak's standard medium speed color negative 16mm film is Eastman EXR 7248 (100 ASA Tungsten). EXR 7293 (200 ASA Tungsten) and 7298 (500 ASA Tungsten) are both high speed color negative stocks, and EXR 7245 (50 ASA Daylight) is their standard daylight color negative stock. Kodak also offers two "Vision" stocks, with slightly improved resolution: the 7277 (320 ASA Tungsten) and the 7279 (500 ASA Tungsten). Fuji manufactures five main 16mm color negative stocks: 8621 (64 ASA Daylight), 8651 (250 ASA Tungsten), 8661 (250 ASA Daylight), 8631 (125 ASA Tungsten), and 8671 (500 ASA Tungsten). (For the addresses of Fuji and Kodak, see "Equipment and Services" in appendix 3.)

Because Super-8 is a format in decline, many of the film stocks that were manufactured in its heyday are no more. The three principal stocks still available today are Kodachrome 40 (40 ASA Tungsten-balanced color reversal), Plus-X (50 ASA Daylight, 40 ASA Tungsten, black-and-white reversal) and Tri-X (200 ASA Daylight, 160 ASA Tungsten, black-and-white reversal). Additionally the company Super-8 Sound (see "Equipment and Services" in appendix 3) offers a complete line of color negative Kodak film, which they cut down from the latest 35mm stocks. The following stocks are preloaded onto 50-foot cartridges: 5245 (50 ASA Daylight), 5248 (100 ASA Tungsten), 5293 (200 ASA Tungsten), 5287 (200 ASA Tungsten, ultra-high latitude), 5296 (500 ASA Tungsten), and 5298 (500 ASA Tungsten, Fine Grain). The purchase cost of the film includes processing, which takes place on the premises.

Video tape is made by a wide range of manufacturers, and new stocks are constantly being released. It's best to stick with the same stock for any one production, or else differences of color and quality may be visible in the final video. Check the latest consumer and professional ratings before purchasing it.

ACCESSORIES

Special battery belts, as well as a whole array of film and video equipment, are manufactured by Cine 60 in New York. Disposable lithium-based batteries, suitable for remote or climatically harsh conditions, are available from Automated Media Systems. K & H Products makes a heated "Portabrace Polar Bear" camera case. For addresses, see "Equipment and Services" in appendix 3.

FILMOGRAPHY

For distributors' addresses, see appendix 3.

Allah Tantou, David Achkar
1991 California Newsreel;
62 mins.

An American Family, Craig Gilbert
1972 NET, Video Verité; 12 one-
hour episodes.

*And Statues Also Die (Et les statues
meurent aussi),* Alain Resnais and
Chris Marker
1953 Intermedia Audiovisuel
Documentaire—Ministère des
Affaires Étrangères (France);
21 mins.

Apocalypse Now, Francis Ford
Coppola
1979; 150 mins.

L'arroseur arrosé, Lumière Bros.
1895 MoMA; 3 mins.

The Ax Fight, Timothy Asch and Napoleon Chagnon
1975 (Yanomamo Series), Documentary Educational Resources;
30 mins.

A Balinese Trance Seance, Timothy
Asch, Patsy Asch, and Linda
Connor
1979 (Jero Tapakan Series),

Documentary Educational Resources; 30 mins.

Baseball, Ken Burns
1994 PBS Video Finders;
18 hours.

Battle of San Pietro, John Huston
1944 Facets Multimedia Inc.;
33 mins.

Before We Knew Nothing, Diane
Kitchen
1988 U.C. Extension; 62 mins.

Birth of a Nation, D. W. Griffith
1915 MoMA; 180 mins.

Black Harvest, Robin Anderson and
Bob Connolly
1992 Direct Cinema (U.S.), Film
Australia (Australia); 90 mins.

Black Panther, Newsreel (San
Francisco)
1968 California Newsreel, Third
World Newsreel; 15 mins.

A Brief History of Time, Errol Morris
1992 New Yorker Films; 84 mins.

"Cannibal Tours," Dennis O'Rourke
1988 Direct Cinema (U.S.),
O'Rourke & Associates—Filmmakers (Australia); 70 mins.

Carnival in Q'eros, John Cohen
1990 U.C. Extension; 32 mins.

Celso and Cora, Gary Kildea
1983 Icarus / First Run Films;
109 mins.

The Chair, D. A. Pennebaker, Richard Leacock, George Shuker
1962 Pennebaker Assoc., Direct Cinema; 76 mins.

Chronicle of a Summer (*Chronique d'un Été*), Jean Rouch and Edgar Morin
1960 Corinth Films (U.S.), Argos Films (France); 90 mins.

The Civil War, Ken Burns
1990 PBS Video Finders; approx. 12 hours.

Cochengo Miranda, Jorge Preloran
1974 Distributed by Jorge Preloran; 58 mins.

A Country Auction: The Paul V. Leitzel Estate Sale, Robert Aibel, Ben Levin, Chris Musello, and Jay Ruby
1984 Penn. State; 56 mins.

Dead Birds, Robert Gardner
1963 Phoenix Films; 83 mins.

"Decisions" Series (*Steel, Oil, Rates*), Roger Graef
1975–76 Granada Television International Ltd.; 3 films of 52 mins. each

Deep Throat, Gerard Damiano
1972; 73 mins.

Diaries, Ed Pincus
1971–76 Distributed by the filmmaker; 200 mins.

Don't Look Back, D. A. Pennebaker, with Howard and Jones Alk
1966 Kino International Pictures; 96 mins.

Double Indemnity, Billy Wilder
1944; 106 mins.

Dreaming Rivers, Martina Attille
1988 Women Make Movies (U.S.); Sankofa Film / Video Collective (U.K.); 30 mins.

Drifters, John Grierson
1929 British Film Institute; 40 mins.

Eze Nwata—The Small King, Sabine Jell-Bahlsen
1982 Ogbuide Ltd.; 29 mins.

Familiar Places, David MacDougall
1980 U.C. Extension; 53 mins.

The Fandango Project, John Bishop
1993 Media Generation; 30 mins.

The Feast, Timothy Asch and Napoleon Chagnon
1970 (Yanomamo Series), Documentary Educational Resources; 29 mins.

First Contact, Robin Anderson and Bob Connolly
1984 Documentary Educational Resources; 54 mins.

Forest of Bliss, Robert Gardner
1988 Arthur Cantor Films, Inc.; 90 mins.

Frantz Fanon: Black Skin, White Mask, Isaac Julien
1996, California Newsreel; 49 mins.

Fronterilandia/Frontierland, Jesse Lerner and Rubén Ortiz-Torres
1995 Distributed by the filmmakers; 78 mins.

Fury, Fritz Lang
1936 MGM / UA Classics; 90 mins.

Garbage, Newsreel
1968 Third World Newsreel; 10 mins.

Goodbye, Old Man, David MacDougall
1977 U.C. Extension; 70 mins.

The Good Woman of Bangkok,
Dennis O'Rourke
　　1991 Direct Cinema Ltd. (U.S.),
　　O'Rourke & Associates—Film-
　　makers (Australia); 88 mins.
Grey Gardens, Albert and David
　　Maysles, Ellen Hovde, Muffie
　　Meyer
　　1975 Maysles Films; 94 mins.
Hair Piece: A Film for Nappyheaded
　　People, Ayoka Chenzira
　　1985 Women Make Movies;
　　10 mins.
Handsworth Songs, John Akomfrah
　　1986 Black Audio Film Collec-
　　tive; 52 mins.
The Harder They Come, Perry
　　Henzell
　　1975; 98 mins.
Harlan County, USA, Barbara
　　Kopple
　　1976 Facets Multimedia Inc.;
　　103 mins.
High School, Frederick Wiseman
　　1969 Zipporah Films; 75 mins.
Hoop Dreams, Steve James
　　1994 Fine Line Features; approx.
　　3 hours.
Hospital, Frederick Wiseman
　　1970 Zipporah Films; 84 mins.
The House Opening, Judith Mac-
　　Dougall
　　1980 Australian Institute of Ab-
　　original and Torres Strait Islander
　　Studies; 45 mins.
The Hunters, John Marshall
　　1958 Documentary Educational
　　Resources; 73 mins.
I'm British But, Gurinda Chadha
　　1989 British Film Institute
　　(U.K.); 30 mins.
Imaginero, Jorge Preloran
　　1969 Phoenix Films; 52 mins.

Imagining Indians, Victor Masyesva
　　1992 Documentary Educational
　　Resources; 60 mins.
In and Out of Africa, Gabai Baaré,
　　Ilisa Barbash, Christopher
　　Steiner, Lucien Taylor
　　1992 U.C. Extension; 59 mins.
In the Year of the Pig, Emile de
　　Antonio
　　1969 MoMA; 101 mins.
Ishi, the Last Yahi, Jed Riffe and
　　Pamela Roberts
　　1992 U.C. Extension; 57 mins.
JFK, Oliver Stone
　　1991 Swank; 188 mins.
Jaguar, Jean Rouch
　　1954/1967 Films de la Pléiade;
　　approx. 110 mins.
Jane, D. A. Pennebaker, Richard
　　Leacock, Hope Ryden, George
　　Shuker, Abbot Mills
　　1962 Pennebaker Assoc., Drew
　　Assoc., Direct Cinema; 30 mins.
The *Jero Tapakan* Series, Timothy
　　Asch, Patsy Asch,
　　and Linda Connor
　　1979–83 Documentary Educa-
　　tional Resources.
Joe Leahy's Neighbors, Robin Ander-
　　son and Bob Connolly
　　1988 Documentary Educational
　　Resources; 90 mins.
John Collier, Jr.: A Visual Journey,
　　Stephen Olson and Maria Luiza
　　Abolm
　　1993 Distributed by the film-
　　makers; 30 mins.
Le joli mai, Chris Marker
　　1962 Intermedia Audiovisuel Do-
　　cumentaire—Ministère des Affai-
　　res Étrangères (France); 124 mins.
The Kawelka—Ongka's Big Moka,
　　Charlie Nairn (Andrew Strathern,

anthropologist)
1974 (Disappearing World Series), Films Inc. (U.S.), Granada Television International Ltd. (U.K.); 52 mins.

The Kayapo, Michael Beckham (Terry Turner, anthropologist)
1987 (Disappearing World Series), Films Inc. (U.S.), Granada Television International Ltd. (U.K.); 52 mins.

Kenya Boran, David MacDougall and James Blue
1974 (Faces of Change Series), Documentary Educational Resources; 66 mins.

Land without Bread (Las Hurdas), Luis Buñuel
1932 MoMA; 27 mins.

The Leader, His Driver, and the Driver's Wife, Nick Broomfield
1991 Lafayette Films; 85 mins.

The Life and Times of Rosie the Riveter, Connie Field
1980 Direct Cinema; 65 mins.

Lightning over Braddock: A Dust Bowl Fantasy, Tony Bubba
1988 Zeitgeist Films; 80 mins.

Lorang's Way, David and Judith MacDougall
1979 (Turkana Conversations Trilogy), U.C. Extension; 70 mins.

Louisiana Story, Robert Flaherty
1948 Flaherty Study Center; 77 mins.

Madame L'Eau, Jean Rouch
1993 NFI Productions (Netherlands); 125 mins.

Made in USA, Ilisa Barbash and Lucien Taylor
1990 Distributed by the filmmakers; 10 mins.

Mad Masters (Les maîtres fous), Jean Rouch
1953–54 Interama (U.S.), Les Films du Jeudi (France); 33 mins.

Man of Aran, Robert Flaherty
1934 Films Inc.; 76 mins.

The Man with a Movie Camera, Dziga Vertov
1929 Kit Parker Films; 103 mins.

The *March of Time* Series, Louis de Rochemont
1935–41 Time Inc., Movies Unlimited.

A Matter of Respect, Ellen Frankenstein
1992 New Day Films; 30 mins.

The Meat Fight, John Marshall
1957–58 Documentary Educational Resources; 14 mins.

Meet Marlon Brando, Albert and David Maysles
1965 Maysles Films; 28 mins.

Memories and Dreams, Melissa Llewelyn-Davies
1993 BBC Video Education and Training; 92 mins.

The Mende, Bruce MacDonald (Mariane Ferme, anthropologist)
1990 (Disappearing World Series), Films Inc. (U.S.), Granada Television International Inc. (U.K.); 52 mins.

The Migrants, Leslie Woodhead (David Turton, anthropologist)
1985 (Disappearing World Series), Films Inc. (U.S.), Granada Television International Inc. (U.K.); 52 mins.

Moi, un noir, Jean Rouch
1957 Les Films du Jeudi; 80 mins.

The Mursi, Leslie Woodhead (David Turton, anthropologist)

1974 (Disappearing World Series), Films Inc. (U.S.), Granada Television International Inc. (U.K.); 52 mins.

N!ai, the Story of a !Kung Woman, John Marshall, Adrienne Miesmer, Sue Cabezas
1980 Documentary Educational Resources; 58 mins.

Naked Spaces: Living Is Round, Trinh Minh-ha
1985 Women Make Movies; 135 mins.

Nanook of the North, Robert Flaherty
1922 MoMA; 55 mins.

Natives, Jesse Lerner and Scott Sterling
1991 Filmmakers' Library; 25 mins.

Nawi, David MacDougall and Judith MacDougall
1970 U.C. Extension; 20 mins.

The Netsilik Eskimo Series, Asen Balikci and Guy Mary-Rousseliere
1967–68 Education Development Corporation and National Film Board of Canada; Documentary Educational Resources; 18 episodes, 10 hours.

Night and Fog (*Nuit et brouillard*), Alain Resnais
1955 Budget Films; 32 mins.

Night Mail, Harry Watt and Basil Wright
1936 Kit Parker Films, MoMA; 30 mins.

No Lies, Mitchell Block
1973 Direct Cinema, Phoenix Films; 16 mins.

The Nuer, Robert Gardner, Hilary Harris, and George Breidenbach
1970 Phoenix Films; 75 mins.

Oceans Apart, Frances Peters
1990 Australian Broadcasting Corporation; approx. 30 mins.

Of Great Events and Ordinary People (*De grands événments et des gens ordinaires*), Raul Ruiz
1979; 65 mins.

On the Pole, D. A. Pennebaker, Richard Leacock, William Ray, George Shuker, Abbot Mills, Albert Maysles
1960 Drew Assoc., Direct Cinema; 53 mins.

Paris Is Burning, Jennie Livingston
1990 Films Inc.; 78 mins.

The Passion of Remembrance, Maureen Blackwood and Isaac Julien
1986 Women Make Movies (U.S.); Sankofa Film/Video Collective (U.K.); 82 mins.

Photo Wallahs, David and Judith MacDougall
1991 U.C. Extension; 82 mins.

Point of Order, Emile de Antonio and Dan Talbot
1963 MoMA, New Yorker Films; 97 mins.

Poto and Cabengo, Jean-Pierre Gorin
1979 New Yorker Films; 77 mins.

Primary, D. A. Pennebaker and Richard Leacock, with Terence Macartney-Filgate and Albert Maysles
1960 Direct Cinema; 60 mins.

La pyramide humaine, Jean Rouch
1958–61 Les Films du Jeudi; 90 mins.

Reassemblage, Trinh Minh-ha
1982 Women Make Movies; 40 mins.

Rivers of Sand, Robert Gardner
1974 Phoenix Films; 83 mins.

Roads End, Robert Gardner
(in progress)

Roger and Me, Michael Moore
1989 Swank; 87 mins.

Rush to Judgment, Emile de Antonio
1966 MoMA; 110 mins.

Ryan's Daughter, David Lean
1970 MGM/UA Classics;
176 mins.

Salesman, Albert and David Maysles
and Charlotte Zwerin
1969 Maysles Films; 90 mins.

Sans Soleil, Chris Marker
1982 New Yorker Films;
100 mins.

The Sharkcallers of Kontu, Dennis
O'Rourke
1982 Direct Cinema Ltd. (U.S.),
O'Rourke & Associates—Filmmakers (Australia); 54 mins.

Sherman's March, Ross McElwee
1985 First Run/Icarus Films;
155 mins.

Song of Ceylon, Basil Wright
1934 MoMA; 40 mins.

The Sorrow and the Pity (*Le chagrin et
la pitié*), Marcel Ophuls
1970 Viewfinders; 60 mins.

Southeast Nuba, Chris Curling
(James Faris, anthropologist)
1982 BBC Video Education and
Training; 60 mins.

Strike, Sergei Eisenstein
1925 MoMA; 97 mins.

Surname Viet Given Name Nam,
Trinh Minh-ha
1989 Women Make Movies;
108 mins.

Takeover, David and Judith
MacDougall
1980 U.C. Extension; 90 mins.

Tempus de baristas (*Time of the Bar-*

men), David MacDougall
1993 U.C. Extension; Istituto
Superiore Regionale Etnografico,
Nuoro (Italy); Royal Anthropological Institute (U.K.); 100 mins.

Testament, John Akomfrah
1988 Black Audio Film Collective; 90 mins.

The Thin Blue Line, Errol Morris
1987 Movies Unlimited, Films
Inc.; 115 mins.

The Things I Cannot Change, Tanya
Ballantyne
1966 National Film Board of
Canada; 58 mins.

Three Horsemen, David and Judith
MacDougall
1982 U.C. Extension; 54 mins.

Titicut Follies, Frederick Wiseman
1967 Zipporah Films; 89 mins.

To Live with Herds, David and Judith
MacDougall
1972 U.C. Extension; 90 mins.

Tongues Untied, Marlon Riggs
1989 Frameline; 45 mins.

Trance and Dance in Bali, Gregory
Bateson and Margaret Mead
1952 (Character Formation in
Different Cultures Series), Penn.
State; 20 mins.

Triumph of the Will, Leni Riefenstahl
1934 Budget Films; 107 mins.

*Trobriand Cricket: An Ingenious Re-
sponse to Colonialism,* Gary Kildea
and Jerry Leach
1976 U.C. Extension; 54 mins.

*The Trobriand Islanders of Papua
New Guinea,* David Wason
1990 (Disappearing World Se-
ries), Films Inc. (U.S.), Granada
Television International Inc.
(U.K.); 52 mins.

Truth or Dare, Alex Keshishian
1991 Swank; 118 mins.
Under the Men's Tree, David and
Judith MacDougall
1974 U.C. Extension; 15 mins.
Unfinished Diary (Journal inachevé),
Marilu Mallet
1983 Women Make Movies;
55 mins.
Valencia Diary, Gary Kildea
1992 Ronin Films; 108 mins.
Vernon, Florida, Errol Morris
1988 New Yorker Films; 60 mins.
The Village, Mark McCarty and Paul
Hockings
1968 U.C. Extension; 70 mins.
Waiting for Fidel, Michael Rubbo
1974 National Film Board of
Canada; 59 mins.
Warrendale, Allan King
1966 Canadian Broadcasting
Company; 100 mins.
The Wedding Camels, David and
Judith MacDougall
1980 (Turkana Conversations
Trilogy), U.C. Extension;
108 mins.
Welfare, Frederick Wiseman
1975 Zipporah Films; 167 mins.
Why We Fight Series, Frank Capra
and Anatole Litvak
1942–45 U.S. War Department;
MoMA; 7 films, various lengths.

A Wife among Wives, David and
Judith MacDougall
1981 (Turkana Conversations
Trilogy), U.C. Extension;
70 mins.
The Wizard of Oz, Victor Fleming
1939; 100 mins.
The Woman's Film, Newsreel (San
Francisco)
1971 Third World Newsreel;
40 mins.
The Women Who Smile, Joanna Head
(Jean Lydall, anthropologist)
1990 Filmmakers' Library (U.S.),
BBC Video Education and Training (U.K.); 50 mins.
The Women's Olamal: The Organiza-
tion of a Maasai Fertility Cere-
mony, Melissa Llewelyn-Davies
1984 BBC Video Education and
Training; 113 mins.
The "Yanomamo" Series, Timothy
Asch and Napoleon Chagnon
1969–76 Documentary Educational Resources.
Zerda's Children, Jorge Preloran
1978 Phoenix Films; 56 mins.
Zulay, Facing the 21st Century, Jorge
and Mabel Preloran
1993 Distributed by Jorge Preloran; 117 mins.

NOTES

INTRODUCTION

1. With digital video, the indexical relation to an original is objectively lost. However, so long as video continues to have the *connotation* that it is an unadulterated denotation of the real world, then it will be read as a trace of it, *as if* it were an actual indexical sign; and that, of course, is what counts.

2. David MacDougall, "Unprivileged Camera Style," *RAIN* (*Royal Anthropological Institute News*) 50 (1982): 9.

3. André Leroi-Gourhan, "Cinéma et sciences humaines—Le film ethnographique, existe-t-il?" *Revue de geographie humaine et d'ethnologie* 3 (July–Sept.): 42–51, cited in Luc de Heusch, "The Cinema and Social Science: A Survey of Ethnographic and Sociological Films," *Visual Anthropology* 1, no. 2 (1988): 118. See also David MacDougall, "A Need for Common Terms," *SAVICOM Newsletter* 9, no. 1 (1981): 5.

CHAPTER 1

1. These are the words of Henri de Parville, a famous contemporary journalist, cited in Siegfried Kracauer, *Theory of Film: The Redemption of Physical Reality* (New York: Oxford University Press, 1960), pp. 31–32.

2. E.g., Kracauer, *Theory of Film*, p. 246.

3. Lucien Taylor, "A Conversation with Jean Rouch," *Visual Anthropology Review* 7, no. 1 (Spring 1991): 101.

4. Bill Nichols has developed a fivefold distinction between expository, observational, interactive, reflexive, and performative films, which is considerably more nuanced and discerning than the crude framework presented here. See Nichols, *Representing Reality* (Bloomington: Indiana University Press, 1991), and *Blurred Boundaries: Questions of Meaning in Contemporary Culture* (Bloomington: Indiana University Press, 1994).

5. John Grierson, *Grierson on Documentary,* ed. Forsyth Hardy (1946; London: Faber and Faber, 1979), p. 19.

6. Elizabeth Sussex, *The Rise and Fall of the British Documentary* (London: Faber and Faber, 1979), p. 29, cited in Brian Winston, "The Tradition of the Victim in Griersonian Documentary," in *New Challenges for Documentary,* ed. Alan Rosenthal (Berkeley: University of California Press, 1988), p. 271.

7. Paul Rotha, *Documentary Film,* London: Faber, 1936, cited in Siegfried Kracauer, *Theory of Film: The Redemption of Physical Reality* (New York: Oxford University Press, 1960), p. 247.

8. Rotha, *Documentary Film,* p. 106, cited in Kracauer, *Theory of Film,* p. 247.

9. Frances Flaherty, *The Odyssey of a Film-Maker* (Urbana, IL: Beta Phi Mu, 1960), p. 11, cited in Stephen Mamber, *Cinema Verite in America: Studies in Uncontrolled Documentary* (Cambridge: MIT, 1974), p. 9.

10. Flaherty, *The Odyssey of a Film-Maker,* p. 11, cited in Mamber, *Cinema Verite in America,* p. 9.

11. Emile de Antonio, "The Politics of Documentary: A Symposium," ed. Barbara Zheutlin, in *New Challenges for Documentary,* ed. Alan Rosenthal (Berkeley: University of California Press, 1988), p. 45.

12. Cited in Erik Barnouw, *Documentary: A History of the Non-Fiction Film* (New York: Oxford University Press, 1983), p. 45.

13. Larry Gross, John Stuart Katz, and Jay Ruby, "Introduction: A Moral Pause," in *Image Ethics: The Moral Rights of Subjects in Photographs, Film, and Television,* ed. Larry Gross, John Stuart Katz, and Jay Ruby (New York: Oxford University Press, 1988), p. 21.

14. Dai Vaughan, "The Space between Shots," in *Movies and Methods,* vol. 2, ed. Bill Nichols (Berkeley: University of California Press, 1985), p. 706.

15. Barnouw, *Documentary: A History of the Non-Fiction Film,* p. 251.

16. Colin Young, "Observational Cinema," in *Principles of Visual Anthropology,* ed. Paul Hockings (The Hague: Mouton, 1975), p. 71.

17. *Cinéma Vérité* is often considered to be altogether different from Direct Cinema, and even from observational cinema as a whole. In retrospect, however, it is clear that there is more that they share than that sets them apart. The history of the two terms is actually more intricate than our synoptic outline would suggest. Oddly enough, American pioneers of Direct Cinema like Richard Leacock and D. A. Pennebaker initially favored the gallicized "vérité." Conversely, except when referring to *Chronicle of a Summer* or Dziga Vertov's "Kinopravda," Jean Rouch tends to prefer the anglicized "cinéma-direct," by which he means observational filmmaking in general. Rouch's wariness of the word "vérité" stems from his fear that it has been taken (largely by Americans) to imply that the camera can record objective reality. On the contrary, he believes that the camera creates a "truth" that is irreducibly cinematic. As Gilles Deleuze puts it, in a formulation that unfortunately begs the question as to the relationship between the two, this is not "a cinema of truth but the truth of cinema." *Cinema 2: The Time*

Image (Minneapolis: University of Minnesota Press, 1989), p. 151. Despite these semiotic intertwinings, the practice of Rouch and Morin is generally characterized as *Cinéma Vérité*, and the American movement as Direct Cinema, and it is this usage that we follow here.

18. Louis Comolli, "Machines of the Visible," in *Film Theory and Criticism,* ed. Gerald Mast and Marshall Cohen (Oxford: Oxford University Press, 1985), p. 759.

CHAPTER 2

1. The video is by Kandece Brown, Elizabeth Roberts, and Miriam Telles and is called *Ladies & Gentlemen, Kiki & Sandra.*

2. Paul Hockings, "Gone with the Gael: Filming in an Irish Village," in *Anthropological Filmmaking,* ed. Jack R. Rollwagen (New York: Harwood Academic Publishers, 1988), p. 144.

3. Ibid., p. 145.

4. David MacDougall, "The Ethnographic Film as Inquiry: An Interview with David MacDougall (by Daniel Bickley)," in *Lifelong Learning* 50 (9 February 1981): 1.

5. Gross, Katz, and Ruby, "Introduction: A Moral Pause," p. 21.

6. David MacDougall, interview with authors, Berkeley, California, 1993.

7. David MacDougall, "Experiments in Interior Commentary," unpublished manuscript, p. 6.

8. Craig Gilbert, "Reflections on *An American Family,*" parts 1 and 2, in *New Challenges for Documentary,* ed. Alan Rosenthal (Berkeley: University of California Press, 1988), p. 301.

9. Ibid., p. 302.

10. Ibid., p. 293.

11. Hockings, "Gone with the Gael," pp. 149–50.

12. Mariane Ferme, interview with authors, Berkeley, California, 1993.

13. Gilbert, "Reflections on *An American Family,*" pp. 199–200.

14. Solveig Freudenthal, "What to Tell and How to Show it: Issues in Anthropological Filmmaking," in *Anthropological Filmmaking,* ed. Jack R. Rollwagen (New York: Harwood Academic Publishers, 1988), p. 128.

15. Thanks to Paco Ferrandez for this point.

16. "Statement on Ethics: Principles of Professional Responsibility," adopted by the Council of the American Anthropological Association, May 1971 (as amended through October 1990), pp. 1–2.

17. Winston, "The Tradition of the Victim," p. 278.

18. Vaughan, "The Space between Shots," p. 713.

19. Calvin Pryluck, "Ultimately We Are All Outsiders: The Ethics of Documentary Filming," in *New Challenges for Documentary,* ed. Alan Rosenthal (Berkeley: University of California Press, 1988), pp. 261–62. (Italics in original.)

20. Alan Rosenthal, "*Salesman:* An Interview with Albert Maysles," in *The New*

Documentary in Action: A Casebook in Film Making (Berkeley: University of California Press, 1971), pp. 81–82.

21. Alan Rosenthal, *Writing, Directing, and Producing Documentary Films* (Carbondale, IL: Southern Illinois University Press, 1990), p. 201.

22. Pryluck, "Ultimately We Are All Outsiders," p. 258.

23. Robert Aibel, "Ethics and Professionalism in Documentary Filmmaking" in *Image Ethics: The Moral Rights of Subjects in Photographs, Film, and Television,* ed. Larry Gross, John Stuart Katz, and Jay Ruby (New York: Oxford University Press, 1988), p. 115.

24. Jean Rouch, conversation with authors, Berkeley, California, 1992.

25. Timothy Asch, "Collaboration in Ethnographic Filmmaking: A Personal View," in *Anthropological Filmmaking,* ed. Jack R. Rollwagen (New York: Harwood Academic Publishers, 1988), p. 19.

26. Lecture at the University of Southern California, 1988.

27. Ivo Strecker, "Filming among the Hamar," *Visual Anthropology* 1 (1988): 373.

28. This is our impression from classes we have both attended and taught at the University of Southern California and the University of California, Berkeley.

29. Jay Ruby, "The Ethics of Image Making," in *New Challenges for Documentary,* ed. Alan Rosenthal (Berkeley: University of California Press, 1988), p. 310.

30. See Karl Heider, *Ethnographic Film* (Austin: University of Texas Press, 1976).

31. J. Stephen Lansing, "The Decolonization of Ethnographic Film," *SVA Review* 6, no. 1 (Spring 1990): 16.

32. Hortense Powdermaker, *Stranger and Friend: The Way of an Anthropologist* (New York: W. W. Norton, 1966), p. 63.

33. Hockings, "Gone with the Gael," p. 149.

34. Linda Connor, Patsy Asch, and Timothy Asch, *Jero Tapakan: Balinese Healer, an Ethnographic Film Monograph* (Cambridge: Cambridge University Press, 1986), pp. 48–49.

35. Ibid., p. 48.

36. John Marshall, "Filming and Learning," in *The Cinema of John Marshall,* ed. Jay Ruby (New York: Harwood Academic Publishers, 1993), pp. 102–5.

37. David Wason, "A Guide for Anthropologists," unpublished manuscript, Granada Television, p. 5.

38. David Turton, "Anthropological Knowledge and the Culture of Broadcasting," *Visual Anthropology Review* 8, no. 1 (Spring 1992): 117.

39. Mariane Ferme, interview with authors, Berkeley, California, 1993.

40. Mariane Ferme, personal communication, letter, 1995.

41. David MacDougall, personal communication, letter, 1995.

42. Connor, Asch, Asch, *Jero Tapakan,* p. 44.

43. Lynn Silverman, "Maurice Godelier: An Interview," in *Anthropological Filmmaking,* ed. Jack R. Rollwagen (New York: Harwood Academic Publishers, 1988), p. 138.

44. David MacDougall, interview with authors, Berkeley, California, 1993.

45. David MacDougall, interview with authors, Berkeley, California, 1993.

46. Jean Rouch, "The Camera and Man," in *Principles of Visual Anthropology,* ed. Paul Hockings (The Hague: Mouton, 1975), p. 91.

47. The "fly-" phrases are Peter Crawford's. See his "Film as Discourse: The Invention of Anthropological Realities," in *Film as Ethnography,* ed. Peter Ian Crawford and David Turton (Manchester: Manchester University Press, 1992), p. 67.

48. George Marcus, for instance, makes this argument in "The Modernist Sensibility in Recent Ethnographic Writing and the Cinematic Metaphor of Montage," in *Visualizing Theory,* ed. Lucien Taylor (New York: Routledge, 1994), pp. 37–53.

49. David MacDougall, interview with authors, Berkeley, California, 1993.

50. Silverman, "Maurice Godelier," p. 136.

51. Asch, "Collaboration in Ethnographic Filmmaking," p. 4.

52. Mariane Ferme, personal communication, letter, 1995.

53. Mariane Ferme, interview with authors, Berkeley, California, 1993.

54. James C. Faris, "Southeast Nuba: A Biographical Statement," in *Anthropological Filmmaking,* ed. Jack R. Rollwagen (New York: Harwood Academic Publishers, 1988), p. 118.

55. Linda Connor, "Third Eye: Some Reflections on Collaboration for Ethnographic Film," in *Anthropological Filmmaking,* ed. Jack R. Rollwagen (New York: Harwood Academic Publishers, 1988), p. 99.

56. Ibid., p. 103.

57. Ibid., p. 107.

58. Mariane Ferme, interview with authors, Berkeley, California, 1993.

59. Ellen Frankenstein, personal communication, letter, 1994.

60. Asch, "Collaboration in Ethnographic Filmmaking," p. 12.

61. Turton, "Anthropological Knowledge and the Culture of Broadcasting," p. 115.

62. Jean Lydall, "Filming *The Women Who Smile,*" in *Ethnographic Film Aesthetics and Narrative Traditions,* ed. Peter I. Crawford and Jan K. Simonsen (Denmark: Intervention Press, 1991), pp. 147–48.

63. Allison Jablonko, "New Guinea in Italy: An Analysis of the Making of an Italian Television Series from Research Footage of the Maring People of Papua New Guinea," in *Anthropological Filmmaking,* ed. Jack R. Rollwagen (New York: Harwood Academic Publishers, 1988), p 172.

64. Connor, "Third Eye," p. 104.

65. Hockings, "Gone with the Gael," p. 154.

66. Ellen Frankenstein, personal communication, letter, 1994.

67. Asch, "Collaboration in Ethnographic Filmmaking," p. 9.

68. Ibid., p. 10.

69. Timothy Asch, "The Ethics of Ethnographic Filmmaking," in *Film as Ethnography,* ed. Peter Ian Crawford and David Turton (Manchester: Manchester University Press, 1992), pp. 201–2.

70. Robert Flaherty, cited in Jay Ruby, "Speaking For, Speaking About, Speaking With, or Speaking Alongside—An Anthropological and Documentary Dilemma," in *Visual Anthropology Review* 7, no. 2 (Fall 1991), p. 51.

71. David MacDougall, "Media Friend or Media Foe?" *Visual Anthropology* 1, no. 1 (1987): 56–57.

72. Dorothy Todd Hénaut, "Video Stories from the Dawn of Time," in *Visual Anthropology Review* 7, no. 2 (Fall 1991), p. 85.

73. Ibid., p. 86.

74. Ibid.

CHAPTER 3

1. Thanks to David MacDougall for this point.

2. Dziga Vertov, *Kino-Eye: The Writings of Dziga Vertov,* ed. Annette Michelson, trans. Kevin O'Brien (Berkeley: University of California Press, 1984), pp. 17–18.

3. Rouch, "The Camera and Man," p. 93–94.

4. John Bishop, *Home Video Production: Getting the Most from Your Video Equipment,* (New York: McGraw-Hill, 1986), p. 109.

5. Rouch, "The Camera and Man," p. 93.

6. John Bishop, "Video Self: !Kung and Khmer," in *Eyes across the Water: Essays on Visual Anthropology and Sociology,* ed. Robert M. Boonzajer-Flaes and Douglas Harper (Amsterdam: Het Spinhuis, 1993), p. 34.

7. *American Cinematographer Manual,* edited by Rod Ryan, David Heuring, Stephen Pizzello, and Marji Shea (Hollywood, CA: American Society of Cinematographers, 1993).

CHAPTER 4

1. Dennis O'Rourke, personal communication, letter, 1995.

CHAPTER 5

1. Bishop, *Home Video Production,* p. 40

2. John Bishop, personal communication, letter, 1994.

3. Bishop, *Home Video Production,* p. 307.

4. Digital cinematography, or digital image manipulation, is an expanding field, letting you recompose body parts, add one actor's face to another's hair to another's body, simulate shadows, computer-generate clothes, and so on—leading some to wonder if flesh-and-blood actors will soon be a thing of the past. But this is very different from digital postproduction, and has made few inroads into 16mm.

5. Thanks to Jesse Lerner for this information.

6. *American Cinematographer Manual,* edited by Rod Ryan et al.

7. Thanks to John Bishop for this information.

CHAPTER 6

1. Anthony Lane, "Style Wars," *The New Yorker,* 11 September 1995, p. 96.

2. Hockings, "Gone with the Gael," p. 153.

3. Timothy Asch, "The Ethics of Ethnographic Filmmaking," p. 199.

4. Alan Rosenthal, "*High School:* An Interview with Frederick Wiseman," in *The New Documentary In Action: A Casebook in Film Making* (Berkeley: University of California Press, 1971), p. 67.

5. Barbara Kopple and Hart Perry, "*Harlan County, USA,*" in *The Documentary Conscience: A Casebook in Film Making,* ed. Alan Rosenthal (Berkeley: University of California Press, 1980), p. 305.

6. Ellen Frankenstein, personal communication, letter, 1994.

7. Jesse Lerner, personal communication, letter, 1994.

8. Kopple and Perry, "*Harlan County, USA,*" p. 305.

9. Louis Massiah and Alrick Riley, "Using Archives," *Black Film Bulletin* 1, nos. 3–4 (Autumn–Winter 1993–94), p. 27.

10. Timothy Asch, "Sequence Filmmaking and the Representation of Culture," unpublished manuscript.

11. Kopple and Perry, "*Harlan County, USA,*" p. 312

12. Ellen Frankenstein, personal communication, letter, 1994.

13. James, D. Walsh, John McCarthy, and V. Glenn McIninch, "Airport X-Rays and Camera Films," an unpublished technical report for the National Association of Photographic Manufacturers, Inc., October 1993.

14. Ellen Frankenstein, personal communication, letter, 1994.

CHAPTER 7

1. Edgar Morin, preface to *The Cinema and Social Science: A Survey of Ethnographic and Sociological Films,* by Luc de Heusch (New York: UNESCO 1962), reprinted in *Visual Anthropology* 1, no. 2 (1988): 102.

2. Documentary Educational Resources, "D.E.R.'s Collection: The Netsilik Series, brochure. (Italics added.)

3. Bill Nichols uses these examples in "'Getting to Know You . . .': Knowledge, Power, and the Body," in *Theorizing Documentary,* ed. Michael Renov (New York: Routledge, 1993).

4. Alan Rosenthal, "*Harlan County, USA:* An Interview with Barbara Kopple and Hart Perry," in *The Documentary Conscience: A Casebook in Film Making* (Berkeley: University of California Press, 1980), p. 309.

5. Bishop, "Video Self," pp. 34–35.

6. David Wason, personal communication, letter, 1995.

7. Rosenthal, "*Salesman,*" p. 82.

8. Eric Michaels, "For a Cultural Future: Francis Jupurrurla Makes TV at Yuendumu," in *Bad Aboriginal Art: Tradition, Media, and Technological Horizons* (Minneapolis: University of Minnesota Press, 1994), p. 115.

9. Jablonko, "New Guinea in Italy," p. 186.

10. Gabriel Marcel, "Possibilités et limites de l'art cinématographique," *Revue internationale de filmographie* 5, nos. 18–19 (July–December 1954): 168–69, cited in Siegfried Kracauer, *Theory of Film: The Redemption of Physical Reality* (New York: Oxford University Press, 1960), p. 264.

11. Ibid.

12. Quoted in "The Art and Politics of the Documentary: A Symposium," *Cinéaste* 11, no. 3 (1981), p. 18.

13. Quoted in Mark Singer, "Predilections," *The New Yorker,* 6 February 1989, cited in Jeffrey K. Ruoff, "Conventions of Sound in Documentary," in *Sound Theory/ Sound Practice,* ed. Rick Altman (New York: Routledge, 1992), p. 223.

14. For more advice on conducting (ethnographic) interviews, see, e.g., James P. Spradley, *The Ethnographic Interview* (New York: Holt, Rinehart and Winston, 1979).

15. Quoted in Louis Marcorelles, *Living Cinema: New Directions in Contemporary Filmmaking* (New York: Praeger, 1973), p. 55.

16. Rosenthal, "*Salesman,*" p. 83.

17. Lecture at School of Cinema-Television, University of Southern California, fall 1989.

18. Karel Reisz and Gavin Millar, *The Technique of Film Editing* (London: Focal Press, 1981, 2nd ed.), p. 195.

19. Washington Area Lawyers for the Arts, "Answers to Common Legal Questions of Independent Film and Video Makers," 1991.

20. David MacDougall, personal communication, letter, 1995.

21. Hockings, "Gone with the Gael," p. 151.

22. Rosenthal, "*Harlan County, USA,*" p. 309.

CHAPTER 8

1. Vertov, *Kino-Eye,* p. 72.

2. Rouch, "The Camera and Man," p. 94.

3. Sergei Eisenstein, "The Cinematographic Principle and the Ideogram," in *Film Form* (New York: Harcourt Brace Jovanovich, 1949), p. 38.

4. André Bazin, *Qu'est-ce que c'est le cinéma?* vol. 1 (Paris: Editions de Cerf, 1958), p. 127.

5. André Bazin, "La Strada," *Crosscurrents* 6, no. 3 (1956): 20.

6. Luc de Heusch, *The Cinema and Social Science: A Survey of Ethnographic and*

Sociological Films (New York: UNESCO, 1962), reprinted in *Visual Anthropology* 1, no. 2 (1988): 113.

7. See Bill Nichols, *Ideology and the Image* (Bloomington: Indiana University Press, 1981), for a very incisive consideration of the differences between direct and indirect address in documentary.

8. Rouch, "The Camera and Man," p. 95. We have slightly altered this translation in order to be true to Rouch's original, which is as follows: "[L]e Monteur . . . ne doit jamais participer au tournage, mais être le second "ciné-oeil"; ne connaissant rien du contexte, il ne voit et entend que ce qui a été enregistré (quelles qu'aient été les intentions du réalisateur)." "Le Camera et les Hommes" (ms. of paper presented at the IXth International Congress of Anthropological and Ethnological Sciences, Chicago, 1973), p. 14.

9. Nichols, *Ideology and the Image,* p. 212.

10. Quoted in Rosenthal, *Writing, Directing and Producing Documentary Films,* p. 200.

11. Quoted in Mamber, *Cinema Verite in America,* p. 118.

12. Rosenthal, "*Salesman,*" p. 88.

13. David MacDougall, "Experiments in Interior Commentary," unpublished manuscript, p. 10.

14. Jablonko, "New Guinea in Italy," p. 175.

15. Hockings, "Gone with the Gael," p. 155.

16. Vaughan, "The Space between Shots," p. 712.

17. Jablonko, "New Guinea in Italy," p. 182.

18. Ibid., p. 184.

19. Dai Vaughan, "The Aesthetics of Ambiguity," in *Film as Ethnography,* ed. Peter Ian Crawford and David Turton (Manchester: Manchester University Press, 1992), p. 109.

20. Ibid., p. 110.

21. Ibid., p. 111.

22. Sol Worth, "The Uses of Film in Education and Communication," in his *Studying Visual Communication,* ed. Larry Gross (Philadelphia: University of Pennsylvania Press, 1981), p. 128.

23. See Vsevolod Pudovkin, *Film Technique and Film Acting* (London: Vision Press Ltd., 1929).

24. Quoted in Nichols, *Ideology and the Image,* p. 218.

25. Toby Alice Volkman, *A Guide to "N!ai, the Story of a !Kung Woman,"* vol. 1 of *The San in Transition* (Cambridge, MA: Cultural Survival, Inc. and Documentary Educational Resources, 1982), p. 34.

26. Quoted in Reisz and Millar, *The Technique of Film Editing,* p. 155.

27. Ibid., pp. 157–58.

28. Trinh Minh-ha, *Framer Framed* (New York: Routledge, 1992), pp. 227–28.

29. Alan Rosenthal, "Grey Gardens: An Interview with Ellen Hovde," in *The Docu-*

mentary Conscience: A Casebook in Film Making (Berkeley: University of California Press, 1980), p. 384.

30. Dai Vaughan, "Television Documentary Usage," in *New Challenges for Documentary,* ed. Alan Rosenthal (Berkeley: University of California Press, 1988), p. 35.

31. Trinh, *Framer Framed,* p 215.

32. Ibid., p. 3.

33. Marshall, "Filming and Learning," p. 90.

34. Hockings, "Gone with the Gael," p. 154.

35. Heider, *Ethnographic Film,* p. 74.

36. Quoted in Richard Dyer, "Entertainment and Utopia," in *Movies and Methods,* vol. 2, ed. Bill Nichols (Berkeley: University of California Press, 1985), p. 223.

37. Peter Bates, "Truth Not Guaranteed: An Interview with Errol Morris," in *Cinéaste* 17, no. 1 (1989): 17.

38. Jablonko, "New Guinea in Italy," p. 188.

39. Ibid., p. 191.

40. Jacqueline Urla and Frances Peters, "Breaking All the Rules: An Interview with Frances Peters," *Visual Anthropology Review* 9, no. 2 (Fall 1993): 102.

41. Jeffrey K. Ruoff, "Conventions of Sound in Documentary," in *Sound Theory/Sound Practice,* ed. Rick Altman (New York: Routledge, 1992), pp. 227–28.

42. Trinh, *Framer Framed,* pp. 127–28.

43. David MacDougall, "Subtitling Ethnographic Films," *Visual Anthropology Review* 11, no. 1 (Spring 1995): 89.

44. Ibid., p. 87.

45. Trinh, *Framer Framed,* p. 114.

46. David MacDougall, "Notes on the Making of *Lorang's Way,*" in *A Retrospective of the Ethnographic Films of David and Judith MacDougall,* ed. Gerald O'Grady (Buffalo: Buffalo Media Study, 1980), p. 8.

47. David Wason, personal communication, letter, 1994.

48. Sabine Jell-Bahlsen, "On the Making of *Eze Nwata—The Small King,*" in *Anthropological Filmmaking,* ed. Jack R. Rollwagen (New York: Harwood Academic Publishers, 1988), pp. 208, 220.

49. Thomas Ohanian, "The Evolution of the Post-Production Facility: The Emergence of Digital Media Solutions and the Digital Nonlinear Online Post Facility," p. 4, available from Avid Technology (see app. 3).

CHAPTER 9

1. Technically, of course, your film's social life got off the ground the moment you started working on it. Once the film goes into distribution it acquires, additionally, a social life as a free-floating entity.

2. Ayoka Chenzira, "The Joys and Pitfalls of Self-Distribution," in *The Next Step:*

Distributing Independent Films and Videos, ed. Morrie Warshawski (New York: Foundation for Independent Film and Video, 1989), p. 32.

3. Julia Reichert, *Doing It Yourself: A Handbook on Independent Film Distribution,* (New York: Association of Independent Video and Filmmakers, 1977), p. 11.

4. Ibid., p. 58.

5. Chenzira, "The Joys and Pitfalls of Self-Distribution," p. 33.

6. Debra Zimmerman, "How to Find A Distributor (And Not Cry Yourself To Sleep After The First Year)," in *The Next Step: Distributing Independent Films and Videos,* ed. Morrie Warshawski (New York: Foundation for Independent Film and Video, 1989), p. 28.

7. Robert Freedman, "Distribution Contracts," in *The Next Step: Distributing Independent Films and Videos,* ed. Morrie Warshawski (New York: Foundation for Independent Film and Video, 1989), p.137.

8. Mitchell Block, "The Non-Theatrical Market," in *The Next Step: Distributing Independent Films and Videos,* ed. Morrie Warshawski (New York: Foundation for Independent Film and Video, 1989), p. 80.

9. Beverly S. Freeman, "The Domestic Broadcast Market," in *The Next Step: Distributing Independent Films and Videos,* ed. Morrie Warshawski (New York: Foundation for Independent Film and Video, 1989), p. 53.

10. Karen Thorsen, "Foreign Sales: Doing It Yourself," *The Independent* 15, no. 10 (December 1992): 20.

11. Ibid., pp. 20–24.

12. Julia Reichert, *Doing It Yourself: A Handbook on Independent Film Distribution* (New York: Association of Independent Video and Filmmakers, 1977), has an excellent section on organizing such screenings.

13. Alan Gadney, *How to Enter and Win Film Contests* (Glendale, CA: Festival Publications, n.d.).

14. Trinh, *Framer Framed,* p. 218.

15. B. Ruby Rich, "The Future of 16mm Distribution," in *The Next Step: Distributing Independent Films and Videos,* ed. Morrie Warshawski (New York: Foundation for Independent Film and Video, 1989), p. 17.

ACKNOWLEDGMENTS

This handbook has benefited inestimably from innumerable individuals other than its authors. Patricia Adler, Bennetta Jules-Rosette, Kelly Masterson, Rosalind Morris, Jay Ruby and Jorge Preloran all commented solicitously on the original proposal, spurring us on to actually write the book. John Cohen, Mariane Ferme, Emily James, David MacDougall, and Liz Roberts graciously consented to be interviewed at length about their filmmaking experiences. John Bishop, Ellen Frankenstein, Nelson Graburn, Tom Hutcheson, Jesse Lerner, Peter Loizos, David MacDougall, John Quick, Dennis O'Rourke, David Turton, David Wason, and Julie Wright generously contributed their own keen insights and knowledge at different stages along the way. Nancy Goldman, Edith Kramer, Steve Seid, and especially Kathy Geritz, all of the Pacific Film Archive, were extremely helpful in furnishing facts and figures about distribution. Alec Raffin undertook research on the latest video technology, and Emily James, Liz Roberts and Stacy Rowe amended an earlier manual out of which this handbook grew. John Bishop, Cynthia Close, Bob Gardner, Gary Kildea, Jesse Lerner, David MacDougall, Dennis O'Rourke, Jay Ruby, Trinh Minh-ha, David Turton, and David Wason sought out (and, in the case of Bishop, even went out of his way to shoot) many of the photos that appear in the preceding pages. Steve Feld helped us disentangle the twisted histories of the words "Vérité" and "Direct." Faye Ginsburg and Fred Myers offered both intellectual inspiration and infrastructural support in the form of library access. John Bishop, Jesse Lerner, Bob Templer, and Sergei Frankin of Earth Video in New York City (Tel. 212 228 4254) all gave freely of their technical and editorial expertise in criticizing considerable chunks of the manuscript. And the long-suffering Paco Ferrandez, Julian Gerstin, Peter Redfield, and Silvia

Tomášková were kind enough to go over the whole book with a fine-tooth comb, improving it immeasurably in the process. Additionally, and at the drop of a hat, Sandra Murray and Chad Vaughan put their lives on hold to design the technical illustrations and figure drawings.

This handbook originated as a teaching manual for the Anthropological Film Program, founded by Jack Potter, at the University of California, Berkeley. That manual was sponsored by the UC Berkeley Academic Senate's Committee on Teaching and the Office of Educational Development. The Département des Etudes Pluridisciplinaires at the Université des Antilles et de la Guyane in Martinique, under the directorship of Jacques Coursil, and the Department of Anthropology at UC Berkeley were both supportive environments for the writing of this book. We have also learned far more from students at the University of Southern California, San Francisco State University, and UC Berkeley than we could ever conceivably have taught them. Moreover, were it not for the Center for Visual Anthropology and the School of Cinema-Television at the University of Southern California, where we were both students, and in particular for Patsy and Tim Asch, Tomlinson Holman, Steve Lansing, Doe Mayer, Alexander Moore, John Morrill, and Michael Renov, this book would simply never have been written—at least, not by us. And were it not for the encouragement and forebearance of Stan Holwitz, our editor at the University of California Press, as well as that of Scott Norton, our production editor, Steve Gilmartin, copy editor, Janet Wood, the book's designer, and Danette Davis, production coordinator—were it not for all their dedication and professionalism the book might never have been finished.

Though in places we have inevitably ridden roughshod over their ideas, and while the very idea of a filmmaking handbook must inspire trepidation in them all, this book is indebted from start to finish to the writings on documentary by Faye Ginsburg, David MacDougall, Bill Nichols, Alan Rosenthal, Jay Ruby, and Dai Vaughan. Needless to say, we alone are responsible for all the prescriptions and proscriptions contained, wittingly and unwittingly, within.

Finally, we would like to thank all collaborators on our films, past, present, and future—and particularly Gabai Baaré and Christopher Steiner.

PHOTO CREDITS

Fig. 1. Courtesy David MacDougall and Judith MacDougall, Fieldwork Films.

Fig. 2. Photo by Lucien Taylor.

Fig. 3. Courtesy Museum of Modern Art, New York, Film Stills Archive.

Fig. 4. Courtesy David Wason, Disappearing World, Granada Television.

Fig. 5. Courtesy Documentary Educational Resources (Marshall Family Collection).

Fig. 6. Courtesy Documentary Educational Resources (photo by Napoleon Chagnon).

Fig. 7. Courtesy University of California Extension Center for Media and Independent Learning (photo by John Cohen).

Fig. 8. Courtesy Gary Kildea.

Fig. 9. Courtesy Documentary Educational Resources.

Fig. 10. Photo by Dennis O'Rourke.

Fig. 15. Courtesy Film Study Center, Harvard University (photo by Jane Tuckerman).

Fig. 16. Courtesy Documentary Educational Resources (photo by Napoleon Chagnon).

Fig. 18. Courtesy Film Study Center, Harvard University.

Fig. 22. Courtesy Film Study Center, Harvard University (photo by Susan Meiselas).

Fig. 23. Courtesy Museum of Modern Art, New York, Film Stills Archive.

Fig. 24. Courtesy Center for Visual Communication.

Fig. 27. Courtesy Film Study Center, Harvard University.

Fig. 28. Courtesy John Bishop, Media Generation.

Fig. 29. Courtesy Jesse Lerner and Scott Sterling.

Fig. 30. Courtesy Museum of Modern Art, New York, Film Stills Archive.

Fig. 33. Courtesy Arriflex Corporation.

Fig. 34. Courtesy Film Study Center, Harvard University (photo by Robert Gardner).

Fig. 36. Courtesy John Bishop, Media Generation.

Fig. 38. Courtesy Lowel-Light Manufacturing Inc.

Fig. 39. Courtesy Museum of Modern Art, New York, Film Stills Archive.

Fig. 40. Courtesy John Bishop, Media Generation.

Fig. 41. Courtesy Kudelski SA.

Fig. 43. Photo by Lucien Taylor.

Fig. 45. Courtesy John Bishop, Media Generation.

Fig. 46. Courtesy John Bishop, Media Generation.

Fig. 47. Courtesy John Bishop, Media Generation.

Fig. 48. Courtesy Gary Kildea.

Fig. 49. Courtesy John Bishop, Media Generation.

Fig. 50. Courtesy Jean-Paul Bourdier, Moongift Films.

Fig. 51. Courtesy John Bishop, Media Generation.

Fig. 52. Courtesy Documentary Educational Resources (Marshall Family Collection).

Fig. 53. Courtesy Film Study Center, Harvard University (photo by Susan Meiselas).

Fig. 54. Courtesy Museum of Modern Art, New York, Film Stills Archive.

Fig. 55. Courtesy Documentary Educational Resources (Marshall Family Collection).

Fig. 56. Courtesy Film Study Center, Harvard University.

Fig. 57. Courtesy David MacDougall and Judith MacDougall, Fieldwork Films.

Fig. 58. Courtesy Museum of Modern Art, New York, Film Stills Archive.

Fig. 59. Courtesy Gary Kildea.

Fig. 64. Courtesy David MacDougall and Judith MacDougall, Fieldwork Films.

Fig. 65. Photo by Dennis O'Rourke.

Fig. 66. Courtesy ImMIX™ (photo by Bill Santos).

Fig. 67. Courtesy John Bishop, Media Generation.

Fig. 68. Courtesy David MacDougall and Judith MacDougall, Fieldwork Films
(photo by Judith MacDougall).

Fig. 69. Courtesy David Turton.

INDEX

Abolm, Maria Luiza, 424

Achkar, David, 332–33

Actualities, filming: cinematic conventions in, 337–39; close-ups in, 335–37; comprehensive coverage in, 334–37; crew dynamics and communication in, 328; directing subjects in, 331–34; not directing subjects in, 328–31; recording sound in, 340–41; reenactment in, 332–34; shot lists (storyboarding) for, 327; staging in, 331–32; what to shoot, 334–39; whole events, 285–86

Adair, John, 401

Addresses: for archival materials, 501; for art theaters and alternative exhibition sites, 505–6; for distributors, 507–11; for equipment and services, 498–501; for festivals, 502–5; for funding, 496–97; for legal assistance, 497–98; for media organizations, 494–95; for publications, 495–96; for television, 511–13; for travel organizations, 501

Aibel, Robert, 56–57

Akomfrah, John, 22, 358

Allah Tantou, 332–33

Ambience, 209–10, 340, 349, 350

American Anthropological Association, 48, 53, 465

American Family, An, 43, 47, 420

Amplitude, 174–76

Anderson, Robin, 6

And Statues Also Die, 19

Anthropologists: collaboration with filmmakers by, 74–85, 336, 364; contrasted with filmmakers, 78–79, 81–83; as aid to funding, 292

Aoi, 108, 405, 427 (fig. 65)

Aperture: depth of field and, 140, 144; f-stops, 142–44, 259; image sharpness and, 144; lens speed as relative, 142; T-stops, 142 (fig. 33), 144, 259, 266

Apocalypse Now, 402

Archival materials, 357–58; addresses for, 501; copyright of, 361–63; music, 359; reproducing, 363; sources of, 361; still photographs, 360–61; stock footage, 358, 359–61

Arroseur arrosé, L', 16

Asch, Patsy, 64, 76, 80, 84, 311

Asch, Timothy, 29, 60, 67, 76, 114, 271, 305–6, 311, 422; on collaboration with an anthropologist, 82, 84–85; on compensating subjects, 64, 65; on knowing subjects, 41; on need for contract with organizations, 86; photo of, 45 (fig. 6); on research vs. educational footage, 77; on shooting footage too distressing to watch, 58; on shooting whole events, 285–86; use of intertitles by, 426; work in Bali of, 80, 81 (fig. 9). See also *Ax Fight, The*

Aspect ratio, 243

Assemble editing, 446

Assembly, 429–30; edited, 432; log footage, 431; master list, 430; paper, 431; screening all footage, 430; transcripts, 430

Association of Independent Video and Filmmakers (AIVF), 470–71, 480

Attille, Martina, 22

Audience: as agents in film's meaning, 60; editing for, 386–88; identifying in film treatment, 287; reaction of, 51; sensing filmmaker's point of view, 50

Audio tape, 27, 182, 184 (fig. 41), 204, 212, 514–15

Ax Fight, The, 49, 69, 114, 306, 383; structure/story of, 31–32, 285–86

anthropologist, 74–85, 336, 364; in
editing, 84, 386; with organizations,
185–86; with subjects, 24, 61, 86–89,
386
Color temperature: conflicting, 154; control in video, 240–41; correcting, 153–
54; meter, 275
Comolli, Louis, 32
Compensation. *See under* Subjects
Composition: camera height, 103–4, 111;
center of interest, 102–3; depth, 100,
102 (fig. 17); diagonals, 99, 100 (fig. 15),
101 (fig. 16); headroom, 97, 98 (fig. 13),
347; noseroom, 98, 99 (fig. 14); rule of
thirds, 96–97, 347; screen dominance,
104; storyboarding, 104–6; symmetry,
avoidance of, 97. *See also* Shots
Coniston Story, 339
Connolly, Bob, 6
Connor, Linda, 64, 285; collaboration with
filmmaker by, 76, 80, 81 (fig. 9), 84;
photo of, 81 (fig. 9)
Consent, 52, 53–54; of minors, 54. *See also*
Release Forms
Continuity: avoiding jump cuts, 391; camera angle and, 130, 391, 394 (fig. 61);
camera movement and, 395; cinematic
conventions of, 337–38; crossing screen
axis and maintaining, 127–28; cutaways
and, 396–97; in expository documentary style, 18, 93; focal length and, 391;
ignoring conventions of, 399–402; image size and, 128, 130; interviewing and,
345–46; leaving the frame and, 395,
396 (fig. 63); maintaining consistency of
screen axis for, 124–27, 395; maintaining focal length for, 391; matching action for, 128, 129 (fig. 27); matching
eyelines for, 395 (fig. 62); matching lighting for, 395; overlapping action for, 391,
392 (fig. 60); rules/tips for, 390–
97; in sound, 172–73, 406. *See also*
Transitions
Contracts: between filmmaker and anthropologist, 84–85; distribution, 471–74;
with organizations, 86
Contrast range, 145, 146
Copyright: on archival materials, 361–63;
sharing with subjects, 65
Corporation for Public Broadcasting, 475
Country Auction, A, 56
Crew, 46–47, 71–72, 83, 328
Cutaways, 127, 128, 338, 396–97
Cutting. *See* Continuity; Editing;
Transitions

Damouré, 41, 386
Dead Birds, 37, 76, 103 (fig. 18), 116, 318
(fig. 53), 381; matching action in, 129
(fig. 27); slow disclosure in, 110–11;
symbolism in, 404
de Antonio, Emile, 25, 30-31, 410, 414
"Decisions" series, 55
Deep Throat, 403
de Heusch, Luc, 376
Depth of field: aperture size and, 140, 144;
camera-to-subject distance and, 140;
circle of confusion and, 138–39; depth
of focus and, 141–42; focal length and,
140; hyperfocal distance and, 140–41;
light intensity and, 140; rule of thirds
and, 138, 139 (fig. 31); short, 132, 133
(fig. 28)
Depth of focus, 141–42
de Rochemont, Louis, 18
Dialogue, formal. *See* Interviews
Dialogue, informal: allowing camera to
roam during, 356; contrasted with interviews, 355–56; editing, 409; transcribing, 364; "unnatural" feel of, 357
Diaries, 31
Diegesis/diegetic, 9, 420. *See also*
Extradiagetic
Diffraction, 180
Digital Video (DV) format: audio tracks of,
229; distribution outlets for, 221; editing, 229; expense of, 216–17; horizontal
resolution of, 232; portability of, 216;
technical quality of, 221, 229; video recording on, 229
Direct Cinema, 28–29, 286, 382, 528n.17
Directing, 328–34
Director, 71–72
Disappearing World series, 69, 410; collaboration between filmmakers and anthropologists in, 76, 84, 336, 364; compensation of subjects in, 65; subtitles in, 437
Dissolves, 398
Distribution, 461–62, 483; addresses for,
507–11; budget, 307–8; contracts,
471–74; by direct mailing, 464–66;
film festivals, 479–83; foreign, 475–77;
guidelines for doing business, 467–70;
outside, 470–74; publicity, 463–64;
self-, 462–70; to television, 474–78;
theatrical, 478–79
Documentary film, 2; contrasted with ethnographic film, 4; contrasted with fiction
film, 3–4, 8, 95; cross-cultural, 4–5;
cultural differences in, 5–7; defined, 16;
evaluating, 8; filmography, 520–26; his-

2; using to best advantage, 36. *See also* Documentary film; Exposure; Fiction film; Film structure or story

Film, 16 mm, 2; aesthetics and social relations of, 222–23; aspect ratio of, 243; circle of confusion of, 139; conforming edited version to original, 458–59; contrasted with video, 2, 222–23; distribution outlets for, 221; ease of use, 216, 247; editing on video, 247–48; editing technology and costs, 218; expense of, 217; image quality of, 242; international standards for, 219–20; latitude, 149; lighting contrast ratio of, 164; longevity of, 219; natural focal length for, 136, 137; printing original, 459; processing of, 215, 250, 317, 453–54; sound, 181, 216, 246–47; technical quality of, 221; workprint, 454. *See also* Film cameras, 16 mm

Film, 35 mm, 136, 242, 243

Film cameras: effects of temperature and humidity on, 323; makes and models of, 516–17; mechanics, 248–50

Film cameras, 16 mm: Aaton, 256 (fig. 49); Arriflex BL, 217; Arriflex SR, 249 (fig. 48), 256–57; Beaulieu R16, 258 (fig. 50); film magazines for, 247, 255, 256 (fig. 49); handholding ease of, 251–52; lenses for, 257–60; lens mount for, 257; lens shades and matte box for, 255–56; maintenance of, 218,265; makes and models of, 516; motor of, 254–55; portability of, 216; registration pin of, 256–57, 263–64; sync sound and camera noise of, 252; tests for, 257, 263–65; video assist on, 257; viewfinder of, 252–54. *See also* Film, 16mm

Film festivals: addresses of, 502–5; distribution to, 479–83

Film formats, 242–43; Super-16, 248. *See also* Film, 16 mm; Super-8 film

Filmmaker: concerns of compared to anthropologists, 81–82; differences from subjects of, 385–86; effect of personality upon film pace, 388; invisible hand of in observational documentary style, 30; as narrator, 410–11; and self-consciousness about role, 46; non-intervention in events by, 328–31; presentation of to subjects, 328; qualities of revealed in film, 50; represented by interviewees, 412, 413; represented by narrator, 412

Film speed, 149, 261–62

Film stock: black-and-white vs. color, 244,

261; characteristic curve of, 147–48; contrast range, 145; daylight, 154, 262; high contrast, 438; magnetic sound (mag), 26–27, 182; negative vs. reversal, 243–44, 261; ordering, 262; processing, 215, 250, 317, 453–54; protecting/storing, 263, 316–17, 323–24, 367; speed, 261–62; tungsten, 154, 155, 262; types, 518–19

Film structure or story: biography or portraits, 286; "journey," 284–85; multiple stories, 286–87; single event, 285–86; time, 285. *See also* Treatments

Filters: color, 267–68, 269; color temperature correction/conversion, 153–54, 155, 268–69; low contrast, 152; neutral density (ND), 267; polarizing, 267; retrofocus attachments, range extenders and reducers, 269–70

Fine cut: composing narration, 434–36; dubbing, 437–38; editing and mixing sound, 440–42; intertitling, 438–39; subtitling, 436–37; using music, 439–40

First Contact, 6

Flaherty, Frances, 24, 119 (fig. 23), 325 (fig. 54)

Flaherty, Robert, 9; casting of films, 40; collaboration with subjects by, 24, 87; film language of, 23–24; photo of, 119 (fig. 23), 325 (fig. 54), 369 (fig. 58); as romantic, 25–26; sponsors of, 85, 290; use of long lens by, 136, 137 (fig. 30). *See also Louisiana Story; Nanook of the North*

Fluorescent lighting, 153, 166

Focal length: angle of view and, 134, 135 (fig. 29); continuity and, 391; depth of field and, 140; hyperfocal distance and, 141; long, 121, 136, 137 (fig. 30); natural perspective and, 136; perspective and, 135–36; short, 135 (fig. 29), 136; of zoom lenses, 134–35

Focussing, 131–34; video, 232–33

Forest of Bliss, 22, 100 (fig. 15), 421

Foundation Center, 291

Frankenstein, Ellen, 81, 84, 294–95, 306, 323

Frantz Fanon: Black Skin, White Mask, 21 (fig. 2), 191 (fig. 43)

Freedman, Robert, 472–73

Frequency, 176–77

Freudenthal, Solveig, 47

Fronterilandia/Frontierland, 22, 118

F-stops, 142–44, 259

Fund-raising, 289–91; addresses, 496–97;

Low, Colin, 87
Luke, Lorrain, 191 (fig. 43)
Lumière, Louis and Auguste, 15–17
Lydall, Jean, 83

MacDougall, David, 87, 337: camera harnesses of, 365–66 (fig. 57); on casting, 40–41; on differences between filmmaker and subjects, 385–86; on dubbing, 425; on misunderstandings between anthropologists and filmmakers, 75; photo of, 366 (fig. 57), 455 (fig. 68); on starting shooting immediately, 70; on subtitles, 424
MacDougall, David and Judith, 6, 14 (fig. 1), 39, 65, 68, 317, 322, 330, 378, 383–84; collaboration with subjects by, 87; pace of films of, 388; style of, 29; use of interior commentary by, 411; use of subtitles and intertitles by, 421–22, 423, 428. See also *Lorang's Way;* Turkana Conversations Trilogy
Madame L'Eau, 41; contrast in, 403; end of, 384; location of, 6, 38; pace of, 388
Made in USA, 195, 292–93, 353
Mad Masters (Les maîtres fous), 255
Madonna, 43
Magazines, 247, 255, 256 (fig. 49)
Mallet, Marilu, 39, 410
Man of Aran, 40, 136, 137 (fig. 30)
Man with a Movie Camera, The, 31
Marcel, Gabriel, 341–42
March of Time series, 18
Maring series, 399–400, 419
Marker, Chris, 9, 19
Marshall, Arthur Calder, 290
Marshall, Elizabeth, 76
Marshall, John, 65, 76, 422; on narration, 411; photo of, 335 (fig. 55); on shooting events, 29, 327; style of, 29–30. See also *Hunters, The; N!ai, the Story of a !Kung Woman*
Marshall, Lorna, 76, 280 (fig. 52)
Masayesva, Victor, 22
Matte box, 255–56
Matter of Respect, A, 294–95
Maysles, Albert, 53, 334, 338, 378, 380. See also *Salesman*
Maysles, David, 378, 380. See also *Salesman*
McCarty, Mark, 37, 63
McElwee, Ross, 31, 350, 410
Meat Fight, The, 29
Meet Marlon Brando, 286
Memories and Dreams, 350
Mende, The, 46, 65, 79
Michaels, Eric, 339

Microphones: bass cut switch on, 201; condenser, 196; directionality in, 194; double breath screen on, 198, 201; dynamic, 195–97; frequency response on, 197; handholding, 198; impedance level on, 197–98; lavalier or clip-on, 200–201; location of relative to sound source, 173; "low Z," 197–98; makes and models of, 515–16; mounts for, 199–200; "omni," 194, 195; on-camera, 182; placement of, 172–73, 207–8, 350; recording music with, 210–11; transducing mechanism on, 195–96; "uni," 194–95; wind noise and, 198–99, 200; wireless, 200–201
Microphone windscreens, 181 (fig. 40), 198–99
Migrants, The, 460 (fig. 69)
Minh-ha, Trinh, 347, 417; on film festivals, 481; in independent filmmaking, 460; on not translating dialogue, 429; photo of, 258 (fig. 50); plays with subtitling conventions, 424; on silence, 408; on translation, 420, 421; use of filmmaker-as-narrator approach by, 411. See also *Naked Spaces: Living is Round; Reassemblage; Surname Viet Given Name Nam*
Minipini, Thomas Woody, 455 (fig. 68)
Mirrors, 100
Mixer, 179, 201–3
Moi, un noir, 20, 418–19
Monitors, 273–75
Moore, Michael, 350, 381
Morin, Edgar, 330. See also *Chronicle of a Summer*
Morris, Errol, 159, 418; use of interviews by, 30-31, 346, 351, 414, 416. See also *Thin Blue Line, The*
Moves: camera head, 116–17; camera mount, 118; and continuity, 395; need to rehearse, 117; pan, 116–17; tilt, 116, 117; zoom, 107, 114–18, 138
Mursi, The, 460 (fig. 69)
Musello, Chris, 56
Music: archival, 359; between diegetic and extradiegetic, 420; editing, 439, 440; extradiegetic, 417–19, 439; negative aspects of, 416–17; original, 419–20, 439–40; recording with microphone, 210–11

N!ai, 41, 42 (fig. 5), 405, 411, 426
N!ai, the Story of a !Kung Woman, 49; beginning of, 109; dubbing of, 426; heroine of, 41, 286; structure of, 286; use of leitmotif in, 405
Nairn, Charlie, 41, 382

Reflection, 177–80, 349, 350
Reflexive documentary style: in Cinéma Vérité, 31; first-person approach of, 31–32; problems of, 32
Refraction, 180
Registration pin, 256–57, 263–64
Reichert, Julia, 465, 469
Release forms, 52–53, 54, 304; examples of, 485–87
Resnais, Alain, 19, 360
Retrofocus attachments, range extenders, and reducers, 269–70
Reverberation, 178
Rich, B. Ruby, 483
Riefenstahl, Leni, 104
Riggs, Marlon, 22
Riley, Alrick, 303
Ritchie, Claire, 65
Rivers of Sand, 58, 336 (fig. 56), 402
Roads End, 37, 114 (fig. 22)
Roger and Me, 163, 381, 478
Rotha, Paul, 23, 123
Rouch, Jean, 9, 24, 37, 65, 255, 411, 418–19; on choosing an editor, 378; on cinema as intervention into time, 17; and Cinéma Vérité, 29, 31, 57, 528n.17; on editing during filming, 370–71; ethno-poetic films of, 20–21; on film crews, 71; on handholding camera, 120–21, 122 (fig. 24); on music, 416; pace of films of, 388; photo of, 122 (fig. 24); on zoom lenses, 136. See also *Chronicle of a Summer; Jaguar; Madame L'Eau*
Rough cut, 430, 432–34, 449
Rubbo, Michael, 378, 382
Ruby, Jay, 56, 59–60, 61
Ruiz, Raul, 124
Ruoff, Jeff, 420
Rushes, 24, 318–19, 328, 454
Rush to Judgment, 414
Ryan's Daughter, 37

Salesman, 28, 49, 338; casting of, 384–85; coercion of subjects in, 53; monologue in, 356; shooting of, 53, 334
Scheduling, 310–11
Screen axis (direction): consistency of, 124–27, 395; how to cross, 127–28; more than one, 127
Screenings: of rough cut, 433–34; of rushes to subjects on location, 24, 318–19, 328
SECAM standards, 220, 221, 232; list of countries using, 488–93
Sharkcallers of Kontu, The, 212
Sherman's March, 31, 410

Shots: camera height, 103–4, 111; center of interest of, 102, 103; cutaway (insert), 112, 338, 348, 396–97, 400; close-up, 107 (fig. 20), 108, 110, 126, 130, 136, 335–37, 371–72, 373, 377; "Dutch," 99; establishing, 110, 338; extreme close-up, 106–7 (fig. 20); long and extreme long, 107 (fig. 20), 109, 377; medium, 107 (fig. 20), 109; medium close-up, 107 (fig. 20), 109; number of people in, 111; over-the-shoulder and reaction, 112–13, 114 (fig. 22); selection of, 397; sequence and meaning of, 372–73; slow disclosure, 23–24, 110–11; wide angle, 136. See also Composition
Shutter speed, 236
Silence, 354–55, 408
Slating, 190–92
Slow disclosure, 23–24, 110–11
Song of Ceylon, 20, 407–8
Sorrow and the Pity, The, 412
Sound: absorption, 177, 350; amplitude and loudness, 174–76; in boomy interiors, 179; change in when moving, 173; "cocktail party effect," 178–79; cultural component to hearing, 179; diffraction, 180; dynamic range of, 175–76; frequency and pitch, 176–77; fundamentals and harmonics, 176–77; inverse square law of, 208–9; as montage element, 407–8; priority of in expository documentary style, 17–18; propagation, 174; reflection, 177–80, 349, 350; refraction, 180; reverberation, 178; and silence, 408; types, 173. See also Editing, sound
Sound equipment accessories: boom, 181 (fig. 40), 199–200; cables and connections, 203–4, 205 (fig. 44); headphones, 179, 201, 203, 204; mixer, 179, 201–3; pre-amplifier, 203; tools, 206; windscreen, 181 (fig. 40), 198–99. See also Microphones
Sound mixing, 440–42, 458
Sound recorders: analog vs. digital, 192–94; bias, 183–85; cleaning, 206; de gaussing, 206; digital audio tape (DAT), 192–94, 212; equalization, 188; magnetic (mag), 26–27, 182; maintenance of, 206–7; Nagra IV-S, 184 (fig. 41); Nagra SN, 212; noise reduction on, 189; recording mechanism, 183; single- vs. double-system, 180–82; synchronous, 18, 27–28, 189–90; tape, 182, 184 (fig. 41), 204, 212, 514–15; tape heads, 185; tape speed, 185–86, 188; video,

182, 188; volume unit or peak program meters on, 186–88, 202, 203, 204, 212, 234; Walkman Pro, 212

Sound recording: ambience track, 209–10, 340, 349, 350; background, 349, 350; change in sound through movement, 173; "cocktail party effect," 178–79; continuity and, 172–73, 406; guidelines, 340–41; interview, 349–50; maintaining consistent recording level, 208–9; mike placement, 172–73, 207–8; minimizing background noise, 207–8, 210; monitoring sound quality, 212; music, 210–11; reducing reflections, 207, 210; reference tone and recording data, 209; slating in, 190–92; in solo shooting, 212; stereo, 183; use of lavalier for, 207, 208; wild, 340–41. See also Interviews; Narration

Sound recordist: communication with camera operator, 211; location of, 207–8, 340; and need to stay alert, 211

Southeast Nuba, 79

Staging, 331–34

Steadicam, 118, 223, 228, 273, 274 (fig. 51), 518

Steiner, Christopher, 38

Sterling, Scott, 135 (fig. 29)

Stone, Oliver, 358

Storyboarding, 104–6, 327

Strecker, Ivo, 58–59

Strike, 402–3, 404

Subjects: anonymity of, 50; coercion of, 53–54; collaboration with, 24, 61, 86–89, 386; compensating, 62–69, 80–81; consent of, 52, 53–54; deception of, 54; directing, 331–34; disguising identity of, 416; editing for, 385–86; editing with, 386; effect of camera on, 16; finding and gaining access to, 40–44, 367–68; identification of, 415–16; issues of intervention, 56–58; narration by, 411; need to know, 41; not directing, 328–31; preparing for interview, 351–52; rapport with, 44–47; reciprocity between filmmaker and, 62–69; recognition of through close-ups, 337; screening rushes to, 318–19, 328; sharing copyright with, 65; sharing royalties with, 64, 65. See also Release forms

Subtitles, 421–24, 428, 436–37

Super-8 film format: advantages and disadvantages, 244, 245; aspect ratio, 243; cameras, 251; distribution, 221, 245–46; ease of use of, 216; editing and processing, 245; film stocks, 519; image size

and speed, 243; longevity, 219; makes and models, 516–17; sound, 244–45; technical quality, 221

Super-VHS video format, 182; audio channels, 226; compared to Hi-8, 226; expense, 217; horizontal resolution, 232; minicassette model, 228; portability, 216; technical quality, 226; on television, 221; time code, 226; video track, 225, 226

Surname Viet Given Name Nam, 333, 424, 426

Syncing up, 192, 250, 456, 458

Synchronous sound, 18, 27–28, 189–90, 252

Takeover, 87, 411

Takes: long, 50, 77, 123–24, 374, 376, 377; short, 123

Tapakan, Jero, 64, 80, 81 (fig. 9)

Tape recorders. See under Sound recorders

Television: addresses, 511–13; distribution to, 474–78; high definition, 224, 248; as source for funds, 293–94; video on, 221. See also International television standards

Television standards, international, 220, 221, 232, 488–93

Tempus de baristas, 70

Testament, 21

Tests, camera, 257: lens, 266; light leak, 265; registration, 263–64; scratch, 264–65; viewfinder, 265

Thin Blue Line, The, 31, 56, 163, 414; interviews in, 351, 414; music in, 418; re-enactment in, 333, 414

Things I Cannot Change, The, 49, 56

Thorsen, Karen, 476

Three Horsemen, 411

Tilting, 116, 117

Time code, 431, 452; generator on video camera, 241–42; Hi-8 video format, 225–26; linear video, 448; SMPTE, 225, 226, 227 (fig. 46), 229, 445, 446, 448; Super-VHS video format, 226

Titicut Follies, 28, 290–91, 380, 404

Titles and credits, 283–84, 449

To Live with Herds, 37, 39, 421–22

Tongues Untied, 22

Topic, selecting a, 35–36

Trance and Dance in Bali, 417

Transitions: discontinuous, 126; dissolves, 398; fades, 398; need to keep in mind while shooting, 123; screen axis and, 124–27; types of, 398–99; wipes, 398–99. See also Continuity

Indexer:	Andrew Christenson
Designer:	Janet Wood
Compositor:	G & S Typesetters, Inc.
Text:	Adobe Garamond
Display:	Runic, Helvetica
Printer:	R.R. Donnelley
Binder:	R.R. Donnelley

Ilisa Barbash and Lucien Taylor are award-winning documentary and ethnographic film- and videomakers, whose works include *In and Out of Africa* (1992). They live and teach in Berkeley, California.